Shakespeare's Festive World

This book offers an exciting new perspective on Shakespeare's relation to popular culture. Shakespeare drew extensively on the Elizabethan world of festival and holiday, including in his plays many of its events and traditions. He mingled popular culture with aristocratic and royal forms of entertainment in ways that combine or clash to produce new meaning, offering surprises which anticipate the Stuart Masque. This process evolved from the early, romantic festive comedies into the late plays which recover the celebrations and patterns of renewal initiated in the 'green world'. The values of festivity are inverted in the comedy of misrule and of the world turned upside-down, and finally perverted in the darker forms of the history plays and tragedies. François Laroque reconstructs the principal events, customs and games of the Elizabethan festive tradition and demonstrates the need for reconsideration of Shakespeare's techniques of amalgamating literary traditions with the folklore and ceremonies of popular pastimes and seasonal celebrations.

European Studies in English Literature

SERIES EDITORS
Ulrich Broich, Professor of English, University of Munich
Herbert Grabes, Professor of English, University of Giessen
Dieter Mehl, Professor of English, University of Bonn

Roger Asselineau, Professor Emeritus of American Literature, University of
    Paris-Sorbonne
Paul-Gabriel Boucé, Professor of English, University of Sorbonne-Nouvelle
Robert Ellrodt, Professor of English, University of Sorbonne-Nouvelle
Sylvère Monod, Professor Emeritus of English, University of Sorbonne-Nouvelle

This series is devoted to publishing translations into English of the best works
written in European languages on English and American literature. These may be
first-rate books recently published in their original versions, or they may be
classic studies which have influenced the course of scholarship in their field while
never having been available in English before.

TRANSLATIONS PUBLISHED
Walter Pater: The Aesthetic Moment by Wolfgang Iser
The Theory and Analysis of Drama by Manfred Pfister
*The Symbolist Tradition in English Literature: A Study of Pre-Raphaelitism and
    'fin de siècle'* by Lothar Hönnighausen
The Rise of the English Street Ballad 1550–1650 by Natascha Würzbach
Oscar Wilde: The Rebel as Conformist by Norbert Kohl
The Fall of Women in Early English Narrative Verse by Götz Schmitz
The Eighteenth-Century Mock Heroic Poem by Ulrich Broich
Romantic Verse Narrative: The History of a Genre by Hermann Fischer
*Shakespeare's Festive World: Elizabethan Seasonal Entertainment and the
    Professional Stage* by François Laroque

TITLES UNDER CONTRACT FOR TRANSLATION
Redeformen des englischen Mysterienspiels by Hans-Jürgen Diller
L'être et l'avoir dans les romans de Charles Dickens by Anny Sadrin

Shakespeare's festive world

Shakespeare's festive world

Elizabethan seasonal entertainment and the professional stage

François Laroque

Professor of English,
Université de la Sorbonne-Nouvelle, Paris III

Translated by Janet Lloyd

CAMBRIDGE
UNIVERSITY PRESS

Published by the Press Syndicate of the University of Cambridge
The Pitt Building, Trumpington Street, Cambridge CB2 1RP
40 West 20th Street, New York, NY 10011-4211, USA
10 Stamford Road, Oakleigh, Melbourne 3166, Australia

Originally published in French as *Shakespeare et la fête*
by Presses Universitaires de France 1988
and © Presses Universitaires de France
First published in a revised and enlarged form in English by Cambridge
University Press 1991 as *Shakespeare's Festive World*

English translation © Cambridge University Press 1991

First paperback edition 1993

Printed in Great Britain at the University Press, Cambridge

British Library cataloguing in publication data

Laroque, François
Shakespeare's festive world: Elizabethan seasonal
entertainment and the professional stage.
1. Drama in English. Shakespeare, William, *1564–1616*.
Influence of English seasonal festivals. England. Seasonal
festivals. Influence on drama in English by Shakespeare,
William, *1564–1616*
I. Title   II. Laroque, François, Shakespeare et la fête
822.33

Library of Congress cataloguing in publication data

Laroque, François.
[Shakespeare et la fête. English]
Shakespeare's festive world: Elizabethan seasonal entertainment
and the professional stage / François Laroque; translated by Janet
Lloyd.
    p.   cm.
Translation of: Shakespeare et la fête.
Includes bibliographical references.
ISBN 0 521 37549 5
1. Shakespeare, William, 1564–1616 – Knowledge – Manners and
customs.   2. Shakespeare, William, 1564–1616 – Knowledge – Folklore,
mythology.   3. Festivals – England – History – 16th century.
4. Holidays – England – History – 16th century.   5. Theater – England –
History – 16th century.   6. England – Social life and customs – 16th
century.   7. Literature and folklore – England – History – 16th
century.   8. Folklore in literature.   9. Seasons in literature.
10. Manners and customs in literature.   I. Title.
PR3069.M3L37   1991
394.26'42'09031 – dc20   90-33537 CIP

ISBN 0 521 37549 5 hardback
ISBN 0 521 45786 6 paperback

In memory of my parents and for my wife, Yolande

Contents

Illustrations

Foreword

In exploring the contribution made by the popular culture of Elizabethan England to the themes and motifs of Shakespeare's plays, François Laroque follows in a well-established tradition. Sir Edmund Chambers' great studies of *The Mediaeval Stage* (1903) and *The Elizabethan Stage* (1923) gave original and authoritative treatment to the calendar customs and festivals which still retained their vitality in Shakespeare's lifetime. Charles Read Baskerville's study of medieval folk festivals and Enid Welsford's investigation into the social and literary history of the fool helped to relate the dramatist's work to conventions of calendrical misrule. What Northrop Frye called the 'green world', to which Shakespeare's characters so often escape, can be related to the periodic emancipation afforded by traditional holidays, and in C.L. Barber's *Shakespeare's Festive Comedy* (1959) the saturnalian pattern of festive release became a central principle of interpretation. A few years later, the English translation of Mikhaïl Bahktin's *Rabelais and his World* inaugurated two decades of critical writing in which the debt of the carnivalesque to the folk humour of popular ritual and spectacle would became a commonplace.

François Laroque's book, however, has two particular strengths. The first is that it rests upon a close acquaintance with the numerous studies of popular culture which have been made in recent years by historians of early modern England. This has enabled him to replace vague invocations of 'carnival' and 'misrule' by a precise reconstruction of the festive calendar of Shakespeare's time and a nuanced understanding of its social implications. Professor Laroque freely acknowledges his debt to the pioneering work in this area of Charles Phythian-Adams. But his own extensive reading in the primary sources of the period and his close acquaintance with the *Annales* school of historians enable him to bring an individual, and in some ways distinctively French, perspective to his subject.

François Laroque's other strength is that he is a critic as well as an historian; and he uses his historical material to illuminate the whole range of Shakespeare's dramatic writing. His readers will be able to judge as well as I how far his distinctive approach has resulted in a new interpretation of the plays. My own feeling is that his demonstration of the ubiquity of festive themes and images in Shakespeare is admirably successful, not just in the case of the comedies, where we might have expected it, but also in the tragedies, where we are convincingly shown how festivity can take on a disturbing and sinister aspect. Professor Laroque is particularly instructive on the way in which Shakespeare's dramatic work reveals conflicting attitudes to the whole festive system, a conflict of values which mirrored changes in society at large.

It is very satisfying to see historical writing put to such effective use. Historians have long been indebted to Shakespearean scholars, who, in the course of their unceasing efforts to discover more about the dramatist's work or to illuminate some obscure passage in his works, have turned over thousands of unpublished documents, thereby generating, almost incidentally, an enormous amount of fresh historical information about the Elizabethan age. It is pleasing to see that on this occasion some of the debt has been repaid and that, through François Laroque's skilful mediation, historians have been able to make an unintended contribution to literary understanding.

Corpus Christi College, Oxford,
Twelfth Night 1991

                                                            Keith Thomas

Preface

This book is the product of several years of work and research pursued in France, England and the United States. Festivals were fleeting affairs but, paradoxically enough, the shorter they were, the longer the time necessary to reconstruct them turns out to be. Studying them also involves moving about from one place to another, from outdoors to indoors, from the street or village square to a desk in a library or some other archive. So my work would not have been possible without the welcome assistance that I received from the British Library in London, the Bodleian in Oxford, the library of the Shakespeare Institute in Birmingham, the libraries of the University of Texas at Austin, the Folger Shakespeare Library and the Library of Congress in Washington, the library of the Centre d'Etudes et de Recherches Elisabéthaines of the Université Paul-Valéry in Montpellier and the Bibliothèque Nationale in Paris.

I am also grateful for the advice and suggestions that I have received from many colleagues: Professor Jean Fuzier and Professor Jean-Marie Maguin at the Université Paul-Valéry in Montpellier, Professor Louis Lecocq of the Université de Lyon II, Professor Bernard Paulin of the Université de Saint-Etienne and Professor Michèle Willems of the Université de Rouen. I should also like to express my gratitude to Professor Emmanuel Le Roy Ladurie of the Collège de France and Sir Keith Thomas of Corpus Christi College, Oxford, for their assistance and encouragement in the areas of historical background and the analysis of mentalities. I am especially indebted to Professor Stanley Wells, the director of the Shakespeare Institute, for his invaluable advice and suggestions and for the material aid that he afforded me, in the shape of a research scholarship at Stratford-upon-Avon. This greatly facilitated the revision of and the additions to this book, originally published in France in 1988 under the title *Shakespeare et la fête*. I am furthermore indebted to him for being so kind as to read over the proofs.

My thanks go to Dr Levi Fox for the hospitality of the Shakespeare Centre, which provided me with a study in which to work as well as with all the resources of the library, and to Dr Susan Brock and Dr Marian Pringle, the librarians of the Shakespeare Institute and the Shakespeare Centre, and the rest of their staff for all their help and unfailing kindness.

Finally, I am grateful to Professor Jacques Berthoud of the University of York, whose remarks and suggestions were most useful and helped me to clarify and complete some points in the book for this revised and enlarged edition.

A note on texts

Unless otherwise specified, all the quotations from Shakespeare come from *The Complete Works*, Compact edition, edited by Stanley Wells and Gary Taylor (Oxford, 1988).

Translator's note

Translating such polysemic terms as *la fête* poses problems in English, for reasons grounded in history, religion and modes of thought. As Michael Bristol shrewdly remarked in his review of the French version of François Laroque's book in *Shakespeare Quarterly*, 40: 3 (Autumn, 1989), '*La fête* is an expression with a somewhat broader range of meanings than feast or festivity. Both these ideas are included in *la fête*, but *la fête* also contains the Latinate sense of 'solemnity' or formal observance and ... has the additional meaning of a "Saint's day".'

Part I

Introduction: Festivity during the Elizabethan age

The theme of festivity is clearly not a *topos* or subject for which there already exists an established critical tradition. The first part of this study concentrates on documents and evidence of both a historical and a literary nature. The second pursues the ramifications and transformations of the theme within Shakespearian drama. Festivity is a social manifestation linked with natural and seasonal cycles and rooted in a so-called archaic vision of time and the cosmos. It is not necessarily fundamentally connected with the written word. Oral transmission was the rule in popular festivity. Not until the second half of the eighteenth century did 'antiquarians', the precursors of the folklorists of today, set about collecting and writing down the texts of ballads, mimed dramas and other festive performances that had been sung and acted in the English countryside since very ancient times. In the case of civic and princely festivals, the archives have preserved not only the texts of pamphlets and the speeches that various personages delivered but also accounts, in which the price of costumes and the artists' fees are all minutely recorded. But the essence of these festivals lay elsewhere: in the music, the dancing, the movement and colour and also – as we should remember – in the shrieks of joy and boos of derision from the crowd of spectators in the background. It is true that a number of writers of the period set about re-creating these festivals, representing them in spicy and colourful sketches, and that in Shakespeare's works the pomp and magic of the theatrical production are sometimes successful in recapturing something of that lost splendour. But we shall never really know what the performance of a Masque at the court of Elizabeth or James I was like. We should also remember that most of the contemporary documentation on the many local or seasonal festivals is drawn from parish registers, judicial or ecclesiastical court hearings, sermons and homilies or other books of a solemn and joyless nature. Modern anthropologists have cameras and sound-recorders at their disposal, but to try to become a *historian* of something that is essentially ephemeral and intangible, the protean phenomenon *par excellence*, may well seem a paradoxical and risky, not to say foolhardy, undertaking. Conscious of the dangers as well as the inevitable limits of this undertaking, I have nevertheless decided to take up the challenge and venture forward along

3

paths still barely charted in a field of study in which sociological and literary elements are closely intertwined.

My decision to investigate forms of behaviour that have now died out, surviving only as traces scattered through a wide variety of documentation, was prompted by a deep conviction which constituted my point of departure. It was the belief that the Renaissance as a whole and the Elizabethan age in England in particular were indissolubly linked with a notion of periodic celebration and rejoicing for which all and sundry prepared and in which all took part: the age was, in short, pervaded with the spirit of festivity. That spirit, generally expressed in traditional and conservative forms, may well have constituted one aspect of the rising liberalism and individualism of the age, but it no doubt also served the purposes of a monarchy now endowed with powers both temporal and spiritual, since it won it the approval and gratitude of the masses. However, by about the last two decades of the sixteenth century, voices on all sides were being raised against the waste and immorality of festivals, whether princely or popular, and darker days were in the offing, days that were to hasten their decline. Under the Stuarts, people set about retrospectively re-creating the myth of 'Merry England' and began to hark back nostalgically to a joyful, festive England in which the morose boredom of Sundays had been a thing unknown.[1] The fact that, already at this early date, it was more a matter of images and collective representations than of social or historical reality in the strict sense of the expression shows clearly enough that the history of festivity has belonged from the start to the domain of imaginary representation and what historians of today call 'mentalities'. So if this history has tended to be set apart from the strictly literary field, it is not on account of any real separation between the two domains but rather as a result of an artificial distinction made between two areas of specialist studies.

The first scholar to attempt to do away with that distinction was Jean Jacquot, the organizer and leader of a series of colloquia in the 1950s on the subject of Renaissance festivals. His three volumes on the subject opened up the way for interdisciplinary studies in a domain where the marking out of subjects for research projects could best be done through collective discussions.[2] I must, however, confess that my own project did not emerge directly from the possibilities envisaged in the course of those discussions. Rather, its obscure, almost secret, origin is to be found in a remark by Jean Jacquot at the end of his Introduction to what he appositely called his 'joyous and triumphant entry' when he observed that it

would have been interesting to explore what palace and castle entertainments (particularly at the New Year and Carnival time) owed to popular festivals. A fine study could be made of folklore's contribution to the aristocratic festival, its role in the pastoral and the 'fairyland' element that the little rural deities, intermingled with the nymphs and dryads of classical mythology, added to the Masques or comedies performed at court.[3]

The idea that festivals, poor and rich alike, draw upon the same mythical and imaginary stock is an attractive one, for it could blow apart the watertight compartments set up by ideologies and call into question the idea that the class struggle is universal. Nor does the suggestion of a mutual interaction and influence between the various manifestations of festivity of the period necessarily imply an old-fashioned, paternalistic view of the situation. Festivity is profoundly ambivalent and, for that very reason, tends to repel dialectical interpretations.

As for my method for analysing texts which are bound to raise the delicate question of how adequately festivity can be reflected within a written corpus of literature to which it does not necessarily belong, I decided to distinguish between two main categories of texts: those used as sources of evidence or documentation (which might be economic, juridical or literary in character) and texts in which the subject of festivity plays a structural, metaphorical or symbolic role. Of course, in practice, the dividing line between these two types of texts is not all that clear or easy to draw: informative texts are frequently also metaphorical, and *vice versa*. All the same, it seems safe to assume that the meaning of the second type of text depends upon our knowledge and understanding of the first type. The corpus of the material on festivity as a whole comprises a vast range of data – networks of imagery and symbolic systems – that provided for the Elizabethan dramatists a language of allusion, a whole panoply of rhetorical devices and a pattern of symbolic references. So the first thing to do is to identify and classify the disparate and scattered data available to us (even if, as some historians have insisted, it will probably never be complete).[4] In the first part of the present study, which will be historical and anthropological in character, I shall try to present a synthesis of the documentation that I have read or to which I have referred, within the general framework of a calendar classification. This should make it possible to define the questions to be asked and determine a method of approach to the literary and imaginary representation of festivity in the theatre of Shakespeare.

I have chosen to limit this study to the period that coincides with Shakespeare's dramatic activity, covering the last fifteen years of Elizabeth's reign and the first ten of James I's, that is to say 1590 to 1613. The reason for that decision is my desire to emphasize the close relationship I detect between festivity and literature during this period. Of course, this does not mean ignoring the continuity of festive folklore and traditions,[5] for it will clearly be necessary to look back at the past to discover elements that influenced the young Shakespeare and are to be found later, in transposed form, in his works. Nor should we underestimate the importance of changes that took place during those years as a result of decisions taken by the secular authorities. Festivals undeniably convey messages about time that are not restricted to the usual historical points of reference, but they were also affected by many changes that took place over these years in the religious, political and administrative domains, both nationally and locally, as a result of decisions made by the authorities. Thus, the royal decrees issued by Henry VIII put a stop to religious festivals that had been observed for centuries. But even as the old Catholic calendar was being changed and purged, new festivals of a civic or national nature were being created. Furthermore, although many local festivals were encountering the hostility of municipal authorities, magistrates and Puritan worthies, at the same time the theatres of London were enjoying a considerable boom and more theatrical companies were touring the provinces. On the other hand, we should, albeit somewhat circumspectly, bear in mind the publication of works such as *The Anatomie of Abuses* (1583) by Philip Stubbes. This was a passionate diatribe against the mores of the period and what the author presents as so many evils affecting society, ranging from the enclosures to the extravagant fashions and costumes paraded at court, and taking in the 'satanism' of the festivals of May and those of the Lord of Misrule.[6] The undeniable popularity of this work points to the existence, among the élite and the educated, of quite a strong movement of opposition to festivity, while at the same time testifying indirectly to its persistent vitality and popularity among the masses. On the other hand, it is fair to suppose that, as I shall be showing later, this violent yet inspired diatribe is just as likely to have exerted a seductive fascination upon certain minds as to have inspired others with a salutary reaction of repulsion. That is frequently the way with works devoted to evil and depictions of hell: instead of ridding the soul of its poisons, they tend to sow the seeds of disturbance there. But the reason why Stubbes is still read and often cited even today is, paradoxically enough, because his denunciation of the abuses of his time constitutes one of the most useful contemporary anthropological sources of evidence on traditions that – certainly unwittingly – he helped to salvage from oblivion. Furthermore, it is perfectly reasonable to suppose that Shakespeare himself may have had the work in mind while writing certain passages of *A Midsummer Night's Dream*, *Twelfth Night* and *Othello*.

All the same, sixty years later, Stubbes' ideas were posthumously realized when a law was passed banning all the great religious festivals of the calendar: the festival of Christmas was replaced by a day of fasting on

25 December 1644 and, in 1647, the celebrations of Easter and Whitsun were banned. It is hard to ignore these events on the threshold of the Elizabethan age, for retrospectively they are bound to affect any analysis of festivity during this period. It would nevertheless be mistaken, I think, to see things purely in relation to the zero degree of festivity represented by Cromwell's Commonwealth, for that would lead to our looking everywhere and prematurely for the signs of a decline all the more inevitable given that we know the end of the story. The period that interests us abounds in difficulties, tensions and contradictions, but nothing seems to have been a foregone conclusion at the time. Festivity continued to punctuate the days and seasons in the countryside, to animate civic processions in the towns and to enliven court life with celebrations of unprecedented pomp. Of course, there were protests from the Puritans and sermons and pamphlets rained down, but there was nothing particularly exceptional about these recriminations: they were part of a long tradition of homilies delivered from the pulpit, castigating excesses of all kinds and condemning the abandonment of spiritual duties in favour of the satisfaction of desire and appetite.

Yet, the Renaissance festival was no longer quite the same as the medieval one, especially in England, where the emancipation of the national Church from the domination of Rome speeded up a break with the spirit of medieval religion and led to the suppression of the traditional cults of saints and also of certain religious festivals. The changes made in the liturgy, services and ceremonies of the Church tended towards a general anglicanization (Latin services being replaced by the Book of Common Prayer), simplification (the spectacular aspect of religion being toned down) and a reduction in the number of the feast days that had studded the old calendar of pre-Reformation days.[7] Thus Corpus Christi, which had been instituted in England in 1264 and was the occasion for dramatic performances and processions in many provincial cities (such as York and Chester) was suppressed by Edward VI in 1547, and the pageant of Saint John's Day (the Midsummer Watch) created by Henry III in 1253, which took place in more and more places after the tragic 'Ill May Day' of 1517,[8] was abolished by Henry VIII in 1539.[9]

It is hard to gauge the real impact of these prohibitions that upset the pattern of secular practices. The decisions of the Privy Council were certainly not implemented immediately, for these were troubled times when, in the absence of any centralized bureaucracy, only patience and vigilance could hope to overcome the many pockets of local resistance. To make the point simply, it was certainly not until well into the second half of the sixteenth century that the reforms adopted at the end of the first half can have been applied and assimilated. In the sixteenth century, the notion of change spelt more anxiety than hope and the considerable effects of the inertia of popular mentalities were also something that had to be taken into account. After the upheavals of the period from 1535 to 1558, Elizabeth's reign was to introduce greater stability and moderation in the face of the two extremes of Catholic reaction, on the one hand, and iconoclastic Puritan zeal, on the other.

In the towns and among the educated élite, the changes may have brought some people to recognize the precarious nature of festivals and a few to regard them as pointless. In the countryside, however, they appear to have influenced customs passed down from one generation to the next hardly at all.[10] On the other hand, those customs were soon to be affected by the socio-economic evolution of Elizabethan England, which was to give rise to numerous satirical couplets on subjects such as the all-powerful nature of money, the attraction of the cities and the landed aristocracy's lack of respect for the traditional duties of charity and hospitality which used to make it a moral obligation to receive the parish poor at one's table during the Christmas festival period.

However, just because tradition was fighting a losing battle in late-sixteenth-century England, we should not assume that festivals were everywhere on the defensive. Even as the great religious festivals of the Catholic calendar were banned and decline set in for the saints' festivals associated with the corporations, clerks and youth organizations (such as those of Saint Nicholas, Saint Clement and Saint Catherine), new popular festivals of an essentially national and Protestant nature were coming into being. Two of the best-known examples are the celebration of the anniversary of Queen Elizabeth's accession to the throne on 17 November and the commemoration of the Gunpowder Plot on Guy Fawkes' Day, 5 November.

Then, in some cases, the prohibition affecting a festival would result not in its extinction, but in its transformation or transfer to another date in the calendar. Thus, the Midsummer Watch, officially suppressed in 1539, survived in the form of the Lord Mayor's Show, thenceforth celebrated in London on 28 October, on the feast day of Saint Simon and Saint Jude.[11] The rulers of the land, now also the supreme authorities over its religious affairs, seem to have been at pains to encourage the constitution of an Anglican calendar markedly different from the Roman one. In this connection, England's refusal to ratify the Gregorian reformed calendar that was adopted by the countries of mainland Europe in 1582 was a negative manifestation of that same concern.

As well as favouring the perpetuation of the civic bourgeois festival now liberated from its former dependence upon the Church, Elizabeth's accession to the throne ushered in a veritable rejuvenation of festivity. Court activities and the queen's visits to the provinces were timed to coincide with various symbolic dates situated at the cardinal points of the calendar, producing the impression that it was royal festivity that provided the general impulse and rhythm for all the different rites and celebrations that took place in the various provinces and at all social levels. The monarchy usurped the place of the Church, with the result that the erstwhile cult of the Virgin and saints was now transferred to the sovereign and her entourage. The activities and daily amusements of the queen and the court followed a quasi-ritual order based upon the division of the year into two. The winter season (the 'season of the revels') began on 17 November, the day when the queen returned to Whitehall to celebrate the anniversary of her accession to the throne, and this was followed by the twelve days of Christmas. Candlemas or Shrove Tuesday were the days for the court to set off for Greenwich or Richmond, where the ceremony of the washing of the feet of twelve poor people took place on Maundy Thursday. The Garter ceremony, on Saint George's Day, 23 April, took place at Windsor. The summer half of the year, known as 'high summer', was devoted to 'progresses' through the provinces, in the course of which the queen received the homage of her subjects and at the same time enjoyed the lavish receptions that the great aristocratic families laid on for her.[12] The entertainments organized for these progresses are well known thanks to the texts and evidence collected by John Nichols.[13] These seasonal festivities were complemented by occasional celebrations – entries, coronations and royal christenings, weddings and funerals – all of them pretexts for displays of liberality and rejoicing much appreciated by the masses. All this pomp and ceremony, connected with the Tudor myth and a revival of Arthurian chivalry, reflected a trend towards absolute monarchy that was to speed up under the Stuarts.

Festivity had always been an outlet for popular energies; under Elizabeth and James I, it became an instrument of government as much as a means of amusement. The genealogical tree that was displayed for the multitude to see on the occasions of royal entries justified the sovereign's legitimacy in the eyes of the masses,[14] while the encouragement of local festivals to mark a royal progress in the provinces was a way of making trouble for the Puritan municipalities who strove to ban them.[15] These festivals furthermore gave the supernatural new associations with the person of the sovereign, for a cult of the 'virgin queen' gradually superseded the old festivals devoted to the Virgin Mary.[16]

Elizabethan festivity is thus marked by secular trends that tended to remove many traditional celebrations from the orbit of religion. In Coventry, for example, the day for the mayor's induction was switched after the Reformation. Until then, it had taken place on the day of the Purification of the Virgin Mary (that is to say, Candlemas, 2 February); now it was moved to 1 November, a date with fewer suspect connections with papist idolatry.[17] But the most general consequence of these trends was probably the progressive eclipse of the extrovert religious feeling that had hitherto been demonstrated in the streets at the high points of the religious year, to the encouragement of a religion of a more austere and individual nature. The rise of the spectacular coincided with an internalization of the sacred.

The movement away from demonstrative religious manifestations was accompanied by a tendency if not to centralization, at least to a relocation of the more grandiose festive occasions. In the Middle Ages, celebrations of the Mysteries and Corpus Christi processions were to a large extent a feature of the towns of the provinces (the most famous, in this connection, being Coventry and Chester); the Elizabethan age saw such creative initiatives decline in the provinces but increase in the capital.[18] In London, the Midsummer Watch was replaced by a Lord Mayor's Show that became ever more lavish as the years passed, but no such replacement for it was introduced in the provinces. Furthermore, the dissolution of the guilds and corporations that used to be responsible for financing and organizing religious festivals and performances was also a factor that hastened the end of these spectacular ceremonies. The traditional calendar festivities probably remained unaffected, for they were the preserve of amateurs (artisans, fraternities or youth associations) and were occasions more for making money than for lavish spending. In the larger cities and in London, in particular, it was at this juncture that, thanks to aristocratic or royal protectors there, permanent troupes of players and professional artists sprang up and began to cater for a paying public by putting on daily performances which took the place of the erstwhile seasonal religious spectacles that used to provide free entertainment for all and sundry.[19] The existence of these troupes of players, who also toured in the provinces, inevitably dealt a fatal blow to the village folk plays and 'May games', which began to decline from 1580 onwards.[20]

The contrast between London and the provinces was increasingly accentuated by the astounding urban and commercial boom that subsequently spread to affect the whole of Elizabethan England. Yet the town/country opposition still lay at the heart of the whole phenomenon of festivity, for even if it was through the towns that festivals were developed, embellished and enriched, essentially the festival was the product of a rural civilization whose seasonal rhythms and magico-religious beliefs were linked with the mysteries of natural fertility. Furthermore, for Shakespeare's contemporaries, the countryside (whether cultivated or fallow or forest), lying *extra muros*, beyond the town walls, was still the object of ancient beliefs and deep-rooted fears. The forest, linked with royal privileges, was the domain of hunting, wildness and the sacred, as is testified by the ballads and legends of Robin Hood, the wealth of iconographic variants on the grotesque theme of the *homo sylvarum*, or wild man, and the juridical treatises of John Manwood.[21] Symbolic flowers and plants were gathered at Christmas time, on 1 May or Saint John's Day, to be arranged in people's houses or displayed in the village squares. These were ritual gestures that moved from the outside inwards, betokening a twofold desire: to overstep boundaries and to appropriate wild nature. At other periods of the year, this town/countryside relationship was reversed, particularly when pastoral festivals were celebrated. These took place during the secular half of the year[22] and were a pretext for urban dwellers to flock out of their towns to take part in the labour and amusements of the fields. Consider, for example, the following complaints expressed by the city of Westminster, bewailing the fact that its inhabitants deserted it in even greater numbers during the summer than at the end of each of the four annual terms:

Those throwes of sorrowe come uppon mee four times every yeare, but at one time more, (and with more paines) than at all the rest. For in the height and lustiest pride of Summer, when every little Village hath the Bachilers & her Damsels tripping deftly about Maypols; when Medowes are full of Hay-makers: when the fields upon the workidaies are full of Harvesters singing, and the town greenes upon Hollydayes, trodden down by the Youthes of the Parish dancing . . . Then (even then) sit I like a Widdow in the middest of my mourning: then doe my buildings shew like infected lodgings, from which the Inhabitants are fledde . . .[23]

It is interesting to note how the festivities that at regular intervals or on special occasions emptied the town of its inhabitants, who all flocked to the countryside, are here indirectly assimilated to the plague ('infected lodgings, from which the Inhabitants are fledde').

The general opposition between town and countryside, which during the Elizabethan period gave way to an increasingly marked opposition between London and the provinces, was compounded by the great regional diversity that characterized all festive or folkloric ceremonies. Most festivities had a distinctly local character, in some cases one peculiar to the area around the church or to a particular part of a town or village. This made for a quasi-protean diversity in the customs, rites and traditions associated with every major calendary ceremony. England was a veritable mosaic of local customs reflecting a multitude of cultural enclaves and local peculiarities, but the most striking disparities were usually to be found in the Celtic fringes and in the northern regions of the country. Unlike the counties of the South-East, which were better served by roads and more receptive to continental influences, those regions still, in the sixteenth century, remembered their own secular traditions and retained a taste for them. One gains a particularly striking impression of the seething pluralism of festive customs and practices by perusing the pages of such scholarly yet popular journals as *The Gentleman's Magazine*, *Notes and Queries* and *Folklore* or by leafing through a volume or two of the copious *Victoria County History*. Apart from these, works of compilation such as those by T.F. Thiselton Dyer, A.R. Wright and, more recently, Christina Hole, list a by no means negligible number of the more important local variants of major festive customs and practices.[24] The diversity is such that it soon makes the researcher's head whirl. If he tries to retain all this picturesque local colour, he is in danger of becoming bogged down in a plethora of concrete details; if, on the other hand, he decides to ignore it, his account of the festive scene is likely to be dry and abstract. Sensing these perils, for the first part of this study I adopted the general rule of confining myself to festive data borrowed, insofar as possible, either from the folklore of Warwickshire and the Cotswolds or else from the traditions of the London region, for it is not only chronologically but also geographically that the present work is connected with the development of Shakespeare's oeuvre. In view of the inertia of collective mentalities, upon which it is so difficult for history to seize, it would clearly have been absurd systematically to eliminate all references that either pre-dated or slightly post-dated the selected period. However, I also adopted as a guiding principle the need to concentrate upon sources that are contemporary, those that either fall within the Elizabethan period or, failing that, are manifestly connected with it. But despite these methodological decisions, we should certainly not forget that the various regions of Elizabethan England were far from being closed in on themselves, nor were their cultures hermetically sealed from one another. They were, on the contrary, for the most part open to the impact of the other traditions and ideas that were in circulation and to that of travellers from other regions and new types of merchandise. The celebration of the various annual festivals provided an opportunity for the spread of culture on the wing and for the ideological peddling of what Jean Duvignaud has neatly termed 'la parole errante' (the wandering word).[25] In the late sixteenth and early seventeenth centuries, the spread of all this festive diversity is likely to have been further speeded up by the many local bans that authorities of Puritan persuasion were imposing.[26] This was probably one of the reasons why the partisans of Sunday observance, who favoured total respect for the day of rest, not only banned activity of any kind on the Lord's Day but also categorically forbade movement from one place to another.[27]

Despite the corrective and levelling effect of nomadic traditions and troupes of entertainers touring with their shows, local disparities remained great. They were, nevertheless, contained within a common spatio-temporal framework. The fact that the places of symbolic importance were identical wherever they were and that everywhere time was ordered by the same seasons and calendar makes it possible to study Elizabethan festivity as a whole within a single framework of space and time. In the villages and small towns of Elizabethan England, the church and its churchyard lay at the heart of ritual space. While the inside of the church was devoted to worship and prayer, the outside was the scene of many festive activities: fair stalls and makeshift stages would often be propped up against the church walls and the cemetery was the scene for all kinds of jollifications (Morris dancing, carousing, feasting and so on). According to Charles Phythian-Adams, such activities were concentrated in the northern part of the cemetery, known as the 'devil's side', which was kept free of tombstones.[28] The festive and the sacred were to be found in similar proximity in the larger towns and even in London itself where, according to John Stow, a maypole loomed over the church of Saint Andrew in Cornhill.[29] The route followed by parades and processions was always the same and everyone knew the spots at which they would pause and the places where shows could be put on: these would be at the churches, triumphal gateways and public fountains or 'conduits'. On the occasions of royal entries and major civic festivals, it would be at these same gates and conduits that certain pageants would take place, in all probability for the entertainment of the general public.[30] At other times of the year (for example, Christmas or May Day), the façades of the houses lining the route would be adorned with holly, ivy or honeysuckle.[31] Nor should we forget the role played by waterways, bridges and ships for, in London, the Lord Mayor's Show could also take the form of a great festival afloat.[32]

The custom of solemnly plotting out the urban space at regular intervals in this way made it possible to imprint its topography on the popular memory just as, in the country, the Rogation ceremony, preserved by the Anglican Church in a simplified form,[33] each year gave the villagers the chance to make a tour of the parish and physically impress the knowledge of its boundaries upon their children by beating them or tripping them by the heels or having the boundary posts struck, a ceremony known as the 'beating of the bounds'.[34] This way of periodically pacing out the parish boundaries, marking out the frontiers between different plots of land and acknowledging the paths and passageways provided a useful set of references in the domain of the customary common law, just as the cadastral register did in that of written law. In this instance, the religious festival represented a ritualization of space and a consecration of property. But there were other festivals too, such as those of Palm Sunday, May Day and Midsummer Day, whose function was precisely the opposite, affording

Oberon and Puck stealing a flower to make the love potion [handwritten annotation]

people licence to commit 'crimes against the vert', that is to say to steal flowers, timber and trees from the forests and their adjacent parks.[35] This provides us with a particularly striking illustration of the ambivalence of the festival: sometimes it served as a solemn ratification of boundaries, points of reference and dividing lines; at other times, it gave a community licence to transgress those boundaries and abolish those dividing lines.

A similar ambivalence or contradiction emerges in connection with the timing of a festival, for a festival was both a commemoration of an event, in many cases unique of its kind, and simultaneously a manifestation of the annual cycle. In the third volume of his *Early English Stages, 1300 to 1660*, Glynne Wickham acknowledges that the festivals of medieval and Tudor England expressed what he calls a 'sense of occasion', but he also establishes an opposition between the cyclical character of the great religious festivals, on the one hand, and the non-recurrent civic ceremonies and court festivities, on the other.[36] Although the latter were organized on the same dates every year, each year the entertainment was stamped with a character all its own, since there was no stereotyped pattern to follow. Instead, the programme would vary according to the plans of the artists to whom the mayor or sovereign, as the case might be, had entrusted the organization of the festivities. The same ambiguity seems to characterize the festivals or rites of passage connected with the celebration of the various stages of life – baptism, marriage and burial. Each of those ceremonies was clearly unrepeatable from the point of view of the individual in whose honour it was held, but at the same time, seen as a virtually inevitable stage of social life, there was a more or less repetitive and unexceptional aspect to it.

In contrast, where the religious and popular festivals of the calendar are concerned, the temporality involved does appear to be fundamentally cyclical, even if each calendary festival corresponds to the perpetuation and celebration of a unique event that once took place in the 'olden days' of the origins of things.[37] In that sense, it is true to say that every major popular calendary festival represented both an expectation and a return.[38] Gradually cyclical festivals became a substitute for figures and dates in the popular memory and eventually came to serve as a temporal point of reference. In the Elizabethan age, legal annals, accountancy books and parish and corporation registers, as well as most of the major events in political, economic, religious and military life, systematically referred in this fashion to the saints of the calendar and the annual feast days, in order to establish their own dates and to set up temporal points of reference. Here, for example, is an extract from the account books of Henry Best, a farmer in charge of a piece of land in the county of York:

It is usual, in pasture groundes wheare they take not upp theyre tuppes, for them to ride about a fortnight or three weekes before Michaellmass; and these lambes that are gotten then will fall aboute Candlemasse, and sometimes a weeke afore...[39]

And in the fort of Berwick, on the Scottish border, Captain Robert Hitchcock provided the soldiers of his garrison with 'Ling... 13 days in Lent, and 1 day in Rogation Week...'.[40] It is clear that, despite the official abolition of the cult of saints, the old dating system was still used to refer to the events of secular life. The old calendar of feast days was still central to the life of the nation, being used more or less universally as a system for measuring time.

Clearly, the calendar as established by the Church, with its series of days consecrated to saints and its fixed and moveable feasts, still played a role of major importance in Elizabethan England (see the calendars in the Appendices, below). It constituted a veritable matrix of time, the effect of which was to subordinate the events of secular life to those of the sacred cycle and to commemorate, as so many configurations that corresponded to the high points of that cycle, a whole host of popular beliefs and folkloric traditions that had developed over the centuries. A whole set of particular rites and festive customs were associated with the Advent and Christmas festivals, while quite different festivities were timed to coincide with the cycle of the moveable feasts of Easter. As we shall see later in more detail, the meanings and functions of the Elizabethan festivals varied depending upon which calendar cycle they belonged to. I may come to see the odd festival, here or there, as having no associations with the calendar and proceed to treat it as a non-recurrent, isolated event. However, the overwhelming majority of the cases that I shall be examining will be found to have their place in the calendar. Within the framework of English society in the late sixteenth and early seventeenth centuries, the calendar seems to me to constitute the basic structure for festivities. Only with a thorough knowledge of its mechanisms and prescriptions can we hope to recover the lost meaning of many celebrations that must have been as splendid as they were ephemeral.

A further, miniature, cycle is incorporated within the wider structural device constituted by the calendar: it consists of the twenty-four hours of the day, divided into two sub-units whose respective importance varies with the seasons and which stand in contrast to one another as day to night. In a sense, day corresponds to the summer half of the year, night to the winter half, the half that, as we shall be seeing, is far richer in festivals (see pp. 93–141). Night seems suited to festivity. Itself a kind of mask, it provokes illusions and stimulates the imagination, constituting a natural invitation to disguise. Besides, during the winter season, nights are longer and there is less work in the fields, so it is understandable that it should give rise to many traditions and festive games whose primary function must have been to fill the long, empty hours.

1 Festivity and popular beliefs in the Elizabethan age

Modern historians all reject the vagaries of the genetic approach to the phenomena of folklore, although all agree that these traditions date back to the earliest antiquity and to pagan times. In the first volume of his study of *The Mediaeval Stage*, E.K. Chambers paid tribute to A. Tille's attempts to reconstruct the primitive calendar of the ancient Celto-Teutonic peoples, but went on to warn the reader of the somewhat conjectural nature of his work, later also criticized by the Swedish scholar, Martin Nilsson.[1] The huge gaps in the documentation relating to the period prior to 1200 combined with the extraordinary confusion occasioned by successive waves of races invading the British Isles[2] have so far thwarted the efforts of scholars researching in this field. So I shall, as far as possible, steer clear of the uncertain paths of genealogy and, in the main, stick to examining the facts and commenting on the texts that I use as evidence.

The many volumes of Migne's *Patrologia Latina* are full of texts in which the Church Fathers express their horror at the persistence of pagan festivals and beliefs (Saturnalia, Calends and so on) and censure the abominations that they foster. In the course of its history, the Church has certainly adopted a wide range of attitudes to this matter, but it would appear that, circumstances permitting, it strove to integrate pagan celebrations into its own calendar, in the hope of unobtrusively changing their immediate meaning. It was thus banking on their progressive assimilation. Just such an attitude seems to have underlain papal policy at the point when England was undergoing christianization, for Gregory the Great sent the following instructions to the mission at Canterbury:

Do not, after all, pull down the fanes. Destroy the idols; purify the buildings with holy water; set relics there; and let them become temples of the true God. So the people will have no need to change their place of concourse, and where of old they were wont to sacrifice cattle to demons, thither let them continue to resort on the day of the saint to whom the church is dedicated, and slay their beasts no longer as a sacrifice, but for a social meal in honour of Him whom they now worship.[3]

Such tolerance allowed the pre-Christian cults to survive, if only in the watered-down form of jollifications and festive traditions that took place close to the dates when the Christian feasts themselves were celebrated,

16

and in the same localities. In Glynne Wickham's view, such co-existence was only possible in towns of some size:

This arrangement was much easier to accommodate in towns than in small villages where practically the only place of public assembly boasting a roof was the parish church; and there, the Christian and the pagan expressions of the same holiday frequently continued to meet each other face to face in the same building.[4]

Nevertheless, evidence of this pagan influence is certainly detectable in the iconographic theme of the 'Green Man', which seems to go back to the fourth or fifth century AD. It is quite frequently to be found in the form of ornamental sculpture on cathedral capitals or church pews.[5] Illustrating the way that ancient pagan beliefs managed to survive within the framework of the Christian faith, the famous legend of Lady Godiva of Coventry provides a good example of the perpetuation of an old cult in a relatively thinly disguised form. It appears that the name 'Godiva' originally referred to an Anglo-Saxon fertility goddess known as Cofa or Goda. In the twelfth century, at the instigation of a local convent, the cult of this ancient founding deity was replaced by the story of a pious benefactress who volunteered to ride naked through the streets of Coventry in order to absolve the inhabitants from the heavy tribute they were supposed to pay to the invaders.[6] Another example of the persistent vitality of the pagan gods is provided in a domain that is particularly revealing in the context of the present study, namely that of the divisions of time. The etymology of the names of the days of the week indicates that after those named for Saturn, the sun and the moon (Saturday, Sunday, Monday), the days are respectively consecrated to Anglo-Saxon gods – Tiw (Tuesday), Woden (Wednesday), Thunor (Thursday) and Frig (Friday). It is also worth noting that two of the chief festivals of the Christian year, Christmas, or Yule, and Easter are known by old names of Saxon origin which refer, respectively, to a period of festivity (*giuli*) and a goddess from a Germanic pantheon (Eostre).[7] Similarly, the Church did not suppress the names of the popular festivals of New Year's Day, May Day and Midsummer's Day, but it did rebaptize them as the Feast of the Circumcision, the Feast of Saint Philip and Saint James and the Feast of the birth of Saint John the Baptist.

Both this etymological accommodation and the attempts that were made to absorb the festivals of the earlier religion reflect the policy of gradual assimilation that the English Church adopted in accordance with the pope's instructions. But they also testify to the limitations of that policy, since we are bound to wonder how far pagan influences continued to affect Christianity even after the latter had gained the upper hand and managed to supplant the earlier cults. It would certainly appear that the

1.1   The 'Green Man' was a variant of the wild man: he too appeared in
       the London pageants and also in the festive shows involving bonfires
       and fireworks.

only ways the Christians were able to prove their superiority over the old
cults was by resorting to the very same spectacular weapons that
involved the supernatural and magic:

> The claim to supernatural power was an essential element in the Anglo-Saxon
> Church's fight against paganism, and missionaries did not fail to stress the
> superiority of Christian prayers to heathen charms.[8]

Gradually, people came to regard relics, holy water and prayers as the
modern equivalents of the old amulets, fetishes and incantations. The
saints, who interceded with God, became healers who could be invoked
to cure all kinds of ills:

> *S. Valentine* excelled at the falling ill! *S. Roch* was good at the plague, *S. Petronill*
> at the ague ... For mad men and such as are possessed with devils, *S. Romane*
> was excellent, and frier Ruffine was also pretilie skilful in that art. For botches
> and boils, *Cosmus* and *Damian*; *S.* Clare for the eies. *S.* Apolline for teeth, *S.* Job
> for the pox. And for sore breasts, *S.* Agatha was as good as Ruminus.[9]

What the ultra-Protestant and ultra-sceptical Reginald Scot is attacking
here is none other than the popular cult of miracles, encouraged by the
hagiography of Jacobus de Voragine, whose *Golden Legend*, published
by Caxton's press in 1483 in an English translation, was to be reprinted
no less than eight times before being banned at the beginning of the
Reformation.[10] According to Charles Read Baskervill, the saints of the
Christian calendar, ostensibly simply intercessors between man and God,
in fact took over the powers of the ancient pagan deities:

> The cult of the saint seems to have sprung up largely as a substitute for that of the
> god of the local shrine, and the liturgy of the saint led to the early miracle play in
> connection with the saint's cult.[11]

Similarly, the old beliefs attached to stones, trees, springs and wells had by no means disappeared[12] and are sometimes detectable in certain religious rites, as John Aubrey points out:

New Yeares Day (Blessing of Fields). To this, seemes to answer, the walking of the young men & maydes who receive the Sacrament on Palme-Sunday, and after dinner walke about the Corne to bless it.[13]

Clearly the Church had taken over the rites of agricultural fertility, whose memory was also preserved in the peals of church bells and the use of fire and candelabra for purificatory purposes (to expel evil spirits). Thus when Bishop Bonner, at the behest of the Archbishop of Canterbury, wrote to the bishops of the province of Canterbury on 28 January 1548, to tell them 'that no candles shall be borne upon candlemas day, nor also from henceforth ashes or palms used any longer . . .',[14] he was expressing not only a desire to simplify the services of the new Anglican Church but also, more fundamentally, a wish to divest it of anything that could be associated with the magic practices of the past. However, the pagan veneration of wells and springs does not seem to have been altogether forgotten even in the seventeenth century, to judge by the following information provided by the same John Aubrey:

In Processions, they used to read a Ghospell at the springs to blesse them, wch hath been discontinued at Sunny-well in Berkshire, but since 1688.[15]

This is probably an allusion to the Rogation of the past, which seem to have retained a style dating from before the royal Injunctions of 1559.[16] That is to say, they continued to be celebrated by spectacular processions organized to incorporate many ecclesiastical chants, banners and ornaments, at the end of which the priest would give his solemn blessing to the fruits of the earth and the flocks. A.L. Rowse cites the case of a priest summoned to Braunton in 1556, 'to come and say masses when our cattle were plagued'.[17] If it is the case that the representatives of the Church traditionally played a double role in the countryside, operating both as the spiritual leaders of the community and as exorcists, it is fair to wonder which of these two functions was more important in the eyes of the local population. To judge from the examples given below, of the two roles that of exorcist seems to have been by far the more highly valued:

there were exorcisms to make the fields fertile; holy candles to protect farm animals; and formal curses to drive away caterpillars and rats and to kill weeds. At the dissolution of the Abbey of Bury St Edmunds there were discovered 'relics for rain, and certain superstitious usages for avoiding of weeds growing in corn'.[18]

Such deviations from the official Christian religion, more or less tolerated in the countryside by the Church but later criticized by Sir

Thomas Browne as 'vulgar errors' and by Aubrey as 'remains of gentilisme' testify to the persistent vitality of pagan superstitions and ancient magical beliefs right down to a relatively late date (the end of the seventeenth century). These survivals in rural regions were the vital source of what William John Thoms was in 1846 to dub 'folklore',[19] a word which was to enjoy considerable future success. They underlay many seasonal and popular festivals which, with the complicity or active collaboration of the parish,[20] made it possible once again to celebrate rites, games and practices that stemmed directly from age-old animism: wells and springs, revered for their miraculous and curative powers, would be visited by the parish on particular feast days and the collective celebration organized around wells (with floral decorations, food, drink and dancing) were an amalgamation of magic and popular festivity. At first glance, the following custom, reported once again by Aubrey, probably simply looks like a jollificatory or Bacchic rite typical of the festivity of the Christmas period:

at Twelve-tyde at night they use in the Countrey to wassaile their Oxen and to have wassaile-Cakes made.[21]

However, the *OED* defines the word 'wassail' as 'the spiced ale used in Twelfth Night and Christmas Eve celebrations' (sense 2) and defines the verb 'to wassail', used transitively (sense 2), as 'to drink to (fruit-trees, cattle) in wassail, in order to ensure their thriving'. One cannot fail to be struck by the parallelism between this popular Epiphany custom and the religious ceremony of the Rogation. It truly looks as though the religious tolerance manifested by Gregory the Great at the time of the conversion of England by Saint Augustine resulted in the amicable cohabitation of a popular religion, or what might be termed folklorized paganism, with the official religion, making it possible for folkloric festivals and ones that were religious in the strict sense of the word to exist in harmony side by side.

Some historians and anthropologists, such as Margaret Murray and Arno Runeberg, have suggested that all these folkloric beliefs and practices might constitute a coherent and autonomous religious corpus. In their view, the chief deities of this popular religion were the fairies and the devil, the worshippers being the witches and wizards who periodically gathered at Sabbaths to celebrate their religion.[22] They suggest that this parallel religion, centred upon the cult of Dianus, the horned god, and based upon initiation into the mysteries of fertility, had been passed down from generation to generation in the greatest secrecy. They claim that Christianity resolved upon a major and direct confrontation with these covert heresies only after the denunciations of the Inquisition and the witchcraft trials that broke out more or less everywhere in Europe towards the end of the sixteenth century. For about thirty years, Margaret Murray's theories gave rise to doubts. Today, however, hardly any historians take them seriously, pointing not only to the lack of method and critical appraisal in her treatment of primary sources (statements given by the accused in witchcraft trials) but also to a generally inadequate grasp of the data of European history.[23] Margaret Murray's chief error seems to have been the somewhat cavalier fashion in which she overstepped the boundaries between periods, cultures and religions for the purposes of her own demonstration. Much of the evidence she used was selectively marshalled in support of a theory which often looks suspiciously like a prefabrication.[24]

For instance, on the subject of fairies, in chapter 2 ('The Worshippers') of her book entitled *The God of the Witches*, she in all seriousness suggests that they were an ancient neolithic race that disappeared early on but was very much alive in the memories of the people of the Middle Ages:

If then my theory is correct, we have in the medieval accounts of the fairies a living tradition of the Neolithic and Bronze Age people who inhabited Western Europe . . . The last authentic account of the fairies occurs in Scotland at the end of the seventeenth century, but in England they had disappeared long before. This strange and interesting people and their primitive civilization degenerated into the diminutive gossamer-winged sprites of legend and fancy, and occur only in stories to amuse children . . .[25]

In making the fairies the representatives of a race and civilization long vanished rather than the imaginary survivors of ancient deities or a pagan ancestor-cult,[26] Margaret Murray was, after all, doing no more than following the story told by Chaucer's Wife of Bath:

> In tholde dayes of the King Arthour,
> Of which that Britons speken greet honour,
> All was this land fulfild of fayerye.
> The elf queen, with hir Ioly companye,
> Daunced ful ofte in many a grene mede;
> This was the olde opinion, as I rede.
> I speke of manye hundred yeres ago;
> But now can no man see none elves mo.
> For now the grete charitee and prayeres
> Of limitours and othere holy freres,
> That serchen every lond and every streem . . .
> This maketh that ther been no fayeryes.[27]

We should no doubt read some irony into the last four lines of this passage, especially bearing in mind that, at the end of the Middle Ages, folklore and magical beliefs really did co-exist without clashing with piety and Christian reverence. It would indeed appear that believing in fairies was not simply a thing of the past or something limited to children. A large proportion of the population of Scotland and the other Celtic fringes of the realm shared these beliefs. In 1605, Pierre Le Loyer wrote as follows:

Les Escossais . . . ont esté diffamez jusques à present d'avoir eu des Nymphes ou Fees visibles, appellees Belles gens, Elfes ou Fairs, foles qui aiment les homes, & cerchent de converser avec eux comme Demons Succubes, & depuis qu'une fois elles les ont amadouez & iouy d'eux, c'est chose fort perilleuse de se pouvoir departir de leur conversation.[28]

(The Scots . . . have until now been maligned as having sensible apparitions of Nymphs and Fairies, known as Fair ones, Elfes or Fairs, mad creatures which dote on men and seek to converse with them as Demons or Succubi, & once they have seduced and enjoyed them, it is a very dangerous thing to try to part company with them.)

As for the peasants of Wales, they displayed 'an astonishing reverence' for the fairies, according to John Penry, writing at about the same time as Reginald Scot.[29] Such superstitious fears can no doubt be explained by the fact that, as M.W. Latham points out, in the sixteenth century fairies were classed as evil spirits: they stole children, dispensed sudden illnesses,[30] destroyed the crops and flocks and were believed to live in hell.[31] The Scots considered apparitions of fairies almost as ominous as those of ghosts, for fairies were the souls of people who died as infants or prematurely or who had not been baptized.[32]

In late-sixteenth-century and early-seventeenth-century England, these beliefs seem to have been much less widespread, although they had not died out completely since Spenser's reference to 'friendly fairies' in the June eclogue of *The Shepheardes Calender* prompted the following gloss from 'E.K.', who produced a commentary on the work:

The opinion of faeries and elves is very old, and yet sticketh very religiously in the minds of some. But . . . the truth is, that there be no such things, nor yet the shadow of the things. But only by a sort of bald friars and knavish shavelings so feigned; which as in all other things, so in that, sought to nurse the common people in ignorance, lest, being once acquainted with the truth of things, they would in time smell out the untruth of their packed pelf, and masspenny religion.[33]

This fervent Protestant polemicist seems to have been taking up the opposite position to Chaucer, despite the fact that the latter was the author upon whom 'E.K.', in the preface of his book, claimed to have modelled himself.[34] But it seems fair to suppose that the hints, antiphrases and irony of the author of *The Canterbury Tales* may well have constituted more effective weapons against the shadows of popular superstition than 'E.K.''s impatient gloss! Besides, even if Spenser was not himself responsible for it, an attack against the fairies such as this was rather ill-judged given that Spenser was soon to situate the world of the fairies, admittedly metamorphosed into poetic imagery and political allegory, at the heart of his major work, *The Faerie Queene*.

All the same, the vehement position adopted by Spenser's commentator does seem to reflect the general attitude towards fairies held by intellectuals in the Elizabethan age, for it is shared by thinkers with views as diametrically opposed as Reginald Scot and James VI of Scotland, whose *Daemonologie*, published in 1597, attacked the fierce scepticism of Scot's *Discoverie of Witchcraft* (1584). Scot refers to the belief in fairies only to support his relativist argument and to rid his contemporaries of the new fear of witches which was in the process of supplanting the old fear of fairies:

And know you this by the waie, that heretofore Robin goodfellow, and Hob gobblin were as terrible, and also as credible to the people, as hags and witches be now: and in time to come, a witch will be as much derided and contemned, and as plainlie perceived, as the illusion and knaverie of Robin goodfellow.[35]

The future James I of England, speaking through Epistemon, claims that he does not take beliefs in fairies seriously either, but does so in order to lay even more emphasis upon the real power of witches and their infamous conspiracy with the powers of evil:

That fourth kinde of spirites, which by the Gentiles was called *Diana*, and her wandring court, and amongst us was called the *Phairie* ... or our good neighboures, was one of the sort of illusiones that was rifest in the time of *Papistrie* ... To speake of the many vain trattles founded upon that illusion: How there was a King and Queene of *Phairie*, of such a iolly court & train as they had a teynd, & dutie, as it were, of all goods: how they naturallie rode and went, eate and drank, and did all other actiones like naturall men and women ... [36]

In the seventeenth century, Robert Burton was to return to the subject in *The Anatomy of Melancholy*, in the chapter entitled 'A Digression of the Nature of Spirits'. He placed fairies in the category of 'terrestrial devils' and enumerated their main characteristics, basing his remarks on a number of authorities and trying hard to preserve a relatively neutral and impartial attitude to the subject:

Some put our fairies into this rank, which have been in former times adored with much superstition, with sweeping their houses, and setting of a pail of clean water, good victuals, and the like, and then they should not be pinched, but find money in their shoes, and be fortunate in their enterprises. These are they that dance on heaths and greens, as Lavater thinks with Trithemius, and as Olaus Magnus adds, leave that green circle, which we commonly find in plain fields ... they are sometimes seen by old women and children.[37]

The note of pseudo-naivety and charming irony on which he concludes this passage constitutes both a cloaked confession of his own incredulity and an indirect recognition of the specific nature of folklore which, as he sees it, belongs to the domain of legends and beliefs handed down through stories and the spoken word. In the disenchanted world of the seventeenth century, fairies no longer had any place except in those despised 'old wives' tales', as John Aubrey nostalgically remarks:

Before Printing, Old-wives Tales were ingeniose, and since Printing came in fashion, till a little before the Civil-warres, the ordinary sort of People were not taught to reade. Now-a-days Bookes are common, and most of the poor people understand letters; and the many good Bookes, and variety of Turnes of Affaires, have putt all the old Fables out of doors: and the divine art of Printing and Gunpowder have frighted away Robin-goodfellow and the Fayries.[38]

This splendid text is not really out to condemn progress, more to give popular culture and the domain of marvels the praise that was due. It reads as a farewell to a vanishing world. The same note of nostalgia for the past is sounded in John Selden's regret that 'There was never a merry world since the Fairies left Dancing, and the Parson left Conjuring.'[39]

We are a long way from those earlier imprecations against papist superstitions. By the end of the seventeenth century, the Anglican Church no longer felt threatened by a possible return to Catholicism, as it constantly had in the Elizabethan period, and proclamations of independence from Rome were no longer fashionable. Now, the overwhelming mood was regret for what had been lost. The favourite theme was the old one of a Golden Age, or rather of a 'Merry England' whose praises were already beginning to be sung at the outset of the Jacobean age. The fact is – and it is an important point to note – that the period when people still believed in fairies was somehow equated with the merry festivals of yesteryear. In the collective mentality, that image was to continue to be associated with the old days, before the divisive civil war and Cromwell's Commonwealth, and in particular with the reign of good Queen Bess.

But perhaps too, as fairies became a part of folklore, they shed the sinister and threatening aspect that credulous rural villagers used to try to appease with nightly offerings of milk and food. Perhaps all that now remained were memories of the 'trooping fairies' of Celtic romances, passing their time with aristocratic entertainments in their palaces under the ground or at the bottom of the sea and delighting in their music and dancing,[40] and of the 'merry wanderer of the night',[41] Robin Goodfellow, the well-loved spirit of the woods and fields and a friendly figure in the cottages that he frequented, far away from castles and princes.[42] Their infernal abode, so familiar to the writers of the Middle Ages, who would compare them to the Proserpina and Pluto of the ancient world,[43] was now forgotten; forgotten too, their ghostly apparitions, their abductions of children and the disappearance of men and women whose company they sought.[44] John Aubrey tells us, in this connection that:

some were led away by the Fairies, as was a Hind riding upon Hapken with corne ... So was a Shepherd of Mr Brown of Winterburn-Basset: But never any afterwards enjoy themselves. He sayd that the ground opened, and he was brought into strange places underground, where they used musicall instruments, violls and Lutes ...[45]

However attractive it is made to seem here, such a descent to hell could be protracted, as we learn from the Scottish ballad of 'Thomas Rhymer', in which the young Thomas accepts the invitation of 'the Queen of fair Elfland' to follow her to her dwelling and disappears for years from the face of the earth:

> He has gotten a coat of the even cloth,
>   And a pair of shoes of velvet green;
> And till seven years were gane and past,
>   True Thomas on earth was never seen.[46]

Katherine Briggs tells us that fairy seducers who lured mortals to their kingdom belonged to the category of 'water spirits and nature spirits' generally considered to be dangerous.[47] And, on the subject of 'water devils', Robert Burton writes:

Olaus Magnus hath a long narration of one Hotherus, a king of Sweden, that having lost his company, as he was hunting one day, met with these water-nymphs or fairies, and was feasted by them; and Hector Boethius, of Macbeth and Banquo, two Scottish lords that, as they were wandering in the woods, had their fortunes told by three strange women.[48]

Such variations on the theme of travellers losing their way and encountering fairies show, in this case through the example of Macbeth and Banquo, that fairies were sometimes closely connected with witches[49] or were indeed one and the same by another name. What established the connection between visits to an underworld of sensual delights and witchcraft was probably the belief that mortals who visited the land of fairies were possessed by them and initiated into diabolical practices. Margaret Murray cites many texts, drawn from primary sources, that testify to the close relations supposed to exist between some witches and the fairies[50] and she also notes a number of coincidences between dates when fairies were sighted and those on which the witches' Sabbaths were believed to take place:

The original celebrations belonged to the May–November year ... The chief festivals were: in the spring, May Eve (April 30), called Roodmas or Rood Day in Britain and Walpurgis Nacht in Germany; in the autumn, November Eve (October 31), called in Britain Allhallow Eve.[51]

As for the dates favoured by fairies to show themselves to human beings, M.W. Latham notes that in Scotland, 'All Hallow Even seems to have been regarded as the period in which they were most active', while in England, 'the first day of May and Midsummer Eve were the two periods when they were most powerful and most enjoyed themselves'.[52] There is really nothing surprising about these coincidences between, on the one hand, the dates of the key festivals of the calendar, on the threshold of either the winter or the summer halves of the year, and on the other the times when the supernatural erupted and irrational forces were unleashed. They testify to the survival of animist beliefs of the pre-Christian era, beliefs that would periodically surface on dates which coincided with those of the old Celtic festivals.[53] Festivals had the effect of triggering the collective memory. Magical beliefs that had lain dormant for most of the year were suddenly reawakened and came back to life for the duration of the festival.

These temporal coincidences aside, it is worth noting that the tradition of devilry had, since the Middle Ages, been a source of comedy that figured in Mystery and Morality plays as well as in the Mummers' burlesque sketches in which the character of Beelzebub would be played by a clown.[54] Robert Weimann makes the same point in connection with the figure of Harlequin:

> The pagan *Herlekin* (like the more modern *Erl-könig*) was 'connected with the fairies' and was followed by a train of witches and hide-covered creatures; he was branded a 'devil' by mediaeval theologians, and made his early appearance on the stage as a comic devil and prince of the fairies in the *Jeu de la Feuillée* (1262).[55]

This distant association of the burlesque with agricultural fertility rites[56] that underlay beliefs in fairies and witches perhaps to some extent explains this remarkable conjunction of laughter and devilry. But more fundamentally, as Stuart Clark points out, the effect of both satanic rites and festive practices is to call into question the established order and the everyday world and both phenomena obey a logic of inversion: 'Renaissance descriptions of the nature of Satan, the character of hell and, above all, the ritual activities of witches shared a vocabulary of misrule . . . '.[57]

Now, this term 'misrule' was used to refer both to the anarchy and disorder that resulted from tyrannical and arbitrary government and also to the joyful pandemonium that ensued when the world was turned upside-down and festive confusion reigned.[58] In fact, Puritan pamphleteers such as Stubbes were to exploit this linguistic ambiguity and represent the May festivals as diabolical pastimes and the 'Lord of Misrule' as a rival Satan.[59] But such attempts to assimilate popular festivity to the Devil's Sabbath were less influential in England than in France, for example, where Jean Savaron launched an attack against Carnival masquerades, claiming that 'the Devil is the author of masques and mummery', both of which he regarded as 'festivals of Satan'.[60] In England they were less successful as, here, the mythology of the witches' nocturnal Sabbath had exerted less fascination than on the continent.[61] In the cases of witchcraft and possession brought to trial in England at the end of the sixteenth century, the emphasis tended to be laid upon the malice of the witch or the spells that she had cast upon her victim, rather than upon her dealings with evil spirits. Keith Thomas accounts for this remarkable difference by pointing to the autonomy of the Church of England and its distrust of exorcists and other Catholic inquisitors and also the fact that the infamous *Malleus Maleficarum*, published in 1486 by two Dominican inquisitors, Heinrich Kramer and Jacob Sprenger,[62] had made little impact in England.

What John Aubrey has to say on this matter is extremely revealing. On the subject of the customs of the month of May, he refers to assemblies of witches only in the context of Germanic beliefs which he immediately contrasts to the much less alarming customs of the youth of England:

'Tis commonly sayd in Germany, that the witches doe meet in the night before the first of May upon an high Mountain, called the Blocks-berg, situated in Ascanien, where they together with the Devils doe dance, and feast, and the common People doe the night before ye said day fetch a certain thorn, and stick it at their house-door, believing the witches can doe them no harm.
Mdm. at Oxford the Boyes doe blow Cows horns & hollow Canes all night; and on May-day the young maids of every parish carry about their parish Garlands of Flowers, wch afterwards they hang up in their Churches.[63]

The nocturnal orgy of the witches' Sabbath is a far cry from this pastoral celebration, in which the purpose of the gathering of greenery and flowers is precisely to guard against the evil spells that might be cast by witches. Reginald Scot also comments upon these May customs which turned the festival into, among other things, an operation against witchcraft and an exorcism:

To be delivered from witches, they hang in their entries hay-thorn, otherwise white-thorn, gathered on May-day.[64]

The world of devilry and witchcraft was thus seen as quite the reverse of festivity. More often than not, furthermore, witches were represented as kill-joys who wrecked the jollifications with confusion and cacophony.[65] Just as signs of fairies at work were feared at the time of christenings, so too was the presence of witches at weddings, particularly on account of the dreaded spell which killed desire, preventing the husband from acquitting himself as he should on his wedding night.[66] In some remote provinces where these superstitions were still very strong, would-be bridegrooms had to take precautions against evil spells of this kind and perform a rite of exorcism. In the Isle of Man, custom demanded that they should walk thrice around the church before the marriage ceremony.[67] Even ceremonies of a private and occasional nature, such as weddings, were thus considered dangerous periods for the individuals concerned, for they exposed them to hostile influences. In circumstances such as these, customs and traditions meant more than simple loyalty to the past and the rules of community life: it amounted to the best way of averting misfortune.

One of the reasons why curses and evil spells were often in evidence on the occasion of family or village celebrations of this kind is that a particular individual or several of those present were likely to be the victims of the vengeance of some old woman who had not been invited to the party. Keith Thomas tells us that the exclusion of certain people from the traditional festivities to which everybody normally had a right to be invited frequently lay behind incidents of witchcraft:

Another cause of offence was a failure to invite the witch to some common celebration. In a village community a man had a social duty to invite his neighbours to participate in his christenings, funerals, sheep-shearings or harvest homes. Guests attended such occasions as of right, and it was a positive slight to refuse an invitation to anyone who was eligible.[68]

However, the indications are that in late-sixteenth-century and early-seventeenth-century England it was not just that particular individuals deemed to be undesirable would be subject to a kind of local or occasional ostracism. There are examples to show that a conflict existed between two different codes of behaviour that now clashed: on the one hand, a system of traditional obligations, in which hospitality and charity were regarded as sacred duties; on the other, a new spirit of individualism that tended more and more to reject those obligations as customs by now outdated. In the old days, it had been customary for the village poor to be invited to eat at the Manor table during the period of the twelve days of Christmas. Now, the local aristocracy turned its back on the simple festivities of the countryside, including its own charitable obligations, preferring the more egoistical and sophisticated pleasures of the towns. During the Elizabethan period, voices are raised on all sides to deplore this state of affairs.[69]

Keith Thomas, like Alan Macfarlane, sees this clash between two different ethics as one of the elements that encouraged witchcraft trials. These were frequently fuelled by the hatred that existed between close neighbours.[70] The guilt and anxiety felt by those who had failed to respect the old code of behaviour (by failing to give alms or by not inviting some individual to some celebration) was such that the slightest sign could change it into hatred for the person whom (from the point of view of tradition) they had wronged. The withholding of charity or hospitality led those who felt guilty to imagine themselves the victims of the person they had wronged, at the first sign of inexplicable illness or other unexpected phenomena. It may be that, indirectly, the seasonal festivals, which some regarded as a source of heavy obligations and as occasions likely to unleash the forces of evil and resentment, came to seem increasingly undesirable. Perhaps that is one reason why members of the élite sometimes supported the recriminations of the Puritans, in whose eyes there was no doubt at all that Satan himself was calling the tune on these festive occasions.[71] In truth, the Puritans were not altogether mistaken, since festivals did encourage a periodic return of old pagan beliefs, reactivated in the rites, games and ceremonies of folklore that were prompted by every celebration in the calendar. But before embarking upon a more detailed analysis of all these beliefs and the festivities that they occasioned, we should pause to consider the general attitude of the period and the superstitions that affected it.

We know that, according to the Ptolemaic view of the world that still prevailed during the Renaissance, the course of earthly things, situated in the sublunary zone below the sphere of the fixed stars, was subject to accident and change ('mutabilitie'). The moon with its cycles therefore exerted a particularly important influence upon everything to do with agriculture, medicine and magic and many other spheres of human activity too.[72] Furthermore, the belief in a system in which the microcosm and the macrocosm were intimately related made every individual directly dependent upon the movements of the planets and bestowed the first importance upon astrological pronouncements and predictions. Hence the vogue for almanacs which listed the dates of the moveable feasts and those of the feast days and fast days, as well as the days that were propitious for blood-letting, purging or bathing and the periods that were good or bad for planting, sowing and castrating animals.[73] They also purveyed information concerning the different phases of the moon, forthcoming eclipses and predictions of a meteorological nature.[74] Time, far from being regarded as a measurable quantity or a simple factor in observable physical phenomena, remained an uneven element which was subject to mysterious fluctuations. The existence of long periods, such as Lent, that were subject to various prohibitions affecting eating and sexual behaviour[75] helped to make the quality of time seem to vary from one part of the year to another. It was proverbial, for instance, that the relationship between the sexes changed in leap years, when tradition had it that women should take the initiative in matters of love.[76] Then there was also a host of days that were either propitious or unpropitious, and dangerous periods when it was safer not to venture upon any enterprise at all. Holy Innocents' Day (28 December), for example, was reputed to bring bad luck to anyone who went back to work then.[77] The twelve days of Christmas were, in general, not favourable for work; and it behoved one to beware of the three black Mondays in the year, as Lord Burghley warned his son, in a letter crammed with good advice:

Though I think no day amisse to undertake any good enterprize or businesse in hande, yet have I observed some, and no meane clerks, very cautionarie to forbeare these three Mundayes in the yeare, which I leave to thine owne consideration, either to use or refuse, viz. 1. The first Munday in April, which day *Caine was born, and his brother Abel slaine.* 2. The second Munday in August, which day *Sodome and Gomorrah were destroyed.* 3. The last Monday in December, which day *Judas was born,* that betrayed our Saviour Christ.[78]

One day, among others, considered as taboo or unlucky was Saint Mark's Day, which fell two days after Saint George's Day, on 25 April. In his biography of Shakespeare, Samuel Schoenbaum argues that this explains why Shakespeare, believed to have been born on 23 April, was not christened until three days later, on 26 April 1564:

if Shakespeare was born on the 23rd, he should, according to the Prayer Book, have been baptized by the 25th. But perhaps superstition intervened – people considered St Mark's Day unlucky. 'Black Crosses' it was called; the crosses and altars were almost to Shakespeare's day hung with black, and (some reported) the spectral company of those destined to die that year stalked the churchyard.[79]

Saint Swithin's Day (15 July) was a key date in the domain of weather predictions or rather forecasts. It was believed – as in France of Saint-Médard – that if it rained on that day, it would continue to do so for the next forty.[80]

In general, these superstitions concerning both time and the weather, still rife in Shakespeare's England, reflected the predominance of the agricultural way of life, in which the rhythm of daily activities was directly linked with climatic factors and the seasonal cycle. On that account, the old religious calendar that continued to be used, with very little modification, until well after the Reformation, was better adapted to a rural society and the ritual of court ceremonies and festivals than it was to the needs of urban chronology. In the country, the points of reference provided by nature, backed up by the village church bells, were all that were needed. Sunrise and sunset sufficed to mark the beginning and end of a shepherd's day, for, as Spenser reminds us in his *Shepheardes Calender,* he would wake at cock-crow and drive his beasts homeward at dusk. On the other hand, town life called for a more precise measurement of time, and the rhythm of the working week concluded by a day of rest on Sunday became increasingly accepted, as industry and trade expanded. Keith Thomas tells us that it was the invention of the pendulum clock in 1657 that made it possible to replace the old seasonal routines definitively with a stricter and more rational chronological system.[81] The changeover encountered resistance and was by no means smooth, even though it did not happen overnight. It only took general effect from the end of the seventeenth century on. But in the Elizabethan period, people were already keenly aware of the opposition between, on the one hand, the natural rhythms of the countryside and the forest, where there were no clocks to register the passing of the hours ('there's no clock in the forest', Orlando reminds Rosalind, who probably still fancied herself to be at court[82]), and on the other the carefully recorded time of the towns. For a peasant, the nights were punctuated only by the random cries of animals or birds and in the daytime he established his bearings from the position of the sun in the sky or from a sundial. But a town-dweller could not afford such vagueness with regard to time. During the day, the church bells and clocks that struck the hour kept him regularly informed of the time; at night, the 'bellman', whose task was to protect the sleeping townsfolk from the dangers of the dark and to raise the alarm in case of fire.[83] As well as the services of the 'bellman' and the patrols normally detailed to mount the watch, the larger towns could call upon troupes of ambulant musicians whose twofold function was to make music at municipal festivals and to mount watch for part of the year, at the time of the 'waits':[84]

Every wait during the times anciently accustomed to watch and walk in the nights through the streets of his honourable city (that is to say) from the Monday next following after Allhallows day until the week before Christmas; and from the first Monday in . . . Lent until our Lady-day, shall be ready and meet at . . . eleven of the clock, at the furthest [of] the places heretofore usual and accustomed.[85]

The function of these 'waits' was in part to lay on a show and promote festivity, but their role as night watchmen drew attention to the considerable differences in respect of the structuring of time that existed, in this period, between the towns and the countryside. The qualitatively differentiated time of the countryside, with its succession of sharp contrasts,[86] that set the rhythm for village life, stood in contrast to the notion of a more homogeneous temporality, based on the regular units of the day and the week, that governed the lives of town-folk. The more primitive organization of time, based upon observance of the plant and animal cycles and the phases of the moon had, over the centuries, become perfectly co-ordinated with the calendar framework imposed by the Church: the positioning of the saints' days in the calendar frequently synchronized the marvels of religion with seasonal events and popular traditions.[87] But that system was now to be replaced by the more strictly quantitative division of time that was imposed by the expansion of the towns and industry. One result was that magical beliefs about time began to disappear and this, in its turn, led to the gradual decline of seasonal festivities.[88]

2   Festivity and society in Shakespeare's time

We shall later be studying bourgeois festivals, the festivals of school-children and students and aristocratic or royal festivity during the Elizabethan period, but we must begin with the popular festivals of the lowest rung of the social ladder, which also happens to be the category in which the traditions of festivity were the richest and the most vigorous. It was at the popular level that the memory of these customs was most faithfully preserved for, as we have seen in connection with superstitions about time, at this level festivals were still invested with certain magical properties as well as functioning as safety valves in the domains of sexual behaviour and eating and drinking habits. We should certainly not underestimate the contributions that scholarly, clerical, chivalric and other esoteric elements made to festivity in general; however, popular memories do seem to have remained extremely close to the origins and vigorous sources of these traditions.

Popular festivity

It is impossible to give a brief, clear definition of the scope of the adjective 'popular' as applied to festivals and culture. Any accurate definition would involve us in a lengthy digression for, by reason of both the complexity of the subject and differing ideological attitudes, specialists in this domain are a long way from unanimous agreement.[1] In any event, the criteria of class suggested by certain sociologists do not seem appropriate for the situation in Elizabethan England, where the prosperous urban artisans and the small-scale landowners formed a group economically distinct from the popular strata, yet continued to identify fully with their culture. In the domain of popular festivity and culture, oppositions between different age-groups (children and groups of unmarried people as opposed to married and older people), between the sexes and between the towns, on the one hand, and the countryside on the other, form the bases for solidarities of a horizontal nature which render null and void attempts to identify these things exclusively with any particular social category. At a time when, under the influence of Puritanism, gravity was beginning to be regarded as a virtue, the devotees of popular festivity were first and foremost those who were fundamentally attached to laughter. This was a point made by Keith Thomas in a long article in *The Times Literary Supplement*:

The new cult of decorum thus meant that it was only the vulgar who could go on laughing without restraint. In 1649 a contemporary observed that those 'most apt to laughter' were 'children, women and the common people' . . .[2]

There are other aspects to the popular culture of Elizabethan England and we shall be returning to them later. But it is characterized first and foremost by its general commitment to a world of merriment. The American anthropologist Robert Redfield has tried to define this popular culture by establishing an opposition between two very distinct traditions: 'The great tradition is cultivated in schools or temples: the little tradition works itself out and keeps itself going in the lives of the unlettered in their village communities . . .'.[3] In his book on popular culture, Peter Burke lists many of the elements of this 'little tradition':

There are folksongs and folktales; devotional images and decorated marriage chests; mystery plays and farces; broadsides and chap-books; and above all, festivals, like the feasts of the saints and the great seasonal festivals such as Christmas, New Year, Carnival, May and Midsummer.[4]

As can be seen, festivals quite rightly figure prominently in this inventory, for it is in the Masques, music, dancing and cuisine of the various festivals that this culture, which was so much a part of everyday behaviour, was most fully expressed. It is primarily because English popular culture of the Renaissance is so closely associated with festivals that it appears as a commitment to a joyous world and way of life.

Let us now turn to the testimony of contemporary witnesses of the many manifestations of this popular culture. It comes as no surprise that we can detect a note of scorn in the remarks of people who prided themselves upon their refinement and education, as they comment upon popular entertainments. Thus, in *A Discourse of English Poetrie* (1586), William Webbe has some harsh things to say about ballads, jigs and other doggerel:

If I let passe the uncountable rabble of ryming Ballet makers, and compylers of senceless sonets, who be most busy, to stuffe every stall full of grosse devises and unlearned Pamphlets: I trust I shall with the best sort be held excused. For though many such can frame an Alehouse song of five or six score verses, hobbling uppon some tune of a Northern Jygge, or Robyn hoode . . . yet if these might be accounted Poets . . . surely we shall shortly have whole swarmes of Poets . . .[5]

This predictable attack against the rhymesters who curried favour with the masses shows the low esteem in which popular culture was held so far as poetry was concerned and perhaps also betrays a certain jealousy on the part of the author regarding the facile, but no doubt profitable, success enjoyed by these composers of ballads. The text also tells us indirectly which were the popular favourites of the period ('Alehouse song', 'Northern Jygge', 'Robyn hoode'...). Puttenham provides us with information of an equally satirical nature in *The Arte of English Poesie*, where he mentions:

small & popular Musickes song by these *Cantabanqui* upon benches and barrels heads where they have none other audience then boys or countrey fellowes that passe by them in the streete, or else by blind harpers or such like taverne minstrels that give a fit of mirth for a groat, & their matters being for the most part stories of old time, as the tale of Sir *Topas*, the reportes of *Bevis of Southampton, Guy of Warwicke*, and *Clymme of the Clough* & such other old Romances or historicall rimes, made purposely for recreation of the common people at Christmasse diners and *brideales*, and in tavernes & alehouses and such other places of base resort, also they be used in Carols and rounds and such light or lascivious Poemes, which are commonly more commodiously uttered by these buffons or vices in playes then by any other person.[6]

It is interesting, first, to note that the titles of the 'old Romances' that Puttenham mentions also figured in the library of a rich artisan of Coventry. This Captain Cox was famous for having put on a 'Hock Tuesday Play' for Queen Elizabeth's entertainment in the course of the festivities organized in her honour at Kenilworth, in July 1575. The play was preserved for posterity thanks to a letter from one Robert Laneham to his friend Humphrey Martin, in which Laneham gives a detailed description of the royal festivities at which he was fortunate enough to be present.[7] It is also worth noting that in Puttenham's work every title cited is mentioned in association with the celebration during which the ballad was sung (either Christmas or a marriage feast). Finally, Puttenham also refers to the considerable licence of the language used in these popular songs, remarking that they were almost as coarse as the jokes of a theatre clown. It is thus hardly surprising that on the Elizabethan stage it was the clown who became one of the major representatives of popular culture.

Indeed, a succession of men of letters and writers of satire, from Philip Sidney to Joseph Hall,[8] expressed their distaste for scenes in which the clown was represented alongside personages of great dignity. This is the kind of popular vulgarity that Marlowe seems to be trying to get away from when he writes, in the prologue to *Tamburlaine*:

> From jygging vaines of riming mother wits,
> And such conceits as clownage keepes in pay,
> Weele leade you to the stately tent of War:
> Where you shall heare the Scythian Tamburlaine,
> Threatning the world with high astounding tearms
> And scourging Kingdoms with his conquering sword.[9]

Here, tragedy is clearly considered a noble and 'high' art in which the rustic antics of the clown are out of place. The 'jig' to which Marlowe alludes was a burlesque interlude which was frequently overtly obscene[10] and sometimes incorporated personal attacks of a satirical nature much appreciated by the famous 'groundlings' of the public theatres.[11] For other reasons than Marlowe's, that is to say in the interests of public order rather than simply on aesthetic grounds, a number of Justices of the Peace had occasion to ban such jigs, as in the 1612 order cited below:

An order for suppressinge of Jigges att the end of Playes – Whereas Complaynte have [sic] beene made at this last Generall Sessions, that by reason of certayne lewde Jigges songes and daunces used and accustomed at the play-house called the Fortune in Gouldinglane, divers cutt-purses and other lewde and ill disposed persons in greate multitudes doe resorte thither at th'end of everye playe, many tymes causing tumultes and outrages . . .[12]

The popularity that these jigs enjoyed brings to mind that of some of the satirical May games[13] that were staged in the villages as part of the May Day festivities. It shows how much the public theatre in London had inherited from the spirit and traditions of popular provincial festivals. William Harrison's *A Description of England* (1577) has left us a picture of similar forms of popular behaviour relating to the culinary tastes and table manners in the English towns and countryside:

The artificer and husbandman make greatest accompt of such meat as they may soonest come by . . . (except it be in London when the companies of every trade meet on their quarter daies, at which time they be nothing inferior to the nobilitie) . . . In feasting also, this latter sort, (I mean the husbandmen), doo exceed after their maner: especially at brideales, purifications of women, and such od meetings, where it is incredible to tell what meat is consumed & spent, each one bringing such a dish, or so manie (with him), as his wife & hee doo consult upon . . .[14]

Harrison draws a contrast between the public and regular jollifications of corporations that were held on Quarter Days[15] and the festivities of a family or occasional nature enjoyed by those who worked on the land. The second aspect of his opposition focuses upon the contrast between quality and quantity, the refinement of the city banquet as opposed to the gluttony of the countryside. He then elaborates his comparison in relation to table manners and conversation on these special occasions:

To conclude, both the artificer and the husbandman are sufficientlie liberall & verie freendlie at their tables; and when they meete, they are so merie without malice, and plaine without inward (Italian or French) craft and subtilitie, that it would doo a man good to be in companie among them. Herein onelie are the inferior sort (somewhat) to be blamed, that being thus assembled, their table is now and then such as savoureth of scurrilitie and ribaldrie, a thing naturallie incident to carters and clowns, who thinke themselves not to be merie & welcome, if their foolish veines in this behalfe be never so little restrained.[16]

After criticizing the gluttony of these popular banquets, Harrison censures the ribaldry that they occasion, joining his voice to those raised in condemnation of the obscenity of jigs and the jokes of clowns in general. Nicholas Breton, the author of a short text entitled *The Mother's Blessing* (1602), passes similar judgement in a scene where a mother gives her son the following advice:

> Make not thy musique of a Country Jigge,
> But leave the Lout, to tread the Morris-daunce...[17]

As the simple pleasures of the countryside and the villagers' imperfect renderings of traditional songs and dances began to seem uncouth to upwardly mobile social strata in quest of more refinement, the popular festival became synonymous with vulgarity. Thus, in James Shirley's *The Lady of Pleasure* (1637), a fine lady, ironically named Lady Bornwell, declares herself to be far above these poor country junketings:

> To hear a fellow
> Make himself merry (and his horse) with whistling
> Sellinger's round! To observe with what solemnity
> They keep their wakes, and throw for pewter candlesticks,
> How they become the morris, with whose bells
> They ring all into Whitsun ales, and sweat,
> Through twenty scarfs and napkins, till the hobbyhorse
> Tire and the Maid Marian, dissolved to a jelly,
> Be kept for spoon meat...[18]

To tell the truth, in Shirley's play it is Lady Bornwell who is made ridiculous by her snobbishness, rather than the Morris dancers about whom she is so scathing; nevertheless, her attitude is typical enough of the desire for distinction that was already increasingly marked among the provincial élites of the Elizabethan period. It is, however, interesting to note that no such disdain is expressed in Castiglione's treatise on society behaviour and good manners, *The Book of the Courtier*, considered indispensable bedside reading for anyone with pretensions to belonging to smart society. Indeed, Pallavicino, one of the interlocutors in this book (which is written in the form of a dialogue), tells Federico:

In Lombardy we are not so fussy. On the contrary, many of our gentlemen are to be found, on holidays, dancing all day in the open air with the peasants...

At which Federico remarks:

I think he should be allowed to ... dance the morris and the *brando* as well, but not in public unless he is at a masked ball.[19]

Other features that critics deplored in the popular taste displayed in games and festivals were their cruelty and violence. In the text cited earlier, Sidney waxes indignant that people should laugh at cripples and beggars and so contravene the laws of hospitality as to make fun of foreigners.[20] Thomas Fuller for his part deplores the violence and excessive boisterousness that villagers deploy in their Sunday sports:

It is no pastime with country-clowns that cracks not pates, breaks not shins, bruises not limbs, tumbles and tosses not all the body. They think themselves not warm in their gears, till they are on fire; and count it but dry sport, till they swim in their own sweat.[21]

Accidents must have been common in these veritable jousts and the case of the actor who played the young husband in the 'Brydeale' performed for Queen Elizabeth at Kenilworth, of whom Robert Laneham writes that he was 'lame of a leg, that in his youth was broken at football',[22] was certainly no exception. Festivity, like warfare, had its casualties.

But one of the most common criticisms of popular sport and festivities was that they fostered practices linked with paganism and distracted the faithful from the proper respect due to Sunday services and prayers. The records of ecclesiastical courts for this period abound in examples of irreverence shown towards religion at festival time. People are found guilty of dancing the 'morice' in church in the middle of the sermon, fixing a pair of horns over the church door and even, as in the case of a certain Catherine Banckes of Graies Thorock, attending church dressed as a man.[23] In a sermon preached in Saint Paul's Cathedral on Saint Bartholomew's Day in 1578, John Stockwood was already complaining over such practices:

There be not many places where ye word is preached besides the Lords day ... yet even that day the better part of it is horriblie prophaned by devellishe inventions, as with Lords of Missrule, Morice dauncers, Maygames, in somuch that in some places they shame not in ye time of divine service, to come and daunce about the Church, and without to have men naked dancing in nettes, which is most filthie ...[24]

The encroachment of popular culture and festivity upon the strictly religious festivals was frequently to be deplored during this period. Preachers of Puritan persuasion went so far as to call upon the judicial and municipal authorities to ban all these practices, which they considered to be profanatory.[25] In one famous case, recounted by Bishop Latimer in a sermon preached on 12 April 1549 in the presence of King Edward VI, it was the popular festival of Robin Hood that had ousted the religious one and the church had remained closed throughout the merrymaking:

I came once myself to a place, riding on a journey homeward from London, and I sent word over night into the town that I would preach there in the morning because it was holy day . . . The church stood in my way, and I took my horse, and my company, and went thither. I thought I should have found a great company in the church, and when I came there, the church door was fast locked. I tarried there half an hour and more, at last the key was found, and one of the parish comes to me and says: 'Sir, this is a busy day with us, we cannot hear you, it is Robin Hood's day. The parish are gone abroad to gather for Robin Hood. I pray you let them not.' I was fain there to give place to Robin Hood; I thought my rochet should have been regarded, though I were not, but it would not serve, it was fain to give place to Robin Hood's men.[26]

The bishop's rancour on this May Day (which was probably the festival that he refers to as 'Robin Hood's day') seems to be occasioned more by the open flouting of his own authority in preference for Robin Hood, whom he goes on to call a 'traitor and thief', than by the fact that Christians were indulging in pleasures of pagan origin and neglecting their religious duties. But if we are to credit the allegations made in one of the Marprelate Tracts entitled *Hay any Work for Cooper*, which shows Puritan inspiration, it was sometimes the priest himself who set the example, abandoning his pulpit in the middle of the service, to join in the Morris dance:

There is a neighbour of ours, an honest priest, who was sometime . . . a Vice in a play, for want of a better. His name is Glibbery of Halstead in Essex. He goes much to the pulpit. On a time, I think it was the last May, he went up with a full resolution to do his business with great commendations. But see the fortune of it. A boy in the church, hearing either the Summer Lord with his May-game, or Robin Hood with his Morris dance, going by the church – out goes the boy. Good Glibbery, though he were in the pulpit, yet had a mind to his old companions abroad (a company of merry grigs, you must think them to be, as merry as a Vice on a stage), seeing the boy going out, finished his matter presently, with John of London's Amen . . . and so came down, and among them he goes.[27]

The good Glibbery, whose guilty frivolity is fastened upon by this Puritan pamphlet written against the improprieties of the Anglican clergy and the corruption of bishops, was no doubt one of those humble, poorly educated parish priests who were close to the people and saw no contradiction between the celebration of religious ceremonies and participation in popular merrymaking. The churchwardens' registers of many parishes testify to the fact that the Church itself was often the organizer and main beneficiary of these festivals. But by the end of the sixteenth century voices were being raised on all sides in protest at these confusions and to decry the ignorance of the holy scriptures among the people. In 1606, Nicholas Bownd wrote of these popular strata of society:

they are more cunning in a tale of Robin Hood, than they are in the histories of the Bible . . . .[28]

The general truth of that remark is borne out by the fact that at this time the common people tended to swear 'by Robin Hood' or 'by Maid Marian', as others swore 'by God' or 'by Saint George', as a number of Jest Books show.[29] The name of Robin Hood was also sometimes invoked as a rallying cry by those bent on defying the power of the Church and its teachings, as in the case of the widow, Margerie Stubbes, who, on 11 July 1633, made the following statement before her judges:

Stubbes told examinate that she might tell them a taile . . . of Robin Hoode, worth foure and twentie of that, meaninge of the catechisme.[30]

Richard Axton cites the case of a Calvinist polemicist who claimed that he would rather spend a penny or two to see a play about Robin Hood, or some other Morris dance, than be present when priests were aping around.[31] It would probably be an exaggeration to speak of popular heresy in connection with all these manifestations of irreverence towards religion, for the anthropological theories that turned Robin Hood into some kind of pagan deity of vegetation are nowadays dismissed by all serious historians.[32] Apart from these folkloric manifestations, there really are no indications of any organized cult running parallel to the official religious ceremonies. Because he was seen as a righter of wrongs, a champion archer and a hunter of distinction as well as a merry fellow who enjoyed life, Robin Hood was the very epitome of a popular hero. The ballads that celebrated his exploits and the Morris dances of May Day and Whitsun, later taken up by the popular theatre, kept his memory everywhere alive.[33]

The sources that inform us about the popular festivals and culture of the Elizabethan period and the tastes and preferences of simple folk which we have been citing should be interpreted with a measure of caution, given that they express essentially negative and critical attitudes. This was the period when, as L.B. Wright points out, 'the differentiation in literary taste as well as in the social structure became more clearly marked'.[34] Even an author such as Thomas Nashe who, in his satirical sallies, frequently refers to the traditions and language of the common people, adopts an ironic and condescending tone toward the humble Humphrey King, a writer who produced verses to mark particular occasions and an enthusiast of the Morris dance, to whom Nashe dedicated his short satirical work entitled *Lenten Stuff* (1599):

To his worthy good patron, Lusty Humphrey according as the townsmen do christen him; Little Numps, as the Nobility and Courtiers do name him; and Honest Humphrey, as all his friends and acquaintance esteem him, King of the Tobacconists *hic & ubique*, and a singular Mecaenas to the Pipe and the Tabour.[35]

Humphrey King, in a pamphlet entitled *An Halfe-penny Worth of Wit*, stands up for the popular festivals and heroes, in the face of the attacks of the Puritans then bent on discrediting them. He takes the opportunity to launch into a veritable paean of praise for popular culture:

> Let us talk of *Robin Hoode*,
> And Little *John* in merry Shirwood,
> Of Poet *Skelton* with his pen,
> And many other merry men,
> Of May-game Lords, and Summer Queenes,
> With Milke-maids, dancing o'er the Greenes,
> Of merry *Tarlton* in our time,
> Whose conceite was very fine,
> Whom Death hath wounded with his Dart,
> That lov'd a May-pole with his heart.
> His humour was to please all them
> Hee talks and prates he knows not what,
> Of May-poles and of merriments
> That have no spot of ill pretence.
> But I wonder now and then,
> To see the wise and learned men,
> With countenance grim, and many a frowne
> Cries, Maisters, plucke the May-pole downe.
> To heare this news, the Milke-maid cries,
> To see the sight, the Plough-man dies.[36]

In this passage, the author proves himself worthy of the title 'Mecaenas to the Pipe and the Tabour' with which, on the strength of his fondness for Morris dances and maypoles, Nashe had honoured him. At the same time, he somewhat heavy-handedly stresses that festivals were indissociable from the popular culture in general. It is hardly surprising to find the poet Skelton, an author of anticlerical satires and a hero of the Jest Books, together with the actor Tarlton, renowned for his clown roles in the public theatres, rubbing shoulders here, alongside the inevitable Robin Hood.[37]

There are other examples too that testify to the deep attachment of humble folk to their own traditions and periodic festivals, in particular to the right to dance and wrestle on the village green after the Sunday service, as Wye Saltonstall reminds us, in a vignette entitled 'A Poore Village':

Their Church is a great way off, whether they goe on Sundayes, that they may talke in the Church-yard and their zeal hangs so after the Taber and Pipe, that they will not be perswaded from dauncing after Service; for they say tis an old custome and therefore lawfull.[38]

In another collection of vignettes, presented as 'characters' and published about fifteen years before Saltonstall's work, Sir Thomas Overbury's description of the Franklin had already pointed to the loyalty that country folk felt for the old customs and calendary celebrations:

He allowes of honest pastime, and thinkes not the bones of the dead any thing brused, or the worse for it, though the Country Lasses daunce in the Church-yard after Even-Song. Rocke Monday, and the Wake in Summer, shrovings, the wakefull ketches in Christmas Eve, the Hoky, or Seed Cake, these he yearly keepes; yet holdes them no reliques of Popery.[39]

The two passages are close in spirit, both confirming the strategic importance of the churchyard at this period. It was here that the major popular festivals of the year took place, partly for geographical reasons – since the churchyard performed the same functions as did the *agora* for the ancient Greeks, and was the natural place to meet – but also for reasons connected with current beliefs and superstitions: festivals were still more or less consciously regarded as occasions when the world of the spirits came into contact with that of the living.[40] The other feature that the two texts display in common, namely a stubborn rejection of Puritan attacks ('they will not be perswaded from dauncing' and 'yet holdes them no reliques of Popery'), is indicative of an early-seventeenth-century popular awareness that was already making people defensive and anxious to preserve their festive traditions.[41] In many of the towns of England, such pleasures were already a thing of the past, belonging to the bygone world of Merry England. In 1577, in *The Practice of the Divell*, Lawrence Ramsey was already sounding the following nostalgic note in a refrain on the subject of the merrymaking of the good old days:

> And howe it was merrie, when Robin Hoods playe
> Was in everie Towne. The Morrice and the foole,
> The Maypoll & the Drum, to bring the Calfe from schoole,
> With *Meege*, *Madge* and *Marian*, about the poll to daunce.[42]

This wave of nostalgia for popular culture, in which laughter, the urge to turn the world upside-down, irreverence and the grotesque were all moving forces, represented a reaction against the rising tide of gravity and efforts to purge religion of all frivolous and folkloric excrescences. As Keith Thomas has explained, it was a state of mind that reflected the gap separating the medieval type of Catholicism from religious practice after the Reformation. At the same time, the emphasis that élite circles now laid upon the control of the normal functions of the body encouraged a tendency to regard as vulgar and tasteless kinds of comic behaviour accepted only yesterday by all and sundry.[43] Now the lewd, cruel, cheerfully obscene laughter of the clown was increasingly unacceptable to the more refined social strata and those moving in that direction. Not only was it censured by writers such as Sidney, who favoured a particular type of poetic and dramatic classicism, but it was also disparaged by those – both men and women – who took offence at the clown's free and biting tone. In the prevailing atmosphere of gravity, even his flights of language were no longer acceptable and a new sense of propriety, in some cases but recently acquired, was no longer content with individual attacks on the jig and the May game. Yet what was really so reprehensible about the sallies of the clown, whom people were now attempting to banish from the church precinct and the village square at the very moment when he was enjoying great success on the stages of the Elizabethan theatres?

The clown is one of the foremost representatives and spokesmen of popular culture. He embodies the triumph of what Bakhtin has called 'the carnivalesque vision of the world', which is composed of three fundamental elements: (1) the setting of the world upside-down, which Bakhtin also calls uncrowning or parody; (2) the predominance of preoccupations of a material and physical nature in the context of what he calls 'grotesque realism'; and (3) ambivalence, that is to say the accepted co-existence of contraries (e.g. life and death, affirmation and negation, and so on).[44] The clown was different from the fool, whose madness (real in some cases, simulated in others) was to some extent professional, designed to afford kings and the high and mighty in general a chance to laugh. The clown, in contrast, was first and foremost a comical country bumpkin, an earthy creature close to the material things of life and a great one for *faux pas*, verbal bloomers and obscene puns.[45] His appetite for both food and sex was voracious and, in his simple naivety,[46] he expressed it quite openly, for he was noted for his forthrightness[47] and his total lack of inhibitions or complexes. His function was to draw attention to the limits of the world of the intellect, speculative or mystical lyricism and high-minded discourse, and to speak for what Bakhtin calls 'the material bodily lower stratum', that is to say the sordid and human, all too human, world of instinct, self-interest and the lower appetites.[48] In many Elizabethan dramas, his role is to act as a comic foil rather than to denounce hypocrisy and sham. He expresses a truculent kind of realism, allowing the spectator to distance himself slightly from the sphere of high-minded activities and discourse. At the same time, he introduces an element of confusion and ambivalence that allows for certain grotesque effects. The clown's humour, still redolent of the countryside, seems to have been indispensable for winning the favour of the popular section of the audience, who would split their sides in great bursts of laughter and applause. The unfortunate John Fletcher, whose *The Faithful Shepherdess* set out to be a pastoral tragicomedy that did not bow to the popular taste, was forced to admit that his play was a total flop. The 'note to the reader', which he subsequently wrote as a justificatory preface to the play, runs as follows:

It is a pastoral tragi-comedy, which the people seeing when it was played, having ever had a singular gift in defining, concluded to be a play of country hired shepherds in gray cloaks, with curtailed dogs in strings, sometimes laughing together, and sometimes killing one another; and missing Whitsun-ales, cream, wassail, and morris-dances, began to be angry.[49]

Elizabethan pastoral at this period was supposed to be full of rustic amusements. Representing the peasant in the grotesque guise of the clown was a way for dramatists to please the popular element in their audiences[50] as well as a good pretext for letting themselves go and spicing their language with grotesque references. Undermining everything high and mighty and expressing a gut reaction against scholarly talk, as they did, such scenes disingenuously allowed all the baser instincts to come to the surface.

   The purpose of incongruous word associations, ambiguities in which scholarly terms are naively reinterpreted in their basic, material sense and linguistic howlers generally is, of course, to introduce into discourse, supposedly of a reasonable and seemly nature, suggestions of revolt and other disruptive proclivities. A clown who goes by the name of People hears the Latin word *Respublica* as 'Rice-pudding cake'; the Latin expression *ad unguem* turns into 'ad dunghill' as spoken by Costard; the name of Sir Roger Oatley (deformed into 'Oatmeal' by Firke, the Rabelaisian apprentice to Simon Eyre, the Master Shoemaker) evokes culinary puns that conjure up gluttonous feasts of rich fare. In each case, we are presented with a clumsy or disrespectful distortion of language usually regarded as the prerogative of the élite (Latin words or phrases, long words and the names of people highly placed).[51] And that is surely the precise purpose of so-called 'Latin de cuisine' (dog-Latin)[52]: it represents a popular disintegration of the language of erudition, in which the latter is dismembered piece by piece and chopped into chewy morsels, to add spice to the incorrigible discourse of material appetites. The body of fine language is sliced, slivered and minced, to be served up as a hotch-potch or 'gallimaufry' fit for the illiterate palate.[53] Couched in the clown's popular speech, verbal symbolism is always something of a balancing act. What the clown puts into words only acquires a symbolic force if, like Mother Stork producing a crowd of little children from beneath her skirts, his signifier immediately gives birth to other elementary signifiers which convey their symbolic meaning through a register confined to the physical or culinary domains. Thus, in the comedy by Robert Greene and Thomas Lodge entitled *A Looking-Glass for London and England* (1590), a character called Alcon speaks of 'arsymetry' instead of 'arithmetics';[54] and in *Mucedorus* (1590), the clown, Mouse, confuses the three-syllable adjective 'solitary' with the noun 'saltcellar'![55] To judge by the clown of the Elizabethan theatre, it would seem that, in the sphere of popular culture, the only way to assimilate the world through language was to (re)convert it into food. Considered from this angle, the act of speaking becomes a symbolic kind of consumption.

One reason for these mutual interactions between the sphere of speech and that encompassing physicality and eating habits (in which we should include behaviour associated with festivity)[56] is possibly to be found in the popular tendency to regard the body, with all its humours and appetites, as a yardstick for the universe. In such a view, assimilation can only take place after a process of consumption and digestion. Painting seems to me to provide some good illustrations of the way in which popular speech and the popular imagination operated in this respect. Consider Arcimboldo's composite heads representing Spring, Summer, Autumn and Winter (1573; see Illustration 2.1). As one looks at these striking, highly-coloured faces, amalgamations of grotesque if not fantastic bumps and curves, they soon dissolve away leaving flowers, fruits, vegetables, fish and game.[57] Scanning the picture close-to, the spectator sees only banal, material details and things to eat. But if he steps back, adopting a different perspective and a change of focus, the shattered, decomposed portrait, as if by magic, comes together again. In a similar fashion, the clown's ridiculous short sight reduces ideal and complex structures to a collection of elementary sub-categories, usually ones connected with eating. His vision is of a shattered world, subject to some irrepressible force that reduces it to tiny particles, creating hybrids and monsters – a world which, like the paintings of Hieronymus Bosch and Pieter Brueghel, leaves an impression of perpetual, teeming and festering proliferation. The seething movement that the painter's optical skills of deception conjure up imbues the painting with a grotesque dynamism. In the most direct and apprehendable fashion, the picture reveals to us the process of metamorphosis that is such a feature of the popular culture of the Renaissance. Furthermore, this kind of painting seems to exert its fascination upon the beholder within the space of a mere glance, through the spectator's hesitation between the complex and the simple and the sense of vertigo that this engenders. In his paintings, Arcimboldo managed to capture and reconstitute the ambivalent element in popular culture that Bakhtin has analysed in his book on Rabelais.

One characteristic of the popular language of the Elizabethan period is this ambiguous bipolarity, which encompasses the comic disintegration of erudite language through the real or feigned clumsiness of the clown. Other distinctive marks are its power of parody and its ability to turn the world upside-down.[58] Sometimes through pastiche, sometimes by mixing things up in a jumbled pot-pourri,[59] it exploits its shortness of vision to foster confusion, surrendering with delight to the temptation to disorient

2.1   'Autumn', by Giuseppe Arcimboldo (1573).

the senses and make an etymological hash of things.[60] All these reversals
and shifts of meaning that in normal circumstances would betray a
failure of comprehension, a mis-hearing or some other sensory malfunc-
tion here, on the contrary, betoken a spirit of mockery and irreverence
vis-à-vis the speech of officialdom or of the sacred sphere. The clown is a
figure with a warped, or rather a one-track mind. His interpretations of
things tend to be regressive or demeaning; they drag the erudite language
of the élite down to earth and translate it into the vernacular of a meaty,
material sub-language, thereby subverting its content.

By way of summing up some of the major aspects of this language of festivity unleashed upon the market places and greens of the towns and villages of Elizabethan England at certain points in the calendar, you might say that it welled up from the depths of popular culture and everyday customs to encompass the cosmic forces of life and death, physicality and sexuality, within a chain of grotesque symbols totally unaffected by any notion of contradiction or the rules of decency and seemliness. It was current tender in communities that were closed in on themselves and where life was hard and comfortless; and it reflected the mentalities and daily customs peculiar to them. But we should not allow the spicy, imagistic verve and freedom of this popular language to blind us to its relative poverty. It depended almost entirely upon stereotyped, proverbial, even dialectal expressions, leaving little room for subtlety or for any complex elaboration. Thus, terms such as 'maypole', 'bagpipe' and 'green gown', used in the context of the spring or May Day country festivals, constituted so many ready-made popular emblems that conjured up an entire scene in which the carefully coded symbols were familiar to everyone except perhaps the very young, not yet fully initiated. These terms also lent themselves to a combination of reversed, switched or shifting meanings that could accommodate satirical allusions and sexual or scatological *sous-entendus*. This made the clown's work of improvisation easier, for, like the compositions of jazz musicians, his jokes could be grafted on to a number of ready-made expressions and well-known themes. It was a language of rural origins, and it excelled at what Hamlet called 'country matters'.[61] The term 'maypole' could be used as a mocking epithet for a gawk, or given an overtly phallic meaning. As for the word 'Hobby-horse', it acquired a succession of meanings, beginning as 'gee-gee', 'pet hobby' or 'childish fancy' and ending up as 'woman of easy virtue or dissolute morals'.[62] Limited though its range was, this popular language was strong in imagery, making up for its lexical limitations with its wide range of connotations and derivations.

I have been drawing my examples from the vocabulary of festivity, but it would be wrong to reduce this popular language to a collection of expressions used to refer to the customs and traditions connected with the various festivals of the calendar and celebrations of a private or family nature. Lexical research in the domain of festivals and folklore can undeniably be of great interest because it sometimes provides definitions and precise concrete descriptions now forgotten or discontinued.[63] However, such formalism may seem too reductive in this area, for its technical rigour could well obscure the all too frequently approximate or uncertain nature of our understanding of popular culture. We have defined popular culture, in the widest sense, as a collection of rituals, practices and beliefs transmitted orally and, for the most part, collectively. So I believe that it would be simplistic to suggest that the popular language which expresses it merely reflects the material and physical world. Behind those popular practices, there lay a whole symbolic system that provides the key to behaviour and scenarios whose general meaning might well escape even the author or actor involved. Behind every custom, many of them handed down from generation to generation, more mechanically than in a religious spirit, there lurks a whole constellation of beliefs and myths. It is magic or superstition that explains the survival of many rituals and practices that cannot, without distortion, be classified simply as resulting from either economic pressures or lapses of the human libido. The rituals recorded by specialists of folklore and historians only assume their true significance when seen as part of the general configuration of religion and popular mythology to which they belong. By way of example, let me now borrow the three main categories of popular symbolism that Claude Gaignebet has analysed in connection with Carnival, namely: (1) the 'circulation of blasts of air', (2) the 'mystical bestiary' and (3) 'hearty eating'.[64]

The 'circulation of blasts of air' comprises the custom of consuming flatulent foods on Shrove Tuesday and then breaking wind in a way that suggested a correlation between the microcosm of the human body and the cosmic forces as a whole. During this festival period, people were recommended to stuff themselves to bursting point, so as to be at one with the natural elements. It is an attitude that reflects the popular adoption of a vulgarized form of Hippocratic medicine, which led to a superstitious belief in certain notions culled from Hippocrates' work entitled *The Winds* (*De flatibus*): which runs as follows:

The spirits [*pneuma*] which live in the bodies are called winds, and those outside are called air. The latter is the greatest master of all and everything and it is important to consider its strength . . . But air must also enter with many foods . . . This is obvious from the fact that many persons belch when eating or drinking, doubtless because the imprisoned air escapes . . .[65]

The importance popularly attached to wind and the circulation of blasts of air at carnival time was also connected with a number of supernatural beliefs, for gusts of wind were associated with the return of dead souls, who were thought to roam around freely during the period of the new moon that ushered in the cycle of the moveable feasts.[66] In popular astrology, the moon was said to control the movements of the souls of the dead in the human world.[67]

What Gaignebet calls the 'mystical bestiary' consists of three main categories of animals that played an important part in Carnival festivities. The first category was that of animals for sacrifice such as the

cock, which in England was ritually stoned to death in the course of a
Shrove Tuesday practice known as 'cock-throwing'. The second category
consisted of horned animals – the stag and the ox (the latter being, as it
were, the domesticated equivalent of the former). Finally, the third
category was that of animals without horns, to wit the donkey, the horse
and the bear. Grotesque enactments of animal behaviour – by the
Mummers, in England, for example – with the aid of masks, animal hides
and horns, were probably supposed to be magical means of triggering the
reawakening of natural human and animal forces. Originally, the dances,
masquerades and music were designed to revive the sleeping forces of
fertility, at the end of the winter. There was a direct link, in popular
belief, between the beginning of carnival and the end of the bear's
hibernation which was liable to take place on Candlemas Day (February
2).[68] As the beast emerged from its lair, it was thought to look around to
see what the weather was like. If it was fine, it went back in, which was a
sign that winter would continue for another forty days, that is to say until
about 10 March; if, on the other hand, the weather was overcast, the
bear emerged for good, thereby marking an early end to winter.[69]
Candlemas fell on the day before Saint Blaise's (also called Saint Blaze's)
Day, 3 February, which was traditionally the earliest possible day for
Shrove Tuesday. This is confirmed by the Book of Common Prayer
which, in its 'Table of Moveable Feasts', gives 4 February as the earliest
possible date for the first day of Lent, which follows Shrove Tuesday.
Every popular festival was associated with its own particular bestiary in
which animals, which had long ago played the role of totemic ancestors,
guardian gods or sacrificial victims, now served as designs for masks, as
pretexts for dressing up and games and also as social or sexual
emblems.[70] Animal sacrifice survived in the Elizabethan period in the
indirect and sporting forms of cock-throwing and various games that
took place inside a ring or pit (bull-baiting, bear-baiting and cock-fights),
but in the grotesque gambols and prances of the Hobby-horse, the roast
goose of Michaelmas and even the Christmas turkey, the idea of sacrifice
had been totally obscured by the aspects of entertainment and traditional
conviviality. Similarly, the horns of the stag-man, an avatar of the ancient
Celtic god Zeus-Cernunnos, were more likely to be seen by Elizabethans
simply as the ridiculous emblem of the cuckold, rather than as a symbol
of strength and potency.[71]

   The third major symbolic aspect that, in Gaignebet's view, characterizes the popular culture of festivity is that of 'hearty eating', naturally
indissociable from 'heavy drinking'. Carnival and Martinmas were first
and foremost times for feasting, a paradise for gluttons and drunkards.
That is why popular Renaissance iconography represents these festivals
by a pot-bellied individual astride a barrel of wine, his neck garlanded

with strings of sausages and black puddings, preceded by a crowd of people brandishing poultry and sucking-pigs on spits.[72] These gluttonous excesses, which were the rule throughout Europe, could certainly be justified by the need to store up heat and energy before the long Lenten period of abstinence. But at a symbolic level, it looks as though the underlying reason was an impulse to distend one's body as sleekly as a full wine-skin so as to fend off the malignant winds and influences believed to be at large in the world at this period. By keeping busy the orifices through which these might insinuate themselves, the human body was turned into a veritable wind instrument. At festival time bodies became bagpipes, as they are depicted in the canvases of Hieronymus Bosch or in Brueghel's scenes of peasant celebrations.[73] In the latter, whether the subject be Carnival, a fairground or a wedding, the swelling of the instrument's bag seems to pass on the breath of fecundity to the dancers, by contagion, puffing the women's billowing skirts, the tipplers' round paunches, the bursting flies of the men's breeches and the greedy cheeks of lovers, as they kiss.[74] This universal rotundity, which is the counterpart to the skeletal emaciation of the observers of Lent, is a sign of renewed abundance and a promise of births to come. The atmosphere of contagious fertility that surrounds the dancing and festivity affects even the men, whose bellies, full of wine, beer and sausages, are almost as round as those of the pregnant women, as if they too were soon to undergo the pains of childbirth! It is an illustration of the side of Carnival and popular lore in which the grotesque element stems from sexual role-reversal.[75] In the exuberance of the festival, ambivalence and metamorphosis can triumph, bestowing a positive and creative power to what is normally alarming or deformed, and transcending sexual differentiation along with the usual oppositions between what is above and what is below, suffering and pleasure and life and death. Now everything comes together and distinctions disappear in the omnipresent and universal image of the horn of plenty. It is in this vision of the Land of Cockaigne (an imaginary country, the abode of luxury and idleness, according to the OED), where the yeast of festivity works upon every form, in this image of what Hegel in his Aesthetics has neatly called 'Life's Sunday', that the symbolism attached to popular festivity and culture reaches its culmination.

The above analyses show that the epithet 'popular', which the Elizabethan élite and educated classes often associated with the somewhat vague idea of vulgarity and ignorance, on the contrary betokened a very specific and living culture which flourished 'at the meeting-point of art and life', as Bakhtin aptly puts it: a culture that was rooted in a basic fund of primitive religion and that expressed an indefatigable curiosity in the material side of everyday life and an insatiable appetite for it. Such a culture is a complex, contradictory and virtually unclassifiable mixture, at once an art of living and a world vision, incorrigibly down-to-earth and materialistic yet, at another level, haunted by superstition. In the Elizabethan period, it was thanks to the clown of the public theatres that this culture was represented and diffused even in the heart of major cities, so that fashion, mutual influences and a desire for popularity abetting, it came to provide the inspiration for some of the greatest scenes created by Shakespeare and his contemporaries.

This rapid survey of popular taste and culture in the Elizabethan age would be incomplete without an analysis of the principal popular productions still being performed in Shakespeare's day, that is to say those relatively primitive seasonal plays generally referred to as 'folk drama'. It is some time since interest in these survivals of popular culture began to be shown. (The first transcription, of the 'Revesby Sword Play', was made in 1779.) But it was not until the late nineteenth century that scholars of folklore and anthropologists began to write books about them. The first studies of the subject, which appeared in Germany, were J. Grimm's works on *Teutonic Mythology* (4 volumes, translated and published in English in the 1880s) and G. Tille's *Yule and Christmas* (1899). These were followed, in England, by the research of the folk-lorist G.L. Gomme, who produced two important works, *The Village Community* (1890) and *The Christmas Mummers* (1897). But it is to Edmund Chambers that most of the credit must go for collecting together, in a scholarly synthesis, all the extant documents, at the same time pointing out how useful these non-literary sources could be to specialists and historians of the Elizabethan theatre. His two main books have since become indispensable works of reference in this domain. They are *The Mediaeval Stage* (in two volumes, Oxford, 1903) and his study entitled *The English Folk Play* (Oxford, 1933). Chambers' analyses and those of the Frazerian and post-Frazerian schools nowadays incur the criticism of many historians. These scholars prefer to study texts (even if they come from sources of late date) and the context of the plays, and tend to reject the interpretations of Frazer and his disciples, who laid much emphasis on the ritualistic aspect of these dramas,[76] regarding them as mimetic performances designed to ensure the renewal of plant-growth in the springtime and based on belief in a type of ancient sympathetic magic, deeply rooted in peasant mentalities. Nevertheless, Chambers' two works remain the obligatory starting point for anybody wishing to study these matters.

But what exactly does the – after all – rather vague expression 'folk play' really mean? It is a general term used to refer to a number of extremely diverse popular spectacles and modes of expression, some of which are known as 'Mummers' plays', others as 'Robin Hood plays' and yet others as 'Sword dances' or 'Morris dances'. All involve interludes of dancing, complemented by grotesque dialogue, frequently of a stereotyped nature but with many variants from one region to another.[77] What is common to all of them is the fact that they were spectacles performed by amateurs and were handed down orally from one generation to the next. It would nevertheless be naive to suppose that over the centuries these popular entertainments remained completely unaffected by the written word. The magnitude and nature of scholarly influences upon the popular domain have been the subject of ceaseless controversy between different schools of thought.[78] Some extremely early transcriptions exist, such as the fragments of popular plays, centring upon the figure of Robin Hood and performed during the May games, that William Copland collected and published between 1553 and 1569.[79] These were probably marginal forms of the 'folk play', in which some cleric or educated townsman may have taken a hand.

To concentrate, for a moment, upon definitions, it is possible, following Thomas Pettitt and Alan Brody,[80] to distinguish three main types of folk play: (1) the 'Hero Combat plays', (2) the 'Sword dance ceremony' and (3) the 'Wooing play'. Let us begin with the Sword dance, which is the most ancient and the least well known since there are so few texts to which to refer. It is certainly the type that remained closest to the original 'folk dance' and contained the least dialogue and the fewest dramatic elements.[81] The traditional Sword dance was probably introduced into England by the Danes and Saxons, for traces of its existence are chiefly to be found in the northern part of the country, where the cultural influence of these peoples remains quite strong. *Beowulf* contains an allusion to the Sword dance (*sweorda-gelac*), used metaphorically to refer to armed combat.[82] But any martial character it may have had disappeared over the centuries and by the late Middle Ages and the Renaissance, the dance had incorporated a grotesque element in the form of two madmen. One, called Tommy, is dressed in skins and sports a fox's brush; the other, Bessy, is a man disguised as a woman.[83] Jehan Tabourot, *alias* Thoinot Arbeau, describes the dance in his *Orchésographie*. He believes it to be distantly connected with the Pyrrhic dance of the ancient Greeks:

From these two types of dance there has been evolved one which we call the buffens or mattachins. The dancers are dressed in small corslets with fringe epaulets and fringe hanging from beneath their belts over a silken ground. Their helmets are made of gilded cardboard, their arms are bare and they wear bells upon their legs and carry a sword in the right hand and a shield in the left. They dance to a special tune played in double time and accompanied by the clash of their swords and shields.[84]

According to Chambers, the use of swords or staves and the presence of grotesque figures link this dance with the famous Morris dance which

→ Not represented in MSD

was much more common in southern England and was connected with the May festivities celebrated between 1 May and Whitsun in Elizabethan times.[85] Despite the warrior implications of the name 'Sword dance', at a deeper level its significance seems to have been that of a parodied or symbolic sacrifice.[86] The hexagon, or squared rose (*quadrata rosa*) formed by the interwined swords or staves placed around the neck of one of the dancers represented a beheading 'in fun', after which the executed man would set to dancing again as if raised from the dead. On 7 August 1814, Walter Scott described the performance of a Sword dance in his journal. It took place on one of the Shetland Isles and he tells us that there were eight dancers, seven of whom represented the Seven Champions of Christendom.[87] The text of this performance is published by J.Q. Adams under the title 'Shetland Sword Dance'. The text is followed by a 'Figuir', explaining the movements and figures of the dance.[88]

Although there are plenty of differences, it would probably be unreasonable to draw a radical distinction between the Sword dance and the second form of folk play, known as the 'Hero Combat play' or the 'Mummers' play'.[89] The best example is the 'Revesby Sword Play', the first folk play ever written down. It combines elements of both the 'Plough play' and the 'Morris dance', as the sub-title of the Adams edition indicates:

Acted by a set of Plow Boys or Morris Dancers in riband dresses, with swords, on October 20th 1779, at Revesby Abbey, in Lincolnshire, the seat of the Right Hon. Sir Joseph Banks.[90]

This play, like the Sword dance, revolves around the cycle of death and resurrection and, in the same fashion, features an execution carried out by a figure called 'the glass', whose function is simply to make it easier to arrange the swords around the 'victim's' neck:

The swords were locked together so that all might be lifted by the hilt of one.[91]

Chambers analyses this play in *The Mediaeval Stage*, at the beginning of Chapter 10, which is devoted to the Mummers' play. He suggests that it was simply a rather more elaborate and dramatic form of the Sword dance.[92] It was performed by seven dancers, six of them male (the madman and his five sons), the other a woman, called Cicely. The madman introduces the play and then goes on to fight first a Hobby-horse (a man carrying round his waist a wickerwork contraption representing a horse, covered with material that fell to the ground, hiding his legs), then a 'wild worm' or dragon. Then the sons decide to kill their father whom they force to kneel down and make his will, with their swords interlocked around his neck. The madman is killed and then brought back to life by his son, Pickle Herring, stamping his feet hard on the ground. The entertainment ends with Sword dances and a Morris dance.

The other type of Mummers' play that Chambers analyses is the Plough play. This was a short mimed drama performed in the country by players moving from house to house at the end of the Christmas festivities. The play involved a dozen characters whose names and callings varied from one region to another. In the two texts from the east Midlands that Chambers analyses, we find a madman called Tom, a recruiting sergeant, a new recruit, three farm-hands, a doctor and two women: one is a young Lady, the other Dame Jane, no longer in her first youth. After the madman has introduced the play, the young recruit is seen being rejected by the young Lady. He then seeks consolation from the madman, upon which Dame Jane claims that the madman is the father of her child. Beelzebub thereupon lays her out with a blow of his cudgel. The miraculous doctor is fortunately at hand to bring her back to life. The play then ends with a hat being passed around the audience. As Chambers sees it, the only difference between the Sword play and the Mummers' play is that the latter includes no heroic characters.[93] In all the twenty-nine versions studied, the basic schema can be reduced to three main parts. Every performance consisted of an introduction, the action or drama itself and a money-collection.[94] The presenter's role would usually fall to the madman, but was sometimes taken on by extra characters so as to adapt the performance to the relevant season of the year. At Christmas time, when a Mummers' play was one of the traditional seasonal entertainments, 'Old Father Christmas' would introduce the play.[95]

The performance would consist of a number of variations on the central theme of death and resurrection and the name of the chief character would vary from region to region: in place of the madman of the 'Revesby Sword Play', we sometimes find Saint George or Saint Patrick or other figures such as 'King Cole' or 'Captain Slasher'.[96] As for the collection, it would usually come after the curtain-call, when the actors would each step forward to wish joy and prosperity to the household or castle in which they had found a welcome. It would fall to Beelzebub, armed with his frying pan or ladle, to make the rounds of the spectators to collect contributions towards the expenses of the evening meal that would reward the actors' efforts. In Chambers' opinion, the combination of all these elements testifies beyond doubt to the existence of an authentic popular dramatic tradition. Rooted in the seasonal festivities as they were, these performances constituted the vestiges of a pagan cult of vegetation:

They [Sword dances and St George's plays] are properly called folk drama, because they are derived, with the minimum of literary intervention, from the dramatic tendencies latent in folk festivals of a very primitive type. They are the outcome of the instinct of play, manipulating for its own purposes the mock sacrifice and other debris of extinct ritual. Their central incident symbolizes the *renouveau*, the annual death of the year or the fertilization spirit and its annual resurrection in spring.[97]

Such generalizations, admittedly purely speculative, are today widely criticized.[98] All the same, they provide a perfect summary of the general tendencies of these extremely ancient traditions of festivity which testify to the existence of a bedrock of autonomous popular culture and also to the fact that the villages and small towns of Elizabethan England were certainly familiar with dramatic spectacles, rudimentary though they may have been.

The last category of folk play, labelled the 'Wooing play' by Brody and Pettitt, does not appear radically different from the Mummers' play which, as we have noted above (in connection with the 'Revesby Sword Play'), sometimes incorporated the theme of rivalry in love. Reginald Tiddy, in his study of the Mummers' play, establishes a distinction between the Mummers' play and the Sword play, on the one hand, and what he calls the Robin Hood play, on the other, and he goes on to remark, 'The latter may have comprised a good deal of love-making of the popular kind.'[99] Charles Read Baskervill, in contrast, clearly considered the Wooing play to be an integral part of the Mummers' play, since he entitled the article in which he published the text of five Wooing plays transcribed in the early nineteenth century 'Mummers' Wooing Plays in England'.[100] In his view, the Wooing play was simply a form of the Mummers' play, essentially a drama of a grotesque nature about the rivalry between two or more suitors for the favours of the Fair One.[101] The identities of the suitors vary from one play to another and from one region to another, but the theme of rivalry between a father and his eldest son, both from the social category of farmers, seems to be a common one. Sometimes, though, the rivals are a country bumpkin (or clown) on the one hand and a member of a wealthier class on the other, as in the pastoral of Adam de la Halle.[102] The theme of rivalry in love presented in a burlesque manner reappears in the famous May game that was traditional entertainment for the villages of medieval and Elizabethan England between May Day and Whitsun. In the sixteenth century, a contamination of the Morris dance by the legend of Robin Hood made its appearance. In this, Maid Marian is the object of the grotesque or obscene attentions of the madman.[103] The Robin Hood play was thus a summer version of the Mummers' play, centred sometimes on the theme of combat (with Robin Hood pitted against Guy of Warwick or George-a-Greene), sometimes on that of rivalry in love.

The last type of folk play to be considered is quite closely related to the Mummers' play as regards both the theme and the season during which it was traditionally presented. The Plough play was performed on the Monday following the feast of the Epiphany, which brought the festivities of the Christmas period to a close. It was, as its name suggests, essentially a ceremony associated with rural England and it concerned either a fight (between Saint George and the Dragon, for example) or the theme of the madman's wooing of the Fair One.[104] It was an entertainment at once burlesque and fantastic (the village boys performing it would sometimes don animal masks) and it constituted both an ancient fertility rite (the plough was dragged around the village to 'bring luck' to the new year's harvests) and an opportunity for the fraternity of young unmarried men to earn themselves a good evening meal with plenty to drink.

The various forms of folk plays that survived in late-sixteenth-century England, the Sword dance, the Hero Combat play and the Wooing play, all incorporate a number of recurrent elements and stereotyped themes, though these may be combined in different ways depending on the region, season of the year or period in which they were performed. The complexity of the various plays depended upon the length or richness of the dialogue, the type closest to mimed drama being the Sword dance of northern England. But most of them were genuine popular spectacles performed by amateurs in the context of seasonal celebrations rather than for profit (in contrast to the professional companies of players whose dramatic activities frequently brought them large profits). In fact, the question of the means adopted to finance the festivities, at a time when the relatively affluent city strata were still officially described as 'popular', is the basic criterion that distinguishes the truly popular festival from the bourgeois or corporative one. (The artisans who produced and acted scenes from the Old Testament and the Gospels were not professionals either.) The Elizabethan period saw the rapid rise of a middle class that was becoming wealthy and even acceding to public positions of great influence. In these circumstances, city and civic festivity assumed a new importance. It provided the bourgeoisie with the means of both differentiating itself and publicly demonstrating its prosperity and power.

Bourgeois festivity

Underlying the many parades and processions that periodically enlivened the life of most of the major towns of Elizabethan England, we find a concept as ubiquitous as it is obscure – namely, the pageant. According to the *OED*, which devotes a relatively long passage to this word, the etymology derives from the Anglo-Latin *pagina*, which could mean either 'a scene displayed on a stage' or 'a stage on which a scene is exhibited or acted'. It is a perfect example of mutual metonymy in which the name of the place of the performance is also used to denote the performance itself. Another possible etymology is that of the Latin *pagina*, meaning the page of a text or manuscript. And when one reflects on the nature of a page from a medieval manuscript, with all its illuminations, the shift from writing to spectacle seems quite a natural one.[105] The word 'pageant' seems thus to have come to denote any form of spectacle presented on a mobile platform mounted on a waggon: 'The root of a "moving show" is obviously the procession ... Giants, animals, figures of saints, and wagons bearing characters dressed up to represent something that they are not in real life, give these processions a pageantic aspect.'[106]

Interestingly enough, the term was at first specifically attached to the celebration of the religious festival of Corpus Christi, created in the thirteenth century by papal bull and introduced in England at the beginning of the following century (the first known reference to it is in 1324, in Ipswich).[107] At this date, the word 'pageant' was used to refer to the Mystery plays staged in towns such as Chester, Coventry, Wakefield and York. That continued to be the case until the Reformation when, in 1547, the Corpus Christi celebrations were suppressed and the Corpus Christi guilds dissolved. Since these guilds were made up of the various corporations responsible for the financing and organization of 'pageants', this amounted quite simply to decreeing the abolition of the religious festival. Despite the ban, the Mysteries of Corpus Christi Day continued to be celebrated, circumstances permitting, until well into the 1570s.[108] But the performances represented no more than sporadic bursts of resistance, at a time when Queen Elizabeth was taking steps to ensure the triumph of the new Protestant calendar over the old cycle of Catholic feasts. Yet, even now, these festivals did not disappear altogether. The towns and municipal authorities quite simply cashed in on the funds formerly earmarked for the Church [109] and the religious festival was secularized. To take the place of the biblical characters who featured in the old pageants, secular figures from legend or folklore were introduced. After the fashion of the famous Saint George's Day processions of 23 April, which inevitably boasted a dragon, the civic pageants would feature various more or less fabulous animals (unicorns, elephants and dromedaries) as well as giants and other 'wild men' (such as the famous 'woodwoses'; see Illustration 2.2).[110] The inclusion of Morris dances, officers in full uniform and minstrels or travelling musicians testifies even more clearly to the purely recreational purpose of these post-Reformation pageants. Furthermore, to remove all possible ambiguity once and for all, the date of the pageants was changed: in the case of Coventry (studied by Charles Phythian-Adams[111]), it was moved

2.2   The woodwose or 'wodehouse' was a wild man dressed up in animal
skins and foliage, who brandished torches in the Midsummer pageants.
He was a both frightening and comical figure and he became a popular
representation of madness.

to the summer Feast of Saint John, or Midsummer's Day: 'The sacred
plays, for which these theatrical waggons had originally been designed,
were last acted in 1579. For a few years, however, they were replaced by
a safe Protestant substitute which, in 1591 at least, seems to have been
performed at Midsummer.'[112]

In provincial towns such as Worcester, Chester and Coventry, these
Midsummer shows seem to have taken over smoothly from the old
Corpus Christi pageants, with only a few short interruptions.[113] In
London, in the mid-sixteenth century, it was a case of one civic
procession replacing another: many sources of evidence show that the
traditional Midsummer Watch or Saint John's Day parade was moved to
29 October, Saint Simon and Saint Jude's Day, to coincide with the
festivities to celebrate the annual enthronement of the Lord Mayor.[114] It
was a date that could justifiably be considered as the day of glory of the
bourgeoisie and corporations, since the Lord Mayor of London was
picked from one company or another according to a system of rotation.
One of our earliest sources of evidence on this ceremony is the work of a
burgher of London, an ardent Catholic and an undertaker by profession,
whose diary contains a detailed account of the various festivals that he
attended between July 1550 and August 1563.[115] His descriptions provide much interesting information on the organization and programmes
of these municipal celebrations and also testify to their fundamental
eclecticism.[116]

Despite the idiosyncratic spelling and elliptical style of this private
diary, never destined for publication, its author Machyn provides a clear
account of the successive stages of the itinerary of the Lord Mayor's
procession and the main attractions of this great civic festival. First came

the waits, groups of municipal musicians recruited in theory to mount guard on the city ramparts, in practice to enliven the corporative festivities; they were followed by the standard-bearers, the lancers bearing arms, the wild men and the escort for the new Mayor. Added to all this, there was a pageant of Saint John the Baptist – probably the patron saint of the company from which the Mayor had been elected – which was remarkably reminiscent of the old Corpus Christi pageants. Another feature worth noting has to do with both the topography of London and the sea-faring traditions of the English. This was the nautical part of the parade which with its banners, trumpet calls and cannon salvoes must have been every bit as impressive as the ceremonies on land.[117] Later, in the 1580s, these Lord Mayor's Shows were to become even more sumptuous, thanks to the collaboration of dramatic authors such as George Peele, Anthony Munday, Thomas Dekker and Thomas Middleton. Clearly, the secularization of the bourgeois festival rapidly led to its professionalization, at any rate in the capital, where the wealth of the corporations made it possible to enlist the services of theatrical experts. It is also noticeable that dramatic performances loomed increasingly large in the pageant, incorporating increasingly elaborate dialogues, whereas in the earliest pageants the visual and spectacular element had been far more important. The *tableaux vivants* retained their allegorical flavour but, bit by bit (perhaps under the influence of the theatres and the court Masque), turned into *tableaux parlants*. However, the main difference between the pageant and the Masque, that is to say between bourgeois entertainments and aristocratic ones, lay in the public character of the former (although there was, admittedly, also a public side to the festivities that surrounded coronations, royal entrances and some of the ceremonies connected with the sovereign's tours of the provinces, the famous royal progresses).[118]

Now that we have considered the pageants and the Lord Mayor's Show, the high points of bourgeois and corporative festivity in sixteenth- and seventeenth-century England, we must turn to one of their institutional components, a group which could be described, both literally and metaphorically, as their principal instrument: namely, the waits. According to the *OED*, the waits were

a small body of wind instrumentalists maintained by a city or town at the public charge ... They played for daily diversion of the councillors on ceremonial and festive occasions, and as a town or city band they entertained the citizens, perambulating the streets, often by night or in the early morning.[119]

The waits' duties as night watchmen in London had been defined by two decrees. The first excepted them from the rule that prohibited the playing of musical instruments during the night between the hours of 10 p.m. and 5 a.m. The second established their calendar of duties.[120]

During the summer period that stretched from 25 March (Lady Day) to 29 September (Michaelmas), the waits had to give concerts every Sunday and on feast days.[121] Furthermore, they took part in the Midsummer Watch and played for the Mayor and municipal councillors on Christmas Day and Candlemas (2 February).[122] In other towns, we find them taking part in other festivals. In Nottingham, in 1558, the waits took part in the festivities marking Queen Elizabeth's accession to the throne and in 1569 they joined in the merrymaking of the May Day procession. In Oxford in 1590, and in Norwich in 1618, they enlivened the celebrations held to mark the anniversary of the sovereign's coronation.[123] These musicians, virtually omnipresent in the larger towns, truly were the life and soul of town and city festivals, a fact that testifies to the essential relation between music and festivity.

This leads us on to study in greater detail a section of the population that was particularly active in the various festivals of the calendar: namely, the fraternities of young men. In France and other countries in continental Europe, these youthful groups seem to have been more highly developed than they were in England, where they are seldom mentioned or described. However, a document in the archives of Norwich Cathedral associates the 'Shrovetide festival' with a local 'bachery guild' and it is probably one such youth association that Philip Stubbes is castigating when he refers to 'all the wilde-heads of the Parish' in his pamphlet attacking the festivals of May.[124] Although it may seem unmethodical or even muddle-headed to include what is in effect an age-group in an analysis of the social spectrum, the fact is that the horizontal strata represented by the young (schoolchildren, apprentices and students) to some extent cut across the diverse vertical social strata, intermingling popular and aristocratic groups and rural and urban traditions. In reality, the situation was not as complex as it may seem since, at this point, most schoolchildren and apprentices were closer to the popular strata, while the students of London, Oxford and Cambridge seem to have had closer connections with the aristocracy (notwithstanding the presence of a small popular meritocracy of which Marlowe is perhaps one of the most illustrious representatives). Another factor also made for cohesion in this age-group, simplifying still further the mixed impression of the group that is suggested above: the almost total absence of girls. The fact that the sexes were kept segregated does not mean that women were excluded from festive games and ceremonies, for quite the reverse was true. However, there were different sets of celebrations and rites of passage for the boys on the one hand and the girls on the other. The historian Charles Phythian-Adams stresses the importance of sex-segregation at this time and also underlines the particularly wretched position of widows, who were excluded both from working and from taking part in festivities.[125] This segregation of the sexes may to some extent account for the intensity of the symbolic encounters during the Hock Tuesday festival held in Coventry and also the excitement engendered by the reunions that occurred during spring festivals devoted to lovers (Saint Valentine's Day and May Day).

Given that such distinctions existed, it comes as no surprise to learn that the boys' festivals were extrovert and rowdy, while the girls observed rituals of a far more discreet nature, which took place indoors. The most important festive occasion for young people, particularly for schoolchildren, fell on Saint Nicholas' Day (6 December), when it was traditional to elect a 'Boy Bishop' whose burlesque reign lasted until the Feast of the Holy Innocents (28 December).[126] Although officially suppressed in 1541, the custom was revived under Mary Tudor and various sources of evidence [127] suggest that it continued to be observed for a few years under Elizabeth. It resembled the low-Church Feast of Fools held between the Feast of Saint Stephen (26 December) and the Feast of the Holy Innocents in mainland Europe. The festival consisted of a parody of ecclesiastical rituals in the course of which children, wearing grotesque fancy-dress, would go from house to house collecting a few coins:

And whereas heretofore dyverse and many superstitions and childysshe observations have been usid, and yet to this day are observed and kept in many and
sundry parties of this realm, as upon sainte Nicholas, sainte Catheryne, saint
Clement, the holye Innocentes and such like; children be strangely decked and
apparelid to counterfaite priestes, bysshopps and women; and so ledde with
songs and daunces from house to house, bleassing the people, and gatherynge of
moneye ...[128]

The anticlerical connotations of the festival should have been pretty much to the taste of the new Anglican Church, which had recently modernized the weighty ritual of the Catholic tradition and denounced the religious institutions defended by Rome.[129] But apart from those connotations, this burlesque ceremonial is on the whole not unlike the rounds of the Mummers at Christmas time and the rural festivities of Plough Monday. Keith Thomas does not think that these schoolchildren's saturnalia survived beyond Mary's reign and suggests that under Elizabeth the traditional festivities of the Boy Bishop were replaced by the custom known in English schools as 'barring out the schoolmaster'.[130] It involved the pupils temporarily locking the schoolmaster out of the classroom, thereby enacting a reversal of authority. Apparently, they would only readmit him when he granted them some extra holidays, for school vacations were few and far between in those days and each school was responsible for fixing its own.[131] The only periods of the year when the school authorities would tolerate such wayward behaviour on the part of the pupils were the days leading up to Christmas and Shrove Tuesday.[132] As well as 'barring out the schoolmaster', pupils enjoyed a number of other rights and other kinds of fun. Shrove Tuesday was the day devoted to cock-fights, an occasion for fun and games and other forms of licence at a time when discipline was generally remarkably severe.[133] The rules of cock-fighting were as follows:

Item, for Cock-fighting, the Schoole-boies continue their Custome still: and have their Victors, that is, he whose cock conquers or beates the rest, is Victor, and *eo nomine*, he hath the Priviledge, during that Lent, to save what Boy he pleases from whipping.[134]

Thanks to the punishment taken by proxy by the cock that lost the match, the fortunate Victor acquired rights to bestow favours that must undoubtedly have afforded him considerable prestige and authority among his schoolfellows. When the fight was over, he was carried in triumph through the streets:

On Shrove Tuesday shroving when the Victor Boy went thrô ye streetes on triumph decked with ribbons, all his school fellowes following with drum and a fiddle to a Feast at their Masters Schoole house.[135]

The feast organized in the school, after the games, set the seal upon the reconciliation effected between the pupils and their master, in just the same fashion as the meals shared by employers and employees on Corpus Christi Day effected a social reconciliation under the sign of commensality.[136] In *The Shoemaker's Holiday*, the playwright Thomas Dekker produced an inspired evocation of these occasions, when amicability and collaboration prevailed between masters and their apprentices.[137] The fine spectacle of harmony presented in this play certainly contrasts sharply with the violence that apprentices traditionally perpetrated on Shrove Tuesday and that the municipal authorities had to put up with as well as they could.[138] Dekker himself alludes to it in *The Seven Deadly Sinnes of London* (1606):

They presently (like Prentices on Shrove Tuesday) take the lawe into their owne handes and doe what they list.[139]

A number of sources suggest that the favourite targets of apprentices on the rampage were brothels (where they roughed up the occupants) and theatres, which they would on occasion completely demolish. The paradoxical nature of these attacks against places of pleasure, which seem more like punitive raids than festive rejoicing, can perhaps be explained by the imminence of Lent, when all dramatic presentations would be banned and, as is well known, any hint of physical pleasure (particularly of a venal nature) was severely proscribed.

The riotous behaviour of apprentices was certainly sometimes extreme and spectacular, but it seems at least to have been limited to London and was not a feature of English towns in general. We might have expected to find that the same applied, *a fortiori*, to students' disturbances and that these would be confined within the thick walls of the London law schools and the Oxford and Cambridge colleges. In fact though, a document dated 9 June 1598 shows that student festivals sometimes degenerated into clashes between the students and the town inhabitants. The incident reported below took place in Oxford, where hostility between town and gown was already a feature of local life, about ten days before Ascension Day, that is to say probably the Sunday before 1 May and the Sunday following it:

The inhabitants assembled on the two Sundays before Ascension Day, and on that Day, with drum and shot and other weapons, and men attired in women's apparel, brought into the town a woman bedecked with garlands and flowers, named by them the Queen of May. They also had Morrisshe dances and other disordered and unseemly sports, and intended the next Sunday to continue the same abuses. Details the proceedings taken by the University officers, and the riotous conduct of the inhabitants, in armed resistance to arrest, discharging volleys of shot, and using seditious speeches. The Vice-Chancellor on his return sent to entreat the Mayor to meet him, to which message the Mayor made a frivolous and dilatory answer, and in the meantime preferred an unjust and scandalous complaint against the University.[140]

The somewhat startling contrast between the pastimes of the town and the more studious activities of the university (which in this case seems to have adopted a position in line with some of the Puritan municipal authorities of the period) is echoed in the following few lines that Thomas Crosfield, a fellow of Queen's College, Oxford, entered in his diary on 1 May 1633:

May Day/Sermon at Magdalen upon Phil. & Jacob after New Colledge men have visited Bartholomewes & *the Vulgar a Maying*.[141]

Such brushes with the local populace were no more than sporadic and it was only during the Christmas festivities that the students of the three universities gave free rein to their improvisational talents. At this period they would organize all kinds of spectacles, dramatic entertainments and parodies, encouraged by a 'Christmas Lord' whom they elected to preside over the orderly celebration of the end-of-year festivities.[142] The titles given to this figure, who is reminiscent both of the schoolboys' Boy Bishop and the courtly Lord of Misrule, varied from one college to another, as did the duration of his reign. In London, where his mandate lasted from the Monday before Saint Thomas' Day (21 December) to the Saturday after Epiphany, he was called 'Prince of Purpoole' (at Gray's

Inn), 'Prince d'Amour' (in the Middle Temple) and 'King of the Cockneys' (at Lincoln's Inn). In Oxford, the custom had already lapsed thirty years earlier, but in 1607–8 the students of Saint John's College revived it:

This motion for that the person of a Prince or Lorde of the Revells had not bine knowen amongst them for thirty yeares before, & so consequentlye the danger, charge, and trouble of such iestinge was cleane forgotten was p'sentlye allowed, and greedilye apprehended of all.[143]

The Christmas Prince chosen that year (a certain Thomas Tucker) reigned throughout the festive period that stretched from Saint Andrew's Day (at the beginning of Advent, 30 November) to Shrove Tuesday (9 February). The festivities included eight plays put on between 30 November and 13 February. They were, in the order in which they were staged: *Ara Fortunae, Saturnalia, Philomela, Time's Complaint, The Seven Days of the Week, Philomathes, Ira Fortunae* and *Periander*.[144] Most of these dramatic entertainments were, furthermore, preceded or followed by banquets and concerts held in the college hall. The festivities of the London colleges, those of Gray's Inn, organized in the winter months of 1594–5, and the Middle Temple (in the winter of 1635–6), are also recorded in detailed descriptions published under the titles *Gesta Grayorum* and *Le Prince d'Amour*.[145] So they are quite well known, particularly since they are believed to have influenced several of Shakespeare's plays.[146]

The most grandiose of these student festivities appear to have been those of Gray's Inn. They included parades through the streets of London, a banquet at the residence of the Mayor and the performance of a Masque in Whitehall, in the presence of the queen.[147] This particularly lavish example, later imitated by the organizers of the festivities of the Prince d'Amour at the Middle Temple,[148] bears out my earlier remarks concerning the close relations between certain student festivities and the aristocratic amusements of the court. But there are also a number of common points that link the luxurious London amusements with the 'Christmas Prince' festivities celebrated at Saint John's College, on a less lavish scale and with more modest personages involved. In both cases, we find the same mixture of dramatic performances (speeches of parody, Masques and comedies) and festive activities of other kinds (banquets, parades and balls). The prevailing spirit of these student festivities reflected an atmosphere inherited from the ancient Saturnalia: the tendency was to hold all the authorities up to ridicule by aping them in a burlesque and mocking manner. England at this time of year was pervaded by a general wave of subversive mockery aimed to undermine authority with fun and 'just for fun':

At colleges and inns of court there were Christmas princes and lieutenants elected from among the students; they burlesqued authority in the same way as did mockmayors in many towns or lords of misrule in the countryside. Even the universities had their licensed buffoons; the 'Terrae Filius' at Oxford and the Prevaricator at Cambridge, young MA's appointed annually to make a speech at the chief academic ceremony of the year...Their orations...consisted of outspoken jests and insults directed at the morals and private lives of the vice-chancellor, heads of houses and other dignitaries...[149]

This passage represents an excellent analysis of what Shakespeare and his contemporaries called 'misrule', namely the whole collection of rites of inversion practised during the season of Christmas festivals. Since this was traditionally the time when everything was supposed to be the wrong way round, as under the reign of Saturn, it was permissible, even required, to contravene all the normal daily customs. The only equivalent term in French seems to have been the 'Abbaye de Maugouvert' (or Maugouverne or Malgouverne), meaning bad government, which was a feature of the Carnival period.[150] It is hardly surprising to find the young making the most of the atmosphere of tolerance that prevailed during the festive period. It was a time when they could freely play the fool and make a mockery of the authority of those in power. Historians have pointed out that such subversiveness was not really a challenge to authority but rather a means of rendering it bearable, at a time when there was no possibility of ousting or undermining it through the ballot-box.[151] Furthermore, these conflicts were no doubt a source of inspiration to the authors of comedy, for their dramas often revolve around similar themes, allegorically expressed as a clash between Old Man Winter and the fresh-faced youth, Summer,[152] or rivalry over love and marriage between the older and the younger generations.[153]

Aristocratic and royal festivity

Let us now move on from the joyful domain of youthful celebrations to the subject of aristocratic and royal festivity. Here, I shall be considering two main categories of celebrations, one more repetitive and seasonal than the other. A distinction should, after all, be made between, on the one hand, what one might call ceremonial occasions, such as the festivities that surrounded royal entries or coronations and, on the other, the amusements that were organized at court in the course of the year, which was divided into two halves: winter, the 'Season of the Revels' and summer, that of the summer progresses. Although these amusements were of many kinds, there was an immutable and cyclical aspect to them, for they were governed by quite a strict calendar which fixed the order in which they took place and the form that they should take.

Royal entries and coronation celebrations were obviously unique occasions involving pomp and spectacles not to be compared with the other festivals to which the inhabitants of the capital and larger towns were accustomed. But royal entries, which marked the sovereign's official accession to the throne[154] or visits from foreign Heads of State, appear to have differed very little from the ceremonies that marked a coronation. On the occasion of a royal entry, the streets through which the procession passed would be richly decorated, bridges would be painted and perhaps adorned with symbolic emblems[155] and town gates and monumental fountains would be the scenes of *tableaux vivants*. Frequently, as a sign of abundance, the fountains would run with wine or milk.[156] Finally one or several pageants presented to the monarch a series of flattering shows endowed with a fairly transparent allegorical meaning.[157] All that we know about the festivities organized in London for the coronations of Elizabeth and James VI of Scotland is altogether in line with these spectacular rites and amusements. On the occasion of Elizabeth's coronation, for example, the queen was presented with a pageant staged in front of the 'Little Conduit'. The scene consisted of two hillocks, the one representing 'a decayed Commonweal', the other a 'flourishing Commonweal'. In the space between them, a pantomime was enacted between two characters, Time and his daughter, Truth. It was a dramatization of the Latin adage to be found at the bottom of many emblems depicting the powers of time, 'Filia temporis Veritas'. When Truth presented Elizabeth with a Bible in English, as a sign of her allegiance to Protestantism, Elizabeth kissed her, clasping her to her bosom in a gesture that spoke far louder than words to the people.[158] The young queen was clearly not slow to understand the potential instrument of political propaganda that festive proceedings of this kind represented. The celebrations held to mark the coronation of James I followed a similar pattern. His entry to London, originally fixed for 25 July 1603, was put off to the following 15 March on account of an epidemic of the plague. As the traditional procession crossed the town from London Bridge to Temple Bar, seven scenes or pageants were put on for the king, each one designed to compliment the new sovereign. Glynne Wickham tells us that these allegories were more contrived and much less political than those performed for Elizabeth's coronation, a fact that seems, on the face of it, somewhat paradoxical, given that writers such as Ben Jonson and Dekker were responsible for the text of these allegories.[159] Glynne Wickham regards it as the sign of a new trend in aristocratic festivals, which were losing their popular audience[160] and becoming purely formal spectacles.[161] It is, in any event, worth noting that these festivals certainly retained their pomp and ceremony and, above all, their hierarchical character and this gave them an atmosphere very different from that of the popular or student festivities which, for their part, were marked by disorderly behaviour and shows of parody expressing disrespect towards all forms of authority.

Tournaments of a hierarchical and sumptuous nature constituted another form of aristocratic entertainment at this period. These medieval sporting events came back into fashion in Elizabeth's reign, along with the rebirth of chivalry occasioned by a combination of the Tudor myth[162] and the Virgin Queen's accession to the throne.[163] In itself, the tournament was not a cyclical event connected with a specific date in the calendar, as is shown by the entertainment in the form of a tournament entitled 'The Four Foster Children of Desire' which was organized in May 1581, to mark the visit of the duc d'Alençon, who had come to make an offer for the queen's hand.[164] But it became customary for a tournament to constitute the cornerstone of the ceremonies held each year on 17 November, to celebrate Elizabeth's accession to the throne. Furthermore, after the defeat of the Armada in 1588, similar entertainments were regularly organized to take place a couple of days later, on 19 November, Saint Elizabeth's Day.[165] The fact that illustrious figures such as Sir Henry Lee and George Gifford, Earl of Cumberland, were known to take part in these tournaments[166] combined with the many literary and artistic allusions that were made to them created a reputation of splendour and sophistication for the 'Accession Day Tilts' or 'Triumphs' or 'Joustes of Peace', as they were also known.[167] They were not altogether closed to the populace, although a financial barrier operated since it cost twelve pennies to gain admittance to a tournament, and that was twelve times more than the price for a place (admittedly a standing one) in a public theatre.[168] Nevertheless, a tournament was an essentially aristocratic festival to the extent that only those of gentle birth could take part.[169] The costs of participation must, in any event, have been high, for tournaments involved not only virile trials of strength but also veritable parades, to judge by Francis Bacon's remarks in his essay entitled 'Of Masques and Triumphs'.[170]

The preliminary formalities leading up to the tournament were so elaborate that they constituted a kind of pageant in themselves. Every contestant who entered the arena was preceded by a procession of retainers dressed in fine costumes, to an accompaniment of fanfares. The knight himself then presented his compliments to the queen (or employed actors or students to do so on his behalf).[171] Only then did the tournament, which could take various forms, commence. Distinctions were made between the different forms of combat. There was the 'jousting' or 'tilting' in which two mounted horsemen would ride at each other separated by a barrier consisting of a long horizontal pole: each would try to unseat the other with a well-directed jab from his lance. This might be followed by the 'tourney', in which the two adversaries, armed with swords, continued the combat on foot. There were also other, less dangerous, events[172] which involved no adversary, such as 'running at the ring', in which the aim was to thread a ring on to the tip of one's lance, and the 'quintain' in which the target was a dummy.[173] The latter exercises were feats of skill rather than martial jousts, but the spectacle as a whole amounted to more than an ordinary entertainment. A tournament was a grandiose spectacle or celebration incorporating elements from the civic pageant and the Lord Mayor's Show, as well as from the courtly Masque.[174] Under James I, tournaments apparently continued to be just as magnificent occasions, but they were reallocated first to 5 August (the anniversary of the discovery of Gowrie's Plot in 1600) then, after 1605, to 5 November, in commemoration of the foiling of the Gunpowder Plot.[175] The changing circumstances in which these aristocratic festivals took place indicate that from being glorifications of the Virgin Queen they turned into rituals of a more expiatory nature. There appear to have been two reasons for the king's desire to change the date of the tournament after 1605. One was to associate the festival with his English reign as well as his Scottish one, the other to eclipse the memory of Elizabeth's lavish ceremonies by replacing them with new rituals timed to take place at almost the same dates of the year. However, perhaps because he never enjoyed the same popular acclaim as Elizabeth, James I seems to have been more partial to the private splendours of the Masque, which enjoyed an unprecedented success in his court, than to the public pomp surrounding the annual tournament. It was chiefly thanks to Henry Frederick, the Prince of Wales, the most popular figure at court, that the tournament owed its shortlived burst of favour under the first Stuart monarch.

Tournaments were moveable feasts, but most aristocratic festivals were cyclical in nature, being court entertainments that were fixed by the calendar, in the same manner as religious, popular and civic celebrations. Each of these courtly festivities was associated with one or other of two distinct periods of the year: the season of the 'Revels', in the winter, and that of the 'Progresses and Entertainments' which took place during the summer months. The transition between the two seasons was marked by a number of ceremonies specially designed for the purpose. In Elizabeth's reign, 17 November, the anniversary of the sovereign's accession to the throne, inaugurated the 'Season of the Revels'. On this date, the court, which would have been visiting Windsor, Richmond or Hampton Court, returned to London for the winter.[176] The tournaments held on that day thus served two functions: they commemorated a political anniversary and also celebrated the queen's return to the palace of Whitehall. It was here that the Christmas festivities began, just over a month later. They included many entertainments of the most varied and lavish kind: music, dancing, Masques and theatrical productions. Most took place in the evening, after supper, in the course of the first three days following the feasts of Christmas, New Year and Epiphany. Sometimes they continued right up to the beginning of Lent, the high points being Candlemas (2 February) and Shrove Tuesday.[177] The task of organizing the festivities devolved upon a specially appointed 'Master of the Revels', who was responsible for assembling troupes of actors and choosing which shows to put on at court. The actors would either be professionals, who would receive payment, or amateurs such as the students of the Inns of Court, who would perform purely for the honour of it and at their own expense, although the costumes and scenery were often provided by the court.[178] The early Tudors, Henry VII and Henry VIII, also seem to have called upon the services of a Lord of Misrule, newly appointed each year to a reign that (according to Stow) lasted from All Saints' Day up to Candlemas.[179] In the universities, this figure appears to have retained his popularity until well after 1550, but he did not last at court beyond Edward VI's reign, probably because his functions to some extent overlapped with those of the Master of the Revels. In the court world of intrigue and rivalry, this must have caused friction and jealousy of a kind unlikely to enhance the quality of the entertainments.[180]

The period of Christmas festivities was the time for symbolic gift-giving so that, on top of all the lavish entertainments organized for the court, on New Year's Day there would be a ritual procession for the offering of presents. It was an occasion that was particularly important under Elizabeth's reign. The custom was encouraged by the veritable cult that was devoted to the queen and the atmosphere of flattery fostered by intriguing courtiers, all anxious to dazzle with the lavishness of their generosity; nor was it discouraged by the acquisitiveness of the queen herself, who could never refuse any gift, however modest. John Nichols meticulously reproduces the interminable lists of presents that she received on these occasions.[181]

When the festivities of Christmas, *stricto sensu*, were over, that is to say after Epiphany, the court would move to Hampton Court, Greenwich or Richmond, to the accompaniment of pealing church bells wherever it passed.[182] At Easter, on Maundy Thursday, the queen would perform a penitential sacrifice at the ceremony of the washing of feet. Then, on Saint George's Day, dazzling festivities would be organized at Windsor, where she received the knights of the Order of the Garter.[183] Equally opulent were the summer festivities, when the entire court progressed through the provinces, receiving hospitality in the castles and country houses of the peers of the realm. Now, however, the bill was footed by those honoured with the prestigious duty of receiving their sovereign. According to Lord Burghley, to whom this expensive honour fell a dozen times, the cost of all this hospitality over periods which sometimes stretched to a month or six weeks would amount to between two and three thousand pounds sterling, an altogether exorbitant sum.[184]

There were many of these summer progresses in the course of the first twenty years of Elizabeth's reign, when she needed to make herself known to her people. In 1561, she visited the counties of Hertfordshire, Essex and Suffolk; then, after two years (during which she made but one visit, to Eton, in 1563), she visited Cambridge, in 1564, and Oxford, in 1566. She was in Warwickshire and Gloucestershire in 1572, in Sussex and Kent in 1573. In 1575, she paid a famous visit to the Earl of Leicester, at Kenilworth Castle, where she stayed for close on three weeks. The poet, George Gascoigne, one of the organizers, has left us a detailed description of the festivities, another account of which appears in a long letter written by Robert Laneham, which has also come down to us.[185] The packed programme included mythological and pastoral entertainments, fireworks, water pageants, banquets followed by Masques, hunting and other rural pastimes.[186] In the 1580s, political problems both at home and abroad (in particular, the war with Spain) led Elizabeth to discontinue her annual travels. But after the victory over the Spanish Armada in 1588, they were resumed with new enthusiasm. The receptions at Cowdray and Elvetham given by Lord Montagu and the Earl of Hertford in 1591 were among the most brilliant, as was that organized the following year at Ditchley by Sir Henry Lee, who was the queen's champion in the yearly tournaments of 17 November.[187] These progresses through the provinces continued into the very last years of Elizabeth's reign, for the queen seemed bent on trying to forget her age and physical debilities in a mad round of parties and amusements. Not content with continuing to throw herself into the dancing at various balls, she was 'fetching in the May' on horseback at Highgate in 1601 and at Lewisham in 1602, less than a year before her death.[188]

In the reign of James I there appear to have been few significant changes in the general programme of annual court festivities apart from the changes of date that we have noted above, in connection with the tournaments. The custom of summer progresses was continued throughout his reign,[189] the main innovation during the winter period of festivities being the development of the court Masque at the hands of Ben Jonson and Inigo Jones.[190] For the rest, E.K. Chambers, who describes the court of James I as 'murky', prefers to cast a discreet veil over the unpopular monarch's vices and degeneracy (his immoderate drinking, his violent passion for hunting, not to mention his weakness for favourites) rather than listing all the respects in which his reign was easily eclipsed by

Elizabeth's.[191] But we should not forget that James I on a number of occasions defended the traditional values of the festive hospitality and generosity dispensed in earlier days by landlords over the twelve days of Christmas, as well as outdoor sports and amusements and popular festivities in general.[192] It is true that in this domain Elizabeth set more store by practice than by preaching, but James I's *Book of Sports* (1618) was an intellectual's way of defending the festivals and customs that in many localities found themselves under threat as a result of the measures to ban them taken by municipal authorities and Justices of the Peace of Puritan persuasion.

It is quite clear that for the monarchy and the aristocracy as a whole the sports, games, amusements and spectacles that went to make up these seasonal festivities were by no means simply a matter of more or less frivolous entertainments and pastimes. Festivity, whether in the guise of civic pageants, tournaments or court spectacles, had a particular importance all its own. It seems to have been regarded as a specially effective means of propagating the national, religious and monarchical ideology of the period. In E.K. Chambers' view, Elizabeth's encouragement of festivals and other contemporary amusements was prompted by political motives and, above all, a desire for popularity.[193]

One reason why it proved relatively easy for Elizabeth to acquire the popularity she seemed so much to covet was probably the more or less spontaneous identification of the personal tastes of the sovereign with those of her people, for the latter were loath to accept the practical consequences of the Reformation, in particular the whittling away of feast days and other occasions of rejoicing. The Puritans who sought to apply the new religious edicts in the strictest fashion inadvertently encouraged the close ties being established between the sovereign and her people. For example, on a visit to Coventry in 1566, Elizabeth was told by a certain John Throgmorton of the traditional festival known as 'Hock Tuesday', which the municipal authorities had abolished six years earlier.[194] Nine years on, as Leicester's guest at Kenilworth, she asked to see an out-of-season performance of that Hock Tuesday play that she had heard about, and thereby indirectly set the seal of legitimacy upon it. The queen thus assumed the role of arbiter or mediator in the clashes that developed between her people and the local authorities. Furthermore, sometimes, as in this case, she took the part of the former against the latter. James I adopted a similar policy of encouragement *vis-à-vis* the local traditions and festive customs of Merry England when he officially echoed criticisms directed at an aristocracy guilty of no longer respecting the old traditions of the twelve days of Christmas:

let us in Gods Name leave these idle forreine toyes, and keepe the old fashion of *England*: For it was wont to be the honour and reputation of the English

Nobilitie and Gentry, to live in the countrey, and keepe hospitalitie . . . Therefore
as every fish lives in his owne place, some in the fresh, some in the salt, some in
the mud: so let every one live in his owne place, some at Court, some in the Citie,
some in the Countrey; especially at Festivall times, as Christmas and Easter, and
the rest.[195]

The purpose of these lines was not so much to reaffirm a profoundly
conservative ideology that opposed social mobility of any kind. Rather,
they constituted an appeal to English idiosyncrasy. They were designed
to support English values in the face of fashions imported from abroad,
which were dividing and undermining the nation. Encouraging local
festivals and rural traditions was a first step towards strengthening
national unity. Such declarations must have found sympathetic ears
among the people, especially at times of crisis, such as the attack of the
Spanish Armada under Elizabeth and the Gunpowder Plot in the reign of
James I. A double reflex of insularity and xenophobia (or rather
anti-Catholicism) helped to rally the people to the policies of the
sovereign and to arouse their animosity against the expansionist and
subversive efforts of countries in the pay of the Pope. The tournament of
17 November 1589 and the firework display of 5 November 1606 must
have enhanced the rejoicing in that they exorcized the people's fears and
inspired them with a nationalistic fervour and hostility towards all papist
countries. In a treatise entitled A Discourse touching the Reformation of
the Laws of England, published in the 1530s, Sir Richard Morison had
already clearly noted the huge propaganda potential that festivity
represented for the authorities, pointing out how much greater an
impression they made upon the people's attitudes than long speeches ever
did. He suggested, even then, replacing 'folk mummings' by plays that
presented the Pope in an unflattering and satirical light, in order to win
over the popular strata to the national cause of Anglicanism, observing in
passing that:

into the common people things sooner enter by the eyes, then by the ears:
remembering more better that they see then they hear.[196]

Once they were turned into an expression of triumph over foreign
powers, festivals thus helped the sovereign to win the people's support
both for himself (or herself) personally and for his (or her) policies, a task
that became all the easier when, following the Reformation, the
sovereign became the embodiment of powers both spiritual and
temporal.[197] An Elizabethan festival was not only a vehicle of political
and religious nationalism, but furthermore took on the character of a
veritable cult devoted to the person of the queen.[198] It was more or less
inevitable that the sudden suppression of devotion addressed to the saints
and the Virgin Mary and the elimination of the many votive festivals

through which that piety was spectacularly expressed at a local or corporative level should leave a sense of emptiness. The popular strata were naturally enough tempted to compensate by switching their adoration to the figure of the Virgin Queen. But even at the educated, aristocratic level, a similar adoration existed, as is demonstrated not only by the neo-Arthurian ceremonies of the tournament held on 17 November and the splendid receptions for the knights of the Order of the Garter on 23 April, but also by the mythological entertainments that presented Elizabeth as a new incarnation of Astraea, the ancient goddess of justice who used to reign alongside Saturn in the Golden Age.[199] Frances Yates is convinced that the institution of the tournaments held to commemorate Elizabeth's accession to the throne was seen as a chivalrous Protestant festival designed to supplant the old religious festivals of the Catholic calendar.[200] In support of this view she cites the words that the hermit of Woodstock addressed to the queen in 1592:

Now most gracious Queen, as they were of late making melody with this homely melody they have brought with them, one that came from the Church told them, how the Curate had showed his parishioners of a holiday which passed all the Pope's holidays, and that should be on the seventeenth day of November.[201]

This short passage tellingly evokes many aspects of the Elizabethan aristocratic festivals that centred around the cult of the queen. It is quite clear that, for the Anglican Church, that is to say the official ideology, the aim was not simply to do away with the festivals of the Roman calendar. It was also to replace them, bit by bit, with a collection of civic, national and monarchical festivals which would encourage the people to transfer their fervour to a new set of ideals. The authorities' use of festivity as a means of rallying the people to the support of their queen, the embodiment of both spiritual and temporal power, was no doubt facilitated by the many points of resemblance between popular and aristocratic festivals.

The fact is that the same dates were celebrated at court *and* in the villages: the twelve days of Christmas, May Day and, of course the festival of 17 November. Moreover, the upper and the lower strata displayed a common taste for masquerade and disguise,[202] dancing and music, and carousing and feasting.[203] The wilful and popular sovereign Henry VIII enjoyed dressing up as Robin Hood, the rustic champion of the May games and Morris dances, and riding forth to gather May in the woods, as Elizabeth also did at the end of her life, thereby demonstrating her loyalty to May Day, one of the principal popular festivals of the calendar.[204] Entries, pageants, coronations and other progresses were certainly aristocratic and costly but they always attracted large crowds. These entertainments (most of them free and accessible to all and sundry) thus clearly had a popular side to them, if only through the presence of the public that flocked to see them. The queen herself was not above enjoying the simple and, no doubt, clumsy shows performed by artisans: they appear to have afforded her considerable pleasure, even amid the far grander amusements organized when she was received at Kenilworth by the Earl of Leicester in 1575.[205] It was only in the reign of James I, not nearly so popular a figure, that luxurious private entertainments, presented behind the closed doors of the palace, began to supplant the public spectacles which all and sundry could attend.[206]

No doubt the coincidence of such tastes at different levels, the logical result of which was to foster an atmosphere of mutual sympathy between the queen and her subjects, reflected a backward-looking ideology that was encouraged by the élites who were close to power and by court circles. However, it surely also testifies to the sentiments of a considerable proportion of the population: all those, for instance, who, when they went to see Shakespeare's comedies and romances, would applaud the scenes that showed craftsmen and shepherds living in harmony with princesses and kings. Of course, it is important not to confuse social reality with the world of imaginary representations, but the myth of the Golden Age and the pastoral dream recur so insistently in the 1590s after the publication of Sidney's *Arcadia* and Spenser's *The Faerie Queene*[207] that it is impossible to explain their success solely by the existence of collective subconscious attitudes. Between the nostalgia and the ideal and underlying the archetypes and conventions, there must have been something that made it possible for what started off as a policy to turn into an aesthetic.

As for the repercussions that all these festive practices may have had upon social relations and the political scene in general, interpretations vary considerably on the matter. Some scholars, such as Mervyn James, see the festivals as rites of inversion that may have served either as models or as excuses for revolt or subversion.[208] On the other hand, others, such as Keith Thomas and Charles Phythian-Adams, regard these sometimes aggressive and violent parodies of the existing authorities as psychodramas that operated as safety valves to deflect the forces of political conflict and revolution.[209] Clearly, it is important to assess each case on its own, for festivals came in different guises and they were at once so numerous and so diverse within both the temporal framework (the calendar) and the regional one that we should not generalize where they are concerned, as will appear in the detailed survey of the principal Elizabethan festivals that now follows.

3   The calendar

Time, festivals and the calendar

All festivals are naturally related to time, whether they are designed to divide sacred time from profane periods or set out to deny the process of change with annual repetitions of rituals that are hoped to be immutable.[1] Festival time is defined by a break with everyday time, but it is also cyclical, structured by the revolving seasons. Hence the idea that, in the beginning, the fluctuations of time could be gauged within the context of a natural calendar based on empirical observation and an understanding of the various harbingers that forecast the approach of the four seasons.[2] To find evidence of this belief in a natural rhythm of time, we need look no further back than the sixteenth or seventeenth centuries, since popular almanacs, shepherds' calendars and much of the pastoral literature of that period constantly appeal to it. Many proverbs and popular sayings about the weather also refer to it implicitly, as if daily life could hardly make do with purely quantitative divisions of time.[3]

In general, the most obvious reference points of periodicity seem to be provided by the phases of the moon, since most so-called primitive calendars adopt a lunar system for counting out the months, making empirical adjustments when the mismatch between the lunar year and the real (that is to say solar) year becomes too great. It is interesting to note that the shortfall between the solar and the lunar years amounts to roughly twelve days, a figure that corresponds to what the Elizabethans called the twelve days of Christmas, that is, the period stretching from Christmas to the eve of Epiphany (or Twelfth Night). It is not hard to see how this period of what were originally simply intercalary days which were wedged between one year and the next became particularly associated with festivity. From time immemorial they had been considered as extra days, over and above the normal, banal flow of time – days which, on that account, eluded the ordinary logic of things. It was probably that special ontological status of theirs that accounted for the particular atmosphere associated with all these Christmas festivities, whether they involved Saturnalia, the *Libertas Decembris* of the ancient world, or the 'misrule' of the Elizabethan period.

Other civilizations, where knowledge of astronomical matters was more advanced (as among the Babylonians, the Egyptians and the Maya) had certainly already produced solar calendars calculated on the basis of reference points, such as the solstices and equinoxes, that were more abstract but more accurate than those constituted by immediately observable natural phenomena (such as the phases of the moon). However, even when the solar calendar was recognized as the official measure of time, in reality it simply co-existed alongside the old lunar calendar which continued to be used to determine the dates of the various religious feast days and ceremonies of the year. That system holds good even today: the profane time of the working world is governed by a fixed, solar, calendar while the cycle of religious festivals stretching from Ash Wednesday to Corpus Christi (known as the moveable feasts) is traditionally determined by the moon. The solstices and equinoxes are not immediately perceptible unless the position of the sun is calculated, but they are, nevertheless, linked with seasonal phenomena and the climatic variations that these produce. In contrast, the lunar cycles, which recur without variation throughout the year, without occasioning any particular meteorological changes, are relatively indistinguishable. Accordingly, the religious festivals and ceremonies that intervened in certain lunar cycles were regarded as celebrations connected with the Greater Time of origins as much as occasions designed to differentiate and punctuate time as perceived by the collective memory.[4] We know that festivals are a means both of marking repetitions and also of anticipating time.[5] But another of the functions of festivals is to establish qualitative distinctions within duration. As Roger Caillois writes,

festivals open the gates to the world of the gods; when men take part in them, they undergo a metamorphosis and attain to a superhuman existence. They allow one to accede to Greater Time and also serve to mark out workaday time. Between one festival and the next, the calendar consists of hollow, anonymous days which only exist in relation to the more meaningful dates of the festivals . . . [6]

Because one of the functions of festivals is to mark out time, they assume an almost immutable character, as if they were detached from time itself and protected from all erosion. Recurring as they did at regular intervals, they helped to dispel the feeling of 'mutability' which seems generally to have characterized the Elizabethan view of the passage of time in the sublunary world. Festivals thus seemed to achieve the impossible synthesis that the Renaissance Neo-platonists so yearned for, namely the fusion of the one and the many which was supposed to set the seal upon Pan's union with Proteus.[7] It is hardly surprising that, albeit for different reasons, popular and aristocratic circles should simultaneously have subscribed enthusiastically to the myth that festivals protected them from the precariousness and erosion of time. Popular time is defensive: despite the abrupt variations to which it is, in reality, subject (what

Edmund Leach has called 'the pendulum view of time'[8]), it seeks to eliminate both chance and change.[9] Aristocratic time is by definition conservative – even reactionary – to judge by the attempts made to restore the Arthurian ideals of chivalry under Elizabeth. The queen's masterly political handling of festivals made it possible, at least to some extent, to make her contemporaries believe that the period of her reign truly did coincide with a return of the Golden Age. Only the rising bourgeoisie and the Puritans seem to have looked to the future and changes in both the political and the religious sphere in the hope of improving the material and spiritual existence of the kingdom's subjects. After Cromwell's victory over the Royalists, he got the Long Parliament to abolish most of the festivals and feast days in the calendar. The popular resentment that these measures provoked[10] shows clearly that festivals remained a key element in a vision of the world and of time for which the Puritans had no substitute to offer, apart from a strictly individualistic and abstract piety.

It would nevertheless be absurd to claim that this illusion of stability and perenniality prevailed at any level except at that of popular mentalities and a collective imaginary view of the world, or that the festivals themselves and the calendar of which they were a part were subject to no change. The refusal to ratify the Gregorian reform of the calendar in 1582 certainly testifies to the conservative nature of mentalities as much as to a reaction both nationalistic and religious against the papacy. But in what historians call 'la longue durée', one cannot help but notice that to a certain extent customs, rituals and sometimes even the dates of festivals within the calendar do shift. Such movements and shifts are, of course, a consequence of historical accidents to which nothing, not even modes of structuring time, is immune.[11] Sometimes, alterations in the calendar can be dated to within a few years (say, to the space of a single generation). That is precisely the case of the Elizabethan period during which, following decisions made at the time of Henry VIII's Reformation, certain festivals such as 'Corpus Christi' were abolished, while other, new ones, such as the anniversary of Elizabeth's accession to the throne, were introduced. As a general rule, however, changes of this kind come about so gradually and imperceptibly that they are registered so to speak automatically by the collective mind. People do not really seem to be individually aware that changes are taking place, as they inevitably do. Festivals seem to suffer the same fate as language: they continue to communicate a message over the centuries, but people do not necessarily notice the evolution of the vehicle of that communication (except, of course, in cases of foreign invasion, when the enemy tries to impose its own language upon the invaded people). The comparison between festivals and language is the more pertinent in the case of Elizabethan England given that changes affecting the calendar and festivals were taking place at the precise time when the vernacular, English, was taking the place of Latin, the traditional language of religious ritual. The process that eventually culminates in the festive calendar shifting from one state of equilibrium to another may have involved many years of erosion and deposit and, without documentation, it is impossible for historians and experts in folklore to determine the successive stages in the evolution of customs in different regions and at different times.

The situation clearly presents grave problems for any scholar researching in the field. He or she must choose between, on the one hand, a laborious reassessment of the evidence, which is bound to be of a disparate nature, and, on the other, working with material collected at a later date, much of which may constitute a bastardized form of the original rituals. If the scholar's essential interest is the continuity of festivals, ideally he should seize upon a network of festivals from the point of view of their stratification over the years, undertaking a kind of archaeology of festivity. If, on the other hand, he seeks to understand the place of a group of festivals within a particular cultural or temporal framework, he should seize upon it in its present state and study it in the context of a known calendar structure. Michel Meslin's study, *La fête des kalendes de janvier dans l'empire romain*, sets out the problem clearly, leaving the reader in little doubt as to the author's own preferences:

I am not sure . . . that the method of regressive erosion adopted by folklorists, a progession upstream through time, does not lead them into error for, as a result of the inevitable gaps in their information, it may conceal the distant origin of these rituals. It is not a matter of denying the evolution, transformation or even deliberate modifications that certain rites undergo. But the contribution of a historian of ancient religions might well be precisely to reveal the logical system of thought or magical actions to which those rites are connected – a system upon which most folklorists can only seize in a state of *membra disjecta*.[12]

In Meslin's view, the regressive approach rules out seizing upon the corpus of festivals except through some arbitrary reconstruction of its scattered parts. To borrow an image from Egyptian mythology, the fear is that the folklorist or ethno-historian may find himself in the position of Isis trying to reassemble all the pieces of her brother Osiris' body, dispersed in the waters of the Nile: only at the end of her long and difficult task does she perceive that one vital part is missing.[13] In the case of the period stretching from the Reformation to Cromwell's revolution in England, we at least know that the festive calendar that survived, after the purge imposed by the break with Rome, was the product of a fusion between two pagan calendars, that of the Graeco-Roman world and that of Celto-Teutonic civilization.[14] On the basis of that knowledge, it seems tempting to study the refraction of the various festive rites within the framework imposed by the Church from the eighth century on and to analyse the points at which the festivals of the two groups were amalgamated or superimposed upon one another or, alternatively, diverged and separated. For instance, it is surely not simply by chance that the birth of Christ coincides exactly with the end of the lunar year and also with the winter solstice (known in ancient times as the *Sol Novus* or *Invictus*) [15] and it is also the starting point dividing the year into two equal halves, since six months later comes the summer solstice or Saint John the Baptist's Day.[16] According to Bede, the ancient pagan year, which was divided into two equal halves, thus began on 25 December.[17] Furthermore, the two principal festivals of the Christian calendar – the one, Christmas, fixed and connected with the solar year; – the other, Easter, a moveable feast connected with the lunar year – happen to coincide with the two great festivals of the ancient Germanic year. Christmas took the place of the mid-winter festival (whose name has not come down to us) and Easter was substituted for the spring festival devoted to the goddess of fertility, Eostre (a connection that is reflected in the word 'Easter') (see Appendix 3, below, p. 309).[18] Moreover, in all probability, the festivals of 24 and 29 June (the Midsummer Watch processions), sanctified though they were by the names of Saints John and Peter, were in truth survivals from the ancient pagan cult of the sun that used to be celebrated at the summer solstice (see Appendix 2, below, p. 308).[19] With masterly skill backed up by many examples, E.K. Chambers charted the long process in the course of which the pagan calendar was replaced by a Christian one, showing that the switch from the former to the latter was a matter of changing not so much dates as names and rituals.[20]

More recently, Glynne Wickham has adopted Chambers' conclusions, presenting them in the synthetic form of a comparative calendar indicating the dates, rituals and general meaning of all the principal festivals, both pagan and Christian, that were held at each solstice and equinox.[21] The first two columns record the gods and festivals of the pre-Christian (Graeco-Roman, Celtic and Teutonic) calendar alongside the festivals of the Christian calendar (both the fixed and the moveable feasts). Then come analyses of the nature and function of the various feast days and the type of celebration (whether sacred or profane) associated with them. The last two columns note the principal specific features of medieval theatre and certain characteristic examples taken from medieval and Renaissance theatre, showing their association with the dates, rituals and general spirit of the festivals mentioned in the other columns. A synoptic table such as this makes it possible to show clearly how much medieval theatre appears to owe to, on the one hand, pagan rites of vegetation, and on the other the folklore and festivals of the Christian calendar. It also conveys a fairly clear, if extremely simplified, idea of the long process of gestation that led to the elaboration of the calendar of the Elizabethan period. Wickham, with great skill, superimposes the various cultural strata vertically one upon the other, in the chronological order in which they appeared (first the Graeco-Roman, then the Teutonic and Celtic festivals), arranging them within each of the periods of the year that correspond to the solstices and equinoxes. In this way, he avoids the headache of working out how the dates from calendars calculated on different bases related to one another.

Wickham's method has the merit of clarifying the problem, but the interest of his table seems to me limited to the extent that this kind of tabulation is capable of establishing only immediate and single connections: thus, for the festival of 1 May, Wickham produces only one antecedent, namely the Celtic feast of 'Beltane', making no reference either to the Greek Thargelia or to the Roman festivals of the 'Bona Dea'. Similarly, he makes no mention of the coincidence between the Celtic festival of 'Dimelc', held on 1 February, and the Feast of the Purification of the Virgin (Candlemas) which was celebrated on the following day. In an article which appeared some time before Glynne Wickham's study, I too had felt the need to try for a clearer understanding of these genealogical approximations and this confused welter of dates and different traditions.[22] My (altogether immoderate) ambition had been to try to piece together a picture that would show the general lines along which the Elizabethan calendar had evolved, under the impact of the various pagan influences by which it had successively been affected. My starting point was the fact that the Greek, Roman and Celto-Teutonic calendars were all lunar ones, governed by religious imperatives that resulted in a college of priests being made responsible for fixing the order and dates of the festivals. (I should, however, point out that, in the case of the Roman calendar, that was only true up until the Julian reform of 46 BC.) The difficulties involved in such an attempt at comparison only emerge when one becomes aware of the great discrepancies between the subdivisions of the year in the first two calendars, on the one hand, and those adopted by the Celts and Teutons, on the other (see Appendix 1, below, pp. 306–7).

For the latter, the year seems to have consisted of, not a series of twelve months, but sequences of sixty-day periods each of which began around the middle of the Julian calendar. Thus, the new year began in mid-November (the start of the winter festival), not with the Calends of March nor on 1 January, as in the Gregorian calendar. As Wickham quite correctly suggests,[23] the various pagan traditions, whether Roman or Celtic or Teutonic, must have evolved a *modus vivendi* in the regions of England where all these cultural influences were at work at the time of the country's Christianization (the early seventh century AD). But when the Roman calendar, reorganized by the Church, was subsequently imposed upon these different localities, the people living there were obliged to adapt their own festive customs to the new system and shift the timing of their celebrations to bring them into line with the new dates of the Christian festivals. Thus, the great Festival of the Dead (of which the popular feast of Saint Martin on 11 November is likely to have been a survival), which used to mark the beginning of both winter and the year as a whole and was probably situated in mid-November in the old calendar, had to be rescheduled in part to early November (Hallowe'en and All Saints' Day), in part to late December (Christmas and New Year's Day). The six great festivals of the Celto-Teutonic calendar, which inaugurated the six major sixty-day periods that made up the year, were thus reduced to four principal festivals which were situated at the beginning of the months of November (Samhain), February (Dimelc), May (Beltane) and August (Lugnasadh). The year, formerly split into two equal halves, each of one hundred and eighty days, was reorganized, for civil and juridical purposes, into four terms, each of ninety days.[24] Once these major axes are established (or rather, in view of their general and hypothetical character, tentatively pencilled in), we can see that the principal points at which the festivals of the old calendar are concentrated fall within four periods of festivity. First, a number of convergences appear between the Roman festival of the January Calends, the Celtic 'Yule' festival and the Christian festivals of Christmas and the New Year, all of which fall within a period of twelve days.[25] Next, a possible conjunction emerges between the Greek festival of the Anthesteria, the Celtic festival of Dimelc and the Christian festival of Candlemas, and a number of other convergences are detectable around 1 May. The last major point of convergence is 1 November, the date of coincidence between the Greek Thesmophoria, the Celtic festival of Samhain and the great Christian Festival of the Dead. Furthermore, each of these great poles of festivity turns out to have other, complementary, meanings which arise out of their position in relation to the major seasonal and agricultural cycles. A festival of birth stands in opposition to a festival of the dead; a festival of purification balances a festival for the renewal and liberation of energies after hibernation.

But that is about as far as we can go in this domain. The existence of such points of convergence shows that different religions and cultures share a common tendency to anchor the religious, festive and civic year in the cycles of nature, whether lunar, solar or simply seasonal. But it proves nothing about the possible links that may connect the various pagan festivals with the festivals of the Christian calendar, for these can only be interpreted within their own respective contexts. The genetic or diachronic perspective thus ends in an impasse. The remaining solution is the synchronic approach. In the context of the present study, this means attempting a detailed analysis of the structure of the calendar of the Elizabethan period.

A synchronic analysis: the structure of the calendar

(a) The division of the year into two halves

At first sight, the Elizabethan year looks extremely complicated: the proliferation of local festivals introduces many regional disparities; processes of transformation introduced by the Reformation have not yet become established custom; and fixed feasts stand in traditional opposition to moveable ones. In reality, however, the Elizabethan year was organized on the basis of the old division into two halves adopted by the Celts and the Saxons. In a short work entitled *Local History and Folklore*, Charles Phythian-Adams shows clearly that the year was divided into two equal halves, each of 182 days and a half, the dividing line running between the solstices of 24 December and 24 June, that is to say the festivals celebrating the births of Christ and his precursor, John the Baptist. The first half is composed of the twelve days of Christmas together with the collection of moveable feasts encompassed by Shrove Tuesday and Corpus Christi. Shrove Tuesday, which fell after the first new moon of February, oscillated between 3 February and 9 March. Corpus Christi, which was officially abolished in England in 1547 but whose traditions persisted for many years in certain towns, fluctuated between 21 May and 24 June. So clearly, in extreme cases, the dates could vary by more than a month from one year to the next. However, the uncertainty hanging over the exact length of this festive half of the year was no more than theoretical since people knew perfectly well how far apart the moveable feasts were from one another and, from the point of view of their individual perception of time, this offset the variability of the calendar position of these festivals: Easter fell forty days after the beginning of Lent, Whitsun came fifty days after Easter, Corpus Christi twenty days after Whitsun. If the moveable feasts were late, the first half of the festive year could end on the very day of the summer feast of Saint John but, on the other hand, it was equally likely to end over a month before the official beginning of summer. In the latter eventuality, as in the case of the short month between the festivals of Christmas and the start of the cycle of moveable feasts, in all likelihood the interval was punctuated by a number of traditional feasts that served to link the different cycles together (see Appendix 3, below, p. 309).[26] We should also bear in mind the many local variations and the fact that in some regions Christmas began on 21 December, while in others the fireworks that marked the arrival of summer and that were usually a feature of the celebrations of the Feast of Saint John were not set off until the eve of Saint Peter and Saint Paul's Day (29 June).[27] So we should avoid setting up inflexible demarcations in this domain, however helpful it may be for establishing boundaries and clarifying the analysis.

The second half of the year was bounded by 25 June and 24 December and was characterized by an absence of major religious festivals (the Feast of the Assumption of the Virgin Mary on 15 August was not celebrated in the Anglican Church), the presence of a few fixed festivals and a predominance of working days over holidays (since most agricultural activities were concentrated into the summer and the early autumn). However, we should beware of leaping to hasty and simplistic conclusions here, since most labour in the fields (which would be carried out collectively, with neighbours helping one another out) gave rise to major celebrations in the countryside and most villages when the tasks were completed. In the calendar that is found in Appendix 2 (below, p. 308), the names of these festivals appear in italics, for they were necessarily moveable feasts, not on account of their relationship to any lunar cycles, but because of climatic factors and variations in topography, regions and local traditions. First came the 'sheep-shearing' festival, generally held before the summer celebrations for Saint John's Day, then the 'rush-bearing' festival in mid-July, when the rushes were cut, then the harvest festivals ('harvest-home') towards the end of August. Finally, there would be a parish festival (the 'wake') sometime around Michaelmas, although the date would vary from one parish to another.[28] The two halves of the year present a strong contrast. The first half, which included most of the major religious festivals, constituted what Phythian-Adams calls the 'ritualistic half'; the second, punctuated by fixed festivals of a civic nature and merrymaking associated with the completion of agricultural labours, represented the 'secular half'.[29] Those labels may seem surprising nowadays when, in the context of our industrial societies, most festivals have lost any sacred or ritualistic character they may once have had, but they seem suitable enough applied to the concepts of medieval or Renaissance mentalities.

In the ritualistic half of the year, from Christmas to Saint John's or Midsummer's Day, most festive behaviour and traditions seem to have been connected with starting off symbolic systems that involved either the elements and forces of nature or else the major phases of the cycle of

birth, death and resurrection. Rituals involving fire ('fire charms') are
much in evidence (Christmas candles, the bonfires of Saint John's Day) as
are the symbolic use of vegetation (Christmas holly and mistletoe, later to
be burned at Candlemas; branches of leaves to decorate the churches on
Palm Sunday) and the practice of inaugurating various festivals with
peals of bells.[30] As for the rites attached to the cycle of birth, death and
resurrection, they centred mainly upon the principal poles of the
Christian liturgy: the festivals of Christmas and Easter, in which the
faithful were bidden to commemorate Christ's birth, death on the cross
and resurrection. Finally, those same ritualistic phases were still finding
burlesque or even grotesque expression in the Mummers' plays which
were performed in the villages of Elizabethan England at Christmas and
Easter, and also in the processions organized on 23 April in honour of
Saint George. These represented the national saint's fight against the
dragon in comic, mimed dramas. The symbolic schema even extended to
the football matches between neighbouring villages on Shrove Tuesday
or at Easter and the ritualistic confrontations that took place between the
two sexes on Hock Tuesday in Coventry. Another major feature of this
ritualistic half of the year is the collection of prohibitions by which it is
marked: dietary ones (during the period of Lent) and sexual ones too
(marriages were forbidden both in Lent and in the month of May, or,
more exactly, from the Sunday before Ascension Day to the Octave of
Pentecost). This had been imposed by the Church in the Middle Ages and
the tradition was fully preserved by the Church of England after the
Reformation. These periods of prohibition tended to be preceded or
followed by explosions of licence. The last feature to note in this half of
the year is the series of processions in which the corporations and other
official bodies (both civil and military) paraded in public.

During the secular half of the year, which stretched from Saint
John's Day to Christmas, the only great parade was the Lord Mayor's
Show, organized to mark the enthronement of the new Lord Mayor of
London. On this occasion, the festivities and celebrations held by the
various official bodies were private affairs (balls, banquets and
Masques); and the only other ceremonies held by the guilds were when
they elected their new masters. For the rest, this period, essentially one of
agricultural activity, was not broken up by long periods of festivity or
marked by the kinds of excess that were such a feature of the other half of
the year. The only occasions when energies were to some extent liberated
were the festivities and libations that crowned the completion of the
various agricultural tasks and parish festivals held in the villages and
countryside. The dearth of festivals no doubt explains why it was that
most of the great annual fairs were held during the summer or early
autumn. At the fairs of Saint Bartholomew, Saint Luke and Saint Giles,

the people of the towns and those of the countryside came together to do business. It is also because no other festivals were scheduled for this period that the great political festivals that were created in the towns were slotted into November (one to mark Elizabeth's accession to the throne, another to celebrate the foiling of the Gunpowder Plot on Guy Fawkes' Day). If the first half of the year was marked by behaviour and symbolism that belonged to a ritualistic and sacred concept of the world, the secular half was devoted to the economic side of life as opposed to the religious, the private as opposed to the public and the rational as opposed to the mystical.

(b) Fixed feasts and moveable feasts

Let us dwell a little longer on the fundamental opposition between the moveable and the fixed feasts, for it established a veritable cleavage between the two half-years that we have distinguished. That opposition conferred an essential quality upon time, as a result of which no year was quite the same as the last, since the ten great moveable feasts strung out between Shrove Tuesday and Corpus Christi never fell on the same dates. In the calendar provided in Appendix 2 (see below, p. 308), all those festivals appear in italics and we can see at a glance that by far the greater number fell in the first half. In the second, those that are in italics (for the sake of clarity) were in truth only 'moveable' in the sense that their dates were indeterminate: they varied from place to place and also from year to year. Indeed, a distinction needs to be made between lunar festivals which are cyclical and festivals whose timing is determined by climatic and regional variables. There can be no doubt that festivals which were essentially secular were not in fact confused by those who took part in them with festivals which marked a sacred or ritual time. Finally, in all likelihood, the dates of local festivals did not vary all that much from one year to another, so their mobility only raises problems for an external observer when he is faced with phenomena of regional variation.

The matter of the moveable feasts of the ritualistic half of the year was obviously more complex and the successful sales of calendars and almanacs at this period were probably due as much to curiosity over the festivals' timing as to mere superstition. It was no doubt only the literate and the educated urban élite who thought to make use of the tables provided in the Book of Common Prayer for establishing the date of Easter from one year to the next (epact and golden number).[31] Once Easter was fixed, it was easy to establish the dates of Shrove Tuesday, Ascension Day and Whitsun, by tracking back for forty days or moving forward forty or fifty days, as the case might be. Whatever the system adopted, we may be sure that these temporal fluctuations (in conjunction with a number of other elements that vary according to whether one lived in a town or in the country) made a strong impact upon both the individual and the collective perception of time in the Elizabethan age for this was a period when, in the countryside and other popular circles, the concept of months and years was not so clearly defined as it is today. At that time, the major natural and seasonal cycles, together with all the events that were associated with them and the recurrent festivals that punctuated them, constituted reference points that were universally recognized, even if we today might consider the temporal demarcations that they established to be somewhat vague.

The question of the moveable feasts does not seem to have bothered Shakespeare's contemporaries unduly, accustomed as they were to a relatively vague concept of time. However, it is complicated enough to make it difficult to give a clear representation of the situation. In an attempt to clarify the matter, I have noted the earliest possible occurrence of the various moveable feasts (3 February, Saint Blaise's Day, for Shrove Tuesday, for example) and also the very latest dates upon which they might fall. This will enable us to form a clear picture of the series of major moveable feasts and see exactly whereabouts they occurred in the calendar. As I have also indicated the maximum variations, we can get some idea of the possible disparities from year to year. The system operates on the principle of a sliding scale within which the various festivals fall into line once the starting point is determined. This is Shrove Tuesday, traditionally situated on the first Tuesday after the first new moon in February. The advantage of this method of orientation, which leaves open the dates situated between the beginning and the end of the festival period as a whole, is that it also reveals the coincidences between on the one hand the moveable calendar used to date the religious festivals and on the other the calendar reflecting the cycles of nature. The 'primary key',[32] that is to say the first possible date for Shrove Tuesday, coincides almost day for day with the date popularly believed to mark the beginning of spring.[33] Ash Wednesday falls two days after the celebration of the Purification of the Virgin (or Candlemas) and Easter falls the day after the spring equinox. As we have already noted, if it fell on the latest possible date, then Corpus Christi, the last in the string of moveable feasts, could coincide with Saint John's Day, that is say the beginning of summer (see below, p. 308). All this confirms the division of the year into two equal parts, a basic division that might otherwise be masked by the variable dating of the string of moveable feasts: the first half of the year stretched from the mid-winter festival of Christmas right to the mid-summer festival of 24 June; the second half consisted of the rest of the year.

Now, the notion of the year falling into two distinct halves was deeply rooted in popular mentalities and in folklore, as we know from all the evidence of ritual combat between Old Man Winter and a youth representing Summer or, in the version recorded in George Waldron's history of the Isle of Man, between a queen of May and a queen of Winter:

In almost all the great Parishes they chuse from among the Daughters of the most wealthy Farmers a young Maid, for the *Queen of May*. She is drest in the gayest and best manner they can, and is attended by about twenty others, who are called Maids of Honour: she has a young Man, who is her Captain, and has under his Command a good number of inferiour Officers. In opposition to her, is the *Queen of Winter*, who is a Man drest in Woman's Clothes with woollen Hoods, Furr Tippets, and loaded with the warmest and heaviest Habits one upon another . . . Both being equipt as proper emblems of the Beauty of the Spring, and the Deformity of the Winter, they set forth from their respective Quarters; the one preceded by Violins and Flutes, the other with the rough Musick and the Tongs and the Cleavers. Both companies march till they meet on a Common, and then their trains engage in a Mock-Battle . . .[34]

As can be seen from the calendar of the principal festivals of the year provided in Appendix 2, the secular half of the year (the right-hand column) is essentially made up of fixed festivals: the only variations here are regional, either depending upon when the various agricultural tasks are completed (essentially climatic factors) or upon the influence of particular local traditions or cults (parish festivals or wakes). As those dates are variable, I have used italics to indicate the festivals connected with them, in the right-hand column of the calendar (see Appendix 2, p. 308).

Another opposition to be taken into account is the one between night and day, for this constitutes a micro-system within the macro-system of the calendar and is extremely important as an element to distinguish between the type or specific nature of the various festive occasions. The nocturnal character of many festivals is attested by their very names: they are known as 'vigils' or 'eves' (e.g. Saint Agnes' Eve or Saint Bridget's Eve) (see below, p. 96) as are certain occasional festivals to mark, for instance, the eve of a battle (e.g. the battle of Agincourt in *Henry V*) (see below, p. 207).

Multiple calendars

The separation of the fixed from the moveable feasts, which reflects variations inherent in the cycles of the moon and seasonal changes, is not the only source of error and confusion nor the most complex problem posed by a study of the calendar. On top of the problem of the mobility of festival dates from one year to another, we must cope with the difficulties created by the fact that the official calendar is a product of many different systems of reference superimposed one upon another. We are here entering upon confusing terrain which a rigorous study of the history of time and the successively adopted instruments for measuring its duration might usefully clear. Such a study would make it easier to understand the considerable difference between our habits of today and those of Shakespeare and his contemporaries. But we should no doubt be surprised at the need to revise some of our assumptions as to our own superiority (thanks to the advances made by modern technology) over the people of the Renaissance. The fact is that we have achieved absolute precision in the measurement of time and the synthesis of various systems of reference only at the cost of alienating ourselves from the bio-cosmic rhythms with which pre-industrial societies kept close contact, thanks to their long-lived memories and their familiarity with tradition. In those days, time and duration were felt to be relatively harmonious, which is not always the case today.[35]

The diversity of the calendar did not present the Elizabethans with insurmountable problems, for they were familiar with various forms of calendar computation. On the one hand, there were the written and official calendars (those of the civic and religious festivals, for example), on the other, a non-written calendar based upon regional, family or guild customs or people's day-to-day familiarity with the rhythms of the seasons (the times for sowing and for harvesting, for example). The co-existence of all this data of a relatively diverse and at times contradictory nature was probably regarded as a form of richness rather than as an inconvenience. However, it is worth noting that the Reformation introduced a great many disruptions that had the effect of undermining age-old customs. On that account it was, in a sense, one of the early causes of the intellectual and spiritual crisis that continued until Cromwell and the Puritans seized power in the mid-seventeenth century. Those disruptive changes, introduced in the course of the 1530s, made a profound impact upon both the religious and the civic calendars.

We have already noted a number of examples of the changes made in the religious calendar. They were generally represented by the bishops as an improvement and a welcome simplification for, over the years, the number of festivals had so increased as to produce a somewhat chaotic situation in which the time left for working was much reduced. Among the official Church documents of the Tudor period, we find, for example, the following request:

And also where a great number of holy days which now at this present time, with very small devotion, be solemnized and kept throughout this your realm – upon the which many great, abominable, and execrable vices, idle and wanton sports, be used and exercised – which holy days, if it may stand with your gracious pleasure, and specially such as fall in the harvest, might, by your majesty, by the advice of your most honourable council, prelates and ordinaries, be made fewer in number...[36]

The author of this particular request urged the suppression of more festivals and was in favour of reorganizing the calendar to include more working days. The theme was to become a leitmotif of the Puritans from 1580 on. According to William Harrison's *Description of England*, published in 1577, the upshot was that the number of festivals and non-working days was reduced by two-thirds.[37]

The reformers were determined to abolish the medieval laxity that was claimed to encourage sloth, drunkenness and vice and also to disrupt the smooth accomplishment of agricultural work upon which the people depended for their sustenance. Official documents of the period emphasize the need to stamp out the festive activities of this period of the year and reserve it totally for work on the land:

Forasmuch as the nombre of holydays is so excessively grown, and yet dayly more and more by mens devocyion, yea rather supersticyon, was like further to encrease, that the same was and should be not onely prejudiciall to the common weale, by reason that it is occasion...of...unthriftynesse and inconvenyency as of decaye of good mysteryes and artes, utyle and necessarye for the common wealthe, and loss of mans fode many tymes, beyinge clene destroyed through the superstitious observance of the said holydaes, in not taking th'opportunitie of good and serene weather, offered upon the same time in harvest...[38]

Having explained the reasons for suppressing summer festivals, the author of this text goes on to specify the areas that it would affect.[39] He also expresses his earnest wish that the dates of the various local 'wakes' should all be brought into line, his reason no doubt being that this would put an end to people prolonging the time set aside for this kind of local rejoicing by moving on from one village celebration to the next.[40] However, we should also note that the same text urges that the custom of fasting in Lent and the particular dietary prohibitions associated with it should continue to be observed. The passage is headed 'A proclamation for the absteyning from flesh in the Lent time. Dated the 16th day of January 1547' and it testifies to the reformers' desire not to upset the Elizabethan parishioners' daily customs altogether nor to jeopardize the important economic activity of fishing.[41] But these are written texts and it is legitimate to wonder how much impact they had upon behaviour in practice, for in the domain of popular mentalities and daily or seasonal customs, people are circumspect and nothing changes overnight. Given such inbuilt resistance and the spirit of compromise between tradition and change that characterized the English Reformation, it is not too surprising to learn from Bishop White Kennett that some of these injunctions were never applied.[42]

Now let us turn to the civic calendar. This too testifies to a wide diversity of customs. The first source of difficulties is the fact that, at this period, the official start of the civic year was fixed for 25 March, Lady Day. This seriously complicated the task of dating during the first three months of the year. On the other hand, the dates of the starts of terms remained uniform for schools, universities, courts and all other major administrative departments. Another text sets them out in detail:

And for further declaracyon of the premyses, be it known that Easter terme begynneth always the 18. day after Easter, reckoning Easter day for one, and endeth the Monday next after th'Ascension day. Trinity terme begynneth always the Wednesday next after th'octaves of Trinitie Sunday, and endeth the 11. or 12. day of July. Mighelmas terme beginneth the 9. or 10. day of October, and endeth the 28. or 29. day of November. Hillary terme begynneth the 23. or 24. day of January, and endeth the 12. or 13. day of February.[43]

As well as these term days, used above all by universities and the judiciary, there were the Quarter Days. These were the dates of the terms for new mayors and municipalities. (In Nottingham, the mayor was installed on Saint Michael's Day, in Coventry this happened at Candlemas, in York on the following day, Saint Blaise's Day). Quarter Days were also the dates when rural leases ran out and rents had to be paid.

According to the *OED*, which provides a detailed list of Quarter Days, the dates were different for England and for Scotland. This divergence between the customs of the two countries is but one instance of the many differences that separated Scotland from England and Ireland, differences that might have constituted an extra problem for us in the present work had not Scotland lain mainly beyond its scope.

There is a further distinction to be made between the payment of rents in the towns, where it was simply a matter of money changing hands, and in the countryside, where it was customary to accompany the rent due to the landlord with some gift in kind appropriate to the particular term day. George Gascoigne mentions these customs in a poem in which he evokes the difficult lives of tenant farmers under pressure from landlords who were themselves in dire financial straits:

> And when the tenauntes come to paie their quarters rent,
> They bring some fowle at Midsommer, a dish of Fish in Lent,
> At Christmasse a capon, at Mighelmasse a goose:
> And somewhat else at Newyeres tide, for fear their lease file loose.[44]

The obligation to make such payments in kind over and above the farm rental must have been bitterly resented, particularly if we are to believe a satire by Joseph Hall, which suggests that in former times tenant farmers could acquit themselves of their debt with no more than a purely symbolic gesture:

> When *Titios* grounds, that in his Grand-sires daies
> But one pound fine, one penny rent did raise,
> A sommer-snow-ball, or a winter rose,
> Is growne to thousands as the world now goes . . .
> Yet he must haunt his greedy Land-lords hall,
> With often presents at ech Festivall;
> With crammed Capons every New-yeares morne,
> Or with green-cheeses when his sheep are shorne
> Or many Maunds-full of his mellow fruite . . . [45]

These strange symbolic payments with their back-to-front timing (a snowball on Midsummer's Day, a rose at Christmas) underline the mismatch that could occur between the civic calendar and the natural calendar of shepherds and tillers of the soil. The subject has been studied by G.C. Homans in his book *English Villagers of the Thirteenth Century*, in particular in chapter 23, entitled 'The Husbandman's Year'. Three centuries later, these traditions and customs remained virtually intact – an indication of the gentle rhythm at which change takes place in the countryside, where people are no doubt more attached to tradition than in the towns. Homans presents a graphic picture of the quasi-ritualistic importance that peasants attached to the performance of every task or celebration, each one associated with the special time and place allotted to it by the calendar. [46]

But before considering the various festivals that were celebrated in between the periods of labour, some of which were totally peculiar to the country way of life, we need to form a more exact picture of the calendar of labour in the fields. Homans tells us that in the thirteenth century the year was divided into four major zones of activity, each one specifically associated with one of the seasons:

Winter (*yems*) was then the name given to the working season from Michaelmas to Christmas. This was the season of the sowing of wheat and rye; therefore these grains were called winter seed (*semen yemale*). The forty days before Easter were kept in much the same way they are now, but the name Lent was loosely given to the whole time from the end of the Christmas holidays to Holy Week. The grains sown in this season – oats, barley, vetches, peas and beans – were the lenten seed (*semen quadragesimale*). The time from Hocktide, after Easter Week, to Lammas (August 1) was summer (*estas*). Accordingly, a May Queen was also a 'summer queen'. And the time from Lammas back to Michaelmas again was harvest (*autumpnus*). [47]

Alongside this division into four major periods of work, another method of structuring the year can be established: one period began at

Candlemas, the date when serious agricultural labour started again and the pastures were closed to the herds, and lasted until Lammas Day; during the other half of the year, from Lammas Day to Candlemas, the reverse obtained and beasts could be pastured freely once the harvest had been stored away.

After describing the major phases of annual activity in the English countryside in the thirteenth century, Homans comes to the subject of holidays and festivals celebrated by those who worked on the land. The dates were determined by the religious calendar:

Easter Week, that is, the week after Easter, together with Whitsun Week and the twelve days of Christmas, were the villein's three long holidays. We must suppose that they were real holidays, that the villein then ceased work on his own lands as well as on the lord's demesne . . . Comparing Easter with Christmas reveals that the celebration of these great feasts of the husbandman's year fell into a single pattern. They began with a feast of the Church. There followed a week or more in which a villein was set free from working for his lord . . . Then the end of the vacation and the resumption of work was marked by another festival, which this time was not a feast of the Church but a feast of the folk. This pattern is clear in the celebration of Christmas. It began with the feast of Christmas itself. There followed the twelve days of holiday, and then work began again after Plow Monday. The same pattern was followed at Easter. First came the great feast itself. There followed a week of holiday, and then the resumption of work was marked by a festival of the folk – Hocktide.[48]

The tripartite structure that Homans discerns (the religious feast, the vacation and the secular feast) is both interesting and revealing. This was probably an extremely ancient pattern of festivity, still followed in the countryside after it had gradually disintegrated in the towns: a pattern that might well underlie many of the major annual festivals.

Having considered the rural world's calendar in the Elizabethan period, let us, finally, turn to the question of how the time of the artisans and the workers was organized. They too had their own festivals, and during the Middle Ages these were quite splendid affairs, thanks to the involvement of the various guilds. The days of these urban workers seem to have been full enough, to judge by the dispositions of the Statute of Artificers of 1563, but possibly not every master applied these to the letter.[49] One would like to think that there were many like Simon Eyre, the cheerful and sympathetic Master Shoemaker of Dekker's comedy, *The Shoemaker's Holiday*: small-scale employers who enjoyed a close relationship with their apprentices and workmen, setting them an example with their own zest for work and their relish for merrymaking or feasting when the chance presented itself.[50]

As for the workers, here is a quotation from an article by Lawrence Stone, which suggests that, in the case of the miners of Sheffield at least, the restrictions on festivals ordered at the Reformation were certainly not observed:

Contemporaries recorded with despondency that the dark and dangerous lives of the miners induced in them a conservative superstition that made them adhere rigidly to the old holiday system. At the turn of the century, George Owen lamented that the miners 'observe all abolished holie daies and cannot be wayned from that follie'.[51]

The implication here seems to be that for miners there were more feast days than for country folk. One explanation might be that those whose work deprived them of direct contact with nature and vegetation were in need of more frequent periodic festivals; another, the existence of strong guild traditions that were much attached to the customs of folklore.[52]

This brief survey of the various calendars and calendar references used in the Elizabethan period in connection with types of activity both religious and secular and in different regions and social circles (essentially either rural or urban) gives an idea of the vast diversity of the customs that were observed at the time. Now let us study them in greater detail.

4   The cycle of calendary festivals

The ritualistic half of the year

From a chronological point of view, it might seem reasonable to begin an analysis of the various festivals of the calendar with the date of 1 January, in spite of the fact that the year was still officially then considered to start on 25 March, Lady Day. In a proper appreciation of the real festive calendar, which falls into clearly defined periods, the date of 7 January must be regarded as marking a return to work in the countryside. At the end of the twelve festive days of Christmas, the resumption of labour seems to have been signalled by the women and was placed under the sign of the spinning-wheel or distaff.

Herrick, the nostalgic bard of the 'Works and Days' of the Elizabethan age, remarks that

> Partly worke and partly play
> Ye must on S. *Distaffs day*...[1]

In the Elizabethan period, the other name for this festival was Rock Monday. The *OED* defines it as follows:

The day after Twelfth Day was called Rock Day...because women on that day resumed their spinning, which had been interrupted by the sports of Christmas...The Monday following Twelfth Day was for the same reason denominated Rock Monday.[2]

It was a festival day much observed in the countryside, to judge from Sir Thomas Overbury's picture of the 'Franklin':

Rocke Monday, and the Wake in Summer, shrovings, the wakefull ketches in Christmas Eve, the Hoky, or Seed Cake, these he yearly keepes; yet holds them no reliques of Popery.[3]

Similarly, in his portrait of the 'Ploughman', Wye Saltonstall writes: 'Hee prayes onely for a faire seedtime and of all days will bee sure to keep Plough-munday';[4] and G.C. Homans also draws attention to this key point in the rural year that marked the end of the twelve days of Christmas.[5]

As on other occasions, it was the women who set the example and led the way, for the men's celebration of the return to work in the fields came four days later, on the first Monday after Epiphany, known as Plough Monday. In the calendar of the Elizabethan countryside, Plough Monday was the day that marked the switch from the early to the later winter festivals. Originally, Plough Monday was the male version of the Festival of Labours, just as Saint Distaff's Day was the female version. Such separations of the two sexes were frequent in the festivals of antiquity, having in the first instance probably been occasioned by the requirements of initiation. But that factor constituted no more than an ancient vestige in Elizabethan England, where Plough Monday soon became a day of competition between men and women, as can be seen from the following lines of Thomas Tusser:

> Plough Munday, the next after Twelftide be past, biddeth out with the plough, the worst husband is last
> If Ploughman get hatchet or whip to the skreene maydes loseth their Cocke if no Water be seene.[6]

The customs mentioned here seem somewhat obscure, so the gloss that 'Tusser Redivivus', the commentator, provides is helpful:

If the ploughman can get his whip, ploughstaff hatchett . . . to the fireside (as proof he is up and about) before the maid hath got her kettle on, the maid loseth her Shrovetide cock, and it belongs to the men.[7]

The game, one of forfeits, was a competition in industriousness (who would be up and about first) and it looked forward to the next festival in the calendar, namely Shrove Tuesday.

Plough Monday was also an occasion for dancing and singing, particularly in Scotland and northern England.[8] The remainder of the day was taken up in all kinds of jollifications:

The peasantry contrived to go about in procession collecting money, though only to be spent in the public-house. It was . . . a very gay and rather pleasant-looking affair. A plough was dressed up with ribbons and other decorations – the *Fool Plough*. Thirty or forty stalwart swains, with their shirts over their jackets, and their shoulders and hats flaming with ribbons, dragged it along from house to house, preceded by one in the dress of an old woman, but much bedizened, bearing the name of *Bessy*. There was also a Fool, in fantastic attire. In some parts of the country, morris-dancers attended the procession; occasionally too, some reproduction of the ancient Scandinavian sword-dance added to the pockets of the lieges.[9]

Naturally enough, the name given to the plough and likewise the details of the ceremony varied from region to region,[10] but a number of features recur everywhere. There was always a Fool accompanied by clowns with traditional names ('Pickle Herring' for instance, and 'Pepper Breeches'), all of whom would fight either a Hobby-horse or a dragon. The Fool would usually be killed in the fight, but would be brought back to life a few minutes later either by Pickle Herring or by a Doctor.[11] The play would in many cases end with a Morris[12] or a Sword dance, which would bring the performance to an end on a cheerful note and give the actors a chance to make a collection.[13] But what is interesting about Robert Chambers' account is that it emphasizes that the conscious aim of these Ploughboys or 'Bullocks' as they were sometimes called, was to entertain the spectators with a view to collecting as much money from them as possible, thereby making sure of a good evening meal with plenty of drink to wash it down. It is a feature that is also common to the charivari, which would not come to an end until payment in coin or kind was forthcoming. Yves-Marie Bercé has shown that in sixteenth-century France these practices were regarded as a right by fraternities of young men, who counted on them as a means of topping up their 'Bacchic funds'.[14]

In the opinion of the Puritan pamphleteer, Philip Stubbes, these rights claimed by youthful associations constituted so many intolerable abuses; and he condemns them each in turn in a chapter he devotes to the 'Lords of Misrule in Ailgna' (an anagram of Anglia, i.e. England):

They have also certain papers, wherin is painted some babblerie or other of Imagery woork, & these they call 'my Lord of mis-rules badges'; these they give to everyone that wil give money for them to maintaine them in their heathenrie, devilrie, whordome, drunkennes, pride, and what not. And who will not be buxom to them, and give them money for these their devilish cognizances, they are mocked and flouted at not a little. And so assoted are some, that they not only give them monie to maintain their abhomination withall, but also weare their badges & cognizances in their hats or caps openly . . . Another sort of fantasticall fooles bring to these hel-hounds (the Lord of mis-rule and his complices) some bread, some good ale, some new-cheese, some olde, some custards, & fine cakes; some one thing, some another; but if they knew that as often as they bring any thing to the maintenance of these execrable pastimes, they offer sacrifice to the devil and sathanas, they would repent and withdraw their hands . . .[15]

The text makes it clear that all this licence to tease and insult, which was part and parcel of the idea of a popular festival, was not simply a consequence of the temporary suspension of normal prohibitions and the general emotional anarchy of festival time. Sometimes it was used as a means of extracting alms (money, food or drink) through intimidation from the spectators, passers-by and the occasional unwilling burgher.

However, in the particular case of the Plough Monday festival, the money collected, known as 'Plough money', came from collections that were made at each of the houses visited rather than from random bullying and blackmail. There is no reason to believe that the Ploughboys' entertainment was welcomed eagerly by all and sundry, but it is safe to suppose that these popular troupes were adept enough at forcing the hands of misers and getting them to dip into their purses, even to the point of staging noisy demonstrations against those who were close-fisted, or roughing them up a bit. According to Glynne Wickham,[16] it was essentially because the Plough play[17] constituted primarily a very effective means of collecting money that the custom persisted in the English countryside, despite being attacked repeatedly for immorality by the Puritans and the authorities of law and order.

About two weeks after the masquerade of Plough Monday, essentially a daytime and masculine festival, came the traditional vigil of Saint Agnes' Eve, on the night of 20 January. This was specifically reserved for unmarried girls and women.[18] It is worth noting that Saint Bridget's Day, which fell on 1 February, used to be the day that corresponded to the great Celtic festival of Dimelc, which marked the beginning of the second half of the winter part of the year ('Earrach'). It was probably abolished quite early on, as there is no evidence of it being celebrated during the Elizabethan period. The following day, 2 February, was the Feast of Candlemas which, in Catholic liturgy, marked the date of the Purification of the Virgin, as the word 'February', derived from the old *februum*, meaning 'purification', reminds us. The religious ceremony consisted of processions of the faithful carrying torches and candles (hence the name 'Candlemas'). The candles symbolized purifying flames and also recalled an ancient pagan festival of light, that used to be celebrated just as the days began to lengthen. On the day of these rites of purification,[19] it was also the custom to burn all the festive greenery that had been used for Christmas decorations; and the right thing to do was to spread the floor with freshly culled reeds and straw.

The main festival in this festive cycle of transition represented by the 'Ploughing feast' was, of course, Shrove Tuesday, which marked the beginning of Carnival time in other European countries. Theoretically, the earliest that it could fall was Saint Blaise's Day (3 February),[20] so it could come either before or after Saint Valentine's Day on 14 February.[21] Thus, some years it was Shrove Tuesday, others Saint Valentine's Day that marked the changeover from winter to spring symbolized by many beliefs connected with the end of the bear's hibernation. Shrove Tuesday fell on the first Tuesday after the first new moon of February and it dictated the dates of all the other moveable feasts of the calendar. It was thus in a pivotal position between two festive cycles, the Ploughing feast which was just over and the period of Lent which was about to start.[22]

Unlike the countries of mainland Europe, Elizabethan England did not lay on the masquerades and processions that were organized in towns there on this date.[23] The reason for this dissimilarity may have been the weather: spring tends to come late in England, so it would not have seemed appropriate to celebrate its return symbolically as early as the month of February. In London and a number of other large towns such as Chester, the high season for parades was Saint John's Day, in the summer.[24] But the fact that were no processions on Shrove Tuesday does not mean that English towns languished in apathy. Shrove Tuesday was a joyous and boisterous festival, chiefly thanks to the fraternities of young men, first and foremost the apprentices. Several games allowed them to give a free rein to their aggressive penchants, among which the sport of throwing at cocks or 'cock-throwing' (that is, pelting to death a poor bird tied to a stake) was particularly popular at this season.[25]

One Shrove Tuesday custom, in London, often led to violence and rioting. The apprentices would band together and raid the brothels and theatres.[26] Thus Rafe, the apprentice grocer in Beaumont and Fletcher's *The Knight of the Burning Pestle*, bids a solemn farewell to his companions as follows:

> Farewell all you good boies in merry London
> Nere shall we more upon Shrove-tuesday meete
> And plucke down houses of iniquitie.[27]

And in Ben Jonson's *Bartholomew Fair*, Lanthorn Leatherhead, the hobby-horse vendor and puppeteer, speaks of all the shows that he has laid on for the Fair in his time:

O the *motions*, that I Lanthorn Leatherhead have given light to, i' my time, since my master *Pod* dyed! *Ierusalem* was a stately thing; and so was Ninive, and the citty of *Norwich*, and *Sodom* and *Gomorah*; with the rising o' the prentises; and pulling downe the bawdy houses there, upon *Shrove-Tuesday*...[28]

The pretext for such excesses was probably the idea that the city should be delivered from its haunts of vice before Lent, the season for penitence, set in. But, under the pretext of attacking sin and lust, the apprentices would give free rein to their inclinations with relative impunity. That is the point that Ben Jonson seems to be making in *Time Vindicated*, in which Ears, Eyes and Nose, who figure in the antimasque, express their desire to let their imaginations run riot and do crazy things, and are promptly rebuked by Fame, as follows:

> You doe abuse the *Time*. These are fit freedomes
> For lawless Prentices, on a Shrove tuesday,
> When they compell the *Time* to serve their riot:
> For drunken Wakes, and strutting Beare-baytings,
> That savour only of their owne abuses.[29]

Another Masque, entitled *The Inner Temple's Masque or the Masque of Heroes*, by Middleton, also reflects this violent festivity in the lawsuit brought against a character by the name of Shrove Tuesday:

> Stand forth, Shrove Tuesday, one o' the silenc'd bricklayers:
> 'Tis in your charge to pull down bawdy houses,
> To set your tribe a-work, cause spoil in Shoreditch
> And make a dangerous leak there, deface Turnbull
> And tickle Codpiece Row, ruin the Cockpit –
> The poor players ne'er thriv'd in't, o' my conscience,
> Some quean piss'd upon the first brick . . .[30]

The festival's reputation for disorder and popular licence is similarly reflected in the following dialogue:

NEW YEAR: Ha, Doctor, what are these?
TIME: The rabble that I pity. These I have serv'd too,
But few or none have ever observ'd me
Amongst this dissolute rout. Candlemas Day!
I'm sorry to see him so ill associated.
DOCTOR: Why, that's his cause of coming to complain
Because Shrove Tuesday this year dwells so near him;
But 'tis his place, he cannot be remov'd.
You must be patient, Candlemas, and brook it.
This rabble, sir, Shrove Tuesday, hungry Lent,
Ill May Day, Midsummer Eve, and the first Dog Day,
Come to receive their places due by custom,
And that they build upon . . .[31]

This passage is somewhat reminiscent of certain tirades in old popular dramas or interludes, in which verbal altercations would take place between the various seasons, months or festivals of the year; but it also reflects the equally popular tradition of almanacs and predictions of all kinds concerning the coming year. Here, Candlemas plays the part of a person of quality who is forced into company that he despises ('dissolute rout', 'rabble') since, as luck would have it, the calendar has positioned Shrove Tuesday right next to him. It was probably on account of some of the excesses that took place that a marked distinction tended to be made between, on the one hand, the religious festivals, which were respectable and well-behaved (Candlemas, Easter and Whitsun) and, on the other, the festivals of a profane and popular nature (Shrove Tuesday, May Day and Midsummer's Eve) which had a much more dubious reputation.

A text by John Taylor provides a detailed account of these raids perpetrated by the apprentices of London on Shrove Tuesday:

Then Tim Tatter (a most valliant villaine) with an Ensigne made of a piece of Bakers mawkin fixt upon a Bromme-staffe, he displaies his dreadfull colours, and calling the ragged Regiment together, makes an illiterate Oration stuft with a most plentifull want of discretion the conclusion whereof is, that somewhat they will doe, but what they know not. Untill at last comes marching up another troope of Tatter-demalions, proclayming wars against no matter who, so they may be doing; then these youths arm'd with cudgels, stones, hammers, tules, trowels, and handsawes, put Playhouses to the sacke and Bawdyhouses to the spoyle . . .[32]

This 'illiterate Oration stuft with a most plentifull want of discretion' puts one in mind of the ridiculous orders issued at the Roman Saturnalia and also during the period of misrule of the Christmas festivals. In connection with rowdy gatherings (this time of barbers), Dekker similarly writes that 'like Prentices upon Shrove-tuesday [they] take the lawe into their owne hands and doe what they list'.[33]

The selected victims of the London apprentices were the theatres and the brothels of the city. Their assaults upon the theatres can perhaps be explained by a kind of rite of passage prior to these being closed for the duration of Lent.[34] According to Edmund Gayton, on Shrove Tuesday the public made the most of certain rights which allowed them to arraign the actors with requests that they should play extracts from their favourite plays:

I have known upon one of these Festivals, but especially at Shrove-tide, when the Players have been appointed, notwithstanding their bils to the contrary, to act what the major part of the company had a mind to; sometimes *Tamerlane*, sometimes *Jugurth*, sometimes *The Jew of Malta*, and sometimes parts of all of these, and at last, none of the three taking, they were forc'd to undresse and put off their Tragick habits, and conclude the day with the merry milk-maides.[35]

If the actors refused to comply with the peremptory requests of the crowd, the audience grew restive and might well set about sacking the theatre:

And unlesse this were done, and the popular humour satisfied, as sometimes it so fortun'd, that the Players were refractory; the Benches, the tiles, the laths, the stones, Oranges, Apples, Nuts, flew about most liberally, and as there were Mechanicks of all professions, who fell everyone to his owne trade, and dissolved a house in an instant, and made a ruine of a stately Fabrick . . . Nothing but noise and tumult fils the house . . .[36]

The theatres were not the only victims of these flare-ups of festive violence. Brothels suffered too, as did performing animals:

then to the Bawdy houses and reforme them; and instantly to the Banks side, where the poor Beares must conclude the riot, and fight twenty dogs at a time beside the Butchers, which sometimes fell into the service; this performed, and the Horse and Jack-an-Apes for a jigge, they had sport enough that day for nothing.[37]

John Earle bears all this out in his *Microcosmography*, remarking of the actor 'Shrove-Tuesday he fears as much as the bawds, and Lent is more damage to him than the butcher.'[38]

On Shrove Tuesday, it was apparently common for the inmates of brothels to be seized, dragged from their lodgings and even paraded through the town in carts, for all to see, as is suggested by the expression 'the carting of the whores' used on these occasions. The *OED* gives the following definition of the verb 'to cart' (second meaning):

To carry in a cart through the streets, by way of punishment or public exposure (esp. as the punishment of a bawd).

In Dekker's *Northward Ho*, the prostitute says:

The Doctor told me I was with child, how many Lords, Knights, Gentlemen, Citizens, and others promised me to be godfathers to that child: twas not God's will: the prentises made a riot upon my glassewindowes the Shrove-tuesday following and I miscaried.[39]

Shrove Tuesday seems to have been the preferred day for carrying out such acts of popular justice. Henry Machyn's diary contains a description of a 'charivari' or 'Skimmington riding' which took place on the Shrove Tuesday of 1562–3:

The xxij of February, was Shroyff-monday, at Charyng-crosse ther was a man cared of iiij men, and for hym a bagpype playhyng, a shame [shawn] and a drum playhyng, and a xx lynkes bornyng abowtt hym, because ys next neybor['s] wyff ded bett [beat] her husband; ther-for yt [is] ordered that ys next neybor shall ryd a-bowtt the plasse.[40]

In mainland Europe, these charivaris were used to monitor marriages, in particular second marriages.[41] But in England, the Skimmington riding was brought into action when marital relations deviated from the norm imposed by the code of community behaviour[42] (when a husband was beaten by his wife, for example). A French visitor to England, Misson de Valbourg, has left us a colourful description of this popular ceremony, usually performed on Shrove Tuesday:

I have sometimes met in the streets of London a woman carrying a figure of straw representing a man, crown'd with very ample horns, preceded by a drum, and followed by a mob, making a most grating noise with tongs, gridirons, frying-pans and saucepans. I asked what was the meaning of all this; they told me that a woman had given her husband a sound beating for accusing her of making him a cuckold, and that upon such occasions some kind neighbour of the poor innocent injured creature generally performed this ceremony.[43]

The Swiss traveller, Thomas Platter, who visited England in 1599, also notes this custom in his diary, but provides fewer details:

Now the women-folk of England . . . have far more liberty then in other lands . . . and the men must put up with such ways, and may not punish them for it; indeed the good wives often beat their men, and if this is discovered, the nearest neighbour is placed in a cart and paraded through the whole town as a laughing stock for the victim, as a punishment – he is informed – for not having come to his neighbour's assistance when his wife was beating him . . .[44]

This popular ceremony was a 'shaming ritual', the purpose of which was to humiliate the husband who was downtrodden or deceived by his wife (an 'unruly woman') for having allowed the traditional social order and sexual hierarchy to be turned upside-down. There is another reference to these customs, more or less contemporary with Misson's, in a long poem by Marvell entitled 'The Last Instructions to a Painter'.[45]

Charivaris, raids on brothels and theatres, cock-throwing – all these goings-on give Shrove Tuesday a penitential or even sacrificial character. But they were excesses that the townsfolk did not necessarily tolerate cheerfully. Thus, in Ben Jonson's *Epicoene*, Clerimont tells us, of his uncle, that:

He would have hang'd a Pewterers' prentice once upon a shrove tuesdaies riot, for being o' that trade, when the rest were quit.[46]

The municipal authorities were also on the qui vive and were likely to intervene when things went too far. The repression that followed the particularly violent Shrove Tuesday rioting in 1617 testifies to the fact that their warnings were not to be taken lightly.[47]

However, the Shrove Tuesday festival should not be reduced to these images of disorder and violence. It was also a day renowned for its gaiety. The taverns would be crowded and, according to Donald Lupton, the landladies would be particularly encouraging:

Shee is merry and halfe made upon Shrove Tuesday, May daies, Feast days and Morrice-dances . . .[48]

As on the continent, it was an occasion for heavy eating and drinking and convivial merrymaking, in anticipation of the long Lenten period of abstinence. At the sound of the 'pancake bell', everyone would rush to table and the feasting and carousing would begin. This stampede to food and drink is evoked by Dekker in *The Shoemaker's Holiday*, the setting for which is, precisely, the celebrations of Shrove Tuesday:

ALL: The Pancake bell rings, the pancake bel, tri-lill my hearts . . .
FIRKE: O musical bel stil! O Hodge, O my brethren! theres cheere for the
         heavens, venison pasties walke up and down piping hote, like sergeants,
         beefe and brewesse comes marching in drie fattes, fritters and pancakes
         comes trowling in in wheele barrowes, hennes and orenges hopping in
         porters baskets, colloppes and egges in scuttles, and tartes and custardes
         comes quavering in in mault shovels.[49]

All this evidence of unbridled appetites and gluttony suggests that in England Shrove Tuesday was a festival of abundance and feasting rather than a pretext for fancy dress and masquerades, as it was in Italy (notably in Venice). In *The Popish Kingdome*, Naogeorgus (Thomas Kirchmeyer) associates the festival with Bacchus,[50] and in an anonymous text, *Vox Graculi*, attributed to Nicholas Breton, Carnival appears in the guise of an obese, pot-bellied monarch:

But now stand off (my friends) give roome I say: for here must enter that waddling, stradling, bursten-gutted *Carnifex* of all Christendome; vulgarly entitled *Shrove-Tuesday*, but more pertinently, sole-monarch of the Mouth, high Steward to the Stomack, chiefe Ganimede to the Guts, prime Peere of the Pullets, first favourite to the Frying-pans, greatest Bashaw to the Batterbowles, Protector of the Pan-cakes, First Founder of the Fritters, Baron of Bacon flitch, Earle of Egg-baskets, and in the least and last place, lower Warden of the Stinke-ports.[51]

The purpose of this burlesque enumeration of all the titles of the sovereign ruler of Carnival, who puts one in mind of the continental tradition of the Carnival king, appears to be to offset the banality of his name that is deemed to be too humble (he is 'vulgarly entitled *Shrove-Tuesday*'). But in reality the list incorporates a whole series of variations on the theme of 'Pancake Day'. This was the profane and popular name for Shrove Tuesday, and it provides proof, of an oratorical kind at least, that the religious name of the festival (literally, 'Confession Tuesday') was simply a label used to mask appetites and entertainments of an essentially pagan nature. However, as we shall see in connection with Martinmas and Christmas, the frankly gluttonous aspect of Shrove Tuesday represents an essential feature of all the winter festivals. A Masque by Thomas Nabbes entitled *The Spring's Glory* (1638) presents a confrontation between 'Christmas' and 'Shrovetide', based on the principle of the duel between different seasons that is such a constant feature of folk plays. The struggle for supremacy between the allegorical representatives of these two great popular festivals is played out in a very familiar context, that of hearty eating:

SHROVETIDE: I say, Christmas, you are past date, you are out of the almanac. Resign, resign. Let the oven give place to the frying-pan, and minced pies yield superiority to pancakes and fritters.

CHRISTMAS: Resign to thee! I that am the king of good cheer and feasting, though I come but once a year to reign over baked, boiled, roast, and plum-porridge, will have being in despite of *thy lardship*. Thou art *but my fag-end*, and I must still be before thee.

SHROVETIDE: But thou wilt never be beforehand. Thou art a prodigal Christmas; and Shrovetide hath seen thee many times in the poultry.

CHRISTMAS: Dost scorn my liberality, thou reasty bacon, tallow-faced scullion? Though thou be as fat as a Fleming, I'll have Lent choke thee with a red herring.

SHROVETIDE: I'll arm myself for that. In three days I can victual my garrison for seven weeks; and it shall go hard but I will domineer in Lent despite of the thin-chapped surgeon that makes men skeletons.[52]

The puns on 'thy lordship'/'thy lardship' would not have been out of place in the parodic list quoted above from *Vox Graculi*; and the fact that Christmas calls Shrovetide 'my fag-end' confirms that Shrove Tuesday was still regarded as belonging to the cycle of the festivals of Christmas.[53] Meanwhile, Shrovetide's boast that in three days he will be able to stow away enough rations and fat to be able to face the seven Lenten weeks in the offing shows that the gluttony in which people indulged at this time was prompted by their greedy apprehension on the threshold of the mortifications and deprivations of Lent.[54]

Lent did indeed begin the very next day, with the austere religious festival of Ash Wednesday. In accordance with the pendulum rhythm that marked the festive calendar, which oscillated between two poles (abundance and deprivation, joy and sadness, etc.), Ash Wednesday was the day that ushered in a return to penitence and abstinence[55] in the period of Lent.[56] Fast days thus followed feast days and fish replaced meat at table[57] (which is precisely the point of Christmas' sarcastic sally at the expense of Shrovetide in the passage cited above: 'I'll have Lent choke thee with a red herring'). While, at a religious level, the beginning of Lent was marked by rites of penitence and mortification, in the domain of folklore and popular tradition it was associated with making a puppet or scarecrow decorated with the emblems of Lent and known as 'Jack of Lent' or 'Jack-a-Lent':

Jack of Lent was a puppet set up on *Ash Wednesday* and decorated with fish-emblems of the penitential season, used as a target for missiles during the six weeks of Lent, and finally destroyed on *Palm Sunday*.[58]

A ballad dated 1570 and entitled 'Lenten Stuff' contains the following description:

> When Jakke a' Lent comes justlynge in,
>   With the hedpeece of a herynge,
> And saythe, repent yowe of yower syn,
>   For shame, syrs, leve yowre swerynge:
> And to Palme Sonday doethe he ryde,
>   With sprots and herryngs by his syde,
> And makes an end of Lenton tyde![59]

As the symbol of a period of fasting and penitence, this figure brought with him Lenten fare and, like the cocks of Shrove Tuesday, he was made the target in a pelting game, as the *OED* reminds us in its definition of 'Jack-a-Lent':

A figure of a man set up to be pelted: an ancient form of the sport of 'Aunt Sally' practised during Lent.

Possibly this dummy stuffed with straw or rudimentary effigy made from a leek and a herring[60] served as a playful substitute for the sacrificial victim of ancient times. His role was clearly an ambivalent one, for he was both a manifest and ubiquitous symbol of the long period of austerity and at the same time operated as a kind of safety valve, allowing people to give vent to the rancour and frustration engendered by the prospect of Lenten abstinence. In other words, he acted as a scapegoat. At the end of Lent, he, like the Carnival giants of mainland Europe, would be solemnly ejected from the town or village and burned on Easter Sunday.[61] Jack-a-Lent, the community scapegoat, heralded the end of winter and the approach of the great spring festivals.

Now we must consider the prohibitions that affected the forty days of Lent for, quite apart from the fact that they stamped this period of the calendar with a character all its own,[62] it should also prove interesting to investigate festivity in reverse.[63] It is worth noting that the Church of England retained the traditional Catholic prescriptions affecting eating habits, to the horror of the Puritans.[64] As Thiselton Dyer suggests, the prohibition on the consumption of meat at this time had probably survived chiefly for economic reasons.[65]

However, as the entire corporation of butchers could hardly be left idle for forty days, there were all kinds of dispensations and special cases to allow for the needs of the sick, and of pregnant women.[66] Doctors were authorized to make these exemptions and to give expectant mothers permission to satisfy their cravings. Of course, there was plenty of cheating, such as the subterfuges for getting round the ban employed by 'Shrovetide' in Thomas Nashe's Masque:

SHROVETIDE: . . . I will domineer in Lent despite of the thin-chapped surgeon that makes men skeletons.
CHRISTMAS: As how?
SHROVETIDE: At any nobleman's house I can lick my fingers in a privy kitchen. Though I be out of commons in the hall, there's flesh to be had sometimes in a chamber, besides a laundress. The very three-penny ordinary will keep me in an upper gallery, and I can be invisible even in the pie-house. Should all fail, the wenches I got with child shall long, and have the physician's ticket.[67]

And, in fact, these periods of Lent do seem to have been particularly favourable to conception, by virtue of the aphrodisiac powers of fish and sea-food:

CHRISTMAS: . . . Children, children, thou parched starveling: thou canst get nothing but anatomies.
LENT: Children! I get more (I maintain not their lawfulness) than Christmas and Shrovetide. O the virtues of oysters, lobsters, sturgeon, anchovies, and caviare![68]

Nevertheless, we should beware of generalizing from these few lines, for there is a paradoxical aspect to them and they are no doubt deliberately provocative. After all, Lent remained a period of sexual abstinence too and, as Keith Thomas notes, was marked by all kinds of taboos.[69]

It is true, though, that in Nabbes' Masque, Lent lays claim to the festival of Saint Valentine, 14 February, as his own, and this was placed under the sign of amorous desire and passion.[70] It was proverbially the day when the birds chose their mates, a belief that was no doubt connected with the mystical bestiary which served to symbolize the movements of the stars and human emotions in popular astrology and the calendar of festivals.[71] But despite the legend the poet Herrick, in his poem entitled 'To his Valentine, on S. Valentine's Day' (in *Hesperides*, 1648), ironically confesses his own ignorance on this matter:

> Oft have I heard both Youths and Virgins say,
> Birds chuse their mates, and couple too, this day:
> But by their flight I never can divine,
> When I shall couple with my Valentine.[72]

The date of this fixed festival coincides, give or take a day, with that of the Roman Lupercalia,[73] one of the most ancient of the Latin festivals, connected with the myths about the founding of Rome by Romulus and Remus. The Luperci used to gather in the cave where the she-wolf was believed to have given suck to the twins. After sacrificing some goats, they would dress up in their skins and, armed with straps cut from those same skins (the *februa*), would rush down the Palatine Hill, lashing out at any women they met on their way, in order to render them fertile. This festival illustrates the fecund powers ascribed to 'wild men' (the Luperci were half-goat, half-wolf)[74] who would appear on the scene just as the energies of Spring were reviving. Similarly, in England, Saint Valentine's Day was an occasion for games amid an atmosphere heavily impregnated with eroticism, and it is certainly by no mere chance that Thomas Nashe used this festival with all its customs as the setting for his libertine poem, 'The Choice of Valentines':

> It was the merry month of February
> When young men in their jolly roguery
> Rose early in the morn 'fore break of day
> To seek their valentines so trim and gay,
> With whom they may consort in summer-sheen
> And dance the heidegeies on our town-green,
> At Ale's, at Easter or at Pentecost
> Perambulate the fields that flourish most
> And go to some village arbordering near
> To taste the cream and cakes and such good cheer,
> Or see a play of strange morality

Showen by bachelry of Manningtree;
Whereto the country franklins flock-meal swarm
Even on the hallows of that blessed saint
That doth true lovers with those joys acquaint.
I went, poor pilgrim, to my lady's shrine
To see if she would be my valentine...[75]

In Ben Jonson's *Tale of a Tub* (1596, revised in 1633), also placed under the patronage of Saint Valentine, there is a similar atmosphere of erotic rejoicing, full of sexual *double entendre*.[76] Saint Valentine's is also the festival that Ophelia sings of, but in this case the lewdness of some of the allusions does not occasion laughter since it is a sign of her madness. The ballad that she sings destroys her image as a pure young girl and is yet another indication of the process of moral and spiritual degeneration that is sapping the kingdom of Denmark:

Tomorrow is Saint Valentine's day
    All in the morning betime,
And I a maid at your window
    To be your Valentine.

Then up he rose and donned his clothes,
    And dupped the chamber door;
Let in the maid, that out a maid
    Never departed more...

By Gis, and by Saint Charity,
    Alack, and fie for shame!
Young men will do't if they come to't,
    By Cock, they are to blame.

Quoth she 'Before you tumbled me,
    You promised me to wed'.
'So would I 'a' done, by yonder sun,
    An thou hadst not come to my bed'.[77]

The disenchantment of the betrayed young girl, a victim of Saint Valentine's Day and male cynicism, is simply expressed in this tale that is as old and as sad as the world itself. It echoes the bitterness of so many 'mornings after the night before'.

The fact is that Saint Valentine's Day was a promiscuous festival in those days, when the choice of a sexual partner was left to the chance of a lottery in which lovers were paired for the day. Misson de Valbourg describes the procedure as follows:

On the Eve of the 14th of *Feb. St Valentine's Day*, a Time when all living Nature inclines to couple, the young Folks in *England*, and *Scotland* too, by a very ancient Custom, celebrate a little Festival that tends to the same end: An equal Number of Maids and Batchelors get together, each writes their true or some feigned name upon separate Billets, which they roll up, and draw by way of Lots, the Maids taking the Mens Billets, and the Men the Maids; so that each of the young Men lights upon a Girl that he calls his Valentine, and each of the Girls upon a young Man whom she calls hers... Fortune having thus divided the Company into so many Couples, the Valentines give Balls and Treats to their Mistresses, wear their Billets several Days upon their Bosoms or Sleeves, and this little Sport often ends in Love.[78]

As well as Saint Valentine, we should mention Saint Oswald, the Leap Year saint, whose festival was linked with other traditions of sexual behaviour. This Saxon saint was only celebrated every four years, in leap years, when the Elizabethan custom was that it should be the women who made the advances. The following lines from *The Maydes Metamorphosis* (1600), attributed to John Lyly, indicate as much:

IOCULO: Maister, be comforted, this is leape year
          Women wear breeches, peticoats are deare.[79]

Another allusion to leap year, in a text dating from 1601 entitled *Treatise Against Judicial Astrologie*, is so elliptical as to suggest that these beliefs were so proverbial that no more than a hint was required for people to get the point:

If the nature of anything change in the leap-year, it seemeth to be true in men and women, according to the answer of a mad fellow to his mistress, who, being called knave by her, replied that it was not possible, 'for', said he, 'if you remember yourself, good mistress, this is leap-year, and then, as you know well, knaves wear smocks'.[80]

V.S. Lean, who cites this passage in his collection of proverbs, offers this explanation:

This alludes, I think, to the saying that in leap-year women woo and propose to the men, and is a play on the double sense of knave, i.e. rogue and young man.[81]

Once Saint Valentine's Day was over, there was about a month to wait for the next festival to brighten up the gloomy Lenten days. Not until the cycle of Easter festivities began were there any celebrations of importance, although here and there there may have been a few local occasions for merrymaking.[82] The first of the chain of Easter festivals was Palm Sunday, when there were processions in which (in default of palms) willow branches were carried.[83] The custom was retained by Henry VIII even after the Reformation.[84] The other high points of this cycle were, of course, 'Shere' or 'Maundy' Thursday and Good Friday, followed by Easter Sunday and Monday. But these were religious festivals which were still characterized by reflection and purification (except in the case of the Puritan of whom a satirical author quipped 'Good-Fryday is his Shrove-Tuesday').[85]

Easter, however, was regarded popularly as one of the great yearly festivals, as is suggested by the references to 'Yule and Pasch and high tide', cited by Tilley in his collection of proverbs.[86] Easter Day was set on a par with Christmas, and both festivals retained their ancient names (the origin of the term 'Pasch'[87] being biblical, that of 'Yule' Germanic). The similarity between them was not fortuitous for, as T.G. Crippen points out, in England the two festivals shared a number of common features:

In England, Christmas and Easter, especially the former, have been the favourite seasons of the Mummers . . . It was customary, though not universal, for the girls to dress as boys, and the men as women: and thus disguised to visit the neighbours' houses, singing, dancing, and partaking of good cheer. In many places, the performers . . . would execute a sword dance.[88]

When they performed during the Easter festival, the Mummers were known as 'Paskers':

. . . the Paskers and Mummers make the merry sport.[89]

Alongside these entertainments, there are frequent references to the figure, or rather grotesque effigy, of Jack-a-Lent, solemnly ejected at the end of the Easter festivals. The place of this emblem of the penitence of Lent would then be taken by another effigy made from plants, known as Jack-in-the-Green.[90] We should not forget that in Elizabethan times 25 March was the date fixed for the start of the new year and it coincided with the earliest possible date for Easter. It was probably this switch from the old to the new that was expressed, on an individual level, by the custom of donning new clothes on this day.[91] The atmosphere of youth, gaiety and freshness associated with this festival is strikingly reflected in Nicholas Breton's lyrical picture of 'Easter Day'.[92] According to Philip Stubbes, Easter Day was one of the three occasions when parish celebrations were organized. They were known as church ales and were designed to raise funds for the purpose of repairing the church or providing charity for the poor.[93]

In Coventry, the second Monday and Tuesday after Easter were marked by Hocktide celebrations. According to the *OED* (see 'Hock-day'), these had been grafted on to what had originally simply been a 'term-day'. Here is a brief description of the capers that recurred on this calendar festival:

Hock Monday was for the men and Hock Tuesday for the women. On both days they, alternately, with great merriment intercepted the public roads with rope and pulled passengers to them, from whom they exacted money to be laid out in pious uses . . .[94]

The evident sexual discrimination that was an integral part of these customs, establishing between men and women a rivalry that was sanctioned by the competitive levying of ransom-money, is reminiscent of the Plough Monday customs mentioned earlier.[95] Similar practices were also associated with Easter Monday and Tuesday, constituting as it were a general rehearsal for the rites of Hocktide:

On Easter Monday, the women forming parties of six or eight each... surround such of the opposite sex as they meet, and either with or without their consent, lift them thrice above their heads into the air, with loud shouts at such elevation. On Easter Tuesday, the men do the same to the women.[96]

Like the charivari, these festival customs ritualized the war between the sexes, converting it into a series of parodic skirmishes, occasions for jokes including, no doubt, many obscene ones.[97] But it was not long before they incurred the disapproval of the religious and civil authorities. In his letter describing the festivities at Kenilworth, Robert Laneham holds the Puritans responsible and calls them:

men very commendabl for their behaviour and learning, & sweet in their sermons, but sume what too sour in preaching awey their pastime...[98]

In the course of these celebrations, Captain Cox and his 'merry men' had staged a Hock Tuesday play, in Coventry, for the entertainment of Queen Elizabeth:

And héertoo folloed az good a spot (me thooght) prezented in an historicall ku, by certain good harted men of Coventrée, my Lordes neighboors thear: who, understanding amoong them the thing that coold not bee hidden from ony, hoow carefull and studious hiz honour waz, that by all pleazaunt recreations her highnes might best fynd her self welcom, and bee made gladsum and mery... made petition that they moought renu noow their olld storiall sheaw: Of argument, how the Danez whylom héere in a troublous seazon wear for quietness born withall, & suffeard in peas, that anon, by outrage & importabl insolency, abuzing both Ethelred, the king then, and all estates everie whear byside: at the grevoous complaint & coounsell of Huna, the king chieftain in warz, on Saint Brices night, AD 1012... And for becauz the matter mencioneth how valiantly our English women for loove of their cuntrée behaved themselves: expressed in actions & rymez after their manner, they thought it mooynght moove sum myrth to her Maiestie the rather.[99]

Just as Robert Dover, in the reign of James I, was to revive the Cotswold Games, this Captain Cox had successfully set out to draw the sovereign's attention to ancient national traditions that were dying out, under pressure from municipal authorities and Puritans alike. George Wither was later to scoff at such attempts, ridiculing 'those presumptuous fellows... who... in defence of Hock-tide custome stood'.[100]

In a poem written in praise of the Cotswold Games revived by Robert Dover, published twenty-three years after Wither's work (1636), one John Trussel confirms the continuing decline of the Hocktide customs:

the Hocktide pastimes are
Declin'd if not deserted...[101]

23 April was the date of another festival that was undergoing a certain decline in the Elizabethan period, namely that of Saint George, the patron saint of England. Up until the mid-sixteenth century, it had been celebrated with jollifications and parades in the towns and by perform-ances of stereotyped popular dramas similar to the Mummers' play or the Sword dance. The Saint George plays obviously enough featured Saint George himself and his dragon, as well as the 'Seven Champions of Christendom'.[102] But after the Reformation, the latter, along with Saint George himself, disappeared from these processions.[103]

The festival of Saint George, which was celebrated by bonfires[104] and coincided with the celebrations for the Order of the Garter at court, was officially abolished by Queen Elizabeth in 1567.[105] However, Saint George and the dragon still did not disappear completely.[106] They reappeared in the May Day games and processions. We have two essential testimonies on this subject. The first comes from Machyn's diary. The author notes that on 24 June 1554, in London,

ther was a May-game . . . and Sant John Sacerys [Zachary's] with a gyant, and drumes and gunes [and the] ix wordes [worthies], with spechys, and a goodly pagant with a quen . . . and dyvers odur, with spechys; and then Sant Gorge and the dragon . . .[107]

The second is drawn from a poem entitled 'William Gamage's Idle Brains'; it describes a May game at Wells, and four verses are devoted to Saint George:

(12)
Our gallant mynded marshall trayne
did in the crosse our sporte mayntayne
and yeke St George did greatly grace
with thundering peaces in that place
yet I doe live in quiett rest
and thinke my hooling game the best.

(13)
Then did St George of Wells proceade
with all his knights most brave in deed
theyr Irishe footemen did attende,
and all men did the same amende
yet &c.

(27)
This being done which then is sayed
all then repayer homewards made
the gyery dragon laye in wayte
for to devoure the princes streight
yet &c.

(28)
but I St George of Wells comende
and all his knights that did attende

that wrought the dragons great decaye
and saved the princes lief that day
yet &c.[108]

Saint George and the dragon were also key figures in the spectacular and popular pageants of the period. They used to be part of the religious Corpus Christi Day processions and when these were suppressed at the Reformation, they found refuge in the May games.[109] Soon, however, they were to be found only on tavern- or inn-signs.[110] Their presence on such signs had probably long co-existed along with their pageant appearances. Finally confined within this restrictive framework, Saint George and the dragon made this their last home, ending a career that speaks volumes about the continuous decline undergone by the great popular festivals ever since the Middle Ages. First they were the subjects of the Mummers' folk plays, with a place in religious and secular processions, then they appeared in dramatic spectacles of the profession-al theatre, later in fairground entertainments. But they wound up ending their days as the painted figures of tavern-signs. It is an image that sums up the decline and paralysis of folklore and popular festivity that set in in the seventeenth century, in England. Still, in the case of Saint George and the dragon, at least the notion of festivity did not vanish altogether, since they continued to serve the cause of rejoicing and the art of merry-making, hoisting high the colours of Merry England and summoning all and sundry to eat, drink and be merry.

In contrast to the fortunes of Saint George, the May Day festival still retained all its appeal and prestige in the Elizabethan period. The comparative calendar at the end of this volume (see Appendix 1, pp. 306–7) shows that the date of this festival fell at a crucial point in the calendar, coinciding with the ancient Greek festival of the Thargelia (in honour of Apollo) and with the ancient Roman celebrations of Bona Dea, the goddess of flowers and fecundity. These included strictly female rites involving dances and other practices frequently condemned as licentious. (Bona Dea was, in fact, also the goddess of prostitutes.) May Day also corresponded to one of the four great Celtic festivals. These were Dimelc (1 February), Beltane (1 May), Lugnasadh (1 August) and Samhain (1 November). Frazer describes the festival of Beltane as an ancient Druid festival, characterized by rites involving fire and practices designed to protect people from the harmful influence of witches.[111]

Such beliefs were still detectable in some of the English rituals of May Day, whose nocturnal traditions were regarded by some as smacking of witchcraft. The Puritan Philip Stubbes describes them as follows:

Against May, Whitsonday, or other time, all the yung men and maides, olde men and wives, run gadding over night to the woods, groves, hils, & mountains, where they spend all the night in pleasant pastimes; & in the morning they return, bringing with them birch & branches of trees, to deck their assemblies withall, and no mervaile, for there is a great Lord present amongst them, as superintendent and Lord over their pastimes and sportes, namely Sathan, prince of Hel...[112]

Perhaps Stubbes was influenced by the legends according to which witches would gather together for a 'Sabbath' during the night of 'Walpurgis' (leading into May Day). In any event, he certainly does not hesitate to associate the popular merrymaking with diabolical practices.[113] Thomas Nashe anyway mocked at Stubbes' somewhat overheated imagination, egging him on to represent in the blackest colours amusements which, while perhaps less innocent than some would have had them believed, were certainly in no sense diabolical.[114]

In any event, countless ballads, songs and poems refer to the amorous games for which this festival was a pretext as, like Saint Valentine's Day, the amusements of May Day were highly prized by the young since they made it possible for lovers to meet or to renew their relations. Thus, in *A Midsummer Night's Dream*, Lysander arranges to meet Hermia in the woods, at the very spot where they first met during the May Day Festival (i, i. 165–8).[115] In fact, the misadventures of Lysander and Hermia in the forest provide a good illustration of the temporary and inconstant nature of many of these unions, for it would appear that many of the amorous idylls initiated in May were just as fleeting as those of Saint Valentine's Day.[116] The anonymous piece (attributed to Nicholas Breton) *Vox Graculi or Jacke Dawes Prognostication* (1622) contains this description of the rites of May Day:

May is the merry moneth, and may not be put beside his iocund humour: yet the first day betimes in the morning, shall young Fellowes and Mayds be so inveloped with a mist of wandring out of their wayes, that they shall fall into ditches one upon another, and there shall the young men lie for a little while, not being able to stand, while the Maids after their downe-falls, being astonied, shall rise sooner than they would doe...[117]

This text shows that, like Saint Valentine's Day, May Day was permeated with an atmosphere of erotic licence and made exciting by its many amorous games and pitfalls.[118] Woe betided any girl who did not understand what was meant by a 'green gown' for, as Richard Brathwait remarks, her good name, if not her virginity, was then likely to suffer:

> For Maids that know not what is to consent
> To a lost Maiden head, nor what is meant
> By giving of a greene gowne, sooner will
> Assent to ill, because they know no ill
> Then such as have of active pleasure store,
> For well were they experimented in't before,

Yea such will never deale unless they smell
Some hope of gaine, or like the trader well...[119]

The 'green gown' is mentioned in Thomas Nashe's *Last Will and Testament*, in the list of pleasures that the character called Ver claims to be part and parcel of the spring festivals.[120] It was one of the emblems of the May Day festival, along with the maypole, the Morris dance and the Robin Hood of ballad and pastoral. To some extent it symbolized the rite of spring. But the Puritans understood it differently and refused to turn a blind eye to what they considered to be shocking debauchery. On the contrary, they did their utmost to warn people by drawing their attention to abuses that they portrayed as intolerable and scandalous. A pamphleteer such as Fetherston, for instance, has no illusions at all as to the consequences of all these licentious games and cites figures of a kind to make even the most bird-brained girl stop and think:

The third [abuse committed in ... May games] is, that you (because you will loose no tyme) doe use commonly to runne into the woodes in the night time, amongst maidens, to fet bowes, in so muche as I have heard of tenne maidens which went to fet May, and nine of them came home with childe.[121]

Two years later, Philip Stubbes' words were to echo Fetherston's as he launched into a similar diatribe against these nocturnal games of the young:

I have heard it credibly reported (and that 'viva voce') by men of great gravitie and reputation, that of fortie, threescore, or a hundred maides going to the wood over night, there have scarcely the third part of them returned home again undefiled. These be the frutes which these cursed pastimes bring forth.[122]

Note, in passing, the discrepancy between the figures cited by the two authors, for it suggests that in order to bring home their point, these zealots made no bones about blackening the truth. Fetherston's figure of 90 per cent illegitimate pregnancies really does seem somewhat incredible – 'of tenne maidens which went to fet May ... nine ... came home with childe'; whereas Stubbes, himself not generally a man inclined to moderation, arrives at a tally of over 60 per cent – 'the third part of them ... returned home again undefiled'. Stubbes, furthermore, uses a much vaguer term to describe the outcome of the nocturnal dalliance: he says the girls are 'defiled', where Fetherston declares them to be 'with childe'. Such significant variations reflect the relatively conjectural nature of their sources – in effect, no more than pure and simple rumour: 'I have heard ... '.[123] On the other hand, one could not go so far as to suggest that these accusations contain not a grain of truth, for there does seem to be general agreement on this particular point. From Brathwait's warnings to the mischievous hints of *Vox Graculi*: 'the Maids after their downe-falls, being astonied, shall *rise* sooner than they would doe', in which the emphasized '*rise*' refers as much to the girls' swelling silhouettes as to their getting up from the ground, everything combines to suggest that these May games were not necessarily totally innocent pastoral frolics.

However, May Day, with all its rites, recurs as a theme in pastoral poetry so constantly as to become something of a cliché in the literature of the period.[124] Here is one example, a poem attributed to Nicholas Breton, 'Phillida and Coridon', which appeared in *England's Helicon*, the famous anthology of lyric verse published in 1600:

> In the merry moneth of May
> In a morne by breake of day,
> Forth I walkèd by the Wood side,
> When as May was in his pride:
> Then I spièd, all alone,
> *Phillida* and *Coridon*.
> Much-a-doo there was, God wot,
> He would love, and she would not.
> She sayd never man was true,
> He sayd, none was false to you.
> He sayd he had lov'd her long,
> She sayd, Love should have no wrong.
> *Coridon* would kisse her then,
> She said, Maides must kisse no men,
> Till they did for good and all.
> Then she made the Sheepheard call
> All the heavens to witnesse truth,
> Never lov'd a truer youth.
> Thus with many a pretty oath,
> Yes and nay, and faith and troth,
> Such as silly Sheepheards use,
> When they will not Love abuse;
> Love, which had beene long deluded,
> Was with kisses sweete concluded.
> And Phillida, with garlands gay,
> Was made the Lady of the May.[125]

Other examples are the many madrigals composed by Weelkes and Morley; here, the combination of the simple theme of love and springtime with the refinement of the musical setting shows how successful pastoral poetry sometimes was in achieving the difficult synthesis of popular and aristocratic tastes.

In the poem quoted above, as in many others like it, the May festivities provide a framework for the amorous idyll as they do for the poem itself, appearing in both the first and the last lines. G.B. Harrison, in the *Elizabethan Journals*, imagines it being sung in the presence of Queen

Elizabeth as part of the entertainments organized for her at Elvetham on 25 September 1591.[126] Harrison remarks that the emotion that the queen displayed on hearing it testifies to the strength of the impact made by such madrigals and pastoral poetry upon people's imaginations and sensibilities at this period.

In his May eclogue in *The Shepheardes Calender* (1579), Spenser had already criticized these frivolous pleasures in the dialogue between Piers and the young shepherd Palinode:

> Sicker this morrowe, no lenger agoe,
> I sawe a shole of shepheardes outgoe
> With singing and shouting, and jolly chere:
> Before them yode a lusty Tabrere,
> That to the many a Horne-pype playd,
> Whereto they dauncen, eche one with his mayd.
> To see those folks make such joysaunce,
> Made my heart after the pype to daunce:
> Tho to the greene Wood they speeden hem all,
> To fetchen home May with their musicall:
> And home they bringen in a royall throne,
> Crowned as king: and his Queene attone
> Was Lady Flora, on whom did attend
> A fayre flocke of Fairies and a fresh bend
> Of lovely Nymphs.

But Palinode's picture of joy and dancing is countered by the cold criticisms of the older Piers, who speaks for Spenser himself in this allegorical pastoral, expressing the attitude of the faction of the Church of England clergy most hostile to all these pagan customs.[127]

Spenser seems to associate himself with the condemnations of the Puritans, taking up his position alongside those whom Ben Jonson was later to call 'the sourer sort of shepherds', and about whom he was to complain bitterly, putting his words into the mouth of Lionel:

> They call ours, *Pagan* pastimes, that infect
> Our blood with ease, our youth with all neglect,
> Our tongues with wantonnesse, our thoughts with lust.
> And what they censure ill, all others must . . .[128]

The play entitled *The Sad Shepherd or A Tale of Robin Hood* (1637) reads as a late rejoinder to Spenser. It is full of melancholy and nostalgia, imbued with a presentiment that the excesses of the Puritans and the economic and social upheavals that had been taking place since the beginning of the seventeenth century were to toll the knell for Merry England and its great pastoral dream.

But for Merry England enthusiasts, the rallying symbol was none other than the maypole, ceremoniously erected by the village youths early on May Day morning and the focal target of the Puritans' attacks against the seasonal festivals.[129] As Fetherston tells us, the maypole would be felled at the end of the nocturnal visit to the forest:

What adoe make our yong men at the time of May? Do they not use nightwatchings to rob and steale yong trees out of other men's grounde, and bring them home into their parishe with minstrels playing before? when they have set it up, they will decke it with floures and garlandes, and daunce round (men and women togither, moste unseemly and intolerable, as I have proved before) about the tree, like unto the children of Israell, that daunced about the golden calfe that they had set up . . .[130]

This text of Fetherston's provides an excellent gloss on the word 'Idol' that is used in the *Vox Graculi* passage cited earlier. It explains the Puritans' fierce hostility towards these inoffensive trees. As they saw it, the maypole was just like the Golden Calf worshipped by Moses' people in his absence, and they had come to regard it as the symbol of a reversion to paganism. Hobbes was also to be alive to those associations, for in his *Leviathan* he likens the maypoles to the fertility symbols known as the Priapi, of Graeco-Latin antiquity.[131]

It is, furthermore, impossible to miss the note of concern that expresses Fetherston's respect for private property: 'to rob and steale yong trees out of *other men's grounde*'. The purpose of the possessive construction used here is juridical as well as grammatical. Indeed, such incursions into private property, for which 'gathering the May' provided a pretext, was taken extremely seriously by the authorities of the period, as is clear from the following passage taken from the diary of Robert Woodfill:

Sept. 18 (1637): At the Justice sent: 'when men were fined cutting down maypoles in the forest, it was told them by one for the king's part that they were not fined for having maypoles but for cutting them down in the forest'.[132]

However, alongside Fetherston's text, which does not specifically use the word 'maypole', the fullest and most colourful account that we possess of these festive practices is certainly that of Philip Stubbes, in his *Anatomie of Abuses*:

Against *May, Whitsonday,* or other time, all the yung men and maides, olde men and wives, run gadding over night to the woods . . . where they spend all the night in pleasant pastimes: & in the morning they return, bringing with them birch & branches of trees . . . But the chiefest iewel they bring from thence is their May-pole, which they bring home with great veneration, as thus. They have twentie or fortie yoke of Oxen, every Oxe having a sweet nose-gay of flowers placed on the tip of his hornes; and these Oxen drawe home this May-pole (this stinking Ydol, rather) which is covered all over with floures and hearbs, bound round about with strings from the top to the bottome, and sometime painted with variable colours, with two or three hundred men, women and children, following it with great devotion. And thus beeing reared up with handkercheefs and flags hovering on the top, they straw the ground rounde about, binde green boughes about it, set up sommer haules, bowers and arbours hard by it; And then fall they to daunce about it like as the heathen people did at the dedication of the Idols, wherof this is a perfect pattern, or rather the thing itself.[133]

In his eagerness to denounce all such abuses, Stubbes skilfully paints an animated and detailed picture of these village scenes, a picture which is somewhat reminiscent of Pieter Brueghel's paintings of Flanders.

The jollifications and dances that took place around the maypole involved the entire community, irrespective of age or gender. It was a joyful time when, as Milton puts it in 'L'Allegro':

> young and old come forth to play
> On a sunshine holiday.[134]

The popularity of May Day traditions and of the maypole[135] was by no means confined to the countryside. It was also a feature of most of the larger towns of Elizabethan England and even of London, as Stow remarks:

I find also, that in the month of May, the citizens of London of all estates, lightly in every parish, or sometimes two or three parishes joining together, had their several mayings, and did fetch in maypoles . . .[136]

But the author immediately goes on to note that since the 'Black' or 'Ill May Day' of 1517, of sinister memory, the authorities had kept a careful eye on all these festivities.[137]

Stow's text also mentions a maypole that was taller than the steeple of the church of Saint Andrew Undershafte, a very symbolic state of affairs. The fact that a maypole could overtop a church steeple and give it its name could be interpreted as an image of the general situation of the Church, obscured by the shadow of an emblem of paganism triumphant. The same idea seems to be quite forthrightly expressed at the beginning of an anonymous poem called 'Pasquil's Palinodia and his Progress to the Tavern . . . ' (1619):

> Fairly we marched on, till our approach
> Within the spacious passage of the *Strand*
> Objected to our sight a *sommer-broach*
> Ycleap't a *May-pole*, which in our land
> > No citty, towne, nor street, can parallell;
> > Nor can the lofty spire of *Clarken-well*,
> > Although he have the vantage of a rock,
> > Pearch up more high his turning weather-cock.[138]

The Puritans vociferated furiously against this 'abomination'. Thus, in Beaumont and Fletcher's *Women Pleased*, Bomby exclaims:

'Twas the fore-running sin brought in those tilt-staves
They brandish 'gainst the church, the devil calls May-poles.[139]

The Puritans' fulminations against maypoles are skilfully satirized in *Vox Graculi*:

This day shall be erected long wooden *Idols* called May-poles; whereat many greasie Churles shall murmure that will not bestow so much as a Faggot-sticke towards the warming of the Poore: an humour, that while it seemes to smell of *Conscience*, savours indeed of nothing but *Covetousness*...[140]

It is an ironical sally against the Puritans for which there appears to be some justification for, in the archives of Chancery Lane, Leslie Hotson has discovered an allusion to a 'Maypole destroyed by a Puritan Parson in Bermondsey, in 1615, after which the preacher kept the wood for his own use...'.[141] There is certainly an ironical aspect to the fact that some Puritans, a group often suspected of miserliness, derived a measure of sordid profit from the spoils of the festival.

The 1893 edition of *The Roxburghe Ballads* contains a seventeenth-century woodcut showing villagers dancing round a maypole (see Illus. 4.1).[142] It is not a particularly skilful engraving but the maypole is clearly shown at the centre, still flourishing a few tufts of foliage at the top, with a man playing the fife and drum, to the rhythm of which two people opposite him are dancing. The faces are wreathed in smiles, the general atmosphere one of revelry, so far as one can tell from this somewhat crude picture. To the left of the woodcut are a couple of passers-by, hand in hand and clearly separate from the dancers. When such passers-by failed to join in the revelry and showed no liking for it, they were probably viewed askance or even taken to task.[143] We have already seen

4.1   The dance round the maypole, an engraving from *The Roxburghe Ballads* (1893).

how easily popular festivity could give rise to teasing and sarcasm. It did not take very much to turn these into taunts.[144] The most common whipping-boys were, of course, the carping burghers and Puritans and it must be said that they often displayed no little courage in openly braving vindictive popular derision.[145] Gradually, however, the iconoclasts became bolder, strengthened by the support of certain Justices of the Peace or municipal authorities. Manifestations of what had begun as a manic obsession of a few fanatics soon increased in both number and frequency in the villages of Elizabethan England. The maypoles that adorned the village squares and the city streets were pulled down and chopped up for firewood and the grim creak of maypoles splintering beneath the axe took the place of the erstwhile merry sound of bells, pipes and tambourines.[146] Eventually, on 8 April 1644, Parliament definitively banned the maypoles, at the same time closing down the theatres of London:

And because the profanation of the Lord's day hath been heretofore greatly occasioned by Maypoles (a heathenish vanity, generally abused to superstition and wickedness), the Lords and Commons do further order and ordain that all and singular Maypoles that are, or shall be erected, shall be taken down and removed.[147]

Actually, the legislative action simply legitimized a turn of events that had already to a large extent taken place and, to judge by certain lines from 'Pasquil's Palinodia', it would appear that maypoles had already disappeared from most of the village squares of England:

> Alas, poore *May-poles*! what should be the cause
> That you were almost banish't from the earth?
> Who never were rebellious to the lawes;
> Your greatest crime was harmless honest mirth:
> What fell malignant spirit was there found,
> To cast your tall *Piramides* to ground?
> To be some envious nature it appears,
> That men might fall together by the eares.[148]

The main reason why the maypole became such an emotive symbol of the pleasures of a bygone age was that it always had been a rallying point. Around it people had gathered for the May Day dances, the spontaneity of which did not exclude a measure of organization, as Baskervill explains:

Of course, such revelry was often of the most informal sort . . . But there was a special group of entertainers representing the talent of the community. Some of these prepared a group dance like the morris . . .[149]

The Morris dance was one of the great attractions of May Day; in fact it seemed impossible to envisage the proceedings of the day without it. In *All's Well That Ends Well*, the clown Lavatch remarks that his answers can fit all questions and are 'As fit as . . . a morris for May-day'.[150] The Morris dance around the Maypole had indeed become the most universal and commonly represented image of English festivity in the Elizabethan period. It looms large, for instance, in one of the Shirburn ballads, 'The Merry Life of the Countriman':

> And then in *may*, by breake of day,
>   with morris daunces trime
> his men and he dothe quickly agree
>   to fetch their may-powle in.
> With pipe and with tabor, in very good order,
>   you knowe,
> throughout the towne, bothe up and downe,
>   their may-game they will sho.[151]

Stubbes saw the nocturnal capers of May, the erection of the maypole and the ensuing revelries all as part of the 'May game', but others identified the May game (see below, pp. 138–9) as the Morris dance.[152] I agree with E.K. Chambers who thinks that there were, in truth, two separate forms of entertainment, and I propose to consider them separately, one after the other. Concerning the origin of the term 'Morris dance', Chambers, who classifies it as a particular variation of the Sword dance, provides the following information:

The earlier English writers call it the *morisce*, *morisk* or *morisco*. This seems to imply a derivation of the name at least from the Spanish *morisco*, a Moor. The dance itself has consequently been held to be of Moorish origin, and the habit of blackening the face has been considered as proof of this . . .[153]

It was certainly an etymology with which the Elizabethans were familiar, for Thomas Heywood refers to it in the second part of his *Fair Maid of the West, or A Girl Worth Gold* (1631). Mullisheg, the Moorish king of Fez, who wants to marry Bess, the 'Fair Maid', says of the revelries that he plans for his wedding:

In wild moriscos we will lead the bride.[154]

And having danced himself off his feet, Clem, the Clown, expresses his exhaustion as follows:

CLEM: Fie upon't! I am so tir'd with dancing with these same black she-chimney sweepers that I can scarce set the best leg forward; they have so tir'd me with their moriscos, and I have so tickled them with our country dances, Sellenger's round and Tom Tiler. We have so fiddled it! . . .[155]

The question that remains to be resolved is how this Moorish dance came to penetrate even the remotest hamlets of England. Gāmini Salgādo has an attractive explanation to offer. He suggests that it was the gypsies, famed in England for their dancing expertise, who introduced it:

It is possible that Morris dancing, that archetypal survival of English folk life, was originally 'Moorish' dancing, brought to the village greens of England by the wandering strangers. Thomas Dekker explicitly compares the appearance of gypsies with that of Morris dancers:
'Their apparel is odd and fantastic, though it be never so full of rents: the men wear scarves of calico or any other base stuff, having their bodies like Morris dancers, with bells and other toys, to entice the country people to flock about them.'
With their many coloured scarves flying in the wind and the music of their bells lilting upon the summer air, these 'Egyptians' brought colour and theatricality to many an English village, creating a larger-than-life spectacle which, as we have seen, Ben Jonson thought fit to set before a king.[156]

Jonson's Masque to which Gāmini Salgādo refers is *The Gypsies Metamorphosed* (1621). In it, one character, known as 'Cock', hails another as follows:

COCK: ... Come hether, Come hether, dicke, didst thou ever see such? the first olive-colourd sprites, they have so danced and gingled here, as if they had beene a sett of overgrowne ffayries.[157]

To which Clod replies:

They should be Morris dancers by their gingle, but they have no napkins.[158]

However, the absence of certain regular features of the Morris dance makes them realize that they were mistaken and that, in truth, 'These are a Covie of Gipsies.'[159]

However close the gypsy dances and the Morris dances may have been, each group thus possessed enough distinctive features to avoid confusion. E.K. Chambers, for his part, would not agree with Salgādo's interpretation, for he goes on to say:

Such a theory seems to invert the order of facts. The dance is too closely bound up with English village custom to be lightly regarded as a foreign importation; and I would suggest that the faces were not blackened because the dancers represented Moors, but rather the dancers were thought to represent Moors because their faces were blackened. The blackened face is common enough in the village festival. Hence ... May-day became proper to the chimney-sweeps ...[160]

Then there is also the fantastical etymology of the term 'Morris' provided by Gerrold, the schoolmaster in *The Two Noble Kinsmen*:

Upon this mighty 'Moor' – of mickle weight –
'Ice' now comes in, which, being glu'd together,
Makes 'morris' ...[161]

The number of participants in this dance and their identities constituted as vexed a question as that of the etymology of the term 'Morris'. Initially, the Morris dance was performed by a limited number of characters, as we learn from Laneham's cut-and-dried description of the performance laid on for the queen at Kenilworth on 17 July 1575:

Well, syr, after théez horsemen, a livelý morisdauns, according too the auncient manner, six daunserz, Mawdmarion, and the fool . . .[162]

In his *Glossographia*, Blount provides an even more restrictive definition, which includes only six participants, as opposed to the eight that Laneham mentions:

Morisco (Span.): a Moor; also a Dance so called, wherein there were usually five men and a Boy dressed in a Girls habit, whom they call the Maid Marrion . . . Common people call it a *Morris Dance*.[163]

However, in the stained-glass window known as 'Tollet's Window',[164] there seem to be many more performers than in the descriptions cited above, for here we find eleven different characters (see Illus. 4.2). They are arranged in groups of three characters, each figure being contained in a lozenge-shaped frame, as was dictated by the stained-glass window technique, and they are set out in four rows. The bottom row consists of (no. 2) a female figure holding a carnation in her left hand, who is probably Maid Marian. Next to her is a stout and jovial friar (no. 3), probably Friar Tuck from the legend of Robin Hood. Above Maid Marian, in the middle of the second row up, is a 'Hobby-horse' (no. 5) mounted by a figure wearing a cape and a crown and whose cheeks are pierced with daggers. Above the Hobby-horse is the maypole, alongside a musician with a fife and a drum (no. 9). In the fourth and top row, to the left, is a Fool (no. 12), represented in profile and recognizable from his bauble[165] and his coxcomb. The other six figures depicted in this engraving bear no particular distinguishing marks apart from the bells tied around their ankles or knees: they probably represent the six dancers mentioned by Laneham. It is interesting to note that Maid Marian, Friar Tuck, the Hobby-horse and the Fool, all of whom appear in this stained-glass window, are also all mentioned in Jonson's *The Gypsies Metamorphosed*, where it is a matter of distinguishing between a Morris and a Gypsies' dance by spotting the presence or absence of certain key figures:

CLOD: They should be Morris dancers by their gingle, but they have no napkins.
COCK: No, nor a Hobby horse.
CLOD: O, he is forgotten, that's no rule; but there's no Maid-marian nor ffrier amongst them, wch is the surer mark.

4.2   Stained-glass window with quarries (glass panes) from Betley Hall in Staffordshire, showing Morris dancers.

COCK: Nor a foole that I see.
CLOD: Unless they all be fooles.[166]

The reasoning here follows a process of elimination, leading to the conclusion that these are not Morris dancers, but gypsies. The Hobby-horse, for his part (for reasons to which I shall be returning), was increasingly often forgotten from the Elizabethan period onwards and no longer constituted an essential element of the Morris dance. As for the Fool, his role was of no more than secondary importance either. Besides, the Fool was not, strictly speaking, a figure peculiar to the Morris dance, for he appeared in many forms of the folk play: the Mummers' play, the Plough play, Saint George's play and the Robin Hood play. Maid Marian and Friar Tuck, on the other hand, constitute what Clod calls 'the surer mark', that is to say a more or less infallible criterion for identifying a true Morris dance.

Here is what the *OED* has to say about the figure of Maid Marian:

A female personage in the May-game and morris-dance. In the later forms of the story of Robin Hood she appears as the companion of the outlaw, the association having probably been suggested by the fact that the two were both represented in the May-day pageants.

In Nashe's anti-Martinist pamphlet (during the Marprelate controversy of 1588–90) entitled *The Return of Pasquil* (1589), the Puritan opponent whom he satirizes as 'Martin' is dressed up as Maid Marian in a parody of a Morris dance that the author uses to attack the Puritans. The implication is that the very name had become synonymous with the donning of grotesque disguises, by the late Elizabethan period.[167] 'Maid Marian' was, furthermore, frequently used as a grotesque epithet to ridicule the extravagant foppishness of aspiring noblemen such as the courtier whom Robert Greene declares to have been capable of making 'the Foole as faire, forsooth, as if he were to playe Maid Marian in a May-Game or a Morris-daunce'.[168] Barnabe Rich also mocks at the extravagant costumes of the fops of his day, using a similar image:

And from whence commeth this wearing, and this imbrodering of long lockes, this curiositie that is used amongst men, in freziling and curling of their hayre? this gentlewoman-like starcht bands, so be-edged, and be-laced, *fitter for Mayd Marian in a Moris Dance* than for him that hath either the spirit or courage that should be in a gentleman.[169]

Sometimes, however, the image of Maid Marian was reversed, as in Falstaff's address to the Hostess, in *1 Henry IV*, 'for womanhood, Maid Marian may be the deputy's wife of the ward to thee'; as Nares' *Glossary* puts it, he compares her to 'a degraded Maid Marian of the later morris dance, more male than female'.[170] By now the Maid Marian of the

Morris dance had become a parody of Marian, the sweet companion of Robin Hood in Adam de la Halle's *Jeu de Robin et Marion.*[171]

The author of the collection of portraits entitled *The Whimzies, or A New Cast of Characters* (1631; sometimes attributed to Richard Brathwait) suggests that Maid Marian was also used as a generic name for 'the loved one' in the May Day games, to whom little presents would be offered:

Saint Martins rings, and counterfeit bracelets are commodities of infinite consequence: these will passe for currant at a may-pole, and purchase a favor from their May-Marian.[172]

Maid Marian had thus become the embodiment of, in some cases, effrontery and vice, in others of extreme vulgarity. The Puritans denounced her as 'the Whore of Babylon' while others, like Lady Bornwell in Shirley's *The Lady of Pleasure* (1637) suffered from the vapours at the very mention of her name.[173] It is true that the frenzied pace of the dance and the energetic movements of Maid Marian must have made for much perspiration, the odour of which may well have offended people of quality and high-society ladies (as Nicholas Breton's *The Mother's Blessing* (1602), also makes clear in the lines quoted on p. 36, above).[174]

But the major target of all these quips was not so much Maid Marian as another key figure in the Morris dance, namely the Fool, whose verbal obscenities and lewd gestures provoked, as the case might be, either disgust or hilarity. Thus, in the anonymous piece called *The Passionate Morrice* (1593), one character declares of another:

Well, I pittie him, because of his kindness which was so crossed; but if *Honestie* hears of any such kind asses hereafter he will make as good sporte thereat as the boyes doo at the foole of a Morrice.[175]

And *Cobbes Prophecie* (1614) presents this picture of a country Morris dance:

> It was my hap of late by chance,
>   oh pretty chance,
> To meet a Country Morris-dance
>   oh pretty dance.
> When chusest of them all the foole
>   oh pretty foole,
> Played with a ladle and a toole,
>   oh pretty toole . . .
> But when they gan to shake their Boxe
>   oh pretty Boxe,

And not a Goose could catch a Foxe
   oh pretty Foxe,
The piper put up his Pipes
   oh pretty Pipes,
But all the woodcocks looked like snipes
   oh pretty snipes.[176]

This naive song provides an amusing illustration of the Fool's role in a Morris dance. The Fool naturally also reappears in the description of the 'Morris' given by Gerrold, the schoolmaster, in *The Two Noble Kinsmen*:

Then the beest-eating Clown; and next, the Fool;
The babion [Bavian] with long tail and eke long tool...[177]

E.K. Chambers provides the following explanations of the Fool's various attributes: his ladle, his long tail and his long tool:

'Bavian' as a name for the fool, is the Dutch *baviaan*, 'baboon'. His tail is to be noted; for the phallic shape sometimes given to the bladder which he carries, cf. Rigollot, 164. In the Betley window, the fool has a bauble; in the Vinckeboon picture a staff with a bladder at one end, and a ladle (to gather money in) at the other. In the window the ladle is carried by the hobby horse.[178]

The long tail and the phallic-shaped bladder that the Fool carried around drew attention to his fabled hyper-sexuality which was somewhat curiously associated with his mental debility, while at the same time making it possible for him to raise a laugh with various obscene mimes. The ladle, carried, as it happens, by the Hobby-horse in the Tollet stained-glass window, was passed round to collect coins from the spectators when the dance was over and the money thus raised was used to pay the dancers and provide for an evening meal. In *Cobbes Prophecie*, the joke is, precisely, that the crowd of Morris-dance spectators melted away before being asked to cough up, and the author pokes fun at this peasant cunning. But, as Thomas Nashe suggests, this ladle could also be flourished as an obscene symbol in the phallic dance that the Fool would sometimes perform, capering round and round Maid Marian: 'Martin himself is the Mayd-marian, trimlie drest uppe in a cast Gowne, and a Kercher... Wiggenton daunces about him in a Cotten-coate, to courte him with a Leatherne pudding and a wooden ladle...'.[179] Nicholas Breton also alludes to the Fool's erotic capers around Maid Marian: 'Maid Marian of late was got with child in her sleepe, and the Hobby-horse was half mad that the Foole should be the Father of it...'.[180]

The fact that Maid Marian passes over the Hobby-horse like this is symptomatic of the way in which he was in general frequently overlooked in the Elizabethan period, as Ben Jonson's lines attest:

NO-BODY: At this time it doth befall
We are the Huisher to a Morise,
(a kind of Masque) whereof good store is
In the countrey hereabout...
But see, the Hobby-horse is forgot.
Foole, it must be your lot,
To supply his want with faces,
And some other Buffon graces,
You know how; Piper play,
And let no bodie hence away.[181]

Nevertheless, the Hobby-horse is given pride of place in the Tollet stained-glass window and he may even have continued to play an important part in the Morris dance, even if Maid Marian did transfer her favours to the Fool.

Nicholas Breton certainly includes the hobby-horse in his list of the four main categories of horses, automatically associating him with the Morris dance:

There be foure chiefe horses for service: the courser for the Souldier, the Hackney for the post, the Cart horse for the Farmer, and the Hobbi-horse for the Morris-dance.[182]

Stubbes also mentions him, along with the dragon, in what he calls 'the devil's daunce':

Thus al things set in order, then have they their Hobby-horses, dragons & other Antiques, togither with their baudie Pipers and thundering Drummers to strike up the devils daunce withall.[183]

As for Ben Jonson, in his *Masque of Owls* he has the amusing idea of introducing on stage a hobby-horse mounted by the famous Captain Cox, who so distinguished himself in the entertainment organized for Queen Elizabeth at Kenilworth:

Enter Captain Cox, on his Hobby-horse.
CAP. COXE:
Roome, roome, for my Horse will wince
If he come within so many yards of a Prince,
And though he have not on his wings,
He will doe strange things.
He is the *Pegasus* that uses
To waite on Warwick Muses;
And on gaudy-dayes he paces
Before the *Coventrie* Graces;
For to tell you true, and in rime,

He was foald in Q. Elizabeths time,
When the great Earle of Lester
In his Castle did feast her.[184]

William Sampson's *The Vow-breaker or The Fair Maid of Clifton* (1636)
contains a long scene in which Miles, the miller, has to persuade Ball, the
cobbler, to let him play the part of Hobby-horse.[185] As to Ben Jonson's
Every Man Out of His Humour it sheds a little light on the tricks that
were performed in the course of the Morris dance by the dancer
representing the Hobby-horse:

CARLO BUFFONE: 'Sbloud, you shall see him turne morris-dancer, he ha's got
him bels, a good sute, and a hobby-horse.
SOGLIARDO: Signior, now you talke of a hobby-horse, I know where one is,
will not be given for a brace of angels.
FASTIDIOUS BRISKE: How is that, Sir?
SOGL.:   Marry, sir, I am telling this gentleman of a hobby-horse, it was my
fathers indeed, and (though I say it –
CAR.:   That should not say it) on, on.
SOGL.:   He did dance on it, with as good humour, and as good regard, as any
man of his degree whatsoever, being no gentleman; I have danc't in it
my selfe too.
CAR.:   Not since the humour of gentilitie was upon you? did you?
SOGL.:   Yes once; marry, that was but to shew what a gentleman might doe, in a
humour.
CAR.:   O, very good . . .
SOGL.:   Nay, looke you, sir, there's ne're a gentleman i' the country has the like
humours, for the hobby-horse, as I have; I have the method for the
threeding of the needle and all, the . . .
CAR.:   How, the method?
SOGL.:   I, the leigeritie for that, and the wigh-hie, and the daggers in the nose,
and the travels of the egge from finger to finger, all the humours incident
to the quality. The horse hangs at home in my parlor. I'le keepe it for a
monument, as long as I live, sure.
CAR.:   Doe so; and when you die, 'twill be an excellent trophee, to hang over
your tombe.[186]

The tricks that Sogliardo mentions here seem to have demanded the
agility and 'leigeritie' of a veritable conjuror; and if that is the case, the
role of Hobby-horse must necessarily have been played by a professional.
I have not come across any representation of what Sogliardo calls 'the
threeding of the needle'[187] or the 'travels of the egge from finger to
finger', which seem to have been two of the well-known tricks that
everyone expected to see performed. But the 'daggers in the nose' are
shown in the Tollet window (albeit piercing the Hobby-horse's cheeks
here, rather than his nose). Brand and Ellis explain that this custom was a
survival from the 'pyrrhic or Sword dance'.[188] However, the crowds
seem to have been getting tired of the Hobby-horse, as is suggested by a

passage from Massinger's *A Very Woman* (1634) in which the Slave-master paints the following picture of the follies of the French:

MASTER: ... Nay, never wonder
    They have a City, Sir, I have been in't,
    And therefore dare affirm it, where, if you saw
    With what a load of vanity 'tis fraughted,
    How like an everlasting Morris-dance it looks;
    Nothing but Hobby-horse and Maid-marrian;
    You would start indeed ...[189]

The general reputation for vulgarity attached to Maid Marian and the Hobby-horse is confirmed by Nicholas Breton, who lumps them together in his disdain:

    The puffing fat that shewes the Pesants feede,
    Proves *Jack a Lent* was never Gentleman;
    The noble Spirit hath no power to reede,
    The raking Precepts of the Dripping pan;
    A Hoppy horse best fits maid *Marian* ...[190]

Attacks rained down on the unfortunate Hobby-horse from all sides, and he was also a major target for the Puritans, in their campaigns against the Elizabethan festivals.[191]

However, during Elizabeth's reign, it was more likely to be the lone Puritan who was mocked and taunted. His 'martyrdom' might even include being forced, clearly much against his will, to play the role of the Hobby-horse. Puritans were indeed often used as whipping-boys when they were in the minority and refused to take part in popular revels. Richard Baxter writes as follows of his childhood memories:

I cannot forget, that in my youth in those late times, when we lost the labours of some of our conformable godly teachers for not reading publicly the *Book of Sports* and Dancing on the Lord's Days – one of my father's own tenants was the town piper, hired by the year (for many years together), and the place of the dancing assembly was not an hundred yards from our door, and we could not on the Lord's Day either read a chapter, or pray, or sing a psalm, or catechise, or instruct a servant, but with the noise of the pipe and tabor, and the shoutings in the street, continually in our ears and even among a tractable people, *we were the common scorn of all the rabble* in the streets, and called *Puritans, Precisians* and *hypocrites*, because we rather chose to read the Scriptures than to do so they did ... And when the people by the book were allowed to play and dance out of public service time, they could so hardly break off their sports, that many a time the reader was fain to stay till the piper and players would give over; and sometimes the morrice dancers would come into the church in all the linen and scarfs, and antic dresses, with morrice bells jingling at their legs. And as soon as Common-prayer was read did haste out presently to their play again.[192]

But even if the Puritans were, without doubt, often the butt of popular sarcasm, we must remember that this was a spontaneous popular reaction to the zealous excesses of some who posed as the scourges of vice. Furthermore, as we shall see a little later, as soon as the Civil War broke out, these martyred Puritans themselves became the oppressors and persecutors of the popular sports and festivals. At all events, even in the Elizabethan age, their intolerance in the face of what they regarded as the unacceptable vestiges of paganism was already leading to a decline in some of the old popular traditions.

Thus, the Hobby-horse often came to be left out of the Morris dance and his rejection may have been due to the defection of many people who, like Bomby in *Women Pleased*, were suddenly overtaken by fits of fanaticism and transports of piety (what the character called Farmer colourfully terms 'zeal-sweats').

The literature of the period contains many references to the eclipse of the Hobby-horse. As the *OED* notes, the extremely popular ballad 'The Hobby-horse is forgot' assumed a quasi-proverbial force at this time, as is confirmed by numerous contemporary texts ranging from the end of the sixteenth century down to the beginning of the Puritan revolution. Shakespeare himself alludes to it in *Love's Labour's Lost*:

ARMADO: But O, but O
MOTE: 'The hobby-horse is forgot' . . .

and does so again in *Hamlet*.[193] As the Hobby-horse's star waned in the context of the Elizabethan festive traditions and the Morris dance, the expression became overlaid with more and more negative connotations, as can be seen from the *OED*:

a frivolous or foolish fellow . . . Lustful person: loose woman, prostitute.

The last clearly identifiable figure on the Tollet window is he whom Shakespeare, in *The Two Gentlemen of Verona* (IV, i, 35) calls 'Robin Hood's fat friar'. This is Friar Tuck, recognizable from his rough, homespun habit, his tonsured head and the rosary in his right hand. As Malcolm A. Nelson points out, in his case too it was his association with the Morris dance that brought about his decline, for it demoted him from a position of relative respectability to that of a figure of fun.[194]

Friar Tuck was surrounded by a number of secondary characters such as Scarlet, Stokesley and Little John. All three are mentioned in an old ballad cited by Brand and Ellis:

> I have heard talk of Robin Hood,
>   Derry, Derry, Derry, down,
> And of brave Little John,
> Of Friar Tuck and Will Scarlet,

Stokesley and Maid Marrian,
    Hey down, &c.[195]

This description of the various interpreters of the Morris dance, whether as principal attractions or in supporting roles, would be incomplete without one other indispensable figure who made it possible to turn the spectacle into a dance, namely the player of the fife and drum, generally known as 'Tom the Piper'. A single individual acquitted himself simultaneously upon the two instruments which, together, beat out the tune and rhythm for the dancers. The engraving printed as frontispiece to William Kempe's work entitled *Kemps Nine Daies Wonder* (1600) shows Tom the Piper to the left (see Illus. 4.3). The piper's costume appears to have been as colourful as that of the Fool and, like the Fool, he sometimes collected contributions from the audience, as Drayton indicates:

Myself above Tom Piper to advance,
Who so bestirs him in the Morris-dance
    For penny-wage.[196]

Another interesting account of Tom the Piper is found in an anonymous

4.3   Tom the Piper and the Fool, from the frontispiece of William Kempe's *Kemps Nine Daies Wonder* (1600).

prose pamphlet of 1608 entitled *Old Meg of Hereford-shire for a Mayd-Marian and Hereford-towne for a Morris-Dance*:

The people of Hereford-shire are beholding to thee, thou givest the men light hearts by thy Pype, and the women light heeles by thy Taber: O wonderfull pyper, O admirable Taber-man, make use of thy worth, even after death, that art so famously worthy in thy life, both for thy age, skill, & thy unbruized Taber, who these threescore yeares has kept her maydenhead sound and uncrackt, and neither lost her first voyce, or her fashion: once for the Countryes pleasure imitate that Bohemian Zisea, who at his death gave his Souldiers a strict command, to flea his skin off, and cover a Drum with it, that alive & dead, he might sound like a terror in the eares of his enemies: So thou sweete Hereford Hall, bequeath in thy last will, thy Velom-spotted skin, to cover Tabors: at the sound of which, to set all the shires a dauncing.[197]

The text reveals the overtly sexual connotations of Tom the Piper's simple instruments: the fife was a phallic symbol, while the tabor was suggestive of the female sexual organs ('has kept her maydenhead sound and uncrackt'). It seems reasonable to suppose that Tom would be likely to include a number of risqué gestures in his many-faceted performance. But in the pamphlet just cited, the emphasis is laid on the great age of the musician and likewise of his instrument, which was made from a water bucket dating from the reign of Edward VI. Age had apparently impaired neither the verve of the musician nor the effectiveness of his drum:

his Tabor hath made Batchelers and Lasses daunce round about the May-poll, three-score Sommers one after another in order, and is yet not worme-eaten.[198]

Although the author dwells with a certain burlesque irony upon the decrepitude of this key protagonist in the popular festival, one detects a sneaking admiration for him, however grotesque his portrayal.

On the other hand, in *The Whimzies, or a New Cast of Characters*, the tone of the description of the piper is clearly satirical. Here this stalwart of the village festival, very much the tavern regular,[199] is portrayed as an individual without rank or dignity, hanging on to a living at society's expense, and furthermore a threat to public order since crowds soon collect around him:

A piper is a very droane, ever soaking and sucking from others labours. In wakes and rush-bearings, he turnes flat rorer. Yet the youths without him can keep no true measure. His head, pipe, and leg hold one consort . . . Hee is never sober, but when hee is either sleeping or piping . . . Hee is generally more carefull how to get a coate for his pipe than his child . . . Hee is a dangerous instrument in the common wealth, for drawing together routs and riotous assemblies; yet so long as they dance after his pipe, there can bee intended no great perilous project of state.[200]

In this vignette, he is made out to be a leech, a sponger and a trouble-maker. But the general opinion of this indispensable parasite, at the time, was that he was really the best fellow in the world! The piper was a wandering musician who hired out his services as he moved from village to village, from festival to fairground ('Hee deserves not his wench, that will not pay for her dance')[201] and on that account he was often seen as a rogue or a vagabond and, when arrested as such, was likely to be pilloried in the stocks or subjected to a whipping.

Also known as a 'piper' was the bagpipe-player who figures so prominently in Pieter Brueghel's paintings. Stubbes, in his well-known and fascinating account of a Morris dance, makes a distinction between on the one hand the 'piper' and on the other the 'drummer'. In larger gatherings in which the entire village community would be assembled, our one-man band might thus be replaced by two separate musicians:

Thus al things set in order, then have they their Hobby-horses, dragons & other Antiques, togither with their *baudie Pipers* and thundering *Drummers* to strike up the devils daunce withall. Then, marche these heathen company towards the Church and Church-yard, their *pipers pipeing*, their *drummers thundring*, their stumps dauncing, their bels iyngling, their handkerchefs swinging about their heds like madmen, their hobbie horses and other monsters skirmishing amongst the route . . .[202]

The colourful atmosphere and cacophony of this May carnival, in which Stubbes detects vestigial traces of the Devil's Sabbath, is somewhat reminiscent of the Dionysiac festivals in which devotees would be induced into trances by the strident sound of pipes accompanied by the insistent beat of drums.

In a Morris dance, the sound of these various instruments would be swollen by the merry jingle of the bells that the dancers wore around their knees and ankles (see Illus. 4.4).[203] These jingle-bells had become one of the distinguishing features of the Morris dance, as is shown by the following lines from Shakespeare's *2 Henry VI*, where York says about Jack Cade:

> I have seen
> Him caper upright like a wild Morisco,
> Shaking the bloody darts as he his bells.   (III, i, 364–6)

The dancers themselves wore brightly coloured costumes and made much play with scarves, to accentuate their gestures, producing a spectacle for the eyes as well as an entertainment for the ears. So far as one can tell from the features of the Morris dance, the festive confusion was likely to produce a kind of 'disorientation of all the senses' ('dérèglement de tous les sens') – if I may be allowed a somewhat anachronistic reference to Arthur Rimbaud's *Saison en Enfer* (*Season in Hell*). Stubbes' description presents us with a veritable fireworks-show of sound and colour:

4.4   Morris dancers, an engraving from *The Roxburghe Ballads* (1893).

First, all the wilde-heds of the Parish, conventing together, chuse them a Ground-Captain (of all mischeefe) whome they innoble with the title of 'my Lord of Misrule', and him they crowne with great solemnitie, and adopt for their king . . . Then, everie one of these his men, he investeth with his liveries of green, yellow, or some other light wanton colour; And as though that were not (baudie) gaudie enough, I should say, they bedecke them selves with scarfs, ribbons & laces hanged all over with golde rings, precious stones, & other jewels: this doon, they tye about either leg xx, or xl bels, with rich handkerchiefs in their hands, and sometimes laid a crosse over their shoulders and necks, borrowed for the most parte of their pretie Mopsies & looving Besses, for bussing them in the dark.[204]

As for the steps of the Morris dance, they seem to have consisted of a series of 'jerks'[205] and 'moulinets', or twirls. In Cotgrave's dictionary, the term 'moulinets' is indeed defined as 'a Morisdauncers Gamboll'.[206] *A Treatise of Daunces*, published in 1581, gives the following description of the steps and movements of a couple of Morris dancers:

When the lusty and fyne man should holde a young damosel, or a woman by the hand, and keeping his measures he shal remove himselfe, whirle, & shake his legges aloft (which the daunsers call crosse capring) for pleasure, doth not she in y^c meane while make a good threede, playing at the Moris on her behalfe.[207]

All the terms used, 'caper', 'jerk', 'gambol', 'moulinet', indicate that the Morris was an energetic if not boisterous dance which could easily take on a suggestive character and project a certain eroticism in the same fashion as the belly dancing of the Arabs and the Flamenco dancing of the Spanish gypsies.[208] Add to all this the comic or obscene wriggling of 'Maid Marian' and the contortions of the Hobby-horse, and it is easy to understand how it was that the whole spectacle must have confirmed the worst fears of the Puritans and scandalized the fine ladies of the time, who had little taste for these popular entertainments. The considerable physical efforts demanded by the Morris dance furthermore caused the dancers to perspire freely, as Thomas Morley notes in one of his madrigals for four voices:

> Ho! who comes here all along with bagpiping and drumming?
> O 'tis the morris dance I see a-coming.
>   Come ladies out, come quickly!
> And see about how trim they dance and trickly.
>   Hey! there again! how the bells they shake it!
>   Hey ho! now for our town and take it!
>   Soft awhile, not away so fast! *They melt them.*
>   Piper, be hanged, knave! see'st thou not the dancers how they swelt them?
> Stand out awhile! you come too far, I say, in.
> There give the hobby-horse more room to play in![209]

There was clearly quite a competitive side to a Morris dance; and this aspect came over even more strongly when competitions between neighbouring villages were organized on 1 May:

On May-day it was the custom for one village to contend with another in dancing matches. 'Hey for our town' was the cry raised on such occasions.[210]

A passage from *The Knight of the Burning Pestle* provides another illustration of the use of the Morris dance as a vehicle of competitive sport between different villages.[211] Their rivalry added spice to the traditional revelry at a time when there was no organized competitive sport and the local youths had few chances to measure their powers or to defend their local colours. Village festivals, organized and enlivened by the various fraternities of young men, thus served a similar purpose to the provincial Sunday football or rugby matches of today.[212] In *Kemps Nine Daies Wonder* and *Old Meg of Hereford-shire*, both already cited, the references to Morris dances are primarily designed to establish certain records: the former work is an account of the feat performed by the actor William Kempe (who travelled all the way from London to Norwich, dancing the Morris for nine consecutive days); the second, which tots up the ages of the eighteen dancers involved, to arrive at the remarkable total of 1,827 years, is designed to evoke the readers' admiration for the staying power of these long-lived dancers.

Having analysed the essential elements of the traditional revelries and entertainments of May Day, in particular the Morris dance, we can now pass on to the next festival to occur, namely the religious feast of Ascension Day. If we consider that the structural pattern for the 'sacred half' (see Appendix 2, below, p. 308) may be brought out by pinning the moveable feasts down to the date of their earliest possible occurrence, then we can understand why Ascension Day is often confused with May Day, since its earliest possible date is 30 April. But in practice its earliest date may be considered as 1 May, since the nocturnal expeditions to fell a maypole and gather the greenery necessary for its decoration took place on the night of 30 April. There are, furthermore, a number of examples to testify to confusion between the festive rites of May Day and those of Ascension Day. Thus, the already cited clash between the students and the townsfolk of Oxford over a procession for the Queen of May took place on Ascension Day:

The inhabitants assembled on the two Sundays before Ascension Day, and *on that Day*, with drum and shot and other weapons, and men attired in women's apparel, brought into the town a woman bedecked with garlands and flowers, named by them the Queen of May.[213]

The main feature of this religious festival was a procession or 'perambulation' right round the parish, in the course of which the animals and the earth's produce were blessed in a manner very reminiscent of pagan rites. These processions were closely connected with the Rogation ceremonies which took place on the three days before either Maundy Thursday or Ascension Day and were usually followed by a dinner, the purpose of which (to judge from the evidence of the parish registers) was to thank the bell-ringers and the standard-bearers for their efforts.[214]

This was followed, ten days later, on the second Sunday after Ascension Day, by the important festival of Whitsuntide, which represented the religious answer to May Day and also constituted one of the key dates in the festive calendar in that it effected the transition from the cycle of winter festivals to that of the summer ones.

Whitsuntide shared enough features with the popular celebrations of May Day for the two dates not always to be clearly distinguished. Thus Stubbes, on the subject of the May game, writes: 'Against *May*,

Whitsonday, or other time . . .', and a poem by William Warner, *Albion's England*, states that, for the people of northern England, 'At Paske began oure Morris, and ere Pentecost our May.'[215] Whitsun, like May Day, was an occasion for Morris dances[216] and also featured other rites and games similar to those of 1 May: for example, the election of a Summer King and Queen:

> And though they do great toyle abide,
> And labour all the weeke,
> Of a sommer lorde, at Whitsuntide,
> They will not be to seeke
> The lorde and the lady, so merry as may be all day
> Like king and queene, will there be seene
> All in their best array . . .[217]

The 'Summer' or 'Whitson Lord' and the 'Summer Queene' are also frequently mentioned separately,[218] no doubt because these titles were awarded in the course of different ceremonies. The Whitsun Lord was elevated to the position of leader of the village youth for the duration of the festival and, in some cases, beyond it, while the Summer Queen was a kind of Beauty Queen.[219]

Whitsun, like Easter, was a time for donning new clothes. It was a pretext for showing off one's finery and competing in elegance,[220] but the custom was also a way of celebrating all the new growth of spring. In Ben Jonson's *Epicoene* (1609), Mrs Otter complains of her husband's slovenly turnout, but makes an exception for his appearance at Easter and Whitsun:

Were you ever so much look'd upon by a lord, or a lady, before I married you: but on the Easter, or Whitson-holy-daies?   (III, i, 46–8)

There is probably a connection between these customs involving the fashions of popular and rural communities and the pastoral comedies that were traditionally performed at this time of the year. Shakespeare alludes to them in *The Two Gentlemen of Verona*, where Julia exclaims:

> for at Pentecost,
> When all our pageants of delight were played,
> Our youth got me to play the woman's part,
> And I was trimmed in Madam Julia's gown.   (IV, iv, 155–8)

And in *The Winter's Tale*, Perdita sports a party-dress to play her role of 'mistress of the feast' and subsequently regrets having made such a spectacle of herself:

> Methinks I play as I have seen them do,
> In Whitsun pastorals . . .   (IV, iv, 133–4)

Perhaps Shakespeare had in mind the shows that he must have seen in Stratford, as is suggested by this entry in the accounts of the town corporation:

Payd to Davi Jones and his companye for his pastime at Whitsontyde . . . xiijs. iiijd.

E.K. Chambers, who cites this in his study on William Shakespeare, goes on to observe: 'Critical eyes may have watched the Whitsun pastoral which David Jones produced in 1583.'[221]

Humbler texts also testify to these practices: a ballad entitled 'In Olde Times Paste' runs:

> Then were there plays att Whitsontyde,
>   And sommer games about.[222]

Similarly, the portrait of the Pedler in *The Whimzies* refers to the 'morrice pastorall',[223] which would appear to suggest that these pastoral entertainments also centred around the Morris dance. Whitsun was thus a favourite time for staging pastoral dramas which must have been the rural and village equivalent of the evening performances given in Elizabethan London during the month of May.[224] It was also, again like May Day, a great time for the 'May game' – a term that should not be defined too restrictively for it seems to have had a somewhat vague application for the Elizabethans. One of the Marprelate Tracts, entitled *Hay any Worke for Cooper*, draws a clear distinction between Robin Hood and the Morris dance on the one hand, and the Summer Lord and the May game on the other. In other texts, in contrast, the two aspects are confused. J.C. Cox's *Churchwardens' Accounts* shows that entries in the Account Books of the town of Yatton in Somerset, for the Whitsun period, appear to make no distinction at all between the Morris dance and the May game:

> 1574. The gatherynge of the wyffes at Whytsontyde for Dauncynge iijs. iiijd.
> 1541 (Culworth). Payntyng of the hoby horse clothes . . . iijs.
> 1558 (St Martin, Leicester). Reed for the mawrys daunce of the chyldren . . . iijs.
> 1594–5. (St Thomas, Sarum). Childrens Daunce . . . 20s. id.
> 1613. (Lowick, Northants). Payd to Rober Brandin for makeinge the Maypole . . . iiijs.[225]

On the other hand, David Wiles is convinced that the May game took place at Whitsun and not on the first of May.[226]

According to Baskervill, the May game continued the pastoral traditions in a farcical mode,[227] which would suggest that the 'Pentecost

... pageants of delight' and the 'Whitsun pastorals' mentioned by Shakespeare do in fact refer to the May game.[228] In the countryside and the small villages, they would probably simply consist of Morris dances, featuring Robin Hood, and other forms of revelry generally associated with him (archery competitions, wrestling, the choosing of a king and a queen, and the consumption of 'cakes and ale'...), while in the larger towns, the May game would take the form of a parade or a pageant.[229] These parades would feature most of the traditional figures from the processions of the Middle Ages, that is to say the Nine Champions, Saint George and the dragon, the Morris dancers and any other topical figure who could be used to caricature carping spirits or locals hostile to the festivities.[230]

Whitsunday was also the day when many parishes would hold a 'church ale',[231] in which the parishioners celebrated and caroused merrily in the churchyard itself.[232] In his *Curiosities of Popular Customs*, W.S. Walsh cites the complaints that a Puritan priest voiced against the 'Whitsun ales' organized in Redbourne in 1597:

These are in their origin bad; they are shamefully abused, having in them piping and dancing, and Maid Marion coming into the church at the time of prayer to move laughter with kissing in the church, and they justly deserve to be called profane, riotous and disorderly.[233]

Feasting and carousing in these circumstances was claimed to be performing a good deed and serving the interests of the Church. But the use of consecrated Church ground for the purposes of what they considered as debauchery was obviously not designed to make the Puritans look kindly upon church ales in general or the Whitsun ale in particular. Henry Burton's collection of instances of divine retribution falling upon these sacrilegious carousers and dancers contains the following example:

A Miller at churchdown, neer Glocester, would needs ... keep a solemn Whitson ale, for which he has made large preparation and provision, even of threescore dozen of cheesecakes with other things proportionable, in the church-house half a mile from his Mill, his musicall instruments were set forth on the side of the Church-house, when the Minister and people were to passe to the Church to Evening Prayer. When Prayer and Sermon were ended, the Drumme is struck up, the peeces discharged, the Musicians play, and the rowt fell a dauncing, till the evening; where all with the Miller resort to his Mill; where that evening before they had supt, about 9 o'clock on Whitsunday, a fire took suddenly in his house over their heads, and was so brief and quick, that it burned down his house and mill.[234]

Before considering Corpus Christi, the last great occasion of this ritualistic half of the year which opens with the series of moveable feasts, a few words about Trinity Sunday would seem to be in place. It fell eight weeks after Easter, its date fluctuating between 17 May and 20 June. According to the testimony cited by the Historical Manuscripts Commission in relation to the county of Wiltshire, the customs associated with this day differed hardly at all from those of the other May festivals:

On Trinity Sunday, June 20 (1641), there was a great riot in Neunton church and places adjoining, in the time of afternoon service, in connection with the custom of carrying a garland; and several depositions were taken before the justices the same evening. Some 40, or as also said, 80, persons of Malmsbury came with Staves, amongst them one John Browne 'sometyme a chymney sweeper', with a hobby horse and bells on his legs, and Davi Tanner is 'a fencer' and the purpose of their going to Neunton was for the garland; and when they saw John Comyn going with the garland, they bid him and his company stand, saying 'Wynn it and weare it, come threescore of you, you are but boies to wee', and thereupon there was a great fight, and many of the Neunton men were sorely beaten.[235]

The Feast of Corpus Christi was of relatively recent date. (This feast of the Blessed Body of Christ had been introduced in 1318 in England, but was abolished in 1547 by Edward VI.) It fell on the Thursday following Trinity Sunday, that is to say eleven days after Whitsun and seventy days after Easter. In the Middle Ages it had been an occasion for lavish festivities which included pageants and also performances of Mystery plays, but it had been severely hit by the Reformation, which had more or less struck it from the calendar. However, following the suppression of this festival in 1547, the custom of performing religious plays on this day seems to have persisted into the late 1570s[236] and from 1580 on the plays were superseded by Midsummer parades of a civic and Protestant character. The replacement of religious activities by secular ones is such a characteristic feature of the Elizabethan period that this particular development should occasion no great surprise. However, it seems that even in the past town guilds used to organize Corpus Christi parades which sometimes served as an alternative to the various dramatic entertainments.[237] This festival marked the end of the ritualistic half of the year. Thereafter the major celebrations would be linked with the completion of the major agricultural tasks (sheep-shearing, harvest-home, etc.). The framework of this economy was essentially rural: the long summer days made it possible to work in the fields and the communal co-operation that was customary in the many agricultural labours helped to oust the anxieties and fears which had haunted people's minds during the dark winter nights.

In England, as in most of the countries of mainland Europe, the advent of summer and the triumph of light over darkness was greeted with a show of bonfires.[238] These bonfires were the focus for all kinds of revelries which perpetuated the memory of superstitions and quite a few magic rites,[239] all of which were associated in popular culture with the particular powers of this, the shortest night of the year. The magical fascination of fire was supplemented by the burning of certain herbs to the accompaniment of incantations.[240] In London and other large towns, the Midsummer festival was also an occasion for grand parades about which contemporaries such as Machyn have left us some precious information. The parades were all the more impressive in that they were staged at nightfall and took the form of torch-light processions.[241] The most popular attractions of these shows included hobby-horses, Saint George's famous dragon ('old Snap'), snaking along at the saint's side as he used to in the parade of 23 April before the revelries of Saint George's Day were suppressed, wild men known as woodwoses (see Illus. 2.2, above) and, above all, the famous giants who were no doubt the equivalent of those paraded at Carnival time on the continent.[242] As many of these figures also appeared in the May game, a certain confusion arose between the rites of May and those of Midsummer's Eve.[243] Thus, when Cantilupo, in John Webster's *The Devil's Law-Case*, speaks of 'a giant in a May game', he is probably in truth referring to the Midsummer Watch rather than to the entertainments of May Day.[244] At all events, Midsummer was a season which became synonymous with confusion and even mental aberration.[245] Midsummer's Eve was traditionally a night of mistakes and wandering wits, popularly attributed more to the influence of the moon than to that of the summer solstice.

Despite the fact that, by reason of its late date, the Midsummer festival is definitely attached to the summer half of the year, from another point of view, through its lavishness and the presence of many familiar rites, it can also be seen as the last in the series of May festivals. For, except when Easter fell particularly late (around 25 April, for example) and it then more or less coincided with Corpus Christi, it had very few features in common with the rest of the summer festivals (Lammas and Michaelmas, for example).

The secular half of the year

The Michaelmas and Lammas festivals were not rich in festive traditions and it was only on account of their function as 'cross-quarter days' and their key position in the calendar that they were still observed at this period. In effect, most of their customs had lapsed, surviving only in the form of proverbs or sayings.[246] In the comparative calendar of pre-Christian festivals and those observed in the Middle Ages and early Renaissance provided as an appendix to *Early English Stages, 1300 to 1660*, vol. III, Glynne Wickham notes in connection with the Lammas festival of 1 August, 'no Christian equivalent'.[247] This festival had probably been a major one in the Celtic and Teutonic calendars, but was reduced in the Christian calendar to no more than a temporal landmark. In the Elizabethan period, its significance was purely secular: it was the date when the pastures were officially opened for common grazing, until they reverted to the private domain at Candlemas.[248] According to Brand and Ellis, the suffix '-mas' meant 'festival time'.[249]

Holyrood Day, 14 September, rates a passing mention. It was associated with the custom of 'going a-nutting' which, like the nocturnal expeditions of May Day, provided an opportunity for the young to meet out in the open air in an atmosphere of freedom. There is a reference to this in William Haughton's play entitled *Grim the Collier of Croydon* (1600), in which Robin Goodfellow declares:

> This day, they say, is called Holy-rood day,
> And all the youth are now a nutting gone.[250]

And a somewhat later work, *Poor Robin's Almanac* (1709), contains the following comment:

> The devil, as the common people say,
> Doth go a nutting on Holy-rood day;
> And sure such leachery in some doth lurk,
> Going a nutting do the devil's work.[251]

Saint Michael's Day or Michaelmas, 29 September, was known principally as the official beginning of term for the colleges of Oxford and Cambridge and the law schools and courts of London. The chief festive tradition associated with it was the Michaelmas goose, which would be eaten by families which observed such traditions. Some sources suggest that this stemmed from the custom of presenting a goose, as payment in kind, when the time came round for paying the rent[252] so as to get into the good books of one's landlord.[253] Other commentators regard the rite as a means of 'bringing luck'.[254] But bearing in mind that the goose was a creature with an initiatory value in a number of ancient religions and which retained a place of importance in popular mythology and folktales,[255] these culinary traditions should perhaps be seen as survivals from ancient sacrificial practices. In later civilizations the cooking of a domesticated goose took the place of the ritual wringing of the necks of the wild, holy geese of pagan religions. Like the Shrove Tuesday cock-throwing, which was interpreted as an expression of hatred for the French, whose national emblem was the cock, the Michaelmas goose was used for purposes of monarchical and patriotic propaganda in the Elizabethan period.[256]

Strategically positioned as it was, at the beginning of the last term of the year and the end of work in the fields, Michaelmas was also taken to be the starting point for a whole collection of secular activities. They are summed up by A.R. Wright:

Michaelmas term was the traditional time for such hiring [of servants] and for the signing of contracts, the trying of lawsuits, the letting of chambers, and of course the harvesting and selling of crops.[257]

As can be seen from the calendar in Appendix 3 (see below, p. 309), the meeting point between the summer hemisphere (south) and the winter one (north) was constituted by Hallowe'en, the eve of the Festival of the Dead (Hallowmas). Whether the religion involved was of Mediterranean or Nordic origin, in the pagan world this festival marked a crucial point in the year, for it was linked with beliefs that this was the time when the souls of the dead returned to haunt the living. Throughout the countryside and villages of Elizabethan England, games were organized on Hallowe'en, partly as a collective means to ward off fear of the dead, partly to exploit the powers of divination proverbially associated with this night, as with Saint Agnes' Eve and Midsummer Eve. The nickname 'nutcrack-night' given to Hallowe'en stemmed from the techniques by which young men satisfied themselves as to the fidelity of their loves.[258] On this occasion, pagan beliefs and popular games intermingled with the atmosphere of the religious festival of All Saints' Day, which the Church had judiciously allocated to the very same date as the pagan *Todtenfest* (Festival of the Dead).[259] Hallowe'en was also the date that marked the start of the reign of the 'Christmas Prince' at Saint John's College, Oxford.[260]

The originally Catholic ritual of tolling the church bell in honour of the souls of the deceased had persisted even after the Reformation and was not banned in England until Queen Elizabeth's Injunction against traditional practices of this kind.[261] As befitted such a period of austerity, the traditional fare of Hallowmas (All Saints' Day) and All Souls' Day was meagre: it consisted basically of 'soul-cakes' and apples,[262] which were the items of food dispensed to the children and paupers of the parish at this time when charity was recommended.

Before Martinmas, the first major popular festival of this winter half of the year, three great civic festivals were held at this time of the year: the Lord Mayor's Show, Guy Fawkes' Day and the celebrations commemorating Queen Elizabeth's accession to the throne of England. The Lord Mayor's Show fell on Saint Simon and Saint Jude's Day, 28 October. Guy Fawkes' Day, the popular festival instituted following 5 November 1605, to commemorate the discovery of the Gunpowder Plot,[263] celebrated the rout of the papists with a great show of fireworks and bonfires. According to Wright, the custom of celebrating the failure of

Guy Fawkes' conspiracy began as early as 1607 in, for example, Bristol.[264] Another of its popular features was the burning of an effigy of Guy Fawkes commonly known as the 'guy'.[265] The third great civic festival, held on 17 November, the anniversary of Queen Elizabeth's accession to the throne, had become a major celebration of the monarchy and Protestantism. In the past, this date had been consecrated to Saint Hugh, the patron saint of shoemakers,[266] but from the 1570s onwards it was celebrated as a national and Protestant festival. In an article entitled 'The Popular Celebrations of the Accession Day of Queen Elizabeth I', Roy Strong writes that 'the solution suggests itself that the Accession Day festivities were the adaptation of an old Catholic festival to the ethos of Protestantism'.[267] The rejoicing, which included bonfires, peals of bells and a special meal, was by no means restricted to the court: 'the Queen's Accession Day was not only a court fête, it was a national festival'.[268]

But however important these civic celebrations may have been, the major festival of early winter was indisputably Martinmas on 11 November. It fell following a gap in the festive calendar and so represented a kind of carnival after the Lenten fare of All Saints' Day. So much is reflected in the Elizabethan expression 'Saint Martin's Lent', one of the three Lenten periods in the liturgical year of the early monks. The first came before Easter, the second between Martinmas and Christmas Eve, the third after the Feast of Saint John the Baptist.[269] Claude Gaignebet explains that this series of Lents was part of the balanced interlocking system of forty-day cycles that was a distinctive feature of the popular calendar. He regards 'these few days of an opposite nature just as one period is ending and another beginning' as 'the exact, symmetrical reverse of the wintry period of the daunting, hail- or frost-bearing saints of early May'. And, in conclusion, he notes that 'the start of each Celtic season is marked by a period of time of a different nature which heralds the return of a new season'.[270] On the continent, particularly in France, this was the great festival of the new vintage of wine, celebrated a few short weeks after the grape-harvest;[271] and meanwhile, in England, the beer was flowing freely and beef was being consumed in quite inordinate quantities. In Elizabethan times, the fact was that the scarcity of fodder and the impossibility of feeding all the herds through the winter forced farmers to slaughter a number of their animals around Martinmas. Not all the meat was eaten fresh; some was set to smoke, up the chimney, some salted away for the winter.[272] But Martinmas or Martlemas beef was a sign of plenty in the rural communities of Elizabethan England. In the popular imagination, it evoked Rabelaisian banquets and a dream of the Land of Cockaigne for folk who led a hard life and seldom got the chance to eat meat. Martinmas beef symbolized days of feasting in the popular English imagination, in the same way as pork products did for the villagers of mainland Europe. The medieval Morality plays often set on stage allegorical representations of the Seven Deadly Sins, among whom Gluttony would be likely to figure prominently. In Marlowe's *Doctor Faustus* (1592), which borrows many features from the Morality plays, Gluttony takes part in the parade organized by Beelzebub to amuse his new follower, announcing:

I come of a Royall Pedigree, my father was a Gammon of Bacon, and my mother was a Hogshead of Claret Wine. My godfathers were these: Peter Pickeld-Herring, and Martin Martlemasse-beefe: But my godmother, O she was an ancient Gentlewoman, her name was Margery March-beere.[273]

The beef of Martinmas thus figures prominently in the grotesque genealogies of the period in which evocative titles ('Peter Pickeld-Herring', 'Martin Martlemasse-beefe', 'Margery March-beere' typical alliterations of names and nicknames) testify to the dynamism of the popular language and imagination which, as we have already seen, tended generally to represent the material world (food, various parts of the body) in a personalized, allegorical form.[274]

William Warner's *Albion's England* contains a curious passage in which the celebrations of Martinmas are associated with the figure of Robin Hood, more generally evoked in connection with the May game:

> At Martlemas wa turned a crabbe, thilke told of Robin hood
>   Till after long time myrke, when blest were windowes, dores and
>   lights,
>   And pails were fild, and hathes were swept, gainst
> Fairie-elves and spirits...[275]

Perhaps the unusual association is due to the fact that the speaker is supposed to be a countryman from the North of England. However that may be, the figure of Robin Hood is here portrayed as a hero of 'romance', as are the fairies and spirits mentioned next, whose high deeds were recounted along with all the other stories and legends told during the long evening hours of Martinmas. Apart from being a major protagonist of the Morris dance and the May game, Robin Hood was often represented presiding at a banquet where the main fare was game (usually venison).[276] On that account, he may well sometimes have been chosen as a patron of the Martinmas festivities.

The last major cycle in the Elizabethan festive calendar was that of the twelve days of Christmas, which started forty days after the period of Martinmas. Before we turn to it, however, there are four other festivals to be considered briefly. These had been extremely popular in the Middle Ages and early Renaissance and continued to be observed under Elizabeth's reign, despite having been banned by Henry VIII at the

Reformation. They were the festivals of Saint Catherine on 25 November, Saint Andrew on 30 November, coinciding with the start of Advent, Saint Nicholas on 6 December and Saint Thomas on 21 December.

Saint Catherine's Day seems to have been honoured by one particular category of the population, defined in terms of age and gender, namely the girls. Brand and Ellis refer to:

Young women meeting on the 25th of November, and making merry together, which they call Catherning.[277]

As on Saint Agnes' Eve and Hallowe'en, these 'young women' would attempt, by means of fasting or other rites and ceremonies, to conjure up an image of their future husbands. In the religious calendar, this was the time of the beginning of Advent and it also served as a point of reference to mark the start of certain secular festivities, as this was the day for crowning the 'Christmas Prince' at Saint John's College, Oxford.[278]

Saint Nicholas' Day, 6 December, used in England to be a time for burlesque rituals and travesties of the religious services which resembled the practices observed in the Feast of Fools in mainland Europe. A selected youth would be dressed up in ecclesiastical vestments and would be expected to parody the liturgical ceremonies and prayers. This 'Boy Bishop', who was elected for the period stretching from Saint Nicholas' Day to the Feast of the Holy Innocents, 28 December, was given full licence to hold the priesthood and the bishopric up to mockery, in the same way as a Lord of Misrule was licensed to mock and parody well-known, highly placed figures of authority.[279] Henry VIII had attempted to put an end to these masquerades in an official proclamation dated 22 July 1541, but Queen Elizabeth was obliged to renew the ban after their reinstatement during the brief reign of Mary Tudor.[280] Brand and Ellis note that the 'Boy Bishop' still refused to die in country villages and schools until the end of the seventeenth century.[281]

Saint Thomas' Day, 21 December, was often regarded as a signal to begin the festivals of Christmas. A.L. Rowse remarks:

Ringing in Christmas often began on St Thomas's Day 21 December, on which day poor women had free licence to beg... and went 'a-gooding' – it was good for the soul to give.[282]

Similarly, in the Inns of Court, in London, the week in which Saint Thomas' Day fell was the first of four weeks of Christmas festivities.[283]

But it is in the city of York that we find the most striking custom associated with Saint Thomas' Day, for here they would parade through the streets the figures of 'Yule' and 'Yule's wife', a spectacle that the Archbishop of York considered indecent. His letter to the Mayor and his

councillors requesting them to ban these proceedings is one of the few
sources of confirmation about this local tradition:

After our hartie commendacons Wheras there hath bene heretofore a verie rude
and barbarous custome mainteyned in this citie. And in no other citie or towne of
this Realme to our knowledge, that yerelie upon St Thomas Daie before christmas
two disguised persons called yule and yules wief should ryde throw the cite verey
undecentlie and uncomelie Drawinge great concourses of people after them to
gaise, often times commitinge other enormities fforasmuche as the said Disguysed
(ydinge) and concourse afforesaid besydes other enconvenientes tendeth also to
the prophanynge of that Daie appointed to holie Uses and also with drawethe
great multitudes of people frome devyne Service and Sermons. We have thought
good . . . to charge and commaunde yow, that ye take order that no such ryding
of yule and yules wief be frome hensfurth attempted or used.[284]

According to another source cited by Alexandra F. Johnston, the
legend underlying these customs went back to the time of William the
Conqueror. While laying siege to York on Saint Thomas' Day, he was
said to have entered the town thanks to the assistance of two monks 'who
had been seeking relief for their fellows and themselves against
Christmas, the one having a wallet full of victualls and a shoulder of
mutton in his hand, with great cakes hanging about his neck; the other
having bottles of ale, with provisions likewise of biefe and mutton in his
wallet'. William the Conqueror thereupon requested the town authorities:

to ask whatsoever they would of him before he went and he would grant their
request; whereupon they (abominating the treachery of the two fryers to their
eternal infamy) desired that on *St Thomas's day* for ever, they might have a fryer
of the priory of *St Peters* to ride through the city on horse-back with his face to
the horse's tayle, and that in his hand instead of a bridle, he should have a rope,
and in the other a shoulder of mutton, with one cake hanging on his back and
another on his breast, with his face painted like a *Jew*, and the youths of the city
to ride with him and to cry and shout YOUL, YOUL, with the officers of the city
rideing before makeing proclamation, that on this day the city was betrayed; and
their request was granted them.[285]

This legend is probably a late rationalization of an old myth
concerning the founding of the town, similar to that of Lady Godiva's
ride though the streets of Coventry. Its chief interest lies in the figure of
the scapegoat made to ride backwards though the town (reminiscent of a
charivari), with his face 'painted like a Jew', a notion presumably
suggested by a pun on 'Yule', the old Saxon term for the festivities of
Christmas. As for the allusion to the shoulder of mutton and the cake,
this seems to be a direct reflection of the hearty eating associated with the
Christmas period, the festival of abundance *par excellence*. The mockery
directed against the monks no doubt expresses the satirical hostility felt
towards the monks in Reformation England.

The twelve days of Christmas, from 25 December to 6 January, was an important period of festivity that was enthusiastically celebrated in town and country alike.[286] Twelve-day periods of festivity recur at various points in the calendar: there were roughly twelve days between All Saints' Day and Martinmas, between Candlemas and Saint Valentine's Day and between May Day and Whitsun (which fell, at its earliest, on 10 May and was regarded as a Quarter Day when it fell on 15 May). For each of the festive mini-cycles, an average period of twelve days separated a religious festival from a secular one (the other way round in the case of May Day and Whitsun). The three principal festivals of the Christmas cycle were held on Christmas Eve, New Year's Eve and the eve of Epiphany, all three very much nocturnal celebrations, a typical characteristic of the festivals of winter. Let us now attempt a more detailed analysis of the customs and celebrations peculiar to each of these three festivals.

The first point to emphasize is the great popularity of this festive period, the longest and most sustained of the whole year.[287] The proverbs cited by Tilley refer more often to 'Christmas' than to any other festival,[288] indicating that Christmas was regarded as the festival *par excellence*. As the following example from *The Merry Devil of Edmonton* (1602), attributed to Dekker, shows, the word 'Christmas' was virtually synonymous with 'holiday':

CLARE: For looke you, wife, the riotous old knight
         Hath o'rerun his annual reuenue
         In keeping iolly Christmas all the yeere.[289]

Christmas had become a veritable myth, in which dreams of the Golden Age came true, when princes visited the humble cottages and the countryside regained the upper hand over the towns:

> The Court in all state, Now opens her gate,
>   And bids a free welcome to most;
> The City likewise, though somewhat precise,
>   Doth willingly part with her cost;
> And yet by report, from City and Court,
>   The Country gets the day;
> More liquor is spent, and better content,
>   To drive the cold winter away.[290]

The idea of observing a period of truce in all social conflicts, which restored a kind of universal fraternity for the duration of these eagerly awaited twelve days, probably stemmed in part from the Roman Saturnalia, with their rites of social inversion. It was also inspired by the feudal, medieval notion of *hospitalitas* which dictated that, over the holy period of Christmas, houses should open their doors to all and sundry

and the poor should be made welcome at the tables of the rich.[291] But
these obligations of hospitality were being increasingly neglected in the
Elizabethan period, a fact that voices on all sides were deploring.

Before embarking upon the games and revelries of Christmas Eve,
decorations had to be put up. For this purpose, evergreens were used –
ivy and holly, for example, which, quite apart from their ornamental
value, symbolized the subterranean persistence of growing plants.
Instead of a Christmas tree, which appears to have been introduced in
England in the nineteenth century only, a large Christmas log, known as
the Yule block, Yule log or Yule clog, was set in the fireplace. There it
was burned according to a rite that constituted the winter version of the
bonfires of Midsummer and appears to have been connected with
celebrating the power of light at the moment of either solstice.[292] George
Wither's 'Christmas Carol' (1622) presents a festive, enthusiastic and
joyous picture of these customs:

> So, now is come our joyfulst feast;
>   Let every man be jolly;
> Each room with ivy leaves is drest,
>   And every post with holly.
> Though some churls at our mirth repine,
> Round your foreheads garlands twine;
> Drown sorrow in a cup of wine,
>   And let us all be merry.
>
> Now, all our neighbours' chimnies smoke
>   And Christmas blocks are burning...[293]

First, Christmas carols – not so much Christian as festival songs[294] –
would be sung to set the atmosphere for Christmas Eve, then it would be
the turn of the pipers and taborers who would play at all the banquets
and balls of the twelve days of Christmas, just as they had enlivened the
festivals of May Day and Whitsun:[295]

> Now every lad is wondrous trim,
>   And no man minds his labour;
> Our lasses have provided them
>   A bag-pipe and a tabor...
> Rank misers now do sparing shun;
>   Their hall of music soundeth;
> And dogs thence with stole shoulders run,
>   So all things there aboundeth.
> The country folks themselves advance
>   With crowdy-muttons out of France;
> And Jack shall pipe, and Jyll shall dance,
>   And all the town shall be merry.[296]

But Christmas Eve was not just a cheerful family affair celebrated in the privacy of one's own home. Neighbours were expected to be included and many visits were paid. The express purpose of customs such as passing the Wassail-bowl and the entertainments of the Mummers was to extend family conviviality to embrace the whole village society. The Wassail-bowl was a large receptacle filled with beer into which small toasted apples were plunged while still smoking.[297] It was carried from house to house by a group of girls who would dispense the drink to everyone present, singing 'Wassail, jolly wassail . . .' and would receive a few coins in exchange.[298]

The Mummers, who also made their appearance at Easter time, likewise moved from house to house to perform their plays and make a collection in return for their pains.[299] The show would generally consist of a folk play, traditionally centred upon a figure such as 'Old Father Christmas' or perhaps 'Saint George'. In some regions of England, particularly the North, these troupes of Mummers would perform a Sword dance.[300] Elsewhere they would don masks and invade the dwellings of certain rich or powerful personages to entertain the company there, but following certain abuses, this tradition was banned by Henry VII.[301] Similarly, in the court Masque, the offspring of these ancient Mummeries,[302] which, along with other plays,[303] had become the favourite entertainment for the Christmas period among the great and the aristocracy, the actors would continue to simulate a brutal invasion into a theoretically startled and unprepared assembly. A sixteenth-century ballad entitled 'A Pleasant Country New Ditty' carefully itemizes all these traditions, underlining the importance of the neighbours' participation:[304]

> To Maske and Mum
> Kind neighbours will come
>   with Wassels of nut-browne Ale,
> To drink and carouse
> To all in his house,
>   as merry as bucks in the pale;
> Where Cake, Bread and Cheese,
> Is brought for your fees
>   to make you the longer stay;
> At the fire to warme
> Will do you no harme,
>   to drive the cold winter away.[305]

When the neighbourly visiting was over and after the dancing, the plays and the hearty eating, the rest of the evening would be passed with various games of chance and feats of skill:

These [sports] being done, the jolly youths and plain dealing plowswains, being weary of cards, fell to dauncing, from dauncing they flew to Gambols. Some ventured the breaking of their shinnes to make mee sport, some the scalding of their lips to catch at apples tyed at the end of a sticke having a lighted candle at the other; some shod the wild Mare; some at hot cockles and the like . . .[306]

These famous Christmas 'gambols' are frequently mentioned along with the other distractions of Christmas, but quite what they were is not made clear.[307]

All these revelries were generally placed under the clownish authority of a Lord of Misrule.[308] This figure had official functions to fulfil throughout the season of the 'Revels' and, as Stow informs us, a similar appointment would be made in the households of the high and mighty of the land.[309] Similar organizers of the Christmas festivities would be appointed by the students of London, Oxford and Cambridge, going by different names in different places: Lord of Misrule, Master of the Revels, King of Christmas or King of the Cockneys, as the case might be.[310] All these student capers, somewhat reminiscent of the Feast of Fools celebrated by the clerks of mainland Europe,[311] were the targets of particularly vigorous attacks from the Puritans, who considered them to be incompatible with a religious education.[312] The fulminations of writers such as Stubbes suggest that such a figure was also to be found at the centre of the rural festivities in the villages of Elizabethan England:

First all the wilde-heds of the Parish, conventing together, chuse them a Graund Captain (of all mischeefe) whom they inoble with the title of 'my Lord of Mis-rule', and him they crowne with great solemnitie, and adopt for their king.[313]

Other contemporary texts contain allusions to a Lord of Misrule presiding over the popular spring festivals. His presence there would appear to be the result of an amalgamation of the burlesque sovereign of the Christmas festivals with the Summer Lord, who used to organize the May game.[314]

The days between Christmas and New Year's Eve, that is to say in particular Christmas Day, Saint Stephen's Day, the Feast of Saint John the Evangelist and the Feast of the Holy Innocents (or Childermas) were the occasions for many other rites and games: Mummers' plays, football matches and, in some villages, church ales.[315]

In the Elizabethan period, time was not conceived as a regular continuum. Certain moments in the year were differentiated qualitatively from others; and these few days of Christmas were invested with a particular quality of their own, which made a decisive impact upon the rest of the year. Christmas Day itself was particularly crucial, except if it fell on a Sunday, which was considered to augur well for the rest of the year.[316] But various taboos were attached to the entire period; for example, working on Childermas was viewed askance, for it was considered an ill-omened day for returning to work.[317] According to Keith Thomas, such ideas were so widespread that, under Charles I, a Puritan preacher was reprimanded by the local authorities for a sermon in which he attacked the belief that whoever worked during the twelve days of Christmas would subsequently be afflicted with lice.[318]

After the amusements of New Year's Eve, basically similar to those of Christmas Eve, including, in particular, a reappearance of the traditional Wassail-bowl, New Year's Day (which the Church, anxious to assimilate all festivals of pagan origin,[319] renamed 'the Feast of the Circumcision'), was essentially a time for giving presents. The practice was apparently observed at all social levels. One of the traditional gifts was an orange (then considered a great luxury) stuck with cloves, another a nugget of golden ginger.[320] Whereas the 'Christmas boxes' of 25 December were presents for the household servants or for apprentices,[321] the gifts of New Year's Day were supposed to get one into the good graces of one's landlord.[322] In similar fashion, litigants were expected to present their judges with delicacies, in the hope of winning their ears:

> Now poor men to the justices
>   With capons make their errants ...
> And if they hap to fail to these,
>   They playne them with their warrants.[323]

At court, there would be a great quantity of New Year's Day presents, each one more lavish than the last, as John Nichols has carefully recorded, for every vassal and courtier would be anxious to attract the favours of the sovereign.[324] Queen Elizabeth, whose coquetry was legendary, received many sumptuous dresses and ornaments on these occasions. Of course, the Puritans fiercely attacked such practices, partly because they considered them scandalously ostentatious and also because, like Prynne,[325] they saw them as a survival of the ancient January feast of the Calends.[326] A similar influence is detectable in the following drinking song dedicated to the god Janus, the two-headed (bi-frons) Roman god of thresholds, who gazed simultaneously out over both the old year and the year to come. It occurs in the pastoral comedy entitled The Thracian Wonder (1599) in a scene where the Shepherds are celebrating Pan's holiday:

Enter TITYRUS *[a merry shepherd], like old Janus, with a coat girt to him, a white beard and hair: a hatchet in one hand and a bowl in the other. He sings.*

Now does jolly Janus greet your merriment;
For since the world's creation,
I never changed my fashion;
'Tis good enough to fence the cold:

My hatchet serves to cut my firing yearly,
My bowl preserves the juice of grape and barley:
Fire, wine, and strong beer,
Makes me live so long here,
To give a merry new year a welcome in.

All the potent powers of plenty wait upon
You that intend to be frolic to-day:
To Bacchus I commend ye, and Ceres eke attend ye,
To keep encroaching cares away.
That Boreas' blasts may never blow to harm you,
Nor Hyems' frosts, but fire you cause to warm you:
Old father Janevere drinks a health to all here,
To give the merry year a welcome in.[327]

In Elizabethan England, the old year was thus buried with revelry and carousing and, from that point of view at least, not much has changed since.

A similar atmosphere marked Twelfth Night, one of the most brilliant and joyful court occasions. Before stepping down, the Lord of Misrule would announce his desire to round off with a kind of apotheosis and a whole succession of spectacular displays of music, dancing and feasting bursting like fireworks, one after the other. Shakespeare's marvellous comedy named after this Twelfth Night preserves the general atmosphere of this period of misrule, characterized by the spicy ambiguity of its intrigues of love and festivity. The students also appear to have amused themselves mightily on this night, electing as 'King of the Bean' whoever came upon a dried bean concealed in his portion of cake. Henry Bourne mentions the custom, calling it 'a Christmas gambol',[328] a description that testifies yet again to the existence of a unifying thread of themes which linked all the festivals included in this twelve-day cycle. The practice of choosing a 'king' by lottery was as popular then as it is now in Europe, and Twelfth Night provided a fine occasion to hand out these titles of king and queen which appear to have been very popular amongst the rites and traditions of folklore. It was a mimetic ritual of royalty that was probably a survival from the old Saturnalia, giving the king of the evening a chance to masquerade as the monarch, derisively aping his authority.[329] Masquerades and fancy-dress mummings are another feature of the lavish amusements of Twelfth Night to which Nicholas Assheton refers in his diary.[330]

Twelfth Night was the festival which brought to an end the long, eventful period of 'Yuletide' revels, although its festive emblems and decorations (ivy, holly and the Yule log) were not taken out of the houses until Candlemas. This was the symbolic counterpart to the Feast of the Purification of the Virgin for the rural communities which continued to observe the traditions[331] and which would ritually eject the 'evergreens' of Christmas on this day. The reversion to outdoor life after the Christmas season, which signalled the end of the festivities, a resumption of labour and an expectation of the coming return of the forces of fertility,[332] would soon be amply symbolized by the rites of Plough Monday.

The pastoral festivals

This chapter examines festive occasions that cannot be fitted definitively into the calendar, either because they do not belong to any of the major cycles of annual popular festivals, or because it was impossible to predict their date in advance (as in the case of festivities to celebrate the completion of particular agricultural labours) or else because the dates for similar occasions would vary from town to town and from one region to another (as in the case of church ales and wakes). It also focuses upon a number of occasional festivities such as the Cotswold Games which Robert Dover organized in the reign of James I, the major annual fairs and family celebrations to mark the passing stages of life (christenings, weddings and funerals).

Let us start by studying the major agricultural and rural festivals strung out through the summer period. First came the festival to mark the sheep-shearing, which was held at different dates in different areas, since one had to be sure that the animals would not suffer from the cold without their wool. According to a proverb cited by Tilley, it could be held as early as the month of May, but in some regions there is no mention of it before June.[1] In an old ballad entitled 'The Merrie Life of the Countriman', the sheep-shearing festival is situated between Whitsun and the beginning of the celebrations for Midsummer. A contemporary text shows that the shearing work had to be completed before the festival, with all its treats to reward the journeymen for their labours, could begin:

My lord Finches Custome att Watton for Clipping Hee hath usually severall Keepinges shorne alltogether in the Hallgarth . . . Hee hath had 49 clippers all at once and their wage is, to each man 12 d. a day, and, when they have done, beere, and bread and cheese; the traylers, have 6 s. a day. His tenants the graingers are tyed to come themselves, and winde the woll, they have a fatter weather and a fatte lambe killed, and a dinner provided for their paines; there will be usually three or four score poore folkes gathering up the lockes, to oversee whom standeth the steward and two or three of his friends or servants with each of them a wadde in his hands; there are two to carry away the woll, and weigh the woll soe soone as it is wounde up, and another that setteth it downe even as it is weighed; there is 6 d. allowed to a piper for playinge to the clippers all the day; the shepheards have each of them his bell weathers fleece.[2]

It is clear from this record, which relates to quite a large flock of sheep, that the shearing was a briskly organized process involving a relatively large team of workers. On top of the forty-nine shearers themselves, there were all the 'graingers' employed on the property as well as a number of journeymen (the 'traylers' and those hired to card and weigh the wool). Several friends or household servants were furthermore entrusted with the supervision of the sixty or so paupers who were allowed to glean the scraps of wool that strewed the ground. Over and above his wage, each labourer could expect a reward in kind in the form of food ('beere, and bread and cheese') or clothes (each shepherd received a ram's fleece). It is interesting to note the presence of a piper, hired to cheer on the shearers through their labours.[3]

That evening, neighbours, friends and all those who had taken part in the day's shearing would be invited to a hearty meal,[4] enjoyed (according to John Aubrey) to the strains of fiddle and tabors:

Sheep-shearings, on the Downes in Wiltshire, and Hampshire &c: are kept with good cheer, and strong beer; but (amongst other dishes) Furmentrie is one. The Fidler and Tabourer attended this Feaste.[5]

Tusser's compendium of precepts for farmers, a veritable handbook of practical agronomy as well as an invaluable source of information on the rural customs of Elizabethan England, lists the sheep-shearing festival among the 'Farmer's feast days' and stresses that it was supposed to be a particularly cordial occasion. Martin Peerson's madrigal, dated 1620, reflects the atmosphere of simple cheer that must have characterized this country celebration:

> Now, Robin, laugh and sing,
> Thy master's sheep-shearing,
> When pies and custards smoke
> Then Robin plies his poke,
> And plays the merry cater,
> My teeth doth run-a-water.
> And when the bagpipes play
> For this the merry day,
> Then comes in little Joan
> And bids strike up the drone.[6]

The sheep-shearing festival, particularly important in the context of the present work as it provides Shakespeare with the setting for Act IV, scenes iii and iv of *The Winter's Tale*, was an opportunity to display one's sense of hospitality and good-neighbourliness at the same time as thanking those who had rallied round and lent a hand to the owner of the flocks.[7] It is one of the pastoral celebrations in which the purpose of the festivities was not simply ostentation or reciprocation, but also to back up working relationships with a convivial sequel and to honour traditional obligations of hospitality.

The second major festival in the agricultural calendar was the ceremony known as 'rush-bearing'. It accompanied, or rather crowned, the gathering of rushes to strew upon the floors of the local church and castle.[8] The gathering generally took place between Midsummer's Day and 1 August, that is to say at haymaking time. The strewing of fresh rushes was a sign of hospitality and festivity.[9] The ceremony of cutting the rushes, then ritually borne to the village in waggons, was an occasion for popular celebrations frequented by all kinds of not particularly respectable characters such as pedlars of various types, pickpockets and cutpurses, similar to the colourful picture painted in *The Whimzies*:

His sovereignty is showne highest at May-games, wakes, summerings, and rushbearings... but these are but his rurall pageants...
A countrey rush-bearing, or morrice-pastorall is his festivall; if ever hee aspire to plum-porridge, that is the day.[10]

The very fact that the festival attracted rather unsavoury or even criminal characters made it easier for the local authorities and Puritans to denounce these occasions for extra licence and public disorder in villages that were not usually at all rowdy places.[11] What is more, these rush-bearings were also a pretext for heavy drinking, as can be seen from the accounts of Chester cathedral:

1595. Gave for wine to the Rushbearers 3s. 8d.
1607. To the rushbearers, wine, ale, & cakes. 6. o d.[12]

In some cases even pillars of the community would get carried away by the festive atmosphere and the dancing and drinking and would stray into wayward behaviour, swiftly to be censured by carping bigots:

Tristram Tildesley, the minister at Rufford and Marsden upon Sundays and hollidaies hath danced emongest light and youthful companie both men and women at weddings, drynkings and rishbearings; and in his dancing and after wantonlye and dissolutely he kissed a mayd... whereat divers persons were offended and so sore grieved that ther was weapons drawn and great dissenssion arose.[13]

Once the rustic pleasures of the rush-bearings, appreciated by some if not by others, were over, the period stretching from Lammas to Michaelmas in the Elizabethan countryside was traditionally devoted to harvesting. These labours lasted much longer than those of sheep-shearing and rush-bearing and only the last day was devoted to celebrating. The festival began with the decoration of the very last wheat-sheaf and the waggon that was to carry it to the barn where it would be stored. The cheery procession that accompanied the last waggon of wheat signalled the end of the harvesting and storage of the crop, the 'harvest-home' as it was known, and opened the public rejoicings. In a short work signed 'N.B.' and attributed to Nicholas Breton, *The Court and Country, or A Briefe Discourse Dialogue-wise set downe betweene a Courtier and a Country-man* (1618), an enthusiast of the pastoral life lists the pleasures of the countryside, noting in particular that:

in July [we have] the peares and the apples ... the beauty of the wide fields, and the labours with delight and mirth, and merry cheare at the comming home of the Harvest cart ...[14]

Two foreigners travelling in Elizabethan England have left us accounts of these customs. The first, one Moresin, the author of a work entitled *The Origin and Increase of Depravity in Religion*, writes that he saw:

in England the country people bringing home in a cart from the harvest field a figure made of corn, round which men and women were promiscuously singing, preceded by a piper and a drum.[15]

The second traveller, Paul Hentzner, was struck by a similar scene that he beheld while staying at Windsor in the summer of 1598:

As we were returning to our inn, we happened to meet some country people celebrating their Harvest Home; their last load of corn they crown with flowers, having besides an image richly dressed, by which perhaps they would signify Ceres, this they keep moving about, while men and women, men and maid servants, riding through the streets in the cart, shout as loud as they can till they arrive at the barn: the farmers do not bind up their corn in sheaves, as they do with us, but directly as they have reaped or mowed it, put it into carts and convey it to their barns.[16]

This cultivated German's suggestion that the festivities of harvest-home reflected vestiges of ancient fertility rites ('by which perhaps they would signify Ceres') was one that was to be taken up later by the founders of the comparative study of religions.[17] Another feature noted by Hentzner was the double promiscuity that characterized these festivities. Men and women mingled together, as did masters and servants, just as they had worked alongside one another in the fields. The meal that followed the harvesting was also a communal one, bringing to mind the egalitarian traditions of the Roman Saturnalia. Brand and Ellis, who indeed cite Macrobius in this connection, emphasize the resemblances between this festival and those of pagan antiquity and conclude their description with a scene of idyllic fraternization:

At this entertainment all are, in the modern revolutionary idea of the word, perfectly equal. Here is no distinction of persons, but master and servant sit at the same table, converse freely together, and spend the remainder of the night in dancing, singing, etc., in the most easy familiarity.[18]

Their observations are confirmed by Tusser, in his *Five Hundred Points of Husbandry*, where he encourages farmers to display good humour at harvest time and make all welcome at their table.[19]

The revelries of harvest-home, marking the combined efforts of the rural population in bringing in and storing the harvest, were followed in the last quarter of this summer period between Michaelmas and Hallowe'en by the hop-picking. As Robert Chambers notes, this took place in the autumn, generally in early October.[20] In all likelihood, it was an occasion for festivities similar to those that marked the grape-harvesting in wine-producing countries, but unfortunately we possess no precise information on the matter and are thus reduced to conjecture. Needless to say, in conclusion, the importance of these diverse agricultural festivals varied from one place to another, sometimes depending upon the kind of crops grown in the region; and no doubt not very many communities would celebrate each and every one of these summer occasions. But, on average, each English peasant community would be involved in at least two in the course of the summer. Once sheep-shearing was over on one's own property, one would go to help one's neighbour. It meant more work, but also more fun.

Church ales and wakes

As well as these summer rural festivities, there were countless local and parish festivals that used to punctuate the year in the little parishes of Elizabethan England. Some were charity affairs known as church ales, the official purpose of which was to raise funds for parish needs or for good works.[21] Wakes, meanwhile, were the church festivals that, in principle, were held one week after the festival of the village patron saint.[22] These two types of celebration, both officially encouraged by the Church, came under constant fire from the Puritans, who could not understand how men of God could possibly contribute to the organization of what they considered to be immoral and seditious gatherings. The wakes, in particular, were the focus of a huge politico-religious debate in the reign of Charles I, in which the supporters of the traditional Church of England, with the backing of the monarchy, clashed with the municipal authorities of Puritan persuasion. First church ales, then wakes, are also the subject of Philip Stubbes' indictments. He mentions several possible dates for the organization of church ales (Christmas, Easter and Whitsun), but in the Elizabethan period they seem to have coincided most often with the Whitsun festival. This is the only date for them mentioned by Carew in *The Survey of Cornwall*, where he gives a detailed account of them.[23]

Texts from the Elizabethan period tend to refer more frequently to Whitsun ales and to bride ales, or wedding feasts, than to church ales.[24] After allowing a defender of the tradition to put his view of the matter, namely that these 'ales' were a means of promoting love and Christian charity, Carew goes on to remark that, to his mind,

the very title of ale was somewhat nasty, and the thing itself had been corrupted with such a multitude of abuses, to wit, idleness, drunkenness, watchings, that the best cure was to cut it clean away ... [25]

Church ales were indeed regarded as occasions of licence and debauchery which encouraged drunkenness in the young and caused the birth of many bastards, responsibility for whose education would fall upon the parish when they were abandoned by their mothers. Church ales are also among the festivals condemned by the Devon Justices of the Peace, in a proclamation dated 1595:

Church or parish ales, revels, May-games, plays and such other unlawful assemblies of the people of sundry parishes unto one parish on the Sabbath day and other times is a special cause that many disorders, contempts of law and other enormities, are there perpetrated and committed to the great profanation of the Lord's Sabaoth, the dishonour of almighty God, increase of bastardy and of dissolute life ... [26]

Along with the rural escapades of Saint Valentine's Day and May Day, the church ales were indeed reputed to encourage illicit love affairs and step up the number of illegitimate births. Thus William Cartwright's play, *The Ordinary or the City Cozener* (1635), alludes to 'a great belly caught at a Whitsunale'[27] and Ben Jonson's antimasque to *The Masque of Queenes* features an infanticide witch who says of the child whom she has despatched:

> 6 [HAG]: I had a dagger, what did I wth that?
> Kill'd an infant, to have his fat.
> A Piper it got, at a Church-ale,
> I bad him, agayne blow wind i' the tayle.[28]

Adultery at this time was considered as a crime that came under the jurisdiction of the 'Bawdy Courts', where those found guilty were severely sentenced. T.G. Barnes cites an example of the type of punishment that would be meted out: 'The dean of Wells and the city's recorder (both county J.P.'s) made a bastardy order in which the parents were to be whipped to the playing of two fiddles to make known that they had begot the child on the "Sabbath" while coming from dancing.'[29] However, this historian is of the opinion that, even if these Whitsun ales were not necessarily shining examples of virtue and decorum ('order was not always preserved at these gatherings, the narrow line between amity and truculence being drawn thin by drink'), the accusations generally brought against them by Puritans and municipal authorities were by no means always well founded: 'The "riots, disorders, murders" and similar in petitions against church ales were formulae, not always relevant or based on fact.'[30] He considers the Elizabethan church ales to have been just like the village fairs depicted by Brueghel, in which, as well as feasting and dancing, there would be sporting activities such as wrestling, for example. Like the sheep-shearings and the rush-bearings, these celebrations would attract many itinerant performers, musicians (fife or bagpipe players), pedlars and hawkers selling songs and almanacs.[31]

The institution of wakes, in England, dated back to the early days of Christianization, for they were a direct result of Gregory the Great's letter to Saint Augustine, urging him to replace the pagan sacrifices by 'love-feasts' in a Christian form. Originally, they had taken place in the church itself, or in the churchyard[32], but were gradually transferred to locations more suitable for secular jollifications – the village square, the taverns or private houses.[33] In theory the dates of these wakes used to vary from village to village, as they fell on the day of the saint to whom the church was consecrated. Later, though, Henry VIII ruled that they should all be held on the first Sunday in October. This reform does not appear to have been very effective,[34] but eventually most of these wakes settled on Saint Michael's Day, for this was the festival that coincided with the end of most of the agricultural labour. This may have been the origin of the 'harvest dinners' situated between Michaelmas and Candlemas which are mentioned by Carew in his work on Cornwall. Stubbes, for his part, paints a somewhat gloomy picture of the excesses and abuses that characterized these occasions and is particularly concerned at the inroads made upon the meagre savings of the poor.[35]

Wakes must nevertheless have been extremely popular, for the wake-day is one of the few festivals that Tusser includes in his limited list of 'Farmers' Feast Days':

> Fil oven ful of flawnes, Ginnie passe not for sleepe,
> To-morrow thy father his wake day will keepe:
> Then every wanton may danse at her will,
> Both Tomkin with Tomlin, and Jankin with Gil.[36]

A groaning board and joyful dancing would invariably produce bursts of popular hilarity, as Joseph Hall notes in *The Triumphs of Rome*:

What should I speak of our merry Wakes and May games, and Christmas triumphs . . . in all which, you may well say no Greek can be merrier than they.[37]

In *The Late Lancashire Witches*, a play written in collaboration by Thomas Heywood and Richard Brome in 1634, act III, scene i shows a wedding feast beset by the evil spells cast by a witch. An interesting exchange takes place in which those present try to console themselves for the unpropitious start to the festivities:

DOUGHTY: I hope the Country wenches and the Fiddlers are not gone.
WIN: They are all here, and one the merriest Wench; that makes all the rest to laugh and tickle.
SEELY: Gentlemen, will you in?
ALL: Agreed on all parts.
DOUGHTY: If not a Wedding we will make a Wake on't, and away with the Witch . . .[38]

The easy transition from one type of celebration to another shows how alike they must in effect have been: both offered the same types of amusement (feasting and dancing); neither was a calendary feast and the fact that the names of both began with W afforded a chance for joking word-play ('Wedding'/'Wake'/'Witch'). Another reason for the association between a wedding and a wake may have been the fact that wakes were opportunities for lovers' meetings, many of which would eventually lead to marriage. Carl Bridenbaugh's study of the customs of the period cites a striking example:

Village dancing provided the ideal opportunity for flirting and match-making, and also for high merriment, considerable drinking, and less innocent pleasures as excitement mounted under the spell of the almost barbaric squirls of the pipes, the shrill squeaking of the fiddle, and the rhythm of the tabor . . . In Lancashire, Adam Martindale's eldest brother fell in love with 'a young wild airy girle, between fifteen and sixteen yeares of age; an huge lover and frequenter of wakes, greenes, and merrie-nights, where musick and dancing abounded'.[39]

Wye Saltonstall's portrait of a 'Ploughman' confirms that Elizabethan wakes were also a means for young people to meet and to fall in love:

His greatest pride is a faire bandpoynt, and to weare a posy in his hat snatcht from the maid Joane . . . If he fall in love, hee'l be sure to single her out at the next Wake to dance with . . .[40]

Finally, it is worth noting that a wake would sometimes incorporate a rush-bearing: new reeds would be strewn on the floor of the church so that the anniversary of its patron saint would coincide with a symbolic refurbishment of the place where he or she was revered.[41] In such cases, the rites and celebrations typical of a rush-bearing would be combined with the revelries of these cheerful parish 'love-feasts'.

Occasional festivals: summer games and fairs

So far, we have considered the principal moveable occasions of the Elizabethan festive calendar, that is, on the one hand, the major rural festivals linked with agricultural labours (sheep-shearings, rush-bearings, harvest-home and hop-picking), on the other the church ales, Whitsun

ales and the wakes. Now we must turn to other occasional festivals of a
public nature such as the Cotswold Games organized by Robert Dover,
the major annual fairs and the private functions held to mark the various
stages of life – christenings, weddings and funerals.

Each year, the Cotswold Games attracted large crowds of people from
the Cotswolds and further afield, who flocked to the games organized by
the indefatigable Robert Dover, an 'attorney' of Barton-on-the-Heath,
Warwickshire.[42] These gatherings, which took place at Whitsun,[43] dated
from the last quarter of the sixteenth century, but towards the end of
Elizabeth's reign, after a few years of success, they were suspended,
possibly on account of the attacks and bans of local Puritans. Only after
James I's accession to the throne did Robert Dover obtain the king's
permission to revive them, after which they were held under his aegis for
the next forty years, that is to say until Oliver Cromwell came to
power.[44] The games consisted essentially of athletic competitions, to
which girls' dances and greyhound-racing were later added,[45] and they

5.1   Frontispiece engraving for the original edition of *Annalia Dubrensia*
(London, 1636), illustrating the Cotswold Games organized by Robert
Dover.

may be seen as being remotely inspired by the Greek Olympic Games.[46] The sports represented at these games were wrestling, jumping, 'cudgel-plays', 'pitching the bar' and 'throwing the sledge'. Other entertainments included an open-air banquet and salvoes fired from a wooden 'castle' specially erected for the purpose.

Quite apart from the attraction that these games held for sporting enthusiasts, the open-air festivities had become an annual rallying point for those opposed to the Puritans' policy of banning all Sunday occasions of fun and distraction. Apart from the allusions that occur in one or two contemporary plays,[47] our main source of information on this sporting festival is the *Annalia Dubrensia* (1636), an anthology of poems specially written in its honour.[48] Alongside the well-known names of such writers as Ben Jonson and Drayton, it contains quite unknown authors like John Trussel, whom the editor Vyvyan introduces simply as 'a Warwickshire man', who instantly hits the keynote:

> The Hocktide pastimes, are
> Declin'd, if not deserted; so that now
> All Publike merriments, I know not how,
> Are question'd for their lawfulnesse; whereby
> Societie grew sicke; was like to die.
> And had not Joviall DOVER well invented
> A meanes whereby to have the same prevented,
> Love, Feasts, and friendly intercourse had perrished,
> Which now, are kept alive by him, and cherished.[49]

Another poem, by Thomas Randall, gives a good idea of the general tone of the collection, in which an atmosphere of pastoral nostalgia is combined with anti-Puritan satire:

> These [melancholly Swaines] teach that Dauncing is a *Jezabell*,
> And Barley-breake the ready way to Hell;
> The Morrice, *Idolls*; Whitson-ales can bee
> But profane Reliques of a Jubilee:
> These in a Zeale, t'expresse how much they doe,
> The Organs hate, have silenc'd Bagg-pipes too,
> And harmless Maypoles, all are rail'd upon,
> As if they were the towers of *Babilon*:
> Some thinke not fit, there should be any sport
> I' the citie, 'Tis a dish proper to the Court;
> Mirth not become 'um, let the sawcie swaine
> Eat Beefe and Bacon and goe sweate againe.
> Besides, what sport can in their pastimes bee
> When all, is but ridiculous fopperie.[50]

The author pokes fun at the hyperbolic biblical language used by the Puritans to discredit popular sport and amusements and indirectly champions the cause of ordinary people against those who, by denying them their Sunday fun, sought to reserve such vicious pleasures for the court and the aristocracy.

Among the other annual events that perpetuated festive traditions and popular games in the towns, fairs were of the first importance. The link between popular festivals and fairs dated back a very long way, for every village festival would attract a host of hawkers and pedlars as well as tumblers, jugglers and other fairground performers. Brand and Ellis even suggest that most fairs were a direct offshoot of the wakes,[51] pointing out that the etymology of the word 'fair' stemmed from the custom of tucking into 'good fare' on these occasions.[52] In the Middle Ages, hawkers used to proffer their wares within the very precinct of the churchyard until, that is, the municipal authorities decided, following various excesses, that to avoid disorders such activities should be confined to particular locations on the outskirts of the larger towns. Here, magistrates were in a better position to keep an eye on the situation than in the further reaches of the kingdom and could more easily call out the mounted constabulary when things got out of hand. It is tempting to interpret such an attitude as a desire to isolate or clamp down upon social elements regarded as dangerous, subversive or quite simply undesirable. But such tendencies were by no means new and it would be unfair and mistaken to see them as a direct political reflection of a desire on the part of local authorities to begin by containing popular excesses and then proceed to the systematic repression of everything to do with a culture that they wished to disappear. All the same, the very fact of granting popular celebrations as it were extra-territorial rights could be seen as a symbolic rejection that pushed them out to the periphery in an attempt to control manifestations which, if they were truly to flourish, needed to take place at the very centre of village or town life. Once these festivities were confined to particular localities, all that needed to be done was precisely what the Puritans were demanding, namely to prohibit Sunday travelling so that they would gradually be forced out of existence.

In the Elizabethan period the survival of large fairs to some extent testified to the continuing vitality of the popular culture and its festivals. Most of the major fairs appear to have taken place in summer rather than winter, no doubt for climatic reasons. Whitsuntide, already the occasion of particular rituals and, in many villages, a church ale, was a favourite date for fairs. In Manningtree, Essex, Whitsunday had for many years been the date of a large fair.[53] It offered dramatic performances (Mystery plays, mainly) and plenty of good fare, to judge by the traditional roasting of a whole ox stuffed with black pudding and sausage meat:

> Just so the people stare
> At an ox in the fair
> Roasted whole with a pudding in's belly.[54]

Greenwich Fair, which began on Whit Monday, was famous for its goose market[55] and for various other jollifications, the most popular of which was a ball in which you had to change partners for every dance.[56] But Puritans deemed these to be licentious activities and managed to get the fair banned.

But the best known of all was undoubtedly Saint Bartholomew's Fair, which began on 24 August in Smithfield, London. This was a huge gathering of travelling fairground folk whose booths were set up alongside stalls selling grilled pork,[57] gingerbread or hobby-horses for the children. A text dated 1641, entitled *Bartholomew Fair*, provides a detailed description of its entertainments and also of all the ruses that were devised to attract passers-by. By and large, it reproduces the picture that Ben Jonson painted in his satirical comedy of 1614 featuring the general atmosphere of the fair and the regulars who took part in it. The popular fascination with freaks and deformities that Phineas Taylor Barnum was later to exploit with his circus in America was amply catered for here, to judge by the list of sideshows recorded by Wasp:

I ha' beene at the *Eagle*, and the blacke *Wolfe*, and the *Bull* with the five legges, and two pizzles; (hee was a calfe at *Uxbridge* Fayre, two yeeres agone) and at the dogges that dance the *Morrice*, and the Hare o' the *Taber*.[58]

The fair was a kind of distorting mirror that reflected in miniature a grotesque image of village festival traditions or rehashed certain scenes from the repertoire of classical drama in the form of puppet shows (one of the principal fairground attractions).[59] The relatively inoffensive nature of most of these amusements did not prevent the Puritans from inveighing mightily against them. Thus Busy, by his own admission, was

one that reioyceth in his affliction, and sitteth here to prophesie the destruction of *Fayres* and *May-games*, *Wakes*, and Whitson-ales, and with sigh and groane for the reformation of these abuses.[60]

The 'Zealous Brother', a character mocked in *The Whimzies*, is equally intolerant:

No season through all the yeere accounts hee more subject to abomination than Bartholomew faire: their drums, hobbihorses, rattles, babies, Jewtrumps, nay pigs and all, are wholly Judaicall. The very booths are brothels of iniquity, and distinguished by the stamp of the beast.[61]

The last comment here might well have been applied to Ursula, the purveyor of roast sucking-pig in Jonson's comedy, who acted as a go-between on the side. Easily scandalized Puritans would have regarded her as living proof that the fair was a place of debauchery. There can be no doubt that, like most public places in those days, a fairground was a venue for a whole shady world of beggars, cutpurses, charlatans, 'cony-catchers', prostitutes and pimps, who tended to give it the air of the court of some Beggar-king.[62] Respectable folk who went to the fair knew full well that they risked losing their wallets or falling prey to some other misfortune. But in those days, such perils were common enough: they lay in wait for anyone foolhardy enough to travel alone or to venture out unaccompanied after dark. Isolation was even more dangerous than a crowd.

The last major fair of the year was held after Saint Bartholomew's Fair, at Charlton, in Kent, on Saint Luke's Day (18 October). In the Middle Ages, it had been a pretext for all manner of masquerades reminiscent of the traditions of the ancient Roman festival of the Calends of January: the men would go dressed up as women, or wearing stags' antlers on their heads.[63] Such disguises also call to mind the Mummers' plays generally performed at Christmas and Easter and the famous Horn dance of Abbots Bromley in Staffordshire.[64] By the Elizabethan period, the latter was no more than a curious local survival, but it remained a potent enough memory to fuel some effective symbolism and to elicit numerous literary allusions.[65]

Private ceremonies: christenings, weddings and funerals

Let us now turn to the other kind of occasion which the Elizabethans marked with amusements and feasting and drinking: the principal private ceremonies constituted by christenings, weddings and funerals. I have chosen to examine these family ceremonies within the framework of the non-calendar festivals, since their timing obviously depended on the initiative of individuals or particular social groups, not on the seasons or prescriptions laid down by the calendar.[66] The fact that these ceremonies were special occasions is more important than their private aspect for in those days any celebration, even of a family nature, would be a community affair.[67] I shall not so much be concerned to analyse the nature of the ceremonies that accompanied the three major stages of human life, but will attempt rather to indicate the particular features of their rites and festive forms at this specific period. The fact is that births, marriages and deaths seldom go unmarked by any ceremony at all, so it is only the quality and intensity of the festivities that surround these occasions that vary from one region or period to another.

In the painting of *The Life and Death of Sir Henry Unton* (see Illus. 5.2), the christening is illustrated by an infant swaddled as tightly as a mummy and sporting a scarlet bonnet. Christenings[68] were certainly occasions for eating, drinking and rejoicing after the religious ceremony, throughout the day and well into the night too. They were not reserved solely for the well-to-do,[69] for even the poorest families would organize

5.2   Detail from *The Life and Death of Sir Henry Unton* (c. 1596), by an
       anonymous artist.

collections so that they could cover the cost of a party (most guests
making contributions in kind, in the form of a loaf of bread, a cake, some
cheese, and so on). A christening would also be an occasion to have the
minstrels in, as John Aubrey notes in his childhood memories, 'the tabor
and pipe were commonly used, especially Sundays and Holydayes, and at
Christenings, and Feasts'.[70] Contrary to the claims of the French visitor
to England, Misson de Valbourg,[71] christenings prompted a considerable
outlay of funds and were certainly convivial occasions. *A Looking-Glass
for London and England*, a comedy by Robert Greene and Thomas
Lodge (1590), contains the following protestation from a poor man by
the name of Alcon:

Nay, an please your majesty-ship, for proof he was my child, search the
parishbook; the clerk will swear it, his godfathers and godmothers can witness it;
it cost me forty pence in ale and cakes on the wives at his christening.[72]

As for the traditional christening gifts presented to the infant, these seem usually to have taken the form of 'Apostle spoons'.[73] Another present might be what was known as a 'crisome pye', a covering for the baby's head, such as that discernible, bottom right, in *The Life and Death of Sir Henry Unton*.[74]

Weddings were also accompanied by a host of customs and jollifications. One popular tradition that was very popular was strewing the bride and groom's path to the church with rushes or flowers, and it is often mentioned by contemporary writers.[75] Fragrant plants such as bay and rosemary would also be used as decorations as well as to perfume the air. The festivities that followed the marriage ceremony sometimes continued for as long as a fortnight, if the hosts had sufficient means and the guests sufficient leisure. They would include banquets, music, Masques and so on. Of course that would be more likely in the case of wealthy families, but the popular strata would not lag far behind, for, according to Harrison's *Description of England*, weddings for them too were pretexts for veritable orgies of food and drink.[76]

The system of having each guest make a contribution in kind that seems to have been the general rule for christenings probably also operated for weddings, as it did for Whitsun ales. A wedding would be enlivened by the presence of Morris dancers,[77] who would provide a joyful escort to the church for the bride and groom, play during the banquet and also provide the music for the dancing that followed. The combination of all these entertainments might make for quite a spectacular occasion, as the example of the Kenilworth 'brydeale' shows. A prose text by Breton entitled 'Choice, Chance and Change' describes a bride ale in which the groom's father starts off by encouraging the whole company to dance ('Son, take your Bride and call in your Friends, and about the house, bestirre your stumps a little, come on . . . '). He is then subjected to a burlesque address given by a member of the Masque's cast, which is abruptly interrupted by the arrival of a band of Morris dancers. The father is angered by the tawdry nature of this entertainment, so it is hardly surprising to find him expressing heartfelt relief when eventually the Masquers and guests decide that it is time to depart, leaving their host in peace:

but thus, after they had masked and mummed; away they went, and lefte it by this time, about the hower of sleepe, when every one taking leave of the other, my mistris gave me a kinde good night, which made me sleepe never the worse.[78]

Puttenham also mentions the minstrels who performed at popular festivals and appears to hold a similarly mediocre opinion of the quality of their performance.[79] Other descriptions of weddings lay particular stress on the excesses and ribaldry likely to rise to the surface at most country weddings.[80]

The dancing into which the company would throw itself with abandon on these occasions naturally contributed to the excitement of the general atmosphere created by all the food and drink.[81] The jokes, smutty stories and risqué songs of the village wedding banquet would lead on to a general freedom of behaviour in the Rabelaisian ambiance of levity so well captured by Brueghel.[82] But it is really not surprising to find such revelry and even loose behaviour on the occasion of wedding celebrations, for they in truth perpetuated ancient fertility rites designed to smooth the way for the transgression of the taboo of virginity represented by the wedding night.[83] Besides, these country weddings also fulfilled a sexually initiatory function with regard to the village adolescents, in the same fashion as the amorous rites of Saint Valentine's Day and May Day.[84]

The idea of a funeral being an occasion for festivity and a well-primed banquet may seem shocking today, although in some districts the tradition of a funeral feast still continues. The attitude of modern societies is in reality indicative not so much of a Puritan revival, but rather of a veritable taboo where death is concerned. Today's discreet, lugubrious occasions, in which all external signs of mourning are deliberately understated, are symptomatic of the embarrassment that is provoked by death and an underlying desire to purge its image from social life. However, as we have seen, in the Middle Ages and in the Elizabethan period, death was obsessionally omnipresent as was the indissoluble link that bound it to the forces of the world of the living, in the context of a popular tradition that was still laden with superstition and belief in magic.

In circumstances such as these, a death provided an opportunity for the family and social group concerned to make a solemn affirmation of their own system of values and beliefs, by observing various rites and customs (laying out the corpse, watching over it, burying it, reading the will), while at the same time honouring the memory of the deceased by bringing forth 'the funeral baked meats' mentioned by Hamlet.[85] In some regions, it was still the custom to hold a convivial night-long wake, while watching over the corpse.[86] And everywhere it was customary to follow the burial with feasting and libations that in some cases lasted for days on end.[87] Brand and Ellis cite an amusing text from 1665 concerning a glutton who, on the point of death, bemoans the fact that funerals are no longer what they used to be.[88] All this is reminiscent of the tales of Rabelaisian feasting and the drinking songs in which even those who die of over-eating and drinking are immediately called back to life by the singing of the assembled carousers, the pervading smell of alcohol and the popping of corks. In this cheery popular vision, death simply meant moving on to a drinker's paradise, some realm of Cockaigne where the beer and wine flowed freely and quails fell ready-roasted from the skies. Joyful funerals such as these were characterized by the same ambivalence as the festive laughter that, according to Mikhaïl Bakhtin, had the power to bring you back to life after sending you to your grave. Death was not nothingness, simply the other side to life, which it prolonged and with which it communicated during the long winter nights and the celebrations of Hallowe'en and All Saints.

For the aristocracy, a funeral was a matter of honour and old families felt in duty bound to lay on as grand a show as possible. In his book on the critical times faced by the aristocracy of the Elizabethan period, Lawrence Stone shows that the conspicuous expenditure (in some cases amounting to as much as the family's income for a whole year) covered not just the funeral ceremony but a banquet too. Custom dictated that the domestic servants should be treated to a feast, no doubt to thank them, in the name of the deceased, for services rendered and, as a result, the occasion would sometimes take on the air of some Saturnalia:

At the funeral of Bess of Hardwick in 1607 some of her servants, a prey to conflicting emotions of relief at the death of the tyrant and anxiety about the future, indulged themselves very freely and there were orgiastic scenes below stairs of the Old Hall that day. The funeral was also an occasion for the distribution of largesse on a gigantic scale. Between 3,000 and 4,000 poor people are said to have been fed from the left-overs from the funeral of Edward Earl of Rutland in 1587.[89]

However, these two examples must have been exceptions, for Stone notes a falling-off in such traditions after 1580, due to the relative austerity introduced by the Reformation and also the spread of insolvency and the decline of the aristocracy that was already perceptible at this time.[90] Lured by the attractions of the capital, many of the local lords were abandoning their land and the aristocracy's consequent loss of influence in the countryside in part explains how it was that traditions of charity and hospitality died away and the community system deteriorated. At the same time, a strong belief existed in a community of the dead, which could be held up as a model for that of the living, and this would periodically come to the fore on the occasion of particular festivals or at funerals.[91]

Now that we have considered the major private celebrations of the Elizabethan period, let us pause on this note of profound ambivalence in which life and death come together and laughter and tears are intermingled, for it brings to a close the first part of this study, which has been devoted to the major manifestations of festivity in sixteenth- and seventeenth-century England. Our survey of the festivals of this period has been partly based on the customs and traditions observed in the various spheres of society (in particular the popular strata and the youthful fraternities, in which they were still very much alive), and partly seen from the point of view of the mentalities of those concerned. It has enabled us to dig out from the collective memory a whole collection of rites, obligations and superstitions all of which were still operative in the Renaissance. But what conclusions should we draw from these observations and what can we learn from them to enrich our understanding of Shakespeare's plays?

At the point when Shakespeare was beginning to write for the theatre, festivity was a subject that had become the focus of an ideological and religious debate, as a result of the vehement attacks of the Puritans against what they regarded as intolerable vestiges of paganism and a source of disorder and violence. We should remember that his early work for the theatre coincided with the decade that saw the publication of Philip Stubbes' *Anatomie of Abuses*. But festivity was still very much alive among the popular classes in town and country alike and at about this time it also became an instrument of political propaganda for a sovereign anxious for popularity and keen to add lustre to the Tudor myth. The many artists who were to help her delved into Graeco-Latin mythology in their search for material that could be elaborated in these didactic entertainments; but they also turned to folklore, thereby reviving images and themes buried deep in a marginal culture, as well as themes from the scholarly domain. As a result, festivity, already such an important element in the popular imaginary representation of the world and temporality, became the key factor in an ethos that was to triumph not only in the countryside, but also at court.

The ideological and religious battle between the Puritan reformers and the Merry England enthusiasts was waged from the 1570s until the beginning of the Civil War, one side seeking to topple the whole edifice of popular superstition, the other, on the contrary, delighting in everything to do with fairies, festivals and folklore. Not many of Shakespeare's contemporaries in the literary world, apart from the Puritan pamphleteers, seem to have inclined to a sweeping rejection of the system of community obligations in which festivals represented a veritable cornerstone in the parish life of Elizabethan England. One reason was probably England's newly developed taste for national roots and domestic traditions and its rejection or fear of everything continental, particularly anything from papist countries. The revival of the ideals of chivalry encouraged by writers such as Sidney and Spenser, and a thirst for luxury, pomp and entertainment among an aristocracy besotted with pleasure, also contributed toward the vogue for festivity that is so much in evidence from 1580 onwards. On top of all the autumn tournaments and the winter balls and masquerades at court, in her summer visits to the provinces Queen Elizabeth was promoting the image of a Virgin

Queen descended from Astraea. Small wonder, then, that the young Shakespeare drew upon his memories and the information of his friends to write certain passages not only in his two historical tetralogies (for example, Bolingbroke's triumphant entry into London in *Richard II* or the crowd scenes of *1* and *2 Henry VI*) but also in some of the Roman plays, in which the ancient world is to some extent portrayed as a transposition of Elizabeth's England. The country was gradually shifting from a ritualistic and relatively static system to a more secular one that made it possible for the themes and images of festivity to be disseminated at every level; and for an author who had always made free and abundant use of a wealth of different sources, the change opened up a field of information and inspiration that was as wide as it was varied. And the rich theme of festivity offered another advantage: it attracted the interest and imagination of the popular strata, which perhaps partly explains the unusual conjunction of simple folk and aristocracy in the theatre audiences of the period. A comedy such as *A Midsummer Night's Dream*, in which ordinary artisans perform a play at court to mark the sovereign's wedding, made just such a situation possible through the popular appeal of its very title.

Another interesting avenue of research, clearly indicated by this survey of Elizabethan festivals, would be a study of the various basic dramatic structures that emerge from seasonal mimes and dramas such as the folk plays and the Morris dance – structures that could then be adapted for the professional theatre by the playwright and his company of actors. Among these many stereotyped scenarios, which nevertheless often varied from one region to another and which expressed basic themes such as time, fertility and the cohesion of the social group, Shakespeare clearly found the kernels of many dramatic plots that could easily be adapted for the professional stage. Such correlations must indeed have been invited by the quasi-ritual association that still existed between the dates of the major performances at court and the great calendary festivals. In many a dramatic scene, the mention of a particular date in the calendar would trigger a particular response in the collective mind. And it might well provoke a combination of hilarity, on the one hand, and on the other unease, for a sudden appearance of supernatural figures (such as fairies or ghosts), which would usually be frightening, might at the same time prompt a feeling of liberation connected with memories of the kicking-over of conventional traces (for example, nocturnal forest expeditions for the purloining of greenery for May Day). Festivals were experienced essentially as two-edged affairs, with a joyful side but also a foreboding one, an ambivalence that Shakespeare's plays certainly do not fail to exploit: tragedy and comedy follow fast one upon the other, sometimes intermingling to grotesque effect (as in the Jack Cade scenes in

2 Henry VI, or Caliban's revolt in *The Tempest*).

Festivals also expressed a vision of time that was on the wane in the late sixteenth century. Festive time was qualitatively differentiated, a mixture of taboos and beliefs, a confection of brutal contrasts. But it was beginning to give way to a more neutral temporality that would be divided up more rationally in relation to both work and religion. The opposition between the measured time of the towns and the business world, on the one hand, and on the other the golden moments of dreams, pastorals and festivals is one that lies at the very heart of Shakespeare's dramas and is a contradiction that frequently underlies the trials and tribulations of his travellers through a world of change.

In this respect, I consider Shakespeare to belong to the camp of the traditionalists. In similar fashion, his dramatic work dignifies the place of the old calendar customs and festivals, associating the irreverence and uncouthness of the clown with the topsy-turvy world and the spirit of parody attached to the notion of misrule, at the precise moment when the figure of the clown was being dropped in the professional theatre generally.

So it has been worthwhile to note the dates and itemize the scenarios of all the different festivals, for this will make it possible to assess the importance of what I regard to be a veritable code whose specific temporal signposts and points of reference indicate a whole symbolic system. These festive traditions combine to chart an imaginary representation of the world, mapped out by *topoi* such as those that we have mentioned in connection with Carnival: 'the circulation of blasts of air', the 'mystical bestiary' and 'hearty eating' (see above, pp. 47–9).

At the lexical level of verbal creation and dynamic imagery, Shakespeare must surely have found inspiration in the popular themes of the major festivals of the time, whether the Lord Mayor's Show, the village Morris dance or the jollifications connected with the period of misrule at court or in the London law schools and the colleges of Oxford and Cambridge. A knowledge of these *topoi* and stereotyped scenarios will help us to move on to an, as it were, archaeological examination of Shakespeare's plays, attempting to discern the influence of these archaic survivals both in the structure of his dramas and in the obsessive recurrence of a series of expressions and images. It may also be legitimate to consider whether Shakespeare was accepting or rejecting this body of customs and traditions or whether he was simply making use of them to beguile his audience.

For one aspect of festivity and respect for tradition was that it was a way of shielding oneself against bad luck and social ostracism at a time when individualism was still tainted with impiety and was considered blameworthy on that account. Somehow, comedy and romances illustrated the theme of first a break with the old order, then a resolution of the contradiction by means of the founding of a new order deeply in harmony with a number of fundamental laws: the inevitable succession of the generations, the alternation of winter and summer, sterility and fertility. In the historical plays, these themes are played out around the vital question of the possession and passing on of power. As for the world of tragedy, it presents the individual at odds with his group, with no possibility of resuming a harmony with the fundamental rhythms of the universe. Here, festivity loses its power of natural symbiosis and instead becomes a vehicle of discord, exclusion and chaos.

Part II

Introduction: Some anthropological and historical perspectives on literary analysis

The Elizabethan literary texts to which Part I of this study refers have been mostly drawn from minor authors, and selected for their documentary value as sources of evidence rich in detailed descriptions and images of festivity. Our task now is to see how our findings on the place and functions of festivity apply to an artistic production as highly elaborated as Shakespeare's plays.

I should make it clear at the outset that I have no intention of considering these intellectual and artistic works as reflections of the social, economic and ideological conditions of the period. The Elizabethan theatre was in no way bound to illustrate the particular problems of any class or any ideological pressure group, nor yet to do the queen's bidding. In moving on from the first stage (the phenomenon of festivity) to its dramatic representation, our original subject matter has to be remoulded, for the sources are impossible to use until they are interpreted. A play may well hold a 'mirror up to nature', as Hamlet says (III, ii, 22), but it never represents reality exactly, so we seldom find a May game, a Morris dance or a jig reproduced on stage in a completely realistic fashion. Elizabethan dramatists were not interested in *reportage* or *théâtre-vérité*; rather, they felt in general that they were taking part in and contributing to a form of ritual.

On the other hand, there is no point in denying the very real impact that their environment made upon the dramatic productions of the period. Elizabethan theatre was far from being a sealed-off refuge devoted to playing out a strictly defined liturgy dictated by tradition and convention. On the contrary, responsive to the demands and tastes of the public, whose favours the rival companies of players were bent on winning, the theatre of this period was decidedly geared to the popular element of society. Rather than drawing their subjects from classical antiquity, as Racine and Corneille, writing for an educated élite in France, were soon to do, the Elizabethan dramatists often preferred to tap 'romances', medieval legends or the traditions and myths attached to celebrating the calendar festivals.[1]

It is patently clear that, far more than poetry and prose, which reached only a limited educated circle, the theatre constituted *the* popular medium. The very plan of public theatres, designed to be easily reconverted into arenas for various kinds of animal fights,[2] is a clear indication of the close rapport of the theatre to the other entertainments of the popular masses. It is also clear that the theatre was not necessarily first and foremost a temple of high culture, but might be primarily a place for having fun, rather than an instrument of privileged communication. Terence Hawkes' study of Shakespeare demonstrates the audio-oral nature of the dramatic experience, in which the written text is not necessarily the most important element.[3] This is a matter Andrew Gurr analyses in detail, taking as his starting point the opposition between two common terms used to refer to the public, namely 'audience' and 'spectators', the etymologies of which refer respectively to the sense of hearing (Latin: *audire*) on the one hand, that of sight (*spectare*) on the other. He uses a number of examples and texts from the Elizabethan period to show that the common crowd was considered to be more susceptible to the sense of sight, while hearing was important particularly for educated people, as he goes on to show in the section entitled 'Learned Ears'.[4] We should also remember that the visual aspect of dramatic performances likened them both to the pageants of the Tudor period, with their parades of banners and grotesque giants, and also to the seasonal festivals, with all their special costumes and symbolic paraphernalia. However, that does not necessarily mean that all three should be set on the same level, for they represent responses to different kinds of motivation, involve different degrees of elaboration and attract different degrees of popular participation. That participation seems to have been more direct in the context of festivals, when all that was demanded from the public was that it should stop to watch the dramatic performances and parades that were laid on.[5]

As for the dramatic performances themselves, according to the testimony of Shakespeare's contemporaries they in themselves constituted veritable festivals, where people would eat, drink, even smoke, and make all kinds of contacts of a more or less respectable nature.[6] The shady but colourful crowd that thronged to the performances at the Globe or to other theatres, composed for the most part of artisans and workers,[7] was the very same that would flock to cheer the pageants or to join in the May Day Morris dances. Admittedly, this picture has been seriously questioned by the American Ann Jennalie Cook, in an article published in *Shakespeare Studies* and also in a book entitled *The Privileged Playgoers of Shakespeare's London*.[8] Her starting point is that there were probably not as many workers as has been claimed in the audiences of the public theatres and that dramatists were in fact addressing a less diversified audience than is often believed. Her historical evidence for this thesis is quite solid and relates to the question of the different social classes of Elizabethan London. It indicates that neither apprentices nor artisans nor domestic servants in truth had either the time or the money to go to the theatre, except on holidays. These must necessarily have been days such as Shrove Tuesday or Midsummer's Day, for instance, rather than Sundays, since in London plays were banned on the Lord's day. On the other hand, if prostitutes were regularly to be found in theatre audiences, that indicates above all that they were likely to find rich clients there, in particular 'gentlemen' with the kind of leisure, money and hedonistic attitudes that would allow them to spend an afternoon at the theatre. Michael Hattaway also notes that the term 'working class' has all too often been used inappropriately to refer to the Elizabethans who made up what was in truth an extremely diversified society.[9]

In the appendix to his *Theatre and Crisis, 1632–1642*,[10] Martin Butler returns to this question and also recognizes that Harbage's class definition is anachronistic since it fails to reflect the incredible diversity of the popular social strata of this period. This section of society was a rag-bag of 'dissolute and suspect persons', 'serving men', 'butchers', 'Thrift the citizen', 'applewives', 'Chimney boys', the 'meaner sort of People', 'chambermaids', 'merchant factors', 'apprentices', 'barbers', 'tailors', 'tinkers and cordwainers', 'sailors', 'yeomen and feltmakers' .... Butler sums up this list as 'a splendid panorama of the under-privileged'.[11] In his conclusion, he again underlines the multi-dimensional nature of this type of theatre, with its references to the court and university worlds but also to the popular, festive, disrespectful and parodic tradition, in which kings cohabited with clowns. Only theatre that attracted such a wide variety of social strata could embrace perspectives multiple enough to give rise to the expression of so many contradictory themes and points of view. Neither Harbage's idealized picture of an artisan public nor Ms Cook's of a cosmopolitan, privileged one does justice to the real complexity of the situation. Dramatic performances were not just distractions or entertainments; they constituted festivals of a kind, to be enjoyed on holidays.[12] And this was even more true of the court, where dramatic productions in the 'Season of the Revels' were in principle put on to coincide with some feast day (such as New Year's Day, Twelfth Night or Candlemas).[13]

For all these festive occasions, whether they involved pageants, theatre or regular annual celebrations, the divisions between the various social strata that made up the public were carefully drawn and levels kept distinct, so it would be quite mistaken to speak of a social melting-pot in this connection. However, the fact remains that the populace and the aristocracy did manifest similar enough tastes when it came to entertainment, did sometimes go to see the same productions and hence, without truly making contact, certainly were brought face to face on these occasions.

So one does come to wonder just where the popular festival ended and the aristocratic one began. For one of the properties of festivals seems to be the way they had of blurring the established dividing lines between the different social classes, sexes and age-groups, linking them in new relationships of an altogether unpredictable nature. In the case of the theatre, the situation was sufficiently undefined and open for a dramatist to be able to seize the opportunity to promote either a coming-together or a separation. In practice, there must have been four main sets of circumstances possible for festive occasions or ceremonies.

(1) The populace could remain passive, reduced to the role of spectators, as in the case of court entries, official ceremonies, various civic processions and pageants. The aristocracy or urban oligarchy would parade their wealth, power and *esprit de corps* while the populace would look on with curiosity. (2) The common people were assigned a protagonists' role and came to perform before the aristocracy, as part of the official programme of progresses and entertainments laid on for the monarch, as in the Kenilworth festivities.[14] (3) The popular strata, whether urban or rural, had fun among themselves, on the periphery of a private celebration or a calendar festival (for example, apprentices on Shrove Tuesday, country folk on Plough Monday or wake days). But as they were, by definition, not their own masters (and this applies not only to workers, servants and journeymen, but equally to various age-groups such as schoolchildren, students and apprentices), to do so they would have to obtain some relaxation of the surveillance to which they would normally be subjected. (4) The court and the aristocracy would indulge themselves in their own way in the privacy of their palaces, away from the eyes of the populace. That is what increasingly happened after James I came to the throne. This type of festivity, which deliberately excluded the people, who would only learn of it through hearsay, if at all, was generally looked upon askance in circles and in a period in which the notion of privacy was associated with egocentricity more than with freedom. Making merry in private betrayed a desire to take liberties, for why be clandestine if not to conceal wicked debauchery? Festivity that excluded the populace thus earned its disapproval.[15] The masses wanted to see so as to know, and condemned whatever went on in their absence. Festivity in which the community played no part was inevitably regarded as ill-omened, even harmful.[16]

But the situation was seldom really as cut and dried as that, and the above classification may well seem arbitrary and over-theoretical. In real life, as on the stage, such radical compartmentalization did not often occur, at least not in the period we are examining, in which it is more usual to find themes and elements of an essentially more popular nature infiltrating educated and aristocratic culture or, alternatively, the popular culture taking over the old ideals of aristocratic chivalry[17] (for example, the vogue for 'romances', particularly the old Arthurian legends). It was no doubt a two-way exchange, effected via the 'wandering word'. But, having made those reservations, it truly does seem to me that the four situations described above by and large represented the cardinal factors that determined the orientation of festivity in the Elizabethan period and on the basis of which authors would elaborate their scenarios and dramas. These would represent popular festivals designed to provide a welcome for the aristocracy (as in *The Winter's Tale*), entertainments presented by artisans in the course of private court festivities (as in *A Midsummer Night's Dream*), popular festivity aimed at flouting official disapproval (synonymous with revolt or anarchy, as in the scenes representing Jack Cade's or Caliban's rebellions in *2 Henry VI* and *The Tempest*) or aristocratic festivities that had no popular approval (such as the bloodthirsty drinking-parties and orgies of tragedy, as in *Hamlet*, *Othello* and *Macbeth*, where festivity is painted in its darkest colours). There are many possible combinations of these four scenarios and to claim to be exhaustive on this point would be presumptuous. I have accordingly decided to limit my analysis to a few significant examples selected from Shakespeare's canon.

6 Festivity and dramatic structure: methodological problems

[William Shakespeare] though his genius generally was jocular, and inclined him to festivity, yet he could (when so disposed) be solemn and serious, as appears by his tragedies.[1]

Archaic survivals

In the first part of this book I have tried to show that the festive traditions of the calendar still flourished in the Elizabethan period, continuing to be honoured in towns and villages the length and breadth of England, according to the seasons. The body of beliefs that underpinned them was still very much alive in the more remote parts of the country and in counties such as Lancashire, where the influence of recusant Catholics was strong; but it played little more than a marginal role in regions pervaded by the influence of the Puritans (in southern England). It is not possible to come to general conclusions in a country and at a time in which so many local diversities existed, but it is safe enough to say that the spirit of the Reformation had by no means penetrated every corner of the countryside or the peasant mentalities that still clung to the way of life and the traditions of Merry England. Despite the efforts of preachers and local dignitaries to impose a measure of moderation and seemliness upon popular celebrations, Puritanism had made little impact except upon the élite of the workers in the towns. The spirit of the festivals of yesteryear endured unimpaired, the maypole continued to cock a snook at the church steeple and the sometimes violent games of Shrove Tuesday, Hocktide and May Day still drew the crowds, to the delight of some and the scandalized indignation of others. What had changed since the Middle Ages was above all the development of a new awareness of what festivals and popular games and sports represented, for they now seemed to establish an ideological division between two rival Englands.

Shakespeare cannot have been unaffected by this conflict, for his plays certainly bear the stamp of it. The early festive comedies are deeply imprinted with popular traditions and folklore; in the great tragedies of the middle period the meaning of festivity is reversed, coming to signify chaos and darkness; then in the 'romances' of the later years the seasonal celebrations resume their importance. There can clearly be no question of

184

denying the importance of Shakespeare's classical heritage and of his use of the works of Plutarch, Ovid and Seneca. But it is certainly worth noting the often underestimated influence of local and oral traditions upon him. As Muriel Bradbrook has suggested, his dramatic writing owed much to its popular, British roots.[2]

How should we explain this attraction, or indulgence, towards the manifestations of such a primitive, if varied, culture in one who was to become the peerless master of the dramatic art of his time? In the first place, we should remember that Shakespeare's native county, Warwickshire, situated close to the Cotswolds and at the heart of historic England, was a region particularly rich in festive rites and traditions of all kinds. It would have been strange if a child born in Stratford had not been present on many occasions when the various rites accompanying the calendary festivals were performed. Writing of the shadowy years that Shakespeare passed in Stratford after marrying Anne Hathaway, about which the legends are as persistent as they are unverifiable,[3] Samuel Schoenbaum suggests that his first contact with the theatre may have come through the amateur performances that were staged as part of many traditional celebrations.[4]

Hypothetical as it is, the suggestion has the merit of drawing attention to the existence of intermediate dramatic forms which, when developed, eventually led the way to the professional London stage. The old seasonal festivals must to some extent, and somewhat paradoxically, have served as antiquarian repositories which the theatrical avant-garde sometimes plundered in quest of inspiration. Admittedly, Shakespeare's references to popular beliefs and masquerades are often somewhat ironical or farcical, but in the last plays they strike an authentically pastoral note.[5]

Shakespeare's use of these archaic survivals in his work to some extent puts one in mind of techniques employed in modern painting – the Cubists' borrowings from African culture, Paul Klee's from naive painting and Jean Dubuffet's from 'art brut', all three examples of the way in which professionals take over artefacts of zero-degree sophistication (created by 'savages', children or the insane) and proceed to elaborate them. In a similar fashion, transposing folkloric practices to the stage was a way of transforming 'the primitive mind', turning it into a spectacle yet at the same time eradicating the visible traces of art so as to bring to life a host of characters, themes and images, hitherto unexploited, which reinforced the impression of spontaneity. The combination of all these elements made up an extremely rich artist's palette that was equally well suited to creating comic, realistic or symbolic effects.

It made, first and foremost, for an immediacy of impact; for by adapting popular festivals and legends for the theatre stage, the

Elizabethan dramatist could be sure of catering for the tastes of a public that was itself drawn largely from popular strata and was consequently unaffected by the tyranny of rules imposed by scholars and pedants. Plays were written with a view to bringing in enough funds to provide a living for the troupe of players, and the first concern was to please. What, then, did this popular public, whose fluctuating tastes seem to have affected Shakespeare's dramatic production so strongly, particularly relish?

The Elizabethan public seems to have shown a marked taste for scenes of horror and cruelty, to judge from the success of plays such as Kyd's *Spanish Tragedy*, Marlowe's *Jew of Malta* and Shakespeare's *Titus Andronicus*. Scenes of high melodrama were much appreciated, as were farce and grotesque comedy combined with a 'pot-pourri' of jigs, songs and dancing. So much is indicated by the success of a comedy such as *Mucedorus* (often performed by Shakespeare's own company of players), many elements of which find an echo in *The Winter's Tale* and *The Tempest*.[6] Finally, and above all, there survived an insatiable nostalgia for all the magical bric-à-brac inherited from the Arthurian legends and popularized through stories to be told on long winter evenings and ballads devoted to the adventures of valiant knights in quest of dragons and lost in labyrinthine forests, tales of abducted children, princesses imprisoned or persecuted, and abominable men of the woods. Peele was to exploit this vein in *The Old Wives' Tale*, while Shakespeare[7] and Beaumont and Fletcher were to mock at it, presenting it in a burlesque light. But in truth, the presentation of the theme is less significant than its almost obsessively constant appeal. However, the 'groundlings' were not alone in appreciating what was really simply the spectacle of festivity brought back to life in places where it was threatened with extinction, namely the larger towns. Without the connivance of the court and the aristocracy, the actors would never have dared to brave the displeasure of the municipal and religious authorities. In principle, popular entertainments did not upset the monarchy, which preferred jollifications, even when rowdy, to seditious plots. The existence of such festivity provided a guarantee that the people would find no grounds on which to object to its own pleasures and, besides, there was also the satisfaction of seeing derision heaped upon those whom it considered not so much as kill-joys but as promoters of a body of opposition to its own policies, namely the Puritans. The unanimity of feeling against this group established between the people and the aristocracy a sort of complicity that could sometimes create the illusion that festivity did away with class barriers, allowing a kind of fraternization to develop between them. A certain convergence of tastes does indeed appear to have developed between these two social strata, even if the tone, attitudes, style and means obviously differed from one level to the other when it came to handling common themes. It was a delicate balance that Shakespeare managed to convey in, for example, *A Midsummer Night's Dream*.[8] Such a measure of sympathy between the people and the aristocracy, however paradoxical or equivocal it may seem, is reflected, at a political level, in a historical play such as *Henry V*. Here it is nationalistic fervour and anti-French feeling that makes it possible to transcend both regional and class differences. On the eve of the battle of Agincourt, which is assimilated to a great warrior festival,[9] a melting-pot in which social cleavages disappear, the disguised king can slip unrecognized among his troops, talking with them man to man, on equal terms.[10] Many of Shakespeare's plays make dramatic use of themes apparently directly inspired by the egalitarian myths of the Saturnalia which possess a cutting edge whose sharpness is not really blunted even when they are parodied or made the object of irony.

Before examining the dramatic and symbolic functions of what I have called the archaic survivals in Shakespeare's work, let us undertake a rapid survey in order to appreciate them in all their diversity. This is a heterogeneous body of material made up of a whole collection of festive customs which to some extent constitute the settings for the plots of some of the plays and which the spectators would recognize for what they were, whatever their dramatic context. Whether it be songs, dances, disguises or spectacles of a more elaborate kind, the effect is always the same and it provides a new perspective on the whole theatrical process. In the most complex case what we witness, in the action on the stage, is something like a 'double-take' or rather a 're-take', in which the playing recedes to a vanishing point: the character in the play becomes once more what he really is – an actor, the forest reverts to being just scenery, or, as in the performance of 'The Murder of Gonzago' in *Hamlet*, the actors become the spectators of a play within a play. Many dramatic critics concur in hailing the modernity of such procedures, seeing them as a prefiguration of Pirandellian theories on dramatic illusion, or Brechtian techniques of alienation. Sometimes archaism can assume the guise of modernity.[11]

Such double-takes or plays within plays were very common in the Elizabethan period, when the stage presented an image of the world in miniature (see, in particular, the word-play on 'globe', used to evoke both the terrestrial globe and the Globe Theatre). They are always somewhat ambiguous devices. They may equally well be employed to clarify the situation to an uncomprehending audience (for example, Snug, at the end of *A Midsummer Night's Dream*, feels obliged to explain that he is not really a lion, just an actor dressed up to look like one, in order to set at rest the minds of the court ladies present) as to quicken the interest of blasé spectators by means of burlesque at one remove. Such techniques were by no means new: they can be traced back to medieval play cycles that were far richer in spectacular processions than in subtle psychological plot developments. They are attached to theatre of a ritualistic origin, fragmentary survivals of which appeared within plays set in a formal framework that included a prologue or induction. Popular comedies such as Robert Greene's *Friar Bacon and Friar Bungay* made use of these techniques to mark out the difference between, on the one hand, the various narrative forms of the tale on which they drew and, on the other, the dramatic spectacle in the strict sense of the expression. However subtle and imaginative Shakespeare's use of these techniques, he never seeks to obscure its connection with a more primitive vein or its deep roots in old popular traditions.[12]

The use of archaic survivals of this kind is not limited to copying ancient dramatic techniques, for they frequently also surface in the form of themes to which scattered references are made throughout the play. A whole body of Celtic or Teutonic rites and legends could be reconstructed from the clues provided by, for example, 'the deer song' in *As You Like It*, the episode of Herne the Hunter at the end of *The Merry Wives of Windsor* or the scenes portraying the 'death' and comic resurrection of Falstaff in *1 Henry IV*. It is as if the masquerades of the Mummers' plays performed in the course of village festivals at Christmas and Easter were being transposed to the professional stage. We should bear in mind that the actors of those folk mimes and dramas were often clad in foliage, animal skins and antlers and they would perform burlesque and obscene dances that reflected ancient fertility rites.[13] Shakespeare's plays also contain numerous references to seasonal festivals and occasions of rejoicing such as the 'Pentecost pageants of delight', the 'Sheep-shearing Feast' and 'Harvest Home'.[14] Alongside these, we find mentions of eating customs, culinary traditions, floral games and songs and dances such as the dance of the shepherds and satyrs or Morris dances such as those featured in *The Two Noble Kinsmen* (III, v, 120–36), for example. All these interludes serve to draw attention to the pastoral nature of the setting in which they appear, a setting which seems to have been closely associated with the representation of popular rejoicing on the Elizabethan stage. But in these cases, the corpus of rites and traditions is portrayed at an intermediary level, at just one remove from the main, strictly dramatic plot.

In other circumstances, these pastoral and popular celebrations took on the more elaborate and official form of the Masque which, after James I's accession to the throne, became the court spectacle *par excellence*. It started off as a form of festivity akin to the shows put on by the Mummers, a term that designated the troupes of decked-out musicians who would suddenly invade homes – usually those of the aristocracy – in the course of the festival of the twelve days of Christmas.[15] They would present a short show of songs and dances after which custom demanded that they be invited to join in the feast and take part in the dancing.[16] Shakespeare alludes directly to these customs in *Romeo and Juliet* and *Timon of Athens* and in *Henry VIII*, in which the king is disguised as a shepherd.[17] Another such allusion is constituted by the famous Masque of Ceres in *The Tempest*, a fertility rite as well as a wedding celebration and a faithful reflection of the ceremonies that attended royal marriages.

The function of the Masque in Shakespeare's plays is not the main focus of this book, so I will limit myself to a few general remarks on the subject. The first point to make is that the Masque constituted a fashionable genre at this time and that, in order to find favour in the eyes of the court, a dramatist might well deem it expedient to incorporate one in his play, in a more or less elaborate form. At the same time, to introduce Masque scenes in productions given even in private theatres was a way of giving the spectators at least some idea of the splendour of royal entertainments that they would otherwise never have the chance of seeing.[18] Furthermore, Shakespeare also uses the Masque to counterbalance the popular scenes with which his plays are studded. The aristocratic entertainment in this way functions as a counterpoint to the popular festival, a contrast and a counterweight, as well as an indirect means of expressing the major themes of the play. All this can be observed in comedies such as *Love's Labour's Lost* and *A Midsummer Night's Dream*, where court entertainments are intertwined with elements of popular farce and grotesque comedy.

It is significant that in some of the scattered allusions Shakespeare makes to various calendar and seasonal festivals, he associates some of his characters from the popular strata with the world of the theatre as, for example, in 'The Pageant of the Nine Worthies' in which Moth and Costard take part in *Love's Labour's Lost* (v, ii, 518–717), and in the scenes where Bottom and the artisans of Athens rehearse and perform 'Pyramus and Thisbe'. In both cases, the show put on is inept and clumsy[19] and the effect produced is burlesque, especially in the eyes of the somewhat supercilious aristocrats who regard it as a second-grade kind of amusement in which the genre rules are stood on their heads. It is certainly worth noting the sarcasms with which the spectators greet the unintentional buffoonery of these performances, but it is also important to see that the situation here is a topsy-turvy one, the reverse of normality. Instead of dutiful common folk passively applauding the ostentatious monarchy, in the first instance we see the nobility being entertained by an unpretentious and sympathetic show put on by the populace to mark the occasion of a princely marriage. The shift admittedly involves passing from the splendid to the burlesque, but it represents a form of role-reversal and also a reversal of the rules of normal behaviour that is in line with the general spirit of Shakespeare's festive comedies. In *A Midsummer Night's Dream*, Shakespeare seems indirectly to acknowledge his debt to this theatre of amateurs, at the same time adding a dimension of parody that as it were constitutes the reverse, grotesque side to his elegant comedy. The clownish performance of 'Pyramus and Thisbe' continues the line of Shakespeare's reflection on the limits of dramatic illusion (to some extent the playlet exemplifies the failure to create such an illusion), revealing to the spectator the 'in-between' world of the theatre. At the same time this helped him to appreciate the gap that separated its more rudimentary forms from theatre at its most sophisticated.[20]

Furthermore, in the case of *Love's Labour's Lost*, a play whose sources are not known, one cannot but be struck by its similarities to Nashe's *Summer's Last Will and Testament*, a comedy which has an air of improvisation[21] and seems closer to a carnival show than to a formally elaborated play.[22] The presence in Shakespeare's comedy of self-contained entertainments, many of them inspired by popular festivities, owed much to the improvisation of actors such as William Kempe, the members of his company who would play the roles of 'clown' or 'fool'.[23] Such actors seem to have been disinclined to accept the constraints of ready-made roles and to have been prone, carried on the crest of the public's applause, to ad lib upon the script with repartees and sallies of their own invention. However popular those improvisations may have been, the author would not be likely to appreciate having the rhythm of the production upset in this way, as we see in the famous passage where Hamlet makes it quite plain to the actors who are to perform his play that it is no part of his plan for them to indulge in such flights of buffoonery:

And let those that play your clowns speak no more than is set down for them; for there be of them that will themselves laugh to set on some quantity of barren spectators to laugh too, though in the mean time some necessary question of the play be then to be considered. That's villainous, and shows a most pitiful ambition in the fool that uses it.
(III, ii, 38–45)

Such warnings to actors who manifested an unfortunate tendency to upstage others pose the whole problem of individual responsibility in dramatic creation. A dramatic creation does depend partly upon the style of the theatre company and the suggestions contributed by its members, so the end product is bound to result from a fusion of collective efforts with the work of the author. So many plays from this period have been lost, and pastiche and direct plagiarism were so common at a time when the juridical notion of literary property was not nearly as strong as it is today, that it would be risky to be too categorical in this domain. Plays were written to be performed rather than to be read, as is attested by the fact that Shakespeare never bothered to have his plays published. In these circumstances, interpreting the initial text was a relatively flexible matter, allowing for a measure of adaptation.[24] The popular culture of the Renaissance was characterized by a similar open-endedness. It manifested a great capacity for amalgamation that enabled it to fuse together elements of the most heterogeneous and contradictory nature. What Philip Sidney, in *The Defence of Poesie*, castigated as disfigurements and ineptitudes in the theatre of his day seem to me, on the contrary, to provide living proof of the extraordinary powers of synthesis and adaptation which I regard as marks of Shakespeare's genius. By allotting such an important place to the kaleidoscope of the festive world, Shakespeare managed to root his plays in the popular culture of his day, at the same time imprinting upon them what we might regard as the stamp of modernity. The archaic and primitive elements that he skilfully organizes and integrates in his plays add a strange fascination to their beauty and also to their universality. In this respect, the dramatist's artistry puts one in mind of what Claude Lévi-Strauss has to say about 'mythical thought':

It builds up structured sets, not directly with other structured sets, but by using the remains and débris of events: in French 'des bribes et des morceaux', or odds and ends in English, fossilized evidence of the history of an individual or a society.

The technique of the *bricoleur** or resourceful craftsman who 'builds ideological castles out of the débris of what was once a social discourse', to quote Lévi-Strauss again,[25] is closely related to the kind of artistic creation that seems to stem, not from a process of prefabrication, with a desired end constantly in view, but from the happy chance of a 'bricolage'. From this point of view, Shakespeare is a genius at making dramatic use of all the flotsam and jetsam of myth and the vestiges of folklore and might be described as an inspired and lucid *bricoleur* who had the vision to realize how useful to his plays these generally despised elements would be and, at the same time, the skill to weld them together into a new whole. He gave form to his aesthetic vision by constructing it upon an archaelogical framework of theatrical remains and achieved the impossible, fusing primitive elements from popular culture together with all the refinement needed to please the aristocrats upon whom his own protection and that of his company of actors depended. However, the

* Translator's note: *bricoleur* might be translated as a 'resourceful craftsman who makes use of whatever comes to hand'. But the term is more or less internationally understood and there is no near English translation for it.

image of *bricolage* is not really a valid simile that can be made to apply to a dramatic production in itself, or to the profession of an actor (even if the role of the clown did afford experienced artists a certain latitude for improvisation). All the same, according to Gary Taylor and Stanley Wells, some of the discrepancies between the 'Good quartos' and the 'Folio' may have been attributable not to errors of transcription on the part of copyists or printers, but to different stages in the construction of the text, which Shakespeare kept on correcting as his plays were repeatedly performed.[26]

From the contributions of tradition to the concept of 'festive comedy'

In a book entitled *An Essay on Shakespeare's Relation to Tradition*,[27] Janet Spens has attempted to relate the early roots of popular drama to the theatre of the English Renaissance in general and Shakespeare's plays in particular. Seeking what she calls 'The Traces of Folk-Plays in Shakespeare', she tries to establish correspondences between Shakespeare's comedies and the major popular festivities of the calendar. She thus suggests that *Twelfth Night* was a dramatic illustration of the winter festival which stretched from All Saints' Day to Epiphany, while *All's Well That Ends Well* echoed the festive customs of the Ploughing Feast which, according to E.K. Chambers, lasted from Candlemas to Shrove Tuesday. A pastoral comedy such as *As You Like It* reflected the traditions and amusements of the summer period (which began on 1 May); *The Winter's Tale* was tailored to fit in with the harvest festival. In short, Janet Spens' thesis is that 'Shakespeare did as a practice found his comedies on popular games . . . '.[28] In the second part of the book, she tries to apply this method to the major tragedies, claiming to detect in them traces of rituals of pagan origin which determined their basic structure. Seeing the folk play as a survival of the agricultural ceremonies of ancient Greece, she analyses the recurring theme of the death and resurrection of the burlesque hero of these seasonal mimes and dramas as a ritual that symbolized the sequence of the seasons.[29]

Applying this schema to Shakespearian tragedy next, she has no qualms about identifying a character such as King Lear, symbolically dismembered by his daughters, as a dramatic avatar of the Frazerian 'Mock-King', the buffoon representing the old year set up as a king, to be ritually sacrificed at the end of the festival.[30]

This critical approach was subsequently pursued and refined by Northrop Frye, who applied it to Shakespeare's comedies and 'romances'. In an article entitled 'The Argument of Comedy', Frye explains that Shakespeare was turning away from the model of Menander's comedies and finding inspiration in the dramatic traditions of medieval England without, however, limiting himself to the genres of Mystery and Morality plays and interludes, for he also drew upon local traditions that Frye describes as follows:

This is the drama of folk ritual, of the St George play and the mummers' play, of the feast of the ass and the Boy Bishop, and of all the dramatic activity that punctuated the Christian calendar with the rituals of an immemorial paganism. We may call this the drama of the green world, and its theme is once again the triumph of life over the waste land, the death and revival of the year impersonated by figures still human, and once divine as well.[31]

What Frye calls 'the drama of the green world', thinking of the forest of Arden in *As You Like It*, the pastoral 'shores' of the mythical Bohemia of *The Winter's Tale* and Portia's enchanted land of Belmont in *The Merchant of Venice*, constituted Shakespeare's version of the pagan and ritualized vision of the world that found expression in the parodic games of the Mummers' play and the rites of inversion in operation when a Boy Bishop was elected. In Shakespearian comedy, this 'green world', in the form of a pastoral refuge or an enchanted forest, balances the world that Frye calls 'the red and white world of history' (probably an allusion to Book I of Spenser's *Faerie Queene*). The green world is a place of change and metamorphosis, where the reinvigorating contact with nature enables people to free themselves from the constraints and injustices of society and to find fulfilment and, having gone through a series of trials and tribulations, in most cases also true love. This is also a world in which the forces of youth and love prevail over the crippling authority of the father, who here embodies the traditional *senex* of Plautus' comedies. The tension between these two worlds in which the characters of Shakespeare's comedies live reappears in the pastoral plays as a tension between the court and the countryside, culture and nature. The green world thus symbolizes a different style of life – contemplation instead of action, the happy harmonies of music and love instead of the metallic clash of arms and the discordances of conspiracy. But, even more, it is a magic place, where a new world is secretly gestating. That is why the various characters who pass through it seldom stay there any longer than the time it takes for their own regeneration or rehabilitation. Except for those who are misanthropic or malevolent (such as Jaques, Malvolio and Shylock) they all return eventually to the real world, in some cases the world of the court, at peace with themselves and society, like the old Duke in *As You Like It* or Beatrice and Benedick in *Much Ado About Nothing,* or united with a wife or a husband after a marriage symbolizing the triumph of love and bearing the seeds of new birth.

But the green world does not stand only for the world of the forests and green meadows; it also represents the house with the three caskets,

Portia's Belmont in *The Merchant of Venice*, and Falstaff's tavern in *Henry IV*. Frye underlines the carnivalesque aspect of the scenes that take place in Mistress Quickly's inn, The Boar's Head, and he considers their place and function in the historical plays to be parallel to those of the green world in the comedies.[32]

In the comedies, the green world is an alternative to and a reversal of the normal world. As a result of some incident, which is either pure chance or provoked by someone's despotic or jealous temperament, that forces the heroes to seek refuge in flight or exile, a new world gradually takes the place of the old one and eventually constitutes a reversed image of it. In *Henry IV*, on the other hand, the two worlds constantly alternate. We keep passing from one to the other as if they were two adjoining territories. In the one case the two worlds are mutually exclusive, in the other they co-exist.[33]

But whichever relationship is predominant, Northrop Frye considers that the final effect of the presentation of the two different places is to draw attention to the place of the dream world within the world of every day. The movement of comedy achieves a sense of relativity and perspective so that, at the end of the play, neither is seen as predominant. In the more open view of life and love, holiday and everyday, imagination and reason must somehow combine.[34]

The creation of this kind of perspective does not induce a Baroque sense of illusion in which everything appears to be theatre and life seems an illusion. On the contrary, it has a debunking effect that leads to detachment and lucidity.

In the light of these remarks, we can appreciate the theses that C.L. Barber puts forward in his analysis of the importance of the theme of festivity in Shakespeare's comedies. In a sense, Barber seems to take up the thread where Frye leaves it. Barber's view is very much in line with Frye's as he sets out to explore the festive structure of plays such as *A Midsummer Night's Dream* and *Twelfth Night*, but he goes on to concentrate upon an analysis of the dramatic function of the various festive nuclei that he uncovers. At the beginning of his study he declares:

To get at the form and meaning of the plays, which is my first and last interest, I have been led into an exploration of the way the social form of Elizabethan holidays contributed to the dramatic form of the festive comedy. To relate this drama to holiday has proved to be the most effective way to describe its character.[35]

Barber is thus not in the least concerned to portray the theatre as continuing or mirroring para-dramatic popular traditions such as the spectacles laid on in the village or on the occasions of various calendar festivals. Comedies cannot be confused with ritual, even if they do sometimes borrow the settings of certain games or popular festivals, for their role is as different from the archaic edifice of magic as it is from the platitudes of everyday life. For Barber, the key to symbolism lies in art, not popular festivals and traditions, which simply provide a supporting framework.[36] Furthermore, in his view, theatre in general and comedy in particular directly affected the evolution of popular mentalities and encouraged the emergence of a more rational concept of existence among the élites and the educated.

According to Barber, the term 'festive' qualifies both the atmosphere and the structure of the Shakespearian comedies that he analyses. The function of the festive elements these contain is to trigger an emotional release and help to create an atmosphere of joyful liberation in the face of the representatives of an archaic law and the forces of a constricting moral order. The oppositions that they bring out serve as dramatic mechanisms and at the same time help everyone to define and understand themselves better.

This is what Barber calls the movement of clarification, which is a consequence of triggering the mechanisms of festivity:

The clarification achieved by the festive comedies is concomitant to the release they dramatize: a heightened awareness of the relation between man and 'nature' – the nature celebrated on holiday. The process of translating festive experience into drama involved extending the sort of awareness traditionally associated with holiday, and also becoming conscious of holiday itself in a new way.[37]

Festive hilarity furthermore proffers a bonus of pleasure, in the generosity of the moment, as, according to him, 'the celebrants also got something from nothing, from festive liberty – the vitality normally locked up in awe and respect'.[38] This welcome bonus brought by the festive current of emancipation is expressed first in a loosening of attitudes and tongues, even a shedding of inhibitions, that is reflected in people's speech. Under the influence of festivity, words begin to bubble and fizz like a fermentation, producing what Barber calls 'the wine of wit': 'in wit, it is language that gives us this something for nothing; unsuspected relations between words prove to be ready to hand to make a meaning that serves us'.[39]

In its state of intoxication, festive language begins to stumble in unexpected directions and into unexpected images.[40] But this is not the world of grotesque improvisation so dear, for example, to Rabelais, for here reason is on the watch to fasten upon these new and apparently effortless flashes of meaningful wit. The wit in *Love's Labour's Lost* operates at the level of verbal repartee within a closed circuit that exploits the external world to which it refers but is not particularly concerned to serve it.[41]

The wit that spurs forth in the effervescent emotional and intellectual atmosphere of the *fêtes galantes* depicted in this youthful comedy corresponds, in Barber's view, to an emotional release followed by clarification, that is to say the dawning of a new awareness. In the case of Bottom's metamorphosis, Barber is convinced that this is no awakening from a fantasy of erotic bestiality;[42] rather, it is a variation on the theme of the grotesque that belongs to a precise symbolic code.[43]

Whether popular or princely, a festival's precise function, beneath its aesthetically or historically determined exterior, was to take over and translate the impulses of desire and the fantasies of the collective imagination.

In the conclusion to his book, Barber justifies the limited number of comedies that he analyses to support his theses, explaining that the concept of festive comedy ceased to operate after *Twelfth Night*:

After *Twelfth Night*, comedy is always used in this subordinate way: saturnalian moments, comic counterstatements, continue to be important resources of his art, but their meaning is determined by their place in a larger movement. So it is with the heroic revels in *Antony and Cleopatra*, or with the renewal of life, after tragedy, in *The Winter's Tale*.[44]

There can be no question of fundamentally challenging Barber's eminently reasonable view that it is comedy that most frequently uses the theme or pretext of festivity, playing upon all its registers ranging from the simple entertainment through more boisterous forms of merrymaking, to satire, the burlesque and the grotesque. Sometimes it certainly is the case – as Barber well demonstrates – that a particular comedy functions in itself as a festival, presenting us with a transposed representation of the clash between Carnival and Lent or of the march of the successive seasons. But it seems to me a pity that, even though his book is about the comedies, he should not have at least sketched out the function of festivity in Shakespeare's other plays. Even if it is true that in tragedy festivity plays a less exuberant role, it still has an important place. In tragedy, the function of festivity is quite simply reversed: it is no longer beneficent but harmful, no longer an antidote to the forces of darkness but their accomplice. As for the last group of plays (the 'romances'), they encompass a return to folklore and festivity which are now invested with a positively regenerating mission, not just with the function of orchestrating the dominant theme of the forces of youth triumphing over paternal tyranny, through the symbolism of the green world. Barber is certainly right to say that, in *The Winter's Tale*, the place of festivity is, when all is said and done, marginal since in this play it simply appears at a particular moment in a much vaster whole: the sheep-shearing feast of Act IV, scenes iii and iv is there to balance the tragedy of the first three acts. However, working on that analogy, it could be argued that in the romances, which are plays that pass through a number of different stages, each of the panels that combine to make up the whole could, in itself, in turn be considered as supplementary features.

However that may be, Barber's remains a pioneering book, which has opened up new avenues for the analysis of Shakespeare's dramatic works as it suggests an extremely fertile method of approach to comedy, orienting it in an ethno-historical direction. In the analyses that follow I shall be trying to extend the field of enquiry in order to survey the whole of Shakespeare's dramatic production to study the ramifications of festivity in the context of the calendar, social relations, dramatic vocabulary and the dynamics of the imagery. Indeed, the theme of festivity, treated from many different angles, seems to me to occupy a place of central importance in Shakespeare's plays.

In *Shakespeare and the Traditions of Comedy*, Leo Salingar returns to Barber's main theses, in his chapter entitled 'Comedy as Celebration'. He gives precise examples, essentially drawn from *Love's Labour's Lost* and *A Midsummer Night's Dream*, to illustrate the idea that 'pastime and revelry constituted a kind of borderland between everyday life and the stage',[45] and he associates the concept of festivity only in strict subordination to the notion of the marriages which bring the comedies to a happy end, crowning all the initiatory trials to which the lovers have been subjected in the course of their tribulations. In Salingar's view, the concept of festivity is not really relevant to the serious comedies and the tragicomedies, even if the plays do incorporate many elements borrowed from seasonal celebrations and civic pageantry. The fact is that festivity is but one facet of existence, even in comedy, but Shakespeare's plays are, above all, 'representations of life'.[46] So other traditions, such as those of classical and Italian comedy, also deserve to be taken into account. In putting out feelers in other directions in which festivity is also important (as Carnival is for the conventions of Italian comedy) but where it is not the dominant element, Leo Salingar has indeed to some extent complemented Barber's work. However, it seems to me a rather too restrictive view of festivity to limit it to its licentious and carnivalesque aspects. As soon as one considers festivity in all its different manifestations, as a calendar phenomenon that expresses a particular vision of time in a language of its own, making use of a vast repertory of images and dramatic nuclei, the whole picture becomes more diverse, taking off in all kinds of directions. In so doing, it offers us a number of keys to a fuller interpretation of certain aspects of the genesis of Shakespeare's plays.

But before moving on to analyse the texts themselves, we still have to distinguish the different facets of festivity detectable in Shakespeare's work.[47] This introduces us into a teeming, kaleidoscopic domain linked with the powers of illusion and imagination – a domain which, in the Renaissance, had as much to do with the margins of politics and religion as it did with aesthetics. Festivity in the theatre is fantasy in the realm of illusion, where it offers the god of spectacle the choice of a thousand and one additional masks to don.

Dionysus beneath the masks of Proteus

Festivity in the theatre produces an intoxication endowed with the power of metamorphosis. When Shakespeare/Proteus[48] takes over this multiform, fluctuating scene, he takes good care not to limit it within any constricting categories whether of an ideological or a symbolic nature. Festivity is dynamic because it is a veritable ravishment, but it is always elusive, impossible to pin down.

Our first task is to make a rapid survey of the genres that make up Shakespeare's dramatic work, to see how the theme of festivity is used in different contexts. Of the thirteen plays that it is customary to include in the group of comedies, three main categories are distinguishable: the minor comedies (*The Comedy of Errors, The Taming of the Shrew, The Two Gentlemen of Verona, The Merry Wives of Windsor* and *Love's Labour's Lost*); the major comedies (*A Midsummer Night's Dream, The Merchant of Venice, Much Ado About Nothing, As You Like It* and *Twelfth Night*); and the so-called 'problem plays' (*The History of Troilus and Cressida, All's Well That Ends Well* and *Measure for Measure*). In the first group, the most interesting comedies, from the point of view of the theme of festivity, are *The Taming of the Shrew* and *Love's Labour's Lost*. The second group divides into two: one in which festivity is a major theme (*A Midsummer Night's Dream* and *Twelfth Night*), the other in which it is a minor one (*The Merchant of Venice* and *Much Ado About Nothing*), while *As You Like It* falls into a class of its own, as it were at a kind of crossroads. In the 'problem' comedies, which almost entirely eliminate the perspective of the green world, festivity is above all remarkable for its absence.[49] In this category, which raises the problem of the exclusion of the ceremonial aspect of existence, the central play is without doubt *Measure for Measure*, where all that is passed over, all that is repressed or suppressed in the end turns out to be more important than whatever is clearly shown.[50] The price to be paid for the suppression of any outlay of a festive or sexual kind is the establishment of a climate of fear that gradually falls prey to the very fantasies that it set out to eject.

The historical plays also find a large place for various festive themes that are thus intertwined with great happenings in the history of England. *Henry VI* and *Henry V* present us with a mixture of battles, revolts and festivals in a varied sequence of images in which the grotesque vies with the epic. Apart from the revolt and the battle scenes, *Henry IV*, through Falstaff, suggests a carnivalesque festival that keeps petering out before reaching its climax; and at the end of *Henry VIII* we are shown the palace taken over by a joyful popular mob running wild.

In the tragedies, festivity is stamped with a negative mark. Estranged from its collective, popular roots, it is portrayed essentially as a bloodthirsty orgy, a refuge in which the criminal can forget his crime, a precarious moment of truce and oblivion. Allied as it is to the forces of destruction and operating as an agent of chaos, it is stripped of its power of symbolically averting evil and violence. It sets its seal upon a world committed to destruction (Egypt, in *Antony and Cleopatra*, and the kingdom of *King Lear*) and as the supporters of Lent and the tyrants approach in a rising tide, it seems no more than a final gesture of bravado.

After this dive into an underworld of shadows, where it loses all power as an explosive libertarian force for life, festivity makes a late reappearance in the group of tragicomedies or 'romances'. These plays, *The Winter's Tale* and *The Tempest* in particular, are about the revenge that seasonal symbolism and the cycles of nature win over the forces of anti-nature and perversion. The festivity which was rendered impotent or destroyed in the no man's land of tragedy, miraculously re-emerges here in an atmosphere of freshness and innocence. And, significantly enough, most of the rejoicings evoked in this last group of plays are of a pastoral nature, falling into the summer half of the festive calendar. They are a way of celebrating nature's new-found fertility, but also of giving the danger of violence as wide a berth as possible.

Over and above the categorization and classification of genres, which often have the effect of concealing the continuity of themes and images from one play to another, the thread of festivity is interwoven throughout virtually all Shakespeare's plays. Admittedly, at some points – of which we should take account – it breaks off or goes back over the same ground. But essentially, Shakespeare describes festivity in all its diverse calendar forms, thereby linking his festive scenes with a concrete representation of time. Then sometimes the dramatist shows us the seasonal holidays from a more political angle, producing a grating vision of festivity that destroys the comforting dream of unified harmony. On that score, many of the images connected with festivity leave us with very few illusions, stripping bare the elemental urges that are unleashed in a topsy-turvy world beset by frustration, disorder and cruelty. Shakespeare's ambivalent images of festivity underline the disturbing uncertainty of the festive theme in a dramatic oeuvre which constantly lays before us both sides of the coin: on the one hand social reconciliation in the festive form of the conviviality associated with the tradition of hospitality, and on the other its complicity with the nocturnal forces that bring division and chaos.

Anne Righter-Barton is certainly justified in drawing attention to the importance of the nocturnal theme in the festive comedies, where it is associated with shadows, illusions and dreams. Jean-Marie Maguin provides a more systematic analysis of the subject in his thesis 'La nuit dans le théâtre de Shakespeare et de ses prédécesseurs',[51] in which he shows that 'a dramatic entertainment has particular affinities with the night' for 'the night too makes play with masks and curtains'.[52]

7   Festivity and time in Shakespeare's plays

Shakespeare and the representation of time

Enter Time, the Chorus.   (*The Winter's Tale*, IV, i)

The idea that the march of history moves in a particular direction, developing in a linear fashion upward to irreversible progress, is one that dates from the nineteenth century. The nineteenth century, with its belief in the triumph of science and the spread of the catastrophic optimism of Marxist theories, was the period when those ideas superseded a concept of cyclical history characterized by regressions as well as leaps forward.[1] Nowadays the notion of linear, cumulative and irreversible time is dismissed by historians just as is the older concept of time as subject to capricious fluctuations.[2]

The birth of these views of history in the nineteenth century was due to the rise of rationalism and the progress of science which, together, gradually made it possible to establish the idea that time is a neutral quantity that is measurable and is characterized by non-repetition. In the magic, primitive view, in contrast, time is apprehended as discontinuous (periods of disorder or festivity alternate with the everyday), uneven (some days are propitious, some unpropitious) and cyclical (by analogy with natural, organic rhythms). In conjunction with the points of reference constituted by the solstices and equinoxes and by historical anniversaries, seasonal festivals still helped to structure time in the collective consciousness during the Elizabethan period. The year was thus marked out by the whole collection of manifestations and ceremonies I have described in my analysis of the festivals of the calendar. These constituted so many rites of passage that made the transition from one season or temporal cycle to the next. In the traditional festive view, accordingly, time was not perceived as a system of differences that provided a basis for calculating the movements of men, things and capital (giving rise to interest); rather, it was seen as a system of prescriptions and prohibitions that provided a code for social behaviour (dress, food and sexual customs).[3] In the popular view, time was not an undifferentiated interval to be used as desired by individuals and groups planning their activities and leisure. Instead, it was a mysterious space in which forces, now benevolent, now malevolent, interacted, the object either of impatient expectation or of anxiety on the part of individuals and groups alike. In the countryside, time was conceived both as a series of particular rhythms that had to be respected (sunrise and sunset, the seasons, the period of gestation) and also as a sequence of clearly cut contrasts between polar opposites (night/day, summer/winter, life/death). The primitive time of popular culture and of the culture of Christianity spiced with folklore, which continued to predominate in the countryside and the small hamlets of sixteenth- and seventeenth-century Europe, was characterized by just such passages between one extreme and another and by just such pendulum-like swings.

Such a conception of time and duration has two consequences. First, it encourages a tendency to idealize the past and regard the present as a degraded image of a Golden Age now inaccessible, while never quite relinquishing the hope of its returning one fine day. Certainly, those special interludes that the calendar festivals represented made it possible to revert to the days of some founding ancestor or protective saint, through the rites of inversion they incorporated and the promise they held out of establishing some kind of Land of Cockaigne. Secondly, it leads to time being represented as something concrete and material. Thus each season or month of the year is symbolized by specific emblems (plants, foods or animals) that create a type of figurative language in which things are so to speak represented in the flesh through words. The heraldry of the seasons led on to festive and dramatic practices, prompting jousts of rhetoric and symbolic skirmishes such as those commemorated in Nashe's *Summer's Last Will and Testament* (1592).

As an Elizabethan dramatist, Shakespeare reflects that pendulum-like vision of time in his plays, just as he adopts the main lines of the medieval cosmogony.[4] Conscious though he certainly is of the demands of dramatic rhythm, he does not appear to conceive of time as a unifying factor, except perhaps in *The Tempest*. Time was, on the contrary, disseminated within a calendar which was certainly complex but which, when considered from the point of view of its overall structure, revealed a profound logic of resonances and connections. The meaning of these may escape the modern mind, but their ancient significance was perfectly familiar to the people of the Renaissance. The success that the sellers of almanacs and predictions of all kinds enjoyed testifies to the importance that people in those days attached to this type of knowledge about time: there were probably as many specialists in this field as there were in that of the signs of the zodiac or that of the correspondences through which the microcosm of the human body was linked to the macrocosm of the heavenly bodies.

Once Shakespeare had decided to take up his position at the crossroads of popular and educated culture and to make use of the archaisms of folklore, he was also bound to adopt the traditional system of reference that the seasons and their festivals provided, alongside a quantitative and linear appreciation of the clock and of the civic calendar.[5] The advantage of retaining the old names and the primitive method of structuring time was that this made it possible to preserve a cosmogonic and ideological continuity and to hold on to the fundamental distinction between time that is sacred and time that is profane. In this way, the dramatist was furthermore also provided with a whole set of symbols, images and emblems that enabled him to speak of time in the most concrete and familiar of terms. Given that one of the greatest problems of the theatre and dramatic representation generally is to find visual and gestural equivalents to the abstract categories of thought and speech, it is easy to see how it was that Shakespeare seized upon the idea of adopting a system of transposition that was still in use among the people who made up his public. Finally, through the medium of the calendar linked with the various traditions and games of the major festivals, he could endow his plays with the extra semantic dimension of temporal symbolism. This was one way of exploiting both the more or less stereotyped analogies between the seasons and the various stages of life and also the theme of the clash of contraries (winter/summer, Shrove Tuesday/Lent). Oppositions of this kind, which are the very substance of festive comedies such as Nashe's *Summer's Last Will and Testament*, are certainly particularly used by Shakespeare in his earliest comedies.

Thus *Love's Labour's Lost* ends with 'The Song of the Cuckoo and the Owl', in which the cuckoo and the owl, respectively representing spring and winter, compete with rival themes. This final song is an echo in miniature of the major theme of the play, which could be interpreted as a long struggle between Carnival and the love-making that goes with it on the one hand, and on the other Lenten meditation and study.[6] Berowne (Biron), Dumaine and Longaville swear to turn the court into

> a little academe
> Still and contemplative in living art ...   (I, i, 13–14)

then gradually allow themselves to revert to the pleasures of the flesh and festivity, so that by the time the king of France's death forces them, much against their will, to observe a period of penitence lasting a year and a day, they have quite forgotten their initial vow. Only when their trial of fidelity is completed will they be allowed to speak of love again:

> QUEEN: ... go with speed
> To some forlorn and naked hermitage
> Remote from all the pleasures of the world.
> There stay until the twelve celestial signs

> Have brought about the annual reckoning.
> If this austere, insociable life
> Change not your offer made in heat of blood;
> If frosts and fasts, hard lodging and thin weeds
> Nip not the gaudy blossoms of your love . . .
> Then at the expiration of the year,
> Come challenge me . . .   (v, ii, 786–97)

This period of penitence and austerity to which Berowne (Biron) and his friends are sentenced at the end of the play is as unexpected in the world of comedy as winter's triumph over summer would be in a folk play. It is a good example of the way Shakespeare has of making use of traditions yet at the same time subverting them.[7] By reversing the expected order of things, he gives new life to scenarios that were after all, rather over-used, obliging the spectator to make an effort of concentration and reconsider the whole question of the dramatic routine.

But then we notice that what Shakespeare has actually done is to have upset the threefold sequence of the festive comedy (festivity; festivity broken off amid confusion; return to normality and reconciliation amid renewed festivity), only to stick more closely to the binary rhythm of the old popular calendar, in which one moves ritually from one extreme to the other, with Lent inevitably taking over from Carnival. It expresses the pendulum-like concept of time, the very same that we also find in the alternation between the figures of the court and the battlefield, on the one hand, and Mistress Quickly's tavern on the other, in *Henry IV*, where the only way of establishing the firm foundations of historical time is to exclude Falstaff and his permanent festivity. And until that linear time can be established, history trips and stumbles in its progress: the altercations between Falstaff and Hal, like the skirmishes between Antony and Octavius in *Antony and Cleopatra*, have the ring of an almost direct echo of ritual oppositions between Carnival and Lent:

> CAESAR: Antony,
> Leave thy lascivious wassails. When thou once
> Was beaten from Modena, where thou slew'st
> Hirtius and Pansa, consuls, at thy heel
> Did famine follow, whom thou fought'st against –
> Though daintily brought up – with patience more
> Than savages could suffer. Thou didst drink
> The stale of horses, and the gilded puddle
> Which beasts would cough at. Thy palate then did deign
> The roughest berry on the rudest hedge.
> Yea, like the stag, when snow the pastures sheets,
> The barks of trees thou browsed. On the Alps
> It is reported thou didst eat strange flesh . . .   (I, iv, 55–67)

A more striking contrast could hardly be imagined between Antony's present sybaritic existence and the nauseating diet he brought himself to stomach in the past, in order to survive in times of hardship. The abrupt shock of this sequence of images, which rudely drags us from the delights of Capua, or Alexandria rather, to confront a régime of horse's urine and tree-bark, builds up a hyperbolic intensification of the antithesis between feasting and fasting, Shrove Tuesday and Lent. But the fundamental opposition in the play remains the contrast between Antony and Octavius: on the one hand, the man of physical exploits – in war as well as in love – the big *spender*; on the other, the ascetic man who renounces the pleasures of material existence and truly relishes only the joys of ambition and power.

But as he makes use of this system of binary oppositions expressed in clashes of words, Shakespeare also exploits the many possibilities offered by the whole network of calendary associations: his technique is to establish a connection between different sequences of the calendar, however far apart, by suggesting the underlying affinities between them that are dictated by the basic rhythms of marriage and childbirth. It would thus be immediately clear to everyone in his audience that a child conceived in May would be born in the course of February, when Shrove Tuesday was expected to occur, that is in Carnival time. No scholarly calculations were needed to reach that conclusion. And such a line of reasoning worked equally well backwards as it did forwards. Thus, in *Romeo and Juliet*, when the nurse refers to the Lammastide festival to work out Juliet's age,[8] the Elizabethan public would, as it counted back nine months, immediately arrive at the implied festival of Hallowe'en (the night of 31 October–1 November) as the likely date of Juliet's conception.[9] In an age accustomed to intellectual efforts of this type, such calculations would have been virtually automatic and Shakespeare makes use of this principally to indicate, quite early on in the play, that a tragic mechanism with the power to abolish the frontiers between love and death may be at work. Indeed, the traditions associated with Hallowe'en were marked by a deep ambivalence. On the one hand, there were ritual games and initiations into love, through which girls would hope to glimpse the face of their future husbands; on the other hand, the customs of Hallowe'en also revived ancient Saxon beliefs that the dead returned to the world of the living during the night before the great annual Festival of the Dead, which was linked to the ancestor-cult of pagan times. To a public still prone to superstition and used to playing the game of calendary associations, the fact that Juliet might have been conceived on that very night constituted a covert hint as to her destiny. Since there was no cheating with time, the calendar was proverbially believed to manifest the truth.[10] Internal correspondences and connections of this kind revealed the secret potential of a calendar that was far from being a fixed, linear structure and possessed its own latent dynamism which, once activated, could be a formidable bearer of messages. In *Romeo and Juliet*, these significant associations and cross-references are used as a means of over-determining the surface theme of Eros devoured by Thanatos: they make it possible to slip in a few covert premonitory hints. The spectator's pleasure thus consists partly in guessing what is going to happen, even as he hopes that his fears will not be realized. By the time they are inexorably confirmed, however, those fears will certainly have helped to create a strong impression of tragic fatality. As a result of the final outcome being carefully prepared at this level of symbolic reasonances, the spectator would emerge from the theatre, at the end of the play, with the feeling that 'it was all predestined'.

The second advantage that stemmed from the use of this interplay of calendary correspondences was that it provided the dramatist with immediate, concrete terms in which to present the problem of the interrelation between a periodic, cyclical type of duration, still sur-rounded by magic and superstition, and the secular time of history, divided up according to objective and quantitative points of reference. What, for example, happens when one passes from a sacred, lunar calendar to a secular, solar one, or when one attempts to substitute the order of daylight for the order of night? These are some of the questions Shakespeare tackles in plays such as *Julius Caesar* and *Antony and Cleopatra*. When Caesar tries to exploit the occasion of the festival of the Lupercalia[11] to get himself proclaimed king by the Roman *plebs* (*Julius Caesar*, I, ii), he is gambling on the indecision of the moment and the ambiguity of a situation in which time is part mythical, part historical, in order to promote his monarchical designs. Had the crowd elected him king-for-a-day, he could subsequently have tried unobtrusively to make permanent and to institutionalize what had been won 'in a moment of fun', with the confusion and euphoria of the festival abetting. If he had been elected king at the carnival, Caesar could have tried to prolong his reign beyond the period allotted for these seasonal rejoicings. But, his attempts having failed, he is toppled one month later (there being thirty days between the Lupercalia, 14 February, and the Ides of March, 14 March), a fateful interval that seals his fall from the heights of myth and knocks him off the pedestal of history. Without the sanction of the people, Caesar had become a mere shadow of the king that he had failed to be and, like the mock-king of end-of-year festivals, he seemed destined to a sacrifice that would mark the end of his carnival reign.[12] In *Antony and Cleopatra*, Antony turns night into day, frenziedly striving to arrest the course of things and history. That is what lies behind his 'Alexandrian revels' and his nights of carousing, in which the purpose of all this festivity, like that of the river Lethe in the underworld, is to make him forget the spectre of his failure.[13] As this inexorably approaches, the orgies become even more frenetic and Antony's excesses increase tenfold:

it is as if they were propitiatory rites designed to stop the machinery of time.

In *Henry IV*, monarchical order once again rises from the ashes of carnival, but not before the pendulum has long continued to oscillate between the court and the tavern, day and night. When, at the end of Part 2, 'the chimes at midnight'[14] toll the knell of festivity rather than a summons to sumptuous rejoicings,[15] it is because now the recorded time of history resumes its precedence over the dissipated time of festivity. To tell the truth, festivity, often arrested at the crucial point when it was just about to take off, seems only to be fully realized either in fantastical projections of the imagination, in fevered expectation or in nostalgic songs that look back to the good old days.[16] Festivity, rushing headlong in the opposite direction to the course of time, repeatedly stopped in its tracks by the principle of reality, is eventually shattered by the machinery of war and reasons of state. Once Prince Hal becomes King Henry V, the only holidays he mentions are meant to raise the morale of his soldiers and to immortalize the memory of military glory. Coinciding as it does with Saint Crispian's Day, the shoemakers' holiday of 25 October, the battle can commence with the promise of England's future gratitude:

> This day is called the Feast of Crispian.
> He that outlives this day and comes safe home
> Will stand a-tiptoe when this day is named
> And rouse him at the name of Crispian.
> He that shall see this day and live t'old age
> Will yearly on the vigil feast his neighbours
> And say, 'Tomorrow is Saint Crispian.'
> Then he will strip his sleeve and show his scars
> And say, 'these wounds I had on Crispin's day'.
> Old men forget; yet all shall be forgot,
> But he'll remember with advantages,
> What feats he did that day . . .   (IV, iii, 40–51)

The English *would*, as a whole, forget. So the Feast of St Crispin or Crispian is accordingly turned into a remembrance day for the high deeds of the English nation on foreign soil. The conversion of a guild holiday into a national festival is facilitated by the magic of warrior valour and also probably by the phonetic proximity of the words 'feast' and 'feats', each an anagram of the other. But, as Alan Brissenden has shown, warfare is itself presented as a festival in the historical plays, through images connected with music, dancing and the celebrations of the calendar[17] – a fact that testifies to the remarkable ambivalence of a theme which, in the hands of other dramatists, such as Dekker, is on every count set in opposition to the theme of corporate conviviality.[18]

With the later romances, this point of view is reversed, for these plays represent a return to myths, festivals and the old calendar. The point is no longer to lay the foundations for some monarchical or imperial enterprise nor to rally energies dissipated amid the din and merrymaking of festivity to serve in some noble conquest. What now is at stake is the regeneration of a world destroyed by jealousy and a mad lust for power. In the plays of Shakespeare's last period, history, having done away with magical thinking and its train of traditions, deemed to be costly and useless, is apparently struck by impotence and sterility and stuck in an impasse. Thus King Leontes' Sicily, a pastoral land if ever there was one, becomes a wasteland. Now it is in the children lost or exiled far afield, long penitence and the magic of art of old rural rituals that lie the youth and hope of a world made sick by violence. That explains why Shakespeare now steps out of the real, official chronology to move into the rhythms of ritual time that beat on the sea-shore or in the forests of strange yet familiar pastoral realms.[19] Nevertheless, in locking into a vague and fantastical passage of time, Shakespeare clearly did not completely disengage himself from the markers of ordinary time for, with his every reference to the structure of the calendar, he demonstrates his familiarity with all the possibilities offered by its devious ramifications.

The reference points of the festive calendar in Shakespeare's dramatic works

A calendar, a calendar – look in the almanac...
(*A Midsummer Night's Dream*, III, i, 48–9)

The essential information on this subject is provided by Nathan Drake's *Shakespeare and his Times*, John Nichols' annals of *The Progresses and Entertainments of Queen Elizabeth* and *The Progresses ... of James I*, Joseph Strutt's *The Sports and Pastimes of the People of England* and T.F. Thiselton Dyer's *Folklore of Shakespeare*, all published in the nineteenth century. However, these simply record a series of individual allusions, without marshalling them into an overall system. Faced with this apparently disparate collection, I thought I should try to bring the information into focus by resituating it within the general framework of the festive calendar, the various aspects of which I have analysed in Part I.

Shakespeare plays freely upon the equivocal subtleties of the obscure area of festivity that flourished on the borders of night and day, the old and the new, and the male and the female, a time which was for him situated during the twelve days of Christmas. He only touches in passing, however, upon the major popular festival of Shrove Tuesday which he mentions in two of his plays.[20] Apart from these two furtive allusions, he keeps very quiet about this strategic point in the festive calendar. But in view of the fact that it was marked by apprentices sacking the London theatres, Shakespeare's silence on this point may have been designed to convey his disapproval of traditions that could be extremely harmful to people of his profession.

Saint Valentine's Day, eleven days after Saint Blaise's Day, which in some years marked the beginning of the Carnival period but in others (when Shrove Tuesday was late) fell in Lent, was a festival situated in the boundary zone between Carnival and Lent. Shakespeare refers directly to it in *Hamlet*[21] and possibly indirectly at the beginning of *Romeo and Juliet*, in the initial slanging match between the minor characters Samson and Gregory:

SAMSON: Me they shall feel while I am able to stand, and 'tis known I am
 a pretty piece of flesh.
GREGORY: 'Tis well thou art not fish. If thou hadst, thou hadst been
 poor-john.   (I, i, 27–30)

Verbal repartee such as this, leading on to skirmishes of sword and dagger, has a more or less emblematic function, suggesting that the clan warfare which rages in Verona might be seen as a counterpoint to the traditional and seasonal clashes between the supporters of Carnival and those of Lent. The friction between the forces of winter and those of spring, as they meet, underlies the festival of Saint Valentine and all the erotic skirmishes leading up to the declaration of sexual warfare which found its full expression in the games of Hocktide during the week after Easter. As such, this looks an adequate introduction to a play in which love and sexual comedy play a central part even though, as fate would have it, Thanatos eventually prevails over Eros, drowning the major protagonists in a tragic whirlpool.

Returning to the words of Samson and Gregory, I would suggest that the language initially used by the two duellists refers indirectly to the rites of Saint Valentine's Day, rites which themselves mark the antithesis between Carnival and Lent. In this mainly verbal altercation, the idea of courage and male strength is conveyed by the verb 'to stand' and the expression 'a pretty piece of flesh': aggressive virility is set in direct opposition to female languor, symbolized by 'fish' and the poor fare of Lent (dried cod, here called 'poor-john').[22] At another level the flesh/fish opposition represents the genital organs of the two sexes as contrary obscene emblems. Finally, set against the background of bloody rivalry between the Capulets and the Montagues, these somewhat insulting allusions to the so-called weaker sex remind us that this sexual acrimony is sparked off by an anorexic response to the gluttonous devotees of Carnival excess that is elicited on the eve of Lent. This verbal duel, a prelude to the crossing of swords in earnest, is continued with the taunts that Mercutio hurls at Romeo on the day after the Capulet feast, sarcasms that constitute a comic counterpoint to the theme of rivalry between the two factions:

BENVOLIO: Here comes Romeo, here comes Romeo.
MERCUTIO: Without his roe, like a dried herring.
               O flesh, flesh, how art thou fishified!   (II, iii, 34–6)

Over and above the echoing effects of 'roe' and 'Romeo', a parody of woeful lamentation, these lines suggest that, having spent a night in Juliet's arms, Romeo has literally betrayed his own fraternity, deserting the ranks of Carnival led by the merry Mercutio to join a fish-like female regiment bearing the banner of Lent. The lover is likened to a Lenten figure, devoid of appetite, whose sexual exhaustion rules him out of warfare and duelling. And Romeo's apathy in the face of repeated provocation from Tybalt does indeed induce Mercutio to take up the challenge on his behalf. Love, undermined by a lack of good fare, might have been seen as a form of anaemia and loss of vigour if, on the other hand, Lenten fare had not also been popularly reputed to have aphrodisiac effects.[23]

Such clashes between the licence of feast days and the forces of penitence are again echoed in *1 Henry IV* in Falstaff's confrontation with Prince Hal, in Mistress Quickly's tavern.[24] And the conflict between Carnival and Lent also plays an essential role at the end of *2 Henry IV* although here the scales are weighted in favour of the forces of abstinence now about to win the day and exclude the jovial representative of Carnival. However, it all starts with a boozy enough Shrove Tuesday celebration in the orchard owned by Master Silence who, being in excellent form, strikes up with joyful drinking songs that hark back to the good old days:

> Do nothing but eat, and make good cheer,
> And praise God for the merry year,
> When flesh is cheap and females dear,
> And lusty lads roam here and there
> So merrily,
> And ever among so merrily ...
>   Be merry, be merry, my wife has all,
>   For women are shrews, both short and tall,
>   'Tis merry in hall when beards wags all,
>   And welcome merry shrovetide.
> Be merry, be merry.   (v, iii, 17–37)

This scene clearly represents both the apotheosis and the swan-song of the defenders of festivity and Carnival, for in the next scene Falstaff is confronted with exile, instead of the triumph that he was expecting:

KING HARRY: I know thee not old man. Fall to thy prayers...
         Leave gormandizing; know the grave doth gape
         For thee thrice wider than for other men...
         Till then I banish thee, on pain of death...   (v, v, 47–63)

After Lent, and in the immediate aftermath of Easter, the Hocktide games ritually took place. As we have seen, they constituted a form of sexual warfare in which men and women in turn took hostages to be set free as soon as they had paid a modest ransom or made some symbolic forfeit. Without ever alluding directly to them, Shakespeare uses as the backdrop to several of his comedies festive practices of this kind, in which men and women could externalize their rivalries, converting their quarrels into light-hearted skirmishes.[25] *The Taming of the Shrew* is *the* Shakespearian play in which the theme of comic sexual warfare is central. Kate and Petruccio's stormy love affair provides the main plot. This revolves around the conquest of a wife, which is presented as the feat of an animal-tamer. That aspect is reinforced by the animal metaphors that are applied to Katherina: as a 'shrew', she is indirectly assimilated to a shrew-mouse, an animal often portrayed in contemporary natural histories as the very embodiment of energy, irascibility and agitation.[26] Furthermore, Petruccio's pseudo-affectionate nickname, 'Kate', assimilates her both to a 'cat' and to a 'kite'.

Petruccio cynically declares that he is only after her money and adopts towards this scold the tactics of a kite-tamer: starve her and deprive her of sleep until she proves more amenable (IV, i, 176–93). The animal imagery applied to both of the main protagonists in this play simultaneously evokes both the medieval and aristocratic bestiary connected with themes of love and at the same time the games and amusements associated with many popular festivals. Viewed in the perspective of Hocktide festivities the first part of the comedy, in which Kate berates and bullies her father and discourages all prospective suitors,[27] can be seen as an equivalent to a 'women's day', when men could be taken prisoners and held to ransom; the second part of the play, which shows how Petruccio tames Kate after taking her home to Padua with him, allows man to regain the upper hand over woman. Act v sets the seal on their final reconciliation and marks the end of hostilities with a sexual peace treaty over which Lucentio rejoices at the beginning of scene ii:

     At last, though long, our jarring notes agree,
     And time it is when raging war is done
     To smile at scapes and perils overblown.   (v, ii, 1–3)

But that reassurance is no more than superficial, as is shown by the reversal which follows when the scold, in a famous speech, declares her new-found total submission to her lord and master while the sweet and loving Bianca turns out to be a sour and disobedient wife. This is the last of the role-reversals depicted in this festive comedy whose Induction (seemingly separate from the rest of the play) through the amusing adventures of Christopher Sly provides the key to all the reversals. As can be seen, there is a vast difference between, on the one hand, the simple, mechanical scenario of the popular festival, which functioned according to the principle of turn and turn about, and on the other the dialectical pirouettes of Shakespeare's comedy.

In several of his comedies, Shakespeare makes use of the general structure of these festive practices through which men and women were able to externalize their quarrels in a playful manner. The first to consider is *All's Well That Ends Well*, one of whose major themes is that of the abandoned woman getting her revenge by means of the famous 'bed-trick', also used in *Measure for Measure*. This play contains a dramatic transposition of the Hocktide games; however, I do not agree with Janet Spens, who reckons that those games constitute the essential symbolic content of this 'problem play'.

Having portrayed sexual antagonisms from a farcical angle, Shakespeare offers another version of the festive rites of Hocktide in *Much Ado About Nothing*. The theme of sexual warfare leading to marriage is here given essentially verbal expression in the acid sparring between Beatrice and Benedick, both past their first prime and old enough to have lost their early illusions about love. Leonato sets the scene at the beginning of the play, as he speaks of 'merry war' between the two:

LEONATO: You must not, sir, mistake my niece. There is a kind of merry war
           betwixt Signor Benedick and her. They never meet but there's a skirmish
           of wit between them.   (I, i, 58–61)

As Anne Righter-Barton points out in her introduction to this play,[28] the interlude at Messina represents a period of carnival during which the court launches itself into a hectic bout of laughter, alcohol and festivity, after the trials and dangers of the war that has just come to an end. But it is not a place for the warrior to drop his guard, for love in Messina is no easy business and, in the case of Benedick and Beatrice, it makes demands upon all the lovers' resources of intelligence and wit as well as upon the impulses of their hearts and emotions. Love-games such as these also form dangerous liaisons beset with risks, even when they are pursued amid the rowdiness of the ball and the carefree festive intrigues of the governor's palace. (I shall return later to the effects of these confusions of love.) At the beginning of the play, the atmosphere of the *fêtes galantes* of Messina is conveyed mainly through verbal images that are full of seasonal echoes:

BENEDICK: ... There's her cousin, an she were not possessed with a fury, exceeds her as much in beauty as the first of May doth the last of December.   (I, i, 180–2)

By using the dates of 1 May and 31 December as the basis of a comparison between Beatrice's looks and those of her cousin Hero, Benedick, usually no more inclined to poetry than to elegant speeches of love, comes up with a conceit which picks up the contrast at three different levels of meaning. The first rests upon the opposition between youth and old age that is suggested by the wide calendar span (two months at opposite poles of the year and two extreme dates, one at the beginning, the other at the end of the month). He assimilates one lady (Beatrice) to the spring festival, indirectly making her the Queen of May, the other (Hero) to the outer darkness of the winter festival, in a movement of relegation that no doubt prefigures her future visit to the underworld, when she shams death.

But it is perhaps in *All's Well That Ends Well* that Shakespeare finds the most successful dramatic equivalent to the ritual rivalries of Hocktide, in the scene where Helena wins back Bertram thanks to the strategy of the 'bed-trick'. Most of Acts III and IV of the play, which is set in Florence within the framework of a war between the French and the Siennese, is structurally organized in alternating scenes in which first only women (Helena, Diana and her mother), next only men (officers in the French camp) are present. In the women's scenes, Helena plans to catch out Bertram in his philandering and make him pay a symbolic ransom, namely accept a marriage that he has been avoiding and swear to be faithful to his wife. In the men's scenes, the plot is publicly to show up the fraudulence of Parolles, Bertram's swaggering lieutenant, and force him to be as good as his word and retrieve the drum abandoned on enemy territory. When Parolles is publicly revealed as a coward who has betrayed his own side, the ransom he is forced to pay is that of his honour but, like Falstaff in *Henry IV*, he does not regard that as so high a price that he would prefer to pay with his life.[29] However, we should note one important difference here from the popular scenario of Hocktide: in the scenes set in the French camp, it is not women but other men, Parolles' own fellow-officers, who set the trap involving the drum, a trap from which Parolles can only escape by losing his 'honour'. This is an instance of how Shakespeare, in his use of calendar rites and festive customs, avoids reproducing them literally, nearly always displaying considerable freedom in his handling of the popular material. As in *Much Ado About Nothing*, the two symbols of the world of martial virility on the one hand, and on the other triumphant femininity are, respectively, a drum and a ring: it is these that set the seal on first Parolles' downfall, then Bertram's, the first of which prefigures the second. As can be seen, the structure of *The Taming of the Shrew* is reversed here, since now it is the woman who triumphs over the man, as in the romances, where the female characters are involved in the salvation and regeneration of a world placed in jeopardy by the pride of men.[30]

After these tugs of war between Carnival and Lent, illustrated in various ways in Shakespeare's comedies, the next major festival that gives rise to festive allusions of any importance is May Day. It is interesting to note in passing that, as with the Christian festival of Christmas, Shakespeare refers no more than fleetingly to the Easter Holy Week, making only one direct allusion to it, in *Romeo and Juliet*.[31] But the festivities of May Day, which marked the junction of the two halves of the calendar, constituted the principal rallying point for popular Elizabethan culture and Shakespeare could not pass over them in silence. An indirect reference to May Day occurs in *Measure for Measure*, when Mistress Overdone mentions the bastard born from Lucio's loves in her establishment. She calculates the age of the child as follows:

His child is a year and a quarter old come Philip and Jacob . . .

(III, i, 460–1)

May Day was indeed also the Feast of Saint Philip and Saint James the Less,[32] so the reference to May Day is relatively oblique. If this child was fifteen months old on 1 May, he must have been born at Candlemas, on the eve of Carnival, and may have been conceived in the course of the nocturnal escapades of May Day two years earlier. The pastoral love affairs consummated in the month of May (when weddings were, in principle, banned) thus came to fruit in Lent. Those May excesses were paid for, nine months later, by a long period of abstinence. The biological rhythms of the body were in step with the calendary timetable and sanctioned the law of the swinging pendulum which dictated the alternations that lie at the heart of festivity. The collective consciousness was no doubt perfectly prepared to accept the law that all things are justly attended by their consequences. However, to judge by Pompey's and Mistress Overdone's declarations in *Measure for Measure*, they appear to have jibbed at Angelo's desire to bring back the old law of Vienna that punished fornication with death. In this instance, the *vox populi* votes against the usurpation of natural justice by a Church or state tribunal but dares to do no more than hint, through the allusion to 'Philip and Jacob', at the pagan festival now banned. However, no sooner is it officially proscribed and the customs associated with it prohibited than it truly begins to haunt people's minds.

The May Day festival is also associated with the atmosphere of joyful confusion that so alarms the palace porter at the end of *Henry VIII*. As soon as news of the christening of young Elizabeth has broken, the people flock to the palace, propelled as much by popular enthusiasm for the royal family as by the hope of being invited to take part in the banquet organized as part of the court's rejoicings:

> ...Do you look
> For ale and cakes here, you rude rascals?

asks the porter, while his assistant, who seems to have a cooler head, intervenes with:

> Pray sir, be patient. 'Tis as much impossible,
> Unless we sweep 'em from the door with cannons,
> To scatter 'em, as 'tis to make 'em sleep
> On May-day morning – which will never be.   (v, iii, 11–14)

The analogy with May Day customs that the porter's assistant draws makes the point that the people's determination is such that it will not be easy to persuade the crowd to depart empty-handed.

As in *Measure for Measure*, allusions to May Day here are also connected with the idea of the procreation of bastards. Panicked by the crowd clamouring to be let into the palace, the porter exclaims:

Bless me, what a fry of fornication is at door! On my Christian conscience, this one christening will beget a thousand. Here will be father, godfather, and all together.   (v, iii, 34–7)

The porter's comic consternation, faced with a mob moved by the process of spontaneous generation, conjures up images of the teeming reproductive powers that figure so largely in popular speech and popular imagination. The grotesque comic impact of a scene in which a psychological reaction (in this instance, fear) is conveyed through a material evocation of vast proliferation is reinforced by the obscene exclamations that lead up to it:

Is this Moorfields to muster in? Or have we some strange Indian with the great tool come to court, the women so besiege us?   (v, iii, 31–3)

In Shakespeare's gallery of grotesque portraits, Caliban,[33] from *The Tempest*, has inherited from the Fool of the Morris dance the insatiable libido that prompts such alarm from the porter in *Henry VIII*. This is a theme that seems to me to be directly related to the somewhat uncontrolled May Day rejoicings in which the collective impulses of lubricity were commonly ascribed to the influence of the moon. Perhaps it is equally the influence of the moon, on top of Puck's blunders, that is supposed to account for the interchanges of partners in the dances of *A Midsummer Night's Dream* and also for Titania's deranged obsession for Bottom when he sports his ass's head! All these mistakes, orchestrated under the aegis of a mischievous 'blind Cupid', here depicted as the blindfolded figure of Chance (also sometimes represented by Night or

Caeca Nox),[34] are tied into the carnivalesque theme of liberated desire, with all its possible hazards. As Leo Salingar observes, 'for Shakespeare, some loss of self-control or deficiency of awareness is an unavoidable incident in "pastime", just as it is necessary for some of the participants to hide or lose their identity under a masquerade'.[35]

Shakespeare thus seems to associate the popular May Day festival with a disordering of the senses and a loss of consciousness of the ridiculous in a situation in which the eruption of the dionysiac element is often as hilarious as it is disturbing.[36] Meanwhile, the Whitsun festival, for its part, is particularly associated with the donning of masks. Here, evidence is provided by the 'Pentecost . . . pageants of delight' mentioned by the disguised Julia in *The Two Gentlemen of Verona* (IV, iv, 158–9), the 'Whitsun pastorals' to which Perdita refers in *The Winter's Tale* (IV, iv, 134) and old Capulet's nostalgic reminiscences in *Romeo and Juliet*, as, for him, the Whitsun festival is synonymous with the masked ball (I, v, 36–8):

> 'Tis since the nuptial of Lucentio,
> Come Pentecost as quickly as it will,
> Some five-and-twenty years; and then we masked.

By associating marriage rejoicings (Lucentio's wedding) with the Whitsun festival, which is more here than just a chronological point of reference, Shakespeare intertwines private with public festivity, princely or aristocratic entertainments with the amusements of the populace. What is suggested by this allusion to Pentecost is that the struggles between the noble families of Verona for supremacy in the city will be held in abeyance for the festive period (for otherwise this could lead to a positive massacre) and that this interlude of rejoicing and intoxication represents a moment of truce in the clan vendetta. The device of wearing masks is a pure convention, for when Tybalt sees through the disguises, old Capulet insists that the rules of hospitality and festivity continue to be respected. In these circumstances, the outsider is, as it were, protected within a magic circle. Unseeing gazes meet. Only love can penetrate the armour of pretence. And it is through this chink made by desire that violence, momentarily checked at the ball, will eventually sweep in and run riot.

In England, Whitsuntide was also the favourite time for Morris dances. Shakespeare duly alludes to these in *Henry V*, in the Dauphin's mocking account to the King of France of the preparations being made by the English troops:

> And let us do it with no show of fear,
> No, with no more than if we heard that England
> Were busied with a Whitsun morris dance.

> For, my good liege, she is so idly kinged,
> Her sceptre so fantastically borne
> By a vain, giddy, shallow, humorous youth,
> That fear attends her not.   (II, iv, 23–9)

In an article entitled 'Shakespeare and the Morris' Alan Brissenden shows that, for the French, who here pour verbal scorn on young Hal, the force of the image of the Whitsuntide Morris dance turns Henry V into a 'make-believe may-game king'.[37] This allusion to the Whitsuntide Morris dance complements the earlier French act of provocation that consisted in sending the young king of England a present of tennis balls (I, ii, 258) and it is justified by the reputation acquired by Prince Hal in his youth from the scenes of nocturnal debauchery in Falstaff's company in the Boar's Head Tavern (I, ii, 249–57).

In *A Midsummer Night's Dream*, Shakespeare played on the similarity between the festivities of May Day and those of Midsummer, deliberately confusing them as if they were more or less equivalent. He seems to have wanted to synthesize all these popular traditions, turning them into a single major festival, the midsummer one, which marked the transition into the pastoral period of summer.

This summer period was, as I have noted in Part I, relatively poor in festive traditions, being marked above all by the kind of rural conviviality that attended the completion of labours connected with herding or bringing in the harvests. Of the four major rural festivals of this type (sheep-shearing, rush-bearing, harvest-home and hop-picking), Shakespeare mentions only the first and the third in his plays, those that incorporated the traditions with the richest symbolical and mythical resonance and those that could be the most effectively introduced into the dramatic framework of pastoral scenes. It is in the last of his plays, *The Winter's Tale* and *The Tempest*, that Shakespeare drew most directly and copiously upon the inspiration provided by these popular summer festivals.

The Winter's Tale is a play remarkable for the importance that it assigns to a literary genre, the pastoral, whose conventions, themes and characters must, in Shakespeare's day, have seemed somewhat passé and which it helped to bring back into fashion. It is also remarkable on account of the place that it allots to the sheep-shearing festival presented in Act IV, scene iv, one of the longest scenes in all of Shakespeare's oeuvre. It is worth noting that in Robert Greene's *Pandosto*, the major source for *The Winter's Tale*, the passage corresponding to the sheep-shearing festival takes up no more than six lines. So it must have been quite deliberately, undaunted by the possibility of *longueurs* and chronological anachronisms, that Shakespeare set the second part of *The Winter's Tale* under the sign of the pastoral and the rural festival.

These scenes are Shakespeare's 'Pastoral Symphony'. The dimensions of the two scenes concerned greatly exceed the quite modest framework of a rustic festival, even one in the form celebrated in the eclogues of Drayton or Dyer. The atmosphere of refound abundance and concord of this festival microcosm makes it possible to modulate the sometimes discordant notes that arise in what is supposed to be a joyful, summer counterpoint to the dominant tragic, winter theme with which the play began. To be more precise, we find first a 'counter-melody', with Autolycus singing the ballad 'When daffodils begin to peer' which heralds the rite of spring, then a 'contra-tempo' when an energetic dance of satyrs takes over from the rather languid rhythms of the dancing shepherds and shepherdesses.[38]

The pastoral festival makes it possible to mark a clear break with the celebrations of winter in which a more radical mix of human beings took part and which were more liable to lead to social transgressions. The opposition that Shakespeare sets up between the kingdoms of Sicilia and Bohemia in a way symbolizes the division between the winter and the summer halves of the calendar. The Sicilian festivities amid which Hermione, at Leontes' request, tries to detain Polixenes, soon turn sour and almost become an occasion for crime, as happens in *Macbeth*.[39] The violation of sacred hospitality soon turns Leontes' court into a place of terror and disorder. Indirectly, it is the festivities themselves (the nine months of Sicilian hospitality offered to Polixenes) that have sparked a mechanism of violence which the gods alone have the power to arrest. By the time the truth is re-established it is too late, for the damage is done (Mamilius is dead, Hermione is supposedly dead and Perdita has been abandoned on distant deserted shores).

The sudden change of scene, the long interval of time and the pastoral festivity make it possible to escape from the impasse. In contrast to Juliet, whose destiny is to some extent decided by the unpropitious circumstances of her birth, Perdita, thanks to what might be called her double birth, is able to elude the tragic whirlpool. Born amid storms and passions and having, like some baby Moses, miraculously escaped a massacre of innocents, her reappearance sixteen years later in the magical land of Bohemia is a symbolic second birth. It is not so much a resurrection, in the manner of Hermione's restoration to life at the end of the play. Instead it is a rebirth, in the sense of an accession to self-awareness, an awakening to the world and other people, an assumption of social existence. Like Proserpina, to whom she is indeed compared,[40] Perdita emerges into the light of day in the summer half of the year, leaving the wintry shadows of the underworld behind her. Not the least of the surprises that this play springs upon us is the fact that it leads us into the midst of the summer celebrations of the shepherds by way of a 'Winter's Tale'. Such an eruption into the fluid time of this summer festival confuses the chronological reference points that link the sequence of events together. As we pass from the first part of the play to the second, the scene and the place change (Sicilia and Bohemia are, so to speak, polar opposites), but we also, and more importantly, pass from one time into another. The function of the sheep-shearing festival is precisely to alert us to this fact, by making the time of the representation of the play coincide with that of the festival. Psychologically, dramatically and symbolically the festival thus operates as a rite of passage.

The ritual and allegorical atmosphere of these scenes should not blind us to their rich diversity, for this makes it possible to read them at a number of different levels. From the points of view of their internal structure, variety of tone and degrees of intensity, perhaps a musical model would be apposite. Not only do these scenes strike a quite different note from the general tone of the first three acts but, in counterpoint, they also provide a constant reminder of a lurking danger, namely that the tragic element might at any moment reappear and convert these delightful rejoicings into a scene of furious discord. The cynical attitude of Autolycus, in whose own personal and metaphorical view of the sheep-shearing it is the shepherds, not the sheep, who are to be 'fleeced' (IV, iii, 120–1), the timidity of Perdita, fearful of entering fully into her role as hostess and organizer of the festival, and the rivalry between Dorcas and Mopsa, competing for the favours of the Clown, are all potentially unsettling elements which could at any moment spoil the good humour and disrupt the festival. The festival itself, as it proceeds, from time to time sounds deep, sinister notes which suggest a threat of disintegration:

> I prithee darken not
> The mirth o' th' feast ...   (IV, iv, 41–2)

says Florizel, anxious to dispel Perdita's dark fears that Polixenes will be angered by this peasant dalliance so unbecoming in a future heir to the throne of Bohemia.

Perdita's lucidity and modesty no doubt do her credit, but they are out of tune with the excitement and abandonment that are indispensable to all festivity. The old shepherd has to heap all his advice on hospitality on top of Florizel's encouragements before she can be persuaded to act more graciously towards her guests and try to enter into the spirit of rejoicing. In counterpoint to her charming bashfulness, Autolycus sounds his note of mockery, jeering at the victims whom he is shamelessly cheating and sneering at the stupidity of Honesty and Trust. The presence of death itself is detectable in the background, in the passage in which Perdita hands round garlands of flowers to everybody present and, more clearly, in the lines in which Florizel commits the sacrilege of looking forward to his inheritance by referring to his father's death:

> One being dead
> I shall have more than you can dream of yet.[41]

Now deeper notes begin to sound while the lively festival airs fade into the distance along with the pipes and tabors. When Polixenes and Camillo remove their masks, the spell of enchantment is broken and the festival rudely halted. Not that the spectator is taken by surprise at this turn of events, for in Act IV, scene ii, Shakespeare has made it clear enough that these two are only attending the festival in order to see for themselves whether what they have been told is true and to get a clear picture of the state of Prince Florizel's loves. Their disguises are essentially tactical, even if, just for a moment, they truly do seem won over by the good-natured gaiety of the festival and the charm of the young shepherdess who greets them with garlands of flowers. But Polixenes' words following the dance of the twelve satyrs soon put us straight, forcing us to recognize the truth.

The joke has clearly gone on quite long enough, for the king: the time has come to pass on to serious matters. At this point the festival organization falters, the medley of voices and laughter becomes confused and a graver note creeps in as attention is gradually focused upon one little group of five people. Chords seem suddenly to clash and the minor key takes over from the major, for the threat looming over the festival has suddenly become reality.

Yet that a halt should be called to the festival is in the order of things. Every festival is by definition circumscribed within a period of limited time laid down in advance. Once it is over, the cacophony and collective madness must cease and things return to normal. That is what marks out a festival from a riot or a revolution, for in the latter cases no one can tell how far things will go or when they will stop. Festival time, theoretically situated on the margins of ordinary duration, is thus subject to tensions of its own that arise from the combination of space in which to rejoice and the clearly defined limits that bound it. At first, festive time seems to expand amid euphoria as the rejoicings get under way, but half-way through it begins to shrink, and eventually gives way to ordinary, everyday time. The principle at work here is that of the hour-glass (the very image that is used by Time, the Chorus, in the transition scene at the beginning of Act IV[42]). Awareness that the sand is trickling away is a factor that helps to plunge the festival first into frenzy, then, as the end approaches, into torpor. Now it is particularly difficult to stage a dramatic representation of a festival gradually falling apart or, on the contrary, acquiring a new lease of life. To interrupt it abruptly, by means of some external intervention (as, for example, the dramatic news of the death of the king of France, in *Love's Labour's Lost*) is more striking and theatrical than staging a rather grey, depressing scene showing the slow winding down into ordinary time. Shakespeare quite often resorts to the device of the interrupted festival[43] and in this case it balances perfectly with the situation in Act I, in which Leontes suddenly cut short the festivities in Sicilia and forced Polixenes to flee. Besides, Polixenes has every reason to wish to part Perdita from his son. If she truly is a shepherdess, she is certainly an unsuitable match for the prince; and if she is a princess in disguise, until such time as he is officially cleared of the accusation of having committed adultery with Queen Hermione, to recognize her is likely to reawaken rumours and bring back those days poisoned by suspicion.

The pastoral festival thus serves here as a long-drawn-out transition between the world of tragedy and the final reconciliation. Its effect is rather like that of the light of dawn dissipating the darkness and, as the sun climbs to its zenith, the play is split in two. Yet the shadows are not completely chased away, for beneath all the talk of hospitality there runs a covert thread of violence and death. Magical though it seems, the festivity does not provide a complete cure for evil. Nature, however strongly reaffirmed, cannot do without the helping hand of art (Hermione's patience and Paulina's cunning) if the hope that flowered timidly during the festival is to take firm root in this wasteland, ravaged by jealousy and tyranny.

As can be seen, Shakespeare accommodates a summer pastoral festival relatively happily within the sophisticated structure of his last plays. Another example, at first sight rather less obvious, is to be found in *The Tempest*. Here, the Masque scene of Act IV appears to have been partly inspired and fuelled by the peasant celebrations and rites of harvest-home.[44] Of course, in a scene such as this, which is presented as a glorification of fertility and abundance, we must take into account an element of mythological transposition and also the fact that the aristocratic genre of the Masque imposed a somewhat stiff solemnity.[45] The parallel that existed between the amusements of the rustic festival and ancient myth was certainly something already detected by the German traveller Paul Hentzner.[46] In the pre-marriage Masque of *The Tempest*, it is again Ceres who, opening her horn of plenty, showers her gifts upon Ferdinand and Miranda and promises them her protection:

> Earth's increase, and foison plenty,
> Barns and garners never empty,
> Vines with clust'ring bunches growing,
> Plants with goodly burden bowing;

Spring come to you at the farthest,
In the very end of harvest!   (IV, i, 110–15)

The interest of the comparison between these lines and the lively little
rustic scene captured by Hentzner in his travel journal is not so much that
it provides another analogue for Shakespeare's passage, but the fact that
it triggers a double reading. Hentzner's diary entry adds a mythological
and scholarly interpretation to his simple record of the customs of
folklore. The ambiguity does not arise by pure chance, for it is in line
with what is sometimes, somewhat vaguely, called the universality of
Shakespeare's message. The scholarly reading must have pleased the
educated public of the period, while the rural rituals delighted the
groundlings, reputed to have had an avid taste for seasonal games and
festivities of all kinds.

In its popular interpretation, Shakespeare's text conjures up a sort of
Land of Cockaigne, where 'vines with clust'ring bunches growing' hold
out a promise of round barrels shortly to be filled with their juice: soon
the wine from a miraculous grape-harvest will be flowing freely and rich
harvests ('barns and garners never empty') of golden wheat will be
converted into crusty loaves. In its aristocratic and scholarly interpretation, the passage celebrates the marriage of Ceres and Bacchus while at
the same time the sacred union of vine and wheat evokes the mystic
combination of wine and bread in the Christian Communion. The space
of a few lines and the fabulous time of festivity thus encompass a whole
sheaf of memories in which references both popular and scholarly, pagan
and Christian, are bound together in an effortless syncretism in no way
heavy or pedantic.[47]

As for the final blessing that Ceres bestows upon the soon-to-be-wed
couple, in which she makes a wish that the springtime will return after
the harvest, it clearly implies a change in the sequence of the seasons. The
perpetual alternation of spring and summer it establishes runs counter to
the calendar and does away with the winter part of the year between
Michaelmas and Lady Day. Ceres' wish is for a return to the Golden Age,
when time ran backwards. The words of this maternal and protective
figure here bring to life old Gonzalo's daydream that

                    nature should bring forth
Of its own kind all foison, all abundance,
To feed my innocent people.   (II, i, 168–70)

But now, amid the beauty of the scene and in conjunction with the strains
of music that confer a solemn and oracular air upon such words, they are
greeted not with the sarcasms of incredulous and cynical listeners but
with cries of delight.

An atmosphere of veritable enchantment surrounds the joyful rites of harvest-home, which are crowned by the graceful dance of the reapers and nymphs:

> You sunburned sicklemen, of August weary,
> Come hither from the furrow and be merry;
> Make holiday, your rye-straw hats put on,
> And these fresh nymphs encounter every one
> In country footing.
> (*Enter certain reapers, properly habited. They join with the nymphs in a graceful dance.*)   (IV, i, 134–8)

Despite the somewhat stiff idealization of the Masque, the sunburned faces of the reapers and the rustic style of the dance testify to the persistence of a popular element here, even if their dance is neither a jig nor a Morris dance.

This last vision of a pastoral Eden brings to a joyful end the revels in the green meadows of Shakespeare's summer festival and it also rounds off the festive calendar. Prospero's line, 'Our revels now are ended' (IV, i, 148), which so many commentators have interpreted as Shakespeare's own farewell to the theatre, also expresses a farewell to festivity.

The calendar nexus situated at the confluence of Michaelmas and Hallowmas corresponded to the beginning of the ancient Celtic year and ushered in a new cycle of festivity (while New Year's Day itself fell in the middle of the twelve days of Christmas).[48] This was an important new departure in the calendar and the blunder made by Simple over this point, in *The Merry Wives of Windsor*, is a clear indication of his weak wits. When asked:

You have not the book of riddles about you, have you?

he responds with another, quite astounding, question:

Book of riddles? Why, did you not lend it to Alice Shortcake upon Allhallowmas last, a fortnight afore Michaelmas?   (I, i, 184–8)

To muddle up the order of the calendary feasts was assuredly proof of simplicity of the highest order. Such a bloomer was bound to provoke hilarity. Not content with reversing the dates of the two festivals, he even halves the interval between them. Clearly, only a simpleton with an addled brain could get the subject of time quite so wrong. But perhaps the allusion to the 'book of riddles' is meant to invite us to see in all this more than a mere tissue of absurdities and to decode some enigmatic meaning. We are, after all, in the realm of comedy, where the whole world can be turned upside-down and time can run backwards. Seen from this angle, Simple's shortening of time might reflect the idea of time speeded up within the space of the dramatic performance or, alternatively, might be an allusion to the sense of acceleration that festivals tend to produce.[49]

The date 2 November, All Souls' Day, is evoked by Buckingham, in *Richard III*, to underline both the bitter irony of his destiny and at the same time the justice of God's wrath, as a result of which he is to be beheaded on the anniversary of the day on which he swore his oath of loyalty to Edward IV and Elizabeth (I, ii, 32–40):

> Why then All-Souls' Day is my body's doomsday . . .
> This, this All-Souls' Day to my fearful soul
> Is the determined respite of my wrongs.
> That high all-seer which I dallied with
> Hath turned my feignèd prayer on my head
> And given in earnest what I begged in jest   (v, i, 12–22).

Quite apart from the fact that the special gravity of this festival is particularly suitable for these meditations on the morality of death, the cyclical structure of the calendar serves to convey the implacable irony of divine retribution, falling as it does exactly a year from the day on which the false oath was sworn. It is a striking example of a Christian reinterpretation of the ancient superstitions that were attached to the calendar.[50]

As for the festivals between All Saints' Day and Martinmas, this period was popularly associated with a last brief flare-up of summer and was often mentioned in this connection.[51] Shakespeare alludes to it in *1 Henry VI*, where Joan tells the Dauphin:

> Expect Saint Martin's summer, halcyon's days,
> Since I have enterèd into these wars.   (I, ii, 110–11)

He mentions it again in both parts of *Henry IV* and, just as Martinmas succeeded Hallowmas in the sequence of calendar festivals, similarly at the beginning of *1 Henry IV*, Falstaff is described as 'All-hallown summer' (I, ii, 156–7), later – in Part 2 – to be described as the very incarnation of Martinmas, in Poins' sarcastic enquiry to Bardolph: 'And how doth the Martlemas your master?' (I, ii, 94–5). This double reference to 'All-hallown summer' is rich in allusions both to middle-age lust and to the Martinmas summer. As we have seen, the latter was a period of inverted time which characterized the beginning of each season of the old Celtic year. It was an apposite image to apply to the scenes that take place in the Boar's Head Tavern, itself an upside-down world in miniature with all such a world's licence, under the patronage of Falstaff, a Lord of Misrule if ever there was one. The allusion also evokes the persistent sprightliness of the aged faun.[52] The second time it occurs, likening Falstaff to the Martinmas ox, it constitutes an ironic dig at his corpulent figure and insatiable appetite. The picture of ribaldry and over-eating is also perfectly in keeping with the pagan atmosphere of the winter festival. Falstaff is the very incarnation of the hearty Martinmas festival, which the Elizabethans had dubbed 'the second carnival'.[53] The reference to the calendar is to some extent obscured by a huge heap of sausages and other rich fare, as if we were suddenly welcomed into the fabulous Land of Cockaigne. The effect of this metonymic shift from the calendary point of reference to the eating habits that it evoked (in particular, the consumption of beef) is to remind us, with great economy of words and still within the framework of festive excess, of Falstaff's corpulence and limitless gluttony. Falstaff is a calendar in himself, for the various parts of his body seem to symbolize a whole string of annual festive traditions. Now a 'Manningtree ox',[54] now a 'Wassail candle',[55] he flaunts the stigmata of his debauchery which, through a curious mimetic effect, have become etched upon his grotesque physique. Such corporeal imprints of festivity are altogether in tune with the concrete imaginary representations of the popular culture, which was constantly representing time, the seasons and the interludes between them with material and down-to-earth imagery.

Forty days after Martinmas came the great festival of Christmas which, as we have seen, was exceedingly popular and which in Elizabethan times retained many echoes of its pagan origins. Curiously enough, Shakespeare's works contain few allusions to it, and those that do occur present it in a relatively unfavourable light, using it as a term to suggest games and entertainments of a rather rudimentary kind.[56] In *Love's Labour's Lost*, in which the vows of penitence and asceticism of the beginning soon give way to the organization of a series of festivities in celebration of love and to what Moth calls 'a great feast of languages' (v, i, 36–7), the amusements of Christmas are described in uncomplimentary terms by Berowne (Biron). When he learns that the Princess and her ladies were laughing at them when they put on their Masque of the Muscovites, he exclaims:

> I see the trick on't. Here was a consent,
> Knowing aforehand of our merriment,
> To dash it, like a Christmas comedy.
> Some carry-tale, some please-man, some slight zany,
> Some mumble-news, some trencher-knight, some Dick . . .
> Told our intents before . . .   (v, ii, 460–7)

What Berowne seems to have in mind here are the Mummers' performances that used to be a feature of the Christmas festivities and, in a sally of exasperation occasioned partly by aristocratic arrogance, partly by his resentment at being the butt of the French ladies' teasing, he heaps upon the amateur actors of these popular entertainments all the worst names he can think of.[57] A similar note is struck at the end of the Induction to *The Taming of the Shrew*. Here, Christopher Sly, the drunken tinker, transformed into a lord for the duration of a prank which seems to be directly inspired by the Saturnalia of ancient times,[58] is addressed as follows by a messenger:

> Your honour's players, hearing your amendment,
> Are come to play a pleasant comedy . . .
> Therefore they thought it good you hear a play
> And frame your mind to mirth and merriment . . .

to which he replies, inelegantly but not without a measure of down-to-earth sense,

> Marry, I will let them play it. Is not a comonty
> A Christmas gambold, or a tumbling trick?   (Induction, ii, 125–34)

Sly's slip of the tongue[59] recalls the clown's way of perverting scholarly talk by introducing grotesque bloomers and involuntary puns that convert it into a popular language full of references to the body, cooking and festivity.[60] The word 'comonty' that, in his still fuddled state, he thickly produces, points up the comedy's 'common' (in the sense of popular or rural) origins; and these help to relate it to the folk play and the festive traditions of the period of the year in which this scene is supposed to be set, that is to say Christmas,[61] to judge by Christopher Sly's expression 'Christmas gambold'. In *The Second Return from Parnassus*, a satirical comedy written between 1601 and 1603 and performed at Saint John's College, Cambridge, during the Christmas festivities there, the Prologue contains a passage which seems a direct echo of this reply of Sly's in Shakespeare's comedy:

MOMUS: What is presented here, is an old misty scene, that hath laine this twelve-moneth in the bottom of a coale house amongst broomes and old shoes . . .
DEFENSOR: It's but a Christmas toy, and [so] may it please your curtisies to let it passe.[62]

Elsewhere in Shakespeare's works, the feast of Christmas is evoked through a metonymic shift from the festival itself to one of its more representative customs, such as the 'wassail', a festive tradition specifically connected with the celebrations of Christmas Eve. The epithet 'wassail' is one that Falstaff, identifying himself with the myth of Merry England, proudly assumes to parry the sneers of the representative of law and order, the Lord Chief Justice:

LORD CHIEF JUSTICE: What! You are as a candle, the better part burnt out.
SIR JOHN: A wassail candle, my lord, all tallow . . . [63]

The fact is that the old rogue is a past master in the casuistic art of presenting his failings as strong points and his obesity as a sign of health, abundance and vitality. The Christian meaning of sin and finitude has apparently never made any impression upon the tough flanks of this rounded bottle of a man who, impervious to any prick of consience, proceeds undaunted on his path, in all his imperturbable rotundity.[64] But in Hamlet,[65] Macbeth[66] and Antony and Cleopatra, where the word 'wassail' also occurs, its connotations are far more negative, rendering it synonymous with, respectively, drunkenness, murderous conspiracy and debauchery.[67] In the context of tragedy, the fundamental ambivalence of festivity is eclipsed, its beneficent aspect submerged by its dark and sinister side. Christmas is the festival of darkness, for it is situated on the threshold of the winter solstice, as the Christian answer to the Mithraic festival of the sol invictus. And here, Shakespeare invokes it in its essentially pagan guise, to symbolize the accursed side of festivity (finitude, impotence and the loss of self-awareness).

The title of Twelfth Night probably owes more to the occasion on which it was performed than to the themes of the play and its internal symbolism. It contains very few allusions to the particular rites that marked the celebration of the end of the twelve-day festival, although the whole comedy is certainly bathed in a generally festive – albeit rather woeful – atmosphere. The rhythm of life in Duke Orsino's court is accompanied by melancholy music, suggesting mournfulness and unrequited love, while in Olivia's household the nocturnal roistering of the clown and the two old rakes, Sir Toby Belch and Sir Andrew Aguecheek, strikes a note hardly any more joyful. Without the sinister Malvolio, at whose expense there is some fun to be had, it would be a relatively gloomy scene. Here, love, festivity and Puritan-baiting have the air of diversions designed to palliate the boredom of a world grown old and grey, rather than to create a general sense of relaxation and liberation through laughter. At all events, that is certainly what is suggested by Feste's song, which brings the play to an end.

However, Twelfth Night does convey the general atmosphere of the 'misrule' that was latent during the Christmas cycle of festivities and that made it possible to turn the world upside-down.[68] That is why the themes and images connected with the idea of reversal are so important to the play. The first is Feste's image of the glove turned inside-out,[69] which perhaps provides one of the keys to this comedy. The theme of inversion here is, after all, closely connected with that of twins. For the image of the glove turned inside-out suggests that, in a period of misrule, in Illyria, the world is nothing but a hall of mirrors. With disguises and misunderstandings abetting, sexes can be swapped, as can identities (but not, except in Malvolio's wishful dreaming, social positions). This was indeed a crossroads in the year, where night won out over day and the interplay of misunderstandings brought forth a comedy of errors and metamorphoses. It was a period that was placed under the aegis of the two-headed Janus, but in this case he is, rather, an androgynous Janus who embodies the junction of two times and two sexes. The theme of an upside-down world is also illustrated, in this interval of mysterious time, by the fact that it is the women who are laying down the law. In circumstances such as these, language too is affected by the passing madness, and words are stood on their heads.

Finally—but this time it is the calendar itself that is stood on its head—we should note Olivia's exclamation at the spectacle of her steward Malvolio dressed up in his yellow stockings and intoning, with an air of complicity, words that mean not a thing to her:

> Why, this is very midsummer madness.   (III, iv, 54)

In the calendar, the Midsummer festival was situated more or less opposite Twelfth Night. This allusion to it, from the depths of the period of festivity that marked the end of the year, seems to me neither as absurd nor as contradictory as some critics have suggested, for it fits in with the logic of an upside-down world. This 'nonsense' logic, which Lewis Carroll was later to develop in the scenes of *Through the Looking-Glass* that take place on the other side of the mirror, boils down to pointing out that, however different things may look on the surface, it's all the same underneath. Festivity takes us into the realm of illusion, a land where contraries seem to keep good company: yet another illustration of the theme of the coincidence of contraries.

Anomalies and deviance

> HAMLET: ... It is a custom
> More honoured in the breach than the observance.   (I, iv, 17–18)

As we have seen, Shakespeare often makes use of the reference points of the festive calendar and the possibilities that it offers for setting up internal relationships that help to structure the representation of time or to reinforce the symbolism inherent in his plays. But we are, at the same time, bound to recognize that there is nothing particularly systematic or orthodox about the way in which he thus draws on tradition and the rites of folklore. Indeed, our analysis has not taken long to show that he was out as much to subvert as to make use of the festive codes and schedules, by muddling up the order of their appearance in the calendar.

A comedy such as *A Midsummer Night's Dream* shows how pointless it would be to expect the sum total of temporal indications to throw the slightest light upon exactly when the play is supposed to be taking place or in what kind of time. For it is placed under the sign of the most utter confusion, as we learn from Titania's long speech at the beginning of Act

II (II, i, 81–117). The festivities that provide a framework to the comedy are present from the start, at the planning stage, and they reappear at the end of the play in the form of entertainments laid on to mark the occasion of the royal wedding. A large chunk of the play thus falls in an 'in-between' time, in between a before and an after – and these are the only points of reference provided to orientate us. It is important to note that the calendar used is a lunar one, as befits the setting of ancient Greece and the framework of popular rejoicings. And it is to the moon that everyone constantly refers – the royal couple, the lovers, the fairies and the artisans alike, whether to bemoan its capricious behaviour or to determine what phase it has reached, in order to calculate the date.

Yet, at the beginning of the play, everything seems quite clear-cut. Theseus, impatient to be wed, tells Hippolyta how long there is to wait before this longed-for celebration:

> Now, fair Hippolyta, our nuptial hour
> Draws on apace. Four happy days bring in
> Another moon – but O, methinks how slow
> This old moon wanes![70]

So we are nearing the end of a lunar cycle, four days away from the new moon, which is to signal the start of the Athenian rejoicings. Meanwhile, though, the artisans tell us that the moon will be shining on the night of Theseus and Hippolyta's wedding:

BOTTOM: A calendar, a calendar–look in the almanac, find out moonshine, find out moonshine.
QUINCE: Yes, it doth shine that night.   (III, i, 48–50)

It just does not make sense. Who has got it wrong? Or is it that time is not the same for princes as for ordinary people?[71]

The only possible explanation at this stage is that Quince has got the date wrong, muddling up Midsummer with May Day, a confusion evident elsewhere in the play too, since its very title does not tally with the festive rites that Theseus mentions at the beginning of Act IV; and the misunderstanding reaches its peak in the last scene of all.[72] When Bottom and his companions give their burlesque performance of *Pyramus and Thisbe*, the moon is shining 'like a sun' – and that is totally farcical. The nonsensical position results in part from the fact that the calendar has been interpreted in two different ways, one popular (it is Midsummer), the other aristocratic (it is May Day). The situation is plunged in absurdity. It is night-time in the middle of the day, with moon and sun both shining at once.[73] Order can only be restored when official time reasserts itself and the 'iron tongue' of the clock has struck twelve. For the lovers, this will signal the start of their honeymoon. But the festival is not over yet for, as Theseus bids the whole company retire to bed, he issues a general invitation to an extra two weeks of celebrations:

> A fortnight hold we this solemnity
> In nightly revels and new jollity. (v, i, 362–3)

The festivities are diluted by being extended into time that fades away in the distance (if they began on May Day, it will be Trinity Sunday by the time they are over). It is a way of making up for their premature interruption, for Theseus has been impatient to wind the festival down so that he can be alone with his bride. Festival time clashes with lovers' time. After the confusion of the night (a period of misrule, which is called in the play 'nightrule' or 'fairy time'[74]) when all spatial and temporal markers are deliberately obliterated, the space for the festival oscillates between two poles represented by on the one hand a frenetic extension, and on the other a premature adjournment.

While the reference to dreams in the title is in itself enough to tip the misunderstandings and intrigues of the forest world into an atmosphere of unreality, the muddle over the calendary reference points and the incompletion of the festival increase still further the doubts raised in the spectator's mind. The festival itself is perceived either as a chimerical dream or as stranded somewhere between the two extremes of postponement and promise and, as such, is rejected as fantasy. It is a pure pastime in the sense that in it time passes as colours fade in the sun. In this play, it is not a matter of liberating festivity from the constraints of the winter calendar or of allowing it to develop freely in the more flexible framework of the pastoral celebrations of summer. The point is to use festivity as a means of abolishing continuous time altogether. In this respect, the festival is the exact equivalent of sleep: a non-time in which awareness of duration and existence is wiped out. When the lovers rub their eyes upon awakening, wondering, incredulously, if they are out of their minds, they are in exactly the same position as the spectators of the Masque in *The Tempest*, in which, as Prospero puts it, the actors

> like this insubstantial pageant faded,
> Leave not a rack behind.[75]

In common with *A Midsummer Night's Dream*, *The Tempest* is a play in which sleep plays an extremely important role partly because it is connected with the action of magic and spells, but also because sleep makes it possible to shake off, or at least relax, the binding grip of time—time that Prospero regulates as strictly as the conductor of an orchestra or a director in the theatre.[76] The famous speech from which the lines cited above are taken ends with an image which expands to include dreams, dramatic illusion and the whole vision of festivity, before being swallowed up in the great ocean that surrounds the fragile island of waking consciousness:

>   We are such stuff
> As dreams are made on, and our little life
> Is rounded with a sleep.   (IV, i, 156–8)

Similarly, in the last act of 2 *Henry IV*, when Prince Hal takes his dead father's place upon the throne, the first thing he does is banish Falstaff and his companions in debauchery, just as one banishes the memory of a bad dream:

> I know thee not, old man. Fall to thy prayers.
> How ill white hairs becomes a fool and jester!
> I have long dreamt of such a kind of man,
> So surfeit-swelled, so old, and so profane;
> But being awake, I do despise my dream.   (v, v, 47–51)

At last awakened to awareness of himself and his duties and seized by a desire to turn over a new leaf, the new king sees his life in a fresh light and rejects the dissipations of his mad youth, which he now considers over. He makes a clean break away from his bad habits, dismisses the sleep of festivity and vows to open his eyes to the virtues of consciousness. By so doing, he deprives himself forever of the healing balm of forgetfulness and condemns himself to the agonies of solitude and sleeplessness.[77] As Macbeth knows, once Carnival and the bloody orgies of festivity are over, the bitter, Lenten price to be paid for royalty is insomnia. A king's lot is the exact opposite to that of the common, carefree Christopher Sly in the Induction to *The Taming of the Shrew*. Surfacing from his vinous slumbers, he awakes to find himself in the lap of luxury and, on hearing that he has been asleep for fifteen years, prefers to enjoy the pleasures now offered him rather than lose them by striving uselessly to understand what on earth is happening. As he sees it, continuing to sleep on his feet is better than taking to a bed of insomniac lucidity. 'Let the world slip'!

Shakespeare's desire to shake free from convention and the constricting framework of strict reference to the unwritten laws of the festive calendar is also detectable in *The Merry Wives of Windsor*. Leslie Hotson tells us that Shakespeare was commissioned by the queen to write this comedy, to mark the celebrations for the Order of the Garter on Saint George's Day, 1597.[78] In this comedy, the allusions to these particular court festivities, which are of a historical rather than a cyclical or popular nature, are complemented by references to the rites of the spring festivals (the cycles of Lent and Easter). In one example, these festive images are used to convey the good spirits of Master Fenton:

HOST: ... he speaks holdiday, he smells April and May.[79]

The most important of these references is probably the one in Act v, where the farce in which Falstaff is made a victim seems to combine elements from both the Mummers' play and the popular May game, whose satirical features I have already mentioned. Falstaff furthermore describes himself as a 'Jack-a-Lent' (v, v, 126), the little scarecrow which symbolized Lent and was stoned and ejected on Easter Day. Yet, alongside these relatively coherent allusions to festivity, we come across others which do not really seem to allow one to reconstruct a truly coherent calendar framework.[80] When Slender asks Mr Page for news of his greyhound, 'How does your fallow greyhound, sir? I heard say he was outrun on Cotswold...' (i, i, 82–3), he is alluding to the competitive sporting events of the Cotswold Games, held on the Thursday after Whitsun. As for Falstaff's 'and there's my harvest-home' (ii, ii, 264–5), this refers us to the pastoral summer festival. Some of Shakespeare's early comedies thus already testify to his tendency to syncretism, which is even more apparent in The Winter's Tale and The Tempest. Shakespeare's method is not that of a ritualist constantly moved by a strict and literal respect for the order of the calendar customs and rejoicings that he uses to construct the backgrounds of his plays. He shows just as much interest in deviance from and exceptions to the rule, in this domain; and this enables him to upset the routines of long-established custom and draw attention to other ways in which the calendar can work and new kinds of associations within it. Yet his attitude is not purely subversive, for he also appeals to the spectator's sense of humour and critical sense and, in the last analysis, tries to produce a perspective on the festive codes as registered (with all their dates, customs and scenarios) in the collective memory. If he moves a calendar date to a different position, deliberately confuses different but analogous festive rituals or produces an anarchical profusion of calendar allusions, it is in every case the action of an artist willing to risk upsetting the conventional pattern of established custom.

Thus As You Like It, in which Shakespeare essentially takes over the pastoral conventions that opposed the freedom of the forest world to the tyranny of court life, incorporates many festive rites and games; in fact, the whole atmosphere of the comedy is a-quiver with pleasures and festivity. Yet these are not attached to any precise date or occasion. The play includes a wrestling match, disguises, a forest banquet, numerous songs and a Masque, a whole series of activities that are no more than vaguely assigned either to the 'everyday' ('working-day world') or to the 'holiday' categories.[81] But after all, the very title of this comedy is an invitation to adopt an easy-going attitude that leaves everyone free to invent his own calendar. The wrestling match of Act i is linked with the traditions of feudal chivalry and constitutes the valiant Orlando's first trial in his quest for freedom and recognition. It is a kind of popular tournament, a ritual spectacle associated with the ballads of Robin Hood, the legendary righter of wrongs of Sherwood Forest. Orlando forces Charles, the professional fighter hired by Oliver to break his neck, to bite the dust. By so doing, he is indirectly assimilated to Saint George, the dragon-slayer. This trial, introduced early on in the play, is particularly important, as it immediately presents Orlando as an athlete who can prove that his virility is no mere façade. As victor in the match that was a traditional feature of the popular Cotswold Games, or the games of Saint Bartholomew's Day, Orlando becomes the rightful champion of the festival. Later on, Orlando repeats one of the exploits of Hercules, when he slays the lioness which is about to kill his sleeping brother. And it is in the aftermath of that valorous deed that he launches himself bravely into the midst of a banquet attended by people whom he believes to be woodsmen, to ask for food for old Adam and himself. In a comical enough reversal, the forest is here made to seem a perfectly civilized place, where a sense of hospitality lives on, while the intruder who springs in from the margins of court life is made to look like a savage:

DUKE SENIOR: Sit down and feed, and welcome to our table.
ORLANDO: Speak you so gently? Pardon me, I pray you.
    I thought that all things had been savage here . . .
    If ever you have looked on better days,
    If ever been where bells have knolled to church,
    If ever sat at any good man's feast,
    If ever from your eyelids wiped a tear,
    And know what 'tis to pity, and be pitied,
    Let gentleness my strong enforcement be.
    In the which hope I blush, and hide my sword.   (II, vii, 105–19)

Even when banished from the towns, communal solidarity still flourishes in the remotest corners of the realm, and the pastoral setting here reaffirms the continuity of those values and traditions in the countryside.

The primitive world is the last refuge of civilization and liberty, even if Jaques' satirical remarks introduce a touch of doubt as to its purity. Unaffected by the measured time of towns,[82] the Forest of Arden contents itself with a series of songs to celebrate the periodic rhythms of the seasons and days.[83] We are presented with a spectacle of 'The Very Rich Hours' (*Très Riches Heures*) of the Duke Senior and his companions, who seem to divide their days of exile between hunting parties and banquets. But the tight organization of these gentlemen of the forest does not quite obliterate the traces of more primitive rituals whose age-old memory was lost in the mists of time, as can be seen from the hunters' famous 'Deer Song':

> What shall he have that killed the deer?
> His leather skin and horns to wear.
> Then sing him home ...   (*As You Like It*, IV, ii, 10–12)

The song evokes the masquerades of the Mummers who used to dress up in animal pelts and antlers for their Christmas and Easter performances. If a man donned animal skins, he identified himself in grotesque fashion with some totemic ancestor, so Shakespeare uses animals, particularly horned ones, as a pretext for introducing farce and buffoonery into his comedies. He also uses them as a focus on which to pin some of his rhetorical and metaphorical strategies.[84] The prevalence of the image of horned creatures furthermore calls to mind the Carnival period with its processions of antlered men and its charivaris.[85]

The other carnivalesque element in the play is Rosalind's disguise as a boy. Girls dressed up as boys were a common feature in Italian Carnivals,[86] but in England such disguises were to be found more generally in the theatre, particularly in Shakespeare's plays. We should, however, note an important difference between animal disguises and Rosalind's masquerading as a man, for the animal disguise is an overtly grotesque costume that fools nobody, whereas Rosalind's disguise, the very essence of the dangerous mimetism of festival-time, operates at quite a different level, leaving a trail of hearts troubled and upset. It reflects yet another aspect of the misrule that is responsible for the confusion of Phoebe, the shepherdess. Wiping out the distinctions between the sexes and the calendary reference points, in this way, produces feelings of disorientation and a state of delectable apprehension. That is why the allegorical figure of Hymen has to come on the scene in the final Masque, for he or she has the power to dispel all these ambiguities:

> Peace, ho, I bar confusion.
> 'Tis I must make conclusion
>   Of these most strange events.   (v, iv, 123–5)

Shakespeare's dramatic works thus contain a number of allusions and references to festivity which are bound to appear atypical when compared with the working system of the calendar, as described in the first part of this study. Without going so far as to consider them simply as exceptions that prove the rule, one could no doubt provide all sorts of reasons to justify their use. But it seems to me more honest to recognize that every literary creation has an irreducible element and that we may here be faced with the limits of what might in shorthand be described as the common denominator to the data provided by the facts and the mentalities involved, on the one hand, and on the other the creative freedom and artistic sense of the dramatic author.

Yet this freedom, the outer limits of which we are attempting to define, by no means implies gratuitousness or anarchy. Ulysses' famous speech in praise of tradition and order (or 'degree'), in *Troilus and Cressida* (i, iii, 74–137), should no doubt be applied to the way that the world and society work, as much as to the microcosm of art; and it would be unreasonable to suppose that the writer would contrive, even in the name of poetic licence, to be the first to break the universal rules that he describes there so eloquently. So to maintain that Shakespeare delighted in systematically muddling the markers provided by the festive calendar would be as short-sighted as to suggest that he scrupulously observes its order. For just as chaos may lurk unseen beneath the conniving cloak of darkness, encouraging confusion and unnatural alliances under the reign of some 'night rule', similarly festivity sometimes conveys an impression of pure disorder. But night gives way to day, festivity to work. The morning after, one has to wake up and resume the daily routine. The festivity in Shakespeare's plays is out of time with everyday routine but does not upset it totally. It is thus circumscribed by an overall rhythm that is expressed in the form of either contrast or succession.

Oppositions and alternations

If all the year were playing holidays,
To sport would be as tedious as to work.

(*1 Henry IV*, i, ii, 201–2)

The great value of festivity is that it ushers in a different kind of time whose limits are set in advance and which stands out against the background of everyday life. The frenzy of Carnival only makes sense in relation to the impending period of Lent and the madness of misrule is simply an inversion of normal rule. Alternation, contrast and reversal are the basic concepts that are always inseparable from the phenomenon of festivity. However, at the same time, particular festivals are inserted into particular temporal cycles and each one combines particular sets of games and entertainments, so this introduces a margin of variability which accounts for the many differences to be found from one region or period to another.

The opposition between special festival time and ordinary, everyday time is one that frequently reappears in Shakespeare's comedies, in *As You Like It* for example, where it reinforces the geographical and symbolic separation between the world of the court and the Forest of Arden:

ROSALIND: O how full of briers is this working-day world!
CELIA: They are but burs, cousin, thrown upon thee in holiday foolery.

(i, iii, 11–14)

Shakespeare seems interested not so much in the actual existence of one festival or another, but rather in preserving the co-existence of these two dimensions, which balance and complement each other. For him, any attempt to do away entirely with one, leaving the other in pride of place, is doomed to failure for it simply precipitates the return in force of whatever it was hoped to annihilate. Characters such as Falstaff and Angelo provide telling illustrations of that point. Falstaff, the apostle of permanent festivity, is pitilessly rejected by his new sovereign and dies in disappointment at not having realized his dream of turning the Boar's Head Tavern into the centre of a new Land of Cockaigne when Prince Hal acceded to the throne.[87] As for Angelo, the great Inquisitor committed to Lent and Puritanism, he is the first to contravene the rule of abstinence that he himself proclaims. If you chase Carnival out through the door, it flies back in through the window. No sooner are festivity and pleasure outlawed than they gather to haunt men's minds as if they derived new power from being proscribed. Denied free expression through festivity, fantasies get diverted into sloughs of slander, as in *Measure for Measure* where, through Lucio, they set out to besmirch the reputation of the absent Duke.

Shakespeare seems to be using absurdity to demonstrate and denounce the imposture of slander, terror or hypocrisy that masquerades as virtue, just as, at the end of *2 Henry IV* and again at the end of *The Merry Wives of Windsor*, he draws attention to the pathetic failure of Falstaff. Ribald roisterers and censorious Puritans alike are sent packing without either being proved right.

In his general concern for balance and symmetry in the calendar periods allotted to festivity and anti-festivity, Shakespeare quite frequently resorts in his plays to the two opposite aspects of private festivity that are represented by weddings and funerals. It is interesting to note that the laws of alternation and contrast operate here too but not in the same fashion as in public festivity. In the case of private festivity, the relation between the two terms in the binary opposition between wedding/burial or joyful festivity/sad festivity seems to be dictated by the internal organization of the play and the particular dramatic genre to which it belongs, rather than by some general cosmological or metaphysical view. In the world of comedy, the ceremonies for weddings and those for funerals are placed in a mutually exclusive relationship[88] that is established at the beginning or the end of the play, for the dramatic tension depends upon a seeming uncertainty as to whether the forces of youth, life, joy and marriage will prevail or whether their opposites will. In the tragedies, weddings and funerals follow more or less quickly upon one another, the effect of which is to shift or correct the atmosphere of festivity into something else. Thus in *Romeo and Juliet* the key scene where we pass from comedy to tragedy is situated at the centre of the play, at the point where the arrangements for Juliet's wedding must suddenly be converted into funeral preparations:

CAPULET: All things that we ordainèd festival
Turn from their office to black funeral.
Our instruments to melancholy bells,
Our wedding cheer to a sad burial feast,
Our solemn hymns to sullen dirges change;
Our bridal flowers serve for a buried corpse,
And all things change them to the contrary.   (IV, iv, 111–17)

When his daughter, who should have gone to bed to dream of her future husband, is discovered dead on her wedding morning, old Capulet naturally feels this to be injustice on the part of fortune, which he attempts to propitiate through the solemnity and pomp of the funeral ceremonies. In reality, this juxtaposition of the rites of marriage and those of burial is a particularly striking and effective theatrical transposition of the contiguity of the ambivalent rites of Hallowe'en, the night on which Juliet was probably conceived as she was born on 31 July. This night vigil was indeed traditionally devoted to games designed to afford girls a glimpse of their future husbands in a dream or a vision; but the following day was devoted to the cult of the dead. In terms of the internal correspondences of the festive calendar, the effect of this tragic juxtaposition, with which the child's conception was as it were stamped, is to make the private, aristocratic ceremonies confirm the underlying beliefs upon which collective popular festivity rested.

A similar notion of juxtaposing the festive rites of marriage and burial, in a shorthand form designed to focus sharply on the human condition, also inspired the work of an anonymous painter whose picture is more or less contemporary with the first performance of *Romeo and Juliet* (in about 1596). The frieze, which depicts the life and death of Sir Henry Unton,[89] is divided into two distinct sections: the one, showing daytime activities, is dominated by the sun and devoted to his life; the other, dominated by the moon, is nocturnal and funereal (see Illus. 7.1). The presence of black and white cupids in the wedding Masque of Diana and Mercury repeats in miniature the picture's general symbolism, based upon the opposition and juxtaposition of the forces of day and night, joy and melancholy. But as one takes in the composition as a whole, what is even more striking is that the long funeral procession, stretched across the entire left panel of the picture, seems to be emerging from the very same house in which the wedding festivities (Masque, torches, music and feasting) are taking place.[90] As in the passage from *Romeo and Juliet* cited above, of which this painting seems in part to be a pictorial version, the funeral seems to be a continuation of the wedding. But telescoping

7.1   *The Life and Death of Sir Henry Unton* (c. 1596), by an anonymous artist.

into one two such radically opposed ceremonies is perhaps, in the last analysis, simply a visual transposition of the rhetorical figure of speech of the oxymoron, of which this play contains many examples.

In *Hamlet*, in contrast, the hurried wedding celebrations that follow close upon the funeral are present right from the outset, like a scandal in the offing that Hamlet seeks to precipitate. Here, the juxtaposition has more than a purely rhetorical function: it sets the general tone of the whole tragedy's symbolism:

HAMLET: Thrift, thrift, Horatio. The funeral baked meats
Did coldly furnish forth the marriage tables.   (I, ii, 179–80)

Young Hamlet considers that Gertrude's hasty remarriage to Claudius desecrates the memory of his father, the dead king who, scarcely cold in his grave, is supplanted by his brother in the warm conjugal bed. As we have noted, in Elizabethan England it was the custom for fraternities of youths to punish over-hasty second marriages and those in which there was too great an age difference between husband and wife, by organizing a charivari (or Skimmington) against them. Prince Hamlet also seeks to draw attention to his mother's remarriage. First, he concentrates on using his own pallor, his black costume and his biting tongue to put the newly married couple in the wrong, then he adopts the device of the play, which gives a mirror-image of events as a means of preventing Claudius from sleeping easy.[91] For a man in Hamlet's social position, the dramatic entertainment, designed both to show up Claudius and to torture him, is the equivalent of the popular Skimmington riding with its din of clashing pots and pans. However, the punishment that Hamlet inflicts through the play is both more surreptitious and more subtle. It skilfully distils the poison of remorse and uncertainty instead of muffling it beneath a vain racket. But Hamlet is not content simply to twist the knife in the wound in this way. The bitter satisfaction of his solitary charivari is only a first stage in the process of vengeance, its purpose to prepare us for the ritual killing that we now realize to be inevitable. It is indeed the image of the wounded stag that Hamlet uses when Claudius, cut to the quick, decides to leave the hall:

> Why, let the stricken deer go weep,
>   The hart ungallèd play,
> For some must watch, while some must sleep,
>   So runs the world away.   (III, ii, 259–62)

Hamlet has seen the light. As for Claudius, he does not yet realize that the light that he calls for will now prevent him from getting a single wink of sleep at night.[92]

In the eyes of Hamlet, the wreaker of justice, all festivity, be it in the form of feasting or carousing, a funeral or a wedding, has a barbarous air. He is not disposed to be lulled by Claudius' mollifying words or by his ingratiating speech at the beginning of the play:

> Therefore our sometime sister, now our queen . . .
> Have we as 'twere with a defeated joy,
> With one auspicious and one dropping eye,
> With mirth in funeral and with dirge in marriage,
> In equal scale weighing delight and dole,
> Taken to wife . . .   (I, ii, 8–14)

For Claudius, everything is a matter of adjustment, balance and delaying tactics. Not only must reality be disguised but festivity ifself must be tricked out with fulsome speeches and carefully adjusted gestures so as to blunt its impact as much as possible. Hamlet, for his part, will tolerate none of these half-measures and contrived phrases in which the specificity of each ceremony is submerged in an amalgamation patched together just like the man whom he indeed considers to be 'a king of shreds and patches'.[93]

The juxtaposition of the two private feasts of the burial and the wedding at the beginning of *Hamlet* is thus premonitory. It hints that Claudius is merely a tragic buffoon, a Carnival Mock King or a Lord of Misrule whose reign closely resembles the interregnum of the king of the Saturnalia. Right from the outset, the festivity is interwoven with violence and its bloody outcome seems inevitable. Claudius' drunken hiccoughs already have the ring of a death-rattle and Hamlet's clowning postures suggest the mask of an avenger.

In *Othello*, it is to vent his hatred that Iago sets everything up to prevent his general from enjoying Desdemona's love. He begins by pushing Roderigo into disturbing the peace of the night to rouse her father from his bed:

> Call up her father,
> Rouse him, make after him, poison his delight,
> Proclaim him in the streets; incense her kinsmen . . .   (I, i, 67–9)

He tells him that there's a thief about and the bell should be sounded, then throws in his face the monstrous secret of the coupling of his daughter with the Moor:

> 'Swounds, sir, you're robbed. For shame, put on your gown.
> Your heart is burst, you have lost half your soul.
> Even now, now, very now, an old black ram
> Is tupping your white ewe. Arise, arise!
> Awake the snorting citizens with the bell,
> Or else the devil will make a grandsire of you.   (I, i, 86–91)

Once the alarm is sounded, Iago gives Roderigo the address of the Sagittary Inn, where the newly wedded couple have found refuge for the night, so that he and Brabantio can wrest the lovers from their bed of love and march them before the Doge of Venice. Iago thus has little difficulty in achieving his primary aim, namely to cut short his master's embraces.[94]

Later, in Cyprus, Iago employs similar tactics when he exploits the rejoicings that Othello organizes to celebrate his wedding and his bloodless victory over the Turkish fleet to provoke a fight between Cassio and Montano, the effect of which is once again to tear the general from the nuptial bed.[95] Jean-Marie Maguin points to yet a third interruption, similar to that of the first night: it occurs when, having restored order, Othello decides to tend Montano's wounds instead of returning to the arms of his young wife.[96] Pierre Janton, for his part, interprets this as a sign of Othello's sexual impotence for which he compensates by other passionate equivalents of orgasm – fits of anger or spasms of hysteria, in the scene in which he collapses in a coma.[97] An alternative hypothesis, similar to Janton's, would be to see all these interruptions as a device to heighten Othello's sexual frustration, since they prevent him from satisfying his desire in the direct and normal fashion. In the state that he is in, the barb of suspicion inserted by Iago's insinuations festers into an increasingly inflamed wound until the strangling of his still-virgin wife in the sheets of their marriage bed provides a deviated and perverse release for Othello's desire. With consummation constantly thwarted, Eros turns into Thanatos.

In my view, the connecting thread to these interruptions of marital consummation is traceable to the model of the charivari, which we noted in connection with *Hamlet*. The festive din is essentially an invasion of privacy aimed at upsetting the progress of the wedding night. In *Othello*, as in *Hamlet*, the collective traditions and rites of bachelor fraternity revels are perverted to serve a private desire for revenge which evolves in devious ways and eventually erupts into an orgy of blood. The disorder thus engendered eventually rebounds against its authors: Iago, like Hamlet, is destroyed by the very process of violence that he himself has triggered.

Shakespeare's dramatization of the theme of private festivity draws upon a combination of different patterns. We have considered a number of different relationships: the mutual exclusion of mourning and marriage in *A Midsummer Night's Dream*, the replacement of marriage by burial in *Romeo and Juliet* (and to a certain extent in *Much Ado About Nothing*), the over-hasty sequence of marriage upon funeral in *Hamlet* and the impossibility of a private consummation of marriage which leads, in *Othello*, to a double funeral. Shakespeare certainly starts out by developing the theme of tragic errors that can lead to the confusion of Eros and Thanatos, but he takes good care to elaborate his description at the level of external and social conventions, that is to say festive rites.

There is yet one more pattern that we should examine. It is to be found, essentially, in the last group of plays, which testify to a measure of uncertainty in the face of these ceremonies. The romances are indeed characterized by their underlying theme of the ambivalence of life and death and the relative lack of differentiation between the two in the festive rituals that accompany them. Thus, in *Cymbeline*, the funeral chant in which Guiderius and Arviragus bid farewell to Fidele/Imogen is reminiscent of certain nuptial songs, such as those composed by Spenser. The pagan prayer in which the two brothers join, by the corpse of their friend Fidele, runs as follows:

GUIDERIUS: No exorcisor harm thee,
ARVIRAGUS: Nor no witchcraft charm thee.
GUIDERIUS: Ghost unlaid forbear thee.
ARVIRAGUS: Nothing ill come near thee.   (IV, ii, 277–80)

This contains echoes of Spenser's *Epithalamion* in which, before passing on to the secret joys of the wedding night, the poet exorcizes the influence of evil spirits:

> Ne let housefyres, nor lightnings helplesse harmes,
> Ne let the Pouke, nor other evill sprights,
> Ne let mischivous witches with theyr charmes,
> Ne let hob Goblins, names whose sence we see not,
> Fray us with things that be not.[98]

In similar fashion, in *The Winter's Tale*, the garlands with which Perdita covers Florizel create a moment of uncertainty in the prince's mind so that, with a somewhat strained laugh, he asks the young shepherdess whether she takes him for a corpse.[99] A little later, Florizel, stung by the old shepherd's words on the subject of the dowry that he intends to give his daughter, reminds him that he happens to be the heir to the throne. He then remarks cynically that in his case marriage and wealth are directly dependent upon a burial:

FLORIZEL: ... One being dead
          I shall have more than you can dream of yet.   (IV, iv, 385–6)

In a sense, he must bury his father in order to be free to marry, a notion to which he appears to resign himself, at least in words, by making such a public allusion to his father's eventual death. It is easy to understand Polixenes' anger at finding himself thus mentally wiped out and excluded in advance from his son's wedding feast:

> Methinks a father
> Is at the nuptial of his son a guest
> That best becomes the table . . .

In Shakespeare's plays, public and popular festivity is generally evoked by being associated with the celebration of some private ceremony: the stampede of the crowd on the occasion of Elizabeth's christening in *Henry VIII* or the plans for Perdita and Florizel's wedding that are made during the shepherds' festival. That might be explained by the dramatist's humanist philosophy, which inclined him to value the individual above the family and the family above the community or city. It also no doubt has something to do with the technical constraints of the theatre in which crowd scenes were naturally more difficult to stage than those involving a smaller group of characters. It seems quite natural that, in plays as complex as Shakespeare's, private festivity should serve as a microcosm of collective and popular festivity since the latter tended to take a somewhat inflexible form, not particularly compatible with the psychological development and subtleties inherent in his plots. Private festivities offered the further advantage of eluding the preordained rhythms of the calendar and could accordingly be more easily woven into the play's own temporality. This might suggest that Shakespeare was inclined to shake off any links with popular culture, were it not for the fact that he went to considerable pains to include in his plays many allusions both to contemporary popular festive practices and also to more ancient ones. Besides, to offset his relative heterodoxy in this domain Shakespeare certainly displays a desire to retain the oppositions, counterbalances and symmetries that are a feature more of the customs related to popular time than of rigorous, precise and quantitative time. Finally, the existence of numerous variations in the pattern of relations between those two major private ceremonies, weddings and funerals, enabled him to adapt the structure of festivity to fit in with the nature of the play in hand (be it a comedy, a tragedy or a romance). He did not often allow popular festivity to erupt on to the forefront of the stage in all its raucous tumult. Often he remodelled it, deconstructing it in the interests of a dramatic transposition that demanded a certain stylization and miniaturization.

Both for technical and for aesthetic reasons, he was determined to arrive at the readjustments necessary to get two different kinds of temporality, the cyclical time of festivity and the linear time of the theatrical representation, to co-exist within the same structure. But in Shakespeare's plays the microcosm of a festival is also linked with the various spheres of Elizabethan society, reflecting their particular archaisms and contradictions and also the changes that were taking place within them.

8   Festivity and society in Shakespeare's plays

The place of popular culture and festivals

The skipping King, he ambled up and down
With shallow jesters and rash bavin wits,
Soon kindled and soon burnt, carded his state,
Mingled his royalty with cap'ring fools . . .
Grew a companion to the common streets,
Enfeoffed himself to popularity . . .   (*1 Henry IV*, iii, ii, 60–9)

Our analysis of the way in which the major moments of the festive calendar are incorporated in Shakespeare's plays has shown that, however great his debt to popular culture and festivals, Shakespeare showed no slavish respect for the exact forms of the seasonal customs. One can sometimes accuse him of deviating from these forms, on occasion with set intent.

We have already noted Shakespeare's tendency to introduce a mismatch between his dramatic representation of a festival and its calendary reality (by altering either date or customs). Also noticeable is his reluctance to portray popular festivity in any way other than as under the control of the aristocracy.[1] Furthermore, either for practical staging reasons or for generally dramatic ones, his plays contain more scenes of private than of public festivity. It is important that we should try to understand the reasons for an attitude which, while not quite implying a desire to reject or repress popular festivals in the strict sense of the expression, nevertheless does lead to a certain marginalization of them.[2]

Let us take as the starting point for our analysis the extract from *1 Henry IV* which serves as epigraph to this discussion. The king is teaching Prince Hal a lesson, citing the bad example set by Richard II ('the skipping King'), whom he himself supplanted on the throne. Henry IV's chief reproach where Richard is concerned is about his dependence upon popularity ('Enfeoffed himself to popularity').[3] Henry, for his part, has retained both his rank and his dignity. His rejection of all forms of flattery coming from the populace is conveyed by his declaration that it is better for a king to make few public appearances and to display a loftiness, albeit unmarked by scorn, towards lowly or mediocre amusements of a popular nature.[4] Coming from a king, such sentiments are certainly not surprising. But in all probability Shakespeare identified

244

himself personally with these views, for in his plays he generally looks with disfavour upon anything that smacks of demagogy.

The plays do, however, contain quite a few scenes in which kings, princes and other great personages try to mingle with the people. It is true that they only do so secretly, in disguise or masked, under cover of night. For Antony, these nocturnal outings are clearly a form of amusement, for he addresses Cleopatra as follows:

> There's not a minute of our lives should stretch
> Without some pleasure now. What sport tonight? . . .
> No messenger but thine; and all alone
> Tonight we'll wander through the streets and note
> The qualities of people. Come, my queen.
> Last night you did desire it.   (*Antony and Cleopatra*, I, i, 48–57)

What Antony hankers after is probably not so much the dangerous and equivocal pleasure of degrading himself, but simply the delight of mingling with the crowd in search of the popular warmth that he remembers from his plebeian youth. This aspect of his character makes him sympathetic and at the same time vulnerable, for his escapades are risks that a man of iron such as Octavius would never take. It is clear to us from the start that, quite apart from the spell that Cleopatra has cast over him and from which he tries to shake free, Antony's taste for festivity and popular jollity and his crazy generosity are also factors that will contribute to his downfall. To govern empires, men of quite a different stamp are needed.

Polixenes, the king of Bohemia, is also prepared to disguise himself as a shepherd, this time in order to attend a pastoral festival. But, unlike Antony, he does not do this for pleasure. His disguise is purely tactical, for he seeks to discover the secret of his son's frequent visits to the old shepherd's hut. As for Florizel, he too certainly sins against his rank, but his excuse is the noble pretext of love and the conventions of the pastoral which dictate that any shepherdess who is loved by a prince must be a princess without knowing it. Finally, in the case of Prince Hal, who decides to make himself up as a tapster to play a trick on Falstaff, he does so for a mixture of motives that include both pleasure and politics:

PRINCE HARRY :   How might we see Falstaff bestow himself tonight in his true colours, and not ourselves be seen?

POINS: Put on two leathern jerkins and aprons, and wait upon him at his table as drawers.

PRINCE HARRY: From a God to a bull – a heavy declension – it was Jove's case. From a prince to a prentice – a low transformation – that shall be mine; for in everything the purpose must weigh with the folly . . .

(*2 Henry IV*, II, ii, 169–76)

As in the ancient Saturnalia, social roles are swapped and the master waits upon his servant. This social metamorphosis[5] is immediately translated into sparkling verbal repartee in which the word-play reflects the role-playing to which Hal is prepared to submit himself. The paronymic association between the words 'prince' and 'prentice' establishes a connection between two social positions which were situated at two extremes of the hierarchy of the period, yet belonged to the same youthful age-group. And, after all, Hal is at this point still serving his apprenticeship for his future profession as king. The term 'apprentice' in this context furthermore puts one in mind of the masquerades of youthful groups and the extremely active role played in London by schoolchildren and apprentices on Shrove Tuesday and May Day. All this suggests that popular festivity was the context in which different social groups could come together, even if the illusion of contact between them was short-lived.

Such an illusion was only possible when kings and princes dressed up as shepherds or tapsters, thereby effacing all marks of their rank. In exchange, and still in conformity with the logic of the world turned upside-down that governs most festive rites, the shepherdess must also become queen for a day, as the drunken tinker must be elevated to the rank of a lord so that the mechanism operates in both directions, upwards as well as downwards. But when Bottom, afflicted with the head of an ass, finds himself in the loving embrace of the queen of the fairies, the situation goes over the top and becomes grotesque. That counter-example is a clear indication that these reversals of fortune, which come about as a result of the games and whims of the festive lottery, are no more than dreams from which one must awake the following day. None of the characters whose position is miraculously transformed in the madness of the festival or through some enchanter's spell can believe the state will last. Bottom is literally spellbound; Perdita protests with charming modesty that Florizel does her too much honour and, despite his reassurances, continues to resist all illusions; while Christopher Sly makes the most of the chance for good living, preferring to remain in ignorance as to what the morrow will bring. In contrast, those such as Malvolio and the Falstaff of *The Merry Wives of Windsor*, who are ambitious or fools, are set on their pedestals only to be promptly toppled and exposed to general derision. Sly and Bottom find themselves suddenly raised to heights to which they would never have dreamed of presuming but are later returned to their former condition as if emerging from a sleep, while Malvolio and Falstaff are both caught out trying to realize their secret dreams. Most people would be mortally wounded at finding themselves publicly exposed with their deepest desires laid bare. But these two characters appear – admittedly to different degrees –

imperturbable to the enlightenment of self-awareness and self-knowledge. Here the festivity has a satirical and anti-utopian function. Not only does it not fuel the egalitarian or vengeful dreams of the populace, but it also provides a means of chastising those who are naive enough to be led into inflated ambition or desire.

Meanwhile, when conquered or laid low by a reversal of fortune, the great should beware of falling into the hands of the populace for the latter will not hesitate to lampoon or trample underfoot the mighty that are fallen, doing so with all the greater aggression and spite since it has always been denied the safety-valve of ambition. Thus when Cleopatra describes to Iras the fate in store for them both if they agree to take part in Octavius Caesar's triumph in Rome, she is under no illusions whatsoever:

CLEOPATRA: Now, Iras, what think'st thou?
              Thou, an Egyptian puppet shall be shown
              In Rome, as well as I. Mechanic slaves
              With greasy aprons, rules, and hammers shall
              Uplift us to the view. In their thick breaths,
              Rank of gross diet, shall we be enclouded,
              And forced to drink their vapour.
IRAS: The gods forbid!
CLEOPATRA: Nay, 'tis most certain, Iras. Saucy lictors
              Will catch at us like strumpets, and scald rhymers
              Ballad us out o' tune. The quick comedians
              Extemporally will stage us, and present
              Our Alexandrian revels. Antony
              Shall be brought drunken forth, and I shall see
              Some squeaking Cleopatra boy my greatness
              I' th' posture of a whore . . .   (*Antony and Cleopatra*, v, ii, 203–17)

This passage is even more striking when set alongside Enobarbus' famous speech in Act II (II, ii, 197–25), to which it forms a perfect foil. The latter depicts Cleopatra as Summer Queen floating down the river Cydnus surrounded by Cupids and Nereids in a refined and sensuous Eastern setting. In contrast, the lines in Act v conjure up a picture of her made the butt of the obscene sallies of the Roman plebs, engulfed in a stream of fetid effluvia and rancid breath.[6] For the first scene, Shakespeare draws closely upon Plutarch, but the second owes him virtually nothing, since it simply picks up one sentence in Thomas North's translation, in which Octavius Caesar explains why he wants to capture Cleopatra alive.[7]

This picture of the Roman populace probably owes much to Shakespeare's observation of the Elizabethan crowds in London. So much is strongly suggested by the allusions to the theatre and its burlesque costumes. It is worth noting, in this respect, that Cleopatra rightly fears that her liaison with Antony would be caricatured by the demeaning spectacle of a drunkard in the arms of a whore.[8] This scenario was no doubt precisely that of some jig, a burlesque and satirical interlude which was an extremely popular feature of the Elizabethan stage.

We should, assuredly, not take this unflattering picture of the populace absolutely literally, for it is painted by a haughty queen who scorns the vulgar masses. On the other hand, Shakespeare may well have been making use of the context of ancient Rome and Egypt, so distant both in time and space, to slip in a few home truths. Remembering the maddened crowd storming the doors of the royal palace at the news of Princess Elizabeth's christening in Henry VIII, one might see in these caustic portraits of the people the hand of a writer visibly exasperated by the crowd's destructive excesses, of which the London apprentices' raids on the theatres on Shrove Tuesdays were but one example.

When it is not presented in a comic light, as in the case of the porter in Macbeth and the engaging, if clumsy, artisans in A Midsummer Night's Dream, the populace of Shakespeare's world does have a somewhat alarming air. Popular characters often appear as monsters or wild men, be they Bottom with his ass's head or Caliban, a hybrid who might turn out to be fish just as easily as flesh.[9] They are clearly creatures of the world of the grotesque and the antimasque, the products of an aesthetic dominated by the fantastic, and this seems to reflect an anxiety and discordance that is also detectable in the styles of Baroque and Mannerist paintings.[10] It is a matter not so much of aversion pure and simple, but rather of a somewhat ambivalent feeling towards the popular strata, a feeling that is expressed in the way that they are presented in two antithetical guises – either as ridiculous or as terrifying.[11] This kind of burlesque fear is exactly what pervades our reactions to Thersites, the common Greek army soldier in Troilus and Cressida. A loud-mouthed braggart and a cynic if ever there was one, he is the very incarnation of the popular version of Rumour and a parody of the Chorus of ancient tragedy. He sees not a scrap of nobility in the actions that he witnesses or is detailed to perform, but invariably denigrates and criticizes everything. As a man with a constant grouse, he is a totally negative spirit, an instrument of the disorder whose effects are described in Ulysses' famous speech on 'degree'. Such rejections of all authority and hierarchy and such permanent dispositions towards revolt are dangerously inclined to explode into violence and chaos. The fact is that festivity, quite apart from its popular aspects, also tends to abolish differences through rites of inversion and the transgression of customary prohibitions, and Shakespeare refuses to take an unqualifiedly sanguine view of it. He realistically shows that festivity often ends in wronged or discontented people taking to the streets in demonstrations that constantly threaten to trigger a social explosion.

Festivity and revolt

YORK: ... In Ireland have I seen this stubborn Cade
Oppose himself against a troop of kerns,
And fought so long till that his thighs with darts
Were almost like a sharp-quilled porcupine;
And in the end, being rescued, I have seen
Him caper upright like a wild Morisco,
Shaking the bloody darts as he his bells.

(2 *Henry VI*, III, i, 360–6)

In the examples that we have studied above, the popular figures in Shakespeare's dramatic oeuvre are presented as a collective Janus with two faces. One is a mixture of slightly bawdy coarseness and resigned bashfulness that makes them adopt a docile and relatively acquiescent attitude towards the princes who govern them. The other, more disturbing, shows the blind and destructive irreverence of an angered mob. In the revolt led by Jack Cade, to which Shakespeare devotes the major part of Act IV in 2 *Henry VI*, the two faces merge together and we are confronted with the full force of the phenomenon of ambivalence. For this bloody revolt of the craftsmen of Kent also has something of the festival about it and is presented as a veritable popular carnival.

True, the revolt is not entirely spontaneous, for it is instigated by Richard Plantagenet, the Duke of York, who is trying to topple Henry VI. Once again, the populace seems to be manipulated by the aristocracy. But with those reservations these scenes of insurrection truly do seem to be the ones in which Shakespeare came the closest to popular mentalities and folklore. It is worth noting that he certainly does not follow Hall's chronicle in his presentation of this episode, for Hall described 'the subtill capitayn named Jack Cade' as a cool-headed leader, 'prohibityng to all men, Murder, Rape or Robbery ... '.[12]

According to Bullough, the source for the atmosphere of grotesque comedy and the frankly popular tone of the revolt depicted by Shakespeare is to be found in Holinshed's and Grafton's accounts of the Peasants' Revolt of 1381 and the claims put forward by Wat Tyler and Jack Straw. But what Bullough describes as 'farcical extravagancies' seem to me to stem from a popular culture and popular fantasies which were always much stimulated and much needed at times of festivity and/or revolt.[13] The promise of fabulous abundance proffered by the festival is overlain by the old utopian dreams of emancipation and communal ownership.[14]

The general tone of these scenes is set in the passage from Act III, cited as the epigraph to this analysis, in which York uses a double comparison to convey the idea that Cade is a devil of a man and one with a vigour quite out of the common run. The two images of the 'sharp-quilled porcupine' and the 'wild Morisco' combine to suggest a heraldic device or emblem which helps the spectator to form an immediate mental image on the basis of what he is told. At the same time, they have a premonitory function, for they represent indispensable keys to any understanding of the scenes of rebellion in Act IV. For example, the vehemence with which Cade shakes the arrows embedded in his thighs is clearly but a foretaste of the energy which he will subsequently devote to shaking off the shackles of popular slavery. Furthermore, these same darts with which his legs are bristling, through the analogy drawn between them and the porcupine quills, assume an overtly phallic meaning which looks forward to the popular leader's loudly proclaimed sexual demands.[15] He was, for instance, to claim for himself the rights of *jus primae noctis* and licence to take his pleasure with other men's wives whenever he wished (*2 Henry VI*, IV, vii, 118–21).

The second image that York uses to characterize Cade is that of a Morris dancer. It introduces an analogy between the animal quills, the arrows lodged in the soldier's flesh and the strings of little bells tied round the dancers' knees and ankles, which jingled so frenetically during the summer festivals. By establishing these correspondences between martial frenzy and the feverish unleashing of popular energies at festival time, Shakespeare reminds us of the close links that initially existed between the Morris dance and the Sword dance, for the jingling of the bells only gradually became distinguishable from the clash of steel in the Sword dance.[16] Emmanuel Le Roy Ladurie tells us that the brawls which led up to the Carnival in Romans in 1580 involved groups of dancers 'with bells on their feet and drawn swords'[17] – providing yet another example of the connections between bells and swords. Similarly, in *2 Henry VI*, Act IV, scene ii, which to some extent serves as a prologue to the revolt, the two actors, George Bevis and John Holland, brandish their wooden swords at each other:

BEVIS: Come and get thee a sword, though made of a lath ...   (IV, ii, 1–2)

These grotesque carnival warriors signal the start of the popular uprising and what is here presented as a heroic-cum-comic version of class warfare:

HOLLAND: Well, I say it was never merry world in England since gentlemen came up.
BEVIS: O, miserable age! Virtue is not regarded in handicraftsmen.

HOLLAND: The nobility think scorn to go in leather aprons.
BEVIS: Nay more, the King's Council are no good workmen.[18]

According to Le Roy Ladurie, in carnivalesque folklore the function of the Sword dance was to put 'an end to the activities of an evil landlord who would terrorize peasants or rape their daughters'.[19] The social and economic emancipation connected with the class struggle is inseparable from the defence of sexual integrity, as Jack Cade reminds his followers after they have cried 'God save the King', upon Clifford's bidding (2 *Henry VI*, IV, vii, 181–5).

The sword seems to have been marked by the same ambivalence as Shakespeare's popular characters: as an instrument of emancipation and insurrection against the authority of the nobility, it is alarming; symbolically whirled around to proclaim the time for carnivalesque revenge and sexual aggression, it is simply comical.

The birth of class revolt among the craftsmen of Kent mustering beneath Jack Cade's burlesque banner seems to herald the province of the Land of Cockaigne. The speeches of the popular leader, who produces a quite fantastical genealogy in support of his insistent claims to the throne occupied by Henry VI, seem inspired by the vein of parodic eloquence that a Lord of Misrule would favour during the Christmas festival, or that would be used by the leader of the vandal apprentices looking for trouble in London on Shrove Tuesday. At this juncture, Cade truly is 'a king of shreds and patches', a Carnival king whose reign ushers in the era of a world set upside-down.[20] He starts off by turning the prices of food and drink upside-down, promising that every dozen shall be thirteen and that he will introduce a wonderful system of prices and measures:

There shall be in England seven halfpenny loaves sold for a penny, the three-hooped pot shall have ten hoops, and I will make it felony to drink small beer.   (IV, ii, 67–9)

And while he is about it, he goes on to decree, striking the London Stone as he does so, that wine shall flow from the fountains throughout the first year of his reign:

And, here sitting upon London Stone, I charge and command that, of the city's cost, the Pissing Conduit run nothing but claret wine this first year of our reign.

From start to finish of his coronation year, the people will be bidden to uninterrupted feasting in a capital that will once more be a drinker's paradise.[21]

Not content with this showy announcement of an era of great drinking and feasting for all, Jack Cade also promises to ease the rigours of fasting and abstinence half-way through Lent, by granting the guild of butchers liberal dispensation to slaughter animals (IV, iii, 6–7). His liberality does not quite extend to establishing a purely carnival kingdom, since the period of Lent is in principle retained, but it does open up the way for more festivity at the expense of the forces of austerity. It is perhaps not altogether irrelevant that Jack Cade himself belonged to the fraternity of drapers and carders, for the Feast of Saint Blaise, the patron saint of this guild, happens precisely to coincide with the earliest date for Carnival, namely 3 February.[22]

For all that he is marked with the seal of carnival and preaches of a licence that is the corollary of permanent festivity Jack Cade is also full of political claims. The popular myth of a Land of Cockaigne lives happily alongside the notion of some communist utopia in which goods and women become common property, as the prophets of revolution announce:

All the realm shall be in common, and in Cheapside shall my palfrey go to grass . . . there shall be no money. All shall eat and drink on my score, and I will apparel them all in one livery that they may agree like brothers, and worship me their lord.
(IV, ii, 70–7)

The notion of founding his own despotism upon a levelling uniformity might indeed evoke the idea of communism were it not for the fact that Jack Cade then flies into a veritable iconoclastic fury against the written word, in which he demands that books be burned and copyists hanged (IV, ii, 78–109). Further on, his diatribe against 'Lord Say' accuses him of having corrupted youth by encouraging education and books.[23]

It might seem tempting to present such an attitude as the revenge of the oral tradition against what might have been regarded as the oppression of written culture, a preserve of the élites. However, the very exaggeration of the scene gives it a grotesque air.[24] It is also interesting that, in the scenes showing Caliban's revolt against Prospero, the first thing that Caliban asks of his new masters, Stephano and Trinculo, is precisely that Prospero's books be seized and burned.[25] The analogy between Jack Cade's revolt and Caliban's goes further. In both cases wine is the Bacchic yeast for a revolt that turns into a dance, either a Morris dance or one performed to the rhythm of a libertarian song beaten out by an invisible musician.[26] On the other hand, while it is hunger that in the end gets the better of Jack Cade's valour (2 Henry IV, IV, ix, 60), it is drunkenness as much as Ariel's mischievous magic that plunges these ridiculous cavorters, rebelling against the tyranny of the enchanter, into the island's bogs, where they are soon hunted down by a pack of hounds (The Tempest, IV, i, 255–9).

This analysis of the connections between festivity and revolt would not be complete without a short look at the scenes depicting the insurrection of the London apprentices which appear in the anonymous play entitled

Sir Thomas More, part of the *Shakespeare Apocrypha*. They are inspired by the historic events of 1 May 1517 (better known as 'Black' or 'Ill May Day'). Detailed critical examination of the part of the manuscript (about one hundred lines) authenticates that these scenes are indeed from the hand of Shakespeare.[27] The scene of the gathering of apprentices, among whom we find a clown, has the burlesque yet frightening ring of Jack Cade's revolt. As in *2 Henry VI*, the popular revolt occurs in festival time. The only difference, really, is that on this occasion the explosion of discontent is sparked off, not by the class struggle, but by xenophobia (foreign merchants being blamed for the high cost of living and the general economic difficulties of the moment).

As these examples show, popular revolt would sometimes erupt on the occasion of a festival or would take on the general air of one and, in the hands of a determined organizer, it could make use of festival rites and customs to give form to demands, half absurd, half serious, for the establishment of a Land of Cockaigne and a carnivalesque 'order', the abolition of all existing laws and all forms of bookish knowledge and for women to be made common property. When that happened, the festival took on what must surely be called a subversive aspect (even if this was partly cancelled out by the comic-grotesque nature of most such scenes), for its end result was to stir up the lower strata of society against their masters.

For it is by no means certain that everyone knew his place and was content to keep to it, even in the vision of a relatively traditional world such as the one that emerges from Shakespeare's plays. It may be true that festivity aimed to promote only playful subversion and that usually it operated as a safety valve for the release of popular energies and demands. But at the same time it certainly did produce an upside-down world whose strictly playful or metaphysical meaning might well be lost on minds of a sour disposition. What would happen if Christopher Sly, after laughing at the spectacle of Kate's taming by Petruccio, refused to climb down and return to his humble market stall? Faced with so much bad faith, the Lord of the Induction scenes might feel that the joke had gone far enough and fail to manifest such a sense of fair play as Sly does. Clearly, the question of power relations cannot altogether be sidestepped when it comes to popular festivity and it is to Shakespeare's lasting credit that he at least sketched in the problem, even if, like most of his contemporaries, he continued to believe that the notion of such an enormity was cause more for laughter than for tears.

Direct conflict between the popular strata and the aristocracy as Shakespeare presents it in the scenes of Jack Cade's revolt, in the ambiguous form of a bloody Carnival, is not really typical of Elizabethan theatre. A far more frequent theme is that of an alliance formed between the people and the nobility on the occasion of a festival or amusements directed against the common enemy, the Puritans. Puritans, who were the declared adversaries of the theatre, festivals and all Sunday sports and other popular games, clashed with both the aristocracy – the leisured class by definition – and also the common people, who were much attached to their traditional jollifications. Likewise, actors and dramatists generally tended not to miss a chance to poke fun at them as sententious and arrogant kill-joys. Such scenes are extremely common in the theatre of the period from 1600 to 1642, as W.P. Holden has shown.[28] Shakespeare and Ben Jonson, for their part, produced anti-Puritan attacks that are far subtler and more complex than such attacks were to become in the years that followed.

In Shakespeare's plays, apart from Malvolio and perhaps Angelo, Puritans are seldom presented as such. Instead, the antagonisms between many of his various characters can be better understood as a struggle between Carnival and Lent, in which the supporters and the adversaries of festivity are brought face to face.

The supporters and the adversaries of festivity in Shakespeare's plays

MARIA: Marry, sir, sometimes he is a kind of puritan.
SIR ANDREW: O, if I thought that I'd beat him like a dog!
(*Twelfth Night*, II, iii, 135–6)

To provide a religious or socio-economic definition of the Puritan in pre-revolutionary England is not my intention. Rather, I will try to seize upon him as a type of character from Shakespeare's dramas who plays, on the Elizabethan stage, a role similar to that of Tartuffe in the world of Molière. However, the various faces of Puritanism are not limited to hypocrisy, be it social, sexual or religious. They also betray a secret ambition and thirst for revenge against the society of the well-off, and these make the Puritans intolerant of all amusements, which they accuse of encouraging an easy-going attitude, prodigality and immorality. Their uncontrollable yearning for social advancement and power, which could not be openly avowed, was driven to find perverse expression in megalomania, moroseness and a phobia of distractions of all kinds: noise, music, singing, bursts of raised voices, festivals. Puritans consequently often present a suspicious, embittered and self-satisfied air which immediately makes them a prime target for rejoicing merrymakers on the look-out for an 'Aunt Sally'. In this particular instance, festivity, far from being a means of liberation, is instead directed towards punishing those who refuse to remain in their place: disorder is used to restore order.

However, even if the festival participants are unquestionably more sympathetic than the Puritans in Shakespeare's plays, they do not always get the last word and some come to quite a pitiful end. These prodigal sons, debauchees, funsters turned tricksters and faded old revellers are in many cases good for nothing except to cock a snook at the grimaces of disapproval that they attract. The supporters of festivity and the Puritans complement even as they oppose one another. If you listen carefully to the clamour of the merry roisterers, you can detect a contradictory echo of the embittered, snooty tones of their critics:

CLOWN: She hath made me four-and-twenty nosegays for the shearers – three-man song-men, all, and very good ones – but they are most of them means and basses, but one puritan amongst them, and he sings psalms to hornpipes...[29]

Frustrated in their impotence to prohibit the roisterers' drinking songs, the Puritans do their best to put an abrupt halt to them, just as in *Twelfth Night* the steward Malvolio interrupts the nocturnal carousing of Sir Toby and Sir Andrew:

My masters, are you mad? Or what are you? Have you no wit, manners nor honesty, but to gabble like tinkers at this time of night? Do ye make an alehouse of my lady's house, that ye squeak out your coziers' catches without any mitigation or remorse of voice? Is there no respect of place, persons, nor time in you?   (II, iii, 83–9)

In his reprimand, Malvolio attempts a role-reversal, identifying his masters with the riff-raff of the tavern. He uses his authority as the defender of his mistress, Olivia, and the shield of his virtue to wreak his vengeance upon people whose social position he envies yet whose behaviour he despises. But Sir Toby will not put up with this and tartly puts Malvolio in his place:

Art any more than a steward? Dost thou think because thou art virtuous there shall be no more cakes and ale?   (II, iii, 109–11)

Sir Toby Belch, presiding in this scene over the festivities of Epiphany and using carnivalesque language to pour scorn upon the vanity and pretensions of the steward, is certainly the equivalent of a Lord of Misrule.[30] Maria, Countess Olivia's maid, makes even less bones about it in the savage picture that she paints of Malvolio for she regards him as a paragon of self-satisfied stupidity, servile and obsequious towards Olivia and disdainful towards everyone else:

The dev'l a puritan that he is, or anything constantly but a time-pleaser, an affectioned ass that cons state without book and utters it by great swathes; the best persuaded of himself, so crammed, as he thinks, with excellencies, that it is his grounds of faith that all that look on him love him.   (II, iii, 141–6)

But Maria, who is always prepared to speak her mind, is equally ready to berate the two nightbirds, telling Sir Toby bluntly 'that quaffing and drinking will undo you' (II, iii, 13). The nostalgic exchanges between the two buffoons are not of a kind to make the spectator indulgent towards them:

SIR ANDREW: . . . I would I had bestowed that time in the tongues that I have in fencing, dancing, and bear-baiting. O, had I but followed the arts! . . . I am a fellow o'th' strangest mind i'th' world. I delight in masques and revels sometimes altogether.
SIR TOBY: Wherefore are these things hid? . . . Why dost thou not go to church in a galliard, and come home in a coranto? My very walk should be a jig.   (I, iii, 89–124)

The spectacle of these idle figures, harking back to their giddy youth and the antics of yesteryear, is almost as depressing as that of the reminiscences of Shallow and Falstaff at the end of *2 Henry IV*:

SIR JOHN: We have heard the chimes at midnight, Master Shallow.
SHALLOW: That we have, that we have; in faith, Sir John, we have. Our watchword was 'Hem boys!'. Come, let's to dinner; come let's to dinner. Jesus, the days that we have seen! Come, come. (III, ii, 211–16)

Festivity, like Shallow's virtually senile babbling, seems doomed to sterile, boring repetition. The veteran champions of festivity have become the pensioners of pleasure. The Puritans may be odious and malicious, but the old merrymakers are plain ridiculous.

In *The Merchant of Venice*, we can detect in the figure of Shylock a kind of amalgamation of the typical Jewish moneylender and the Puritan whose keen desire for profit had become proverbial in the Elizabethan period. Like the Puritan, Shylock is alarmed by festivals. The mad dissipation is an affront to his own austere religion, his manic, almost grotesque avarice and his taste for a private life strictly protected from external intrusions.[31] As soon as he hears rumours of masking and merrymaking, he hastens to give his daughter Jessica lengthy advice as to her behaviour in his absence:

SHYLOCK: What, are there masques? Hear you me, Jessica,
Lock up my doors; and when you hear the drum
And the vile squealing of the wry-necked fife,
Clamber not you up to the casements then,
Nor thrust your head into the public street
To gaze on Christian fools with varnished faces,
But stop my house's ears – I mean my casements.
Let not the sound of shallow fopp'ry enter
My sober house. By Jacob's staff I swear
I have no mind of feasting forth tonight.   (II, v, 28–37)

Shylock the miser bids his daughter see that all his doors are double-locked. Just as Portia is symbolically locked within a lead casket by her father's orders until such time as a Prince Charming appears to release her, similarly Jessica is imprisoned in a house that resembles a safe. The very name Shy-*lock* semantically reinforces the theme of locking up and imprisonment in this play. In opposition to the figures who represent the locking-up (Portia's father, as much as Shylock), the forces of friendship, love and festivity are invested with the power to force those locks. In the case of Portia, who helps Bassanio, her suitor's opening of the right casket takes place to the accompaniment of music and singing. For Jessica, liberation from her father's house involves a break-in to the more insistent beat of the pipe and tabor.

The disguised figures, really Bassanio, Lorenzo and Gratiano, who stand in opposition to Shylock, are in truth hardly more impressive than he, even if they appear to be cast in a more sympathetic role: they are all prodigals who have been living it up and now seek a rich marriage as a means of restoring their fortunes. When Bassanio describes Portia to his friend Antonio, he sets her wealth above her beauty and then makes use of a mythological parallel which provides the key to his plan:

> her sunny locks
> Hang on her temples like a golden fleece,
> Which makes her seat of Belmont Colchis' strand,
> And many Jasons come in quest of her.   (I, i, 169–72)

In sixteenth-century Venice, the voyage of this latter-day Argonaut looks very much like that of a dowry-hunter. As for Lorenzo, who masterminds the nocturnal masquerade beneath the windows of Shylock's house, he exploits festivity as a love ploy that will enable him to make off with Jessica, whom he loves all the more for not forgetting to 'gild' herself with her usurer-father's ducats, as she makes her escape.[32] The festival is far from being simply an occasion for collective and disinterested celebration. Instead, it serves to disguise what is, in effect, both an erotic and a financial theft. Gratiano, who comments cynically upon the whole operation, suggests that the charm of the festival is likely to be soon dispelled, the money soon spent, the brilliant trappings of love soon in shreds:

> How like a younker or a prodigal
> The scarfèd barque puts from her native bay,
> Hugged and embracèd by the strumpet wind!
> How like the prodigal doth she return,
> With over-weathered ribs and raggèd sails,
> Lean, rent, and beggared by the strumpet wind!   (II, vi, 14–19)

It is significant that the operations involved in these conquests of love should be described as more or less fabulous sea-voyages, for this makes the point that in Venice everything revolves around gold and trade. Love and festivity are both circumscribed by economics. They beat to the rhythm of trade and their success too depends upon the return of ships laden with riches and merchandise. The keys to the situation are thus held by characters who are not concerned in the intrigue of love and festivity, namely the merchant and the moneylender, Antonio and Shylock. And once Antonio's somewhat foolish generosity to Bassanio has forced him into the camp of the supporters of festivity, thereby placing him in a very dangerous position, everything in the end turns out to depend upon Shylock. Not the least of the ironies of this comedy, nor the least of Shylock's humiliations, is the fact that it should be precisely this puritanical figure who, at the end of the trial, finds himself obliged to finance the prodigality of a festive Venice, with no foreseeable return on his outlay. The punishment for usury and the chastisement of the Jew who used his money as an instrument first of coercion then of revenge against the Christians appears to involve the triumph of gilded, dissipated youth. Yet this comedy does not directly align itself on the side of the Christians and the supporters of festivity, for the alarming power that Shylock suddenly assumes constitutes as sharp a warning to prodigals as does the lesson in fidelity that the wives teach their flighty husbands at the end of the play. Whether the Jew wins the day or their wives walk out on them, either way for them would spell total bankruptcy and an interminable Lenten life.

Measure for Measure begins where *The Merchant of Venice* leaves off, for the accession to power of the Puritan Angelo immediately tolls the death-knell for festivity.[33] On the pretext of setting the world to rights again and re-establishing the letter of a law no longer respected in Vienna, the Duke decides to withdraw temporarily from the management of the city's affairs (I, iii, 19–31). The partisans of festivity (here caricatured as the proprietors of a brothel) immediately interpret the plan to re-establish order as a decided return of Lent. Just as on Shrove Tuesday, in London, the apprentices gave the signal for the beginning of the period of abstinence by sacking the city brothels, Pompey here tells Mistress Overdone, the go-between, that 'All houses in the suburbs of Vienna must be plucked down' (I, ii, 87–8). This notion that Angelo's reign heralds an abrupt end to a long period of festivity is promptly confirmed by Claudio, a gentleman from Vienna.

Politics simply set an official seal upon the pendulum-like rhythms of festive time, in which periods of fasting and restriction alternate with moments of over-eating and waste. Instead of indulging in the licence that used to prevail, now it is necessary to do penance and repress one's desires. Everybody finds his pleasures reduced by this law and Mistress Overdone suffers from a loss of clientèle (she is 'custom-shrunk': I, ii,

82). However, there is an important difference between the cyclical time of festivity and the linear time of history. In cyclical time, Lent rules only for a period whose limits are set in advance and known, whereas nobody knows for certain how long the new law will be able to enforce its rigours without leading to popular disturbances. The function in the play of grotesque characters such as Pompey and Lucio is precisely to act as the obdurate spokesmen for the baser, corporeal side of a life of appetites of all kinds, appetites that they do not for a moment consider it possible to quell. Pompey fights Escalus every inch of the way to defend the legitimacy of his trade, the oldest in the world, which, he maintains, no caprice of the law will ever manage to abolish:

ESCALUS: How would you live, Pompey? By being a bawd? What do you think of the trade, Pompey? Is it a lawful trade?
POMPEY: If the law would allow it, sir.
ESCALUS: But the law will not allow it, Pompey; nor it shall not be allowed in Vienna.
POMPEY: Does your worship mean to geld and splay all the youth of the city?
(II, i, 214−21)

Popular realism and common sense are, it seems, as tenacious as facts themselves and, despite the austere behaviour prescribed by the law, they cling to the belief that only a nation of eunuchs and geldings could tolerate the suppression of all desire and festivity. Lucio's criticisms to the Duke about Angelo's excessive severity manifest a similar scepticism:

LUCIO: A little more lenity to lechery would do no harm in him . . .
DUKE: It is too general a vice, and severity must cure it.
LUCIO: Yes, in good sooth, the vice is of a great kindred, it is well allied. But it is impossible to extirp it quite, friar, till eating and drinking be put down.   (III, i, 363−8)

These two replies, reminiscent of Sir Toby's and Feste's responses to Malvolio's carping remonstrations in *Twelfth Night*,[34] are reinforced in *Measure for Measure* by the slips of the tongue made by the representative of law and order who comes to arrest the malefactors:

ELBOW: If it please your honour, I am the poor Duke's constable, and my name is Elbow. I do lean upon justice, sir; and do bring in here before your honour two notorious benefactors.
ANGELO: Benefactors? Well! What benefactors are they? Are they not malefactors?
ELBOW: If it please your honour, I know not well what they are; but precise villains they are, that I am sure of, and void of all profanation in the world that good Christians ought to have.   (II, i, 45−54)

It may be hard to make head or tail of Elbow's words, but indirectly what they appear to imply is that human nature's lot is to sin and fall. A good

Christian is aware of that, while a wicked Puritan ('a precise villain') pretends not to be. Whoever presumes to be an angel is liable to become a beast.[35] And this Angelo would indeed be a monster were he not well known to be the first to seek to transgress the law that he imposes upon others. That is what makes him human still – a fact which supports the claims of the advocates of the 'baser instincts' which it seems to be no easy matter to banish. On the other hand, this does not put the latter in the right, for it is also known that by favouring intemperance they have made themselves responsible for spreading diseases which erode the bones and bring on baldness:

LUCIO: ... I have purchased as many diseases under her roof as come to –
SECOND GENTLEMAN: To what, I pray?
LUCIO: Judge.
SECOND GENTLEMAN: To three thousand dolours a year.
FIRST GENTLEMAN: Ay, and more.
LUCIO: A French crown more ... thy bones are hollow, impiety has made a
         feast of thee.   (I, ii, 43–55)

The pun on 'dolours', meaning both 'dolors' (or pains) and 'dollars' (European currency of this period) suggests that libertinage and the frequenting of Mistress Overdone's establishment result not only in a man being bled of his money but also in physical ailments generally considered shameful and here indicated by their conventional symptoms: loss of hair was indeed caused by the treatment for syphilis, known in England as 'the French disease', and, in Lucio's last rejoinder, the word 'feast' suggests the kind of burning infection that consumed one internally. The idea that it would make sense to try to put a stop to the ravages caused by festivity was just beginning to catch on at this point while the subsequent takeover by Puritan extremism was to bring back a nostalgia for the tolerance of the old days. Caught between, on the one hand, the spectacle of degenerate beings sapped by the pox and the abuses of high living and, on the other, the terror imposed by hypocritical rulers, the spectator is prompted to favour a middle way. The libertines and the Puritans, each group trying to impose its own style of life upon the other and both forgetting the need for alternation, emerge from this play as enemy brothers.

The very same lesson is purveyed by *Timon of Athens*. In this play, the two extremes of festivity and anti-festivity are opposed not as two clashing models of society or two enemy camps, but as two sides to the life of a single individual. Timon is the most generously profligate of revellers but, once ruined, he becomes the most misanthropic of Puritans. Prodigal turns preacher. Timon starts out by practising a boundless generosity, hoping that his friends will later repay him in the same coin.

He adopts a position that is at once beyond the merchant society in which he lives and, at the same time, falls short of it as Richard Marienstras has perceived when he writes that 'Timon . . . practises a system of gift and counter-gift, through buying and selling . . .'[36].

In the days of his splendour, Timon refuses to pay the slightest attention to the warnings of those seeking to make him see his folly, whether it be Apemantus (I, ii, 235–8), the cynic philosopher, or his own steward Flavius:

> 'Heavens', have I said, 'the bounty of this lord!
> How many prodigal bits have slaves and peasants
> This night englutted! Who is not Timon's?
> What heart, head, sword, force, means, but is Lord Timon's?
> Great Timon, noble, worthy, royal Timon!
> Ah, when the means are gone that buy this praise,
> The breath is gone whereof this praise is made.
> Feast won, fast lost; one cloud of winter show'rs,
> These flies are couched.'   (II, ii, 161–9)

The expression 'feast won, fast lost' is admirably apposite, for with perfect concision it encapsulates the two poles of Timon's life and the two terms of the antithesis upon which the play is constructed: the blind expansiveness of festivity as opposed to the lucid malediction of anti-festivity and desolation. When the ingratitude of the parasites who have indulged themselves at his orgies is revealed, Timon understands the harsh truth and renounces festivity and all social life forever:

> Therefore be abhorred
> All feasts, societies, and throngs of men.   (IV, iii, 20–1)

Too late: now only hell awaits him, a hell paved with the very gold that he has squandered without counting the cost.

Lear, like Timon, is a prodigal-turned-preacher. Having assured himself (verbally) of the love of his daughters, he proceeds to divide his kingdom, possessions and wealth among them with the idea of thereafter living with each of them in turn, as recipient of their boundless gratitude. He too lives according to the logic of gift and counter-gift and is convinced that if he voluntarily abdicates his power in their favour, his generosity will be returned to him a hundredfold. Like Timon, however, he runs up against a wall of ingratitude when his daughter Goneril slams the door of hospitality in his face (*King Lear*, I, iv, 215–51).

Freed of his kingly duties, Lear imagined that he would be able to live a life of festivity, feasting and junketing amid his peers and friends. But now his noisy parties are held against him and he finds his daughter reading him a lesson in morals. The world has been turned upside-down.

In reality, what is at work is ingratitude under the mask of Puritanism, as Lear well realizes. He storms out, refusing to heed Goneril's suggestion that he should reduce the numbers in his train (I, iv, 225–30). It is a subject to which Goneril subsequently returns, thereby immediately driving her father into a fury (II, ii, 435–7).

But Lear knows that if he complies with such a deal he will soon be stripped bare and left entirely at the mercy of his daughter's good will. He will no longer have a home to call his own – he, who has given everything and is, in return, held to petty account. He refuses even to discuss the matter of what is and what is not superfluous to his needs. The superfluous is his badge of rank, more necessary to him than necessities. Denied his power to spend and even to waste, he would be deprived of an essential part of his royalty. As a prodigal father, he lives in the belief that his noble blood entails the obligation to adopt a showy life-style incorporating feasts, generosity and waste, rather than the obligations that go hand in hand with any relationship of dominator to dominated, or master to servant. In the end, his inflexible attitude leads to madness in which, like Timon, he flings curses at the heedless winds and waste land. Like Antonio, the merchant of Venice, he has gambled away his fortune and delivered himself, trussed hand and foot, into the power of those whom he took for creditors, only to find them executioners. And Cordelia is no Portia, so there is no last-minute salvation for Lear. He must learn the bitter lesson of self-discovery, far from his former flatterers and the festivities which blinded him to self-knowledge. That is the only gift he will ever receive from his ungrateful daughters Goneril and Regan.

We have considered a number of examples: Timon's bitter misanthropy, Lear's madness, the fall of Antony and Cleopatra before the icy efficiency of Octavius, and Falstaff's expulsion once his erstwhile companion in debauchery becomes King of England. All of them seem to convey a similar message. In each case, we witness the fall of those who believed in the value of the festive system and lived by its rules of hospitality, conviviality, gift and counter-gift, generosity and respect for community traditions. Now, all the plays in which these characters appear portray a historical or political situation based upon a contradiction between on the one hand the old order, whose institutional and economic foundations have collapsed, albeit leaving behind them an ideology and set of values that live on and, on the other, a new society in which those who are taking over the positions of authority no longer understand or will no longer tolerate the beliefs and customs of the *ancien régime*. Such, in broad terms, was the position of England between 1600 and 1640. In this situation, Shakespeare uses ancient or medieval history or old legends in order to elaborate models that fuel his own and his contemporaries' thoughts. Falstaff, Mark Antony, Lear and

Timon can each, at his own level, be seen as a Don Quixote defending festivity, as a champion, laughable or sublime as the case may be, of what seems to be useless. For after shamefully exploiting their generosity, goodness and *joie de vivre*, the guests at the feast turn a deaf ear when their turn comes round to foot the bill. That is a misunderstanding that leads to tragedy. Whoever is made the victim of non-reciprocity is bound to come to a bad end.

At this point, the question that arises is: who is responsible for these disasters? To say with Sartre that 'hell is other people' resolves nothing; and it is impossible to lay everything at the door of the 'wicked' Puritans or merchants who block the system by refusing to play the game.[37] So the examples that we have considered would appear to present us with a situation in which it looks very much as if festivity and the values on which it rests are being brought to trial. The fact is that festivity seems to produce the improvidence, prodigality and blindness that propel individuals towards their downfall. The context provided by a network of communal obligations might, in fact, suggest that 'salvation is other people' and that, as a result, it is not indispensable for each individual to take responsibility for his own destiny. But Shakespeare's dramatic works promote above all the idea of self-knowledge rather than any particular mode of behaviour recommended within some ritualized system. To that extent, we may well wonder whether Shakespeare does not intend to cast a certain doubt upon the question of festivity and all its heroes. In the tragedies, after all, festivity was to unleash the forces of chaos and anti-nature. Here Shakespeare would convey the themes of inversion and disorder, in images of violence.

9 Festivity and its images in Shakespeare's plays

The disorders of love

Liking will not be long a dooing; and love that followes is but little, whereby he brings no great harme; but al the mischieefe comes with desire, which swelles the affections, and predominates over love and liking; he makes the misrule, and keeps the open Christmas; he desires the sporte, and maintaines the pastime, so that, though he be long in comming, and staies but little in his Lordship, yet the remembrance of his jolitie is not forgotten a long time after.[1]

In this passage from an anonymous work called *The Passionate Morrice* (1593), desire, assimilated to festivity, is presented as the great troublemaker. He is a king of confusion and disorder who stirs up a great to-do, unlikely to be soon forgotten. Moreover festival time is, *par excellence*, the time for permutations among loving couples and switches of partners, for all such changes are encouraged by the equivocation of carnival masks and the atmosphere of freedom which prevails when the prohibitions and constraints of ordinary life are lifted.

In Shakespeare's plays, as in the upside-down festival world characterized by all the ambiguities and metamorphoses of desire, it was the women who skilfully orchestrated the interchanges in the dance of affinities and passions and, by means of impersonations and acrobatic costume changes, eventually managed to restore the world to rights at the same time as ensuring their own personal well-being. When the pitch of confusion is at its height and everything is upside-down, Rosalind, Viola and Portia all find ways of rectifying the situation and getting what they want. They are past-mistresses in the art of luring on desire only to divert it back to the one forsaken. But *in extremis*, they are confronted with the realization that desire cannot be satisfied unless they themselves undertake to stand in for the male sex. In *As You Like It* and *Twelfth Night*, Phoebe and Olivia, confounded by their mistake of having fallen in love with a woman, are obliged to settle, respectively, for the love of Silvius and Sebastian.[2] In Shakespeare's comedies, the business of seduction frequently involves a third party. So much would seem to be suggested by the mystery of the three caskets of the palace of Belmont in *The Merchant of Venice*. However, things never go irrevocably wrong since those disqualified turn out to be either fools such as Sir Andrew Aguecheek, or kill-joys such as Malvolio.[3]

264

But tragedy is not far away in *Much Ado About Nothing*, where the intrigues of a trickster reshuffle the cards and thereby impede the switch-over from a symbolic triangle to the formation of a real couple. In Messina, all the love affairs proceed thanks to the intervention and good offices of a third party. Thus Don Pedro suggests taking Claudio's place in the wooing of Hero, by passing himself off as Claudio, at Leonato's masked ball:

> DON PEDRO: I know we shall have revelling tonight.
> I will assume thy part in some disguise,
> And tell fair Hero I am Claudio.
> And in her bosom I'll unclasp my heart
> And take her hearing prisoner with the force
> And strong encounter of my amorous tale.   (I, i, 303–8)

It is all supposed to be good fun, even if the involuntary use of an obscene *double entendre* (amorous tale/tail) betrays a secret proclivity to rape, which is quite at odds with the surface proprieties.[4] But Claudio's irresponsibility in entrusting his wooing to another is certainly disconcerting; and Don Pedro's bastard brother, Don John, who is the villain of the play, makes use of that to get his personal revenge (I, iii, 60–4).

It only takes Borachio to adopt Don Pedro's strategy in reverse (replacing, not the suitor but his partner, by arranging for Margaret unwittingly to take the place of Hero) for Claudio's little game to rebound against him, with possibly tragic results. It is true that Hero herself is later party to a similar subterfuge designed to catch out her cousin Beatrice in her love for Benedick, but she is acting in a good cause and only does so in order to get the better of the somewhat masochistic cynicism with which Beatrice protects herself. And besides, she was not the one who started all this. The whole trouble began with the masked ball and the deception that Claudio allowed. The very name of Borachio, derived from the Spanish *borracho* (drunkard), evokes the dangerous intoxication of festivity. Now all that he needs to do is exploit this opening and persevere with his labour of destruction. In the ensuing torrent of misunderstandings which it appears impossible to stem, it seems to be innocence that is the victim and has to pay the price for all this dangerous sport. This is one of Shakespeare's comedies which show just how great the ravages caused by festivity can sometimes be. The superficial gaiety of the moment is no more than a mask that conceals forces of destruction, and if you play with fire, it is quite likely to flare up in earnest, reducing everything to ashes.

The farce of *The Merry Wives of Windsor* also concerns triangular games of desire and seduction. Here Falstaff takes it into his head to win the hearts of both Mistress Ford and Mistress Page. However, in this context the bigamous plan is never taken seriously for it is presented as a manoeuvre inspired more by greed than by lechery. Besides, the two 'merry wives' quickly regain the upper hand and skilfully manipulate Falstaff's schemes in such a way as to have some fun themselves, as well as to teach the male sex a lesson. Each of them sets out to correct in the one case the excessive trust, in the other the morbid jealousy of her husband, at the same time inflicting upon Falstaff, whose overweening arrogance astounds them, a series of comical punishments which reach their apotheosis in the final May game. These comical punishments that Falstaff undergoes at the hands of the 'merry wives'[5] are described as a 'Skimmington' by Anne Parten.[6] Christiane Gallenca, in 'Ritual and Folk-Customs in *The Merry Wives of Windsor*', an article which appeared at the same time as Anne Parten's, pursues the analysis of the images in the play in rather more detail and shows that the English version of the charivari known as 'riding the stang' is a variant to which Shakespeare also alludes in this comedy.[7] The 'merry wives' themselves do not escape scot-free, for in the series of games in which the tricksters are tricked, they are in their turn beaten at their own game, when Master Fenton carries off young Anne Page under the noses of the imbeciles whom the wives had in mind for her. If three-cornered love affairs are essentially the stuff of comedy, they nevertheless do not exclude the possibility of tragic developments. The comic note certainly predominates to begin with when Falstaff, sporting his antlers, expands upon the mythological precedents to his metamorphosis and compares himself to a 'rutting stag':

When gods have hot backs, what shall poor men do? For me, I am here a Windsor stag, and the fattest, I think, i' th' forest. Send me a cool rut-time, Jove, or who could blame me to piss my tallow?   (v, v, 11–14)

Having thus become a lustful deer, Falstaff in advance justifies the lapses of conduct that he hopes he is about to commit, with references to pagan antiquity and the beast whose antlers he bears on his head.[8] He makes the most of this opportunity to indulge rapturously in a flood of sexual fantasies in which aphrodisiacs rain down from heaven, following which he emerges, like some primitive man or savage, at the peak of his virility:

SIR JOHN: My doe with the black scut! Let the sky rain potatoes, let it thunder to the tune of 'Greensleeves', hail kissing-comfits, and snow eringoes; let there come a tempest of provocation, I will shelter me here . . . Divide me like a bribed buck, each a haunch . . . Am I a woodman, ha? Speak I like Herne the hunter?   (v, v, 18–26)

This passage, the theatrical effects of which are bound to intensify the atmosphere of farce and grotesque comedy, is, without doubt, one of the funniest in the play. But, from another point of view, the image of the deer which Falstaff is supposed to embody also strikes a somewhat sinister note. When Falstaff likens himself to Jupiter, he forgets that in order to seduce Pasiphae and to carry off Europa, the god took the form of a white bull, that is to say a holy, sacred animal, whereas a deer first and foremost suggests a beast pursued by a pack of hounds and hunters. The blast of bugles and horns that sounds immediately after the arrival of Mistress Ford and Mistress Page has the effect of presenting Falstaff's punishment as a scene of tally-ho leading up to a kill: the stag at bay, about to be slaughtered, quarry to be flung to the dogs. Having first likened himself to the legendary figure of Herne the Hunter, Falstaff proceeds to identify himself with the mythological Actaeon, the hunter hunted down and devoured by his own hounds after Diana had changed him into a deer.[9] We should not forget that Actaeon's horrible death was his punishment for a transgression both sexual and religious – sexual voyeurism and spying on the female mysteries of the cult of Diana.[10] Shakespeare's grotesque version of the myth of Actaeon here operates as a comic de-metaphorization of the image used at the beginning of *Twelfth Night* by Duke Orsino, to express the agonies of love that he is suffering:

> O when mine eyes did see Olivia first
> Methought she purged the air of pestilence;
> That instant was I turned into a hart,
> And my desires, like fell and cruel hounds,
> E'er since pursue me.   (I, i, 18–22)

In this final scene, Falstaff plays the role of a 'scape-deer', abandoned to the mercies of the fairies and elves by whom he is cornered. Beneath the farce, there clearly lie primitive myths associated with the notions of sacrifice, courage and metamorphosis. The dynamic of the images is intended to reveal 'the accursed side' of festivity in which what Jeanne Addison Roberts calls 'the "innocent" revenge of its night-wandering spirits' in truth masks a scene of ritual sacrifice or sacred lynching.[11]

The torment of Tantalus

The thoughtlessness of festival behaviour, when love becomes a game, thus on occasion lies at the root of deep ravages whose consequences may not be immediately apparent. But festivity itself is also sometimes used as an instrument of torment. It is worth remembering that, in the Elizabethan period, capital executions often took on a festive, popular air, with crowds thronging to watch the execution of criminals or traitors. The elements of sadism and unconscious anthropophagy inherent in these occasions were deliberately fostered by the authorities.

Before tackling the theme of the festival as massacre in Shakespeare's plays, let us analyse its euphemistic formulation in which festivity is used as a lure, a means of taming and a punishment. Such are the tactics employed by Petruccio in *The Taming of the Shrew*. His method is to blow first hot, then cold, allowing his young wife a glimpse of fabulous festivity in order to whet her appetite, then offering her, instead of feasting, nothing but fasting and sleeplessness. Thus, following the burlesque celebration of their marriage, the tables are set up and the company is preparing to enjoy the festivities when Petruccio takes his wife by the hand and announces:

> Go to the feast, revel and domineer,
> Carouse full measure to her maidenhead.
> Be mad and merry, or go hang yourselves.
> But for my bonny Kate, she must with me.   (III, iii, 96–9)

Later, upon their arrival home after an exhausting journey, Petruccio sends the meat back to the kitchen, declaring it to be burnt, and drags away Kate, who is starving, concluding this non-meal with words suitable for the period of Lent: 'And for this night we'll fast for company' (IV, i, 163)

Like a falcon, tamed by being deprived of food, Kate is literally exhausted by the hellish regimen to which Petruccio subjects her and she ends up by complying with the demands of her lord and master. Before the astonished guests, she eventually produces an excellent performance as a meek and docile wife. In this play, festivity and anti-festivity, which Petruccio cynically exploits in the taming of Kate, are essentially reduced to instruments of repression designed to impose normality upon the behaviour of one judged to be deviant.

But the transformation of a festival into a Tantalus-like torment is a tactic not only used to force submission from an adversary (a wife, in this case) in the war between the sexes. It can also be a daunting instrument of revenge. In *Timon of Athens*, Timon the prodigal, the patron of festivity, the Trimalchio of a city mad with desire for gold, has the idea of using this stratagem against the town senators and parasites of all kinds who have enjoyed and abused his hospitality, to give them a taste of a cold dish of vengeance. All the feasts that he has given without counting the cost and opening his doors to all comers are suddenly forgotten by his friends when it is his turn to call upon their generosity.[12] This absence of respect for the unwritten law of reciprocal obligation which is, after all, one of the foundations upon which this oligarchic society rests, makes Timon turn to misanthropy. Before retiring to become a hermit in the wilds, he determines to set the seal on his break with this purulent society by summoning his friends to one last great feast:

TIMON: Each man to his stool with that spur as he would to the lip of his
mistress. Your diet shall be in all places alike. Make not a city feast of it,
to let the meat cool ere we can agree upon the first place. Sit, sit. The
gods require our thanks ... Uncover, dogs, and lap.
The dishes are uncovered and seen to be full of warm water [and stones].
May you a better feast never behold,
You knot of mouth-friends. Smoke and lukewarm water
Is your perfection. This is Timon's last,
Who, stuck and spangled with your flattery,
Washes it off, and sprinkles in your faces
Your reeking villainy.   (III, vii, 65–8 and 87–92)

This is the festive world turned upside-down. In this avenger's furious
Saturnalia, the lure of festivity masks pitilessly Lenten fare. It looks like
an inverted Cana wedding-feast, where the festival wine is turned into
warm water to be thrown in the faces of the guests. The feast, hitherto
supposed to be a sanctuary of conviviality and a sacred refuge from
which envy and violence were banned, is now accursed and likened to a
gathering of rogues and thieves:

TIMON: ... Henceforth be no feast
Whereat a villain's not a welcome guest.   (III, vii, 101–2)

Having thus deliberately violated the laws of festivity and converted
them into a punishment for the ingratitude of his fellows, Timon exiles
himself from the city, subsisting on curses and hatred:

Piety and fear,
Religion to the gods, peace, justice, truth,
Domestic awe, night-rest, and neighbourhood,
Instruction, manners, mysteries, and trades,
Degrees, observances, customs, and laws,
Decline to your confounding contraries,
And let confusion live!   (IV, i, 15–21)

In *The Tempest*, Prospero, the avenger, resorts to magic in preparing
for his enemies a punishment similar to that devised by Timon. After
allowing the lost, shipwrecked band to wander for a while, he conjures
up before their spell-bound eyes the mirage of a magical table spread for
a banquet:

ALONSO: What harmony is this? My good friends, hark.
GONZALO: Marvellous sweet music!
*Enter Spirits, in several strange shapes, bringing in a table and a banquet, and
dance about it with gentle actions of salutations, and, inviting the King and his
companions to eat, they depart ... Thunder and lightning. Ariel [descends] like a
harpy, claps his wings upon the table, and, with a quaint device, the banquet
vanishes.*   (III, iii, 19–20 and after l. 52)

Here, the festival is a phantom designed to punish the wicked, first appearing, then vanishing before their eyes. Through Prospero's magic wand, the enchanted island becomes a purgatory for vice, in which illusions and fantasies, dispelled on the point of being realized, torture the inhabitants of a realm of illusion and will-o'-the-wisps. The purpose of the disappearing banquet is to convert the pangs of hunger into pangs of conscience. The effect of this travesty of a feast is thus exactly the reverse of the alluring attractions of festivity in which fantasies of satiety lead to the dissolution of self-awareness and the effacement of the barriers of self-consciousness.

Macbeth, in contrast, shows a ghost, conjured up by the criminal's guilt, bringing a banquet to a halt. The sight of the dead man's empty seat produces in Macbeth's guilty mind a series of hallucinations which Lady Macbeth dismisses as a symptom of superstitious, childish fears, worthy only of the old wives' tales told on long winter evenings (III, iv, 62–5). Here, the spectre at the feast is Death, intruding upon the brotherly conviviality of the living. The guilty king is cut off from his people and can no longer take part in the communal meal: hence his self-excommunication.[13] Deprived of festivity, as he is of sleep, Macbeth is now denied both rest and relaxation. He is committed to the hell of anti-nature, the perversions of witchcraft and bloody tyranny.

Festivity as massacre

Once it has been cut off from its roots and has forfeited popular approval, festivity is doomed to become an instrument of torment, an occasion of sacrifice, even an abettor of the forces of evil. In these circumstances, the delirium of festivity goes beyond the mere destruction of objects, in the form of property and wealth, and the frenzied consumption of food, and leads on to the unleashing of violence and massacre.

So it is, for example, with the bonfires of Saint George's Day to which the Duke of Bedford looks forward as a feature of a triumphant war against the French, in *1 Henry VI*:

> Bonfires in France forthwith I am to make,
> To keep our great Saint George's feast withal.   (I, i, 153–4)

It is an allusion that warns of atrocity later in the play, when it becomes clear that Joan of Arc, called a witch by the English, is to be burned alive, a mere five weeks after Saint George's Day (29 May, 1431). The covert ambivalence of this festive image reveals the distant horror, beyond the bonfires lit to celebrate patriotic fervour and martial glory: the girl-saint to be martyred as a living torch. Similarly, when René suggests celebrating the recapture of Orléans and the Maid's victory, the nocturnal rejoicing is again to be lit by bonfires:

> Why ring not out the bells aloud throughout the town?
> Dauphin, command the citizens make bonfires
> And feast and banquet in the open streets
> To celebrate the joy that God hath given us.   (I, viii, 11–14)

The Dauphin's response to this suggestion is also significant. Having recognized the victory to be due to Joan of Arc as much as to the French troops, he speaks already of erecting a monument to her after her death:

> A statelier pyramid to her I'll rear
> Than Rhodope's of Memphis ever was.
> In memory of her, when she is dead
> Her ashes, in an urn more precious
> Than the rich-jewelled coffer of Darius,
> Transported shall be at high festivals
> Before the kings and queens of France.
> No longer on Saint Denis will we cry,
> But Joan la Pucelle shall be France's saint.   (I, viii, 21–9)

The allusion to 'ashes' provides sinister confirmation of the hidden meaning of that word 'bonfire', used at the beginning of the play, for it refers us to the aftermath of the burning of Joan of Arc. We are bound to recognize that the Dauphin's foresight, which envisages the remains of a girl of nineteen as a future relic, is somewhat startling. It seems to guarantee in advance that the Burgundians and the English will connive to send the Maid to the stake for the crime of witchcraft and that, once the victim has been sacrificed, they will try to make terms. As in the case of Jack Cade's revolt evoked in 2 Henry VI, we are bound to recognize the premonitory force of images which establish a connection between festivity and massacre.

A similar ambivalence characterizes the images which associate elements of festivity with instruments of torture in Lear's allusion to the 'wheel of fire', when he is reunited with Cordelia:

> LEAR: Thou art a soul in bliss, but I am bound
> Upon a wheel of fire, that mine own tears
> Do scald like molten lead.   (King Lear, IV, vi, 39–41)

Lear is here referring to the torment of the damned in hell (Ixion on his wheel, as much as the punishments envisaged in medieval legends and the Apocrypha of the New Testament).[14] However, unlike the image of the bonfires mentioned above, this one is also connected with the rites of celebration that attended the coming of the summer solstice, on Midsummer's Eve.[15] In similar fashion, when he appears symbolically crowned with flowers betokening both his madness and also his conversion into a Mock King, Lear again evokes the carnivalesque figure of the *homo sylvarum* decked out in greenery and foliage, who would make a ritual appearance in the Midsummer pageants. As John Holloway correctly remarks, 'He is a Jack-a-Green, at once hero and victim of a popular ceremony . . .'.[16]

At this point, it is interesting to note the concomitance specifically indicated in the stage directions ('*Enter Lear, mad, crowned with weeds and flowers*') between the eruption of madness and the wearing of plant emblems. In popular spectacles such as pageants, Jacks-in-the-green and woodwoses would frighten and amuse the crowds by simulating madness and brandishing blazing torches. Similarly, on an Elizabethan stage, the arrival of Lear thus transformed would operate immediately as a visual reference to the connection between madness and festivity.

In the eyes of the Elizabethans, such a return to the state of nature, symbolized by the floral insignia with which Lear is crowned, would in all probability be regarded as the very epitome of madness. On the other hand, a wild, massive invasion of the forces of vegetation such as takes place at the end of *Macbeth* would be interpreted as the natural order taking its revenge against a tyrant's perverted reign. As John Holloway puts it, 'the coming of Birnam Wood to Dunsinane is a dumbshow of nature overturning anti-nature at the climax of the play . . .'.[17] This critic goes on to interpret the coming of Birnam Wood, foretold by the 'weird sisters', as the equivalent of 'a Maying procession, celebrating the triumph of new life over the sere and yellow leaf of winter'.[18] Seen in this perspective Macbeth takes on the air of a Lord of Misrule, draped in clothes too large for him, which make him look a fool. The triumph of festivity of a primitive kind undoubtedly signals cruelty and sacrifice. Nevertheless, in the case of *Macbeth*, the killing of the tyrant represents a defeat for black magic and bloody oppression, so that here festivity in the end resumes its liberating function as a life-affirming force.

Another form of sacrifice connected with the popular May Day festivals may be indirectly perceived underlying the pathetic words that Cleopatra pronounces when she is told of Antony's death:

> O, see, my women,
> The crown o'th' earth doth melt. My lord!
> O, withered is the garland of the war.
> The soldier's pole is fall'n. Young boys and girls
> Are level now with men.[19]

It is furthermore clear, through the phallic symbolism of these pagan emblems of fertility, that Antony's fall is also interpreted as a castration. This emerges discreetly from that final image:

Young boys and girls
Are *level* now with men ...

Once the supreme representative of the virility of days gone by has been laid low, the world is bereft of those glorious erections, the people deprived of its festive insurrections and life as a whole is reduced to a children's game. Cleopatra, who for her part has little taste for a cut-down version of life, chooses to return to her ancestors with the help of the obscene yet exquisite bite of a snake which she presses to her bosom, thereby identifying herself with the medieval image of *Voluptas*, in the final ecstasy of her death-throes.

The cannibal banquet

In its tragic version, festivity produces devastating effects in Shakespeare's dramatic world. The banquet in which one eats covertly evokes a banquet in which one might be eaten.

It is an image that is applied first and foremost to Death, the great devourer, feasting on the human flesh of the world's battlefields. In *King John*, the Bastard waxes ironical on the cost of those fine military victories whose carnage provides rich pickings for Death, which is represented as a monster gnawing away at the corpses of soldiers and kings:

> O, now doth Death line his dead chaps with steel;
> The swords of soldiers are his teeth, his fangs;
> And now he feasts, mousing the flesh of men
> In undetermined differences of kings.   (II, i, 352–5)

This allegory of cannibal Death gives a new slant and intensity to the old commonplace drawn from the Christian notion of death as a great leveller. Death is presented as the eater of flesh gorging at the battle banquet, the great mother of all scavengers.[20]

Alongside this medieval theme of a carnival of the dead, Shakespeare's plays contain a whole collection of images in which the hearty eating of festival time is associated with a cannibal feast. Thus, in *Timon of Athens*, the cynical Apemantus employs a striking image to make his master see that he is allowing himself to be devoured alive by the crowd of parasites who throng every day to his house:

> O you gods, what a number of men eats Timon, and he sees 'em not! It grieves me to see so many dip their meat in one man's blood; and all the madness is, he cheers them up, too!   (I, ii, 38–41)

Here again, the hyperbolic effect of the metaphor makes the theme of the loss of substance and dilapidation produced by festivity particularly arresting.

In *The Merchant of Venice*, Antonio's extraordinary pledge for a loan of three thousand ducats from Shylock makes us realize that this pound of flesh is no mere image. It is true that, for Shylock, money is not simply base inert metal for, as he explains to Antonio through the parable of the sheep of Laban, taken from the Book of Genesis, it too is endowed with the power to reproduce itself:

ANTONIO: Was this inserted to make interest good,
            Or is your gold and silver ewes and rams?
SHYLOCK: I cannot tell. I make it breed as fast.   (I, iii, 93–5)

In the minds of Shakespeare's contemporaries, usury and fornication were two closely associated activities.[21] If money is a living element with the same powers of reproduction as human beings, one can see why Shylock, who in his dealings with Gentiles abides by the Draconian principle of 'an eye for eye, a tooth for a tooth' interpreted literally, is willing to exchange his ducats only for human flesh. His demand stems not so much from a perverted whim but from a terrifying logic. The moneylending Jew is assimilated to a bloodthirsty ogre. Admittedly, Shylock calls the pledge that he is demanding a 'merry bond', (I, iii, 172), but, as is hinted by the word-play on 'kindness' (which can suggest 'payment in kind'), the joke is a macabre one in as bad taste as the cry of the populace at the time of the Carnival at Romans, the little French town near Grenoble in Dauphiné studied by Emmanuel le Roy Ladurie:

The popular faction was so rebellious, Guérin added . . . , that some of them, intending to mock the price list of provisions . . . , continued to cry as formerly [on St Blaise's Day, 3 February]:
    Flesh of Christians, four deniers the pound![22]

Le Roy Ladurie's comments on this passage from the diary of Judge Guérin of Romans are most illuminating:

Once more the theme of cannibalism surfaces . . . Of course, it was nothing but a joke, if a sick one, based on fantasies of eating human flesh. Romans's citizens certainly would not have eaten the liver of some patrician they had just slaughtered. Likewise the 'blood drinkers' of the French Revolution were with few exceptions only metaphorical.[23]

In this counter-Carnival of the poor, exploding into frightening and blasphemous cries, the price set on 'one pound of Christian flesh' is considerably lower than Shylock's evaluation! But the episode certainly constitutes an example of the convergence between popular fantasies, as expressed in festival time, and the deep imaginary preoccupations which resurface in drama of popular inspiration.

In Shakespeare's plays, the theme of the cannibal banquet is, clearly, conveyed in the most direct fashion in *Titus Andronicus*, in the strange menu prepared for the masterpiece of revenge that is represented by the feast organized for the Empress Tamora. In the whole Shakespearian canon, this is the only example of an avenger's massacre-festival, for which the model – frequently imitated by Jacobean and Caroline dramatists – is the ending of Kyd's *Spanish Tragedy* (1587). Titus is bent on avenging the atrocities to which his daughter Lavinia has been subjected by the sons of the Queen of the Goths, who first raped then horribly mutilated her. He captures the violaters, Chiron and Demetrius, executes them, then serves them up in a great pie made from human flesh. When Tamora, his guest at the feast, has eaten liberally of the dish, Titus reveals its secret recipe:

> Why, there they [Chiron and Demetrius] are, both bakèd in this pie,
> Whereof their mother *daintily* hath fed,
> Eating the flesh that she herself hath bred.
>
> (v, iii, 59–61; italics mine)

Quite apart from the macabre refinement in cruelty involved here, the consumption of these helpings of human flesh in a pie represents the transgression of a triple taboo. The first, clearly, is cannibalism; the second and third are indicated by the use of the word 'daintily'. 'Dainty' was also a term currently employed to refer to the testicles, which suggests that two other major taboos have also been transgressed – those of castration and incest, for Tamora has taken in and consumed her own sons' reproductive organs.[24] Born from their mother's body, they re-enter it through a different orifice.[25] Barbarity on this scale produces a 'Grand Guignol' effect. It is so horrific that the excessive cruelty takes on an air of parody. That is no doubt one reason why Shakespeare never returned to the theme of festival as massacre except in a euphemistic and veiled form.

Hamlet is perhaps the tragedy in which these images of cannibal banqueting are the most systematically and carefully reworked. An early example of this 're-metaphorization' is to be found in the exchange between Hamlet and Horatio, at the beginning of the play, in which Hamlet, with pitiless ferocity, denounces his mother's hasty remarriage to his uncle:

HORATIO: My lord, I came to see your father's funeral.
HAMLET: I prithee do not mock me, fellow-student;
      I think it was to see my mother's wedding.
HORATIO: Indeed, my lord, it followed hard upon.
HAMLET: Thrift, thrift, Horatio. The funeral baked meats
      Did coldly furnish forth the marriage tables.   (I, ii, 175–80)

The synecdoche ('meats' for 'feast') operates as a striking shorthand which leads one to conjure up a picture of a funeral march being literally overtaken by the wedding procession. Scarcely was King Hamlet cold in his grave than Gertrude made for the warmth of his brother's bed. The successive meals follow equally hard upon one another, but the menus are reversed: the steaming dishes cooked for the funeral feast are served up cold for the wedding breakfast.[26] If we bear in mind the meaning of 'to cool off' and 'cold meat' in the popular vernacular, it does not take much to see the wedding feast as an avatar of the cannibal banquet in which the king/father, sacrificed by the primitive horde which lusted after his wife, is ritually consumed by his subjects/sons.[27] In this instance, the fantasies of the individual seem to converge with the findings of psychoanalytical anthropology.

But Hamlet, obsessed by this notion of cannibalism tinged with incest, cannot stop there. The same nightmare surfaces in his macabre jokes on the subject of Polonius, whom he has accidentally despatched (mistaking him for Claudius, concealed behind the arras of the queen's chamber):

KING: Now, Hamlet, where's Polonius?
HAMLET: At supper.
KING: At supper? Where?
HAMLET: Not where he eats, but where a is eaten. A certain convocation of politic worms are e'en at him. Your worm is your only emperor for diet. We fat all creatures else to fat us, and we fat ourselves for maggots. Your fat king and your lean beggar is but variable service – two dishes, but one table. That's the end.   (IV, iii, 17–25)

The riddle of Polonius' supper suggests, once again, that the banquet at which one eats may also be the banquet at which one is eaten. There is a pun here on the Diet of Worms (called in 1521 by Charles V), in which Luther refused to retract his doctrine. This is associated with the behaviour of ordinary worms, as content to gorge upon the fat flesh of kings as upon the desiccated corpses of beggars. And when subjected to the dynamics of cannibalism, the chain of living creatures can certainly lead to strange connections, as Hamlet goes on to point out:

HAMLET: A man may fish with the worm that hath eat of a king, and eat of the fish that hath fed of that worm.
KING: What dost thou mean by this?
HAMLET: Nothing but to show you how a king may go a *progress* through the guts of a beggar.   (IV, iii, 27–31)

Once it is realized that the word 'progress' (my italics) also designated the official visits of much pomp and ceremony which the queen or king would pay to the various provinces of the realm, one can appreciate to the full the audacity of Hamlet's remarks, for they paint a picture of festive aristocratic processions progressing through the empty stomach of the populace. Seldom can the image of an upside-down world have had such an explosive force. In retrospect, this also helps us to understand the meaning of the cries of the rabble of the town of Romans and their own particular consummation of a carnivalesque festival. This is the moment when the populace gets to eat the king, having for all too long had to cinch in their belts.

Once subjected to tragic perversion, which produces a macabre alchemy in which Eros and Thanatos cease to be seen as contraries, festivity which involves general hearty eating may thus conjure up the spectre of the cannibal feast. As in Macbeth's feast *manqué*, a back-to-front Communion seems to be taking place, a Black Mass in which fantasies of cannibalism become the stigmata which betray a submission to the laws of anti-nature. When one analyses the ramifications of the theme of wine, another essential ingredient of festivity within Shakespeare's tragic world, a similar perversion may be detected.

The first point here to note is that, although beer may have been the masses' staple drink at festival time, Shakespeare's tragedies refer in the main to wine. The reason for the substitution is made quite clear in *Richard III*, where the assassins sent by the king to murder Clarence throw his corpse into a butt of Malmsey wine, turning it into what was known as a 'sop', a delicacy consisting of cake soaked in wine.[28] Clarence's corpse, drained of blood and impregnated with sweet wine, is thus used to produce a sinister kind of *sangría*. In this concoction, blood is turned into wine and murder becomes a Bacchic and sadistic feast. Similarly, it is after the feast held in Macbeth's palace that the host, violating the laws of hospitality, murders Duncan as he sleeps, Lady Macbeth having taken the precaution of making his guards drunk (*Macbeth*, I, vii, 61–70). And it is only by virtue of Menas' lack of initiative and the cowardice of Pompey, who had been hoping for a *fait accompli*, that Caesar, Antony and their guests were not assassinated during the Egyptian festivities organized aboard Pompey's galley.[29] In the course of this Bacchic orgy it would, after all, have been perfectly easy to drown the blood spilt in floods of wine and lay the entire massacre at the door of drunkenness.

Festival wine may thus be a foreboding metaphor for blood. Shakespeare has no need to spatter blood about the stage in order to imbue his audience with a sense of tragic horror. Cruelty is distilled more effectively by the *sous-entendus* of images which convey the theme of sacrificial blood through a process of re-metaphorization and metonymic links. Disorder, thus heralded yet deferred, explodes with all the more violence once it comes to the boil. Thus, in *Othello*, the Moor's murder of Desdemona is programmed in masterly fashion by Iago, who goads his general into a frenzy by implanting in him a series of darts of suspicion which progressively stir up agonies of sexual frustration and torments of jealousy.[30] When Othello holds a 'night of revels' to mark his victory and to entertain his troops by celebrating his wedding, Iago finds a way to provoke the initial little disturbance whose development will subsequently prove impossible to arrest. Iago makes the most of this chance to get Othello's lieutenant Cassio drunk and, once he is worked up by the wine, it proves easy to involve him in a fight the noise of which does not fail to disturb his general. But it is above all in the conversation between Iago and his dupe Roderigo that the connection between wine and evil is conveyed through an image, in the most unmistakable fashion. Roderigo remarks that Desdemona is 'full of most blessed condition', to which Iago's prompt rejoinder runs as follows:

Blessed fig's end! The wine she drinks is made of grapes. If she had been blessed, she would never have loved the Moor . . .   (II, i, 251–3)

Wine, through the intermediary of (black?) bunches of grapes, which are associated with Othello and his reproductive organs, here takes on a significance laden with sexual implications. In Iago's analogical rhetoric, wine is synonymous with desire and lust, the symbol *par excellence* of coarse pleasures of the flesh. It is a way of insinuating that Desdemona is hot-blooded. Iago does so with the conscious aim of provoking trouble and he proves himself to be a most redoubtable manipulator of people's imaginations and fantasies. It is hardly surprising that wine and festivity here take on a sinister air, indirectly causing ravages which, in other circumstances, would have been put down to madness or witchcraft. Here, festivity, propagating disorder by means of wine and blood, appears in its disturbing and nocturnal guise.

However, it is probably in two complementary images telescoped together, which appear in two very different plays, that the equation established in Shakespeare's tragedies between the liberating intoxication of carnival, on the one hand, and frenzied carnage, on the other, appears most clearly in all its violence. The first part of this double image is to be found in the episode of Jack Cade's bloody Carnival, when Jack promises his followers to open the gates of the Land of Cockaigne to them, in the first year of his reign (2 Henry VI, IV, vi, 1–4). The hidden meaning of what at first sight seems simply a Lord of Misrule's hollow promise is revealed when Jack's words are set alongside Calpurnia's premonitory dream in Julius Caesar:

> CAESAR: . . . Calpurnia here, my wife, stays me at home.
> She dreamt tonight she saw my statue,
> Which like a fountain with an hundred spouts
> Did run pure blood; and many lusty Romans
> Came smiling and did bathe their hands in it.   (II, ii, 75–9)

The connection between, on the one hand, popular fantasies in which streams of blood flow from the mouths of the 'pissing-conduit' and, on the other, the image of Caesar's statue which spouts blood in Calpurnia's dream, seems to me to provide a key to the mysterious ambivalence of popular festivity, to which I have several times drawn attention. When the statue spouting blood is superimposed upon the image of the miraculous fountain, this chimaera of eternal abundance turns into rivers of blood. That was indeed to be precisely the destiny of Jack Cade, for his head ended up set on the tip of a pike. Seen from the opposite angle, the image of the fountain of abundance from which claret wine runs continuously mitigates the alarming symbolism of the dream, seeming to confirm the reassuring interpretation produced by Decius, who presents the vision as a presage of fertility and rebirth for Rome:

> This dream is all amiss interpreted.
> It was a vision fair and fortunate.
> Your statue spouting blood in many pipes,
> In which so many smiling Romans bathed,
> Signifies that from you great Rome shall suck
> Reviving blood . . .   (II, ii, 83–8)

This interchange between the fountain and the statue, in which wine becomes blood and blood wine, is confirmed both by our knowledge of Elizabethan festival customs and also by the testimony of Renaissance iconography. We have already seen, in connection with Jack Cade's fountain, that the conduits or fountains of London were points where people would often gather and also constituted strategic elements in the organization of pageants or other street festivities. In the Midsummer pageants, representations of the fight between Saint George and the dragon would be put on, and Ordish points out that 'the representation of the pageant of St. George invariably took place by a well or water conduit . . . '. Withington, who cites this passage in a note, goes on to comment: 'This may be due to the fact that the conduit, running wine, could be made to suggest *dragon's blood*, and so add verisimilitude to the killing.'[31]

The contiguity and ever-possible interchangeability of the image of blood and that of wine is here illustrated by a pagan Eucharist. At the same time, however, the vision of the statue spouting blood, which is not to be found in Plutarch's text, is probably partly traceable to the influence of iconography. Fountains in the shape of nude female statues spouting forth life-giving liquid from their breasts were a relatively common sight. One example is the engraving by Robert Fludd which is placed at the end of the text of *Julius Caesar* in the Riverside Shakespeare (see Illus. 9.1). Here, a fecund stream pours forth from the solar bosom

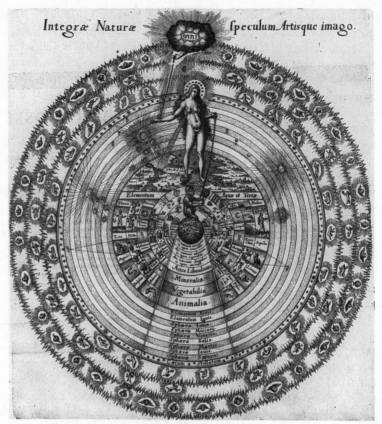

9.1   'Integrae Naturae speculum Artisque imago' ('The Mirror of Nature and the Image of Art'), from Robert Fludd's *Utriusque Cosmi Maioris Scilicet et Minoris Metaphysica Physica atque Technica Historia* (1617).

of Nature.[32] Another is a painting by Antoine Caron entitled *The Emperor Augustus and the Sibyl of Tibur.* The painting is, precisely, of a dramatic performance of *The Mystery of the Incarnation and Nativity of our Saviour and Redeemer Jesus Christ.* The scene represented is that in which:

Augustus questions the Sibyl of Tibur as to the future of his reign. The Sibyl produces a prophetic interpretation of the divine inspiration which has smitten her, pointing heavenwards to where, in a nimbus surrounded by cherubim,

The Virgin gently cradles
Her lovely new-born son,

who is to succeed Augustus as emperor of the world. Sadeth, the servant, who is accompanied by a very realistic monkey, tells the Sibyl of the portents which show that her prophecy is true: the Roman fountain is now gushing with oil 'as yellow as a thread of gold'.[33]

This blessed vision may also be compared to the passage in *The Golden Legend* which is devoted to the hagiography of Saint Blaise. After the martyrdom of the saint, tied to a tree and torn to pieces by metal combs, the women who have piously gathered up the drops of his blood are condemned by the governor of Cappadocia to suffer the same fate:

the governor ordered that they be strung up and that their flesh be torn to pieces by metal combs. But their flesh was as white as snow and, instead of blood, it flowed with milk.[34]

Femininity presided over the days leading up to the beginning of Carnival: 1 February was the feast of Saint Bridget (also known in England as Saint Bride) an Irish saint from Ulster who had displaced an earlier cult of the fertility mother-goddess of the ancient Celts; the following day was Candlemas, the Feast of the Purification of the Virgin and 5 February was the Feast of Saint Agatha, the patron-saint of wet-nurses, who was martyred by having her breasts cut off.[35] Jack Cade's virile Carnival was to change these rivers of milk into rivers of wine and blood. Meanwhile, through a woman's intuition, the wine, seen as blood, which flowed from the statue of Julius Caesar (whose initials, J.C. like Jack Cade's, are the same as those of Jesus Christ!) was to take on a sinister connotation.

A festival can thus be a back-to-front Eucharist. In it we see a counter-Communion in which the wine and bread of carnival are converted into a bloodbath and a cannibal banquet.

In the next and final chapter, I should like to study in greater depth an example of the way in which festival traditions make their way into Shakespearian tragedy, where the use of customs and devices borrowed from the traditions of comedy and popular festivals is disturbing and impels the action along a catastrophic course. In *Othello*, Iago makes an insidious use of carnivalesque devices, symbolism, language and behaviour such as we have noted in chapter 2[36] and he exploits the ambiguity of the grotesque, with all its equivocal images, to drive Othello to commit his irreparable crime.

10   *Othello* and the festive traditions

Shakespeare's dramatic texts sometimes function like a cultural memory in which traditions, both written and oral, learned and popular, surface through some significant image patterns or clusters of meaning. *Othello* is a play marked by considerable complexity and a deep ambivalence, but this enhances rather than detracts from its dramatic effectiveness on the stage, even if it sometimes puzzles the reader. By adopting an archaeological approach, which accommodates rather than reduces cumulative evidence, the critic is able to combine various perspectives, however numerous and contradictory they may be. This is a great advantage, for nowadays it would seem unsatisfactory to adopt any but a pluralist and polysemic reading of *Othello*.

Moreover, it is as a result of replacing *Othello* against its background of festive European traditions, such as those attached to the celebration of Carnival,[1] that I have been led to challenge a number of current ideas about the dramatic genres. One of the paradoxes and difficulties of this great tragedy is that many of its themes, situations and image patterns and much of its symbolism seem to derive from the world of comedy and popular festivals. It cannot be denied that 'the tragic loading of this bed', as Lodovico calls the sorry sight of the three dead bodies of Desdemona, Emilia and Othello at the end (v, ii, 373), conjures up the pathos, if not the horror, normally associated with tragedy; yet it is also true that the tragic ending of this play is a trick of chance and intrigue rather than the effect of fate and necessity: the final disaster is brought about by a perversion of motifs and situations that would normally belong to the world of comedy.

The presence of comic elements in *Othello* has already been analysed by critics such as Emrys Jones, Susan Snyder, John Bayley and others[2] and it is not a particularly new idea. Shakespeare had written a dozen odd comedies and only four tragedies (*Titus Andronicus, Romeo and Juliet, Julius Caesar* and *Hamlet*) when he chose to dramatize Cinthio's novella for the popular stage. But it seems to me that, rather than following the conventions of certain pre-established genres such as comedy or tragedy, the playwright was thinking in terms of a particular dramatic tradition and stage experience (situations already worked out with certain actors, stage properties, musical instruments, emblematic elements and so on). An archaeological approach obliges one to think more in terms of such built-in patterns of performance than according to the notions of conventional dramatic genres, since it lays stress on genetic rather than on generic data. The fact that comic structures are frequently reshaped or reprocessed in *Othello* testifies to a continuous traffic between the world of the comedies and that of the tragedies. This type of analysis tends to deny the existence of watertight boundaries between the comedies and the great tragedies, for its aim is to uncover the deeper, 'archaic' structures common to both types of play.

It is remarkable that *Othello* should open with the theme of the angry old father, the *senex iratus* outwitted by a pair of young lovers, which is one of the archetypes of New Comedy, illustrated by the plays of Menander in Greece (342?–291 BC) and of Plautus (c. 254–184 BC) and Terence (190–159 BC) in Rome. The waking up of the father by two 'ruffians' in the dead of night is an old trick borrowed from *commedia dell'arte* which associates Brabantio with the stock figure of Pantalone, the frantic father.[3] In a 1982 London production of *Othello*, the Young Vic Company tried to use this analogy and to adapt it on the stage, but, according to one reviewer, this was not particularly successful:

Othello began with a dumbshow of masked commedia dell' arte figures acting out, as the programme put it, *the abduction of Pantalone's daughter by the black-masked Arlecchino and her suspected seduction by the braggart-captain* . . . The keynote of the play seemed to be Iago's obscene joking.[4]

The trouble with heightening the potential note of farce in these early scenes is that one thereby risks diminishing dramatic effects which depend for their impact upon a certain ambiguity.[5] Similarly, the pathetic accusations of Brabantio against the Moor, whom he suspects of having practised on his daughter 'with foul charms, / Abused her delicate youth with drugs or minerals' (I, ii, 73–4) are often rightly compared with those of Egeus against Lysander at the beginning of *A Midsummer Night's Dream*.[6] The parallel is also misleading, as Brabantio is no mere carnival bugbear but acts rather as the double or the forerunner of Othello, who will himself later unwittingly echo the words of Desdemona's father when he broods in an unfinished sentence: 'And yet how nature erring from itself . . . '.[7] The theme of love linked to the strong presence of night,[8] moon, delusion, errors, and to the theme of passion's irrationality, is another feature common both to *Othello* and to a comedy like *A Midsummer Night's Dream*. But in *Othello* Shakespeare presents the Moor as lunatic, lover and poet all rolled into one.[9] As lunatic, Othello indeed 'sees more devils than vast hell can hold'[10] when he calls Desdemona 'the fair devil' (III, iii, 481) and when he falls victim to 'the very error of the moon . . . [that] makes men mad' (V, ii,

118–120); as poet, he initially seduces Desdemona with the strange, exotic story of his life and, at the end of the play, he finds a string of flamboyant images and conceits to express his tragic predicament. Many critics have remarked that, until Cassio is cashiered by Othello after the nocturnal brawl in Cyprus, the dominant rhythms in the play correspond to the powerful currents of comic resolution: the wooing described by Othello and Desdemona in front of the Venetian council has succeeded in spite of the barriers of age, colour and conditions of life, the machinations of the villain and the stupid rival have been annihilated, the father who blocks the lovers' way has been overruled by the Duke. Moreover, nature seems to have contributed to the movement that favours love and harmony since the storm has drowned the Turk and preserved the general and his young bride. The climax of this comedy in miniature, as Susan Snyder calls it,[11] is found in the reunion of Othello with Desdemona on the shores of Cyprus:

> OTHELLO: ... If it were now to die,
> 'Twere now to be most happy, for I fear
> My soul hath her content so absolute
> That not another comfort like to this
> Succeeds in unknown fate...
> I cannot speak enough of this content.
> It stops me here, it is too much of joy:
> And this, [*they kiss*] and this, the greatest discords be
> That e'er our hearts shall make.   (II, i, 190–200)

But the passage is fraught with dramatic irony, as the music of the kiss also provides the chord on which the lovers will die. The isle of Cyprus, which could have played the role of some beneficent green world, fails to fulfil its cathartic function (as the grim irony of its being called a 'fair island' by Iago confirms) while love and marriage, the traditional topics of comedy, slowly degenerate into jealousy, misunderstanding and death. The beneficent magic of nature becomes inoperative and there is no providential agent or trick of Fortune to save the situation at the last minute. In contrast to the basic situation in most of the comedies, the women are here left in the dark while a man, Iago, is in control of the whole situation. In this play, sexuality is soon divorced from its usual pastoral environment and is increasingly reduced to the confines of masculine fantasy. The men become estranged from the women whose patience and revitalizing energies are undermined in the unfamiliar world of this distant military garrison. Instead of promoting fertility, love, poisoned by suspicion, leads to destruction. The main reason why nature changes sides in this way, turning into an enemy rather than an accomplice of love, may be a lack of 'sympathy in years', as Iago calls it (II, i, 228). The age difference is certainly important, not so much because, as Iago insinuates, the Moor will soon prove unable to satisfy Desdemona's appetite, but because it unavoidably places Othello in the position of a father.[12] The archetypal betrayal of the father by the daughter seems likely to be repeated later, at the expense of the husband, for the sake of a younger lover.

In Act III, the initial romantic comedy turns into a *fabliau*-like situation, a sort of parody of Chaucer's marriage of January and May in *The Merchant's Tale*. This strengthens the association between the idea of marriage and the bitter, bawdy notion of cuckoldry, making the second an almost inevitable correlative of the first:

> To take a wyf it is a glorious thyng,
> And namely whan a man is oold and hoor . . .
> They [bacheleris] lyve but as a bryd or as a beest,
> In libertee, and under noon arreest,
> Ther as a wedded man in his estaat
> Lyveth a lyf blisful and ordinaat,
> Under this yok of mariage ybounde.
> Wel may his herte in joy and blisse habounde,
> For who kan be so buxom as a wyf? . . .
> And yet somme clerkes seyn it nys nat so . . .
> 'Ne take no wyf,' quoth he [Theofraste]
> And if thou take a wyf unto thyn hoold,
> Ful lightly maystow been a cokewold.[13]

The same idea is found in chapter XXXII of Rabelais' *Tiers Livre*, which is entitled 'How Rondibilis declareth cuckoldry to be naturally one of the appendances of marriage':

There remaineth, as yet, quoth Panurge . . . one small scruple to be cleared . . . Shall I not be a cuckold? By the haven of safety, cried out Rondibilis, what is this you ask of me? If you shall be a cuckold? My noble friend, I am married, and you are like to be so very speedily; therefore be pleased, from my experiment in the matter, to write in your brain with a steel-pen this subsequent ditton, there is no married man who doth not run the hazard of being made a cuckold. Cuckoldry naturally attendeth marriage. The shadow doth not more naturally follow the body than cuckoldry ensueth after marriage, to place fair horns upon the husbands' head.[14]

Shakespeare also found an allusion to this traditional satire of women and marriage in a passage of Kyd's *Spanish Tragedy* which he echoes in *Much Ado About Nothing*[15] and in *As You Like It*:

TOUCHSTONE [to Audrey]: . . . for here we have no temple but the wood, no assembly but horn-beasts. But what though? Courage. As horns are odious, they are necessary. It is said many a man knows no end of . . . them. Well, that is the dowry of his wife, 'tis none of his own getting. Horns? Even so. Poor men alone? No, no, the noblest deer hath them as huge as the rascal . . .

JAQUES: Will you be married, motley?

TOUCHSTONE: As the ox hath his bow, sir, the horse his curb, and the falcon
her bells, so man hath his desires; and as pigeons bill, so wedlock would
be nibbling . . .   (III, iii, 44–74)

Othello will be led by Iago to make such an association between marriage
and cuckoldry, but he is not amused:

OTHELLO: . . . O curse of marriage,
That we can call these delicate creatures ours,
And not their appetites! . . .
. . . Yet 'tis the plague of great ones;
Prerogatived are they less than the base.
'Tis destiny unshunnable, like death.
Even then this forkèd plague is fated to us
When we do quicken . . .   (III, iii, 272–81)

In contrast to the clown who resigns himself, at least verbally, to the
'natural' necessity of cuckoldry (comedy or 'comonty', as Christopher Sly
calls it in the Induction to *The Taming of the Shrew*, is, after all, a
rejection of singleness and a reduction of the individual to the common
lot of mankind), Othello refuses to be made 'A fixèd figure, for the time
of scorn / To point his slow unmoving finger at . . . ' (IV, ii, 56–7). The
difference between the noble Moor and the rest is that, to his eyes, 'A
hornèd man's a monster and a beast' (IV, i, 60) and that he cannot bring
himself to accept what Iago cynically presents as the common plight of
married men:

Good sir, be a man,
Think every bearded fellow that's but yok'd
May draw with you . . .   (IV, i, 64–6)

Iago's words are extremely cold comfort and they only serve to rub salt
into Othello's wounds, as the submerged metaphor of the ox in the
above-quoted lines assimilates him to a tame, castrated animal passively
drawing the matrimonial yoke. Such taunting suggestions are of course
intended to arouse his pride and excite his fury.

By now, the roles of the two men have been clearly established:
Othello is the embodiment of the romantic, idealistic lover, who will be
tortured into insanity by the crude jokes which seem to delight his ensign
so much. Iago, for his part, is the *agon* of the comic in the play,
constantly offering a bawdy, cynical and violently anti-feminist vision of
love reduced to some bestial intercourse, to 'a lust of the blood and a
permission of the will' (I, iii, 334–5). As such, he is less a Machiavellian
than a Rabelaisian character. What is more, as the base, low-born
fellow,[16] he embodies the views of the *demos*, traditionally reputed to be
incapable of accepting the idea of love as a noble, generous or refined
feeling. The struggle between Othello and Iago is also one between

amour courtois and *amour grivois*. An exponent of the voice of the belly and material appetite, Iago is also the instigator of most of the popular traditions and scenarios evoked or indirectly suggested in the course of the play. He initiates a form of rough music, or charivari, in the dark streets of Venice to rouse Brabantio in the middle of the night; he engages in word-play and in a satirical portrait game with Desdemona in the tradition of Venetian *conversazione*,[17] he sings merry drinking songs during the night of revels in Cyprus and possesses a whole repertoire of images of carnivalesque customs.

Iago, throughout the play, masquerades as some black fool or evil buffoon, who conjures up popular games and folk traditions only to pervert them to his own ends. Just as he is a false physician, who uses his art to poison rather than to heal, he endows the festive role of the fool with a destructive instead of a cathartic function. Festivity and ridicule, normally aimed against the blocking figures in comedy (the Shylocks, Malvolios and other spoilsports), are here deployed against the romantic hero and lover.

Once Othello, the romantic hero, falls under Iago's influence he relapses into savage passion and superstition. His verbal magic and music desert him as he indulges in incoherent, grotesque mumblings. Unable to order his confused thoughts and to pull his split selves together, he cuts the sorry figure of a man torn between irreconcilable poles, being now the heroic and ecstatic lover not easily made jealous, now the miserable 'cuckold . . . / Who dotes, yet doubts, suspects yet fondly loves' (III, iii, 171–5).

Throughout the play, one is conscious of this double perspective, alternately comic and tragic, derisive and pathetic. But, since the tragedy is brought about by Iago, using comic elements or situations to reach his evil ends, let us take stock of the various customs and popular traditions to which he turns in his manipulative strategy. An archaeological study of the comic elements will help illuminate the real nature of the tragic effects that are reached at the end of the play.

The first important festive tradition echoed in *Othello* is that of waking someone up or of creating some public disturbance to protest against a marriage of which the local community disapproved, namely the tradition of charivari, better known in England under the names of 'rough music', 'Skimmington riding' or 'riding the stang'.[18] Iago probably has this popular custom at the back of his mind when he says to Roderigo at the beginning of the play:

> Call up her father,
> Rouse him, make after him, poison his delight,
> Proclaim him in the streets, incense her kinsmen.   (I, i, 67–9)

These lines correspond to the definition given by Cotgrave for 'charivari':

A publicke defamation, or traducing of; a foule noise made, black Santus rung, to the Shame, and disgrace of another; hence, an infamous (or infaming) ballade sung, by an armed troupe, under the window of an old dotard married, the day before, unto a young wanton, in mockery of them both.[19]

The foul noise or public uproar raised by Iago is compared to the bell used to provoke alarm or confusion:

> RODERIGO: Here is her father's house, I'll call aloud.
> IAGO: Do, with like timorous accent, and dire yell,
> As when, by night and negligence, the fire
> Is spied in populous cities.   (I, i, 74–7)

Moreover, the image of a 'Black Sanctus' or 'Santus' used in Cotgrave's definition,[20] seems particularly apt for the evocation of the 'old black ram/... Tupping your white ewe' (I, i, 88–9). Rough music or cacophony is used by the satanic Iago to conjure up the frightening vision of some Black Mass superimposed upon images of bestial intercourse which, in turn, evokes the breeding of monsters (see I, i, 91, 110–15). The ensign's idea of resorting to the popular rite of charivari seems apt since this noisy demonstration was, among other reasons, traditionally intended as a form of protest against ill-assorted marriages or against strangers who married local women.[21] It is to be noted, however, that here we have a perversion of the custom, for it is directed against the father of the bride rather than the newlyweds. But this is part of the warping process, which starts early in the play, where the father is placed in a quasi-incestuous position vis-à-vis his daughter (critics have remarked upon the ambiguity of the word 'ewe' [= you] in Iago's allusion to the 'old black ram/... Tupping [his] white ewe').[22]

Conversely, Othello, in his capacity as Desdemona's husband, will later be assimilated to a father-figure and will likewise be roused from his bed in the middle of the night by a similar trick. Iago and Roderigo's initial charivari has introduced an atmosphere of misrule which turns the normal world upside-down and upsets the ordinary sexual and social roles throughout the time-span represented in the play.

A second form of charivari is suggested at the beginning of Act III, in the brief scene where the Clown greets the musicians sent by Cassio to play early-morning music beneath the window of the general and his bride. The choice of wind instruments (bagpipes presumably),[23] which provoke the ribaldry of the Clown (a double of Iago),[24] is not particularly delicate. It is another instance of Othello's loss of musical harmony once he has fallen under Iago's rule. The latter's attempts to cross Othello's marriage are indeed expressed in musical images[25] and his progressive introduction of discordant notes to Othello's music may have been inspired by the prologue of a popular play, which was well known to Shakespeare (it was part of the répertoire of his company), namely the anonymous *Comedie of Mucedorus* (1598). The play is preceded by a debate between Comedie and Envy who challenge each other as to who will prevail in the end:

> COMEDIE: Comedie, play thy part and please,
> Mak merry them that come to ioy with thee...
> Ioy then, good gentilles; I hope to make you laugh,
> Sound forth Bellonas silver tuned strings...
> ENVY: Nay, staie, minion, there lies a block
> What, al on mirth! Ile interrupt your tale
> And make your musicke with a tragicke end.
> Ile thunder musicke shall appale the nimphe,
> And make them shever their clattering strings...
> Sound drums and crie, 'stab', 'stab'!
> Hearken, thou shalt hear a noise
> Shall fill the aire with a shrilling sound,
> And thunder musicke to the gods above...[26]

But as for Cassio's *aubade*, it seems to represent a form of Italian *mattinata*, a custom attached to the popular rites of marriage. It was, in fact, fairly close to charivari as it involved cacophonous music as well as to various obscene songs and words designed to show the local community's disapproval of some atypical marriage. In its Florentine version (one, no doubt, familiar to Michael Cassio), it included bagpipes and trumpets accompanied by various musicians or singers.[27] But the *mattinata* remained an ambiguous custom since it was also a popular tradition to greet the newlyweds with music on the morning following the consummation of their marriage. In Lombardy, which was influenced by German law, it was in fact the moment when family and friends would come to offer their presents (*Morgengabe*) to the bride and groom.[28] Shakespeare may have conflated the two aspects of the *mattinata*. Initially meant by Cassio as a greeting and ingratiating compliment to Desdemona, it turns into a somewhat ill-timed and inappropriate ceremony, as there is a serious chance that the incidents of the rowdy night at the camp prevented Othello and Desdemona from consummating their marriage.[29]

Similar festive traditions probably also underlie the play's general imagery and its rich and complex montage of dramatic nuclei. One is certainly the Morris dance, also called Moorish dancing, because the dancers sometimes had blackened faces.[30] As an illustration of the possible Moorish origin of the folk dance, E.K. Chambers quotes a passage from *Spousalls of Princess Mary* (1508), in which 'morisks' is rendered as 'ludi Maurei quas morescas dicunt'.[31] We may here recall the devil-haunted description of Philip Stubbes, for whom the Morris dance was a form of pagan idolatry and a homage paid to Satan:

Thus al things set in order, then have they their Hobby-horses, dragons & other Antiques, togither with their *baudie Pipers* and thundering *Drummers* to strike up the devils daunce withall. Then, marche these heathen company towards the Church and Church-yard, their *pipers pipeing*, their *drummers thundring*, their stumps dauncing, their bels iyngling, their handkerchefs swinging about their heds like madmen, their hobbie horses and other monsters skirmishing amongst the route.[32]

Although, 'the devils daunce' depicted in these lines is no doubt a product of the over-heated imagination of the Puritan pamphleteer, interestingly enough, Othello's famous 'Farewell' speech (III, iii, 355–62) has a somewhat similar ring:

> O, farewell,
> Farewell the neighing steed and the shrill trump,
> The spirit-stirring drum, th' ear-piercing fife,
> The royal banner, and all quality,
> Pride, pomp, and circumstance of glorious war!
> And, O you mortal engines whose wide throats
> Th' immortal Jove's dread clamours counterfeit;
> Farewell! Othello's occupation's gone.

The strident evocation of the pageantry of war may simply be a rhetorical analogue for the internal tumult which is beginning to ravage Othello's mind and which will reach its climax in the 'savage ecstasy' of Act IV. The visualization of the uproar of the Morris dance and the description of martial music seem to belong to a similar upsurge of 'histerica passio'.[33] Of course, there is no such thing as a Morris dance in *Othello*, but the play does present a Moor with a 'begrim'd' face (III, iii, 392) who repeatedly calls himself a 'fool' (for example at V, ii, 332), mentions a 'handkerchief' or 'napkin' in no less than six passages in the play, and alludes to a light woman called 'a hobby-horse' (IV, i, 152). All this suggests that Shakespeare had a good personal knowledge of this folk dance and also that he had Stubbes' description in mind when he wrote those scenes in *Othello*, where pathos is undercut by a current of black hilarity.

Also significant is the fact that the Morris dance derives from the old martial Sword dance, a connection which makes it particularly relevant to the world of *Othello* where both the opening and the closing lines spoken by the general contain allusions to swords.[34] Jack Cade, the leader of the popular rebellion in *2 Henry VI*, whom York presents as 'a wild Morisco',[35] might well be considered as a grotesque analogue of Othello.

As we have seen above, the Morris or Sword dance was itself simply a particular type of folk play called Hero Combat or the Mummers' play and there is also an echo of this in *Othello*. Indeed, in the scene of Othello's fit of epilepsy, which, as some critics have remarked,[36] has a comic or grotesque effect, the general's blackout is followed by his revival at the hands of Iago. The general's ensign here masquerades as a healer/poisoner figure[37] and this scene may be interpreted as a dramatic variation of the popular shows put on at Christmas and Easter in the villages of Elizabethan England. The Mummers' play ritually presented a battle between a Christian Knight (generally embodied by the figure of St George) against Beelzebub or a Turkish Knight, the latter being both endowed with blackened faces.[38] After the first clash, St George was clubbed to the ground, where he lay unconscious, until he was revived by a miraculous Doctor who emerged from the crowd of spectators. So, according to the scenario imported from the Mummers' play, Iago would appear under the double persona of the medicine man and of the white Christian knight who defeats the dark, pagan African.

At this juncture, Iago may be identified with his Spanish namesake, Sant Iago Matamoros, that is, Saint James the killer of Moors. This national hero was adopted as a patron saint in Spain after winning the battle of Clavijo against the Moors in the eleventh century (see Illus. 10.1).[39] On woodcuts he is represented on his white horse, hacking at the Moorish army opposite him and routing the Infidels.

If we bear in mind this Spanish connection, we see that Iago torments Othello with cuckoldry, the nightmarish green-eyed and horned monster, just as a bull-fighter will bait and tame a savage bull. The fighting of bulls had long been a popular sport in the south of Spain where it was used as a test of strength between Christian knights and the Moorish chieftains.[40] The masters would fight the bulls on horseback, armed with lances, while the *peons*, on foot as befitted their inferior status, would manoeuvre the animals, exciting them with darts or directing them towards the waiting horsemen. These auxiliaries were called *chulos* or *matamoros*.[41] In this perspective, Iago appears as both a vulgar *peon* serving a Moorish general and a *matamoros* baiting his horn-mad master with a strawberry-spotted handkerchief. Like the Spanish bull-fighter, he wounds and gradually dominates a savage animal, until he is in a position to make the kill.

Naturally, the background for the allusions to this sport in the play is not solely Spanish, as the game of bull-baiting was quite popular in Elizabethan England. The reference thus seems all the more relevant to Shakespeare's play as the public theatres, where *Othello* was first performed, had been built as convertible bull-baiting arenas. Iago the

10.1   A 1470 print by Martin Schongauer, showing Sant Iago Matamoros
defeating the Moors.

'Spartan dog', the 'pernicious caitiff',[42] baits a bear-like Othello who is,
as it were, tied to the stake of his honour and John Wain is certainly
correct in saying that Iago 'has bull-ring fever'.[43] Iago describes the pangs
of jealousy in terms of intense physical torments, like the laceration of
teeth biting into the flesh.

Most of the buried popular traditions which we have unearthed so far
derive their significance from the basic antagonism between two worlds,
two cultures, two sensibilities, two perspectives – namely those that lie
behind the characters of Othello and Iago. These were not traditions
related to any specific date in the calendar which, in normal practice,
would account for their association with the imagery or symbolism of the
play. But *Othello* is also deeply marked by the popular games and
traditions of carnival, through the double influence of, on the one hand,
Rabelais and the contemporary theory of humours (in the tradition of
Galen and of astrological medicine), and on the other the popular
mythology of the wild man.

In his book on Rabelais, Mikhaïl Bakhtin has defined the grotesque as
a vision of the body as open and ambivalent.[44] That vision might apply
to Iago, who masquerades in the play as, among other things, the
representative of bodily appetite and of the obscenity of bodily functions.
In Act III, scene i, his double, the Clown, plays with the idea of the

human body as a 'wind instrument' with a 'tail'. Speaking of the courtly exchanges and the kiss between Cassio and Desdemona, he uses the scatological-medical image of the clyster-pipe.[45] Meanwhile, Othello is tormented by the obsessive notion that his wife's body has lain open to another man:[46]

> I had rather be a toad
> And live upon the vapour of a dungeon
> Than keep a corner in the thing I love
> For others' uses . . .   (III, iii, 274–7)

Similarly, when he addresses Emilia as

> You, mistress,
> That have the office opposite to Saint Peter
> And keep the gates of hell . . .   (IV, ii, 94–6)

Othello uses a *double entendre* current in the Elizabethan period, in which hell also designated the female sex. A similar obsession with open gates may be found in Leontes' jealous outbursts at the beginning of *The Winter's Tale*:

> There have been,
> Or I am much deceived, cuckolds ere now,
> And many a man there is, even at this present,
> Now, while I speak this, holds his wife by th' arm,
> That little thinks she has been sluiced in's absence,
> And his pond fished by his next neighbour, by
> Sir Smile, his neighbour. Nay, there's comfort in't,
> Whiles other men have gates, and those gates opened,
> As mine, against their will. Should all despair
> That have revolted wives, the tenth of mankind
> Would hang themselves. Physic for't there's none.
> It is a bawdy planet . . . be it concluded,
> No barricado for a belly . . .   (I, ii, 191–205)

Under the influence of Iago's pathological vision of sex, Othello dismembers the human body into monstrous independent organs,[47] opening the way to some grotesque anatomy of hell as in the paintings of Hieronymus Bosch. Then he becomes convulsed by his epileptic fit.

As to medical knowledge, Iago, the perverted physician, *prescribes* the wrong drugs, which inflame the jealous fancy of his patient instead of providing the expected *remedia amoris*. These inflammatory drugs work in quite the opposite fashion to the remedies used by Doctor Rondibilis, in Rabelais' *Tiers Livre*, to assuage Panurge's lust:

The fervency of lust is abated by certain drugs, plants, herbs, and roots, which make the taker cold, maleficiated, unfit for, and unable to perform the act of generation; as hath been often experimented in . . . agnus castus, willow-twigs, hemp-stalks, woodbine, honeysuckle, tamarisk, chaste tree, mandrake, etc. . . . [48]

One of the ironies of the play is that mandragora is refused to the furious Othello[49] while the willow tree becomes the floral funereal emblem of the chaste Desdemona.[50]

So Iago's poisoned wit functions like some inflammatory agent that reawakens the dormant savagery inside the apparently cool and dignified noble Moor. At the outset Iago had proclaimed him in the streets to be like some lascivious black animal, an old black ram, or a Barbary horse, thereby prefiguring the image of the ugly beast which Othello later becomes.

The elopement of Desdemona with the black stranger at the beginning of the play revives a traditional association between the figure of the Moor and that of the wild man, the bloody savage and rapist found in popular drama and pageantry. A pageant involving 'Homini Selvaggi' pursuing and abducting nymphs is mentioned in an account of the Carnival of Belluno (near Venice) in 1507; and the *intermezzi* of Jacopo de Legname (1517) included nymphs, satyrs, a Silenus, a bear and a wild man.[51] In his article on 'The Wild Man on the English Stage', Robert Hillis Goldsmith says that, in a play by the same author, 'between the fourth and fifth acts, an episode takes place . . . there is a wild dance of Moors, the bear knocks down one of the dancers, and the wild man beats the bear . . .'.[52]

Similar dramatic elements are found in *Mucedorus*, where, after an episode involving a white bear, the Lady Amadine is abducted by Bremo the Wild Man. When Mucedorus, disguised as a hermit, manages to approach the young lady and whisper in her ear he arouses the monster's jealousy ('BREMO [jealous]: What secret tale is this? What whispering have we here?'),[53] and is obliged to resort to lying and cunning to get rid of Bremo so that he can marry Amadine. The lost play of *Valentine and Orson* (recorded in Henslowe's Diary) dealt with a similar story – that of two twin brothers born in the woods and brought up by a she-bear. One of the brothers leaves the forest, later to become a courtier and a warrior, while the other becomes a wild man in the woods. One day, unaware that the latter is his brother, the courtier who is sent to hunt and kill him manages to capture him alive and bring him back to the court. In the end a recognition scene takes place between the two brothers. Othello seems to roll into one the parts of the two warring brothers, for he projects a double image: on the one hand that of the valiant general praised by the Duke of Venice, on the other that of the dark stranger who likens himself to the 'turbaned Turk',[54] whom he symbolically kills in himself, in his spectacular suicide at the end of the play. The story of Valentine and

10.2   The masquerade of Valentine and Orson, from a 1566 woodcut by Pieter Brueghel.

Orson also figured in a folk play performed in a number of European countries during the Carnival period: it is depicted in a drawing by Pieter Brueghel and in a corner of his famous painting of *The Battle of Carnival and Lent* (see Illus. 10.2).[55]

In the French Pyrenees, at Prats-de-Mollo, a bear chase is ritually organized each year on Saint Blaise's Day (3 February), the earliest possible date for Shrove Tuesday. A photograph of the game (see Illus. 10.3)[56] shows the man who plays the part of the bear having his face blackened with soot (sometimes ashes and oil are used); this calls to mind Othello's 'begrim'd face' or Edgar's transformation in *King Lear*.[57] The black-faced bear chases a man-woman called Rosetta and, when he catches her, in turn begrimes her face with dirt – a clear enough symbol of rape and sexual defilement. A similar ritual seems to be echoed in the quarto text of *Othello*, where the Moor says of Desdemona:

> Her [My] name that was as fresh
> As Dian's visage, is now begrimed and black
> As mine own face . . .   (III, iii, 391–3)

It is worth noting that this is altogether in line with the plans of Iago, who has already announced his intention 'to turn her virtue into pitch' (II, iii, 351).

The popular custom at Prats-de-Mollo celebrates the bear's awakening from hibernation, hailing it as a harbinger of spring. *Othello* contains

10.3   The bear chase at Prats-de-Mollo in the French Pyrenees. The 'bear' is
having his face covered with grime.

one image in which the 'lustful Moor' is clearly identified with a bear.[58]
But, in the mock-spying scene, Iago asks him to 'encave' himself (IV, i,
80) – a word used only once by Shakespeare, as the *OED* notes, which
means that he must return into his cave, thereby delaying the arrival of
spring and prolonging the forces of winter. The symbolism is the reverse
of that of the liberating forces of the green world in comedy and this
explains why the carnivalesque here loses its cathartic function and is
perverted into its contrary.

Othello is associated with other carnival animals, as well as the bear.
One is the ass, with which Iago identifies him twice in the course of the
play (I, iii, 394 and II, i, 308). Furthermore, when Iago says that the
Moor 'will as tenderly be led by th' nose / As asses are', he may have in
mind the Carnival custom of making cuckolded husbands ride backwards on a donkey through the streets of the city. This derisive tradition
was part of the Ash Wednesday pageant of the Confrérie des Cornards in
Dijon and of the riding of the Cuckolds in Lyons, as can be seen from a
popular woodcut in the Bibliothèque Nationale in Paris (see Illus.
10.4).[59] It shows the cuckold, or the man who represents him, seated
facing the tail end of a donkey and wearing a cap with cock feathers
(sometimes replaced by ass's ears) which symbolize cuckoldry. This
popular punishment of cuckolds was also a form of charivari, often
included among the 'entertainments' of Shrove Tuesday, and is mentioned in many sixteenth- and seventeenth-century texts.

10.4   *La chevauchée du cocu à Lyon*: anonymous woodcut (1587) in the Bibliothèque Nationale, Paris.

In the above-mentioned print, as in a series of woodcuts by Jacques Callot, the infamous riding through the streets of the city is attended by a reveller blowing bellows into the hind parts of the animal (see Illus. 10.5 and 10.6).[60] The importance of the pair of bellows and of the wind symbolism is also shown in another woodcut depicting the banner of the 'Compagnie de la Mère Folle' in Dijon. Here Mother Folly stands under the clouds holding a pair of bellows in both hands and pressing with her left foot on a third pair lying on the ground (see Illus. 10.7).[61] Gaignebet explains that the association comes from a pun on the supposed etymology of the word 'folly', falsely connected with the Latin *follis*, meaning bellows. Another pun may also be involved on the origin of the name of the patron saint celebrated at Carnival time, Saint Blaise (*Blasius* in Latin), which is akin to the English verb 'to blow', derived from the old Teutonic word *blaejen*.[62] Iago, who seems to find inspiration in the popular rites of Carnival for some of the tricks that he plays on Othello, also mentions clysters – another type of wind instrument used in the infamous donkey rides – when Cassio kisses Desdemona's fingers when the storm, which has blown him ashore, is over.[63]

Iago certainly excels at raising an ill wind which blows nobody good, once the 'wind-shaked surge, with high and monstrous main, [which] /

10.5 and 10.6   Two prints by Jacques Callot showing *commedia dell'arte* scenes.

10.7   Banner of the 'Compagnie de la Mère Folle', from a sixteenth-century painting in the Musée de Puycousin, Dijon.

Seems to cast water on the burning bear' (II, i, 13–14) has calmed down. When Othello disembarks in Cyprus, the tumescence brought about by his desire is indirectly described in cosmic sea imagery which blends heroic and erotic elements in a conceit which may be interpreted as an anamorphosis:[64]

> Great Jove, Othello guard,
> And swell his sail with thine own powerful breath,
> That he may bless this bay with his tall ship,
> Make love's quick pants in Desdemona's arms.   (II, i, 78–81)

In the medical treatises of Galen and Hippocrates, as in the Renaissance theory of humours, the wind is supposed to favour physical intercourse through the action of *pneuma* and *ventositas* (the technical Latin word for the poetic image of swelling the sail in the above-quoted lines). Curiously, Othello's blown up rhetoric (which Iago decries as 'a bombast circumstance / Horribly stuffed with epithets of war' (I, i, 13–14)) is also strongly linked to the wind imagery, as his famous 'Farewell' speech suggests. At the beginning of this, Othello swells himself up; by the graphic last line, 'Farewell! Othello's occupation's gone' (III, iii, 362), he has blown his love away. The descending, trochaic rhythm ends in bated breath, in something that sounds very close to a final whisper. A little later, he exclaims: 'All my fond love thus do I blow to heaven – 'tis gone' (III, iii, 450). It is important to note the dash which should introduce a pause in the actor's delivery of this line – enough for Othello to blow his love away.

This is immediately followed by his strange invocation of vengeance: 'Arise, black vengeance, from thy hollow cell . . .'. The complementary image of Othello puffing out his love to inhale black hate turns him into a kind of wind instrument – a pair of bellows handled by an external agent. Iago manipulates Othello by blowing into his mind suspicions which he himself calls 'exsufflicate', that is, puffed up, and blown (III, iii, 186) or by getting 'trifles light as air' (III, iii, 327) to prey upon his imagination. In the light of what we know of some of the carnival customs of the Renaissance, this reduction of body and mind to some mechanical apparatus is not altogether surprising; it is also congruent with the current medical conceptions of the day.[65]

After the good wind of desire has abated, Othello becomes progressively swollen by a hideous and obscene flatulence. The joy of seeing Desdemona on the shores of Cyprus had the effect of stopping his breath;[66] his later fit of epilepsy (an affliction close to hysteria, then called 'suffocation of the mother') provokes a blackout. This spectacular emotional disturbance may be a form of what Robert Burton in *The Anatomy of Melancholy* calls 'wind melancholy', of which he writes that 'oftentimes it degenerates into epilepsy, apoplexy, convulsions . . .'.[67] Among the symptoms of this form of melancholy, Burton lists 'cold joints, indigestion . . . continual wind in their hypochondries . . . midriff and bowells are pulled up . . . and swell from vapours and wind'.[68]

As to possible cures for this condition, ironically enough, these 'windy flatuous persons', as Burton calls them, 'are luxurious, incontinent, and prone to venery, by reason of wind, *et facile amant, et quamlibet fere amant* (Note: Hypochondriaci maximi affectant coire et multiplicantur coitus in ispis, eo quod ventositates multiplicantur in hypochondriis, et *coitus saepe allevat has ventositates*)' (my italics).[69]

By provoking an influx of black bile into Othello's otherwise sanguine humour, Iago turns him into a saturnine figure suffering from 'wind melancholy'. Simultaneously, by twice interrupting his marital love-making, he deprives the general of the natural outlet which, according to Burton, would alleviate his torment. Iago is a perverted therapist who creates the disease and then blocks all access to cure or even release. Yet, among the possible cures for this form of melancholy, Burton mentions what he himself calls 'a strange remedy: Put a pair of bellows' end into a clyster pipe and applying into the fundament, open the bowels, so draw forth the wind, *natura non admittit vacuum*'.[70]

However, Iago has already perverted the remedy into an indirect means of torment and humiliation through an analogy with the infamous riding of cuckolds in the carnival period. From now on, Othello will be unable to find any means to relieve his diseased imagination and will eventually be led to identify the chaste Desdemona with some ill, infected wind:

> Heaven stops the nose at it, and the moon winks,
> The bawdy wind, that kisses all it meets,
> Is hush'd within the hollow mine of earth . . .   (IV, ii, 79–81)

He will punish her by stopping her wind and stifling her under a pillow, a death in which he sees a form of justice,[71] probably because he regards Desdemona's balmy breath as the bawdy wind of lust. When he realizes his error, he will resort to the same wind imagery to vow himself to an eternal punishment where his soul will be blown about by the winds of hell: 'Whip me, ye devils . . . Blow me about in winds . . .' (v, ii, 284–6). Iago, the fake doctor and real poisoner, has applied the recipes of pre-scientific medical knowledge together with the tricks of folklore and festive traditions, which he knows inside-out, to turn the healthy, tumescent wind of carnival dehibernation into a foul, bawdy wind that corrupts and ultimately kills those it has infected. But this tactic, at the end of the play, turns itself against him when he is betrayed by the tongue of his wife who will blow out the truth when she discovers it after the death of her mistress: "Twill out, 'twill out. I peace? / No, I will speak as liberal as the north [First Quarto: air]' (v, ii, 225–6).

After spreading the ill wind of rumour and slander, Iago is at last confronted with the difficulty of containing the healthy air of truth. When Emilia finally speaks out, this unforeseen change in the wind defeats him and he can only remain in obdurate silence and refuse to speak a word (v, ii, 310).

The dynamics of the grotesque explode the established forms and conventions of the different genres, revealing how the comic and the tragic modes are constantly blended. *Othello* appears as a play partly underpinned by the festive customs of the carnival tradition celebrated by, among others, Rabelais – one of the writers first responsible for grafting medical knowledge onto the farcical elements of French folklore. But Italian, Spanish and English customs also seem to have been woven into the backdrop of analogies and correspondences against which Iago's comic strategy is played out.

Othello is a play characterized by a tug-of-war between the forces of comedy and those of tragedy. Comedy is accommodated here in its full range, from the romantic to the bawdy and the satirical, but it becomes deviated from its true end when, through Iago's manipulations, sex is divorced from love and nature. Tragedy, meanwhile, is prevented from expanding from the private to the public and cosmic levels, and is instead compressed, constricted inside an air-tight space.

In fact, the play only finds its real space within the sphere of fantasy; ultimately, what our analysis reveals is that this perverted comedy or tragedy of errors can only be truly understood at the level of the deeper structures of the imagination.

Conclusion

This book has adopted a resolutely empirical approach to a relatively unexplored domain in which it would be not only difficult but also dangerous to generalize. My aim has been to assemble the major festive data and to trace how these events are echoed in Shakespeare's dramatic work. My sources have included quite a large number of literary texts, mostly drawn from authors generally considered to be of minor importance, who are little read these days (such as Breton, Warner, Earle), travellers' journals (Hentzner, Platter, Misson de Valbourg) and diaries of private individuals (Machyn, Assheton, Crosfield). These have provided me with firsthand information on many festive practices. I have also made use of archival documentation (parish registers, diocesan notes, the minutes of ecclesiastical tribunals and royal decrees) to fill in gaps and provide extra details. Finally, I have consulted the few iconographical sources of evidence that exist in this domain. My collection of sources as a whole is thus of a necessarily heterogeneous nature, but we should remember that syncretism also characterized Shakespeare's own use of sources, for he was as willing to draw his material from folklore as from the many kinds of written texts to which he had access in his own library or in those of his friends and protectors. In analysing the wide variety of documents which I have cited, I detected a considerable interaction between them, and this has made it easier to overcome the major obstacle that confronts a study of this kind, namely the difficulty of proceeding from the basic information provided by the primary sources to the complexity of the literary texts.

In Part II, I have tried to explain the place and function of festive themes and images in some of Shakespeare's plays. In his comedies and his romances, Shakespeare makes direct use of the symbolism attached to festivals. In his histories and tragedies, he reverses the liberating dynamic of festivity, turning it into an instrument of moral perversion, a conveyor of darkness and a herald of chaos. In his historical plays, he also makes use of festive traditions, but introduces an element of calendary vagueness which confuses the situation while still allowing the spectator a taste of the *déjà-vu*. In his tragedies, he proceeds to rework the metaphors of the customs and images of festivity, imbuing them with a new force or even violence. Once it forfeits the sanction of the people, a

303

festival loses its unificatory power and reverts to being, *par excellence*, an occasion for sacrifice and confusion. In these circumstances it becomes a pagan High Mass of disorder in which the cheery jubilations of the masses give way to the vengeful cries of a populace in revolt, the communion of hearty eating becomes a cannibal feast, the festive wine a bloodbath. It is an upside-down world all right, but one which, unlike that of the Saturnalia, does not bode well. In the case of *Othello*, we have seen in greater detail how certain rites which start off as comic or as occasions for rejoicing (such as a charivari, a riding, a Morris dance, the evacuation of wind) can produce disastrous effects when they are used for harmful purposes or when they are perversely interpreted, that is to say taken completely seriously or else tragically. Iago perverts the meaning of festivity, turning it into a nightmare in which it loses the liberating powers and function which, in the normal way, serve to wipe out violence and exorcise evil. In contrast, in Shakespeare's last plays, festivity reassumes its original cathartic powers of reconciliation – or 'recreation', as Leontes puts it in *The Winter's Tale* (iii, ii, 239); for here it serves as a rite of passage between generations, a means of making the transition from the old world to the new.

Festivity held an age-old place of importance in the calendar and was so deeply rooted in people's imaginary representations of the world that it could resurface in the most unexpected places. When hidden from public view or used to promote destructive forces, it became more disturbing, introducing a reversal of values that ran counter to the balance which it was supposed to help to preserve. In these circumstances its dionysiac force could inspire a tragic vision of life. The ambivalence of festivity is the fount of its astonishing power of metamorphosis.

A dramatist's use of popular traditions was not limited simply to transferring them to the stage or superimposing them upon the structure of his play. No doubt a minimum of fidelity to the forms of traditional festive customs was necessary to enable the public to recognize the general references. However, there was also room for him to mask those references and to introduce ellipses, shortened versions of rituals or, on the other hand, to develop correspondences and ramifications of them. Transpositions of this kind led to the creation of distortions – that is understandable enough, since the rituals were being reconstructed in a different space and seen in a different perspective, as in Hans Holbein's famous picture, *The Ambassadors*, in which the enigmatic plaque at the bottom of the canvas only delivers up its secret when the beholder looks at it having assumed a position to one side of the painting. Like the painter, the dramatist may choose to conceal his subject, the better to reveal it.[1] The arcane meanings of the calendar, when taken seriously, can reveal secrets that have been forgotten since our minds lost the habit of making all the possible permutations and establishing the covert correspondences.

When a knowing observer places himself close to the wall on which Holbein's painting hangs and looks at it sideways, what does he see? Thanks to the painter's skilful use of perspective, an oblique view makes it possible for him automatically to convert the oblong plaque into a skull. This anamorphosis is quite simply a variation on the 'vanity' theme which was a commonplace in seventeenth-century painting.[2] Similarly, in the domain of the theatre, an analysis of some of Shakespeare's images which use the theme of the Land of Cockaigne and illustrate the myth of festive abundance uncovers a negative image of torture or the spectre of a fountain flowing with blood. The most exuberant rejoicings take place at the gates of annihilation. The function of the counter-discourse of tragic festivity is to remind us of this, even as we are drawn into the joyous whirlpool of surface pleasures.

As Le Roy Ladurie remarks, in connection with the Romans carnival, the festival feeds on the dead to 'produce living flesh anew'.[3] Such symbolic cannibalism lies at the origin of a strange alchemy in which contraries espouse one another in a *coincidentia oppositorum* which is singularly upsetting to reason. Yet herein lies the mystery of the 'convulsive beauty' of which André Breton speaks at the end of *Nadja* and which other writers such as Artaud and Bataille have tried to capture in their theatre of cruelty and eroticism. To my mind, it is above all because Shakespeare's plays manage to capture the meaning of that fundamental ambivalence of festivity yet at the same time to convey the bewildering multiplicity of its forms that, despite changing fashions and theories, they continue to draw the crowds and to astonish the specialists who study them.

Folk customs	Calendar festivals	Correspondences	Folk customs	Calendar festivals	Correspondences	Folk customs	Calendar festivals	Correspondences
	JANUARY	MISRULE		**15**	Beginning of the Roman year		**MAY**	BELTANE †
Kings and Queens	1 New Year's Day	Calends of January	WINTER FEAST	**MARCH**	LENT	Morris dances / Maypole / Robin Hood (1–15)	1 May Day	BONA DEA O
	6 Twelfth Night						5 Ascension Day (M)	THARGELIA β *(Apollo/Pharmakos)*
Sword dance / Folk play	7 Distaff Day	LENAIA β Greek feast to arouse the slumbering vegetation	PLOUGHING	Palm Sunday (M)	HILARIA O	Morris dances / Ales / Mummers' plays / Summer Lords	Whisun	
	11 Plough Monday			24 Maundy Thursday (M)			Greenwich Fair	(Whit Thursday)
Divination of husbands	20 St Agnes' Eve	PAGANALIA β *(Ceres/Tellus)*	FEAST Official start of the year up until 1752	25 Good Friday (M) (Lady Day) (QD)			Cotswold Games	
				Easter (M)		Ember Days (16, 20, 21)	Trinity Sunday (M)	Summer Feast
	FEBRUARY	DIMELC†		27 Easter Monday (M)			22	
	1 St Bridget	ANTHESTERIA β *(Dionysus/Hermes)*	Hock-tide — 28 Hock Monday (Women's Day) / 29 Hock Tuesday (Men's Day)				26 Feast of Corpus Christi (M)	
	2 Candlemas			**APRIL**	MEGALESIA O *(Cybele/Attis)*	End of Moveable Feasts		
Pancakes / Cock-throwing / Sacking of brothels & theatres	9 Shrove Tuesday (M)	PARENTALIA O	Start of Moveable Feasts	4	SUMMER FEAST	Horse and greyhound races / Wrestling / Dancing	**JUNE**	
Jack-a-Lent	10 Ash Wednesday (M)	LUPERCALIA O	LENT	21	PARILIA O *(Dedication of flocks to Pales)*			
	14 St Valentine's Day	FORNACALIA O (M)	Bonfires / Pageants	23 St George	VINALIA	Bonfires	23 Midsummer Eve	High Summer Feast
(E) 17, 19, 20				28	FLORALIA	Fowl offerings / Pagants in London	24 Midsummer (QD)	

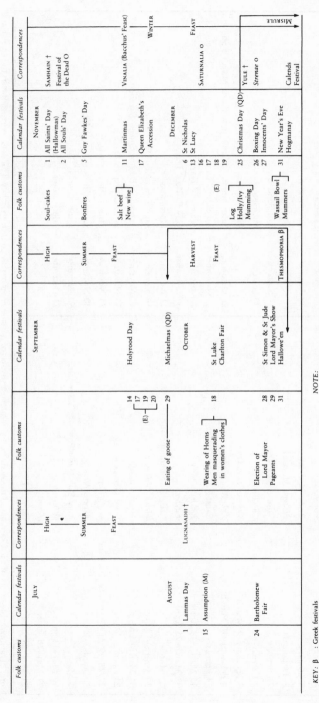

JULY – AUGUST

Folk customs	Calendar festivals	Correspondences
	JULY	HIGH
		SUMMER
		FEAST
	AUGUST	
	1 Lammas Day	LUGNASADH †
	15 Assumption (M)	
	24 Bartholomew Fair	

SEPTEMBER – OCTOBER

Folk customs	Calendar festivals	Correspondences
	SEPTEMBER	HIGH
		SUMMER
14, 17, (E) 19, 20		FEAST
Eating of goose — 29	Holyrood Day	
	Michaelmas (QD)	HARVEST
	OCTOBER	
Wearing of Horns 18	St Luke	FEAST
Men masquerading in women's clothes	Charlton Fair	
Election of Lord Mayor 28, 29, 31	St Simon & St Jude	
Pageants	Lord Mayor's Show	THESMOPHORIA β
	Hallowe'en	

NOVEMBER – DECEMBER

Folk customs	Calendar festivals	Correspondences
	NOVEMBER	
Soul-cakes	1 All Saints' Day (Hallowmas)	SAMHAIN †
	2 All Souls' Day	Festival of the Dead O
Bonfires	5 Guy Fawkes' Day	
Salt beef	11 Martinmas	VINALIA (Bacchus' Feast)
New wine	17 Queen Elizabeth's Accession	WINTER
	DECEMBER	
	6 St Nicholas	
(E)	13 St Lucy	
	16	
	17	
Log	18	SATURNALIA O
Holly/Ivy	19	
Mumming	25 Christmas Day (QD)	YULE †
	26 Boxing Day	Strenae O
Wassail Bowl	27 Innocents' Day	
Mummers	31 New Year's Eve	Calends Festival
	Hogmanay	MISRULE

NOTE:

The dates noted for the principal moveable feasts correspond to those of the year 1864, the reference date for Robert Chambers' *Book of Days*.

a 'Anthesteria' is the name of the month of February in Greek. The festival opened on the 11th of the month and lasted for three days. It was a festival of flowers held first in honour of Dionysus (a celebration of life and Spring), then in honour of Hermes, the guide of the dead in the Underworld, with offerings of pots of cereals to the dead.

KEY: β : Greek festivals
o : Roman festivals
† : Celtic festivals
M : Moveable feasts
E : Ember days
QD : Quarter Days

Appendix 1. A comparative calendar of pagan and Christian festivals and traditions

SACRED OR RITUALISTIC HALF	
25 December	Christmas – Nativity (Midwinter)
26 December	Twelve Days of Christmas
28 December	Holy Innocents
1 January	New Year
6 January	Epiphany
7 January	Rock Monday
7–14 January	*Plough Monday*
21 January	Saint Agnes' Day
2 February	Candlemas
3 February–9 March	*Shrove Tuesday*
4 February–10 March	Ash Wednesday
14 February	Saint Valentine's Day
15 March–18 April	*Palm Sunday*
22 March–25 April	*Easter*
25 March	Lady Day (Annunciation)
30 March–3 May	*Hock Monday*
31 March–4 May	*Hock Tuesday*
23 April	Saint George's Day
27/28/29 April–31 May–1/2 June	*Rogations*
30 April–3 June	*Ascension*
1 May	May Day (Saint Philip & Saint James)
10 May–13 June	*Whitsun*
17 May–20 June	*Trinity*
21 May–24 June	*Corpus Christi*

PROFANE OR SECULAR HALF	
	Sheep-shearing
24 June	Saint John the Baptist (Midsummer)
15 July	Saint Swithin
	Rush-bearing
1 August	Lammas
15 August	Assumption
	Harvest-home
14 September	Holyrood Day
29 September	Michaelmas
	Parish wakes
28 October	Saint Simon & Saint Jude (Lord Mayor's Show)
1 November	All Saints' Day
2 November	All Souls' Day
5 November	Guy Fawkes' Day
11 November	Martinmas
16 November	Saint Edmund's Day
17 November	Accession Day of Queen Elizabeth
23 November	Saint Clement's Day
25 November	Saint Catherine's Day
30 November	Saint Andrew's Day (Advent)
6 December	Saint Nicholas' Day
21 December	Saint Thomas' Day

Note: The moveable feasts of the Church and the main non-calendar festivals (of peasants and parish) appear in italics. The dates correspond to the earlier and later limits for the moveable feasts given in the Book of Common Prayer.

Appendix 2. A calendar of the principal festivals and feast days in Elizabethan England

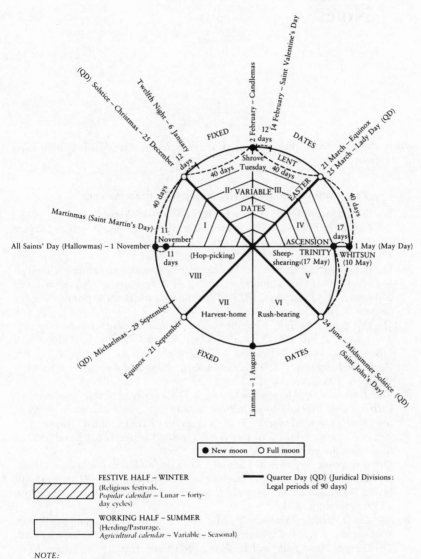

NOTE:
This is an 'early key' calendar, that is, a calendar using the earliest possible dates for the moveable feasts.

Appendix 3. The popular, agricultural and legal calendars

Notes

Where the term 'repr.' has been used, it refers to the date of the edition used for citations.

Part I. Introduction: Festivity during the Elizabethan age

1. See the *Oxford English Dictionary* (*OED*), article 'Merry'.
2. *Les fêtes de la Renaissance*, articles collected and introduced by Jean Jacquot (Paris, 1956). The edition used here is the second edition, 1973.
3. *Ibid.*, vol. i, p. 14.
4. On this point, see Robert W. Malcolmson, *Popular Recreations in English Society 1700–1850* (Cambridge, 1973), p. 3. In *Popular Culture in Early Modern Europe* (London, 1978), Peter Burke tackles these problems in his chapter 3, 'An Elusive Quarry', pp. 65–87.
5. On this point, see E.K. Chambers, *The Mediaeval Stage* 2 vols. (Oxford, 1903), vol. i, pp. 110–15 and *passim*); Charles Phythian-Adams, *Local History and Folklore* (London, 1975), pp. 8–11; and Glynne Wickham, *Early English Stages 1300 to 1660*, vol iii: *Plays and their Makers to 1576* (London, 1981), pp. 11–22.
6. *The Anatomie of Abuses: containing a Discoverie, or Briefe Summarie of such Notable Vice and Imperfections as now raigne with many Countreys of the World; but (especially) in a famous Llande called Ailgna* [i.e. Anglia] . . . Four editions of this book appeared between 1583 and 1595. I have used the edition London, 1877–9.
7. On this point, see Keith Thomas, *Religion and the Decline of Magic* (London, 1971), chapter 3; Charles Phythian-Adams, *Local History*, p. 10; David Wilkins, *Concilia Magnae Britanniae et Hiberniae*, 4 vols. (London, 1737), vol. iii, p. 823.
8. See *OED*, article 'May-day', sense a. See also on this subject Robert Withington, *English Pageantry, An Historical Outline*, 2 vols. (Harvard, 1918; repr. New York and London, 1963), vol. i, p. 19, n. 1, and M.C. Bradbrook, *The Rise of the Common Player* (Cambridge, 1962; repr. 1964), p. 289, n. 9.
9. Withington, *English Pageantry*, vol. i, pp. 39 and 41–2.
10. See Thomas, *Religion*, p. 71.
11. Withington, *English Pageantry*, vol. ii, pp. 11–14.
12. See A.L. Rowse, *The Elizabethan Renaissance: The Life of the Society* (London, 1971), pp. 90–1.
13. *The Progresses and Public Processions of Queen Elizabeth I*, 3 vols. (London, 1788–1807; repr. 1823); *The Progresses, Processions and Magnificent Festivities of King James the First*, 4 vols. (London, 1828).

14. See David Bergeron, *English Civic Pageantry 1558–1642* (London, 1971), p. 268.
15. In this book, I shall be using the words 'Puritan' and 'Puritanism' in their generally accepted sense, limiting them to the somewhat polemical meaning of those who opposed the various folkloric festivals and traditions inherited from both paganism and 'papism', rather than that of 'religious dissenter' or member of any particular movement or sect. As Patrick Collinson shows in *The Elizabethan Puritan Movement* (London, 1967), the evidence shows clearly that as early as the beginning of Elizabeth's reign, the Puritan movement manifested a very wide range of preoccupations. In fact some of the movement's activities took on a somewhat festive air – for instance the meetings held in taverns – or even incorporated a measure of irreverent buffoonery reminiscent of the Feast of Fools of the Middle Ages, as in the case of the 'Martin Marprelate Controversy' (*Elizabethan Puritan Movement*, pp. 392–4).
16. See Roy Strong, *The Cult of Elizabeth* (London, 1977), p. 16; Jean Wilson, *Entertainments for Elizabeth I* (Woodbridge, Suffolk, 1980), p. 21.
17. See Charles Phythian-Adams, 'Ceremony and the Citizen: The Communal Year at Coventry, 1450–1550', in Peter Clark and Paul Slack, eds., *Crisis and Order in English Towns, 1500–1700* (London, 1972), p. 79.
18. See Glynne Wickham, *Early English Stages*, vol. iii, p. 60.
19. *Ibid.*, p. xix.
20. We should not, however, underestimate their importance. Elizabethan theatre, which to some extent supplanted them, remained deeply influenced by the spirit and traditions of this primitive and popular 'theatre'.
21. Malcolm Nelson, *The Robin Hood Tradition in the English Renaissance* (Salzburg, 1973); Kathleen Basford, *The Green Man* (Ipswich, 1978); Richard Marienstras, *New Perspectives on the Shakespearean World* (Cambridge, 1985), pp. 20–30.
22. See below, pp. 141–54.
23. Thomas Dekker, *The Dead Terme* (1608), in *The Non-Dramatic Works of Thomas Dekker*, ed. A.B. Grosart, 5 vols. (London, 1884–6; repr. New York, 1963), vol. iv, p. 22.
24. T.F. Thiselton Dyer, *British Popular Customs* (London, 1981); A.R. Wright, *British Calendar Customs*, 3 vols. (London, 1940); Christina Hole, *A Dictionary of British Folk Customs* (London, 1976).
25. *Le don du rien* (Paris, 1977), p. 131.
26. See *Victoria County History* (*VCH*), vol. viii: *Warwickshire*, p. 219.
27. On this point, see the decree passed by the Long Parliament in April 1643, 'for the better observation of the Lords-Day', cited, with a commentary, by W.P. Baker in the chapter entitled 'The Observance of Sunday' in his *Englishmen at Rest and Play. Some Phases of Leisure, 1588–1714* (Oxford, 1931), pp. 116–17.
28. *Local History*, p. 18.
29. *A Survey of London* (1598), ed. Henry Morley (London, 1890), p. 124.
30. See Alice S. Venezky, *Pageantry on the Shakespearean Stage* (New York, 1951), pp. 93–102.
31. Stow, *Survey*, p. 102.
32. Venezky, *Pageantry*, p. 102.

33. See Thomas, *Religion*, pp. 62–5.
34. See *OED*, article 'beat' (verb), entry 41. See also Bickley's 'Articles for Chichester', in W.P.M. Kennedy's *Elizabethan Episcopal Administration*, 3 vols. (London, 1924), vol. iii, p. 216; John Brand and Henry Ellis, *Observations on the Popular Antiquities of Great Britain*, 3 vols. (London, 1849), vol. i, p. 206; Barry Reay, ed., *Popular Culture in Seventeenth-Century England* (London, 1985, repr. 1988), p. 8; and Richard Marienstras, 'La fête des rogations et l'importance des limites à l'époque élisabéthaine', in *L'Europe de la Renaissance. Culture et civilisations. Mélanges offerts à Marie-Thérèse Jones-Davies* (Paris, 1988), pp. 114–15.
35. See Charles Phythian-Adams, *Desolation of a City: Coventry and the Urban Crisis of the Middle Ages* (Cambridge, 1979), p. 176.
36. *Early English Stages*, vol. iii, pp. xvii, 23–61.
37. See Mircea Eliade, *Le mythe de l'éternel retour* (Paris, 1969), p. 73.
38. See, among others, the two following proverbs cited in M.P. Tilley, *A Dictionary of the Proverbs in England in the Sixteenth and Seventeenth Centuries* (Ann Arbor, 1950; repr. 1960): 'Christmas comes but once a year . . .' and 'They talk of Christmas so long that it comes' (nos. B 701 and C 373).
39. *Rural Economy in Yorkshire in 1641, Being the Farming and Account Books of Henry Best* ed. C.B. Robinson, Surtees Society, 33 (Durham, 1857), p. 3.
40. 'The English Army Rations in the Time of Queen Elizabeth', in *Social England Illustrated*, ed. A. Lang (London, 1877–90), p. 13.

1 Festivity and popular beliefs in the Elizabethan age

1. A. Tille, *Yule and Christmas* (London, 1889); Chambers, *Mediaeval Stage*, vol. i, p. 113; Martin P. Nilsson, *Primitive Time Reckoning* (London, 1920), p. 77. On this point see also Michel Meslin, *La fête des kalendes de janvier dans l'empire romain* (Brussels, 1970), p. 127.
2. See Phythian-Adams, *Local History*, p. 9; Wickham, *Early English Stages* vol. iii, p. 11.
3. Bede, *Ecclesiastical History of the English Nation*, ed. and trans. J. Steevens (London, 1723), Everyman edition, pp. 52–3.
4. *Early English Stages*, vol. iii, p. 15.
5. Basford, *Green Man*, p. 19.
6. *VCH*, vol. viii: *Warwickshire*, p. 246.
7. Phythian-Adams, *Local History*, pp. 10 and 22; see also Nilsson, *Primitive Time Reckoning*, p. 293, and Christine E. Fell, 'Gods and Heroes of the Northern World', in *The Northern World: The History and Heritage of Northern Europe, AD 400–1100* (London, 1980), pp. 34–9.
8. Thomas, *Religion*, p. 26.
9. Reginald Scot, *The Discoverie of Witchcraft* (1584), ed. Brinsley Nicholson (London, 1886), Book xvi, chapter 24, p. 525. This criticism was later made again by Thomas Hall in *Funebriae Florae or the Downfall of May Games* (London, 1661), p. 7.
10. On this point see *A Short-Title Catalogue of Books Printed in England, Scotland and Ireland 1475–1640*, ed. A.W. Pollard and G.R. Redgrave, vol. i

(2nd edn, London, 1976), article 'Voragine, Jacobus de'. Twelve editions of this work appeared between 1483 and 1527, after which there were no more because of anti-Catholic criticism.

11. 'Dramatic Aspects of Medieval Folk Festivals in England', *Studies in Philology*, 17 (1920), p. 61.
12. On this point, see Robert Charles Hope, *The Legendary Lore of the Holy Wells of England* (London, 1893), pp. xx–xxi.
13. *Remains of Gentilisme and Judaisme* (1686–7), ed. James Britten (London, 1881), p. 9.
14. Wilkins, *Concilia*, vol. IV, p. 30.
15. *Remains*, p. 34.
16. See Thomas, *Religion*, p. 63; Archbishop Grindal had stipulated that the Rogation should no longer take the form of 'processions', but should be 'perambulations'. See *The Remains of Edmund Grindal*, ed. W. Nicholson (Cambridge, 1843), pp. 249–51.
17. *Elizabethan Renaissance*, p. 172.
18. Thomas, *Religion*, p. 32.
19. See this word in the *OED*. See also *Peasant Customs and Savage Myths. Selections from the British Folklorists*, ed. Richard M. Dorson, 2 vols. (London, 1968).
20. The parish registers show that the Morris dancers' costumes would be stored in the church, as were other disguises used for festival entertainments. The parish was the principal beneficiary from these festivals, since the money from collections was mostly donated to it, for its good works; and in many cases the parish seems to have been the main organizer of these local festivals. On this subject, see J.C. Cox, *Churchwardens' Accounts* (London, 1913).
21. *Remains*, p. 9. See also Robert Herrick, *Hesperides* (1648), ed. J. Max Patrick (New York, 1968), poem no. H 787, p. 347.
22. Margaret Murray, *The Witch-Cult in Western Europe* (Oxford, 1921) and *The God of the Witches* (London, 1931); Arno Runeberg, *Witches, Demons and Fertility Magic* (London, 1947).
23. See on this point the criticisms of Norman Cohn, *Europe's Inner Demons* (London, 1975), chapter 6: 'The Non-Existent Society of Witches'.
24. On this point see the analysis by Jean Delumeau, *Le peur en Occident* (Paris, 1978), pp. 364–70.
25. Pp. 63–4.
26. On this subject, see M.W. Latham, *The Elizabethan Fairies* (New York, 1930), pp. 44–7; and K.M. Briggs, *The Anatomy of Puck* (London, 1959), p. 117.
27. *The Canterbury Tales*, in *The Works of Geoffrey Chaucer*, ed. Walter W. Skeat, 7 vols. (Oxford, 1894–7), vol. IV.
28. *A Treatise of Specters or Straunge Sights, Visions and Aparitions Appearing Sensibly unto Men* (London, 1605). (*Discours et histoires des spectres, visions et apparitions des esprits, anges, démons, et âmes, se monstrans visibles aux hommes* (Paris, 1605), p. 201.
29. See *A Treatise Containing the Aequity of an Humble Supplication which is to be Exhibited unto his Gracious Maiesty and this High Court of Parliament in behalfe of the Country of Wales, that some Order may be*

taken for the preaching of the Gospell among these people (Oxford, 1587), p. 46.

30. According to Keith Thomas (*Religion*, p. 607), the expression 'elf-shot' was used to refer to individuals smitten with sudden ailments for which there was, at the time, no medical explanation.

31. Latham, *Elizabethan Fairies*, p. 34. See in particular the work by the minister at Aberfoil, Robert Kirk, *Secret Commonwealth, or A Treatise Displayeing the Chiefe Curiosities as they are in Use among diverse of the People of Scotland to this Day* (London, 1691; repr. 1815).

32. Briggs, *Anatomy of Puck*, p. 117.

33. Published in London in 1579. I have used the Everyman edition, ed. Philip Henderson (London, 1932; repr. 1960), p. 55.

34. *Ibid.*, pp. 3–4.

35. *Discoverie*, p. 131.

36. *Daemonologie* (Edinburgh, 1597), ed. G.B. Harrison, The Bodley Head Quartos, 10, 1922–6; repr. 1966, pp. 73–4.

37. *The Anatomy of Melancholy* (London, 1621). I have used the Everyman edition, ed. Holbrook Jackson (London 1932; repr. 1978), Part 1, sect. 2, mem. 1, subs. 2, pp. 192–3.

38. *Remains*, pp. 67–8.

39. *Table-Talk* (London, 1689), in *Table Talk by Various Writers*, ed. J.C. Thornton (London, 1934), p. 74 (article 'Parson').

40. Briggs, *Anatomy of Puck*, p. 13.

41. *A Midsummer Night's Dream*, II, i, 43.

42. Latham, *Elizabethan Fairies*, p. 239.

43. See the anonymous poem *Sir Orfeo* (c. 1300), which transposes the myth of Orpheus into a romantic framework of the fairy world; also 'The Merchant's Tale' in Chaucer's *The Canterbury Tales*.

44. Fairies were reputed to steal children whom they considered to be beautiful, leaving in their place substitutes, usually ugly or deformed: changelings. The *OED* gives the following definition: 'A child secretly substituted for another in infancy; esp. a child (generally stupid or ugly) supposed to have been left by fairies in exchange for one stolen'. Robert Willis, in *Mount Tabor or Private Exercises of a Penitent Sinner* (London, 1639), tells of an episode from his early childhood which shows that in 1564, the year of both his and Shakespeare's births, beliefs in changelings had by no means disappeared:

> When we come to yeares, we are commonly told of what befel us in our infancie, if the same were more than ordinary. Such an accident (by relation of others) befell me within a few daies after my birth, whilst my mother lay of me being her second child, when I was taken out of the bed from her side, and by my suddain and fierce crying recovered again, being found sticking between the beds-head and the wall; and if I had not cryed in that manner as I did, our gossips had a conceit that I had been carried away by the Fairies they know not whither, and some elfe or changeling (as they call it) laid in my room.   (pp. 92–3)

45. *Remains*, p. 30.

46. F.J. Child, *The English and Scottish Popular Ballads*, 5 vols. (London, 1882; repr. 1965), no. 181.

47. *Anatomy of Puck*, p. 15.

48. *Anatomy of Melancholy*, Part 1, sect. 2, mem. 1, subs. 2, p. 192.

49. It is worth noting that Holinshed describes those who were to be called the 'weird sisters' in *Macbeth* as 'goddesses of destinie, or else some nymphs or feiries'. See *Macbeth*, ed. Kenneth Muir, The Arden Shakespeare (London, 1951; repr. 1979), p. 172.

50. *God of the Witches*, pp. 48–50. On this point, see also the article 'Fairy' in the *Encyclopaedia of Religion and Ethics*, ed. James Hastings *et al.* (Edinburgh, 1908–26), and Thomas Davidson, *Rowan Tree and Red Thread* (Edinburgh and London, 1949).

51. *Witch-Cult*, p. 109.

52. *Elizabethan Fairies*, p. 101.

53. On this subject, see the catalogue for the Bibliothèque Nationale's exhibition, *Les sorcières*, ed. Maxime Préaud (Paris, 1973), p. 66.

54. See, for example, 'The Leicestershire St George Play', in *Chief Pre-Shakespearean Dramas*, ed. J.Q. Adams (Boston, 1924), pp. 355–6.

55. *Shakespeare and the Popular Tradition in the Theater* (Baltimore, 1978), p. 32 (first published in German, Berlin, 1967).

56. On this subject, see Enid Welsford, *The Fool* (London, 1935; repr. 1978), pp. 69–71.

57. 'Inversion, Misrule and the Meaning of Witchcraft', *Past and Present*, 87 (January 1981), p. 100.

58. See the word 'Misrule' (entries 1 and 2) in the *OED*. See also Stuart Clark, 'Inversion, Misrule and Witchcraft', p. 103; Keith Thomas, *Rule and Misrule in the Schools of Early Modern England*, The Stenton Lecture 1975 (Reading, 1976), pp. 32–4; François Laroque, 'La notion de "Misrule" à l'époque élisabéthaine', in J. Lafond and A. Redondo, eds., *L'image du monde renversé et ses représentations littéraires et para-littéraires de la fin du XVIᵉ siècle au milieu du XVIIᵉ* (Paris, 1979), pp. 161–70.

59. *Anatomie of Abuses*, pp. 148–9.

60. *Traité contre les masques* (Paris, 1608), p. 3.

61. Thomas, *Religion*, pp. 440–5.

62. *Ibid.*

63. *Remains*, p. 15.

64. *Discoverie*, p. 152.

65. On this point, see *The Late Lancashire Witches* (1634), by Thomas Heywood and Richard Brome, IV, i, ed. Laird H. Barber (New York and London, 1979) pp. 190–1, and also *The Witch of Edmonton* by Samuel Rowley, Thomas Dekker and John Ford (1621), III, iv, 14–67 (ed. Peter Corbin and Douglas Sedge, in *Three Jacobean Witchcraft Plays* (Manchester, 1986), pp. 183–4).

66. See James I, *Daemonologie*, p. 10; Scot, *Discoverie*, p. 31.

67. See George Waldron, *The History and Description of the Isle of Man* (London, 1744), p. 120.

68. *Religion*, p. 556.

69. On this subject, see Thomas Nashe, *Summer's Last Will and Testament* (1600), in Thomas Nashe, *Works*, ed. R. McKerrow, 5 vols. Oxford, 1904–10; repr. 1958, vol. III, pp. 232–95; Joseph Hall, *Virgidemiarum*, (1598), in *The Collected Poems*, ed. A. Davenport (Liverpool, 1949), p. 81; Thomas Dekker, *A Strange Horse Race* (1613), in *Non-Dramatic Works*, vol. III, pp. 335–8.

70. Alan Macfarlane, *Witchcraft in Tudor and Stuart England* (London, 1970), p. 174; Thomas, *Religion*, p. 561.
71. See Stubbes, *Anatomie of Abuses*, pp. 148–9.
72. On this point, see Thomas Tusser, *His Good Points of Husbandry*, ed. D. Hartley (London, 1931), pp. 59, 96; *Lean's Collectanea, Collections by Vincent Stuckey Lean*, 4 vols. (London, 1903), vol. III, pp. 244–9; Thomas, *Religion*, p. 297.
73. See Thomas Buckminster, *An Almanack and Prognostication for the Year 1598*, ed. Eustace F. Bosanquet, Shakespeare Association Facsimiles, 8 (Oxford, 1935), sign. A ii.
74. These are collected together in Part 2 of Buckminster's calendar cited above, n. 73.
75. As is indicated by the following two proverbs cited by Lean, *Collectanea*, vol. III, p. 239: 'Marry in Lent / And live to repent', and 'Marry in May / And you'll rue the day.' Weddings were prohibited during this season. The parish registers of the county of York show that, up until the eighteenth century, the period of Lent was the time when there were the fewest conceptions (see Thomas, *Religion*, pp. 620–1). As Thomas Platter (*Travels in England, 1599* (trans. Clare Williams, London, 1937), p. 188), notes with some surprise, England, which suscribed to the reformed faith, had maintained the rules of Lent, essentially for economic reasons:

> Although England belongs entirely to the reform church, yet on two days a week . . . throughout the year, and also during fast time they eat no meat, by order of the secular government, so that the meat shall not be entirely consumed, especially as a great deal is salted for export. Likewise to keep the fish trade alive . . . and the fishermen would otherwise go short.

76. Lean, *Collectanea*, vol. III, p. 232.
77. Aubrey, *Remains*, p. 63. See also the *OED*, article 'Childermas' (sense 2).
78. Cited by Brand and Ellis, *Popular Antiquities.*, vol. II, p. 48.
79. *William Shakespeare. A Compact Documentary Life* (Oxford, 1977), p. 25.
80. On this point, see *Every Man Out of His Humour* (1600), by Ben Jonson (I, iii, 33–5):

> SORDIDO: O here, S. Swithins, the xv day, variable weather, for the most part raine, good; for the most part raine: why, it should raine forty daies after . . .
> (*Ben Jonson*, ed. C.H. Herford and Percy [and Evelyn] Simpson, II vols. (Oxford, 1925–52), vol. III, p. 453).

81. Thomas, *Religion*, p. 623. According to F. Noël's *Nouveau dictionnaire des origines, inventions et découvertes* (Paris, 1883), pendulum clocks were actually invented a little earlier than that, by Vincent Galileo, Galileo's son, in 1649 in Venice. The pocket watches made in Nuremberg from about 1500 on were imported into England only in about 1576–7. See also the information provided on this subject by John Kerrigan in his introduction to the New Penguin edition of *Shakespeare's Sonnets and A Lover's Complaint* (Harmondsworth, 1986), pp. 34–8. In an article entitled 'Ladies, Gentlemen and Skulls: *Hamlet* and the Iconographic Traditions' (*Shakespeare Quarterly*, 30 (1978), pp. 15–41), Roland Mushat Frye notes that there existed at this time watches in the form of skulls, each of which would serve as a *memento mori*. They were often worn attached to a chain. He reproduces an

engraving showing one of these 'deathhead time pieces' which belonged to Mary, Queen of Scots (p. 20).

82. *As You Like It*, iii, ii, 294–5.
83. On this point, see Robert Chambers, *The Book of Days*, 2 vols. (London, 1864), vol. ii, p. 410.
84. The *OED* defines this word as follows (sense 8a): 'A small body of wind instrumentalists maintained by a city or town at the public charge. They played for the daily diversion of the councillors on ceremonial and festive occasions, and as a town or city band they entertained the citizens perambulating the streets, often by night or in the early morning.'
85. W.L. Woodfill, *Musicians in English Society from Elizabeth to Charles I* (Princeton, 1953), p. 46.
86. These contrasts lie at the heart of what the anthropologist Edmund Leach has called 'the pendulum-vision of time' in 'Two Essays concerning the Symbolic Representation of Time' in his *Rethinking Anthropology* (London, 1961), pp. 124–36. On this subject, see also my article 'Images et figures du grotesque à l'époque élisabéthaine: calendrier, corps, cuisine' (*Cahiers Charles V, Théâtre et Société*, 2 (April 1980), p. 31).
87. In the legend of Saint Lucy, the saint tears out her own eyes, so that her lover will leave her in peace, alone with God. (See *Brewer's Dictionary of Phrase and Fable*, rev. edn by Ivor H. Evans, London 1970; repr. 1977.) The date of the Feast of Saint Lucy, 13 December, made it one of the shortest days of the year, 'the year's midnight', as John Donne calls it in his poem entitled 'A Nocturnal upon St. Lucy's Day, Being the Shortest Day'.
88. We should, however, note that the 1582 Gregorian reform of the calendar was not adopted in England and Scotland until 1752, as a result of religious opposition to the papacy. According to John Kerrigan (*Shakespeare's Sonnets and A Lover's Complaint*, p. 35), fob-watches had been introduced in England under Elizabeth's reign, so that 'clock time invaded men's lives, and was indeed, for city-dwellers like Shakespeare, the matrix of living'.

2 Festivity and society in Shakespeare's time

1. On this subject, see the proceedings of the colloquium organized at Goutelas in September 1979 on 'La littérature populaire aux XV^c et XVI^c siècles', ed. Henri Weber, Claude Longeon and Claude Mont, which have been published in the two volumes of no. 11 (December 1980) of the *RHR* review (*Bulletin de l'Association d'études sur l'Humanisme, la Réforme et la Renaissance*). See also J.C. Schmitt's article entitled 'Religion populaire et culture folklorique' in *Annales* (September–October 1976), pp. 941–53, in which the author shows how difficult it is to give a clear definition of this adjective, for it involves more than a simple distinction between *literati* and *illiterati*.
2. 'The Place of Laughter in Tudor and Stuart England', *TLS* (21 January 1977), p. 80.
3. Robert Redfield, *Peasant Society and Culture* (Chicago, 1956), p. 41.
4. Peter Burke, *Popular Culture*, p. 24.
5. *A Discourse of English Poetrie* (London, 1586), sign. D.

6. George Puttenham, *The Arte of English Poesie* (1589; Scolar Press Facsimile, Menston, 1968), vol. ii, ix, p. 69.

7. Robert Laneham, *A Letter* (London, 1575), pp. 34–36. See also *Robert Laneham's Letter*, ed. F.J. Furnivall, New Shakespere Society, 6th ser., 14 (London, 1890), pp. xii and ff.

8. In *The Defence of Poesie* (London, 1595; repr. as Scolar Press Facsimile, Menston, 1968), Philip Sidney expresses his distaste for plays in which the genres are mixed:

> But besides these grosse absurdities, howe all their Playes bee neither right Tragedies, nor right Comedies, mingling Kinges and Clownes ... so as neither the admiration and Commiseration, nor the right sportfulnesse is by their mongrell Tragicomedie obtained ... But if wee marke them well [the Ancients], wee shall finde that they never or verie daintily matche horne Pipes and Funeralls.   (Sign. I. v.)

On Sidney's ambivalent feelings when confronted by Tarlton and the theatre, and also on the probable source of his expression 'mingling Kinges and Clownes' (probably drawn from George Whetstone's *Promos and Cassandra*), see Andrew Gurr, *Playgoing in Shakespeare's London* (Cambridge, 1987), pp. 122–3. Two years later, Joseph Hall, in *Virgidemiarum* (1598), was to make a similar attack against these incongruous mixtures.

9. *Tamburlaine* (1590), Part 1, Prologue, in *The Complete Works of Christopher Marlowe*, ed. Fredson Bowers, 2 vols. (Cambridge, 1973; repr. 1981), vol. i, p. 79.

10. Thomas Dekker, in 'A Strange Horse-Race' (1613) (*Non-Dramatic Works*, vol. iii, p. 340) calls it both 'nasty' and 'bawdy'.

11. On the jig, which used to round off Elizabethan dramatic performances in the theatres, see also Thomas Platter's remarks, *Travels in England*, p. 166. The translation is by T.S. Dorsch, who cites this passage in his introduction to the Arden Shakespeare edition of *Julius Caesar* (London, 1955; repr. 1977, p. vii):

> After lunch, at about two o'clock, I and my party crossed the river, and there in the house with the thatched roof we saw an excellent performance of the tragedy of the first emperor Julius Caesar, with about fifteen characters; and after the play, according to their custom, they did a most elegant and curious dance, two dressed in men's clothes and two in women's.

For an analysis of the jig, see Charles Read Baskervill, *The Elizabethan Jig and Related Song Drama* (New York, 1929), p. 3; see also David Wiles, *Shakespeare's Clown. Actor and Text in the Elizabethan Playhouse* (Cambridge, 1987), pp. 43–60.

12. 1612, Oct. 1, Order at General Session of the Peace for Middlesex held at Westminster, printed from Session Rolls, in John Cordy Jeaffreson, *Middlesex County Records*, 3 vols. (Clerkenwell, 1886), vol. ii, p. 83. Cited by E.K. Chambers, *The Elizabethan Stage*, 4 vols (Oxford, 1923), vol. iv, pp. 340–1.

13. See my analysis of these festive manifestations within the framework of the May Day celebrations, below, pp. 138–9.

14. William Harrison, *A Description of England in Shakespeare's Youth* (1577) ed. F.J. Furnivall, The New Shakspere Society (London, 1877–81), p. 150.

15. See below, pp. 89–90.
16. William Harrison, *Description of England*, pp. 150–1.
17. In *The Works in Prose and Verse of Nicholas Breton*, ed. A.B. Grosart, 2 vols (Edinburgh, 1879; repr. Hildesheim, 1969), vol. I, p. 7 (1st column).
18. *The Lady of Pleasure*, ed. Ronald Huebert (Manchester 1986) I, i, 8–16. See below, p. 125.
19. First published in Venice in 1528, this book was translated into English in 1561. I have used the edition by George Bull (Harmondsworth, 1967; repr. 1978), pp. 117–18.
20. *Defence of Poesie*, Sign. I v.
21. *The Holy State; the Profane State* (Cambridge, 1642), p. 175.
22. Cited by Nichols, *Progresses of Queen Elizabeth*, vol. I, p. 443.
23. See *A Series of Precedents and Proceedings in Criminal Cases 1475–1660*, ed. W.H. Hale (London, 1847), cases 702, 710 and 724, pp. 226–34.
24. Cited in William Harrison, *Description of England*, pp. 133–4.
25. See Thomas Lupton (?), *Siuqila...Too Good to be True...*(London, 1580), p. 18. On this point, see also David Underdown, *Revel, Riot, and Rebellion. Popular Politics and Culture in England, 1603–1660* (Oxford, 1985; repr. 1987), pp. 43–68; Christopher Hill, *Society and Puritanism in Pre-Revolutionary England* (London, 1964; repr. 1969), in particular the chapter entitled 'The Uses of Sabbatarianism', pp. 141–211; Patrick Collinson, *The Religion of Protestants. The Church in English Society 1559–1625* (Oxford, 1982; repr. 1988), pp. 203–25.
26. *Sermons by Hugh Latimer*, ed. C.E. Corrie (Cambridge, 1844), p. 208. On this point, see Collinson, *Religion of Protestants*, p. 225.
27. *The Marprelate Tracts 1588–1589*, ed. William Pierce (London, 1911), pp. 226–7. See also Andrew Gurr's analysis in *Playgoing*, pp. 142–3, on the subject of the adaptation of 'traditional folk-play May-games against Martin'; Patrick Collinson (*Elizabethan Puritan Movement*, pp. 392–4) observes that, in his opinion, Martin's satire is far superior to that of the 'professional wits' hired to answer him. Martin was also to be called 'a foolish jester' by Josias Nichols, an expression which calls to mind the traditions of the satirical farce of the fourteenth and fifteenth centuries and the Feast of Fools.
28. *Sabbathum Veteris et Novi Testamenti or the True Doctrine of the Sabbath* (London, 1606), p. 339.
29. See in particular *Mery Tales of the Mad Men of Gotham* (1630), in *Shakespeare Jest-Books*, ed. W.C. Hazlitt, 3 vols. (London, 1864; repr. New York, 1964), vol. III, p. 4.
30. *The Acts of the High Commission Court within the Diocese of Durham*, ed. James Raine, Surtees Society, 34 (London, 1858), p. 52.
31. 'Folk Play in Tudor Interludes', in *English Drama: Forms and Development, Essays in Honour of M.C. Bradbrook*, ed. Marie Axton and Raymond Williams (Cambridge, 1977), p. 3.
32. On this point, see Robert Weimann, *Shakespeare and the Popular Tradition*, pp. 267–8, n. 38. For an opposite view, see E.A.M. Colman, *The Dramatic Use of Bawdy in Shakespeare* (London, 1974), p. 80.
33. Quite apart from all the allusions scattered through many plays – *As You Like It*, I, i, 109–11, for instance – the name of Robin Hood appears in the titles of no fewer than fifteen plays written between the fifteenth

and the seventeenth centuries. On this subject, see Alfred Harbage and Samuel Schoenbaum, *Annals of English Drama, 975–1700* (London, 1964), p. 277.

34. *Middle-Class Culture in Elizabethan England* (Chapel Hill, 1935; repr. 1964), p. 95.
35. *Works*, vol. III, p. 147. In this connection, see the note by Jean-Marie Maguin, 'Nashe's *Lenten Stuffe*: The Relevance of the Author's Name', *Cahiers Elisabéthains*, 24 (October 1983), p. 73.
36. *An Halfe-penny Worth of Wit, in a Penny-Worth of Paper* (London, 1613), pp. 21–2.
37. On this point, see Andrew Gurr's analysis (*Playgoing*, pp. 121–8), in which he studies the link between Tarlton and the 'country May-games' and comments: 'Tarlton put the stereotype on stage, dressing himself in country clothes, a buttoned cap, baggy slops in russet, a bag at his side and the pipe and tabor . . . commonly used in country May-games' (p. 127). See also Sandra Billington, *A Social History of the Fool* (Brighton, 1984), pp. 42–4.
38. *Picturae Loquentes or Pictures Drawne Forth in Characters* (1631 and 1635), ed. C.H. Wilkinson (Oxford, 1946), p. 67.
39. *The Overburian Characters* (1614), ed. W.J. Paylor (Oxford, 1936), pp. 78–9.
40. On this point, see E.K. Chambers, *Mediaeval Stage*, vol. I, pp. 229 and 267; Mikhaïl Bakhtin, *Rabelais and His World* (Moscow, 1965; trans. Hélène Iswolsky (Boston, 1968; repr. Bloomington, Ind., 1984), pp. 389–94, 407–9; Emmanuel Le Roy Ladurie, *Carnival in Romans. A People's Uprising at Romans 1579–1580*, trans. Mary Feeney (London, 1980; repr. Harmondsworth, 1981), p. 173.
41. See Underdown, *Revel, Riot, and Rebellion*, pp. 45–7.
42. *The Practice of the Divell* (London, c. 1577), sign. c2.
43. See Thomas, 'The Place of Laughter', pp. 80–1.
44. *Rabelais and His World*, pp. 12–23.
45. See Olive Busby, *Studies in the Development of the Fool in the Elizabethan Drama* (New York, 1923), pp. 22–3; see also Victor Bourgy, *Le bouffon sur la scène anglaise au XVIe siècle* (Paris, 1969), pp. 258–66, and Richard Levin, *The Multiple Plot in Renaissance Drama* (Chicago, 1971), p. 141.
46. According to Bourgy, a clown is characterized by 'a simple mind', a 'naive soul', a 'solid stomach' and a 'generous heart' (*Le bouffon*, pp. 146–58). Levin (*Multiple Plot*, p. 146) compares the mind of a clown to that of a child. On the subject of his sexual appetite, see the analysis by Edward Berry, *Shakespeare's Comic Rites* (Cambridge, 1984), pp. 120–3.
47. On this subject, see Jaques' speech in *As You Like It* (II, vii, 36–61), envying the clown his freedom of speech and the immunity which he enjoyed.
48. Levin, *Multiple Plot*, p. 145.
49. Francis Beaumont and John Fletcher, *Select Plays*, ed. G.P. Baker (London, 1911; repr. 1953), p. 252. To understand the full bitterness of this lament, which may seem somewhat out of place in a public theatre, we should remember, as Andrew Gurr points out, that this tragicomedy had originally been written to satisfy the more pretentious taste of the patrons of the private Blackfriars theatre: 'Fletcher had more grounds for grief than most

since the playgoers at Blackfriars seem to have expected a traditional and populist kind of play with May-games and rural clowns, not at all the usual Blackfriars pretension' (*Playgoing*, p. 95).

50. See Wiles, *Shakespeare's Clown*, pp. 2–23.
51. *Respublica* (by Nicholas Udall?) (1533), ed. W.W. Greg, Early English Text Society, 226 (London, 1952), III, iii, 1, p. 22; *Love's Labour's Lost*, v, i, 73–75; Thomas Dekker, *The Shoemaker's Holiday*, ed. R.L. Smallwood and Stanley Wells (Manchester, 1979), p. 157. See also Levin, *Multiple Plot*, p. 145: 'For the clown's roles as child-idiot-lout, as saturnalian ruler, and as ritual mocker all seem to operate ... by sanctioning the release, through the subplot, of our anarchic impulses and feelings ...'.
52. Dog-Latin; see *OED*, 'Dog', sense 17e (translator's note).
53. In the Preface to his *Endimion*, John Lyly seems to be aware of this phenomenon, when he writes: 'what heretofore hath been served in severall dishes for a feast, now minced in a charger or a gallimaufry. If we present a mingle-mangle, our fault is to be excused, because the whole worlde is become an Hodge-podge' (in *The Complete Works of John Lyly*, ed. R. Warwick Bond, 3 vols. (Oxford, 1902; repr. 1967), III, ii (p. 115).
54. '... I have taught you arsymetry, as *additiori multiplicarum*, the rule of three, and all for the begetting of a boy, and to be banished for my labour?' (III, ii, in Robert Greene, *Complete Plays*, ed. Thomas H. Dickinson, (London, 1909), p. 124).
55. IV, iv; in *The Shakespeare Apocrypha*, ed. C.F. Tucker Brooke (Oxford, 1908), p. 111.
56. The visual and proverbial theme of the clash between Carnival and Lent, in which individuals carrying strings of sausages and chitterlings came to blows with those bearing cod or other dried fish appears in Pieter Brueghel's paintings. It demonstrates clearly enough the semantic inter-dependence between the body (fat/thin), food (pork/beef/fish) and festivity (Carnival/Lent).
57. See André Pieyre de Mandiargues, *Arcimboldo le merveilleux* (Paris, 1977); see also Jean-Claude Margolin, 'Pour une sémiologie historique des nourritures', in *Pratiques et discours alimentaires à la Renaissance* (Paris, 1982), pp. 263–6.
58. This inversion is detectable at the level of the popular etymology of the French word *galimatias* (gibberish). It is supposed to be traceable to the mistake made by a preacher who, having told the story of Matthew's cock so many times, said 'Galli Matthias' (the Matthew of the cock) instead of 'Gallus Matthiae'. On this subject, see *L'image du monde renversé et ses représentations littéraires et para-littéraires de la fin du XVIe siècle au milieu du XVIIe*, ed. Jean Lafond and Augustin Redondo (Paris, 1979), p. 181.
59. It is worth remembering that *Satura*, or satire, etymologically referred to a dish of vegetables and meat cooked together, something like a stew or a more spicy version of a salmagundi.
60. See Claude Gaignebet, *Le carnaval* (Paris, 1974), p. 162.
61. *Hamlet*, III, ii, 111.
62. See, on this subject, the article 'Hobby-horse' in the *OED*, senses 4, 6 and 3.

63. See, for example, Hole, *Dictionary of British Folk Customs*.
64. *Le carnaval*, chapters 7, 8 and 9, pp. 117–52.
65. Cited in Bakhtin, *Rabelais*, pp. 355–6.
66. Shrove Tuesday was fixed by the Church to take place on the first Tuesday after the first new moon of February. On the subject of the presence of the dead and the importance of the community of the dead in popular festivals, see below, p. 143.
67. Gaignebet, *Le carnaval*, p. 32: 'the exchanges between souls of the Earth and those of the Empyrean heavens take place through the doorway represented by the moon'.
68. On this subject, see the article by Thomas Pettitt, 'English Folk Drama and the Early German *Fastnachtspiele*', *Renaissance Drama*, n. s. 13 (1982), pp. 1–34. Pettit mentions a similar English custom involving a 'straw bear' which made its appearance in some regions, such as Lincolnshire, on the Tuesday following Plough Monday, a few weeks after Shrove Tuesday: 'the straw bear was a man completely swathed in straw, led by means of a string and made to dance before people's houses, in return for which money was expected' (p. 33).
69. In this connection see Gaignebet, *Le carnaval*, p. 18 and *passim*. See also the entry 'Ours' ('Bear') in Jean-Paul Clébert, *Bestiaire fabuleux* (Paris, 1971) and Arlette Frigout's article 'La fête populaire' in Guy Dumur, ed., *Histoire des spectacles* (Paris, 1965), pp. 276–8. See also 'Dictons météorologiques' ('Meteorological sayings') in Robert's *Dictionnaire des proverbes et dictons* (Paris, 1989), pp. 210–11.
70. Animal motifs were also very important in pageants, in which they were initially connected with various saints, then with various corporations. See Withington, *English Pageantry*, vol. I, pp. 64–70. See also Emmanuel Le Roy Ladurie's remarks on Carnival 'reynages' in Romans (the kingdoms of the cock, the eagle and the partridge represented the wealthy classes, while those of the bear, the sheep and the hare represented the artisans and the peasants) (*Carnival in Romans*, pp. 182–215).
71. See Clébert, *Bestiaire fabuleux*, pp. 86 and 90; see also in Hastings *et al.*, *Encyclopedia of Religion and Ethics*, article on 'Herne the Hunter'; Meslin, *La fête des Kalendes*, pp. 89ff.; F. Laroque, 'Ovidian Transformations in *A Midsummer Night's Dream*, *The Merry Wives of Windsor* and *As You Like It*', *Cahiers Elisabéthains*, 25 (April 1984), pp. 23–36. See also Colman, *Dramatic Use of Bawdy*, p. 80.
72. On this subject, see Claude Gaignebet, 'Le Combat de Carême et de Carnaval de P. Bruegel (1559)', *Annales*, 27:2 (1972), pp. 313–45.
73. The connection between the grotesque and the paintings of Bosch and Brueghel is analysed by Wolfgang Kayser in *The Grotesque in Art and Literature* (Bloomington, 1963), pp. 32–7.
74. The metaphorical relationship between the lovers' puffed-out cheeks and the bagpipes' pouch is conveyed by the old-fashioned expression 'pipers' cheeks', which the *OED* ('piper', sense 1b) defines as 'swollen, inflated cheeks, as of one blowing a pipe'.
75. Gaignebet, *Le carnaval*, p. 150. See also Daniel Fabre, *La fête en Languedoc* (Toulouse, 1977), pp. 164–5.
76. On this point, see Julia C. Dietrich, 'Folk Drama Scholarship: the State

of the Art', and Thomas Pettitt, 'Early English Traditional Drama: Approaches and Perspectives', both in *Research Opportunities in Renaissance Drama (RORD)*, 19 (1976) and 25 (1982).

77. On this subject, see Charles J. Sisson, *Le goût public et le théâtre élisabéthain jusqu'à la mort de Shakespeare* (Dijon, n.d.), pp. 113–15.

78. On this subject, see E.K. Chambers, *Mediaeval Stage*, vol. I, pp. 224–5, and Dietrich, 'Folk Drama Scholarship', pp. 15–16.

79. Malone Society Collections 109, vol. I, 125, ed. W.W. Greg, repr. by J.Q. Adams in *Chief Pre-Shakespearean Dramas* (Boston, 1924), and *Rymes of Robin Hood. An Introduction to the English Outlaw*, ed. B. Dobson and J. Taylor (London, 1976), nos. 19, 20 and 21.

80. Thomas Pettitt, 'English Folk Drama', p. 1; Alan Brody, *The English Mummers and their Plays* (London, 1969), p. 53.

81. E.K. Chambers, *Mediaeval Stage*, vol. I, p. 190.

82. The most detailed description of this dance is to be found in Olaus Magnus, *De Gentibus Septentrionibus* (Rome, 1555); it is cited in translation by Cecil J. Sharp in *Sword Dances of Northern England*, 4 vols. (London, 1912–13), vol. I, pp. 18–19.

83. E.K. Chambers, *Mediaeval Stage*, vol. I, p. 192.

84. Thoinot Arbeau (an anagram for the author's real name, Jehan Tabourot), *L'Orchésographie, ou Traité en forme de dialogue par lequel toutes personnes peuvent apprendre et pratiquer l'honneste exercice des danses* (Langres, 1589; translated as *Orchesography* by Mary Stewart Evans, London, 1948; repr. ed. by Julia Sutton, New York, 1967), p. 183. Julia Sutton adds some interesting information in a note on this passage: 'The *bouffons*, or *mattachins*, was related to the Morris and Fastnachtspiel Sword dances, and to the English Mummers' Play. It may also have included a "rose" figure (crossed swords) and a symbolic beheading, both old-age customs of agricultural fertility ritual . . . There is a possible connection between the mattachins and the moresca of the mimed-battle type, for they are both lively sword dances . . . Arbeau's dance is nothing more than a mock sword-fight . . . Perhaps it would have been staged as part of a ballet, for mock battles were stereotyped parts of many entertainments of the period' (p. 231). The author of this important treatise on dancing was a deacon in the French town of Langres and he should not be confused with his uncle Etienne Tabourot, the author of *Les bigarrures du Seigneur des Accords* (Paris, 1588).

85. E.K. Chambers, *Mediaeval Stage*, vol. I, pp. 195ff. See below, pp. 120–37 for a detailed description of this dance.

86. E.K. Chambers, *Mediaeval Stage*, vol. I, p. 293. See Sharp, *Sword Dances*, vol. I, pp. 28–9.

87. E.K. Chambers, *Mediaeval Stage*, vol. II, Appendix J II, p. 271.

88. Adams, *Chief Pre-Shakespearean Dramas*, p. 352. The expression 'rosa quadrata' is used by Olaus Magnus in his description (see n. 82). On this point, see Sharp, *Sword Dances*, pp. 18 and 28–9.

89. See Reginald Tiddy, *The Mummers' Play* (Oxford, 1923), p. 72: 'To consider the Mummers' Play in isolation and apart from the Sword Dance Play would be unsuitable and misleading . . .'.

90. Adams, *Chief Pre-Shakespearean Dramas*, p. 57.

91. *Ibid.*, p. 358, n. 3.
92. Vol. I, p. 207.
93. *Mediaeval Stage*, vol. I, p. 270.
94. *Ibid.*, p. 271.
95. *Ibid.*, p. 216.
96. *Ibid.*, pp. 212–13.
97. *Ibid.*, p. 218.
98. On this point, see the studies cited above and also David Bergeron, 'Folk Drama Supplement', ed. Harry B. Caldwell, in Bergeron's *Twentieth Century Criticism of English Masques, Pageants and Entertainments: 1558–1642* (San Antonio, 1972).
99. *Mummers' Play*, p. 93.
100. *Modern Philology*, 21 (1924), pp. 225–72.
101. *Elizabethan Jig*, p. 249.
102. See in particular 'Le jeu de Robin et Marion' in *Théâtre comique du Moyen-Age*, ed. Claude-Alain Chevalier (Paris, 1973; repr. 1982), pp. 148–78.
103. See Baskervill, 'Mummers' Wooing Plays', p. 356.
104. Helena M. Shire and Kenneth Elliott, 'La fricassée en Ecosse et ses rapports avec les fêtes de la Renaissance', in Jacquot *et al.*, eds., *Les fêtes de la Renaissance*, vol. I, p. 342; see also, by the same authors, 'Plough Song and Plough Play', *The Saltire Review*, 2:6 (Edinburgh, 1955).
105. On this point, see Withington, *English Pageantry*, vol. I, p. 20, n. 3. See also Stanley J. Kahrl, *Traditions of Medieval English Drama* (London, 1974), pp. 31–3: '*pagina* or *pageanda* was a rather special sort of stage... the terms *pagina* or *pageanda* are carefully kept separate from the term *ludus*. Later the terminological confusion begins... and the term is clearly synonymous with *ludus*.'
106. Withington, *English Pageantry*, vol. I, p. 3. See also Jean Robertson, 'Rapports du poète et de l'artiste dans la préparation des cortèges du Lord Maire' in Jacquot, *et al.*, eds., *Les fêtes de la Renaissance*, vol. I, pp. 265–72.
107. On this subject, see Mervyn James, 'Ritual, Drama and Social Body in the Late Medieval English Town', *Past and Present* 98 (February 1983), p. 4.
108. See Imogen Luxton, 'The Reformation and Popular Culture', in *Church and Society in England, Henry VIII to James I*, ed. Felicity Heal and Rosemary O'Day (London, 1977), pp. 70–1. See also *VCH*, vol. VIII: *Warwickshire*, p. 217.
109. Luxton, 'Reformation and Popular Culture', pp. 70–1.
110. On this point, see Joseph Strutt, *The Sports and Pastimes of the People of England* (London, 1831), p. 377; see also Withington, *English Pageantry*, vol. I, pp. 72–7.
111. 'Ceremony and the Citizen', pp. 57–85.
112. *Ibid.*, p. 79.
113. Withington, *English Pageantry*, vol. I, pp. 43–7.
114. *Ibid.*, p. 42. See also Stow, *Survey*, pp. 126–8.
115. See entry for Machin, or Machyn, Henry, in the *Dictionary of National Biography*; see also *The Diary of Henry Machyn, Citizen and Merchant-Taylor of London 1550–1563*, ed. John G. Nichols (London, 1848).

116. Cited in Withington, *English Pageantry*, vol. II, pp. 13–14.
117. On this subject, see Thomas Dekker, *Jests to Make You Merrie* (1607), in *Non-Dramatic Works*, vol. II, p. 287. See also Venezky, pp. 102–3.
118. This a fundamental point that is stressed by Alice Venezky (*Pageantry*, p. 91), and also by David Bergeron (*English Civic Pageantry*, p. 2).
119. *OED*, 'Wait', sense 7.
120. Woodfill, *Musicians*, pp. 46 and 74; see also Phythian-Adams, 'Ceremony and the Citizen', p. 70, and Thomas Sharp, *A Dissertation on the Pageants and Dramatic Mysteries Anciently Performed at Coventry* (Coventry, 1825; repr. 1973) p. 211.
121. Woodfill, *Musicians*, p. 50.
122. *Ibid.*, p. 49.
123. *Ibid.*, p. 80.
124. See the quotations from Stubbes, below, p. 134. On this point, see also Pettitt, 'English Folk Drama', p. 21.
125. See *Desolation of a City*, pp. 90–2 and 'Ceremony and the Citizen', pp. 58–9.
126. See Rowse, *Elizabethan Renaissance*, p. 202.
127. Aubrey, *Remains*, p. 40; see also Puttenham, *The Arte of English Poesie*, p. 128.
128. In Wilkins, *Concilia*, vol. III, p. 860.
129. This is perhaps the point at which to note that the very first Masque produced at Elizabeth's court on the eve of Epiphany 1559, which included crows, donkeys and wolves dressed up in ecclesiastical vestments, in a spirit of anti-Catholic satire, met with the queen's displeasure. On this point, see E.K. Chambers, *Elizabethan Stage*, vol. I, p. 155.
130. 'Rule and Misrule', p. 32.
131. *Ibid.*, pp. 16–20.
132. *Ibid.*, p. 22.
133. See Stow, *Survey*, p. 118.
134. Aubrey, *Remains*, p. 41. On this subject, see 'Pasquil's Palinodia and His Progresse to the Taverne...' (by William Fennor?) (London, 1619; in *Illustrations of Old English Literature*, ed. J.P. Collier (London, 1886), vol. I, pp. 29–30.
135. *Ibid.* See also Thomas, *Rule and Misrule*, p. 20.
136. Phythian-Adams, 'Ceremony and the Citizen', p. 65.
137. On this subject, see the edition by Smallwood and Wells, pp. 41–2.
138. A riot occurred on Shrove Tuesday 1617, and James I had several apprentices, considered to be the ringleaders, hanged. See Andrew Gurr, *The Shakespearean Stage, 1574–1642* (Cambridge, 1970; repr. 1980), pp. 13–14.
139. In *Non-Dramatic Works*, vol. II, p. 65.
140. *Calendar of the Manuscripts of the Most Honourable the Marquess of Salisbury preserved at Hatfield House*, p. 201, in the 8th Report of the Historical Manuscripts Commission (London, 1899). See also Saltonstall, *Picturae Loquentes* sign. D5.
141. *The Diary of Thomas Crosfield*, ed. Frederick Boas (Oxford, 1935), p. 63 (my italics).
142. In the particular case of the Christmas Prince of Saint John's College,

Oxford, for the circumstances of his election see the preface of the manuscript of *The Christmas Prince*, new edition by F. Boas and W.W. Greg, Malone Society Reprints (London, 1922), pp. 3–4.

143. *Christmas Prince*, p. 4.

144. On this subject, see F. Boas' introduction to *The Christmas Prince*, p. ix. See also A. Wigfall Green, *The Inns of Court and Early English Drama* (New Haven and London, 1931).

145. *Gesta Grayorum* (1594), ed. W.W. Greg (London, 1914); *Le Prince d'Amour or The Prince of Love* (London, 1635). According to Harbage and Schoenbaum (*Annals of English Drama*), this text, which was presented in the Middle Temple by Benjamin Rudyerd, was at first attributed to William Davenant and was published in J. Maidment and W.H. Logan, eds., *The Dramatic Works of Sir William Davenant*, 5 vols. (Edinburgh, 1872–4; repr. 1964).

146. On this point, see Bradbrook, *Rise of the Common Player*, pp. 258–62; see also Clifford C. Huffman, 'The Christmas Prince: University and Popular Drama in the Age of Shakespeare', *Costerus*, n. s. 4 (1975), pp. 51–76.

147. Bradbrook, *Rise of the Common Player*, p. 260; Huffman, 'The Christmas Prince', p. 56.

148. See *Le Prince d'Amour*, pp. 86–7, in which the author mentions a visit to the Court by '11 Knights, 11 Esquires, 9 Maskers and 9 Torchbearers' on the day of Epiphany. The following Monday, the prince is invited by the Lord Mayor and attended with great pomp ...'.

149. In Thomas, 'The Place of Laughter', p. 78. See also Phythian-Adams, 'Ceremony and the Citizen', pp. 67–8.

150. See Le Roy Ladurie, *Carnival in Romans*, pp. 199–200.

151. See Phythian-Adams, 'Ceremony and the Citizen', p. 69; also F. Laroque, 'La notion de "Misrule" à l'époque élisabéthaine', p. 163. For an opposite view (the subversive role of games and festivity), see James, 'Ritual, Drama and Social Body', p. 27–9. Jean Delumeau devotes one chapter of his major work, *Le péché et la peur, la culpabilisation en Occident, XIII–XVIIIᵉ siècles* (Paris, 1983), to an analysis of these manifestations of an upside-down world, judged by some to be a perverted world, and concludes that these carnivalesque rites had a 'functional' character (p. 199).

152. See E.K. Chambers, *Mediaeval Stage*, vol. I, pp. 187–8.

153. See Northrop Frye, *Anatomy of Criticism* (Princeton, 1957; repr. 1973), pp. 163 and 171.

154. See 'Entry', *OED*, sense 4.

155. See Venezky, *Pageantry*, pp. 94–6.

156. See Withington, *English Pageantry*, vol. I, pp. 185 and 188.

157. *Ibid.*, pp. 200–1. See also Bergeron, *English Civic Pageantry*, p. 269, and Gordon Kipling, 'Triumphal Drama: Form in English Civic Pageantry', *Renaissance Drama*, n. s. 8 (1977), pp. 42 and 53.

158. See Jean Wilson, *Entertainments for Elizabeth*, p. 6.

159. Glynne Wickham, 'The Contribution by Ben Jonson and Dekker to the Coronation Festivities for James I', in Jacquot *et al.*, eds., *Les fêtes de la Renaissance*, vol. I, p. 282. See also Bergeron, *English Civic Pageantry*, p. 268.

160. Wickham, 'The Contribution', p. 282. According to Withington (*English*

Pageantry, vol. I, p. 86), the popular character of the royal entry is in line with the fundamental principle of pageantry.

161. Wickham, 'The Contribution', p. 282.

162. In this myth, the Tudors are represented as the descendants of the Trojan Brutus, the legendary founder of 'Troyanovant' or New Troy, that is to say London. They are also attributed another prestigious ancestor in the person of King Arthur; and the reign of Queen Elizabeth is seen as the accomplishment of Merlin's prophecies and a return to the Golden Age. On this point, see Frances A. Yates, *Astraea, The Imperial Theme in the Sixteenth Century* (London, 1975), pp. 50–1; Roy Strong, *The Cult of Elizabeth* (London, 1977), p. 140; also Jean Wilson, *Entertainments for Elizabeth*, p. 36.

163. On this point, see E.C. Wilson, *England's Eliza* (Cambridge, Mass., 1939; repr. London 1966), pp. 213–29; and Yates, *Astraea*, pp. 69–74.

164. The text of this tournament is to be found in the collection made by John Nichols (*Progresses of Queen Elizabeth*, vol. II, pp. 310–29). Jean Wilson's *Entertainments for Elizabeth* contains a more recent edition of it.

165. On this point, see E.K. Chambers, 'The Court', in a collective work entitled *Shakespeare's England*, 2 vols. (Oxford, 1917), vol. I, p. 96; and Strong, *Cult of Elizabeth*, p. 146. E.C. Wilson notes that this festival, devoted to Saint Elizabeth of Hungary in the Catholic calendar, had been dropped from the Protestant calendar along with thirty-seven others, in 1568 (*England's Eliza*, pp. 221–3).

166. On this subject, see Roy Strong, *Cult of Elizabeth*, pp. 146–51.

167. See E.K. Chambers, 'The Court', pp. 95–6.

168. On this point, see Marcia Vale, *The Gentleman's Recreations* (Cambridge, 1977), p. 15. The sum of twelve pence is mentioned in a description of the 1584 tournament by a German, Lupold von Wedel. Roy Strong cites this text in his *Cult of Elizabeth* (pp. 134–5).

169. Vale, *Gentleman's Recreations*, p. 12–13. We should note, in passing, that there existed a popular variant to these tournaments. It took the form of water jousts between the youths of London, which took place during the Easter festivities (see Stow, *Survey*, p. 118).

170. Francis Bacon, *Essays*, ed. Oliphant Smeaton (London, 1906), p. 116.

171. Strong, *Cult of Elizabeth*, p. 138.

172. On this subject, see Vale, *Gentleman's Recreations*, pp. 13–14.

173. Joseph Strutt, in *Sports and Pastimes* (pp. 112–25), gives a detailed description of these various exercises.

174. Roy Strong (*Cult of Elizabeth*, p. 146) considers the Elizabethan tournament to be the direct ancestor of the court Masques of the Stuarts. Jean Wilson, for her part, writes as follows: 'the Tilts were a courtly equivalent of the tableaux mounted by the cities to welcome Elizabeth' (*Entertainments for Elizabeth*, p. 31).

175. E.K. Chambers, 'The Court', p. 106.

176. Strong, *Cult of Elizabeth*, p. 136.

177. Chambers, 'The Court', pp. 97–9.

178. *Ibid.*, p. 97.

179. *Survey*, pp. 122–3. The position was filled by Sir Edmund Tilney from 1579 until his death in 1610. On this subject, see *Shakespeare de A à Z ou*

presque, ed. Michel Grivelet, Marie-Madeleine Martinet and Dominique Goy-Blanquet (Paris, 1988), under the entry 'Menus Plaisirs', p. 305.

180. On this point, see E.K. Chambers, *Mediaeval Stage*, vol. I, p. 405.

181. In *Progresses of Queen Elizabeth*. See also Rowse, *Elizabethan Renaissance*, p. 101.

182. E.K. Chambers, 'The Court', p. 100. On the role of bells during festivals, see Rowse, *Elizabethan Renaissance*, pp. 213–14.

183. E.K. Chambers, 'The Court', p. 100.

184. *Ibid.*, p. 101, and Jean Wilson, *Entertainments for Elizabeth*, pp. 52–7. According to Rowse (*Elizabethan Renaissance*, p. 91), these figures are probably exaggerated.

185. Gascoigne, *The Princely Pleasures at Kenilworth Castle*, in *The Complete Works of George Gascoigne*, ed. John W. Cunliffe, 2 vols. (Cambridge, 1907; repr. Hildesheim, 1974), vol. II, pp. 91–131.

186. In particular a bride ale and the famous Hock-Tuesday play presented by Captain Cox of Coventry. See Nichols, *Progresses of Queen Elizabeth*, vol. I, pp. 441–6, and *Laneham's Letter*, pp. 26–7. On this point, see Bruce R. Smith, 'Landscape with Figures: The Three Realms of Queen Elizabeth's Country-House Revels', *Renaissance Drama*, n. s. 8 (1977), pp. 68–73.

187. For the texts of these entertainments, see Jean Wilson, *Entertainments for Elizabeth*, pp. 86–95, 96–118 and 119–42.

188. On this point, see E.K. Chambers, 'The Court', p. 105.

189. As is clearly shown by the four volumes of *Progresses of King James I* by John Nichols.

190. E.K. Chambers, 'The Court', p. 111. See also Wickham, *Elizabethan Stage*, vol. I, pp. 399–403, and Cornelia E. Baehrens, *The Origin of the Masque* (Gröningen, 1929), pp. 14–61.

191. E.K. Chambers, 'The Court', p. 110.

192. See *The Political Works of James I*, ed. C.H. McIlwain (Cambridge, Mass., 1918), pp. 343–4, on the encouragement given to the Cotswold Games organized by Robert Dover and the publication of James I's *Book of Sports*, 24 May 1618.

193. 'The Court', pp. 79–80.

194. See *VCH*: vol. VIII: *Warwickshire, The City of Coventry*, p. 218.

195. *Political Works*, pp. 343–4.

196. Cited by Strong, *Cult of Elizabeth*, p. 118. See also below, p. 180.

197. See Jean Wilson, *Entertainments for Elizabeth*, p. 7.

198. See above, p. 9.

199. Yates, *Astraea*, pp. 29–87.

200. *Ibid.*, pp. 100–2.

201. Cited by Yates, *ibid.*, p. 100.

202. The origin of the court Masque seems to be traceable to the rustic customs of the Mummers. On this subject, see E.K. Chambers, *Mediaeval Stage*, vol. I, p. 400, Enid Welsford, *The Court Masque: A Study in the Relationship between Poetry and the Revels* (Cambridge, 1927), p. 30, and Baehrens, *Origin of the Masque*, p. 48.

203. Moryson, in his *Itinerary* (London, 1617; *Extracts* repr. by the New Shakspere Society, London, 1909), p. 277, nevertheless establishes distinc-

tions between the table manners and, in particular, the drinking habits of the populace and those of the aristocracy.

204. On the 'Maying' of Henry VIII and Queen Catherine, see Stow, *Survey*, pp. 123–4. On Queen Elizabeth, see E.K. Chambers, 'The Court', p. 105.
205. On this subject, see the article by Smith, 'Landscape with Figures', pp. 72–3.
206. See Venezky, *Pageantry*, p. 91.
207. In this connection, see Harry Levin, *The Myth of the Golden Age in the Renaissance* (Indianapolis, 1969; repr. Oxford, 1972), pp. 95–136.
208. James, 'Ritual, Drama and Social Body', pp. 27–9.
209. Thomas, 'The Place of Laughter', p. 81, and Phythian-Adams, 'Ceremony and the Citizen', p. 69.

3 The calendar

1. On this subject, see Eliade, *Le mythe*.
2. E.K. Chambers, *Mediaeval Stage*, vol. I, pp. 110–11.
3. On these question, see Gaignebet, *Le carnaval*, pp. 18–29.
4. On this point, see Thomas, *Religion*, p. 618.
5. 'They talk of Christmas so long that it comes' is one of the sayings of sixteenth- and seventeenth-century England that Tilley, in his *Dictionary of the Proverbs in England*, tells us means the same as 'Long looked for comes at last.'
6. *L'homme et le sacré* (Paris, 1939; repr. 1950), p. 225.
7. See the Pico della Mirandola aphorism cited by Edgar Wind in *Pagan Mysteries in the Renaissance* (Oxford, 1958; repr. 1980), p. 191.
8. *Rethinking Anthropology*, p. 133.
9. See F. Laroque, 'Images et figures du grotesque à l'époque élisabéthaine: calendrier, corps, cuisine', *Cahiers Charles V, Théâtre et Société*, 2 (1980), pp. 30–1.
10. On this point, see Godfrey Davies, *The Oxford History of England: The Early Stuarts 1603–1660* (Oxford, 1982; repr. 1988), pp. 307–8.
11. On this point, see Henri Hubert and Marcel Mauss, 'La représentation du temps dans la religion et la magie', in their *Mélanges d'histoire des religions* (Paris, 1909).
12. *La fête des kalendes*, p. 127.
13. See the article 'Osiris' in Jean Chevalier and Alain Gheerbrant, *Dictionnaire des symboles* (Paris, 1969; repr. 1982).
14. According to Michel Meslin, *La fête des kalendes*, pp. 120–1, 'the influence of the Roman rites of the New Year . . . spread with Christianization'.
15. On this subject, see E.K. Chambers, *Mediaeval Stage*, vol. I, pp. 234–6.
16. E.K. Chambers, *Mediaeval Stage*, vol. I, pp. 240–4.
17. See Nilsson, *Primitive Time Reckoning*, pp. 294–5.
18. See Phythian-Adams, *Local History*, p. 22.
19. Wickham, *Stages*, vol. III, p. 18.
20. *Mediaeval Stage*, vol. I, pp. 228–73, chapters entitled 'The Beginning of Winter' and 'New Year Customs'.
21. *Early English Stages*, vol. III, pp. 258–63, Appendix B.

22. 'A Comparative Calendar of Folk Customs and Festivities in Elizabethan England', *Cahiers Elisabéthains*, 8 (October 1975), pp. 5–13.
23. *Early English Stages*, vol. III, p. 11.
24. As we shall see, this original division was maintained by the religious division of the year into fixed feasts (connected with Christmas) and moveable feasts (connected with Easter).
25. See my comparative table in Appendix 1, pp. 306–7, below.
26. On this point, see Phythian-Adams, 'Ceremony and the Citizen', p. 71.
27. See Phythian-Adams, *Local History*, p. 24.
28. The dates for wakes and parish festivals used to be decided by the date of the feast of the parish patron saint. Henry VIII tried to have all these festivals transferred to the first Sunday in October. However, according to Bishop White Kennett (*Parochial Antiquities*, 2 vols. (London, 1818), vol. II, p. 305) his attempt to impose uniformity proved unsuccessful.
29. Phythian-Adams, 'Ceremony and the Citizen', p. 71.
30. On this point, see the analysis by Rowse in *Elizabethan Renaissance*, p. 214.
31. *The Book of Common Prayer. The Elizabethan Prayer Book*, ed. John E. Booty (Charlottesville, 1976).
32. I am here borrowing the expression used by Claude Gaignebet (*Le carnaval*, pp. 17–39).
33. On this point, see Gaignebet *Le carnaval*, pp. 18–19.
34. *The History and Description of the Isle of Man* (London, 1744), pp. 94–6.
35. Some sleep-disorder specialists regard summer-time (which, in France, is two hours out of step with solar time) as the cause of many people's sleep disorders (connected with their own internal clocks) and of the phenomena of nervous stress which apparently increase at this period of the year.
36. Henry Gee and William John Hardy, *Documents Illustrative of the English Church* (London, 1896), p. 150 (document dated 1532).
37. New Shakspere Society edn, pp. 158–9.
38. Wilkins, *Concilia*, vol. III, p. 823.
39. *Ibid.*, p. 824.
40. *Ibid.*, vol. IV, p. 20.
41. On this subject, see the amazement of Thomas Platter, *Travels in England*, p. 188. See the text of the quotation, above, p. 316, note 75.
42. W. Kennett, *Parochial Antiquities* (London, 1695), p. 611.
43. Wilkins, *Concilia*, vol. III, p. 824.
44. 'Flowers', in *Complete Works*, vol. I, p. 72.
45. *Virgidemiarum*, lib. 5, sat. I, lines 22–6 and 73–8, in *Collected Poems*, ed. Davenport, pp. 75 and 77.
46. *English Villages of the Thirteenth Century* (New York, 1941), p. 379.
47. *Ibid.*, p. 354.
48. *Ibid.*, p. 365.
49. This document is to be found in the famous anthology compiled by R.H. Tawney and Eileen Power entitled *Tudor Economic Documents*, 3 vols. (London, 1924), vol. II, pp. 335–42.
50. See my analysis in 'Le Londres en fête du *Shoemaker's Holiday* de Thomas Dekker', in *Les représentations de Londres dans la littérature et les arts*, *Annales du G.E.R.B.* (Bordeaux, 1984), vol. II, pp. 7–33.

51. 'An Elizabethan Coalmine', *Economic History Review*, 2nd ser., 3 (1950–1), p. 101.
52. For example, on 1 May 1984, in Stratford, I watched a performance given on the lawn opposite the theatre by a group of miners who were folklore enthusiasts. (I have forgotten the name of the little town from which they hailed.) The dancers wore red costumes and their faces were painted black, a fact that put one in mind of the figures representing devils or nocturnal forces (the 'blackened faces' which were a feature of the early Morris dances) and at the same time evoked the black faces of miners emerging from the pits. The rich symbolism, the agility and skill of the dancers and of the musicians seemed to me to testify to the persistence or revival of old popular traditions even in heavily industrialized regions.

4 The cycle of calendary festivals

1. 'Saint Distaffs day, or The Morrow after Twelfth Night', in *Hesperides* (1648).
2. See *OED*: 'Rock Day, Monday', quotation from R.T. Hampson (*Medii Aevi Kalendarium, or Dates, Charters and Customs of the Middle Ages* (London, 1841).
3. *Overburian Characters*, p. 79.
4. *Picturae Loquentes*, sign. c5b.
5. See above, p. 91.
6. Tusser, *A Hundreth Points of Husbandrie* (1557), ed. Cedric Chivers, (Bath, 1969).
7. *Ibid.*
8. In this connection, see Shire and Elliott, 'La fricassée en Ecosse'. Also see above, p. 324 note 104.
9. Robert Chambers, *Book of Days*, vol. I, p. 94.
10. E.K. Chambers, *Mediaeval Stage*, vol. I, pp. 298–9, n. 4.
11. *Ibid.*, p. 208.
12. The presence of the 'ploughman' in the Morris dance is alluded to by Dekker in *The Guls Horn-Book* (1609), in *Non-Dramatic Works*, ed. Grosart, vol. III, where he mentions 'talking and laughing (like a Plough-man / performer in a Morris)'.
13. See also Sharp, *Sword Dances*, vol. I, p. 24.
14. *Fête et révolte* (Paris, 1976), p. 17.
15. *Anatomie of Abuses*, p. 148.
16. *The Medieval Theatre* (London, 1974), p. 146.
17. In his *Popular Culture* (p. 193), Peter Burke points out that 'in England, the custom was to perform "Plough Plays", which might include mock weddings, on the first Monday after the Epiphany'.
18. See *The Insatiate Countess*, by John Marston (1610), I, i, 211–18, in his *Works*, ed. A.H. Bullen, 3 vols. (London, 1887), vol. III, p. 141. See also Ben Jonson, *The Entertainment at Althorpe* (25 June 1603; publ. 1604):

ELFE: Shee [Mab, the mistris-Faerie] can start our Franklins daughters,
In their sleepe, with shrikes, and laughters,
And on sweet Saint Anne's night,
Feed them with a promis'd sight,

Some of husbands, some of lovers,
Which an emptie dreame discovers.   (*Works*, vol. vii, p. 123)

In the Notes to the edition, vol. x, p. 396, there is the following commentary on the subject of these customs:

Saint Anne's night, St Agnes' Eve, 20 January. Burton, *The Anatomy of Melancholy*, ed. 1632, p. 542,: ''Tis their only desire, if it may be done by art, to see their husbands picture in a glasse, they'le give anything to know when they shall be married, how many husbands they shall have, by *Cromnyomantia*, a kind of Divination with onions laid on the Altar on Christmas Eve, or by fasting on S. Annes night, to know who shall bee their first husband.'

19. As Charles Phythian-Adams notes in *Local History* (p. 14): 'For both church and people, fire and smoke were important antidotes to evil. Each Candlemas taper was hallowed "that in what places soever tremble for feare, and fly away discouraged".' The fire and smoke of Candlemas was certainly believed to have the magic power to chase away devils and ward off evil. On this point, see also Scot, *Discoverie*, p. 236.

20. Note that Thomas Kirchmeyer, alias 'Naogeorgus', placed his analysis of the 'abuses' of Shrove Tuesday after the festival of Saint Blaise in *The Popish Kingdome or Reigne of Antichrist* (trans. Barnabe Googe, 1570; ed. R.C. Hofe, London, 1880), Book iv, p. 47.

21. See Brand and Ellis, *Popular Antiquities*, vol. i, pp. 63–94.

22. The division between the cycle of Christmas festivals and the cycle which began on Shrove Tuesday seems to me to have been observed to widely varying degrees in the various regions. For example, the records of the city of Norwich mention a certain John Gladman, who apparently paraded through the streets in the costume of 'King of Kirtsmesse' on Shrove Tuesday (see *The Records of the City of Norwich*, published by William Hudson and John C. Tingey, 2 vols. (Norwich, 1906), vol. ii, pp. 345–6.

23. There must have been some exceptions, for on this point the *OED* ('Carnival', sense 3) cites the testimony of Thomas Coryat (*Crudities* (London 1611), p. 315): 'Carnival Shows in Italy like Shrove-Tuesday ones in England . . . Their Carnival day . . . is observed amongst them in the same manner as our Shrove-Tuesday with us in England.' At all events, what struck English people such as Fynes Moryson, visiting Venice, was the custom for certain women to dress up as men at Carnival time. On this subject, see Leo Salingar, *Shakespeare and the Traditions of Comedy* (Cambridge, 1974), pp. 192–3.

24. Charles Phythian-Adams, in *Desolation of a City*, observes that 'the absence of Carnival in England is most marked' (p. 178). See also F. Laroque, 'Le carnaval dans l'Angleterre élisabéthaine', *Eidolon*, 13 (October 1980), pp. 116–17.

25. In this connection see the anonymous poem called 'Pasquil's Palinodia and his Progresse to the Taverne . . . ', among other pieces of contemporary evidence.

26. See above, p. 61.

27. *The Knight of the Burning Pestle*, v, iii, 152–4. (I have used the Aubier edition (1958), with introduction and notes by Professor M.T. Jones-Davies.)

28. *Bartholomew Fair*, v, i, 6–12 (in *Works*, vol. vi, p. 112).

29. *Time Vindicated* (in *Works*, vol. vii, p. 663, lines 253–7).

30. In T.J.B. Spencer, ed., *A Book of Masques, in Honour of Allardyce Nicoll* (Cambridge, 1970), p. 264.

31. Jonson, *Works*, vol. ii, pp. 181–94.

32. *Jack-a-Lent, his Beginning and Entertainment with the Mad Pranks of his Gentleman-Usher Shrove-Tuesday that Goes before him, and his Footman Hunger Attending* (1630), in *All the Workes of John Taylor the Water-Poet*, repr. in 3 parts, Spenser Society (London, 1868–9), p. 115.

33. *The Seven Deadly Sinnes of London* (1606), in *Non-Dramatic Works*, vol. ii, p. 65.

34. These destructive rites performed by the young apprentices are somewhat reminiscent of the erstwhile schoolboys' custom of burning their exercise books at the end of the year and also of the *monômes* of *bacheliers* in France (it was a now lost tradition for secondary-school boys, although some girls did attend too, after sitting the *baccalauréat* exam, to walk in groups through the streets, sing bawdy songs, throw flour at the passers-by and fight with the police).

35. Edmund Gayton, *Pleasant Notes upon Don Quixot* (London, 1654), p. 271.

36. *Ibid.*

37. *Ibid.*

38. John Earle, *Microcosmography, or a Piece of the World Discovered in Essays and Characters* (London, 1628), p. 57.

39. *Northward Ho* (1607), iv, iii, 74–8, in *Dramatic Works*, ed. Fredson Bowers, 4 vols. (Cambridge, 1953–61), vol. ii (1955).

40. Machyn, *Diary*, p. 301.

41. On this subject, see Natalie Zemon Davis, 'The Reasons of Misrule', in her *Society and Culture in Early Modern France* (Stanford, 1965; repr. 1975), pp. 98–123. See also the proceedings of the Paris colloquium (17–25 April 1977) on *Le charivari*, edited by Jacques Le Goff and Jean-Claude Schmitt (Paris, 1981). On Elizabethan England, see Martin Ingram, 'Le charivari dans l'Angleterre du XVIe au XVIIe siècles. Aperçu historique' in Le Goff and Schmitt, eds., *Le charivari*, pp. 251–64. See also Henri Rey-Flaud, *Le charivari, Les rituels fondamentaux de la sexualité* (Paris, 1985).

42. The exact origin of the word 'Skimmington' is unknown but its root may derive from 'skimming' as in 'skimming ladle'. According to the *OED*, it designated 'the man or woman personating the ill-used husband or the offending wife in the procession intended to ridicule the one or the other . . . ' (entry 1) and 'a ludicrous procession, formerly known in villages and country districts, usually intended to bring ridicule or odium upon a woman or her husband where the one was unfaithful to, or ill-treated, the other' (entry 2). For an analysis of the custom, see Violet Alford, 'Rough Music or Charivari', *Folklore*, 70 (December 1959), pp. 505–18. This author writes: '*Rough Music* is the beginning of popular justice, the overture of pots and pans, whistles and bells, outside the house of the culprit . . . ' (p. 505). Henri Rey-Flaud is useful on these questions, as is the article by Christiane Gallenca on the importance of the charivari in *The Merry Wives of Windsor* ('Ritual and Folk Customs in *The Merry Wives of*

Windsor', Cahiers Elisabéthains, 27 (April 1985), pp. 27–41). See also Anne Parten, 'Falstaff's Horns: Masculine Inadequacy and Feminine Mirth in *The Merry Wives of Windsor'* (*Studies in Philology*, 82:2 (Spring 1985), pp. 184–9). On primary sources and contemporary testimony for the charivari, see in particular *Records of the County of Wiltshire*, ed. B. Howard Cunnington (London, 1932), p. 79, which describes 'A Skimmington in Marden' in the year 1626.

43. H. Misson de Valbourg, *Mémoires et observations faites par un voyageur en Angleterre* (The Hague, 1698), p. 70. The English text is cited by Brand and Ellis (*Popular Antiquities*, vol. ii, p. 191) under the title *M. Misson's Memoirs and Observations in his Travels over England*, translated by Mr Ozell (London, 1719), p. 129. There seems to have been some confusion over the Christian name of the author, for the book is sometimes attributed to Henri Misson's brother, François Maximilien (e.g. in the catalogue of the Bibliothèque Nationale in Paris), sometimes to Henri himself (as in the British Library in London).

44. See *Travels in England*, pp. 181–2. More often, it was the husband himself or one of his neighbours who had to ride a donkey, seated to face its tail, to the accompaniment of the 'rough music' of the charivari or 'Skimmington ride', produced by a cacophony of kitchen instruments (pots, ladles and skillets). See also the analysis and documents cited by David Underdown (*Revel, Riot and Rebellion*, pp. 100–3). See also the 'Skimmington' scene in *The Late Lancashire Witches* (1634), by Thomas Heywood and Richard Brome, ed. Laird H. Barber (New York and London, 1979), p. 190:

CRY: A Skimington, a Skimington, a Skimington.
DOUGHTY: Whats the matter now, is Hell broke loose?
SHAKESTONE: At whose suit I prithee is Don Skimington come to town?

(lines 1880–9)

The editor provides the following explanations on the subject of the word 'Skimmington', in a note on p. 190:

An old custom in England villages, which mocked such marital troubles as nagging, bullying, and infidelity. A procession was organized whose chief participants were a couple on horseback – either impersonators or effigies – who were gotten up as the husband and wife involved, and paraded through the village for general amusement. The origin of the word 'skimmington' is unknown, but it seems likely that it derived from the skimming ladle with which the wife in the procession beats her husband.

See also Parten, 'Falstaff's Horns', p. 187: 'in the preposterous world of the skimmington, the new symbols of authority are skillets, pots and ladles'. This is interesting, for Shakespeare uses the term in *Othello*, in a context where the background is a burlesque kind of rite quite like a charivari: the clamour organized by Iago on the occasion of the Moor's secret wedding. On this point, see below, chapter 10, pp. 287–8.

45. Andrew Marvell, 'The Last Instructions to a Painter', lines 375–86; I have used Andrew Marvell, *The Complete Poems*, ed. Elizabeth Story Donno (Harmondsworth, 1972; repr. 1976).

46. *Epicoene*, i, i, 157–9 (in *Works*, vol. v, p. 169).

47. 'The Prentizes on Shrove Tewsday last, to the number of 3. or 4000 comitted extreme insolencies ... such of them as are taken his Majestie

hath commaunded shal be executed for example sake' (cited by A. Gurr, in his *Shakespearean Stage*, pp. 13–14).

48. *London and the Country Carbonadoed and Quartered into Several Characters* (London, 1622), p. 130.
49. v, ii, 177–94, in *Dramatic Works*, vol. I.
50. *Popish Kingdome*, Book IV, pp. 47–8.
51. *Vox Graculi or Jack Dawes Prognostication* (London, 1622), p. 55.
52. In Spencer, *Book of Masques*, pp. 327–8 (my italics).
53. Ben Jonson similarly associates the festivals of Christmas and that of Shrove Tuesday in the Prologue to *The Staple of News* (lines 8–9), where 'Mirth' calls herself 'the daughter of Christmas, and spirit of Shrovetide'. A 1613 Masque by F. Beaumont, entitled *The Masque of Flowers*, also refers to 'such sports as are commonly known by the name of Christmas sports, or Carnival sports' (in Spencer, *Book of Masques*, p. 163).
54. See the description of this feasting by the author (William Fennor?) of 'Pasquil's Palinodia', p. 29.
55. See the proverb cited by Tilley, 'After Christmas comes Lent' (*Dictionary of the Proverbs*) and the following lines from Philip Massinger's play, *The City Madam*:

> HOLDFAST: ...She hath feasted long
> And After a carnival Lent ever follows...

in *The Plays and Poems of Philip Massinger*, ed. Philip Edwards and Colin Gibson, 5 vols. (Oxford, 1976), vol. IV, p. 79.
56. The etymology of the word 'Lent' is rather obscure. See the definition given by Thomas Blount in his *Glossographia* (London, 1658; repr. 1661).
57. On this point see Shakespeare's *Pericles*:

> MASTER [to Pericles]:   ...Come, thou shalt go home, and we'll have *flesh for holidays, fish for fasting-days*, and moreo'er puddings and flap-jacks and thou shalt be welcome...   (scene v, ll. 122–4; my italics)

58. E.K. Chambers, *The English Folk Play* (Oxford, and New York, 1923; repr. New York, 1964), p. 157.
59. Cited by T.F. Thiselton Dyer in his *Folklore of Shakespeare*, p. 280.
60. *Ibid.*
61. See Nicholas Breton, *Fantastickes* (1626), in his *Works*, vol. II, p. 12, col. 1. See also *The Honour of Valour*, p. 6, I, 52.
62. See Thomas, *Religion*, p. 618. We should note, in passing, that the zodiac sign of the fish, attached to the month of February, gives an astrological and emblematic meaning to these dietary prohibitions.
63. This indissociable polar relationship between feast days and fast days is well shown in paintings and engravings illustrating the theme of the struggle between Carnival and Lent.
64. See J. Hitchcock, 'Religious Conflict at Mapperton, 1597–1599', *Proceedings of the Dorset Natural History and Archaeological Society*, 89 (1967), p. 228, cited in a note in Thomas, *Religion*, p. 621. See also the satirical portrait of 'A Zealous Brother' in *The Whimzies, or a New Cast of Characters*, ed. James O. Halliwell (London, 1859), p. 115. At the other extreme, see Harpool's statement in *The Life of Sir John Oldcastle* (1600), IV, iii, in Brooke, ed., *The Shakespeare Apocrypha*, p. 153.

65. *Folklore of Shakespeare*, p. 282.
66. In *Churchwardens' Accounts* (pp. 251–2), J.C. Cox points out that there was a charge for these dispensations and that the money thus raised would go to swell the funds available for parish good works. According to this author, the cost of the dispensations at the end of the sixteenth century was 26 shillings and 8 pence for the nobility, 13 shillings and 4 pence for knights and ladies and 6 shillings and 8 pence for the common people. Parish funds would be further increased by the fines imposed for breaking the Lenten fast: for example, a certain Robert Chamberlain, of Henley-on-Thames, was fined in 1596 'for roasting a pig in his house on 24 March (Lent)' (*ibid.*, p. 252).
67. Thomas Nabbes, *The Spring's Glory*, in Spencer, *Book of Masques*, p. 328.
68. *Ibid.*
69. *Religion*, p. 620.
70. See Spencer, *Book of Masques*, p. 329.
71. See my analysis of the importance of animals in popular symbolism, above, pp. 47–8.
72. *The Complete Poetry of Robert Herrick*, ed. J. Max Patrick (New York, 1963; repr. 1968), p. 202.
73. See in particular Francis Douce, *Illustrations of Shakespeare* (London, 1839).
74. The etymology of the word 'Lupercal' stems from *lupus*. On this point, see Rey-Flaud, *Le charivari*, pp. 23–4.
75. *Works*, vol. iii, pp. 403–4.
76. *A Tale of a Tub*, i, i, 1–50, in *Works*, vol. iii, pp. 13–14.
77. *Hamlet*, iv, v, 47–65.
78. *Mémoires et Observations*, pp. 330–1.
79. *Complete Works*, vol. iii (iv, i), p. 156.
80. John Chamber, *Treatise against Judicial Astrologie* (London, 1601), p. 113.
81. *Lean's Collectanea*, vol. ii, p. 232.
82. For example, Saint David's Day, in Wales (1 March) and Saint Patrick's Day (17 March), in Ireland.
83. According to Reginald Scot (*Discoverie*, p. 231), these consecrated branches of foliage were believed to possess prophylactic powers against curses: 'greene leaves consecrated on Palme Sundaie [as a protection against witches]'.
84. See Brand and Ellis, *Popular Antiquities*, vol. i, p. 128.
85. *The Whimzies*, p. 115.
86. *Dictionary of the Proverbs*, no. y 52.
87. According to the *OED*, one etymology for the word 'Pasch' is the Hebrew word used for the Feast of the Passover, 'Pesakh'.
88. *Christmas and Christmas Lore* (London, 1923), p. 94. A poem by William Warner suggests that May Day and Whitsun games would make their first appearance at the religious festival of Easter:

As Paske began our Morrisse, and ere Penticost our May,
Tho Roben Hood, Liell John, Frier Tuck, and Marian deftly play,
And Lord and Ladie gang till kirke with Lads and Lasses gay.
    (William Warner, *Albion's England* (London, 1612), Book v, chapter 25)

89. Breton, *Fantastickes*: 'Christmas Day' (1626), in *Works*, vol. ii, p. 11.

90. See Hole, *Dictionary of British Folk Customs*, p. 169.
91. See 'Poor Robin's Almanac', cited in Thiselton Dyer, *Folklore of Shakespeare*, p. 284:

> At Easter let your clothes be new
> Or else be sure will it rue.

92. *Fantastickes*, in *Works*, vol. II. We should remember that in *The Figure of Foure* (1636), Breton had already classified Easter among the days welcome to scholars ('5/9. Foure dayes welcome to Schollers: Christmas Day, Shrove-tuesday, Easter-day, and Whitsunday' (in *Works*, vol. II, p. 7)).
93. *Anatomie of Abuses*, p. 150.
94. Brand and Ellis, *Popular Antiquities*, vol. I, p. 187.
95. The collections must have been rather handsome as they were entered on the parish registers. See Cox, *Churchwardens' Accounts*, p. 64.
96. Brand and Ellis, *Popular Antiquities*, vol. I, p. 182.
97. In 'Ceremony and the Citizen' (pp. 66–7), Charles Phythian-Adams makes a detailed analysis of the Hocktide customs: they afforded married women a chance to get their symbolic revenge against their menfolk, by capturing them and holding them to ransom before freeing them. Charles Phythian-Adams also suggests that, contrary to the general customs of the time, women may have taken part in the Hock Tuesday play performed in the presence of the queen at Kenilworth.
98. *Laneham's Letter*, p. 27.
99. *Ibid.*, pp. 26–7. The passage shows that English women played an important part in the popular war against the Viking occupation of England. That was possibly an added reason why Queen Elizabeth was pleased by the performance of this little popular play. As to the origin of the word 'Hocktide', it has been the subject of many historical and philological studies such as that by F.J. Furnivall, the editor of Robert Laneham's letter (pp. 26–7), or the notes on Hocktide customs in Hexton published in nos. 11 and 12 of the tenth series of *Notes and Queries* (1909), pp. 488 and 71–3. It would appear, however, that – as Phythian-Adams suggests ('Ceremony and the Citizen', p. 79) – there was no follow-up to Captain Cox's attempt to revive the folk customs of the past.
100. *Abuses Strippt and Whipt* (London, 1613; repr. 1622), p. 232.
101. In *Annalia Dubrensia* (London, 1636; repr. Cheltenham, 1878, ed. E.R. Vyvyan), as 'To my Noble Friend Mr Robert Dover, on His Annual Assemblies upon Cotswold' (p. 7).
102. See E.K. Chambers, *Mediaeval Stage*, vol. I, pp. 220–3, and vol. II, pp. 164–5.
103. Christina Hole, *Saints in Folklore* (London, 1965), pp. 25, 28.
104. Cf. *1 Henry VI*, I, i, 153–4:

> BEDFORD: Bonfires in France forthwith I am to make
> To keep our great Saint George's feast withal.

105. In *Shakespeare versus Shallow* (London, 1931), Leslie Hotson suggests that the first performance of *The Merry Wives of Windsor*, a play commissioned by Queen Elizabeth I, may have taken place on 23 April 1597, at Westminster.
106. The celebration of Saint George's Day must have outlived its official

abolition, for Moryson notes in his *Itinerary* that this festival was one of the three most important in the kingdom.

107. Machyn, *Diary*, p. 201.
108. Charles J. Sisson, *Lost Plays of Shakespeare's Age* (London, 1936), pp. 178–83.
109. On this point, see Withington, *English Pageantry*, vol. I, p. 24, No. 1.
110. This is but one of many examples of the decline of the ideals of chivalry and the way that they were taken over by the popular culture. Beaumont and Fletcher were to make use of the burlesque aspects of chivalry in their *The Knight of the Burning Pestle*. Another example is provided by the following passage from Shakespeare's *King John*:

BASTARD: Saint George that swinged the dragon, and e'er since
Sits on's horseback at mine hostess' door.   (II, i, 288–9)

111. *The Golden Bough, A Study in Magic and Religion* (London, 1971), p. 814.
112. *Anatomie of Abuses*, p. 149.
113. See also Aubrey, *Remains*, p. 15; Scot, in *Discoverie* (p. 152), refers to similar superstitions in England.
114. *The Anatomy of Absurditie*, in *Works*, vol. I, pp. 22–3.
115. Theseus is the first to associate these two festivals of love. At the sight of the lovers asleep in the woods, he says:

Good morrow, friends. Saint Valentine is past.
Begin these wood-birds but to couple now?   (IV, i, 138–9)

116. In 'Ceremony and the Citizen' (p. 66), Charles Phythian-Adams compares the sexual behaviour of Hocktide and May Day.
117. P. 62.
118. See Gayton, *Pleasant Notes*, p. 79.
119. *A Strappado for the Divell* (London, 1615), pp. 118–20.
120. In *Works*, vol. III, p. 241.
121. *Dialogue Against Light, Lewde and Lascivious Dauncing* (London, 1582), sign. D 7.
122. *Anatomie of Abuses*, p. 149.
123. Patrick Collinson (*Religion of Protestants*, p. 225) writes of 'the anxiety of preachers about the irrepressible sexuality of the young and about the central place of dancing in the economy of pairing and mating'.
124. Apart from Shakespeare and Ben Jonson, English pastoral shows a definite tendency to idealize love and avoid all eroticism. However, if we scanned this literature with the beady eye of one such as Gérard Genette (see 'Le serpent dans la bergerie', in his *Figures I* (Paris, 1966)), we should no doubt discover a whole host of disturbing ambiguities.
125. In *England's Helicon* (1600), sign. D3 and verso. The poem also appears in A. Grosart, ed., *Works*, vol. I, *Daffodils and Primroses* (poems from *Phoenix Nest* and *England's Helicon*), p. 7.
126. *The Elizabethan Journals (1591–1603)* (London, 1938; repr. 1955), pp. 56–7.
127. 5th eclogue, lines 18–32 and 36–41.
128. *The Sad Shepherd*, I, i, iv, 36–9 (in *Works*, vol. VII, p. 16). On this subject, see J.B. Bamborough, 'The Rusticity of Ben Jonson' in *Jonson and Shakespeare*, ed. Ian Donaldson (London, 1983), pp. 148–50.

129. See *Vox Graculi*, p. 63: 'This day shall be erected long wooden *Idols* called May-poles . . .'.

130. *A Treatise against Dicing*, quoted in Marienstras, *New Perspectives on the Shakespearean World*, pp. 175–6.

131. *Leviathan* (London, 1651; Scolar Press, London, 1969).

132. *The Diary of Robert Woodfill, Steward of Northampton*, Book III, cited in the 9th Report of the Historical Manuscripts Commission, vol. VIII, Appendices, pp. 496–9. It is worth remembering that, in this period, the forests were the preserve of the king and that 'crimes against the vert' were punishable offences, as was poaching the wild animals normally reserved for royal hunting parties. On this point, see the analysis of John Manwood's work, *A Treatise on the Lawes of the Forest*, by Richard Marienstras (*New Perspectives*, pp. 20–30). Charles Phythian-Adams ('Ceremony and the Citizen') is, for his part, of a quite different opinion on this subject, and he cites (p. 68) a municipal decree of the city of Coventry.

133. *Anatomie of Abuses*, p. 149.

134. Lines 97–8: John Milton, *Poetical Works*, ed. Douglas Bush (Oxford, 1960; repr. 1983).

135. The maypole was indeed a pillar of popular festivity, as Rousseau recognized in his *Lettre à d'Alembert sur les spectacles* (Paris, 1758; repr. Paris, 1889): 'Plant a pole bedecked with flowers in the middle of a public square, gather the people around it, and there starts a holiday . . .' (p. 268; my translation).

136. *Survey*, p. 124.

137. *Ibid*. According to the *OED*, 'the 1st of May 1517 when the apprentices of London rose against the privileged foreigners, whose advantages in trade had occasioned great jealousy'.

138. 'Pasquil's Palinodia', p. 14.

139. Beaumont and Fletcher, *Women Pleased* (1620), IV, i, 198–9.

140. *Vox Graculi*, p. 62; cited by Brand and Ellis, (vol. I, p. 236).

141. 'Maypoles and Puritans', *Shakespeare Quarterly*, 4 (October, 1950), p. 205.

142. *The Roxburghe Ballads*, vol. VII, ed. W. Chappell and J. Woodfall Ebsworth (Hertford, 1893), p. 81.

143. On this point, see Barnabe Rich, *The Honestie of this Age: Proving by Good Circumstance that the World was Never Honest till Now* (London, 1614; repr. London, 1844 (ed. Peter Cunningham, Percy Society, 11)), p. 11.

144. See *The Diary of John Manningham, 1602–1603*, ed. John Bruce (London, 1868), p. 53.

145. But not all showed such determination, as can be seen from the anecdote told by Nashe in *Have with You to Saffron Walden*, in his *Works*, vol. III, p. 122.

146. In some seventeenth-century Puritan pamphlets, any accident that happened to occur in the course of these festivals was regarded as a divine warning and punishment, leading to the damnation of those who indulged in their pleasures no matter what the preachers told them. The most revealing of the texts is probably the one by Henry Burton. Its full title runs as follows: *A Divine Tragedie lately acted or a Collection of sundrie*

memorable examples of Gods Judgements upon Sabbath-breakers, and other Libertines, in their unlawfull Sports, happening within the Realm of England (London, 1636).

147. Cited by W.B. Whitaker, *Sunday in Tudor and Stuart Times* (London, 1933), p. 148.
148. 'Pasquil's Palinodia', pp. 15–16.
149. *Elizabethan Jig*, p. 7.
150. II, ii, 20–3.
151. *The Shirburn Ballads, 1585–1616*, ed. Andrew Clark (Oxford, 1907), p. 362.
152. See the words of Soto in *Women Pleased*, by Beaumont and Fletcher (p. 193):

> There's ne'er a duke in Christendom but loves a May-game.

Soto, a farmer's son who is extremely keen on May Day sports, is here addressing a recruiting officer who is trying to interrupt the village's Morris dance in Act IV.

153. *Elizabethan Stage*, vol. I, p. 199. See *The Malcontent* (1604), by John Marston:

> MALEVOLE [to Prepasso, a gentleman-usher]: . . . here's a knight of the land of Catito shall . . . do the sword-dance with any morris-dancer in Christendom
>
> (I, i, 100–3), in *Works*, vol. I, p. 214.

154. Second part (1631), I, i, 388; ed. Robert K. Turner (Regents Renaissance Drama Series, London 1967).
155. II, i, 6–10.
156. *The Elizabethan Underworld* (London, 1977), p. 157.
157. *The Gypsies Metamorphosed*, in *Works*, vol. VII, p. 589, lines 744–8.
158. *Ibid.*
159. *Ibid.*
160. *Elizabethan Stage*, vol. I, p. 199. See also Cecil J. Sharp, *Sword Dances*, pp. 35–6; and Cecil J. Sharp and Herbert C. Macilwaine, *The Morris Book. A History of Morris Dancing with a Description of Eleven Dances as Performed by the Morris-Men of England*, 4 vols. (London, 1907–11), vol. I, p. 15.
161. III, v, 120–2.
162. *Laneham's Letter*, pp. 22–3.
163. See under 'Morisco'.
164. The name 'Tollet' is still associated with this stained-glass window from Betley Hall, Staffordshire, now in the Victoria and Albert Museum in London, for Tollet was the first to mention its existence to Steevens and Johnson who, however, forgot to cite their source in their edition of Shakespeare's works. See the *Dictionary of National Biography*, Tollet entry, on this point.
165. In his *Histoire des marionnettes en Europe* (Paris, 1862), Charles Magnin explains that the *marotte* (bauble), or fool's sceptre, topped with an effigy of a little girl, was derived from the name 'Marion', popularly given to the statuettes of the Virgin Mary which used to be set up at crossroads, for the veneration of passers-by. Quite apart from its etymological interest, this

information could also explain the special links between the Fool and Maid Marian, in the Morris dance.

166. *The Gypsies Metamorphosed*, in *Works*, vol. VII, p. 589 (lines 748–55).
167. *Works*, vol. I, p. 82.
168. *A Quip for an Upstart Courtier* (1592), in W. Oldys, ed., *Harleian Miscellany*, vol. V (London, 1745), p. 382.
169. *The Honestie of this Age*, p. 50 (my italics).
170. *1 Henry IV*, III, iii, 114–15; Robert Nares' *Glossary*..., ed. J.O. Halliwell and Thomas Wright, 2 vols. (London, 1888).
171. On this subject, see Malcolm A. Nelson, *Robin Hood Tradition*, p. 61.
172. *The Whimzies*, p. 139.
173. I, i, 8–16. See above, p. 36.
174. See above, p. 36 and note 17, p. 319.
175. New edition by the New Shakspere Society in *A Sequel to Tell-Trothes New Yeares Gift* (1593), ed. N. Trübner (London, 1876).
176. *Cobbes Prophecie* (London, 1614; new edn by A.H. Bullen, in *Ancient Drolleries* (Oxford, 1890)).
177. III, vi, 133–4.
178. *Mediaeval Stage*, vol. I, pp. 196–7. The painting by David Vinckeboon to which Chambers refers is entitled 'The Thames at Richmond' and dates from the early seventeenth century. It is in the Fitzwilliam Museum, Cambridge, and is identified in the catalogue simply as 'No. 61, Flemish School'. It is a magnificent landscape and also a lifelike genre painting in the purest tradition of the Flemish painters of this period. In the top left-hand corner, Richmond Palace overlooks the Thames, while in the lower part of the picture ferries are plying from one bank to the other, carrying passengers. In the foreground is a group of two musicians and five Morris dancers, among whom the Hobby-horse, Maid Marian and the Fool are easily recognizable. The dancers seem to have just finished their perform-ance for the entertainment of the passengers waiting to take the ferry, and the Fool is holding out his ladle towards a rich spectator wearing a red coat.
179. *The Returne of Pasquil*, in *Works*, vol. I, p. 92.
180. Letter no. 43, 'A Merry Letter of News to a Friend', in *A Poste with a Packet of Mad Letters* (n.d.), in *Works*, vol. II, *h*, pp. 44.
181. *The Entertainment at Althorpe*, in *Works*, vol. VII, p. 130 (lines 249–91).
182. *The Figure of Foure*, in *Works*, vol. II, *f*, p. 6.
183. *Anatomie of Abuses*, p. 147.
184. *The Masque of Owls at Kenilworth* (1624). *Presented by the Ghost of Captaine Coxe mounted on his Hobby-horse*, in *Works*, vol. VII, p. 781 (lines 1–14). See also above, p. 109.
185. v, ii, in W. Bang, *Materialien zur Kunde des älteren englischen Dramas*, vol. XLII (Louvain, 1914).
186. *Every Man Out of His Humour*, II, i, 40–71, in *Works*, vol. III, pp. 460–1.
187. Stubbes was probably thinking of a trick of this sort when he wrote: 'all good minstrels may dance the wild morris through a needle's eye...' (*Anatomie of Abuses*, p. 171).
188. *Popular Antiquities*, vol. I, p. 269.
189. III, i, 123–9, in *Plays and Poems*, vol. IV, p. 245.
190. *The Honour of Valour* (1605), in *Works*, vol. I, p. 6. See Carlo Buffone's

irony at the expense of Sogliardo, who declares that he has danced with the Hobby-horse (see p. 128, above). Carlo asks him:

Not since the humour of gentilitie was upon you? did you?

In similar vein, see the passage from James Shirley's *The Lady of Pleasure* cited above, p. 36.

191. See Ben Jonson, *Bartholomew Fair*, iii, ii, 39–42, in *Works*, vol. vi, p. 63.
192. *Autobiography (1615–1633)*, cited in L.A. Govett, *The King's Book of Sports* (London, 1890), p. 6.
193. *Love's Labour's Lost*, iii, i, 27–8; *Hamlet*, iii, ii, 129.
194. *Robin Hood Tradition*, p. 75.
195. *Popular Antiquities*, vol. i, p. 266.
196. *Ibid.*, pp. 266 and 267.
197. *Old Meg of Hereford-shire for a Mayd-marian*, in *Herefordshire, Worcestershire*, ed. David N. Klausner (Records of Early English Drama, Toronto, 1990), p. 125.
198. *Ibid.*, p. 129.
199. Hence the expression, 'drunk as a piper' (*OED*, 'Piper', sense 1b).
200. *The Whimzies*, pp. 142–3.
201. *Ibid.*
202. *Anatomie of Abuses*, p. 147 (my italics).
203. Illus. 4.4 is also reproduced in *Philip Stubbes's Anatomy of Abuses in England in Shakspere's Youth, A.D. 1583*, ed. Frederick J. Furnivall (New Shakspere Society), 2 vols. (London, 1877–9), vol. i, p. 28.
204. *Anatomie of Abuses*, p. 147.
205. In *The Entertainment at Althorpe*, the presenter 'No-body' warns the peasant Morris dancers:

Not a jerke you have shall make
Any Ladie in Love.   (in *Works*, vol. vii, p. 130, lines 279–80).

206. Randall Cotgrave, *A Dictionarie of the French and English Tongues* (London, 1611).
207. Cited in Baskervill, *Elizabethan Jig*, p. 354.
208. Baskervill (*ibid.*) refers in this connection to the publication, on 5 February 1593, of a pamphlet entitled 'A pleasant fancie or merrie conceyt called "the passionat morrys" daunst by a crue of Eight couples of whores, all meere Enimyes to love'.
209. *Madrigals to Four Voyces* (1594) (my italics), in E.H. Fellowes, *English Madrigal Verse, 1588–1632* (Oxford, 1920; repr. 1967), p. 143. The strange conjunction of the sophisticated art of the madrigal and the often popular or rustic character of their lyrics has been studied by Jean Fuzier in 'London and Country Cries: Elizabethan Life in Song and Music' (*Cahiers Elisabéthains*, 8 (October 1975), pp. 31–63). He also mentions the competitive Morris dances, p. 49 (see below).
210. A.H. Bullen, ed., *Lyrics from the Dramatists of the Elizabethan Age* (London, 1901), p. 293.
211. iv, v, 80–2, 91–4.
212. Football was already being played in England in the fourteenth century, particularly on the occasion of festivals such as Shrove Tuesday and May

Day. As for rugby, it offers certain analogies with the folk plays which used to be performed in the countryside at Christmas and Easter. (We should note, in particular, the role played by the medical attendant with his 'magic' sponge, rather like the one carried by the Doctor in the Mummers' Play . . . .) Daniel Fabre (*La fête en Languedoc*, p. 198) comments: 'In some cases, rugby teams seem to have taken over from the traditional youth organizations. Similarly, in the whole atmosphere surrounding the game, it is easy to detect a reworking of carnival elements.'

213. *Calendar of the Manuscripts of the Marquess of Salisbury*, in the 8th Report of the Historical Manuscripts Commission, p. 201 (my italics).
214. On this point, see J.C. Cox, *Churchwardens' Accounts*, pp. 263–5.
215. Stubbes, *Anatomie of Abuses*, p. 149; Warner, *Albion's England*, v, 25. See also above, p. 116.
216. See the following lines from Shakespeare's *Henry V* (II, iv, 23–5):

> DAUPHIN: And let us do it with no show of fear,
> No, with no more than if we heard that England
> Were busied with a Whitsun morris dance.

217. Clark, *The Shirburn Ballads*, p. 363: 'The Merie Life of the Countryman'.
218. In the Prologue to *A Tale of a Tub* (line 8), Ben Jonson mentions: 'antique proverbs drawn from Whitson lords . . .'. Now, thanks to John Selden (*Table-Talk*, p. 10), we know that Ben Jonson was also the author of a pastoral comedy entitled *The May Lord* in which 'Contrary to all other pastoral he bringeth the clowns making mirth and foolish sports.' Unfortunately, this play of Ben Jonson's, written between 1613 and 1619, according to Harbage and Schoenbaum, has not come down to us. On the other hand, Beaumont and Fletcher's comedy, *Women Pleased*, contains a short scene which gives an amusing idea of the popularity of the May Lord in the countryside. Soto, who has been made 'May Lord' addresses the recruiting captain, who is trying to take him off to the wars, as follows:

> Are you a man? Will you cast away a May-lord?
> Shall the wenches in the country curse you?   (IV, i, 121–2)

219. In connection with the 'Summer Queene', it is worth citing the following lines by Thomas Campion (in *The Works of Thomas Campion*, ed. Walter R. Davis (London, 1967, repr. 1969), p. 80):

> Jack and Joane . . .
> Skip and trip it on the greene
> And help to chuse the Summer Queene.

According to C.R. Baskervill ('Dramatic Aspects', p. 50), the Whitsun festival was a particularly solemn and sumptuous occasion in Arthurian literature and hence also for the medieval aristocracy, and popular celebrations reflected its major characteristics, in their own peculiar fashion: 'From the sixteenth century to the nineteenth, the folk May and Whitsun games have been organized in England after the same fashion, with a king and a queen, attendants as sword and mace bearers, feasts in arbors or halls, sports and wooing games or matings.' In some towns, St Ives in Cornwall for example, the king and queen were expected to preside over the organization of 'Summer Games'. The money collected at the games would be handed over to the parish, to be used for the relief of the poor. On this point, see J.C. Cox, *Churchwardens' Accounts*, p. 280.

220. See *The Whore of Babylon* (1607) by Thomas Dekker (in *Works*, vol. II, p. 574; v, ii, 171–9).

221. *William Shakespeare, A Study of Facts and Problems*, 2 vols. (Oxford, 1930), vol. I, p. 9.

222. In *Percy Folio of Old English Ballads* (London, 1910), vol. IV, p. 42.

223. *The Whimzies*, p. 138.

224. Testimony as to the evening performances of plays in London during the summer is provided by Machyn (see his *Diary*, p. 150), who makes a note of a performance of a 'stageplay of goodly matter' between eight o'clock and midnight on 29 July 1557; and also by Stow who, in his *Survey of London*, writes: 'toward the evening [the citizens of London] had stage-plays, and bonfires in the streets' (p. 124). On this point, see the unpublished thesis by Jean-Marie Maguin, 'La nuit dans le théâtre de Shakespeare et de ses prédécesseurs', 2 vols. (Lille, 1980).

225. J.C. Cox, *Churchwardens' Accounts*, p. 286.

226. *The Early Plays of Robin Hood* (Cambridge, 1981), p. 4.

227. *Elizabethan Jig*, p. 288.

228. E.K. Chambers (*Mediaeval Stage*, vol. I, p. 173) writes: 'The May-game is probably intended by the "Whitsun pastorals" of *The Winter's Tale* and the "pageants of delight" of *The Two Gentlemen of Verona*.'

229. On this subject, see Wiles, *Early Plays of Robin Hood*, p. 31.

230. See, for example, the case of the draper John Hole and his action in connection with the organizers of the May game at Wells in 1607, in Charles J. Sisson, *Lost Plays of Shakespeare's Age* (London, 1936), p. 165 and *passim*.

231. On this subject, see the description given by Stubbes (*Anatomie of Abuses*, p. 150); also J.C. Cox, *Churchwardens' Accounts*, p. 289.

232. See Dekker's *The Devils Answer to Pierce Pennyless* (1606), in *Non-Dramatic Works*, vol. II, p. 116:

> Epicures grow as fat there [Venice], as in England, for you shall have a slave eat more at a meale, than ten of the Guard, and drink more in two dayes, than all *Manningtree* do's at a *Whitsun ale*.

233. (Philadelphia, 1898), p. 25.

234. *A Divine Tragedie*, pp. 10–11.

235. 'The Records of Quarter Sessions in the County of Wilts' in the Historical Manuscripts Commission's *Reports on Manuscripts in Various Collections*, vol. I, pp. 107–8.

236. On this subject, see Charles Phythian-Adams, *Ceremony and the Citizen*, p. 79; also *VCH*, vol. VIII: *Warwickshire*, pp. 218–19.

237. See Lawrence M. Clopper, ed., *Chester* (Records of Early English Drama, Toronto, 1979), p. lv.

238. The etymology of the word 'bonfires' has been much disputed. Some scholars believe that they were 'bone-fires' (connected with the fires on which martyrs were burned at the stake), others that they were 'boon-fires', that is to say fires designed to attract blessings from heaven. On this point, see Brand and Ellis, *Popular Antiquities*, vol. I, pp. 301–2. See also the line

from Warner's *Albion's England*: 'At Baptis-Day with Ale and cakes bon fire neighbours stood.' In his *Survey of London*, Stow mentions similar customs in the various quarters of the town (p.126). It is true that Stow's information relates to an earlier period than the one that we are studying but, at least in the case of the Midsummer festivals, it shows that conviviality had by no means disappeared from some quarters of the capital and that the difference that we have noted between the towns and the countryside with respect to hospitality and festive traditions must have been a relatively recent phenomeon (dating from about the middle of Elizabeth's reign). It is interesting to note that Stow sets himself up as a defender of the pacific, civilizing aspects of festivals (which made for neighbourliness and a form of social harmony). See also Aubrey, *Remains*, p. 26.

239. It was a matter of jumping as high as possible over the flames and then dancing round the fire, as is indicated in the ballad entitled 'The Merie Life of the Countriman' in Andrew Clark, *Shirburn Ballads*, p. 363 (strophe 8). Baskervill ('Dramatic Aspects', pp. 51−2) mentions the custom of bowling flaming wheels down hillsides or mounds.

240. Night-time was itself believed to be propitious for divinations and the fires were thought to fertilize the fields. On this point, see Thomas, *Religion*, pp. 240, 648. See also Stow, *Survey*, pp. 126−7. On these Midsummer customs of divination, John Aubrey (*Remains*, p. 26) writes: 'It was a Custome for some people that were more curious then ordinary to Sitt all night in the church porch of their Parish on Midsomer-eve, St John the Baptist's eve; and they should see the apparitions of those that should die in the parish that yeare come back and knocke at the dore . . . '.

241. These torches might be those carried by 'Wild men' or, alternatively, the lanterns known as 'cressets', which were carried by men-at-arms.

242. In *The Arte of English Poesie* (1589) (p. 128), George Puttenham refers to these giants, in an image designed to criticize the excesses of the 'high style':

> But generally the high stile is disgraced and made foolish and ridiculous by all wordes affected, counterfait and puffed up . . . and cannot be better ressembled than to these midsommer pageants in London, where to make the people wonder are set forth great and uglie Gyants marching as if they were alive, and armed at all points, but within they are stuffed full of brown paper and tow, which the shrewd boyes underpeering, do guilefully discover and turne to great derision.

In *A Dissertation on the Pageants and Dramatic Mysteries Anciently Performed at Coventry* (pp. 204−5), Thomas Sharp provides some interesting details about these giants:

> The Giants exhibited by the Drapers' Company in Coventry, were both male and female (a Giant and his wife). No distinction of sex is expressed in the Cappers' Accounts; but we learn from them a very curious fact, viz.: that a candlestick was put into the head of their Giant, containing a wax candle; and when it is recollected that both the Processions were made by night, a light within the head of the figure, it is easy to conceive, might be so contrived as to exhibit the goggle-eyes and terrific looks of the Giant, with greatly heightened effect.

This passage confirms the spectacular nature of these parades lit by candles and lanterns, in which the atmosphere of rejoicing was tinged with a feeling of nocturnal magic. Charles Phythian-Adams tells us that this was a characteristic of London processions which certain provincial corporations tried to imitate: 'As from 1533 the parvenu craft of Cappers aped a custom of the London companies by bearing a carnival-type giant, with illuminated eyes, through the dusky streets at Midsummer and St Peter's' ('Ceremony and the Citizen', p. 63). However, in some towns – Chester, for example – the processions of Giants appear to have been banned, in this case by the mayor in person, who is described in the archives as 'a godlye over zealous man': 'He caused the Gyauntes in the Midsomer show to be put downe & broken and not to goe...' (cited in Clopper, *Chester, The Records*, pp. 71–2.

243. On the subject of civic inauguration ceremonies, Phythian-Adams ('Ceremony and the Citizen', p. 75) points out that although the ritual half of the year (which stretched from Christmas, the mid-winter festival, to Midsummer's Day) began with rites of inversion and parodies of power (Lords of Misrule, Mock Mayors), it ended with parades which restored a kind of hierarchical order, with the installation of a king and a queen.

244. The full quotation, which is intended to underline the gap between fine appearances and a less magnificent reality, is probably inspired by Puttenham's image (cited above, p. 345, n. 242):

> CANTILUPO: What title shall I set to this base coyne?...
> He has no name, and for's aspect he seemes
> A Gyant in a May-game, that within
> Is nothing but a Porter...
>   (IV, ii, 144–7), in *John Webster, The Complete Works*, ed. F.L. Lucas, 4 vols. (Cambridge, 1927), vol. II, p. 293.

245. See proverb no. R 75 in Tilley, *Dictionary of the Proverbs*: 'He spent Michaelmas rent in Midsummer moon.' According to the *OED* ('Midsummer', sense 3), the expression 'Midsummer moon' refers to a 'time when lunacy is supposed to be prevalent'.

246. In connection with the three-monthly subdivisions of the year, we should, however, remember that Lammas and Michaelmas in truth belonged to two distinct systems: the former was adopted in England and Ireland, the latter in Scotland. In the domain of proverbs, we may cite, for example, 'at latter Lammas', with the variant 'at Nevermas', which has a French equivalent in the expression 'Aux calendes grecques'. As regards Michaelmas, the proverb cited above in connection with Midsummer (n. 245) clearly sets out the contradiction between an extreme of spending (summer) and one of obligations (autumn).

247. P. 261.

248. On this subject, see Phythian-Adams, 'Ceremony and the Citizen', p. 70; and Hole, *Dictionary of British Folk Customs*, pp. 178–9.

249. *Popular Antiquities*, vol. I, p. 348. Hence, no doubt, the Puritans' objection to the term:

> He holds all bonds bearing date at Lammasse, Michaelmasse, Candlemasse, or any masse whatsoever, to be frustrate and of no effect; but by changing masse into tide they become of full force and vertue...
>   (*The Whimzies*, 'A Zealous Brother', p. 117)

250. *Grim the Collier of Croydon, or the Devil and his Dame* in *A Select Collection of Old Plays*, compiled by Robert Dodsley 4 vols. (London, 1744; repr. by W.C. Hazlitt, 1874–6, and again in New York, 1964), vol. IV (IV, i, p. 415).

251. Cited in Brand and Ellis, *Popular Antiquities*, vol. I, p. 353. The Day of the Holy Cross was also an important date in the hunting calendar: it was the last day of the deer and roe-buck hunting season (which began on Midsummer or Saint John's Day) and the first day of the season for hunting the females of these two species. See Marienstras, *New Perspectives*, pp. 31–2.

252. The poet George Gascoigne refers to these traditions in 'Flowers of Poesie' (*Complete Works*, vol. I, p. 72).

253. It was also advisable for servants and young men wishing to avoid the rigours of military service to butter up their masters or the recruiting officer with timely presents of poultry, or some other gift in kind. See the text cited and commented upon in Brand and Ellis, *Popular Antiquities*, vol. I, pp. 370–1.

254. See Thomas, *Religion*, p. 71: 'a Michaelmas goose meant good luck for those who ate it'.

255. Clébert, *Bestiaire fabuleux*, pp. 267–70.

256. Brand and Ellis mention but reject as apocryphal (*Popular Antiquities*, vol. I, p. 309) the explanation according to which the custom was started by the fact that Queen Elizabeth learned of the defeat of the Invincible Armada (on 29 September 1588) while she was eating a dish of goose.

257. *British Calendar Customs*, vol. III, p. 80.

258. For an explanation of these divination games which concerned the supposed fidelity of a young couple, see Brand and Ellis, *Popular Antiquities*, vol. I, p. 396: 'as a necessary part of the entertainment [of the night before All Saints' Day] the young folks amuse themselves with burning nuts in pairs on the bar of the grate, or among the warm embers, to which they give their name and that of their lovers, or those of their friends who are supposed to have such attachments, and from the manner of their burning and duration of the flame, &c., draw such inferences respecting the constancy and strength of their passions . . . '; see also vol. I, pp. 377–8. For an example of the use of these customs within the framework of a literary system of symbols and in the context of Celtic traditions in Ireland in the late nineteenth century, see F. Laroque, 'Hallowe'en Customs in "Clay" – A Study of James Joyce's Use of Folklore in *Dubliners*', *Studies in the Early Joyce*, CVE (Montpellier), 14, (October 1981), pp. 47–56.

259. See E.K. Chambers, *Mediaeval Stage*, vol. I, p. 247.

260. *The Christmas Prince*, p. 3.

261. See Brand and Ellis, *Popular Antiquities*, vol. I, p. 394–5. On this point, see also *British Calendar Customs*, vol. III, p. 133. On the commemoration of the souls in purgatory on All Saints' Day, see Jacques Le Goff, *La naissance du purgatoire* (Paris, 1981), pp. 170–3. In Elizabeth's reign, bishops were supposed to make sure that none of the churches in their particular diocese reverted to this papist rite. See Kennedy, *Administration*, vol. II ('Visitations and Injunctions 1575–1582'), p. 30. John Bossy, (*Christianity in the West 1400–1700*, (Oxford, 1985), p. 33) connects these customs (tolling

the bells at night, torchlight, bonfires) with the folklore of Hallowe'en; David Underdown (*Revel, Riot and Rebellion*, p. 70) makes similar comments.

262. See Brand and Ellis, *Popular Antiquities*, vol. i, p. 393; also *British Calendar Customs*, vol. iii, p. 143.

263. On this subject, see the text cited by David Wilkins (*Concilia*, vol. iii, p. 424). See also Walsh, who writes (*Curiosities*, p. 495):

It was in January of the same year (1606) that the British Parliament appointed the 5th of November as 'a holiday for ever in thankfulness to God for our deliverance and detestation of the Papists'. A special service for this day formed part of the ritual of the English Book of Common Prayer until 1859, when an ordinance of the Queen in Council abolished it . . .

264. Wright and Lones, *British Calendar Customs*, vol. iii, p. 145.

265. *Ibid.*, pp. 146–7.

266. See the many references to this day in Dekker's *The Shoemaker's Holiday*, and the interpretation that I put upon them in 'Le Londres en fête de Thomas Dekker', pp. 7–33. These traditions associated with Saint Hugh are also mentioned in Richard Johnson's *The Pleasant Conceits of Old Hobson the Merry Londoner* (1607): 'Upon Saint Hewes Day, being the seventeenth of November, upon which day the triumph was holden for Queen Elizabeth's happy government, as bonfiers, ringing of bells, and such like . . . ' (in Hazlitt, *Shakespeare's Jest-Books*, vol. iii, p. 26).

267. Roy Strong, in *Journal of the Warburg and Courtauld Institutes*, 21 (1959), p. 87. See also, by the same author, *The Cult of Elizabeth*, p. 119. On this point, see also Carl Z. Wiener, 'The Beleaguered Isle. A Study of Elizabethan and Early Jacobean Anti-Catholicism', *Past and Present*, 51 (May 1971), pp. 53–4. As regards the peals of bells characteristic of this day, which took the place of the peals that used to be rung in honour of the souls in purgatory, see the amusing passage by Harsnett cited below, on the subject of a spirit responsible for a case of possession:

Touching that which is written of the pretended spirit name Puffe, is that he should say upon 'St Hughs day' he would go ring for the Queene: she verily beleeveth that eyther those words have been advised by the writer of the booke, or else that if she . . . uttered them, it was because, she heard them speaking of ringing that day, in honour of the Queene . . .

A Declaration of Egregious Popish Impostures, to withdraw the harts of her Maiesties Subjects from their Allegiance, and from the Truth of Christian Religion Professed in England, under the Pretence of Casting out Devils (London, 1603), p. 182.

268. Strong, 'Popular celebration', p. 87.

269. On this subject, see the *OED* ('Lent', sb 1 3b). The meteorological phenomenon of Saint Martin's summer, defined by the *OED* as 'a season of fine mild weather occurring about Martinmas' ('Martin', sense 3) was also connected with this idea.

270. *Art profane et religion populaire au Moyen Age* (Paris, 1985), pp. 64–70.

271. This day corresponded to the ancient Roman festival of the *Vinalia* (Bacchus' Feast). See Drake, *Shakespeare and his Times*, 2 vols. (London, 1817), vol. i, p. 291.

272. *Shakespeare's England*, vol. I, pp. 355–6.
273. *Doctor Faustus* (1593, published 1604), II, ii, 696–700, in *Works*, vol. II, p. 184.
274. See F. Laroque, 'En marge de l'idéologie: antimasque et grotesque dans le *Dr Faustus* et *La Tempête*', in *Théâtre et idéologies: Marlowe, Shakespeare. Actes du Congrès de la Société française Shakespeare (1981)* (Paris, 1982), p. 102.
275. Book v, chapter 25.
276. As we have seen above, in connection with the hunting calendar, the deer-hunting season normally ended on 'Holyrood Day'. This confirms that the Sheriff of Nottingham's sworn enemy, Robin Hood, did indeed transgress a royal prohibition (poaching, in this case).
277. Brand and Ellis, *Popular Antiquities*, vol. I, p. 411.
278. See *The Christmas Prince*, p. 13: 'Y^c Councell table, wth y^c Lord himself mett together to nominate Officers, & to appoynt the day of y^c Princes publicke installment wch was agreed should be on Sr Andrews day at night; because at that time y^c Colledge allso was to chouse their new officers for y^c years following.'
279. Below (pp. 352–3), I shall be studying the functions of a Lord of Misrule during the festivities of the twelve days of Christmas. With respect to the Boy Bishop, there are still a few texts that refer to the custom in the Elizabethan period. One is George Puttenham's *The Arte of English Poesie*:

> me thinks this fellow speakes like the Bishop *Nicholas*, for on Saint *Nicholas* night commonly the Scholars of the Countrey make them a Bishop, who like a foolish boy, goeth about blessing and preaching with so childish termes, as maketh the people laugh at his foolish counterfaite speeches.   (p. 228)

There are also a few known cases where it was a young woman who was elevated to this comic office. See *Cambridge History of English Literature*, ed. A.W. Ward and A.R. Waller, 15 vols. (Cambridge, 1907–10), vol. 5, repr. 1961) 'The Origins of English Drama', p. 8. The very principle of such a parodic institution stemmed from the Saturnalia and the festive themes of an upside-down world, for here serious, even sacred, dignities were conferred upon children (in this connection, see the characteristic expression 'childysshe observation' in the prohibition order cited above, p. 60). See Levin, *Multiple Plot*, p. 142.

280. I have quoted the essential part of the official prohibition order on this festival above, p. 60. On this point, see also Rowse, *Elizabethan Renaissance*, p. 202.
281. Brand and Ellis, *Popular Antiquities*, vol. I, p. 430.
282. *Elizabethan Renaissance*, p. 203.
283. On this point, see Wigfall Green, *Inns of Court*, p. 56.
284. Letter dated 15 November 1572, cited by Alexandra F. Johnston, 'Yule in York', *Records of Early English Drama (REED)*, 1 (1976), p. 5.
285. *Ibid.*
286. On this point, see Michael Harrison, *The Story of Christmas. Its Growth and Development from the Earliest Times* (London, n.d.), pp. 83–110.
287. See Muriel St Clare Byrne, *Elizabethan Life in Town and Country* (London, 1925), p. 250.

288. See, in particular, the three following proverbs: 'Christmas comes but once a year, and when it comes it brings good cheer, but when it's gone it's never the near' (B 701 & C 369); 'After Christmas comes Lent' (C 367) and 'They talk of Christmas so long that it comes' (C 373).
289. *The Merry Devil of Edmonton* (an anonymous play included in Brooke, *Shakespeare Apocrypha*), I, i, 71–3.
290. A song cited by Muriel St Clare Byrne, in *Elizabethan Life*, p. 251.
291. See Tusser, *A Hundreth Good Points of Husbandrie* (1557), p. 68: 'At Christmas, we banket, the rich with the poor.' For example, a large landowner such as Bess of Hardwick would make a point of being particularly generous towards the parish poor at the time of the Christmas festivities. A.L. Rowse writes: 'at Chelsea in 1591 the poor at her gates receive, in addition to the regular 20s, "for Christmas and Twelve days, more 13s"' (*Elizabethan Renaissance*, p. 102). But these traditions were disappearing, for most representatives of the landed aristocracy were now neglecting their charitable and hospitable obligations at Christmas and were instead living in splendour in London. See the remarks of Robert Greene on the decline of this tradition in *A Quippe for an Upstart Courtier* (1592): 'The niggardness of the lord or master is the cause no more chimneys do smoke: for would they use ancient hospitality as their forefathers did, and value as lightly of pride, as their great-grandfathers, then should you see every Chimney in the house smoke' (*Life and Complete Works in Prose and Verse*, ed. A.B. Grosart, 15 vols. (London, 1881; repr. New York, 1964), vol. X, p. 272). Barnabe Rich (*Honestie of the Age*, p. 66) makes similar comments but attributes the cause of such behaviour to the vanity of women who wished to be seen in town instead of staying in their country manors and discharging their traditional obligations there.

An anonymous comedy entitled *A Merry Knack to Know a Knave* (1592) in Dodsley, *A Selection of Old Plays* (vol. III, p. 544), contains an allusion to this decline in hospitality in an amusing scene in which a penniless knight wonders how his father can have managed to hold open house in the castle at Christmas time:

> Neighbour Walter, I cannot but admire to see
> How housekeeping is decayed within this thirty year;
> But where the fault is, God knows: I know not.
> My father in his lifetime gave hospitality
> To all strangers,
> And distressed travellers;
> His table was never empty of bread, beef and beer;
> He was wont to keep a hundred tall men in his hall.
> He was a feaster of all comers in general,
> And yet he was never in want of money . . .

To which the practical and cynical rejoinder of his neighbour Walter runs as follows:

> At a Christmas-time feast none at all,
> But such as yield you some commodity;
> I mean such as will send you now and then
> Fat geese and capons to keep house withal:
> To these and none else would I have you liberal.

According to L.C. Knights, 'the "age of hospitality" seems to have been used as an equivalent for "the good old times" and the decline of the great households became a matter of popular comment' (*Drama and Society in the Age of Jonson* (London, 1937; repr. 1962, pp. 113–14). It is an idea that is confirmed by a passage from the 1613 poem by Humphrey King, *An Halfe-penny Worth of Wit* (p. 19):

> Welcome here must be your Chiefe
> To a friendly peece of Biefe,
> Such was us'd in ancient time
> When house-Keeping was in prime;
> When the Biefe and Brewes flourisht,
> When the silly soules were nourisht,
> Then 'twas a wonder to the poore
> To see a Porter keepe the doore,
> Then were silly harmlesse folkes,
> Plain chimneyes then were full of smoakes:
> Every table then was spred,
> And furnished out with Biefe and bread
> Every man then tooke a pleasure
> In his house to spend his treasure.
> Who was then the Gentries Guest?
> The Widow poore, that's oft opprest,
> The Souldiers with their wounds and skarres
> Bleeding for their Countries warres.
> Then in the Country dwelt true pity,
> Now Christmas is but for the Citty.

The phenomenon of this exodus from the provinces of an aristocracy which abandoned its castles to enjoy the luxury of the towns, and the decline in traditions of local hospitality that this brought about, seemed to James I serious enough for him to issue a proclamation in 1615. It urged the nobility, who were in London to amuse themselves, to return to their country homes: 'to maintain Hospitalitie amongst their neighbours'. (The text of this proclamation is cited above, pp. 70–1.)

292. Brand and Ellis, *Popular Antiquities*, vol. I, p. 471.
293. In *Juvenilia* (1622), ed. T. Wright, Percy Society, 4 (London, 1841), p. 63.
294. Brand and Ellis, *Popular Antiquities*, vol. I, p. 484.
295. The portrait of the 'Piper' in *The Whimzies* (p. 142) refers to this in an amusing if caustic comment on these amateur musicians: 'Hee might bee not altogether improperly charactered, an ill wind that begins to blow upon Christmasse eve, and so continues very loud and blustring all the twelve dayes . . . '.
296. Wither, *Juvenilia*, p. 64.
297. See Thiselton Dyer, *Folklore of Shakespeare*, p. 194.
298. See the description given by John Taylor, the Water-Poet, in a pamphlet entitled *The Complaints of Christmas and the Teares of Twelfetyde* (London, 1631), pp. 22–3.
299. See Wickham, *Medieval Theatre*, p. 146.
300. See Crippen, *Christmas and Christmas Lore*, p. 94. These Mummers' performances seem sometimes to have been replaced by a Morris dance, to judge by a text cited by Brand and Ellis (*Popular Antiquities*, vol. I, p. 492)

which refers to '...the coming into the hall of the Hobby-horse at Christmas'.

301. See John Northbrooke, *A Treatise wherein Dicing, Dauncing, Vaine Plays, or Enterludes, are Reproved* (1577), ed. J.P. Collier (London, 1843), p. 105.

302. Enid Welsford defines it as 'a sophisticated mumming' (*Court Masque*, p. 4).

303. On the importance of plays during the twelve days of Christmas ('Season of the Revels'), see Michael Shapiro, *Children of the Revels* (New York, 1977), pp. 11–12.

304. In *The Whimzies* (p. 80), this point is stressed: '[at Christmas] his neighbours, whom he tenders as members of his own family, joyne with him in this consort of mirth and melody'.

305. Chappell and Ebsworth, *Roxburghe Ballads*, vol. I, pp. 87–8.

306. Taylor, *The Complaints of Christmas*, p. 23. According to Blount's *Glossographia*, 'Christmas gambols are properly games or tumbling tricks plaid with the legs [Ital.: *gamba*]': the game of 'shoeing the wild mare' is defined in the vaguest of terms by the OED ('Mare', sense 2b) as 'some childish Christmas game', while in Nares' *Glossary*, the game of 'hot cockles' is defined as 'an old game, practised especially at Christmas, in which one person knelt down hoodwinked, and being struck behind, was to guess who inflicted the blow'.

307. The ballad cited above, 'A Pleasant Country New Ditty', refers in one of its later verses to what it calls 'some gambole of Christmas play', suggesting that the term could be applied to some kind of rudimentary show. See below, p. 226.

308. John Selden, in *Table-Talk* (p. 31), draws a parallel with the Saturnalia of the ancient world: 'Christmas succeeds the *Saturnalia*, the same number of Holy-days; then the Master waited upon the Servant like the Lord of misrule.'

309. *Survey*, p. 122.

310. See Strutt, *Sports and Pastimes*, p. 343.

311. Polydore Vergil notes, in his *De Inventoribus Rerum* (Venice, 1499; repr. Henry Ellis (London, 1846)), V, 2 (1499), that these 'Christmas Lords of England' were a peculiarly English tradition. See also Strutt, *Sports and Pastimes*, p. 339.

312. Brand and Ellis, *Popular Antiquities*, vol. I, p. 503.

313. *Anatomie of Abuses*, pp. 146–7.

314. In *A Divine Tragedie* (p. 20), Henry Burton mentions a 'May-lord of Misrule'. See also Thomas Lodge who, in his portrait of a jester, is led through an association of ideas to evoke the popular japes of Lords of Misrule in rural festivals:

> The fellow [a 'ieaster'] in person is comely, in apparell courtly but in behaviour a very ape, and no man: his studie is to coin bitter ieasts, or to show antique motions, or to sing baudie sonnets and ballads: give him a little wine in his head, he is continually flearing and making of mouthes; he laughes intemporately at every occasion, and dances about the house, leaps over tables, out-skips mens heads, trips up his companions heeles, burns sacke with a candle, and hath all the feats of a lord of misrule in the countrie.

(*Wits Miserie* (1596), in *The Complete Works of Thomas Lodge*, ed. Edmund Goose, 4 vols. (Glasgow, 1883; repr. New York, 1963), vol. IV, p. 84)

The Lords of Misrule were also a cause for concern to the ecclesiastical authorities, to judge by a diocesan article in which Archbishop Grindal asks whether 'the minister and the churchwardens have suffered any lords of misrule or summer Lords or Ladies, or any disguised persons, or others, in Christmas or at May-games, or any morris-dancers... to come unreverently into the church or churchyard' (*Visitation Articles* (1576), cited in Chambers, *Mediaeval Stage*, vol. I, p. 503).

Still on the subject of Lords of Misrule, an interesting document drawn from the archives of the city of Norwich records a popular uprising which took place on 25 January 1442 and was organized by a certain John Gladman, a merchant of the town. After parading joyfully through the streets, wearing a paper crown, he was proclaimed 'Kyng of Kristmesse':

John Gladman of Norwich... on fastyngong tuesday made a disporte w^t his neighbours having his hors trapped with tyneseule and otherwyse dysgysyn things crowned as King of Kristmesse in token that all merthe shuld end with ye twelve monthes of ye yer, afore hym eche moneth dysgysd after ye season yerof, and Lenten cladde in white with redde herrins skinnes and his hors trapped with oyster shelles after him in token y^t sadnesse and abstinence of merth shulde followe and an holy tyme; and so rode in diverse stretes of ye Cite w^t other pepel w^t hym disgysed making merthe and disporte and pleyes.
(*The Records of the City of Norwich*, ed. William Hudson and John Tingey, 2 vols. (Norwich, 1906), vol. II, pp. 345–6)

This text presents a relatively atypical example of a 'Kyng of Kristmesse' being crowned on a Shrove Tuesday (a good week before Saint Blaise's Day, as the early date of January 25 shows). As the editors point out in a note, 'the mention of "Fastyngong Tuesday", that is, Shrove Tuesday, is perplexing [since] Shrove Tuesday in that year was not until 5 March' (p. xc). Like Jack Cade in *2 Henry VI* and the Captain Paumier described by Le Roy Ladurie in *Carnival in Romans* (pp. 105–6 and 175–6), John Gladman is one of those Carnival kings who illustrate the ambivalence of festivals, in which it is always hard to distinguish fun and parody from revolt and subversion. The Norwich authorities, for their part, were in no doubt as to the dangerous, or at least provoking, nature of these manifestations taking place in between the festivities of Christmas and those of Shrove Tuesday.

Popular revolts disguised as festivals appear to have been not uncommon in this period, as can be seen from the examples cited by D.G.C. Allan in 'The Rising in the West, 1628–1631', *Economic History Review*, 2nd ser., 5 (1952–3), pp. 76–7). Particular mention is made of a popular leader called John Williams, who was known by the somewhat curious title of 'Lady Skimmington'. D.G.C. Allan comments as follows:

He belonged to the tradition of the quasi-comic and quasi-religious leader – combinations, as it were, of biblical saviours and lords of misrule – which had been present in the popular revolts of the sixteenth century or of earlier periods. Jack-o'-the-Style, Piers Plowman, Bartholomew Stere, the four Captains of Penrith and the more concrete but no less magical personality of Ket, had all exercised the same strange appeal, and in Stuart times, their ranks were joined by Captain Pouch, with his female imitator Captain Dorothy Anderson of the Fens and Lady Skimmington himself.

All these examples show that this figure, the Lord of Misrule, who appeared at every level of society on particular festive occasions (Christmas, for instance) sometimes served as a model for many radically different types of behaviour ranging from court entertainments, through the satirization of social customs and of the academic authorities of University colleges, to popular revolt.

315. See Stubbes, *Anatomie of Abuses*, p. 150.
316. See Thomas, *Religion*, p. 239.
317. *Ibid.*, p. 619.
318. *Ibid.*
319. *Ibid.*, p. 47.
320. Brand and Ellis, *Popular Antiquities*, vol. i, p. 11.
321. *Ibid.*, p. 495. See also Crosfield, *Diary*, pp. 68–9.
322. See the lines by Hall (*Virgidemarium*), cited above, p. 90.
323. Wither, 'Christmas Carol' in *Juvenilia*, p. 64.
324. Michel Meslin (*La fête des kalendes*, pp. 32–3) points out that the Roman emperors also received presents from the people on this date. Caligula was the only one cynical enough to ask for money instead.
325. *Histrio-mastix: The Players Scourge or Actors Tragedie* (London, 1633), pp. 757–8.
326. Michel Meslin (*La fête des kalendes*, p. 40) notes that the practice of offering gifts (*strenae* or *handsels*) was originally a private custom which also entailed making an offering to the deity. The present itself thus became a tangible omen of prosperity.
327. *The Thracian Wonder* (1599) [by John Webster and William Rowley?], Act ii, sc. ii, in *The Dramatic Works of John Webster*, ed. William C. Hazlitt, 4 vols. (London, 1857, repr. 1897), vol. iv, p. 149.
328. Cited in Strutt, *Sports and Pastimes*, p. 343.
329. Ian Lancashire ('Records of Drama and Minstrelsy in Nottinghamshire to 1642', *Records of Early English Drama*, 1977 (i), pp. 23–4) cites a speech made by the presenter of a Twelfth Night entertainment, given on that date. The speech concerns the election of a 'King of Wassail'.
330. *Journal*, pp. 74–5: 'Jan. 6. Twelfth-day. At night some companie from Reead came a Mumming; was kindly taken but they were but Mummers.' With regard to the customs of Epiphany, in a curious passage in the *Declaration of Egregious Popish Impostures* (pp. 200–3), Samuel Harsnett cites a statement made by Sara Williams, a young girl involved in an affair of possession at the beginning of the seventeenth century:

Whereas also it is said of her, that 'there appeared unto her in a fit the said 6. of January a Mummery coming in at the doore with a bright eye before them: a drummer sounding, and sixe in number with mostly vizards, which daunced one about her, and so departed'. She answereth that she believeth that it is but a made tale by some of the priests, or that if she told any such her selfe, it was but a dreame, or some such things, as shee had before heard of amongst them, it being Christmas . . . Besides, in Christmas time there was gaming and mumming at the L. Vaux his house, and she saith, she saw the mummers dressed with their vizards: whereby she learned to talke of such things, when they said, the spirit began to ascend out of her foote: that is, when he began from time to time (as they say) to trouble her.

The coincidence of the festival and the possession bears out the author's opinion that both were derived from the same papist superstition, the Epiphany masquerade being an indirect signal for the unleashing of the powers of evil. Although this is not made explicitly clear, the attitude here resembles that of Philip Stubbes, who also descried Satan and all his works in the Lord of Misrule and his colourful May Day parade. In my view, this constitutes an interesting piece of evidence, for it conveys some idea of the internal resonance and the imaginary and phantasmagorical elaboration of the festive rites of this period.

331. See Herrick's poem, 'Ceremony for Candlemas Eve', in *Hesperides*, p. 402.
332. Keith Thomas notes in this connection that the pre-Reformation Church used to organize processions for the purpose of blessing the trees, at Epiphany (*Religion*, pp. 62–3).

5 The non-calendary festivals

1. *Dictionary of the Proverbs*: 'Shear your sheep in May, and shear them right away' (s 311); and Storm Jameson (*The Decline of Merry England* (Indianapolis, 1930), p. 39) writes: 'The sheep-shearing started in June . . .'.
2. Robinson, *Rural Economy in Yorkshire*, pp. 134–5.
3. See *The Whimzies*, p. 144.
4. On this point, see the lines by Joseph Hall, in *Virgidemarium*, Book v, Satire 1, lines 76–7, in *Collected Poems*, ed. Davenport. See quotation above, p. 90.
5. *Remains*, p. 34.
6. Cited in E.H. Fellowes, *English Madrigal Verse, 1588–1632* (Oxford 1920; 3rd edn, 1967, revised and expanded by Frederick W. Sternfeld and David Greer), p. 178.
7. The failure to invite a neighbour to a sheep-shearing festival was regarded as a form of social ostracism and might be followed by curses or other magic means of revenge. See Thomas, *Religion*, p. 556.
8. Nicholas Assheton's journal contains an allusion, dated 25 July, to a rush-bearing ceremony: 'July 25, Saint James's Day. At Whalley; ther a rush-bearing, but much less solemnity than formerlie' (*Journal*, p. 34). John Nichols, who records this remark in *Progresses of King James I* (vol. iii, p. 400), in a note cites quite a detailed description of these festivities.
9. See the following proverb, cited by Tilley *Dictionary of the Proverbs*, no. R 213): 'Strew green rushes for the stranger.' See also the expression used by Nicholas Breton in *Wonders Worth the Hearing* (1692) (in *Works*, vol. ii, p. 5): 'Green rushes, Mister Francisco'. The editor, A.B. Grosart, explains in a note that this was 'a familiar rustic phrase equivalent to "Good morning"'.
10. *The Whimzies* ('A Ruffian', 'A Pedler' and "A Piper'), pp. 82, 138–42.
11. *Ibid.*, p. 115: 'He [the zealous brother] . . . denounceth an heavie woe upon all wakes, summerings and rush-bearings . . .'.
12. Alfred Burton, *Manchester* (Manchester, 1891), p. 19.
13. Cited in A. Tindel Hart, *The Country Clergy in Elizabethan and Stuart Times* (London, 1958), p. 33.

14. (London, 1618), in Grosart, ed., *Works*, vol. II, p. 7.
15. Cited in Drake, *Shakespeare and His Times*, vol. I, p. 187.
16. *A Journey into England in the Year 1598* (Strawberry Hill, 1757, translated from the Latin by Horace Walpole), p. 79.
17. On this point, see in particular Frazer's analysis in *The Golden Bough* (Compact edn, pp. 525–42). Admittedly, the idea of a similarity between certain festive traditions and rites stemming from the old pagan religions was very much in vogue at that time among intellectuals and educated people, following the ideological conflict introduced by the Reformation and Protestantism. It is worth noting that John Aubrey was later to produce an altogether analogous analysis (*Remains*, p. 34).
18. *Popular Antiquities*, vol. II, p. 16.
19. Cited in Brand and Ellis, *Popular Antiquities*, vol. II, pp. 25–6.
20. Robert Chambers, *Book of Days*, vol. II, p. 399 (on the month of October). In *A Perfite Platform of a Hoppe Garden* (London, 1574, p. 29), in the chapter 'Of the Gathering of Hoppes'), Reginald Scot writes: 'In what time (or rather before) that your hoppes begyn to chaunge colour (that is to say) somewhat before Michaelmas, your must gather them . . . '.
21. See the definition given by T.G. Barnes ('County Politics and a Puritan *Cause Célèbre*: Somerset Church-ales 1623', *Transactions of the Royal Historical Society*, 5th ser., 9 (1959), p. 106, n. 4). In *Churchwardens' Accounts* (pp. 289–91), J.C. Cox provides more detailed information on the amounts that these festivals could raise for the parishes that organized them:

> In the sixteenth century it became customary at Yatton to hold three parish ales annually – namely at Whitsuntide, at Midsummer Day, and at Hocktide in the second week after Easter week. In 1524–5 the three ales realised £ 32, and in 1547–8 the great sum of £ 24 2s . . . The church-ale was the great source of income at Mere, Wilts. In 1557 the profits were £ 12 0s 6d . . . The ale profits of 1605 amounted to £ 15 6s, and in 1607 to the great sum of £ 23 6s 8d.

22. Barnes, 'County Politics', p. 106, n. 4.
23. *The Survey of Cornwall* (London, 1602; ed. F.E. Halliday, 1953; repr. 1969) pp. 141–2.
24. See Zeal-of-the-Land Busy's attack against them in *Bartholomew Fair*, IV, vi, 89–92, in *Works*, vol. VI (1938), p. 139.
25. *Survey of Cornwall*, p. 142.
26. Cited in Whitaker, *Sunday*, p. 44.
27. IV, iii, 96, in *The Plays and Poems of William Cartwright*, ed. G.B. Evans (Madison, 1951).
28. In *Works*, vol. VII (1941), p. 291.
29. 'County Politics', pp. 108–9, n. 3.
30. *Ibid.*, p. 107, n. 2.
31. *Ibid.*, pp. 106–7. See also the portrait that John Earle paints of 'The Poor Fiddler', in his *Microcosmography* (p. 39): 'A country wedding and Whitsun ale are the two main places he domineers in, where he goes for a musician, and overlooks the bag-pipe.'
32. The word 'wake' does not refer here to the former Irish custom of the watching of relatives and friends beside the body of a dead person, but to the local annual festival of an English parish, usually the feast of the patron saint

of the church. This refers to the occasion, while an 'ale' designated a festival or merry-making at which ale was drunk (*OED*). See Brand and Ellis, *Popular Antiquities*, vol. II, pp. 226–7.

33. On this point, see *Parochial Antiquities* by Bishop White Kennett, vol. II, p. 303; also Baskervill, 'Dramatic Aspects', pp. 72–4.

34. See Kennett, *Parochial Antiquities*, vol. II, p. 395.

35. *The Anatomie of Abuses*, pp. 152–3.

36. *An Hundreth Good Points of Husbandrie*, cited in Brand and Ellis, *Popular Antiquities*, vol. II, p. 3.

37. Cited by Brand and Ellis, *Popular Antiquities*, vol. II, p. 2.

38. *The Late Lancashire Witches*, lines 1189–1196, p. 170.

39. *Vexed and Troubled Englishmen, 1590–1642* (New York, 1967; repr. Oxford, 1976), p. 110.

40. *Picturae Loquentes*, sign. c5 b.

41. See Brand and Ellis, *Popular Antiquities*, vol. II, pp. 13–15.

42. See Strutt, *Sports and Pastimes*, p. xxxvi.

43. No doubt an elaborated form of the Whitsun ale. On this subject, see Drake, *Shakespeare and His Times*, vol. I, p. 252. See also J.B. Bamborough 'Rusticity', pp. 150–1:

> [Robert Dover] may have inaugurated his 'Cotswold Olympic Games' as early as 1612; most probably what he did was to take over and develop an existing Whitsuntide festival, setting out to aggrandize it, to raise and modernize ancient country sports, and to attract to them the local gentry as well as the labouring population.

44. See Strutt, *Sports and Pastimes*, p. xxxvi. John Arlott (*The Oxford Companion to Sports and Games* (Oxford, 1977), p. 162) notes that these games continued up until 1850, being known as 'Dover's Games'. (Today, they are again celebrated, in the springtime, in the village of Chipping Camden). See also Underdown, *Revel, Riot and Rebellion*, p. 64, and the analysis by Peter Stallybrass in '"Wee feaste in our Defense": Patrician Carnival in Early Modern England and Robert Herrick's *Hesperides*', *English Literary History*, 16: 1 (Winter 1986), pp. 234–52.

45. See *Shakespeare's England*, vol. II, p. 452.

46. Robert Dover himself named them 'Cotswold's Olympic Games'. See also Thiselton Dyer, *Folk-Lore of Shakespeare*, p. 297.

47. See *The Merry Wives of Windsor* (I, i, 82–3); see also the following passage from *A Jovial Crew, or The Merry Beggars* (1641) by Richard Brome:

> VINCENT: Will you go up to the hilltop of sports, then, and merriments, Dover's Olympics or the Cotswold Games?
> MERIEL: No, that wil be too public for our recreation. We would have it more within ourselves.
> (II, i, 83–6; ed. Ann Haaker, Regents Renaissance Drama Series (London, 1968)).

48. This anthology contains thirty-five poems of varying length, composed by various poets, some known, some unknown.

49. 'To my Noble Friend Mr Robert Dover, on His Annuall Assemblies upon Cotswold', *Annalia Dubrensia*, p. 7.

50. In 'An Eclogue on the Palilia and Noble Assemblies Revived on Cotswold Hills by Mr. Robert Dover', *Annalia Dubrensia*, pp. 20–1.

51. *Popular Antiquities*, vol. II, p. 459.
52. *Ibid.*, n. 2 (Brand and Ellis quote Du Cange's *Glossary* on this).
53. See Nashe's allusion to this fair in the passage from 'The Choice of Valentines' cited above, pp. 105–6; also Thiselton Dyer, *Folk-Lore of Shakespeare*, p. 297.
54. Ballad cited in *Nichol's Collection of Poems* (1780), vol. III, p. 204.
55. See p. 7, n. 97 in the Arden edition of *Love's Labour's Lost*.
56. See Robert Chambers, 'Bartholomew Fair', in *Book of Days*, vol. I, pp. 643–5.
57. Bartholomew Fair was not only the largest cloth fair; it was also an important pig market. See also *2 Henry IV* (II, iv, 232–3), where Doll calls Falstaff, '[thou] little tidy Bartholomew boar-pig'.
58. *Bartholomew Fair*, IV, vi, 82–6, in *Works*, vol. VI, p. 109.
59. See the performance of the drama of *Hero and Leander* by a puppeteer, in this same play, V, iii, in *Works*, vol. VI, p. 117–21.
60. *Bartholomew Fair*, IV, vi, 87–9, *Works*, vol. VI, p. 109.
61. *The Whimzies*, p. 117.
62. See Robert Greene, *Second and Last Part of Cony-Catching* (1591), cited in A.V. Judges, *The Elizabethan Underworld* (London, 1930), p. 162.
63. On this point, see Robert Chambers, *Book of Days*, p. 132.
64. The 'Horn dance' of Abbots Bromley, Staffordshire, is described in detail in Cecil Sharp, *Sword Dances*, vol. I, pp. 105–12.
65. On the place of the symbolism of the stag-man, see above, p. 48.
66. Where marriage was concerned, however, some periods were propitious, others taboo; see *Shakespeare's England*, vol. II, p. 148. Keith Thomas (*Religion*, p. 620) notes that, although there were quite a number of taboo periods in the Middle Ages, after the Reformation they were reduced to Lent and Advent.
67. Being left out of this kind of celebration was considered a serious slight and those who were excluded in this way would sometimes seek revenge; see Thomas, *Religion*, p. 556.
68. The christening ceremony was itself criticized by the ultra-Protestant Harsnett, who expressed great indignation over what he considered to be a veritable masquerade (*Declaration*, p. 32).
69. See Waldron, *History and Description*, p. 121.
70. *Aubrey's Brief Lives* (ed. Oliver Lawson Dick, London, 1949; repr. 1950), p. 319.
71. *Mémoires et observations*, pp. 19–20.
72. II, ii, in Greene, *Complete Plays*, p. 122.
73. *Ibid.*, pp. 83–4. See also *Shakespeare's England*, vol. II, p. 143, and John Bossy, *Christianity in the West*, pp. 15–16.
74. Regarding the rites of baptism and the 'churchings' which followed them, see Edward Berry, *Shakespeare's Comic Rites*, pp. 25–6. He notes in passing the considerable expenses incurred by these family ceremonies, at a time when families ran to numerous births.
75. On this point, see *The History of the Two Maids of More-clacke* (1609) (I, i, 1–3), by R. Armin (in *Works of Robert Armin, Actor*, ed. A.B. Grosart (Blackburn, 1880)).
76. *Description of England*, p. 383.

77. See F.G. Emmison, *Elizabethan Life: Morals and the Church Court* (London, 1973), p. 154. The presence of a Morris dance is mentioned by Laneham, in his description of the 'Brydeale' represented in honour of Queen Elizabeth during the festivities at Kenilworth. See *Laneham's Letter*, p. 20, and Nichols, *Progresses of Queen Elizabeth*, vol. I, p. 442. See also above, p. 122.
78. 'Choice, Chance and Change' (1606), in *Glimpses of Merry England*, ed. A.B. Grosart (Manchester, 1881), pp. 45–6.
79. *The Arte of English Poesie*, II, ix, p. 69.
80. Matthew Griffith, *Bethel, or a Forme for Families* (London, 1634), p. 279.
81. On this subject, see *The Christen State of Matrimony* (1541) by Heinrich Bullinger, translated by Miles Coverdale (London, 1542), fo. 51, sign. H I.
82. See Walter S. Gibson, *Bruegel* (London, 1977), p. 159. All these customs and festivities are brilliantly painted in Wye Saltonstall's colourful and delightful description of 'A Country Bride' in his *Picturae Loquentes*, sign. C4 a to C5 b. Edward Berry, who describes these ceremonies and rejoicings in detail, (*Shakespeare's Comic Rites*, pp. 165–71) refers us to another picture of the period, the *Festival at Bermondsey* (by the Flemish painter Hoefnagel). It was painted in about 1569 and is at present at Hatfield House and part of the collection of the Marquess of Salisbury: 'The painting portrays the festive table, bride cup and bride cakes, musicians and representations of all social classes' (p. 166).
83. Apart from this taboo about female virginity, which does not seem to have been taken very seriously in the countryside (see n. 84, below, on this point), the major fear was that that a young bridegroom might be possessed by a witch. If this happened, the evil spell, usually cast as a result of jealousy, would knot the young man's codpiece point, rendering him impotent on his wedding night. A comical illustration is provided by the play by Heywood and Brome cited above, *The Late Lancashire Witches*, in which young Lawrence finds himself unable to satisfy his bride Parnell, who is possessed by the devil:

> SHAKESTONE: . . . the house keepers, *Lawrence* and his late bride *Parnell* are fallen out by themselves.
> ARTHUR: How, prithee?
> SHAKESTONE: The quarell began they say upon their wedding night, and in the bride bed.
> BANTAM: For want of bedstaves?
> SHAKESTONE: No a better implement it seemes the bridegroom was unprovided of, a homely tale to tell.   (lines 1892–8, p. 190)

As a direct consequence of Lawrence's inability to fulfil his marital duties, Parnell loses her temper and beats the unfortunate bridegroom: all of which, with public rumours abetting, leads to a charivari (or Skimmington):

> BANTAM: But has she beaten him?
> SHAKESTONE: Grievously broke his head in I know not how many places: of which the hoydens have taken notice, and will have a Skimmington . . .
>   (lines 1915–18, p. 190)

84. On the basis of an article by C.R. Baskervill, 'English Songs on the Night Visit' (*PMLA*, 36 (1921), pp. 565–614), Jean-Marie Maguin ('La nuit', pp.

395–9) shows that, thanks to the traditional practice of nocturnal visits to the loved one, trial marriages were by no means a new phenomenon in the countryside.

85. See Bossy, *Christianity*, p. 27; *Hamlet*, I, ii, 179.
86. See *Shakespeare's England*, vol. II, p. 151.
87. *Ibid.*, p. 152. On this point, see also the description by Misson de Valbourg (*Mémoires et observations*, p. 133).
88. Richard Flecknoe, *Aenigmatical Characters* (1665), cited in Brand and Ellis, *Popular Antiquities*, vol. II, p. 244.
89. *The Crisis of the Aristocracy (1558–1641)* (Oxford, 1965), p. 575.
90. *Ibid.*, p. 263. However, the long procession stretching from the centre of the picture representing the life and death of Sir Henry Unton, which ends up at a sumptuous funerary monument, would appear to belie this (see Illus. 7.1, p. 238).
91. See Bossy, *Christianity*, p. 32: 'At the tolling of the bell, the neighbourhood was encouraged to drop what it was doing . . . or at least to say a prayer for the soul of the dying.' On the subject of burial rites, Patrick Collinson (*Elizabethan Puritan Movement*, p. 370) notes that the most extreme Puritans attacked even the burial sermon, while the more moderate limited their criticisms to 'the popish ringing and jangling of bells'.

Part II. Introduction: Some anthropological and historical perspectives on literary analysis

1. It may be objected that I seem to be paying scant attention to Shakespeare's Roman plays. However, as we shall see in connection with *Antony and Cleopatra*, Elizabethan England can often be detected underlying Plutarch's texts, the major source for these plays.
2. On this point, see *Shakespeare's England*, vol. II, p. 285, n. 1. See also Platter, *Travels in England*, pp. 167–9, where 'theatre' is the word used to refer to the arenas for cock-fights and bear- or bull-baitings ('place built like a theatre'). See also Louis Adrian Montrose, 'The Purpose of Playing: Reflections on a Shakespearean Anthropology', *Helios*, n.s. 7:2 (Spring 1980), pp. 51–74.
3. *Shakespeare's Talking Animals* (London, 1973); see in particular chapter 12, 'Drama versus Theatre'.
4. See Andrew Gurr, *Playgoing*, pp. 92–6. On this subject, see also the quotation from Sir Richard Morison, above, p. 71. Thomas Heywood makes a similar observation about a London pageant: 'The third Pageant or Show meerly consisteth of Anticke gesticulations, dances, and other Mimicke postures, devised only for the vulgar, who are better delighted with that which pleaseth the eye, than contenteth the eare . . . ' (*The Dramatic Works*, ed. R.H. Shepherd, 6 vols. (London, 1874; repr. 1964), vol. IV, p. 312).
5. According to a number of sources of evidence (including Edmund Gayton, *Pleasant Notes*, p. 271), the spectators were by no means passive. As in Beaumont and Fletcher's *The Knight of the Burning Pestle*, many comments would come from all sides of the auditorium. On this point, see also Alfred Harbage, *Shakespeare's Audience* (New York, 1941; repr. 1961), pp. 92–116.

6. On this point, see Platter, *Travels in England*, pp. 168–75. See also *The Knight of the Burning Pestle*, pp. 66–8.
7. Harbage, *Shakespeare's Audience*, p. 90.
8. 'The Audience in Shakespeare's Plays', *Shakespeare Studies* 7 (1974), pp. 283–305; *The Privileged Playgoers of Shakespeare's London 1576–1642* (Princeton, 1981).
9. *Elizabethan Popular Theatre. Plays in Performance* (London, 1982), p. 44.
10. Cambridge, 1984.
11. *Ibid.*, p. 299.
12. In *Privileged Playgoers*, Cook notes that, curiously enough, Henslowe's company never put on a new play on festival days, which were precisely the times when theatre audiences were largest. As the author suggests, the reason may have been that it reckoned that the vulgar masses would not be up to appreciating a new play correctly. But it may quite simply have been a matter of commercial common sense. Knowing that there would be no problem in attracting a full house on these occasions, Henslowe preferred to keep his new plays up his sleeve, to attract spectators on less popular days.
13. See Shapiro, *Children*, pp. 11 and 31.
14. See Withington, *English Pageantry*, vol. I, p. 209.
15. See Jean Jacquot's Introduction to *Les fêtes*, vol. I, pp. 10–11.
16. In his *Lettre à d'Alembert sur les spectacles*, (p. 267) Rousseau expresses the same popular sentiment when he contrasts the open-air festivities of the cheerful masses with 'those exclusive shows which confine a small number of people within a dark recess...'. For Rousseau, the opposition between indoors and outdoors corresponds exactly to that between innocence (which has nothing to hide) and depravity (which takes refuge out of the sight of curious eyes).
17. In connection with educated culture, see above, p. 345, note 242, on Puttenham's use of the eminently popular giants of the pageants, in his treatise on poetry and rhetoric. As for the aristocracy, the antimasque provided a way of introducing a grotesque and popular note into their sophisticated and dignified spectacles.

6 Festivity and dramatic structure: methodological problems

1. Thomas Fuller, *The History of the Worthies of England*, 3 vols. (London, 1662; repr. 1840).
2. In *The Growth and Structure of Elizabethan Comedy* (Cambridge, 1955; repr. 1973); see also by the same author, 'Shakespeare's Primitive Art', in *Interpretations of Shakespeare*, ed. K. Muir (Oxford, 1986), pp. 16–18.
3. During his years of apprenticeship, Shakespeare is supposed to have acquired the reputation of a regular tavern-goer who was not averse to a bit of poaching. He is even said to have been obliged to flee Stratford and take refuge in London after being caught poaching deer on Sir Thomas Lucy's estates at Charlecote. On this subject, see Samuel Schoenbaum, *William Shakespeare*, pp. 95–109.
4. *Ibid.*, pp. 111–12.
5. On this subject, see Muriel Bradbrook, *The Living Monument, Shakespeare*

and the Theatre of his Time (Cambridge, 1976; repr. 1979), p. 209; and C.J. Sisson, *Le goût public*, pp. 16–18.

6. On this point, see Bradbrook, *Living Monument*, p. 211.

7. See in particular Shallow's memories in *2 Henry IV* (III, ii, 276–83).

8. On this point, see M.C. Bradbrook, 'Folk Festivals', in O.J. Campbell and E.G. Quinn, eds., *A Shakespeare Encyclopedia* (London, 1966; repr. 1974), p. 237.

9. In an article entitled 'The Sense of Occasion: Some Shakespearean Night Sequences' (in *Shakespeare, Man of the Theatre*, ed. Kenneth Muir, J.L. Halio and D.J. Palmer (East Brunswick, N.J. and London, 1983), pp. 98–104), Emrys Jones calls *Henry V* a 'festive history' (p. 102).

10. *Henry V*, IV, i, 36–226. Shakespeare's young king no doubt owed his skill at assuming disguises to his years of dissipation in Falstaff's company. His familiarity with tavern life and the close encounters made at festival-time, described in *1* and *2 Henry IV*, made him feel at home with popular customs and problems.

11. On this point, see Francis Berry, *The Shakespeare Inset, Word and Picture* (London, 1965), pp. 129–37. In his introduction (pp. 12–13), Berry defines five major types of 'inset':

    (1) those which occur at the beginning of the play ('Expository')
    (2) scenes which are described in a narrative sequence but not acted or shown ('Interior Plot Required')
    (3) speeches such as Mercutio's famous description of Queen Mab, in *Romeo and Juliet*, which have no directly dramatic function ('Voluntary Inset')
    (4) songs
    (5) plays within plays.

12. On these questions, see the unpublished PhD thesis (available on microfilm) by W.B. Thorne, 'The Influence of Folk Drama upon Shakespearean Comedy' (University of Wisconsin, 1965), p. 32.

13. On this subject, see the analysis of Robert Weimann in the chapter entitled 'The Folk Play and Shakespeare' in his *Shakespeare and the Popular Tradition*, pp. 39–48.

14. These quotations refer to *The Two Gentlemen of Verona* (IV, iv, 156), to *The Winter's Tale* (IV, iv, 69) and to the 'sunburnt sicklemen' in the Masque in *The Tempest* (IV, i, 134–8).

15. On this point, see Welsford, *Court Masque*, p. 360.

16. On this subject, see Inga Stina-Ewbank, '"These pretty devices". A Study of Masques in Plays', in Spencer, *Book of Masques*, p. 414.

17. *Romeo and Juliet* (I, iv), *Timon of Athens* (I, ii), *Henry VIII* (I, iv). The function of the Masque in each of these plays is analysed by Catherine Shaw ('The Visual and the Symbolic in Shakespeare's Masques', in *Shakespeare and the Arts*, ed. Cecile Williamson Cory and Henry S. Limouze (Washington, 1982), pp. 21–34).

18. See for example Shirley's Masque entitled *Changes, or Love in a Maze* (1631–2) (IV, ii):

    CAPERWIT (a Poetaster):   A masque will be delightful to the ladies.
    DANCER: Oh sir, what plays are taken without these
         Pretty devices?

(James Shirley, *The Dramatic Works and Poems*, ed. William Gifford and Alexander Dyce, 6 vols. (London, 1883), vol. II, p. 339).

19. See the analyses by Allardyce Nicoll in 'Shakespeare and the Court Masque' (in *Shakespeare's Later Comedies*, ed. D.J. Palmer (London, 1971), pp. 160–72), and by Catherine M. Shaw, *'Some Vanity of Mine Art': The Masque in English Renaissance Drama*, 2 vols. (Salzburg, 1979), vol. I, pp. 113–19 and vol. II, p. 338.

20. Berowne (Biron) in *Love's Labour's Lost* does not disguise his scorn for this clumsy drama (v, ii, 460–2).

21. The atmosphere of brilliant improvisation was splendidly caught in the Royal Shakespeare Company's 1975 production. (See *Cahiers Elisabéthains*, 8 (1975), pp. 79–80).

22. On this subject, see the analysis by Francis Berry, *Shakespeare Inset*, pp. 129–30. See also Anne Righter-Barton, *Shakespeare and the Idea of the Play* (London, 1962; repr. 1967) pp. 107–110, and Wiles, *Shakespeare's Clown*, pp. 14–23.

23. See Levin, *Multiple Plot*, p. 141, and Wiles, *Shakespeare's Clown*, chapters 2–6.

24. This is in part responsible for the variants between the quarto and the folio texts, and makes it extremely difficult to establish the texts of some plays (*Hamlet*, for example). See Stanley Wells and Gary Taylor, *William Shakespeare, A Textual Companion* (Oxford, 1987), pp. 20–31.

25. *The Savage Mind* (London, 1966), p. 21.

26. *Textual Companion*, pp. 20–31.

27. Oxford, 1916.

28. *Essay*, p. 42.

29. *Ibid.*, p. 49. See also Douglas Hewitt, '"The Very Pompes of the Divell" – Popular and Folk Elements in Elizabethan and Jacobean Drama', *Review of English Studies*, 25 (1949), pp. 10–23.

30. *Ibid.*, p. 50. See also Frazer, *Golden Bough*, pp. 764–8, and Hewitt, '"Very Pompes"', pp. 18–20.

31. 'The Argument of Comedy', in *Shakespeare, Modern Essays in Criticism*, ed. L.F. Dean (Oxford, 1957), p. 85.

32. *Ibid.*, p. 87.

33. *Ibid.*, p. 88.

34. *Ibid.*, pp. 88–9.

35. *Shakespeare's Festive Comedy. A Study of Dramatic Form and its Relation to Social Custom* (Princeton 1959; repr. 1972), p. 4.

36. *Ibid.*, p. 4.

37. I do not quite follow Barber here for, in my view, the culture which found expression in Elizabethan popular festivity possessed a symbolism of its own, even if Shakespeare did not see fit to reverse or parody it in his festive comedies. Meanwhile, the Masques, pageants and students' festivals held in various universities aimed for a highly aesthetic impression and significance. The principal difference between these and the professional theatre was that the former were directly associated with a particular calendar occasion or with some private celebration.

38. *Festive Comedy*, p. 8.

39. *Ibid.*, p. 7.

40. *Ibid.*, p. 99.
41. See, for example, the passage in *Love's Labour's Lost* in which Berowne (Biron) describes the '"honey-tongued" Boyet' (line 334) as follows:

> He is wit's pedlar, and retails his wares
> At wakes and wassails, meetings, markets, fairs . . .   (v, ii, 317–18)

Clearly, the lexical alliteration results more from a free association of certain sounds (ws and ms) than from the strict meaning of the sentence.
42. On this point, see Jan Kott's analysis of this scene in *Shakespeare Our Contemporary* (London, 1965), in the chapter entitled 'Titania and the Ass's Head', pp. 171–90.
43. *Ibid.*, p. 261.
44. It is strange that Barber leaves out of his analyses two comedies in which festivity plays an altogether central role, namely *The Taming of the Shrew* and *The Merry Wives of Windsor*!
45. Leo Salingar, *Shakespeare and the Traditions*, p. 9. However, in his view, Shakespeare was not simply a folklorist or 'recorder of fêtes'.
46. *Ibid.*, p. 19.
47. The theses of Janet Spens, Northrop Frye and C.L. Barber and many other critics of Shakespearian comedy (including the romances) are analysed and compared in an article by Wayne A. Rebhorn, 'After Frye: A Review-Article on the Interpretation of Shakespearean Comedy and Romance', *Texas Studies in Literature and Language*, 21:4 (Winter 1979), pp. 555–82. The article performs a number of functions: it provides a bibliography with commentary for Shakespearian comedy, a discussion of various different approaches (based on the ritualistic, mythical and festive theses of the above-mentioned three major pioneers in this field) and a recapitulatory synthesis of the various problems raised by the disagreements between these critics. On this question see also chapter 17 in Arthur M. Eastman's *A Short History of Shakespearean Criticism* (New York, 1968), pp. 354–82, in particular pp. 356 and 361.
48. The name given him by the Romantic critics.
49. In a more detailed study, qualification would clearly be called for here, for an equivalent to the 'green world' of romantic comedy could no doubt be found in Mariana's 'moated grange' (*Measure for Measure* iii, i, 266) and in Helena's magic powers and the mysterious knowledge of the women in *All's Well That Ends Well*.
50. The theme of masks, secrets and pretence is clearly central to this comedy, in which the Duke swaps his crown for a monk's habit.
51. Anne Righter-Barton, *Shakespeare and the Idea of Play* (London, 1962), pp. 100–12; Maguin, 'La nuit': see, in particular, the chapter entitled 'La fête interrompue', vol. i, pp. 467–92.
52. 'La nuit', vol. i, p. 471. In vol. ii, p. 1038 (n. 7), Maguin notes that 'of the thirty-eight plays of Shakespeare, eighteen contain a nocturnal festival or features of one. They are *The Taming of the Shrew*, *Romeo and Juliet*, *A Midsummer Night's Dream*, *The Merchant of Venice*, *1* and *2 Henry IV*, *Much Ado About Nothing*, *The Merry Wives of Windsor*, *Twelfth Night*, *Hamlet*, *Troilus and Cressida*, *Othello*, *Macbeth*, *Timon of Athens*, *Antony and Cleopatra*, *Coriolanus*, *Pericles* and *Henry VIII*.

7 Festivity and time in Shakespeare's plays

1. This last tendency is represented in the eighteenth century by a historian such as Giambattista Vico, in his *Principii di una scienza nuova* (1725).
2. On this point, see the article 'Temporalité historique/Temps', in *La nouvelle histoire*, ed. Jacques Le Goff, Roger Chartier and Jacques Revel (Paris, 1978), pp. 558–60.
3. An opposition is set up between two different concepts of time in *The Merchant of Venice*: the measured time of usury ('If you repay me not on such a day', says Shylock to Antonio, (I, iii, 145)) stands in contrast to the time given or squandered by festivity ('you know me well and herein spend but time / To wind about my love with circumstance' (I, i, 153–4) is all that Antonio says to Bassanio before agreeing to help him in his amorous venture.
4. See E.M.W. Tillyard, *The Elizabethan World Picture* (London, 1943; repr. 1967), pp. 11–16.
5. On this subject, see Frederick Turner, *Shakespeare and the Nature of Time* (Oxford, 1971), in particular the chapter entitled '*As You Like It*: "Subjective", "Objective" and "Natural" Time', pp. 29–31.
6. On this point, see Robert G. Hunter, 'The Function of the Songs at the End of *Love's Labour's Lost*', *Shakespeare Studies*, 7 (1974), pp. 55–64. See also Francis Berry, *Shakespeare Inset*, pp. 110–15, and W.B. Thorne, 'The Influence of Folk Drama', pp. 113–15.
7. This strategy of reversing certain expected conventions is used in pastoral comedies such as *As You Like It* and *The Winter's Tale*. In the former play, the conventions inherent in the genre are seen in a new perspective and with a new focus, after undergoing a veritable battery of criticisms. In the latter, Sicilia, *the* land of ancient pastoral, is the place of tragic winter, while springlike and festive rebirth is moved to the distant 'shores' of Bohemia.
8. NURSE: ... How long is it now to
             Lammastide?
    CAPULET'S WIFE: A fortnight and odd days.
    NURSE: Even or odd, of all days in the year
             Come Lammas Eve at night shall she be fourteen.   (I, iii, 15–19)
9. For a non-Shakespearian example of this use of internal calendary correspondences, see, in Ben Jonson's *Epicoene, or The Silent Woman*, Morose's flood of invective against the band of minstrels who have come to disturb the silence of his home: 'Rogues, Hellhounds, *Stentors*, out of my dores, you sonnes of noise and tumult, begot on an ill *May*-day, or when the Gally-foist is a-floate to Westminster! A trumpetter could not be conceiv'd but then' (IV, ii, 124–7; in *Works*, vol. v, p. 227). The deforming vision of satire and the grotesque here provides an example of popular associations between an individual's vocation and the date of his birth, which in this case is insultingly connected with the calendar festivities during which many bastards were conceived. In this popular astrology, in which the zodiac is plotted by the major seasonal festivals, each individual carries within himself, as the emblem of his personality, a 'genetic programme' directly based upon the festive dates which correspond to the time of his conception of birth. The allusion to 'ill *May*-day' and the Lord Mayor's Day (by implication from the reference to Westminster) establishes a connection with disorder and confusion.

10. This is the fundamental notion conveyed by the Latin tag 'Temporis Filia Veritas', which appeared on many emblems during the Renaissance period and which Shakespeare implanted at the heart of *The Winter's Tale*. On this point, see Inga-Stina Ewbank, 'The Triumph of Time in *The Winter's Tale*', *Review of English Literature*, 5 (1964), pp. 83–100, and Clifford Davidson, 'The Iconography of Illusion and Truth in *The Winter's Tale*', in Cory and Limouze, *Shakespeare and the Arts*, pp. 73–91.

11. For Shakespeare's contemporaries, the date of the festival of the Lupercalia coincided with the Carnival period and the rites of Saint Valentine's Day, when a king and a queen would be elected to preside over the jollifications. In an article entitled '"Thou Bleeding Piece of Earth". The Ritual Ground of *Julius Caesar*' (*Shakespeare Studies*, 14 (1981), pp. 175–96), Naomi Liebler analyses the play from the point of view of the rites of fertility connected with the Lupercalia and suggests that they corresponded to certain rural traditions such as 'the beating of the bounds'. On this custom, linked with Whitsun and the Rogations and the Morris or Sword dances see above, pp. 34 and 136. For the relationship between the ritual flagellations of the Lupercalia and the playful lambasting of the spectators by the Morris-dance Fool, see p. 191 of the above article. See also Levin, *Multiple Plot*, p. 144.

12. On these questions, see Richard Wilson '"Is This a Holiday?": Shakespeare's Roman Carnival', *English Literary History*, 54:1 (Spring 1987), pp. 31–44, in particular p. 37:

> [Julius Caesar] is the Carnival King, a Lord of Misrule who governs by exploiting his subjects' desires with his 'foolery' (I, ii, 232), manipulating 'fat, sleek-headed men' (I, ii, 190), as he indulges Antony in plays and music when he 'revels long a' nights' (II, ii, 116). Provoking them 'to sports, to wildness, and much company' (II, i, 189), Caesar is the master of the revels who knows that 'danger' belongs to the 'lean and hungry' who can discipline the body to their purposes. So his Roman carnival becomes a model of authoritarian populism, the true regimen of bread and circuses.

In this sense, if Caesar embodies the forces of Carnival, Brutus, for his part, is consigned to the ranks of the 'lean and hungry', that is to say, the supporters of Lent. On this point, see my analysis above, pp. 204–5, which suggests that Shakespeare expresses the political and personal conflict between Antony and Octavius Caesar in terms of the clash between Carnival and Lent.

13. At the end of *2 Henry IV*, Prince Hal uses this image of Lethe when he learns of the death of his father, whom he must now succeed. He is addressing the Lord Chief Justice and reproaching him for interrupting him in the midst of his feasting and amusements in Falstaff's tavern:

> PRINCE HARRY: ... How might a prince of my great hopes forget
> So great indignities you laid upon me?
> What rate, rebuke, and roughly send to prison
> Th'immediate heir of England! Was this easy?
> May this be washed in Lethe and forgotten?   (V, ii, 67–71)

Here the function of the image is quite the reverse from the situation in *Antony and Cleopatra*, for it is history itself, embodied by the future king, which declares its refusal to forget the festivity and dissipation of its youth. But Henry V will soon take the opposite course and banish Falstaff, his erstwhile companion in revelry (V, v, 47–72).

14. *2 Henry IV*, III, ii, 211–14:

> SIR JOHN: We have heard the chimes at midnight, Master Shallow.
> SHALLOW: That we have, that we have, that we have; in faith, Sir John, we have.

15. On this point, see Maguin, 'La nuit' vol. I, pp. 488–9.
16. On this subject, see Falstaff's regretful words in *2 Henry IV*: 'Now comes in the sweetest morsel of the night, and we must hence and leave it unpicked' (II, iv, 370–1).
17. But there are also examples where festivity and its images are used to express derision (by both the English and the French) in describing the approach of the enemy army. See *King John*, v, ii, 131–6, in the first case and *Henry V*, II, iv, 23–5, in the second.
18. On this point, see the comparison between *Henry V* and *The Shoemaker's Holiday* in 'Le Londres en fête du *Shoemaker's Holiday*', p. 12.
19. See Edward Berry, *Shakespeare's Comic Rites*, pp. 145–8.
20. *All's Well That Ends Well* (II, ii, 22–3) and *2 Henry IV* (v, iii, 35).
21. See above, p. 106; Linda Bamber, *Comic Women, Tragic Men. A Study of Gender and Genre in Shakespeare* (Princeton, 1982, p. 82) describes Ophelia as a 'tragic May queen'.
22. The problem is complicated by the fact that the expression 'poor-john', which is synonymous with 'piece of cod', refers one, through a reversal common at this period, to the word 'cod-piece', an emblem of virility. All the same, conversely, the reverse of 'cod-piece' might undoubtedly suggest a certain phallic apathy. On this point, see Thomas Nabbes' Masque, *The Spring's Glory*, in Spencer, *Book of Masques*, p. 329.
23. See Nabbes, *The Spring's Glory, ibid.*, p. 329.
24. *1 Henry IV*, II, v, 245–51. On this subject, see Barber, who interprets this play in terms of the Saturnalia and Falstaff as a Lord of Misrule (*Festive Comedy*, pp. 192–221). See also Neil Rhodes, *Elizabethan Grotesque* (London, 1980), pp. 99–130.
25. On this subject, see Bradbrook, 'Shakespeare's Primitive Art', p. 55.
26. In this connection, see Brian Morris' introduction to the play in the Arden edition (London, 1980), p. 120.
27. See for example, the following passage (I, i, 52–5):

> BAPTISTA: If either of you both love Katherina,
>   Because I know you well and love you well
>   Leave shall you have to court her at your pleasure.
> GREMIO: To cart her rather. She's too rough for me.

The word-play on 'to court' and 'to cart' is to be noted as it alludes to another festive practice, the charivari, in which notorious harpies used to be punished by being driven through the streets in carts, exposed to the jeers and vindictiveness of the public. This same punishment was meted out to prostitutes on Shrove Tuesday. See above pp. 99–101.

28. In *The Riverside Shakespeare*, ed. G. Blakemore Evans (Boston, 1974), p. 328. See also A.R. Humphreys' introduction to the Arden edition (London, 1981), p. 50.
29. See *1 Henry IV*, v, i, 127–40.
30. This analysis applies first and foremost to *The Winter's Tale*, in which

Paulina, Hermione and Perdita are presented as agents of reparation and renewed fertility, after all the destruction caused by Leontes' madness. It is true that in *Cymbeline* the queen is malevolent, but her role is balanced by Imogen's selflessness. Finally, in *Pericles* and *The Tempest*, Marina and Miranda are both agents of salvation.

31. MERCUTIO: Didst thou not fall out with a tailor for wearing his new doublet before
    Easter...?   (III, i. 26–7)

32. On this point, see Robert Chambers, *Book of Days*, vol. I, p. 569; see also Donald Attwater, *A Dictionary of Saints* (London, 1965), p. 282.

33. PROSPERO: ...I have used thee,
    Filth as thou art, with human care, and lodged thee
    In mine own cell, till thou didst seek to violate
    The honour of my child.
    CALIBAN: O ho, O ho! Would't had been done!
    Thou didst prevent me; I had peopled else
    This isle with Calibans.

Caliban's frustrated dream is a variant on the proliferation associated with the grotesque and imaginary representations of monstrosity. What Caliban would have produced with Miranda would not have been a child, but a litter of baby monsters in his own image. On this question, see Willard Farnham, *The Shakespearian Grotesque, Its Genesis and Transformation* (Oxford, 1971), pp. 151–69. There can be no doubt that Caliban, a hybrid creature, is connected with an ancient tradition of fauns, or the 'wild men' of the late Middle Ages, whom Claude Kappler in *Monstres, démons et merveilles à la fin du Moyen Age* (Paris, 1980, p. 262) analyses as follows:

Virile monsters such as fauns, woodsprites, satyrs and centaurs are also symbols of boundless sexual proliferation. In antiquity, these creatures were associated with orgiastic qualities which came to be regarded as anathema in the Middle Ages. 'Wild men' are sometimes invested with a similar character and thus also come to represent lust.

See also Robert Hillis Goldsmith, 'The Wild Man on the English Stage', *Modern Language Review*, 53:4 (October 1958), pp. 490–1.

34. On this subject, see Erwin Panofsky, *Studies in Iconology* (Oxford, 1939), chapter 4: 'Blind Cupid'. *Caeca Nox* is represented as a blindfolded woman in a miniature, dated ca. 975, now in the Berlin Staatsbibliothek.

35. Salingar, *Shakespeare and the Traditions*, p. 15.

36. See Joseph A. Longo, 'Myth in *A Midsummer Night's Dream*', *Cahiers Elisabéthains*, 18 (October 1980), p. 17.

37. *Review of English Studies*, 117 (1979), pp. 10–11. See also, by the same author, *Shakespeare and the Dance* (London, 1981), pp. 30–1. See also Barton-Righter, *Shakespeare and the Idea*, p. 107, and Emrys Jones, 'The Sense of Occasion: Some Shakespearean Night Sequences', in K. Muir, J.L. Halio and D.J. Palmer, eds., *Shakespeare, Man of the Theatre* (East Brunswick, N.J. and London, 1983), p. 101.

38. The dance of the shepherds occurs after line 166, in Act IV, scene iv; the dance of the twelve satyrs comes after line 341 in the same scene. Shakespeare seems to have borrowed the idea of a dance of satyrs from Ben Jonson's Masque, *Oberon, The Faery Prince* (1611). On this subject, see

J.H.P. Pafford's edition of *The Winter's Tale* (London, 1963; repr. 1968), p. xxii; Robert Hillis Goldsmith, 'The Wild Man', p. 487, and Bradbrook, *Living Monument*, pp. 71–2. This grotesque dance serves as an anti-masque. A similar dance is used by Thomas Campion in *The Lord's Masque*, which was performed at court on the wedding day of Princess Elizabeth and the Elector Palatine (14 February 1613). See *The Lord's Masque*, in *The Works of Thomas Campion*, pp. 250–1.

39. See Camillo's promise to Leontes (I, ii, 344–8).
40. IV, iv, 116–18. On this point, see Linda Bamber, *Comic Women, Tragic Men* (p. 170), who detects in Perdita 'an association between the motif of the feminine return and the figure of the May queen'.
41. IV, iv, 70–108 and 385–6. The symbolism of wreaths of flowers is altogether ambivalent, for they are used to celebrate life and love as well as in funerary rites. The same ambivalence is evident in other Renaissance customs: bunches of rosemary were a feature of both weddings and burials.
42. 'I turn my glass', IV, i, 16.
43. See Maguin, 'La fête interrompue' in 'La nuit', vol. I, pp. 467–92.
44. It is noticeable that, as with the winter festivals, Shakespeare is not exhaustive, for he leaves aside the village rejoicings which used to accompany the rush-bearings. In truth, in this respect, he follows the pastoral tradition, which likewise makes no mention of them. The explanation may be that, since no parallel could be found in the festivals of antiquity, it was not possible to pad them out with mythological trimmings.
45. On this point, see Gary Schmidgall, *Shakespeare and the Courtly Aesthetic* (Berkeley and London, 1981), pp. 150–3.
46. *Journey into England*, p. 79. See above, p. 156.
47. For a scholarly reading of this scene and a meticulous decoding of the references to classical antiquity, see Yves Peyré, 'Les Masques d'Ariel. Essai d'interprétation de leur symbolisme', *Cahiers Elisabéthains*, 19 (April 1981), pp. 53–71.
48. On this point, see John B. Bender, 'The Day of the Tempest', *English Literary History*, 47 (1980), p. 245.
49. One is put in mind of the prologue to *Henry V*, telling the spectators, at the beginning of the play (Prologue, 28–31):

> For 'tis your thoughts that now must deck our kings,
> Carry them here and there, jumping o'er times,
> Turning th'accomplishment of many years
> Into an hourglass . . .

50. See above, p. 143.
51. See above, pp. 143–5.
52. See Bender, ('The Day of *The Tempest*', p. 236) who regards *The Tempest* simply as a dramatic illustration of the rites of Hallowmas. Taking this view, he follows in the footsteps of R. Chris Hassel, *Renaissance Drama and the English Church Year* (Lincoln, Neb., 1979), according to whom those at court saw a correlation between, on the one hand, the themes of the plays performed for particular festive occasions in the course of the Season of the Revels and, on the other, the customs and prayers which the Book of Common Prayer associated with particular feast days. For another indirect

correlation (that is to say one not explicitly indicated in the text of the play) between one of Shakespeare's plays and the customs of Hallowmas, see Jeanne Addison Roberts, 'The Merry Wives of Windsor as a Hallowe'en Play', Shakespeare Survey, 25 (1972), pp. 107–12, and Shakespeare's English Comedy (Lincoln, Neb., 1979). See below, p. 372, n. 80.

53. On this subject, see J. Dover Wilson, The Fortunes of Falstaff (Cambridge, 1943; repr. 1964), p. 30.

54. 1 Henry IV (II, v, 456–8):

> PRINCE: ... that huge bombard of sack, that stuffed cloak-bag of guts, that roasted Manningtree ox with the pudding in his belly ...

On the Manningtree ox, see Nares' Glossary, p. 546. See also above, p. 165.

55. 2 Henry IV, I, ii, 159. See above, p. 150.

56. In Bandello's story 'Romeo and Julietta' (in the second volume of his Novelle, published in 1554), which is one of the sources for Romeo and Juliet, Romeo ventures into the Capulet house on the occasion of a Christmas masquerade. Curiously enough, Shakespeare did not retain this reference to the calendar feast in his play and presents the masked ball simply as a private party. On this point, see Salingar, Shakespeare and the Traditions, p. 192.

57. Leo Salingar (Shakespeare and the Traditions, p. 274), thinks that Shakespeare too is referring to the 'Gray's Inn revels of Christmas 1594–1595' and goes on to say: 'The dramatist turns a fiction elaborated from a real festive performance into a new fiction for his own stage...'.

58. On this subject, see W.B. Thorne, 'Folk Elements in The Taming of the Shrew', Queen's Quarterly, 75:3 (Autumn 1968), pp. 482–3.

59. Note that in The Taming of a Shrew (printed in quarto in 1594 and whose text widely differs from that printed in Shakespeare's 1623 Folio, which is variously considered by critics: some think it may have been a source for The Taming of the Shrew, some consider it as Shakespeare's own earlier play later rewritten as The Taming of the Shrew while others see in it a later play influenced by Shakespeare's comedy), it is the actors who make the mistake. In his comedy Shakespeare attributes it to a character from the popular strata, which is quite a different matter and a significant change, for here the actors are more professional and the bumpkin's role falls to a spectator.

60. See above, pp. 43–5.

61. This is what Barry Kyle did in his production of the play at Stratford, in the autumn and winter season of 1982. See Cahiers Elisabéthains, 24 (October 1983), pp. 107–8.

62. The Second Return from Parnassus in The Three Parnassus Plays, ed. J.B. Leishman (London, 1949), p. 220.

63. 2 Henry IV (I, ii, 157–9). In the view of the Lord Chief Justice, the image of the used-up candle suggests that Falstaff has passed the age for revelry and his vital energy has to a large extent been exhausted in earlier dissipations. Falstaff makes a spirited response, identifying himself with a large Christmas candle ('a Wassail candle being a large, fat candle lighted at festivities and meant to last the night through', according to A.R. Humphrey's note in the Arden edition). Quite apart from Sir John's pride in his corpulence, acquired over a long succession of calendar feast days, this verbal exchange also

conveys a number of *sous-entendus* relating to the sexual powers of the Knight of the 'Boar's Head' (a name, incidentally, which may be a spoonerism and may be construed as a phonetic anagram of the 'Whore's Bed'!). The image of the candle burned at both ends certainly refers to festive dissipation but also evokes the idea of sexual impotence, an idea also conveyed by the very name of 'Falstaff'. On this point, see Jean-Marie Maguin, 'A Note on a Further Biblical Parallel with the Death of Falstaff', *Cahiers Elisabéthains*, 10 (October 1976), pp. 65–6. Falstaff's retort does not seem to refute the suggestion, if we bear in mind the fear that he himself expresses when he dresses up as Herne the Hunter in Windsor Forest: 'I am here a Windsor stag, and the fattest I think, i' th' forest. Send me a cool rut-time, Jove, or who can blame me to piss my tallow?' (v, v, 12–14). The Wassail candle suggests not so much virility as that the old knight is making up for the loss of his sexual powers by over-indulgence in food and drink. He bravely flies the colours of festivity, but covertly corroborates the judge's insinuations.

64. This figure of a pot-bellied Bacchus, untouched by shame or remorse, in itself has something reassuring about it. The same idea is to be found in *Julius Caesar* (I, ii, 193), where Caesar, suspicious of the leanness and pallor of the conspirators, exclaims: 'Let me have men about me that are fat...'. See above, p. 366, note 12.

65. In this play the Christmas period is described as holy and protected from possession or spells cast by evil spirits and from invasion by ghosts (I, i, 138–45). Does that mean that the action of the play takes place at the beginning of the winter festivals, that is to say during the night of Hallowe'en, when the souls of the dead were supposed to return to earth?

HAMLET: The King doth wake tonight and takes his rouse,
          Keeps wassail...   (I, iv, 9–10)

Hamlet immediately adds that he would like to see the festival dropped from the calendar:

                    it is a custom
More honoured in the breach than the observance.   (I, iv, 17–18)

66. In *Macbeth*, a 'wassail' is the means by which Lady Macbeth plunges Duncan's guards into a 'swinish sleep' (I, vii, 67). The expression evokes the powers of metamorphosis possessed by Circe, the enchantress of antiquity, with whom Lady Macbeth here indirectly identifies. The wassail is the equivalent of a harmful magic philtre, used to further the murder of the king. On this point, see F. Laroque, 'Magic in *Macbeth*', *Cahiers Elisabéthains*, 35 (April 1989), pp. 63–4.

67. *Antony and Cleopatra*:

CAESAR: ...Antony,
          Leave thy lascivious wassails...   (I, iv, 55–6)

68. This idea is suggested by one of the etymologies for the prefix 'mis-' proposed by the *OED*: namely, the Sanscrit word *mythia*, which it renders by the adverbs 'contrarily' and 'invertedly'.

69. FESTE: A sentence is but a cheveril glove to a good wit, how quickly the wrong side
            may be turned outward!   (III, i, 11–13)

Feste, who moreover describes himself not as 'her [Lady Olivia's] fool, but her corrupter of words' (III, i, 34–5), plays a part of central importance in all this word-play connected with misrule. On this point, see F. Laroque, 'La notion de "misrule"', pp. 166–7.

70. I, i, 1–4. For Shakespeare, festivity is generally linked with marriage (either as an initiation or as a ceremony). Even in the rural festivities of *The Winter's Tale*, the public rejoicings take on the aspect of a private celebration for the lovers, when Florizel invites Perdita to regard them as a rehearsal for their future wedding (IV, iv, 49–51).

71. According to Jean-Marie Maguin ('La nuit', vol. I, p. 440), the chronological incoherence results from the nocturnal elements which permeate the play. For Jean Paris, the confusion is accounted for by a cosmic extension of the dream-world. See 'Clefs d'un songe', in his *Univers parallèles*, vol. I: *Théâtre* (Paris, 1975), pp. 154–7.

72. See Barber (*Festive Comedy*, p. 119) who rightly remarks that the May game was not specifically linked with May Day, being equally connected with Midsummer (p. 120). See also David P. Young, *Something of Great Constancy. The Art of A Midsummer Night's Dream* (New Haven and London, 1966), p. 24: 'it seems clear that [Shakespeare] has deliberately created a blurring of time in the play in order to dismiss calendar time and establish a more elusive festival time'.

73. The theme of confusion between moonlight and sunlight is a comic device which Shakespeare had already used in *The Taming of the Shrew* (IV, vi, 1–50). In that instance, however, it was not a matter of illustrating chronological confusion, but demonstrating the full effectiveness of Petruccio's taming of Kate. According to Jean Paris (*Théâtre*, p. 157), the grotesque conjunction of sun and moon comes to symbolize the wedding festivities at the end of the play.

74. III, ii, 5, and v, i, 357.

75. Prospero's words (IV, i, 155–6) seem to echo Demetrius' remarks:

> It seems to me
> That yet we sleep, we dream . . .   (IV, i, 191–2)

76. See Marjorie B. Garber, *Dream in Shakespeare. From Metaphor to Metamorphosis* (London, 1974); also Garrett Stewart, 'Shakespearean Dreamplay', *English Literary Renaissance*, 2:1 (Winter 1981), pp. 44–69. See also Ernest B. Gilman, 'Prospero's Inverted Masque', *Renaissance Quarterly*, 33:2 (Summer 1980), pp. 222–4.

77. See King Henry's soliloquy in *Henry V*, IV, i, 230–81.

78. *Shakespeare versus Shallow.*

79. *The Merry Wives of Windsor*, III, ii, 62. See below, n. 80.

80. In '*The Merry Wives of Windsor* as a Hallowe'en Play' (pp. 107–12) and *Shakespeare's English Comedy*, Jeanne Addison Roberts has tried to show the links between this comedy and the beginning of the winter festivals. However, she fails to explain why the play contains not a single example of the games and traditions that characterized the festival of Hallowe'en during the Elizabethan period (love philtres to help girls to glimpse an image of their future husbands, and the return to earth of spirits and dead souls). Nor does she suggest why the play contains no calendar reference, either direct or

indirect, to this period. See *Cahiers Elisabéthains*, 17 (April 1980), pp. 118–19.

81. This opposition emerges clearly from the first dialogue between Rosalind and Celia in *As You Like It* (I, iii, 12–14).

82. ROSALIND: I pray you, what is't o'clock?
    ORLANDO: You should ask me what time o'day. There's no clock in the forest.
    (III, ii, 293–5).

83. Having begun with a winter song ('Blow, blow, thou winter wind' (II, vii, 175)), Amiens rounds off with a merry spring song ('In spring-time, the only pretty ring-time...' (v, iii, 18)), in accordance with the natural cycle of the seasons.

84. On this point, see F. Laroque, '"No Assembly but Horn-Beasts" – A Structural Study of Arden's "Animal Farm"', *Cahiers Elisabéthains*, 11 (April 1977), pp. 55–62.

85. See Misson de Valbourg, *Mémoires et observations*, p. 70 (French edn).

86. See Salingar, *Shakespeare and the Traditions*, pp. 192–3.

87. See Levin, *Multiple Plot*, p. 143; Barber, *Festive Comedy*, pp. 213–21; and Walter Kaiser, *Praisers of Folly: Erasmus, Rabelais, Shakespeare* (London, 1964), pp. 224–6.

88. See the beginning of *A Midsummer Night's Dream* (I, i, 11–14):

THESEUS: Go, Philostrate,
    Stir up the Athenian youth to merriments.
    Awake the pert and nimble spirit of mirth.
    Turn melancholy forth to funerals...

89. See the analysis of this painting by Maurice Hussey, *The World of Shakespeare and His Contemporaries. A Visual Approach* (London, 1971; repr. 1972), p. vi; also Edward Berry, *Shakespeare's Comic Rites*, p. 193, and Angela Cox, *Sir Henry Unton, Elizabethan Gentleman* (Cambridge, 1982).

90. In truth, it is noticeable that whereas the funeral procession follows a straight line, the nuptial Masque evolves as a spiral. It leads into a section outside the house, which depicts Sir Henry Unton's lifetime activities, then continues into the house of the wedding feast, before finally giving way to burial.

91. Hamlet's metaphorical charivari is not directed solely against Claudius. His insulting obscenities against Ophelia and his mention of the hobby-horse in the scene immediately preceding the performance of the 'Murder of Gonzago', should no doubt be associated with the customary burlesque jests and humiliations of the charivari. Ophelia serves as the butt of attacks that he transfers from the queen to her.

92. Maguin sees Hamlet essentially as a kill-joy, like the Lord Chief Justice in *1* and *2 Henry IV* and Malvolio in *Twelfth Night*, regarding them respectively as the *bêtes noires* of the nocturnal revellers represented by Claudius, Falstaff and Sir Toby Belch. Antagonisms such as these are bound to disrupt festivity. Maguin writes: 'This remarkable recurrence of interruptions to nocturnal festivities... reflects an aspect of Elizabethan society (essentially in London) which was due to the preponderance of Puritan ideas amongst the merchant classes from which the city administrators were drawn...' ('La nuit', vol. I,

p. 491). Such binary polarities do no doubt underpin the dynamics of these plays. But similar oppositions are also characteristic of the very way in which festivals work, for they constantly oppose or make fun of the world which denies festivity and the people who attempt to ban it (see the theme of the clash between the seasons, or that between Carnival and Lent, as well as the expression – very common at the time – 'to make a May game of somebody'). But the details of the situation are in reality more complex and ambivalent: for example, Hamlet fights Claudius by using the very weapons of festivity and the upside-down world ('antic disposition', drama, the jester's grating irony, etc.); and similarly, Iago impels Othello towards homicidal mania by using festive and popular traditions which he manages to pervert, the better to bait his victim (see below, chapter 10, pp. 283–302).

93. III, iv, 93. Maguin ('La nuit', vol. I, p. 480) associates the image of the 'king of shreds and patches' with that of the Jack-a-Lent of the beginning of Lent (see also above, pp. 104, 108 and 232). Claudius like Macbeth, Lear and Henry IV thus takes his place alongside the kings whom Anne Righter-Barton calls 'the Player Kings of the flawed rule' (*Shakespeare and the Idea*, p. 109).

Lear indeed appears in Act IV of *King Lear*, wearing a derisory crown made of plants ('*Enter King Lear mad [crowned with weeds and flowers]*', IV, v, 80) and in *Macbeth*, v, ii, Angus describes the hounded tyrant in similarly grotesque terms:

> Now does he feel his title
> Hang loose upon him, like a giant's robe
> Upon a dwarfish thief.   (v, ii, 20–2)

Richard too, although a legitimate king, assimilates himself to this line of carnivalesque kings, in *Richard II*:

> O, that I were a mockery king of snow,
> Standing before the sun of Bolingbroke
> To melt myself away in water-drops!   (IV, i, 250–2)

Referring back to the analyses in Part I of the present work which describe the figures who parodied royal authority in the context of the calendary festivals, we might identify Lear with one of those Lords of Misrule or Summer Lords who were frequently a feature of the festivals of May and Whitsun in the villages of Elizabethan England (see above, pp. 134, 137). As for Macbeth, in the above quotation, he is indirectly assimilated to the giants of the Midsummer Watch, whose stature was out of all proportion to the men hidden inside the dummies and carrying them along. Finally, the image of the 'mockery king of snow' in *Richard II* indirectly evokes the 'Mock King' of the Christmas festivals, the period of misrule. In these three portraits, the imagery of flowers, giants and snow respectively provides an emblematic code which helps the spectator to associate these kings with three separate types of festive ceremonies, all different yet all characterized by similar rites of inversion. See also below, p. 378, note 20.

94. See the analysis of this scene in Chapter 10, below, pp. 287–9.
95. II, ii, 1–7.

HERALD: It is Othello's pleasure – our noble and valiant general – that, upon
certain tidings now arrived importing to the mere perdition of the Turkish
fleet, every man put himself into triumph; some to dance, some to make
bonfires, each man to what sport and revels his addiction leads him; for
besides these beneficial news, it is the celebration of his nuptial.

The word 'triumph' used to describe these rejoicings is worth noticing for as
well as its direct meaning of a celebration to mark a military victory, in the
Elizabethan period it was also used for royal festivities such as tournaments
or martial jousting (see *OED*, 'Triumph', sense 4: 'a public festivity or joyful
celebration; a spectacle or a pageant; esp. a tournament'). However, as a
result of the turn that these garrison festivities soon take under the direction
of the diabolical Iago, the implanter of discord, they turn into a degenerate
version of the Triumph, as it is described by Minoru Fujita (*Pageantry and
Spectacle in Shakespeare* (Tokyo, 1982), p. 69).

96. II, iii, 247–8; see Maguin, 'La nuit', vol. I, p. 531.
97. 'Othello's "Weak Function"', *Cahiers Elisabéthains*, 7 (April 1975), pp.
     47–50.
98. Spenser, *Epithalamion*, lines 340–4, in *The Works of Edmund Spenser*, ed.
     R. Morris (London, 1907), p. 590. See also the blessing which Oberon
     bestows upon the three newly wed couples at the end of *A Midsummer
     Night's Dream* (V, ii, 33–50).
99. IV, iv, 127–32. The death/resurrection cycle serves, through the ambivalent
     symbolism of flowers, as a metaphorical evocation of the *stasis* of passionate
     love and also to celebrate the rites of death and the renewal of desire. See
     C.L. Barber, '"Thou that Beget'st Him that did Thee Beget": Transforma-
     tion in *Pericles* and *The Winter's Tale*', *Shakespeare Survey*, 22 (Cambridge,
     1969), pp. 59–67.

8 Festivity and society in Shakespeare's plays

1. See 'Folk Festivals' in Campbell and Quinn, *Shakespeare Encyclopedia*,
    p. 239.
2. The problem here is to distinguish between on the one hand what might be a
    straightforward, direct representation of popular festivity, and on the other
    an insidious, yet insistent representation of it, which lurks behind a whole
    collection of indirect allusions, puns and images. See, in particular, in *All's
    Well That Ends Well*, the speech in which the clown, Lavatch, replies to the
    Countess of Roussillon with the following amusing chain of images: 'As fit as
    ten groats is for the hand of an attorney, as your French crown for your
    taffeta punk, as Tib's rush for Tom's forefinger, as a pancake for Shrove
    Tuesday, a morris for May Day . . .' (II, ii, 20–3). These lines provide an
    example of a popular kind of grotesque comic language in which a basic
    syntactical construction ('as . . . as . . .', in this case) provides the spring for a
    succession of images linked together according to the laws of analogy or
    simple thought association. In this kind of 'logic', which is deliberately
    arbitrary and absurd, festive traditions clearly play an important part. This
    passage may be compared with the scene of the Saultiers' dance in *The
    Winter's Tale*, announced amusingly by a servant during the sheep-shearing
    festival: 'They call themselves saultiers, and they have a dance which the

wenches say is a gallimaufry of gambols, because they are not in't ...' (IV, iv, 324–7). Apart from its alliterative quality, the expression 'a gallimaufry of gambols', which establishes a connection between the vocabulary of festivity and that of cooking, seems to spring directly from the popular, female ('the wenches') imagination. As for the word 'gambols', it was more specifically associated with the festive traditions of Christmas (see above, p. 151) and is here mixed in with a tasty linguistic mish-mash. In his *Glossary*, Nares suggests the following etymologies for the word 'gallimaufry': 'A confused heterogeneous jumble: from *galimafrée*, a sort of ragout or mixed hash of different meats ... Minshew ... seems to have considered it as a *galley maw fry*, that is a fry made for the maws or mouths in the gallies ...'.

3. At this period, 'popularity' had a number of meanings: 'demagogy', 'popular culture' and also plain 'popularity' (see senses 3a and 4 in the *OED*).

Furthermore, the use of 'enfeoffed', the literal meaning of which is 'given as a fief', adds a political dimension to the alienation. By offering the populace his person to feed on, the king reverses the dominator–dominated relationship. It is tantamount to saying that seeking frantically for popularity is the symbolic equivalent of abdicating one's power (and this serves to justify the position of Bolingbroke, the usurper).

4. See *1 Henry IV* (III, ii, 74–85).

5. The image, drawn from Ovid, of Jupiter's metamorphosis as a bull provides a recurrent leitmotif which accompanies the general theme of disguise, in Shakespeare. See *The Merry Wives of Windsor* (v, v, 3) and *The Winter's Tale* (IV, iv, 25–8).

6. It is worth noting that *Coriolanus*, another play which gives expression to a particularly vigorous scorn for the plebs, sounds a note that closely echoes Menenius Agrippa's address to the tribunes (IV, vi, 99–102). On this point, see Bradbrook, *Living Monument*, p. 179, and Venezky, *Pageantry*, p. 58. Minoru Fujita (*Pageantry and Spectacle*, p. 123) points out that the magnificent *tableau vivant* constituted by Cleopatra's appearance on the river Cydnus, in Enobarbus' speech, was inspired not only by Plutarch but also by the grand water pageant organized in London on the occasion of the Lord Mayor's inauguration.

7. Cited in the Appendix to the Arden Shakespeare edition of *Antony and Cleopatra*, ed. M.R. Ridley (London, 1954; repr. 1971), p. 274.

8. What Cleopatra, deep down, fears most of all is being made to suffer the type of fate traditionally meted out to prostitutes in London on Shrove Tuesday.

9. *The Tempest*, II, ii, 24–36. See G. Schmidgall, *Courtly Aesthetic*, pp. 196–214.

10. In *La peinture maniériste* (Neuchâtel, 1964), Jacques Bousquet shows that this aesthetic movement, which was influential between 1520 and 1620, testifies to a fundamental anxiety which is expressed in its contorted, bizarre or distorted figures (pp. 27–8). He furthermore suggests that, despite its apparent élitism and preciosity, this form of art was in truth not cut off from the popular public. He bases his thesis in particular upon the fact that Shakespeare's plays were appreciated by an audience of "groundlings" composed of craftsmen, members of fraternities and apprentices ... while the more cultivated wits of the time manifested a greater reticence ...' (p. 67).

11. In this sense, the people would be represented by the 'woodwose' or 'wild man', the grotesque figure who appeared in Midsummer pageants (see Illus. 2.2, p. 57). On this point, see Withington, *English Pageantry*, vol. I, p. 72. See also Jacques Le Goff's preface to Marc Soriano, *Les contes de Perrault, culture savante et traditions populaires* (Paris, 1968, repr. 1977), p. xxiii. This image of the common man as a 'threatening animal' is well illustrated by York's symbolic picture of Jack Cade in *2 Henry VI*, where he describes him as 'a sharp-quilled porcupine' (III, i, 363). We should remember that, in political pamphlets of the Renaissance, the populace was represented as a 'many-headed monster'. On this point, see Christopher Hill, 'The Many-Headed Monster in Late Tudor and Early Stuart Political Thinking', in *From the Renaissance to the Counter-Reformation*, ed. C.H. Carter (London, 1966). See also C.S.L. Davies, 'Révoltes populaires en Angleterre (1500–1700)', *Annales* (January-February 1969), pp. 24–60.

12. Edward Hall, *The Union of the Two Noble and Illustre Families of Lancastre and Yorke* (1548), quoted in *Narrative and Dramatic Sources of Shakespeare*, 8 vols. Geoffrey Bullough, ed. (London, 1957–75), vol. III (1960), pp. 114–15.

13. *Sources*, p. 96.

14. On this subject, see Robert Weimann, *Shakespeare and the Popular Tradition*, pp. 39 and 185.

15. On this point, see 'porcupine' in Ad de Vries, *A Dictionary of Symbols and Imagery* (London, 1974; repr. 1976).

16. See the 'dance of the Jesters' ('la dance des Bouffons') described in Jehan Tabourot (*alias* Thoinot Arbeau), *Orchésographie*, p. 97. See also E.K. Chambers, *Mediaeval Stage*, vol. I, p. 195. Alan Brissenden (*Shakespeare and the Dance*) establishes an interesting link between the warrior and the festive elements which are combined in the Morris dance. He draws his evidence from a number of traditions of the Oxford region (p. 21).

17. *Carnival in Romans*, p. 171.

18. IV, ii, 8–16. On this point, see also Stephen Greenblatt, 'Murdering Peasants: Status, Genre, and the Representation of Rebellion', in *Representing the English Renaissance*, ed. Stephen Greenblatt (Berkeley and Los Angeles, 1988), pp. 23–5; Dominique Goy-Blanquet, 'Pauvres Jacques: chroniques et spectacles en Angleterre au XVIe siècle', in Elie Königson (ed.), *Figures théâtrales du peuple* (Paris, 1986), p. 67. In *Carnival and Theater. Plebeian Culture and the Structure of Authority in Renaissance England* (New York and London, 1985), Michael Bristol returns to these scenes (p. 88–90), but is unwilling to limit Cade's speeches to a carnivalesque dynamic, declaring 'the speeches of Cade and his followers constitute a powerful political and discursive indiscretion' (p. 89). Michael Hattaway, whose analysis is rather more nuanced, nevertheless seems to follow Michael Bristol when he writes in a recent article ('Rebellion, Class Consciousness and Shakespeare's *2 Henry VI*', *Cahiers Elisabéthains*, 33 (April 1988), pp. 13–22, that 'York's description of Cade as a "Morisco" . . . also places him in this tradition of revelry . . . I cannot agree however, that the episode is thereby depoliticized' (p. 19). On this point, see also Wiles, *Shakespeare's Clown*, p. 44. The figure of Jack Cade prompts the same kind of arguments as those put forward on the subject of Caliban and other grotesque popular

figures in Shakespeare's plays (see F. Laroque, 'La fonction des artisans dans *The Taming of the Shrew, A Midsummer Night's Dream* et *2 Henry VI*', in *Annales du Groupe d'Etudes et de Recherches Britanniques (GERB)* (Bordeaux, 1987), pp. 7–25). The question is whether the role of these figures is simply to parody the main plot (Hattaway uses the apposite expression 'shadow play' in this connection, 'Rebellion', p. 19), with a comic function verging on the grotesque, or whether they express a truly utopian and subversive vision designed to undermine the existing régime. I believe that the scenes showing Cade's rebellion are designed to strike a grating, carnivalesque note although, at the same time, they certainly play an important and complex role in the context of the organization of the trilogy, for structurally they occupy a central position in it. On the grotesque aspect of these scenes, see Rhodes, *Elizabethan Grotesque*, pp. 93–4.

19. *Carnival in Romans*, p. 296. The author, who cites Paolo Toschi (*Le origini del Teatro italiano* (Milan, 1955), p. 78), points out that sword dances of this type were very common in Italy, France, Germany and England too.

20. That is the meaning of the political programme announced by the actor Bevis, at the beginning of the scene (IV, ii, 4–6): 'Jack Cade the clothier means to dress the commonwealth, and *turn* it, and set a new nap upon it ...' (my italics). On Carnival kings and queens, see also above, pp. 102–3. This notion of a parodic coronation, more or less inspired by the traditions of the festivals of Christmas (Lord of Misrule) or May (Kings of the May and May Queens) is a particularly important leitmotif in Shakespeare's history plays. The first example is that of the paper crown which Margaret sets on York's head in *3 Henry VI* (I, iv, 96–108), to lend weight to the sarcasms with which she taunts him before beheading him. (And this is perhaps the point at which to note that John Gladman, the Norwich 'Kyng of Kristmesse', also donned a paper crown, in mockery, in the course of the Shrove Tuesday festivities. See above, p. 353, note 314). Certainly, the mental torture that Margaret inflicts upon the man who tried to seize the crown of her husband, King Henry VI, goes far beyond the parodic rites of the 'Mock King' and comes much closer to the original meaning of what was later turned into a burlesque game. I refer to the Babylonian custom of executing a slave or a criminal after crowning him king for the duration of an interregnum of twelve days. According to Frazer, this individual was chosen to embody the spirit of the year that was coming to an end (on this point, see *The Golden Bough*, pp. 766–8).

In *Richard III*, it is again Margaret who resorts to this kind of image, waxing sarcastic over the fate of Elizabeth, who is now no more than a 'Mock Queen':

> I called thee then, poor shadow, 'painted queen'...
> A sign of dignity, a breath, a bubble,
> A queen in jest, only to fill the scene.   (IV, iv, 83–91)

In this passage, as in the episode of Jack Cade's rebellion, such parodic coronations produce a travesty of the image of royalty and the ceremonial ritually associated with it by using expressions borrowed from the 'lower' world of the seasonal festivals and the comic languages of carnival traditions. In *Henry VI*, the function of these images and scenes of revolt, positioned at the heart of the trilogy, is clearly to constitute a distorted and distorting microcosm, to reflect the excesses and indignities of the factions of the nobility squabbling over the crown of England. See Righter-Barton, *Shakespeare and the Idea*, pp. 121–38; see also Margaret Loftus Ranald, 'The Degradation of Richard II: An Inquiry into the Ritual Backgrounds', *English Literary Renaissance*, 7:2 (Spring 1977), p. 194.

21. *2 Henry VI*, IV, vi, 1–4. On this point, see Pierre Sahel's analysis, slightly at odds with my own, in '*Henri VI*: le mythe contre l'histoire', in *Mythe et histoire, Actes du Congrès 1983 de la Société française Shakespeare* (Paris, 1984), pp. 51–66, especially p. 61. Cade's promise to have the fountains run with wine is simply a burlesque exaggeration of the tradition of filling the city fountains with wine on the occasions of royal entries or when pageants were put on to mark a sovereign's coronation. Froissart mentions this custom in his account of the ceremonies for Bolingbroke's coronation, in his *Chronicles* (ed. and trans. Geoffrey Brereton, Harmondsworth, 1968), p. 464.

22. In a chapter entitled 'La corde magique', Claude Gaignebet analyses the correspondences between the rites of Saint Blaise's Day and those of Carnival (*Le carnaval*, pp. 65–86). For Le Roy Ladurie, the symbolism relates essentially to the death/renewal dichotomy, which is central to this spring festival: 'The drapers were weaving a shroud for the old world, a shroud they waved like an undertaker's pall' (*Carnival in Romans*, p. 173).

23. *2 Henry VI*, IV, vii, 30–8. As for the bloody puppet game in which he indulges later, with the severed heads of Lord Say and his son-in-law stuck on to the tips of pikes (IV, vii, 147–54), this seems to have been inspired by a sequence in the popular Sword dance which Olaus Magnus calls the *rosa quadrata*, in which the dancers' swords were interwoven around the neck of the individual playing the 'Fool' or the 'Captain'. In the text of a Spanish Sword dance of the seventeenth century, this figure of the dance is, in fact, called the *degollada* (the decapitation). Cecil J. Sharp, who was present at the performance of these customs in the early years of the present century, writes that, at this point, it really did look as if the 'victim' had been•beheaded (Sharp, *Sword Dances*, vol. I, p. 29).

24. On this point, see E.W. Talbert, *Elizabethan Drama and Shakespeare's Early Plays* (Chapel Hill, 1963), p. 58.

25. *The Tempest*, III, ii, 92–6:

> Remember
> First to possess his books . . .
> Burn but his books.

26. *Ibid.*, III, ii, 123–5:

> STEPHANO: Flout 'em and cout 'em,
> And scout 'em and flout 'em!
> *Thought is free.*

27. See G. Blakemore Evans' Introduction to *Sir Thomas More* in *The Riverside Shakespeare*, pp. 1683–5.

28. *Anti-Puritan Satire, 1581–1642* (New Haven, 1954; repr. 1968).

29. *The Winter's Tale*, IV, iii, 39–44. According to W.P. Holden (*Anti-Puritan*

Satire, pp. 102-3), the psalms were sung in a very nasal fashion in Puritan services. The Clown's amusing comment in *The Winter's Tale* ('he sings psalms to hornpipes') may also be intended to poke fun at Puritans who were against festivity. The expression conjures up an image of the Puritans' efforts – as heroic as they were hopeless – to sanctify the pagan sounds emitted by this diabolical instrument, the bagpipes. (See Hieronymus Bosch's monstrous representation of it on top of the tree of knowledge in his painting of 'Hell' in the Millennium triptych in the Prado, Madrid.) See also *Othello*, III, i, 19 ('Clown: ... put up your pipes in your bag'), in which Pierre Iselin ('Les musiques d'*Othello*', in *Autour d'Othello*, ed. Dominique Goy-Blanquet (Amiens, 1987), p. 68) detects a word-play on 'bag-pipes'.

30. On this point, see the analysis by Terence Hawkes in 'Comedy, Orality and Duplicity: *A Midsummer Night's Dream* and *Twelfth Night*', in *Shakespearean Comedy*, ed. Maurice Charney (New York, 1980), p. 161.

31. On this, see the article by Danièle Prudhomme, 'The Reformation and the Decline of Anti-Judaism', *Cahiers Elisabéthains*, 26 (October 1984), pp. 8–9.

32. II, vi, 49–50:

> JESSICA: I will make fast the doors, and gild myself
> With some more ducats, and be with you straight.

33. The Duke himself reveals Angelo's Puritanism, in the portrait that he paints of him (I, iii, 50–3):

> Lord Angelo is precise,
> Stands at guard with envy, scarce confesses
> That his blood flows, or that his appetite
> Is more to bread than stone ...

As the *OED* notes, the adjective 'precise' was then synonymous with 'Puritan'.

34. *Twelfth Night*, II, iii, 109–13:

> SIR TOBY: Dost thou think because thou art virtuous there shall be no more cakes and ale?
> FESTE: Yes, by Saint Anne, and ginger shall be hot, i' th' mouth, too.

Ginger, used to spice beer, possessed proverbial aphrodisiac powers (see de Vries, *Dictionary of Symbols and Imagery*, p. 215). Feste is defending both the rights of the stomach and the persistent joys of bawdy word-play.

35. This is certainly what Lucio seems to be suggesting when he tells the Duke of the extravagant rumours going around about Angelo (III, i, 368–73): 'They say this Angelo was not made by man and woman, after this downright way of creation ... Some report a sea-maid spawned him, some, that he was begot between two stockfishes ... '. This last image is interesting, for it is a typical instance of the popular grotesque tradition, in which, as the example of Juliet revealed, the date and circumstances of an individual's conception were as important as those of his or her birth. Saying that Angelo was conceived between two pieces of dried cod suggests that he is a product of Lent and therefore an upholder of abstinence and fasting (I, ii, 43–55).

36. 'La représentation et l'interprétation du texte' (on Peter Brook's production of *Timon of Athems*, at the Théâtre des Bouffes du Nord, in Paris), in *Les*

voies de la création théâtrale, vol. v, ed. Denis Bablet and Jean Jacquot (Paris, 1977), p. 25.

37. See Maguin, 'La nuit', vol. i, p. 491.

9 Festivity and its images in Shakespeare's plays

1. *The Passionate Morrice*, p. 97.
2. Here, as in *The Merchant of Venice*, Shakespeare was probably inspired by the carnival traditions of Venice, where women frequently dressed up as men. On this point, Leo Salingar cites the testimony of an English traveller in Italy, Fynes Moryson:

   > many times in the Cities (as at Padua) I have seen Courtesans (in plain English whores) in the time of shroving, apparelled like men, in carnation or light coloured doublets and breeches and so . . . at which time of shroving, the Women no less than Men (and that honourable women in honourable company), go masked and apparelled like men in the afternoon about the streets, even from Christmas holidays to the first day in Lent *(Shakespeare and the Traditions*, pp. 192–3)

3. The situation is rather different in *The Merchant of Venice*, which is a more serious if not more complex play than the rest of Shakespeare's romantic comedies. Here, there are on the one hand those of Portia's suitors (the Neapolitan prince, the Count Palatine, Monsieur le Bon) who return home without even undergoing the test of the three caskets (i, ii, 38–62), on the other those who, like the Princes of Morocco and Aragon, made the wrong choice and are obliged to return empty-handed to the prospect of perpetual celibacy (ii, i, 40–2). At the end of the play, when the three couples (Bassanio and Portia, Lorenzo and Jessica, Gratiano and Nerissa) have all been reconciled and are joined for better or worse, Antonio's solitude and celibacy seem hard to bear. This produces a somewhat discordant note amid the general harmony of Act v. Finally, the male disguise that Portia and Nerissa adopt, which produces the same effect of cross-sex duplication as in *As You Like It* and *Twelfth Night*, serves to resolve the apparently inextricable position in which Antonio finds himself and is, at the same time, presented as a trial of fidelity, through the device of the rings. Portia and Nerissa punish their husbands by giving them to believe that they obtained the rings by sleeping with the young judge and his assistant (v, i, 258–65). The confusion can thus be resolved without recourse to a third party and at the same time serves to teach the young husbands a lesson in fidelity. On this point, see the analysis by Linda Bamber (*Comic Women, Tragic Men*, pp. 40–1); she remarks, in particular, that 'the feminine other is Shakespeare's natural ally in the mode of festive comedy'.
4. See Eric Partridge, *Shakespeare's Bawdy* (London, 1947; repr. 1968), p. 197.
5. According to Parten ('Falstaff's Horns', p. 189) and Gabrielle B. Jackson, in her edition of *Ben Jonson: Every Man in his Humour* (New Haven and London, 1969; p. 136, n.), the expression evokes the idea of 'merry tricks', itself an expression based on a pun involving the Latin *meretrix*, meaning 'prostitute'.
6. On these questions, see also Chapter 10, below, pp. 287–9.
7. Pp. 185–8.
8. Ovid's theme of metamorphoses connected with the love affairs of the gods,

382 Notes to page 267

Jupiter in particular, was invoked during the Renaissance to justify deviant or perverted male desire. In *The Merry Wives of Windsor*, however, the references to the myths of pagan antiquity are unlike those in *The Winter's Tale* (see IV, iv, 25–35), where they are connected with the idea of rebirth and the re-creation of the world. In *Merry Wives* they remain associated with an atmosphere of bourgeois farce. Even if Falstaff is at first likened to Jupiter and, above all, to his Gallic avatar, Zeus-Cernunnos, the horned god of fertility, references to his subsequent metamorphoses are intended to be no more than metaphors or puns, as is made particularly clear at the point where, in the course of his exchanges with Mistress Ford and her husband, Falstaff realizes that they have made a fool of him (V, v, 116–20):

MRS FORD: Sir John, we have had ill luck. We could never mate. I will never take you for my love again, but I will always count you my deer.
SIR JOHN: I do begin to perceive that I am made an ass.
FORD: Ay, and an ox, too...

Falstaff's series of metamorphoses are conveyed by a string of puns (deer/dear, deer/ass, ass/ox) which express the progression from ridicule to the pathetic degradation inherent in his position. First he is a stag with a noble head of antlers, then an ass, like Bottom, before he ends up totally stripped of the trappings of virility as a plain ox, the domesticated, castrated version of the wild and royal beast. The transition from stag to ox reflects, through a sequence of potent images, the decline from potential tragedy (the stag being a beast of the hunt, linked with the wild and the sacred) to the domesticated level of bourgeois comedy.

9. On this point, see the analysis by E.A.M. Colman (*Dramatic Use of the Bawdy*, pp. 80–1), which points out the importance of folklore in these last scenes of Shakespeare's play, and at the same time produces a measured appreciation of its influence:

It would be rash to suppose that Shakespeare was consciously basing the comedy on English popular customs. It is far more likely that he was...welding together incompatible incidents and ideas from other plays that he had seen or read about – the Robin Hood plays are the most obvious possibility, just as the stag's head could be that of any Warwickshire or Berkshire mummer.

10. An equivalent of this myth is to be found in Euripides' *Bacchae*, in which Pentheus is torn to pieces by maenads in a state of trance, led by his own mother, as a result of his having tried to encroach upon their exclusively feminine mysteries. On this point, see René Girard on Dionysus and the festival which turns sour, in *Violence and the Sacred* (Baltimore, 1977), chapter 5.

11. '*Merry Wives*', p. 112. On the identification of Falstaff with Actaeon, see the articles of John M. Steadman, 'Falstaff as Actaeon: A Dramatic Emblem' (*Shakespeare Quarterly*, 14 (1963), pp. 231–44), and Leonard Barkan, 'Diana and Actaeon: the Myth as Synthesis' (*English Literary Renaissance*, 10:3 (Autumn 1980), pp. 317–53); see also Parten, 'Falstaff's Horns', pp. 84–99. On the metaphorical links between Falstaff and the popular figure of the wild man, and his progressive dismemberment in the course of the play, see my article 'Ovidian Transformations', pp. 27–9.

12. It is worth noting that the word 'feast(s)' is used fifteen times in this play, far more frequently than in Shakespeare's other plays. See Marvin Spevack, *The Harvard Concordance to Shakespeare* (Olms, 1973).

13. On this subject see the analysis by Herbert R. Coursen in *Christian Ritual and the World of Shakespeare's Tragedies* (London, 1976), pp. 347–52. See also Maguin, 'La nuit', vol. II, pp. 769–77.

14. On this point, see de Vries, *Dictionary of Symbols and Imagery*, p. 498.

15. *Ibid.*: 'fire-wheels rolled downhill at midsummer' (entry 12b). See also Baskervill, 'Dramatic Aspects, pp. 51–2.

16. *The Story of the Night* (London, 1961), p. 97.

17. *Ibid.*, p. 65.

18. *Ibid.*, p. 66. On this point, see F. Laroque, 'Magic in *Macbeth*', pp. 77–8. See also Bamber, *Comic Women, Tragic Men*, p. 82, who sees Ophelia as a 'tragic May queen'.

19. *Antony and Cleopatra*, IV, xvi, 64–8. Here Cleopatra piles up images of dissolution, withering and downfall. For her, the death of Antony is clearly the end of a world, if not the world. With his dying breath, Antony acquires a cosmic dimension: he is 'the crown o' th'earth' and the 'soldier's pole'. The word 'pole' used in association with the word 'soldier' also, as M.R. Ridley suggests in a note to the Arden edition, p. 186, probably refers to the martial standard which fell to the ground when the general died. The allusion to 'young boys and girls' who now find themselves on a par with men suggests that Antony numbered among the 'great' or giants of history and that, with his death, this race of men is no more. This bitter, disillusioned observation is close to the words of Edgar, who rounds off *King Lear* (V, iii, 301–2):

> The oldest hath borne most. We that are young
> Shall never see so much, nor live so long.

As to the allusion to the 'soldier's pole', associated as it is with the presence of a 'wither'd . . . garland' and 'young boys and girls', it is tempting to go along with the Riverside Shakespeare edition (n. 65, p. 1381) and see it also as an allusion to the 'May pole', which was the rallying point for May Day festivals and dancing. Antony's downfall seems to coincide with the end of the old world (the moribund Rome of heroes of his ilk), just as, to the partisans of the old order, the creaking of the maypoles felled on the orders of the Puritans from the end of the sixteenth century onwards in England was to symbolize the decline of Merry England.

20. Such images of festivity in association with death frequently occur in Shakespeare's plays. See, for example, *Romeo and Juliet*, V, iii, 84–6, and *Hamlet*, V, ii, 318–21.

21. On this point, see *Measure for Measure*, III, i, 275–7:

> POMPEY: 'Twas never merry world since, of two usuries, the merriest was put down, and the worser allowed by order of law . . .

According to the Riverside edition, the expression 'two usuries' alludes to 'lending money at interest and fornication, both of which produce increase . . .' (p. 568). Campbell and Quinn, in *A Shakespeare Encyclopedia*, note on the other hand (p. 524) that 'Dante, in his *Inferno*, places usurers in the same circle of hell as the sexual perverts.'

22. *Carnival in Romans*, p. 198.
23. *Ibid*. On Shylock's cannibalism, see Leslie Fiedler, *The Stranger in Shakespeare* (St Albans, 1972; repr. 1974), pp. 91–3. See also my article, 'Cannibalism in Shakespeare's Imagery', *Cahiers Elisabéthains*, 19 (April 1981), pp. 27–38, and my note 'An Analogue and Possible Secondary Source to the Pound-of-Flesh Story in *The Merchant of Venice*', in *Notes and Queries*, 30:2 (April 1983), pp. 117–18. In an article entitled 'Dog, Fiend and Christian, or Shylock's Conversion' (*Cahiers Elisabéthains*, 26 (October 1984), pp. 15–27), Camille Pierre Laurent also alludes to this problem.
24. See *OED*, 'Dainty', sense b: '(a. OF. *deintie, daintie, dainte* pleasure, tit-bit:– L. *dignitatem* . .)'. As Richard Marienstras explains in *New Perspectives on the Shakespearean World* (pp. 33–4), after the kill, the first act in the ritual cutting up of the stag was the removal of its testicles. It should not be forgotten that Lavinia had been raped, then mutilated, in the course of a hunt (ii, iii) and that first Aaron, then Demetrius had referred to her as a '*daintie* doe' (ii, i, 118 and ii, ii, 26, my italics). The framework of Titus' culinary revenge is thus a direct extension of the ritual of the hunt in the course of which the empress' sadistic sons violated and mutilated his daughter, and the punishment that Titus inflicts upon Chiron and Demetrius metaphorically echoes the circumstances in which they raped Lavinia.

   In this play, another metaphorical link is established between images of festivity and the rites of horror and cruelty at the point where, after both her arms and her tongue have been cut off, the mutilated Lavinia is described by Marcus, Titus' brother, as resembling the fountains in pageants, which run with wine, spouting their red liquid as a sign of rejoicing and prosperity (ii, iv, 29–30):

   > And not withstanding all this loss of blood,
   > As from a conduit with three issuing spouts . . .

   On this point, see Venezky, *Pageantry*, p. 185.
25. On this subject, see the article by Jean Fuzier and Jean-Marie Maguin, 'Archetypal Patterns of Horror and Cruelty in Elizabethan Revenge Tragedy', *Cahiers Elisabéthains*, 19 (April 1981), pp. 9–25.
26. See above, pp. 238–9.
27. This is what Freud, in *Totem and Taboo* (London, 1950, p. 142), calls 'the totem meal' which he sees as 'mankind's earliest festival . . . a repetition and a commemoration of this memorable and criminal deed, which was the beginning of so many things – of social organization, of moral restrictions and of religion'.
28. i, iv, 151–5. Later, during the night before the Battle of Bosworth, Clarence's ghost returns to remind Richard of his crimes, as follows (v, v, 85–6):

   > Let me sit heavy on thy soul tomorrow,
   > I that was washed to death with fulsome wine . . .

29. *Antony and Cleopatra*, ii, vii, 80–115. See the analysis by Jean-Marie Maguin, in 'La nuit' (vol. i, pp. 486–7).

30. See chapter 10, below, pp. 282–302, for a development of this idea and above pp. 100–1, on links with ceremonial din and the comic punishments of the charivari.
31. Withington, *English Pageantry*, vol. I, p. 24, n. 1.
32. A good commentary on this engraving may be found in Jean Fuzier's edition of *Les Sonnets de Shakespeare* (Paris, 1970), p. 98. There is another in Joel Fineman, *Shakespeare's Perjured Eye* (Berkeley and London, 1986), pp. 119–20.
33. Jean Ehrmann, *Antoine Caron* (Geneva, 1955), p. 25.
34. Jacobus de Voragine, *The Golden Legend*, vol. I, ed. F.S. Ellis (London, 1892).
35. *Ibid.*, pp. 201–3. On this point, see also Daniel Fabre's review of Gaignebet's *Le carnaval*, in *Annales* (March–April 1976), 'Le monde du carnaval', p. 392.
36. See above, in particular pp. 47–50.

10 *Othello* and the festive traditions

1. In this connection, see Louis A. Montrose, 'The Purpose of Playing', p. 52:

> The professional drama of Shakespeare's London had roots in the late medieval drama; in the polemical drama of the turbulent mid-sixteenth century; and in the hodgepodge of popular entertainments – juggling and clowning, singing and miming, dancing and fencing, cockfighting and bearbaiting – from which it was still in the process of distinguishing itself at the end of the sixteenth century. 'Game' and 'play', 'gamehouse' and 'playhouse', seem to have been used interchangeably well into the century.

2. Emrys Jones, *Scenic Form in Shakespeare* (Oxford, 1971), pp. 119–47; Susan Snyder, *The Comic Matrix of Shakespeare's Tragedies* (Princeton, 1979), essentially in chapter 2, 'Beyond Comedy: *Romeo and Juliet* and *Othello*', pp. 56–88; John Bayley, 'The Fragile Structure of *Othello*' (*TLS*, 20 June 1980), pp. 707–9. See also Helen Gardner, 'The Noble Moor', British Academy Lecture 1956, repr. in *Shakespeare: Othello* (Casebook series), ed. John Wain (London, 1971), pp. 164–6; Alan W. Watt's 'The Comic Scenes in *Othello*', *Shakespeare Quarterly*, 19 (1968), pp. 349–54; Brian F. Tyson, 'Ben Jonson's Black Comedy: A Connection between *Othello* and *Volpone*', *Shakespeare Quarterly*, 29:1 (1978), pp. 60–6; Martha Tuck Rozett, 'The Comic Structure of Tragic Endings: The Suicide Scenes in *Romeo and Juliet* and *Antony and Cleopatra*' [an analysis which is also partly relevant to *Othello*], *Shakespeare Quarterly*, 36:2 (1985), pp. 152–64.
3. See K.M. Lea, *Italian Popular Comedy*, 2 vols. (Oxford, 1934), vol. II, pp. 378–9.
4. *Shakespeare Quarterly*, 34:3 (Autumn 1983), p. 338 (my italics).
5. This is the reason why, though this was the first acknowledgement of the comic aspects of *Othello*, Thomas Rymer's final rejection of the play as a 'Bloody Farce' (in *A Short View of Tragedy* (London, 1693), p. 146) is not acceptable since it amounts to blowing to pieces the play's essential hesitation or contradiction between two modes. It is this built-in ambiguity

which produces the play's complexity as well as the troubling fascination it has always exerted upon its audiences.

6. *A Midsummer Night's Dream*, I, i, 26–35. This is also a theme which, allied to that of jealousy, lies at the heart of *The Comedy of Errors* in the passage where Antipholus of Syracuse, a stranger to the town of Ephesus, declares:

> They say this town is full of cozenage,
> As nimble jugglers that deceive the eye,
> Dark-working sorcerers that change the mind,
> Soul-killing witches that deform the body,
> Disguisèd cheaters, prating mountebanks,
> And many suchlike libertines of sin . . .   (I, ii, 97–102)

7. III, iii, 232. See Brabantio's 'That . . . perfection so could err / Against all rules of nature . . .' (I, iii, 100–1).

8. According to Jean-Marie Maguin ('La nuit' vol. II, p. 939), *Othello* (51 per cent) ranks alongside *A Midsummer Night's Dream* (76 per cent) as the play with the highest percentage of night scenes in the Shakespearian canon.

9. See *A Midsummer Night's Dream*, v, i, 7–8.

10. *Ibid.*, v, i, 9.

11. *Comic Matrix*, p. 74.

12. In this connection, see my analysis in 'Figures de la perversion dans *Othello*', in *Autour d'Othello*, pp. 58–9.

13. *The Canterbury Tales*, vol. IV, 1268–1306, in F.N. Robinson, ed., *The Complete Works of Geoffrey Chaucer* (Oxford, 1957; repr. 1974), pp. 115–16.

14. *Master Francis Rabelais, Five Books of the Lives, Heroic Deeds and Saying of Gargantua and His Son Pantagruel*, translated into English by Sir Thomas Urquart of Cromarty and Peter Antony Motteux, 3 vols. (London, 1653 and 1693; rept. A.H. Bullen, 1904), vol. II, p. 183.

15. DON PEDRO: Well, as time shall try. 'In time the savage bull doth bear the yoke'.
    BENEDICK: The savage bull may; but if ever the sensible Benedick bear it, pluck off
        the bull's horns and set them in my forehead, and let me be vilely painted,
        and in such great letters as they write, 'Here is good horse to hire', let them
        signify under my sign, 'Here you may see Benedick, the married man'.
    CLAUDIO: If this should ever happen thou wouldst be horn-mad.
    DON PEDRO: Nay, if Cupid have not spent all his quiver in Venice, thou wilt quake
        for this shortly.   (I, i, 245–54)

It is interesting to note that Venice is here associated with licentiousness, as in Iago's description of the love habits of his female compatriots which is based upon the fame of Venetian courtesans in the Renaissance as well as upon the pun on the two names, Venice and Venus, which are phonetically so close to each other; it is also worth noting that Benedick's denial of marriage is belied by his future behaviour as wooer of Beatrice, just as is Othello's solemn promise to the senators in I, iii, 268–72 ('. . . when light-winged toys, / And feather'd Cupid, seel with wanton dullness / My speculative and officed instruments / . . . Let housewives make a skillet of my helm') is later contradicted by his neglect of public affairs for the sake of his own private obsession with his wife's alleged infidelity. Finally, just as the image of the marriage yoke was already to be found in Chaucer, the reference to the horned bull as an emblem of cuckoldry was also present in *The Merchant's Tale* in an ironical astrological consideration:

> The moone, that at noon was thilke day
> That Januarie hath wedded fresshe May
> In two of Tawr, was into Cancre glyden . . .   (lines 1885–7)

16. According to J.W. Draper (*The Othello of Shakespeare's Audience* (New York, 1966), p. 165), Iago is a 'Villaine' in the etymological meaning of that interesting word, a low-class person with low-class ideals.

17. J.W. Draper, who analyses the witty and bitter exchange between Iago and Desdemona (I, i, 103–63) in terms of this question-and-answer scheme, remarks (*The Othello*, p. 196) that '*Othello* is the only tragedy to have a *conversazione*'.

18. In this connection, see E.P. Thompson, 'Rough Music: le charivari anglais', *Annales* (March–April 1972), pp. 285–312; Jean-Claude Margolin, 'Charivari et mariage ridicule', in Jacquot, *Les fêtes*, vol. III, pp. 579–601; and my analysis above, pp. 100–1.

19. Cotgrave, *Dictionarie*.

20. According to the *OED* ('Sanctus', entry 3), the expression was synonymous with rough music or charivari:

    Black Sanctus: A kind of burlesque hymn; a discord of harsh sounds expressive of contempt or dislike (formally used as a kind of serenade to a faithless wife); 'rough music'.

21. Thompson, 'Rough Music', p. 295. Natalie Zemon Davis (*Society and Culture*, p. 116), speaks of grotesque disparities in age between bride and groom which could scandalize the city.

22. Michael Neill, 'Changing Places in *Othello*', *Shakespeare Survey*, 37 (Cambridge, 1984), p. 122.

23. See Watts, 'Comic Scenes', p. 352.

24. In this connection, see Lawrence J. Ross, 'Shakespeare's Dull Clown and Symbolic Music', *Shakespeare Quarterly*, 17 (1966), pp. 107–28 and Pierre Iselin, 'Les musiques d'*Othello*', p. 68.

25. See for instance II, i, 201–2:

    > But I'll set down the pegs that make this music,
    > As honest as I am.

26. *A Most Pleasant Comedie of Mucedorus* (1598), in Brooke, *Shakespeare Apocrypha*, p. 105.

27. See Christiane Klapish-Zuber, 'La mattinata médiévale d'Italie', in Le Goff and Schmitt, *Le charivari*, pp. 150–3.

28. *Ibid.*, p. 160. In the Penguin edition of the play (Harmondsworth, 1984), p. 199, Kenneth Muir notes that it was an Elizabethan custom to awaken the newly married couple with music.

29. See T.G.A. Nelson and Charles Haines, 'Othello's Unconsummated Marriage', *Essays in Criticism*, 33:1 (January 1983), p. 7.

30. E.K. Chambers, *Mediaeval Stage*, vol. I, p. 199. See also above, pp. 120–1.

31. *Ibid.*, n. 1.

32. *Anatomie of Abuses*, p. 147.

33. *King Lear*, II, ii, 232.

34. I, ii, 59 and V, ii, 251. For an analysis of the sword imagery in *Othello*, see Pierre Iselin, 'Les musiques d'*Othello*', p. 70.

35. See my analysis above, pp. 249–51.
36. Leslie Fiedler, *The Stranger in Shakespeare*, p. 126.
37. See the line 'Work on; my medicine work', IV, i, 42–3.
38. In *Dramatic Identities and Cultural Tradition. Studies in Shakespeare and His Contemporaries* (Liverpool, 1978), George K. Hunter remarks (p. 38) that 'the English folk-play describes St George's enemy as . . . Black Morocco Dog'.
39. In this connection, see Barbara Everett, 'Spanish *Othello*: the Making of Shakespeare's Moor', *Shakespeare Survey*, 35 (Cambridge, 1982), p. 103.
40. See the entry 'Bull-fighting' in the *Encyclopaedia Britannica*.
41. See Jean Testas, *La tauromachie*, Collection 'Que-sais-je' (Paris, 1974), p. 16.
42. V, ii, 362 and V, ii, 319.
43. Introduction to *Othello*; Casebook, p. 13.
44. *Rabelais*, pp. 316ff.
45. IAGO: . . . yet again, your fingers at your lips? Would they were clyster-pipes for your sake.   (II, i, 178–80)
46. In this connection, see Pierre Iselin, 'Les musiques d'*Othello*', p. 71 and notes 40–1.
47. 'Pish! Noses, ears, and lips' (IV, i, 40–1). In this connection, see Peter Stallybrass, 'Patriarchal Territories: The Body Enclosed', in *Rewriting the Renaissance, The Discourses of Sexual Difference in Early Modern Europe*, eds. Margaret W. Ferguson, Maureen Quilligan and Nancy J. Vickers (Chicago, 1986), p. 138.
48. *Master Francis Rabelais*, vol. II, chapter 31, p. 178.
49. See Iago's

> Not poppy, nor mandragora . . .
> Shall ever medicine thee to that sweet sleep
> Which thou owedst yesterday.   (III, iii, 334–7)

50. In this connection, see Pierre Iselin, 'Les musiques d'*Othello*' pp. 69–70.
51. See Robert Hillis Goldsmith, 'Wild Man', p. 486.
52. *Ibid*.
53. *The Comedie of Mucedorus*, V, i, 35 (p. 121).
54. V, ii, 362.
55. See the analysis of this painting by Claude Gaignebet in 'Le combat', pp. 313–45.
56. Reproduced in Claude Gaignebet's *A plus hault sens. L'ésotérisme spirituel et charnel de Rabelais*, 2 vols. (Paris, 1986), vol. II, p. 118.
57. See *King Lear*, II, ii, 169–72:

> EDGAR: . . . and am bethought
> To take the basest and most poorest shape
> That ever penury, in contempt of man
> Brought near to beast. My face I'll grime with filth.

58. Othello indirectly assimilates himself to a bear when he says of Desdemona: 'O, she will sing the savageness out of a bear!' (IV, i, 184–5).
59. Anonymous woodcut, reproduced in Gaignebet's *A plus hault sens*, vol. II, p. 60.

60. *Ibid.*
61. *Ibid.*, p. 217.
62. *Ibid.*, vol. I, p. 88. See also Gaignebet, *Le carnaval*, pp. 136 and 140; Christiane Gallenca, 'Ritual and Folk Customs', pp. 34–5.
63. See the quotation above, in n. 45, this chapter.
64. Anne Lecercle, 'The "Unlacing" of the Name in *Othello*', in *Autour d'Othello*, p. 75.
65. This striking image of the bellows was to be explicitly used at the beginning of *Antony and Cleopatra* where Philo says that Antony 'is become the bellows and the fan / To cool a gipsy's lust' (I, i, 9–10).
66. 'It stops me here, it is too much of joy' (II, i, 198).
67. *The Anatomy of Melancholy* (1621), edited by Holbrook Jackson (London, 1932; repr. 1978), Part I, sec. 4, mem. 1, 'Prognostics of Melancholy', p. 430.
68. *Ibid.*, p. 411.
69. *Ibid.*, p. 413.
70. Part II, sec. 5, mem. 3, subs. 2 (p. 260).
71. 'Good, good, the justice of it pleases, very good' (IV, i, 204).

CONCLUSION

1. See Ernest B. Gilman, *The Curious Perspective: Literary and Pictorial Wit in the Seventeenth Century* (New Haven, 1978). Gilman applies this pictorial technique to literary analysis and (particularly in the chapter on *Richard II*) produces some extremely convincing results. See also C.W.R.D. Moseley, *Shakespeare's History Plays. Richard II to Henry V. The Making of a King* (Harmondsworth, 1988), p. 166, n. 17. Moseley points out that *The Ambassadors* was designed to be seen from the side and above. (The painting was meant to hang at the foot of a staircase.)
2. On this subject, see the article by R.M. Frye, 'Ladies, Gentlemen and Skulls', pp. 21–4, and the thesis by Marie-Madeleine Martinet, *Le miroir de l'esprit dans le théâtre élisabéthain* (Paris, 1982), pp. 52–3.
3. *Carnival in Romans*, p. 173.

Bibliography

Note: The books or articles quoted below, which I read or consulted for this study, are all mentioned in the Notes. I have, however, added a few titles either because I had initially overlooked them or because they appeared after the French edition was published in 1988 and are relevant to my topic. Where I have used the term 'repr.', this refers to the date of the edition which I have used for citations. Anonymous works are listed in the alphabetical order of their title.

Works of reference

Arlott, John, *The Oxford Companion to Sports and Games*, Oxford, 1977.
Attwater, Donald, *A Dictionary of Saints*, London, 1965.
The Book of Common Prayer, ed. John E. Booty, Charlottesville, 1976.
Brewer's Dictionary of Phrase and Fable (1870), revised by Ivor H. Evans, London, 1970; repr. 1977.
Campbell, O.J., and E.G. Quinn, eds., *A Shakespeare Encyclopedia*, London, 1966; repr. 1974.
Chevalier, Jean, and Alain Gheerbrant, *Dictionnaire des symboles*, Paris, 1969; repr. 1982.
Clébert, Jean-Paul, *Bestiaire fabuleux*, Paris, 1971.
Cotgrave, Randall, *A Dictionarie of the French and English Tongues*, London, 1611.
Dictionary of National Biography [*DNB*], ed. Leslie Stephen and Sidney Lee, Oxford 1882; compact edition, 1975.
Harbage, Alfred, and Samuel Schoenbaum, *Annals of English Drama, 975–1700*, London, 1964.
Hastings, James, John A. Selbie *et al.*, eds., *The Encyclopedia of Religion and Ethics*, 13 vols., Edinburgh, 1908–26.
Hole, Christina, *A Dictionary of British Folk Customs*, London, 1976.
Montreynaud, Florence, Agnès Pierron and François Suzzoni, *Dictionnaire des proverbes et dictons*, Usuels du Robert, Paris, 1989.
Nares, Robert, *A Glossary or Collection of Words, Phrases, Names, and Allusions to Customs, Proverbs etc. which have been thought to require illustration in the Works of English Authors, particularly Shakespeare and His Contemporaries*, ed. James Orchard Halliwell and Thomas Wright, 2 vols., London, 1888.
Noël, François, *Nouveau dictionnaire des origines, inventions et découvertes*, Paris, 1883.
Oxford English Dictionary [*OED*], Compact edition, 2 vols., Oxford, 1971; repr. 1972.
Partridge, Eric, *Shakespeare's Bawdy*, London, 1947, repr. 1968.

Pollard, A.W., and G.R. Redgrave, *A Short-Title Catalogue of Books Printed in England, Scotland and Ireland 1475–1640*, 2 vols., London, 1926; repr. 1976 and 1986.

Spevack, Marvin, *The Harvard Concordance to Shakespeare*, Olms, 1973.

Tilley, M.P., *A Dictionary of the Proverbs in England in the Sixteenth and Seventeenth Centuries*, Ann Arbor, 1950; repr. 1960.

Velz, John W., *Shakespeare and the Classical Tradition. A Critical Guide to Commentary, 1660–1960*, Minneapolis, 1968.

Vries, Ad de, *Dictionary of Symbols and Imagery*, London, 1974, repr. 1976.

Ward, A.W., and A.R. Waller, eds., *The Cambridge History of English Literature*, 15 vols., Cambridge, 1907–16; repr. 1961.

Historical documents

Bede, *Ecclesiastical History of the English Nation*, ed. and trans. J. Steevens, London, 1723.

Buckminster, Thomas, *An Almanack and Prognostication for the Year 1598*, ed. Eustace F. Bosanquet (Shakespeare Association Facsimile, 8), Oxford, 1935.

Calendar of the Manuscripts of the Most Honourable the Marquess of Salisbury preserved at Hatfield House, in *Historical Manuscripts Commission (HMC)*, VIII (1889).

Clopper, Lawrence M., ed., *Chester* [The Records] (Records of Early English Drama), Toronto, 1979.

Cox, J.C., *Churchwardens' Accounts*, London, 1913.

Cunnington, B. Howard, ed., *Records of the County of Wiltshire*, London, 1932.

Gee, Henry, and William John Hardy, *Documents Illustrative of the English Church*, London, 1896.

Hale, W.H., ed., *A Series of Precedents and Proceedings in Criminal Cases 1475–1660*, London, 1847.

Historical Manuscripts Commission [Printed for H.M. Stationery Office], London, 1872–1946.

Hudson, William, and John C. Tingey, eds., *The Records of the City of Norwich*, 2 vols., Norwich, 1906.

Jeaffreson, John Cordy, ed., *Middlesex County Records*, 3 vols., Clerkenwell, 1886.

Kennedy, W.P.M., *Elizabethan Episcopal Administration*, 3 vols., London, 1924.

Kennett, White, *Parochial Antiquities (1695)*, 2 vols., London, 1818.

Kinloch, G.R., *Reliquiae Antiquae Scotiae*, Edinburgh, 1848.

Klausner, David N., *Herefordshire, Worcestershire* (Records of Early English Drama), Toronto, 1990.

Latimer, Hugh, *Sermons by Hugh Latimer*, ed. C.E. Corrie, Cambridge, 1844.

Nichols, John, *The Progresses and Public Processions of Queen Elizabeth I*, 3 vols., London, 1788–1807, repr. 1823.

The Progresses, Processions and Magnificent Festivities of King James the First, 4 vols., London, 1828.

Nicholson, W., ed., *The Remains of Edmund Grindal*, Cambridge, 1843.

Pierce, William, ed., *The Marprelate Tracts 1588–1589*, London, 1911.

Raine, James, *The Acts of the High Commission Court within the Diocese of Durham* (Surtees Society, 34), London, 1858.

[Salisbury, Marquess of], *Calendar of the Manuscripts of the Historical Manuscripts Commission*, vol. VIII, London, 1899.

Tawney, R.H., and Eileen Power, *Tudor Economic Documents*, 3 vols., London, 1924.

Victoria County History, vol. VIII: *Warwickshire*, 3 vols., London, 1904–69.

Waldron, George, *The History and Description of the Isle of Man*, London, 1744.

Wilkins, David, *Concilia Magnae Britanniae et Hiberniae*, 4 vols., London, 1737.

Anthologies

Adams, J.Q., ed., *Chief Pre-Shakespearean Dramas*, Boston, 1924.

Bang, Willy, ed., *Materialen zur Kunde des älteren englischen Dramas*, Louvain, 1902–14.

Brooke, C.F. Tucker, ed., *The Shakespeare Apocrypha*, Oxford, 1908, repr. 1971.

Bullen, A.H., ed., *England's Helicon* (1600), London, 1887.
Ancient Drolleries, Oxford, 1890.
Lyrics from the Dramatists of the Elizabethan Age, London, 1901.

Chappell, W., and J. Woodfall Ebsworth, eds., *The Roxburghe Ballads*, 9 vols., Hertford, 1869–99.

Chevalier, Claude-Alain, ed., *Théâtre comique du Moyen-Age*, Paris, 1973; repr. 1982.

Child, F.J., *The English and Scottish Popular Ballads*, 5 vols., London, 1882; repr. 1965.

Clark, Andrew, ed., *The Shirburn Ballads 1585–1616*, Oxford, 1907.

Collier, J.P., ed., *Illustrations of Old English Literature* (1866), 3 vols., New York, 1966.

Corbin, Peter and Douglas Sedge, eds., *Three Jacobean Witchcraft Plays* (The Revels Plays Companion Library), Manchester, 1986.

Dodsley, Robert, ed., *A Select Collection of Old Plays*, 12 vols., London, 1744: repr. ed. W.C. Hazlitt, 15 vols., London, 1874–6, and repr. New York and London, 1964 (15 vols. in 7).

Ebsworth, J.W., ed., *The Amanda Group of Bagford Poems*, Hertford, 1880.

Harrison, G.B., *Bodley Head Quartos*, 15 vols., London 1923–6; repr. Edinburgh, 1966.

Hazlitt, W.C., ed., *Shakespeare Jest-Books*, 3 vols., London, 1864; repr. New York, 1964.

Oldys, W., ed., *The Harleian Miscellany: A Collection of Pamphlets and Tracts*, 8 vols., London, 1744–6.

Pierce, William, ed., *The Marprelate Tracts 1588–1589*, London, 1911.

Spencer, T.J.B., ed., *A Book of Masques. In Honour of Allardyce Nicoll*, Cambridge, 1970.

Thornton, J.C., ed., *Table Talk by Various Writers*, London, 1934.

Pre-Renaissance and Renaissance authors and works

Annalia Dubrensia, London, 1636; repr. ed. E.R. Vyvyan, Cheltenham, 1878.

Arbeau, Thoinot [anagram of Jehan Tabourot], *L'Orchésographie, ou Traité en forme de dialogue par lequel toutes personnes peuvent apprendre et pratiquer l'honneste exercice des dances*, Langres, 1589, translated as *Orchesography* by Mary Stewart Evans, London, 1948; repr. ed. Julia Sutton, New York, 1967.

Armin, Robert, *Works of Robert Armin, Actor*, ed. A.B. Grosart, Blackburn, 1880.

Assheton, Nicholas, *The Journal of Nicholas Assheton*, ed. F.R. Raines (Chetham Society), 1848.

Aubrey, John, *Remains of Gentilisme and Judaisme*, London, 1686–7; repr. ed. James Britten, London, 1881.

Aubrey's Brief Lives, ed. Oliver Lawson Dick, London, 1949; repr. 1950.

Bacon, Francis, *Essays*, ed. Oliphant Smeaton, London, 1906; repr. 1962.

Beaumont, Francis, and John Fletcher, *Women Pleased*, in *Select Plays*, ed. G.P. Baker, London, 1911; repr. 1953.

Le chevalier de l'ardent pilon (The Knight of the Burning Pestle), ed. and trans. Marie-Thérèse Jones-Davies, Paris, 1958.

Blount, Thomas, *Glossographia*, London, 1658; repr. 1661.

Bownd, Nicholas, *Sabbathum Veteris et Novi Testamenti or the True Doctrine of the Sabbath*, London, 1606.

Brathwait, Richard, *A Strappado for the Divell*, London, 1615.

[Brathwait, Richard?] *The Whimzies, or A New Cast of Characters*, London, 1631; repr. ed. James O. Halliwell (Phillipps), London, 1859.

Breton, Nicholas, *The Works in Verse and Prose*, ed. Alexander B. Grosart, 2 vols., Edinburgh, 1879; repr. Hildesheim, 1969.

Choice, Chance and Change, ed. Alexander B. Grosart, Manchester, 1881.

[Breton, Nicholas?] *Vox Graculi or Jacke Dawes Prognostication*, London, 1622.

See also 'N.B.'.

Brome, Richard, *A Jovial Crew, or The Merry Beggars*, ed. Ann Haaker (Regents Renaissance Drama Series), London, 1968.

Browne, William, *Britannia's Pastorals* (1613–16), ed. W. Thompson, London, 1845.

Bullinger, Heinrich, *The Christen State of Matrimony*, Antwerp, 1541; trans. Miles Coverdale, London, 1542.

Burton, Henry, *A Divine Tragedie lately acted or a collection of sundrie memorable examples of Gods Judgements upon Sabbath-breakers, and other libertines, in their unlawful sports, happening within the Realm of England*, London, 1636.

Burton, Robert, *The Anatomy of Melancholy* (1621), ed. Holbrook Jackson, London, 1932; repr. 1978.

Campion, Thomas, *The Works of Thomas Campion*, ed. Walter R. Davis, London, 1967; repr. 1969.

Carew, Richard, *The Survey of Cornwall* (1602), ed. F.E. Halliday, London, 1953; repr. 1969.

Cartwright, William, *The Plays and Poems of William Cartwright*, ed. G.B. Evans, Madison, 1951.

Castiglione, Baldassare, *The Book of the Courtier*, Venice, 1528; trans. Sir Thomas Hoby, 1561; ed. and trans. George Bull, Harmondsworth, 1967; repr. 1978.

Chamber, John, *Treatise against Judicial Astrologie*, London, 1601.

Chaucer, Geoffrey, *The Works of Geoffrey Chaucer*, ed. Walter W. Skeat, 7 vols., Oxford, 1894–7; repr. 1963.

The Complete Works of Geoffrey Chaucer, ed. F.N. Robinson, Oxford, 1957; repr. 1974.

The Christmas Prince (1607–8), ed. F. Boas and W.W. Greg (Malone Society Reprints), London, 1922.

Cobbes Prophecie (1614), repr. in A.H. Bullen, ed., *Ancient Drolleries*, Oxford, 1890.

Coryat, Thomas, *Crudities*, London, 1611.

Crosfield, Thomas, *The Diary of Thomas Crosfield*, ed. Frederick S. Boas, Oxford, 1935.

Davenant, William, *The Dramatic Works of Sir William Davenant*, ed. J. Maidment and W.H. Logan, 5 vols., Edinburgh, 1872–4; repr. 1964.

Dekker, Thomas, *The Non-Dramatic Works of Thomas Dekker*, ed. A.B. Grosart, 5 vols., London, 1884–6; repr. New York, 1963.

Dramatic Works, ed. Fredson Bowers, 4 vols., Cambridge, 1953–61.

The Shoemaker's Holiday, ed. Robert Smallwood and Stanley Wells, Manchester, 1979.

Earle, John, *Microcosmography, or A Piece of the World Discovered in Essays and Characters*, London, 1628.

[Fennor, William?] 'Pasquil's Palinodia and his Progresse to the Taverne . . .', (1619), in J.P. Collier, ed., *Illustrations of Old English Literature*, New York, 1966, vol. I.

Fetherston, Christopher, *Dialogue against Light, Lewde and Lascivious Dauncing*, London, 1582.

Froissart, Jean, *Chronicles* (1400), ed. and trans. Geoffrey Brereton, Harmondsworth, 1968.

Fuller, Thomas, *The Holy State; the Profane State*, Cambridge, 1642.

The History of the Worthies of England, 3 vols., London, 1662; repr. 1840.

Gascoigne, George, *The Complete Works*, ed. John W. Cunliffe, 2 vols., Cambridge, 1907–10; repr. Hildesheim, 1974.

Gayton, Edmund, *Pleasant Notes upon Don Quixot*, London, 1654.

Gesta Grayorum (1594), ed. W.W. Greg, London, 1914.

Greene, Robert, *Life and Complete Works in Prose and Verse*, ed. A.B. Grosart, 15 vols., London, 1881–6; repr. New York, 1964.

Complete Plays, ed. Thomas H. Dickinson (Mermaid Series), London, 1909.

Griffith, Matthew, *Bethel, or a Forme for Families*, London, 1634.

Hall, Joseph, *The Collected Poems*, ed. A. Davenport, Liverpool, 1949.

Hall, Thomas, *Funebriae Florae or the Downfall of May Games*, London, 1661.

Halle, Adam de la, *Le jeu de Robin et Marion*, in Claude-Alain Chevalier, ed., *Théâtre comique du Moyen-Age*, Paris, 1973; repr. 1982.

Harrison, William, *Harrison's Description of England in Shakespeare's Youth* (1577), ed. F.J. Furnivall (New Shakspere Society) London, 1877–81.

Harsnett, Samuel, *A Declaration of Egregious Popish Impostures*, London, 1603.

Haughton, William, *Grim the Collier of Croydon, or The Devil and his Dame* (1600), in R. Dodsley, ed., *A Select Collection of Old Plays*, New York and London, 1964, vol. IV.

Hentzner, Paul, *A Journey into England in the Year 1598*, trans. Horace Walpole, Strawberry Hill, 1757.

Herrick, Robert, *The Complete Poetry of Robert Herrick*, ed. J. Max Patrick, New York, 1963; repr. 1968.

Heywood, Thomas, *The Dramatic Works*, ed. R.H. Shepherd, 6 vols., London, 1874; repr. 1964.

   The Fair Maid of the West, or A Girl Worth Gold (2 parts, 1610 and 1631), ed. Robert K. Turner (Regents Renaissance Drama Series), London 1967.

Heywood, Thomas, and Richard Brome, *The Late Lancashire Witches*, London, 1634; repr. ed. Laird H. Barber, New York and London, 1979.

Hobbes, Thomas, *Leviathan* (1651), ed. C.B. Macpherson, London, 1971; repr. 1979.

James I, *The Political Works of James I*, ed. C.H. McIlwain, Cambridge, Mass., 1918.

   Daemonologie (1597), in G.B. Harrison, ed., The Bodley Head Quartos, Edinburgh, 1966, vol. x.

Johnson, Richard, *The Pleasant Conceits of Old Hobson the Merry Londoner* (1607), in W.C. Hazlitt, ed., *Shakespeare Jest-Books*, New York, 1964, vol. III.

Jonson, Ben, *Ben Jonson's Masques and Entertainments*, ed. H. Morley, Manchester, 1890.

   Works, ed. C.H. Herford and Percy [and Evelyn] Simpson, 11 vols., Oxford, 1925–52.

   Epicoene, or The Silent Woman (1609), ed. R.V. Holdsworth, London, 1979.

King, Humphrey, *An Halfe-penny Worth of Wit, in a Penny-Worth of Paper*, London, 1613.

Kirchmeyer, Thomas ('NAOGEORGUS'), *The Popish Kingdome or Reigne of Antichrist*, trans. Barnabe Googe, 1570; ed. R.C. Hofe, London, 1880.

Kirk, Robert, *Secret Commonwealth or A Treatise Displayeing the Chiefe Curiosities as they are in Use among diverse of the People of Scotland to this Day*, London, 1691; repr. 1815.

Laneham, Robert, *Robert Laneham's Letter* (1575), ed. F.J. Furnivall (New Shakspere Society, 6th series, 14), London, 1890.

Le Loyer, Pierre, *Discours, et histoires des spectres, visions et apparitions des esprits, anges, démons, et âmes, se monstrans visibles aux hommes*, Paris, 1605.

Lodge, Thomas, *The Complete Works*, ed. Edmund Gosse, 4 vols., Glasgow, repr. New York, 1963.

Lupton, Donald, *London and the Country Carbonadoed and Quartered into Several Characters*, London, 1622.

[Lupton, Thomas?] *Siuqila . . . Too Good to be True . . .* , London, 1580.

Lyly, John, *The Complete Works*, ed. Robert Warwick Bond, 3 vols., Oxford, 1902; repr. 1967.

Machyn, Henry, *The Diary of Henry Machyn, Citizen and Merchant-Taylor of London 1550–1563*, ed. John G. Nichols, London, 1848.

Manningham, John, *The Diary of John Manningham 1602–1603*, ed. John Bruce, London, 1868.

Marlowe, Christopher, *The Complete Works of Christopher Marlowe*, ed. Fredson Bowers, 2 vols., Cambridge, 1973; repr. 1981.

Marston, John, *The Works*, ed. A.H. Bullen, 3 vols., London, 1887.

Marvell, Andrew, *The Complete Poems*, ed. Elizabeth Story Donno, Harmondsworth, 1972; repr. 1976.

Massinger, Philip, *The Plays and Poems*, ed. Philip Edwards and Colin Gibson, 5 vols., Oxford, 1976.

A Merry Knack to Know a Knave (1592), in R. Dodsley, ed., *A Select Collection of Old Plays*, New York and London, 1964, vol. III.

Mery Tales of the Mad Men of Gotham (1630), in W.C. Hazlitt, ed., *Shakespeare Jest-Books*, New York, 1964, vol. III.

Milton, John, *Poetical Works*, ed. Douglas Bush, Oxford, 1969; repr. 1973.

Misson de Valbourg, Henri, *Mémoires et observations faites par un voyageur en Angleterre sur ce qu'il y a trouvé de plus remarquable*, The Hague, 1698.

Moryson, Fynes, *Extracts from Moryson's Itinerary* (1617) (New Shakspere Society), London, 1909.

Nabbes, Thomas, *The Spring's Glory* (1638), in T.J.B. Spencer, ed., *A Book of Masques. In Honour of Allardyce Nicoll*, Cambridge, 1970.

Nashe, Thomas, *Works*, ed. R.B. McKerrow, 5 vols., Oxford, 1904–10; repr. 1958.

'N.B.' [Nicholas Breton?], *The Court and Country, or A Briefe Discourse Dialogue-wise set downe betweene a Courtier and a Country-man*, London, 1618.

Northbrooke, John, *A Treatise wherein Dicing, Dauncing, Vaine Playes, or Enterludes, are Reproved* (1577), ed. J.P. Collier (Shakespeare Society), London, 1843.

Old Meg of Hereford-shire for a Mayd Marian (1608), in Klausner, David, ed., *Herefordshire, Worcestershire*, Toronto, 1990.

Overbury, Thomas, *The Overburian Characters* (1614), ed. W.J. Paylor, Oxford, 1936.

'Pasquil's Palinodia and his Progresse to the Taverne . . .', *see* [Fennor, William?]

The Passionate Morrice in *A Sequel to Tell-Trothes New Yeares Gift* (1593), ed. N. Trübner (New Shakspere Society), London, 1876.

Penry, John, *A Treatise Containing the Aequity of an Humble Supplication . . . in the behalfe of the Countrey of Wales, that some Order may be taken for the preaching of the Gospell among those people*, Oxford, 1587.

Petronius Arbiter, *The Satyricon and the Fragments*, trans. J. Sullivan, Harmondsworth, 1965.

Platter, Thomas, *Travels in England, 1599*, trans. (from the German) and ed. Clare Williams, London, 1937.

Porter, Henry, *Two Angry Women of Abingdon* (1588), in R. Dodsley, ed., *A Select Collection of Plays*, New York and London, 1964, vol. VII.

Le Prince d'Amour, or The Prince of Love, London, 1635.

Prynne, William, *Histrio-mastix: The Players Scourge or Actors Tragaedie*, London, 1633.

Puttenham, George, *The Arte of English Poesie* (1589), Scolar Press Facsimile, Menston, 1968.

Rabelais, François, *Master Francis Rabelais, Five Books of the Lives, Heroic Deeds and Sayings of Gargantua and His son Pantagruel*, translated into English by Sir Thomas Urquart of Cromarty and Peter Antony Motteux, 3 vols., London, 1653; repr. ed. A.H. Bullen, London, 1904.

Ramsey, Lawrence, *The Practice of the Divell*, London, c. 1577.

Rich, Barnabe, *The Honestie of this Age: Proving by Good Circumstance that the*

World was Never Honest till Now (1614), ed. Peter Cunningham (Percy Society, 11), London, 1844.

Rousseau, Jean-Jacques, *Lettre à d'Alembert sur les spectacles* (1758), ed. Léon Fontaine, Paris, 1889.

Rowley, Samuel, Thomas Dekker and John Ford, *The Witch of Edmonton* (1621) in *Three Jacobean Witchcraft Plays*, ed. Peter Corbin and Douglas Sedge (The Revels Plays Companion Library), Manchester, 1986.

Saltonstall, Wye, *Picturae Loquentes, or Pictures Drawne Forth in Characters* (1631), ed. C.H. Wilkinson, Oxford, 1946.

Sampson, William, *The Vow-Breaker or The Fair Maid of Clifton* (1625), in Willy Bang, ed., *Materialen zur Kunde des älteren englischen Dramas*, Louvain, 1902–14, vol. XLII.

Savaron, Jean, *Traité contre les masques*, Paris, 1608.

Scot, Reginald, *A Perfite Platforme of a Hoppe Garden*, London, 1574.

The Discoverie of Witchcraft (1584), ed. Brinsley Nicholson, London, 1886.

Selden, John, *Table-Talk*, ed. R. Milward, London, 1689; repr. ed. J.C. Thornton, London, 1934.

A Sequel to Tell-Trothes New Yeares Gift (1593), ed. N. Trübner (New Shakspere Society), London, 1876.

Shakespeare, William, *The Riverside Shakespeare*, ed. G. Blakemore Evans, Boston, 1974.

The Complete Works [Compact edition], eds. Stanley Wells and Gary Taylor, Oxford, 1988.

Antony and Cleopatra, ed. M.R. Ridley (The Arden Shakespeare), London, 1954; repr. 1971.

Julius Caesar, ed. T.S. Dorsch (The Arden Shakespeare), London, 1955; repr. 1977.

King Henry IV, Part 1, ed. A.R. Humphreys (The Arden Shakespeare), London 1960; repr. 1985.

King Henry IV, Part 2, ed. A.R. Humphreys (The Arden Shakespeare), London 1966; repr. 1987.

Macbeth, ed. Kenneth Muir (The Arden Shakespeare), London, 1951; repr. 1969.

Much Ado About Nothing, ed. A.R. Humphreys (The Arden Shakespeare), London, 1981.

Othello, ed. M.R. Ridley (The Arden Shakespeare), London, 1958; repr. 1984.

Othello, ed. Kenneth Muir (The New Penguin Shakespeare) Harmondsworth, 1968; repr. 1984.

The Taming of the Shrew, ed. Brian Morris (The Arden Shakespeare), London, 1980.

Les Sonnets de Shakespeare, ed. Jean Fuzier, Paris, 1970.

The Sonnets and *A Lover's Complaint*, ed. John Kerrigan (The New Penguin Shakespeare) Harmondsworth, 1986.

The Tempest, ed. Frank Kermode (The Arden Shakespeare), London, 1954; repr. 1970.

The Winter's Tale, ed. J.H.P. Pafford (The Arden Shakespeare), London, 1963; repr. 1968.

Shirley, James, *The Dramatic Works and Poems*, ed. William Gifford and Alexander Dyce, 6 vols., London, 1883.

Sidney, Philip, *The Defence of Poesie* (1595), Scolar Press Facsimile, Menston, 1968.
Spenser, Edmund, *Works*, ed. W.L. Renwick, 8 vols., Oxford, 1930–2.
The Shepheardes Calender: Conteyning Twelve Aeglogues proportionable to the Twelve Moneths (1579), ed. Philip Henderson, London, 1932; repr. 1960.
Stow, John, *A Survey of London* (1598), ed. Henry Morley, London, 1890.
Stubbes, Philip, *Philip Stubbes's Anatomy of Abuses in England in Shakespeare's Youth, A.D. 1583*, ed. Frederick J. Furnivall, 2 vols. (New Shakspere Society), London, 1877–9.
The Anatomie of Abuses (1583), facsimile of 1583 edn, Amsterdam, 1972.
Tabourot, Jehan, *see* Arbeau, Thoinot [anagram of Jehan Tabourot].
Taylor, John, *All the Workes of John Taylor the Water-Poet* (1630), repr. in 3 parts (Spenser Society), London, 1868–9.
The Complaints of Christmas and the Teares of Twelfetyde, London, 1631.
The Three Parnassus Plays, ed. J.B. Leishman, London, 1949.
Tusser, Thomas, *A Hundreth Good Points of Husbandrie* (1557), ed. Cedric Chivers, Bath, 1969.
[Udall, Nicholas?] *Respublica* (1553), ed. W.W. Greg (Early English Text Society, 226), London, 1952.
Vergil, Polydore, *De Inventoribus Rerum* (Venice, 1499), ed. Henry Ellis (Camden Society), London, 1846.
Voragine, Jacobus de, *The Golden Legend* (ed. W. Caxton, London, 1483), ed. F.S. Ellis, 3 vols., London, 1892.
Warner, William, *Albion's England*, London, 1612.
Webbe, William, *A Discourse of English Poetrie*, London, 1586.
Webster, John, *The Complete Works*, ed. F.L. Lucas, 4 vols., Cambridge, 1927.
[Webster, John and William Rowley?] *The Thracian Wonder* (1599), in *The Dramatic Works of John Webster*, ed. William C. Hazlitt, 4 vols., London, 1857; repr. 1897, vol. IV.
The Whimzies, or A New Cast of Characters, see [Brathwait, Richard?].
Whitgift, John, *Works*, ed. John Ayre, 3 vols. (Parker Society), London, 1851–3.
Willis, Robert, *Mount Tabor or Private Exercises of A Penitent Sinner*, London, 1639.
Wither, George, *Abuses Strippt and Whipt*, London, 1613; repr. 1622.
Juvenilia (1622), ed. T. Wright, 4 vols. (Percy Society), London, 1841.

Historical studies

Baker, W.P., ed., *Englishmen at Rest and Play. Some Phases of Leisure 1588–1714*, Oxford, 1931.
Barnes, T.G., 'County Politics and a Puritan Cause Célèbre: Somerset Church-ales 1623', *Transactions of the Royal Historical Society*, 5th ser., 9 (1959).
Bercé, Yves-Marie, *Fête et révolte*, Paris, 1976.
Blomefield, Francis, *The History of the City and County of Norwich*, 6 vols., Norwich, 1745.
Bossy, John, *Christianity in the West 1400–1700*, Oxford, 1985.
Bridenbaugh, Carl, *Vexed and Troubled Englishmen 1590–1642*, New York, 1967; repr. Oxford, 1976.

Burke, Peter, *Popular Culture in Early Modern Europe*, London, 1978.
Burton, Alfred, *Manchester*, Manchester, 1891.
Byrne, Muriel St Clare, *Elizabethan Life in Town and Country*, London, 1925.
Collinson, Patrick, *The Elizabethan Puritan Movement*, London, 1967.
    The Religion of Protestants. The Church in English Society 1559–1625, Oxford, 1982; repr. 1988.
Cressy, David, *Bonfires and Bells. National Memory and the Protestant Calendar in Elizabethan and Stuart England*, London, 1989.
Davies, C.S.L., 'Révoltes populaires en Angleterre (1500–1700)', *Annales* (January–February 1969).
Davies, Godfrey, *The Early Stuarts 1603–1660*, in *The Oxford History of England*, Oxford, 1937; repr. 1967.
Delumeau, Jean, *La peur en Occident*, Paris, 1978.
    Le péché et la peur, la culpabilisation en Occident, XIIIe–XVIIIe siècles, Paris, 1983.
Dumur, Guy, ed., *Histoire des spectacles*, Paris, 1965.
Emmison, F.G., *Elizabethan Life: Morals and the Church Court*, London, 1973.
Hampson, R.T., *Medii Aevi Kalendarium; or Dates, Charters, and Customs of the Middle Ages*, London, 1841.
Hart, A. Tindel, *The Country Clergy in Elizabethan and Stuart Times*, London, 1958.
Heal, Felicity, and Rosemary O'Day, eds., *Church and Society in England. Henry VIII to James I*, London, 1977.
Hill, Christopher, *Society and Puritanism in Pre-Revolutionary England*, London, 1964; repr. 1969.
    'The Many-Headed Monster in Late Tudor and Early Stuart Political Thinking', in C.H. Carter, ed., *From the Renaissance to the Counter-Reformation*, London, 1966.
Homans, G.C., *English Villagers of the Thirteenth Century*, New York, 1941.
Hudson, William, and John C. Tingey, eds., *The Records of the City of Norwich*, 2 vols., Norwich, 1906.
Jameson, Storm, *The Decline of Merry England*, Indianapolis, 1930.
Johnston, Alexandra F., 'Yule in York', *Records of Early English Drama (REED)*, 1 (1976).
Lang, A., *Social England Illustrated*, London, 1877–90.
Le Goff, Jacques, *La naissance du purgatoire*, Paris, 1981.
Le Goff, Jacques, Roger Chartier and Jacques Revel, eds., *La nouvelle histoire*, Paris, 1978.
Le Roy Ladurie, Emmanuel, *Carnival in Romans. A People's Uprising at Romans 1579–1580*, translated from the French edn of 1979 by Mary Feeney, London, 1980; repr. Harmondsworth, 1981.
Luxton, Imogen, 'The Reformation and Popular Culture', in Felicity Heal and Rosemary O'Day, eds., *Church and Society in England. Henry VIII to James I*, London, 1977.
Malcolmson, Robert W., *Popular Recreations in English Society 1700–1850*, Cambridge, 1973.
Redfield, Robert, *Peasant Society and Culture*, Chicago, 1956.
Robertson, Jean, 'Rapports du poète et de l'artiste dans la préparation des

cortèges du Lord Maire' in Jean Jacquot, ed., *Les fêtes de la Renaissance*, Paris, 1956; repr. 1973, vol. I.

Robinson, C.B., ed., *Rural Economy in Yorkshire in 1641, being the Farming and Account Books of Henry Best* (Surtees Society, 33), Durham, 1857.

Rowse, A.L., *The Elizabethan Renaissance: The Life of the Society*, London, 1971.

Shakespeare's England, An Account of the Life and Manners of his Age, 2 vols., Oxford, 1917.

Stone, Lawrence, 'An Elizabethan Coalmine', *Economic History Review*, 2nd ser., 3 (1950–1).

The Crisis of the Aristocracy (1588–1641), Oxford, 1965.

Strong, Roy, 'The Popular Celebrations of the Accession Day of Queen Elizabeth I', *Journal of the Warburg and Courtauld Institutes*, 21 (1959).

The Cult of Elizabeth, London, 1977.

Thomas, Keith, *Religion and the Decline of Magic*, London, 1971.

Rule and Misrule in the Schools of Early Modern England, The Stenton Lecture 1975, Reading, 1976.

'The Place of Laughter in Tudor and Stuart England', *TLS*, 21 January 1977.

Underdown, David, *Revel, Riot, and Rebellion. Popular Politics and Culture in England 1603–1660*, Oxford, 1985; repr. 1987.

Wiener, Carl Z., 'The Beleaguered Isle. A Study of Elizabethan and Early Jacobean Anti-Catholicism', *Past and Present*, 51 (May 1971).

Wilson, Elkin C., *England's Eliza*, Cambridge, Mass., 1939; repr. London, 1966.

Ethnology and folklore

Alford, Violet, 'Rough Music or Charivari', *Folklore*, 70 (December 1959).

The Hobby Horse and Other Animal Masks, London, 1978.

Basford, Kathleen, *The Green Man*, Ipswich, 1978.

Baskervill, Charles Read, 'Dramatic Aspects of Medieval Folk Festivals in England', *Studies in Philology*, 17 (1920).

'English Songs on the Night Visit', *PMLA*, 36 (1921).

'Mummers' Wooing Plays in England', *Modern Philology*, 21 (1924).

The Elizabethan Jig and Related Song Drama, New York, 1929; repr. 1965.

Bourrain-Moerdyk, Rolande and Donald, 'A propos du charivari: discours bourgeois et coutumes populaires', *Annales* (March 1972).

Brand, John, and Henry Ellis, *Observations on the Popular Antiquities of Great Britain*, 3 vols., London, 1849.

Brinkworth, E.R.C., *Shakespeare and the Bawdy Court of Stratford*, Chichester, 1972.

Brody, Alan, *The English Mummers and their Plays*, London, 1969.

Caillois, Roger, *L'homme et le sacré*, Paris, 1939; repr. 1950.

Chambers, Robert, *The Book of Days*, 2 vols., London, 1864.

Clark, Stuart, 'Inversion, Misrule and the Meaning of Witchcraft', *Past and Present*, 87 (January 1981).

Cohn, Norman, *Europe's Inner Demons*, London, 1975.

Crippen, T.G., *Christmas and Christmas Lore*, London, 1923.

Davidson, Thomas, *Rowan Tree and Red Thread*, Edinburgh and London, 1949.

Davis, Natalie Zemon, *Society and Culture in Early Modern France*, Stanford, 1965; repr. 1975.

'The Reasons of Misrule: Youth Groups and Charivaris in Sixteenth-Century France', *Past and Present*, 50 (1971).

Dorson, Richard M., *Peasant Customs and Savage Myths. Selections from the British Folklorists*, 2 vols., London, 1968.

Duvignaud, Jean, *Le don du rien*, Paris, 1977.

Eliade, Mircea, *Le mythe de l'éternel retour*, Paris, 1969.

Fabre, Daniel, 'Le monde du carnaval', *Annales* (March–April 1976).

La fête en Languedoc, Toulouse, 1977.

Fell, Christine E., 'Gods and Heroes of the Northern World' in *The Northern World. The History and Heritage of Northern Europe A.D. 400–1100*, London, 1980.

Frazer, James, *The Golden Bough, A Study in Magic and Religion*, 12 vols., London, 1911–15; repr. 1971 (abridged edition).

Freud, Sigmund, *Totem and Taboo*, trans. from the Vienna 1913 edn by J. Strachey, London, 1950.

Frigout, Arlette, 'La fête populaire', in Guy Dumur, ed., *Histoire des spectacles*, Paris, 1965.

Gaignebet, Claude, *Le carnaval*, Paris, 1974.

Art profane et religion populaire au Moyen-Age, Paris, 1985.

Girard, René, *La violence et le sacré*, Paris, 1972.

Gomme, G.L., *The Village Community*, London, 1890.

The Christmas Mummers, London, 1897.

Govett, L.A., *The King's Book of Sports*, London, 1890.

Graves, Robert, *The White Goddess*, London, 1961.

Grimm, J., *Teutonic Mythology*, trans. J.S. Stallybrass, 4 vols., London, 1880–8.

Hazlitt, W. Carew, ed., *Faiths and Folklore of the British Isles*, London, 1905; repr. New York, 1965.

Hole, Christina, *Saints in Folklore*, London, 1965.

Hope, Robert Charles, *The Legendary Lore of the Holy Wells of England*, London, 1893.

Hubert, Henri, and Marcel Mauss, 'La représentation du temps dans la religion et la magie', in their *Mélanges d'histoire des religions*, Paris, 1909.

Ingram, Martin, 'Le charivari dans l'Angleterre du XVIe et du XVIIe siècles. Aperçu historique', in *Le charivari*, ed. Jacques Le Goff and Jean-Claude Schmitt. 'Ridings, Rough Music and the "Reform of Popular Culture" in Early Modern England', *Past and Present*, 105 (November 1984), pp. 79–113.

James, Mervyn, 'Ritual, Drama and Social Body in the Late English Medieval Town', *Past and Present*, 98 (February 1983).

Klapisch-Zuber, Christiane, 'La mattinata médiévale d'Italie', in J. Le Goff and J.C. Schmitt, eds., *Le charivari* (Proceedings of the Paris Colloquium, 17–25 April 1977), Paris, 1981.

Laroque, François, 'A Comparative Calendar of Folk Customs and Festivities in Elizabethan England', *Cahiers Elisabéthains*, 8 (October 1975).

'Le carnaval dans l'Angleterre élisabéthaine', *Eidolon*, 13 (October 1980).

'Les fêtes populaires à l'époque élisabéthaine' (thesis), Lyons, 1980.

'Hallowe'en Customs in "Clay" – A Study of James Joyce's Use of Folklore in

Dubliners', *Cahiers Victoriens et Édouardiens*, 14: *Studies in the Early Joyce* (Montpellier, 1981).

Leach, Edmund, *Rethinking Anthropology*, London, 1961.

Lean, Vincent Stuckey, *Lean's Collectanea, Collections by Vincent Stuckey Lean*, 4 vols., London, 1903.

Le Goff, Jacques, and Jean-Claude Schmitt, eds., *Le charivari* (Proceedings of the Paris Colloquium, 17–25 April 1977), Paris, 1981.

Lévi-Strauss, Claude, *The Savage Mind*, London, 1966 (translation of *La pensée sauvage*, Paris, 1962).

Lloyd, A.L., *Folk Song in England*, London, 1967, repr. 1975.

Lovejoy, A.O., *The Great Chain of Being*, Cambridge, Mass., 1936.

Macfarlane, Alan, *Witchcraft in Tudor and Stuart England*, London, 1970.

Margolin, Jean-Claude, 'Charivari et mariage ridicule', in Jean Jacquot, ed., *Les fêtes de la Renaissance*, Paris, 1956; repr. 1973, vol. III.

'Pour une sémiologie historique des nourritures', in his *Pratiques et discours alimentaires à la Renaissance*, Paris, 1982.

Marienstras, Richard, 'La fête des rogations et l'importance des limites à l'époque élisabéthaine', in *L'Europe de la Renaissance. Culture et civilisations. Mélanges offerts à Marie-Thérèse Jones-Davies*, Paris, 1988.

Meslin, Michel, *La fête des kalendes de janvier dans l'empire romain*, Brussels, 1970.

Murray, Margaret, *The Witch-Cult in Western Europe*, Oxford, 1921.

The God of the Witches, London, 1931.

Nilsson, Martin P., *Primitive Time Reckoning*, London, 1920.

Phythian-Adams, Charles, 'Ceremony and the Citizen: The Communal Year at Coventry, 1450–1550', in Peter Clark and Paul Slack, eds., *Crisis and Order in English Towns, 1500–1700*, London, 1972.

Local History and Folklore, London, 1975.

Desolation of a City. Coventry and the Urban Crisis of the Middle Ages, Cambridge, 1979.

Préaud, Maxime, *Les sorcières* (catalogue of an exhibition at the Bibliothèque Nationale), Paris, 1973.

Reay, Barry, ed., *Popular Culture in Seventeenth-Century England*, London, 1985; repr. 1988.

Rey-Flaud, Henri, *Le charivari. Les rituels fondamentaux de la sexualité*, Paris, 1985.

Robertson, Jean, 'Rapports du poète et de l'artiste dans la préparation des cortèges du Lord Maire', in Jean Jacquot, ed., *Les fêtes de la Renaissance*, vol. I, Paris, 1956; repr. 1973.

Runeberg, Arno, *Witches, Demons and Fertility Magic*, London, 1947.

Salgādo, Gāmini, *The Elizabethan Underworld*, London, 1977.

Schmitt, J.C., 'Religion populaire et culture folklorique', *Annales* (September–October 1976).

Sharp, Cecil J., *The Sword Dances of Northern England*, 4 vols., London, 1912–13.

Sharp, Cecil, J., and Herbert C. Macilwaine, *The Morris Book. A History of Morris Dancing with a Description of Eleven Dances as Performed by the Morris-Men of England*, 4 vols., London, 1907–11.

Shire, Helena M., and Kenneth Elliott, 'Plough Song and Plough Play', *The Saltire Review*, 2:6 (Edinburgh, 1955).

'La fricassée en Ecosse et ses rapports avec les fêtes de la Renaissance', in Jean Jacquot, ed., *Les fêtes de la Renaissance*, Paris, 1956; repr. 1973, vol. I.

Spence, Louis, *The Minor Traditions of British Mythology*, London, 1948.

Strutt, Joseph, *The Sports and Pastimes of the People of England*, London, 1831.

Testas, Jean, *La tauromachie*, Paris, 1974.

Thiselton Dyer, T.F., *Folk-Lore of Shakespeare*, London, 1883; repr. New York, 1966.

Thompson, E.P., 'Rough Music: le charivari anglais', *Annales* (March–April 1972).

Tille, A., *Yule and Christmas*, London, 1899.

Vale, Marcia, *The Gentleman's Recreations*, Cambridge, 1977.

Walsh, W.S., *Curiosities of Popular Customs*, Philadelphia, 1898.

Whitaker, W.B., *Sunday in Tudor and Stuart Times*, London, 1933.

Wilson, Jean, *Entertainments for Elizabeth I*, Woodbridge, Suffolk, 1980.

Withington, Robert, *English Pageantry, An Historical Outline*, 2 vols., Harvard, 1918; repr. New York and London, 1963.

Wright, A.R., and T.E. Lones, *British Calendar Customs: England*, 3 vols. (The Folk-Lore Society), London, 1936; repr. 1940.

Dramatic and literary studies

Anglo, Sydney, *Spectacle, Pageantry, and Early Tudor Policy*, Oxford, 1969.

Axton, Marie, *The Queen's Two Bodies, Drama and the Elizabethan Succession*, London, 1977.

Axton, Marie, and Raymond Williams, eds., *English Drama: Forms and Development, Essays in Honour of M.C. Bradbrook*, Cambridge, 1977.

Bablet, Denis, and Jean Jacquot, eds., *Les voies de la création théâtrale*, vol. v, Paris, 1977.

Baehrens, Cornelia E., *The Origin of the Masque*, Gröningen, 1929.

Bakhtin, Mikhaïl, *Rabelais and His World* (Moscow, 1965), trans. Hélène Iswolsky, Boston, 1968; repr. Bloomington, Ind., 1984.

Bamber, Linda, *Comic Women, Tragic Men. A Study in Gender and Genre in Shakespeare*, Stanford, 1982.

Bamborough, J.B., 'The Rusticity of Ben Jonson', in Ian Donaldson, ed., *Jonson and Shakespeare*. London, 1983.

Barber, C.L., *Shakespeare's Festive Comedy. A Study of Dramatic Form and its Relation to Social Custom*, Princeton, 1959; repr. 1972.

"Thou that Beget'st Him that did thee Beget": Transformation in *Pericles* and *The Winter's Tale*' (*Shakespeare Survey*, 22), Cambridge, 1969.

Barkan, Leonard, 'Diana and Actaeon: the Myth as Synthesis', *English Literary Renaissance*, 10:3 (Fall 1980).

Bayley, John, 'The Fragile Structure of *Othello*', *TLS*, 20 June 1980.

Beecher, Donald, and Massimo Ciavolella, eds., *Comparative Approaches to Renaissance Comedy*, Ottawa, 1986.

Bender, John, 'The Day of *The Tempest*', *English Literary History*, 47 (1980).

Bergeron, David, *English Civic Pageantry 1558–1642*, London, 1971.

ed., *Twentieth Century Criticism of English Masques, Pageants and Entertainments: 1558–1642*, San Antonio, 1972.

Bernheimer, Richard, *Wild Men in the Middle Ages*, Cambridge, Mass., 1952.

Berry, Edward, *Shakespeare's Comic Rites*, Cambridge, 1984.

Berry, Francis, *The Shakespeare Inset. Word and Picture*, London, 1965.
Billington, Sandra, *A Social History of the Fool*, Brighton, 1984.
Bourcier, Elisabeth, *Les journaux privés en Angleterre 1600–1660*, Paris, 1970.
Bourgy, Victor, *Le bouffon sur la scène anglaise au XVIe siècle*, Paris, 1969.
Bradbrook, M.C., *The Growth and Structure of Elizabethan Comedy*, Cambridge, 1955; repr. 1973.
  The Rise of the Common Player, Cambridge, 1962; repr. 1979.
  The Living Monument, Shakespeare and the Theatre of His Time, Cambridge, 1976; repr. 1979.
  'Shakespeare's Primitive Art', in Kenneth Muir, ed., *Interpretations of Shakespeare*, Oxford, 1986.
Briggs, K.M., *The Anatomy of Puck*, London, 1959.
Brissenden, Alan, 'Shakespeare and the Morris', *Review of English Studies*, 117 (1979).
  Shakespeare and the Dance, London, 1981.
Bristol, Michael, *Carnival and Theater. Plebeian Culture and the Structure of Authority in Renaissance England*, New York and London, 1985.
Bullough, Geoffrey, ed., *Narrative and Dramatic Sources of Shakespeare*, 8 vols., London, 1957–75.
Busby, Olive, *Studies in the Development of the Fool in Elizabethan Drama*, New York, 1923.
Butler, Martin, *Theatre in Crisis 1632–1642*, Cambridge, 1984.
Calderwood, James L., *Metadrama in Shakespeare's Henriad. Richard II to Henry V*, Berkeley and Los Angeles, 1979.
Chambers, E.K., *The Mediaeval Stage*, 2 vols., Oxford, 1903.
  'The Court', in vol. I of a collective work entitled *Shakespeare's England*, 2 vols., Oxford, 1917.
  The Elizabethan Stage, 4 vols., Oxford, 1923.
  William Shakespeare. A Study of Facts and Problems, 2 vols., Oxford, 1930.
  The English Folk Play, Oxford, 1933.
Charney, Maurice, ed., *Shakespearean Comedy*, New York, 1980.
Clubb, Louise George, 'Theatregrams' in D. Beecher and M. Ciavolella, eds., *Comparative Approaches to Renaissance Comedy*, Ottawa, 1986.
Coghill, Nevill, 'Wags, Clowns and Jesters', in John Garrett, ed., *More Talking About Shakespeare*, London, 1959.
Colman, E.A.M., *The Dramatic Use of Bawdy in Shakespeare*, London, 1974.
Cook, Ann Jennalie, 'The Audience in Shakespeare's Plays', *Shakespeare Studies*, 7 (1974).
  The Privileged Playgoers of Shakespeare's London 1576–1642, Princeton, 1981.
Cornelia, Marie, *The Function of the Masque in Jacobean Tragedy*, Salzburg, 1979.
Cory, Cecile Williamson, and Henry Limouze, eds., *Shakespeare and the Arts*, Washington, 1982.
Coursen, Herbert R., *Christian Ritual and the World of Shakespeare's Tragedies*, London, 1976.
Davidson, Clifford, 'The Iconography of Illusion and Truth in *The Winter's Tale*', in C.W. Cory and H. Limouze, eds., *in Shakespeare and the Arts*, Washington, 1982.

Dean, L.F., ed., *Shakespeare, Modern Essays in Criticism*, Oxford, 1957.
Dietrich, Julia C., 'Folk-Drama Scholarship: the State of the Art', *Research Opportunities in Renaissance Drama*, 19 (1976).
Dobson, B., and J. Taylor, *Rymes of Robin Hood. An Introduction to the English Outlaw*, London, 1976.
Donaldson, Ian, ed., *Jonson and Shakespeare*, London, 1983.
Douce, Francis, *Illustrations of Shakespeare*, London, 1839.
Drake, Nathan, *Shakespeare and His Times*, 2 vols., London, 1817.
Draper, John W., *The Othello of Shakespeare's Audience*, New York, 1966.
Eastman, Arthur M., *A Short History of Shakespearean Criticism*, New York, 1968.
Eliot, T.S., *The Sacred Wood*, London, 1920.
Everett, Barbara, 'Spanish Othello: the Making of Shakespeare's Moor' (*Shakespeare Survey*, 35), 1982.
Ewbank, Inga-Stina, 'The Triumph of Time in *The Winter's Tale*', *Review of English Literature*, 5 (1964).
Farnham, Willard, *The Shakespearean Grotesque. Its Genesis and Transformation*, Oxford, 1971.
Ferguson, Margaret W., Maureen Quilligan and Nancy J. Vickers, eds., *Rewriting the Renaissance. The Discourses of Sexual Difference in Early Modern Europe*, Chicago, 1986.
Fiedler, Leslie, *The Stranger in Shakespeare*, St Albans, 1972; repr. 1974.
Fineman, Joel, *Shakespeare's Perjured Eye*, Berkeley and London, 1986.
Frye, Northrop, *Anatomy of Criticism*, Princeton, 1957; repr. 1973.
Frye, Roland Mushat, 'Ladies, Gentlemen and Skulls: *Hamlet* and the Iconographic Traditions', *Shakespeare Quarterly*, 30 (1979).
Fujita, Minoru, *Pageantry and Spectacle in Shakespeare*, Tokyo, 1982.
Fuzier, Jean, and Jean-Marie Maguin, 'Archetypal Patterns of Horror and Cruelty in Elizabethan Revenge Tragedy', *Cahiers Elisabéthains*, 19 (April 1981).
Gaignebet, Claude, *A Plus Hault Sens. L'érotisme spirituel et charnel de Rabelais*, 2 vols., Paris, 1986.
Gallenca, Christiane, 'Ritual and Folk-Customs in *The Merry Wives of Windsor*', *Cahiers Elisabéthains*, 27 (April 1985).
Garber, Marjorie, *Dream in Shakespeare. From Metaphor to Metamorphosis*, London, 1974.
Gardner, Helen, 'The Noble Moor', British Academy Lecture, London, 1956; repr. in John Wain, ed., *Shakespeare: Othello* (Casebook series), London, 1971.
Garrett, John, ed., *More Talking About Shakespeare*, London, 1959.
Genette, Gérard, *Figures I*, Paris, 1966.
Gilman, Ernest B., *The Curious Perspective: Literary and Pictorial Wit in the Seventeenth Century*, Yale, 1978.
  'Prospero's Inverted Masque', *Renaissance Quarterly*, 33:2 (Summer 1980).
Goldsmith Robert Hillis, *Wise Fools in Shakespeare*, Liverpool, 1955; repr. 1958.
  'The Wild Man on the English Stage', *Modern Language Review*, 53:4 (October 1958).
Goy-Blanquet, Dominique, 'Pauvres Jacques: chroniques et spectacles en

Angleterre au XVIe siècle', in Elie Königson, ed., *Figures théâtrales du peuple*, Paris, 1986.

ed., *Autour d'Othello*, Amiens, 1987.

Green, A. Wigfall, *The Inns of Court and Early English Drama*, New Haven and London, 1931.

Greenblatt, Stephen, ed., *Representing the English Renaissance*, Berkeley and Los Angeles, 1988.

'Murdering Peasants: Status, Genre, and the Representation of Rebellion', in his *Representing the English Renaissance* (see above).

Grivelet, Michel, Marie-Madeleine Martinet and Dominique Goy-Blanquet, *Shakespeare de A à Z ou presque*, Paris, 1988.

Gurr, Andrew, *The Shakespearean Stage, 1574–1642*, Cambridge, 1970; repr. 1980.

Playgoing in Shakespeare's London, Cambridge, 1987.

Harbage, Alfred, *Shakespeare's Audience*, New York, 1941; repr. 1961.

Harrison, G.B., *The Elizabethan Journals (1591–1603)*, London, 1938; repr. 1955.

Hassel, R. Chris, *Renaissance Drama and the English Church Year*, Lincoln, Neb., 1979.

Hattaway, Michael, *Elizabethan Popular Theatre. Plays in Performance*, London, 1982.

'Rebellion, Class Consciousness and Shakespeare's *2 Henry VI*', *Cahiers Elisabéthains*, 33 (April 1988).

Hawkes, Terence, *Shakespeare's Talking Animals*, London, 1973.

'Comedy, Orality and Duplicity: *A Midsummer Night's Dream* and *Twelfth Night*', in M. Charney, ed., *Shakespearean Comedy*, New York, 1980.

Hewitt, Douglas, ' "The Very Pompes of the Divell" – Popular and Folk Elements in Elizabethan and Jacobean Drama', *Review of English Studies* 25 (1949).

Holden, W.P., *Anti-Puritan Satire 1572–1640*, New Haven, 1954; repr. 1968.

Holloway, John, *The Story of the Night*, London, 1961.

Hotson, Leslie, *Shakespeare Versus Shallow*, London, 1931.

'Maypoles and Puritans', *Shakespeare Quarterly*, 4 (October 1950).

Huffman, Clifford C., '*The Christmas Prince*: University and Popular Drama in the Age of Shakespeare', *Costerus*, n.s. 4 (1975).

Hunter, George K., *Dramatic Identities and Cultural Tradition. Studies in Shakespeare and His Contemporaries*, Liverpool, 1978.

Hunter, Robert G., 'The Function of the Songs at the End of *Love's Labour's Lost*', *Shakespeare Studies*, 7 (1974).

Hussey, Maurice, *The World of Shakespeare and His Contemporaries. A Visual Approach*, London, 1971; repr., 1972.

Iselin, Pierre, 'Les musiques d'*Othello*', in Dominique Goy-Blanquet, ed., *Autour d'Othello*, Amiens, 1987.

Jackson, Russell, 'A Review of Barry Kyle's *Taming of the Shrew*', *Cahiers Elisabéthains*, 24 (October 1983).

Jacquot, Jean, ed., *Les fêtes de la Renaissance*, 3 vols., Paris, 1956; repr. 1973.

Janton, Pierre, 'Othello's "Weak Function" ', *Cahiers Elisabéthains*, 7 (April 1975).

Jones, Emrys, *Scenic Form in Shakespeare*, Oxford, 1971.

'The Sense of Occasion: Some Shakespearean Night Sequences', in K. Muir, J.L. Halio and D.J. Palmer, eds., *Shakespeare, Man of the Theatre*, East Brunswick, N.J., 1983.

Judges, A.V., *The Elizabethan Underworld*, London, 1930.

Kahrl, Stanley J.,*Traditions of Medieval English Drama*, London, 1974.

Kaiser, Walter, *Praisers of Folly: Erasmus, Rabelais, Shakespeare*, London, 1964.

Kappler, Claude, *Monstres, démons et merveilles à la fin du Moyen Age*, Paris, 1980.

Kernodle, George, *From Art to Theatre*, Chicago, 1944.

Kipling, Gordon, 'Triumphal Drama: Form in English Civic Pageantry', *Renaissance Drama*, n.s. 8 (1977).

Knights, L.C., *Drama and Society in the Age of Jonson*, London, 1937; repr. 1964.

Königson, Elie, ed., *Figures théâtrales du peuple*, Paris, 1986.

Kott, Jan, *Shakespeare Our Contemporary*, London, 1965.

'The Bottom Translation', *Assays*, 1 (1981).

Lafond, Jean, and Augustin Redondo, eds., *L'image du monde renversé et ses représentations littéraires et para-littéraires de la fin du XVIe siècle au milieu du XVIIe*, Paris, 1979.

Lancashire, Ian, 'Records of Drama and Minstrelsy in Nottinghamshire to 1642', *Records of Early English Drama (REED)* (1977).

Laroque, François, '"No Assembly but Horn-Beasts" – A Structural Study of Arden's "Animal Farm"', *Cahiers Elisabéthains*, 11 (April 1977).

'La notion de "misrule" à l'époque élisabéthaine', in J. Lafond and A. Redondo, eds., *L'image du monde renversé et ses représentations littéraires et para-littéraires de la fin du XVIe siècle au milieu du XVIIe*, Paris 1979.

'Images et figures du grotesque à l'époque élisabéthaine: calendrier, corps, cuisine', *Cahiers Charles V, Théâtre et Société*, 2 (1980).

'Cannibalism in Shakespeare's Imagery', *Cahiers Elisabéthains*, 19 (April 1981).

'En marge de l'idéologie: antimasque et grotesque dans le *Dr Faustus* et *La Tempête*', in *Théâtre et Idéologies: Marlowe, Shakespeare* (Proceedings of the Conference of the French Shakespeare Society, Paris, 1981), Paris, 1982.

'An Analogue and Possible Secondary Source to the Pound-of-Flesh-Story in *The Merchant of Venice*', *Notes and Queries*, 30 (April 1983).

'Le Londres en fête du *Shoemaker's Holiday* de Thomas Dekker', in *Les représentations de Londres dans la littérature et les arts*, 2 vols., *Annales du GERB*, Bordeaux, 1984, vol. II.

'Ovidian Transformations in *A Midsummer Night's Dream, The Merry Wives of Windsor* and *As You Like It*', *Cahiers Elisabéthains*, 25 (April 1984).

'La fonction des artisans dans *The Taming of the Shrew, A Midsummer Night's Dream* et *2 Henry VI*', *Annales du GERB*, Bordeaux, 1987.

'Figures de la perversion dans *Othello*', in D. Goy-Blanquet, ed. *Autour d'Othello*, Amiens, 1987.

'Magic in *Macbeth*', *Cahiers Elisabéthains*, 35 (April 1989).

Latham, M.W., *The Elizabethan Fairies*, New York, 1930.

Laurent, Camille Pierre, 'Dog, Fiend and Christian, or Shylock's Conversion', *Cahiers Elisabéthains*, 2 (October 1984).

Lea, K.M., *Italian Popular Comedy*, 2 vols., Oxford, 1934.
Lecercle, Ann, 'The "Unlacing" of the Name in *Othello*', in D. Goy-Blanquet, ed., *Autour d'Othello*, Amiens, 1987.
Levin, Harry, *The Myth of the Golden Age in the Renaissance*, Indianapolis, 1969; repr. Oxford, 1972.
Levin, Richard, *The Multiple Plot in Renaissance Drama*, Chicago, 1971.
Liebler, Naomi Conn, '"Thou Bleeding Piece of Earth". The Ritual Ground of *Julius Caesar*', *Shakespeare Studies*, 14 (1981).
Longo, Joseph A., 'Myth in *A Midsummer Night's Dream*', *Cahiers Elisabéthains*, 18 (October 1980).
McDonald, Russ, 'Othello, Thorello and the Problem of the Foolish Hero', *Shakespeare Quarterly*, 30 (1979).
Shakespeare and Jonson, Jonson and Shakespeare, Lincoln, Neb. and London, 1988.
Magnin, Charles, *Histoire des marionnettes en Europe*, Paris, 1862.
Maguin, Jean-Marie, 'A Note on a Further Biblical Parallel with the Death of Falstaff', *Cahiers Elisabéthains*, 10 (October 1976).
'La nuit dans le théâtre de Shakespeare et de ses prédécesseurs' (thesis) 2 vols., Lille, 1980.
'Nashe's *Lenten Stuffe*: the Relevance of the Author's Name', *Cahiers Elisabéthains*, 24 (October 1983).
Marcus, Leah S., *The Politics of Mirth. Jonson, Herrick, Milton, Marvell and the Defense of Old Holiday Pastimes*, Chicago and London, 1986.
Puzzling Shakespeare. Local Reading and Its Discontents, Berkeley and Los Angeles, 1988.
Margolin, Jean-Claude, and Marie-Madeleine Martinet, eds., *L'Europe de la Renaissance. Culture et civilisations, Mélanges offerts à Marie-Thérèse Jones-Davies*, Paris, 1988.
Marienstras, Richard, 'La représentation et l'interprétation du texte' [about Peter Brook's production of *Timon of Athens*] in D. Bablet and J. Jacquot, eds., *Les voies de la création théâtrale*, vol. v, Paris, 1977.
New Perspectives on the Shakespearean World (Paris, 1981), trans. Janet Lloyd, Cambridge, 1985.
Martinet, Marie-Madeleine, *Le miroir de l'esprit dans le théâtre élisabéthain*, Paris, 1982.
Mehl, Dieter, *The Elizabethan Dumb Show*, Harvard, 1966.
Montrose, Louis Adrian, 'The Purpose of Playing: Reflections on A Shakespearean Anthropology', *Helios*, n.s. 7:2 (Spring 1980).
'Shaping Fantasies: Figuration of Gender and Power in Elizabethan Culture', in S. Greenblatt, ed., *Representing the English Renaissance*, Berkeley and Los Angeles, 1988.
Moseley, C.W.R.D., *Shakespeare's History Plays. Richard II to Henry IV. The Making of A King*, Harmondsworth, 1988.
Muir, Kenneth, ed., *Interpretations of Shakespeare*, Oxford, 1986.
Muir, Kenneth, J.L. Halio and D.J. Palmer, eds., *Shakespeare, Man of the Theatre*, East Brunswick, N.J., 1983.
Mullaney, Steven, 'Strange Things, Gross Terms, Curious Customs: The Rehearsal of Culture in the Late Renaissance', in S. Greenblatt, ed., *Representing the English Renaissance*, Berkeley and Los Angeles, 1988.

Neill, Michael, 'Changing Places in *Othello*' (*Shakespeare Survey*, 37), Cambridge 1984.

Nelson, Malcolm, *The Robin Hood Tradition in The English Renaissance*, Salzburg, 1973.

Nelson, T.G.A., and Charles Haines, 'Othello's Unconsummated Marriage', *Essays in Criticism*, 33 (January 1983).

Nicoll, Allardyce, 'Shakespeare and the Court Masque', in D.J. Palmer, ed., *Shakespeare's Later Comedies*, London, 1971.

Nutt, Alfred, *The Fairy Mythology of Shakespeare*, London, 1900.

Palmer, D.J., *Shakespeare's Later Comedies*, London, 1971.

Paris, Jean, *Univers parallèles*, vol. I: *Théâtre*, Paris, 1975.

Parten, Anne, 'Falstaff's Horns: Masculine Inadequacy and Feminine Mirth in *The Merry Wives of Windsor*', *Studies in Philology*, 82:2 (Spring 1985).

Patterson, Annabel, *Shakespeare and the Popular Voice*, Cambridge, 1989.

Pettitt, Thomas, 'Early English Traditional Drama: Approaches and Perspectives', *Research Opportunities in Renaissance Drama*, 25 (1982).

'English Folk Drama and the Early German *Fastnachtspiele*', *Renaissance Drama*, n.s. 13, (1982).

Peyré, Yves, 'Les Masques d'Ariel. Essai d'interprétation de leur symbolisme', *Cahiers Elisabéthains*, 19 (April 1981).

Prudhomme, Danièle, 'The Reformation and the Decline of Anti-Judaism', *Cahiers Elisabéthains*, 26 (October 1984).

Ranald, Margaret Loftus, 'The Degradation of Richard II: An Inquiry into the Ritual Backgrounds', *English Literary Renaissance*, 7:2 (Spring 1977).

Rebhorn, Wayne, *Court Performances: Masking and Festivity in Castiglione's Book of the Courtier*, Detroit, 1978.

'After Frye: A Review-Article on the Interpretation of Shakespearean Comedy and Romance', *Texas Studies in Literature and Language*, 21:4 (Winter 1979).

Rhodes, Neil, *Elizabethan Grotesque*, London, 1980.

Righter-Barton, Anne, *Shakespeare and the Idea of the Play*, London, 1962; repr. 1967.

Roberts, Jean Addison, '*The Merry Wives of Windsor* as a Hallowe'en Play' (*Shakespeare Survey*, 25), Cambridge 1972.

Shakespeare's English Comedy, Lincoln, Neb., 1979.

Ross, Lawrence J., 'Shakespeare's Dull Clown and Symbolic Music', *Shakespeare Quarterly*, 17 (1966).

Rozett, Martha Tuck, 'The Comic Structure of Tragic Endings: The Suicide Scenes in *Romeo and Juliet* and *Antony and Cleopatra*', *Shakespeare Quarterly*, 36:2, 1985.

Rymer, Thomas, *A Short View of Tragedy*, London, 1693.

Sahel, Pierre, '*Henri VI*: le mythe contre l'histoire', in *Mythe et histoire* (Proceedings of the Conference of the French Shakespeare Society, Paris, 1983), Paris, 1984.

Salingar, Leo, *Shakespeare and the Traditions of Comedy*, Cambridge, 1974.

Schmidgall, Gary, *Shakespeare and the Courtly Aesthetic*, Berkeley, 1981.

Schoenbaum, Samuel, *William Shakespeare. A Compact Documentary Life*, Oxford, 1977.

Shapiro, Michael, *Children of the Revels*, New York, 1977.

Sharp, Thomas, *A Dissertation on the Pageants and Dramatic Mysteries Anciently Performed at Coventry*, Coventry, 1825; repr. 1973.

Shaw, Catherine, '*Some Vanity of Mine Art*'. *The Masque in English Renaissance Drama*, 2 vols., Salzburg, 1979.

'The Visual and the Symbolic in Shakespeare's Masques', in C.W. Cory and H. Limouze, eds., *Shakespeare and the Arts*, Washington, 1982.

'*The Tempest* and *Hymenaei*, *Cahiers Elisabéthains*, 26 (October 1984).

Sisson, Charles, J., *Le goût public et le théâtre élisabéthain jusqu'à la mort de Shakespeare*, Dijon, n.d.

Lost Plays of Shakespeare's Age, London, 1936.

Smith, Bruce, R., 'Landscape with Figures: The Three Realms of Queen Elizabeth's Country-House Revels', *Renaissance Drama*, n.s. 8 (1977).

Snyder, Susan, *The Comic Matrix of Shakespeare's Tragedies*, Princeton, 1979.

Soriano, Marc, *Les contes de Perrault, culture savante et traditions populaires*, Paris, 1968; repr. 1977.

Spens, Janet, *An Essay on Shakespeare's Relation to Tradition*, Oxford, 1916.

Stallybrass, Peter, '"Wee feaste in our Defense": Patrician Carnival in Early Modern England and Robert Herrick's *Hesperides*', *English Literary History*, 16:1 (Winter 1986).

'Patriarchal Territories: the Body Enclosed' in M.W. Ferguson, M. Quilligan and N.J. Vickers, eds., *Rewriting the Renaissance. The Discourses of Sexual Difference in Early Modern Europe*, Chicago, 1986.

Steadman, John M., 'Falstaff as Actaeon: a Dramatic Emblem', *Shakespeare Quarterly* 14 (1963).

Stewart, Garrett, 'Shakespearean Dreamplay', *English Literary Renaissance* 2:1 (Winter 1981).

Talbert, E.W., *Elizabethan Drama and Shakespeare's Early Plays*, Chapel Hill, 1963.

Tennenhouse, Leonard, *Power on Display. The Politics of Shakespeare's Genres*, New York and London, 1986.

Thorne, W.B., 'The Influence of Folk Drama upon Shakespearean Comedy', unpublished PhD thesis, University of Wisconsin, 1965.

'Folk Elements in *The Taming of the Shrew*', *Queen's Quarterly*, 85:3 (Autumn 1968).

Tiddy, Reginald, *The Mummers' Play*, Oxford, 1923.

Tillyard, E.M.W., *The Elizabethan World Picture*, London, 1943; repr. 1967.

Shakespeare's Early Comedies, London, 1965.

Toschi, Paolo, *Le origini del Teatro italiano*, Milan, 1955.

Traversi, Derek, *Shakespeare: The Roman Plays*, London, 1963.

Turner, Frederick, *Shakespeare and the Nature of Time*, Oxford, 1971.

Tyson, Brian F., 'Ben Jonson's Black Comedy: A Connection between *Othello* and *Volpone*', *Shakespeare Quarterly*, 29:1 (1978).

Venezky, Alice S., *Pageantry on the Shakespearean Stage*, New York, 1951.

Wain, John, ed., *Shakespeare: Othello* (Casebook series), London, 1971.

Watson, Donald Gwyn, 'Erasmus' *Praise of Folly* and the Spirit of Carnival', *Renaissance Quarterly*, 32:3 (Autumn 1979).

Watt, Alan W., 'The Comic Scenes in *Othello*', *Shakespeare Quarterly*, 19 (1968).

Weber, Henri, Claude Longeon and Claude Mont, *La littérature populaire aux XVe et XVIe siècles* [Proceedings of the Second Goutelas Conference, 21–3 September 1979], *Bulletin de l'Association d'Etudes sur l'Humanisme, la Réforme et la Renaissance*, 2 vols., 11 (1980).

Weimann, Robert, *Shakespeare and the Popular Tradition in the Theater* (Berlin, 1967), Baltimore, 1978.

Weissinger, Herbert, 'The Myth and Ritual Approach to Shakespearean Tragedy', *The Centennial Review of Arts and Science*, 1 (1957).

Welsford, Enid, *The Court Masque. A Study in the Relationship between Poetry and the Revels*, Cambridge, 1927.

The Fool, London, 1935; repr. 1978.

Wickham, Glynne, 'The Contribution by Ben Jonson and Dekker to the Coronation Festivities for James I', in Jean Jacquot, ed., *Les fêtes de la Renaissance*, vol. I, Paris, 1956; repr. 1973.

Early English Stages 1300 to 1600, 3 vols., London, 1959–72; repr. 1981.

The Medieval Theatre, London, 1974.

Wiles, David, *The Early Plays of Robin Hood*, Cambridge, 1981.

Shakespeare's Clown. Actor and Text in the Elizabethan Playhouse, Cambridge, 1987.

Willeford, William, *The Fool and His Sceptre*, London, 1969.

Wilson, John Dover, *The Fortunes of Falstaff*, Cambridge, 1943; repr. 1964.

Wilson, Richard, '"Is This A Holiday?": Shakespeare's Roman Carnival', *English Literary History* 54: 1 (Spring 1987).

Wind, Edgar, *Pagan Mysteries of the Renaissance*, London, 1958; repr. Oxford, 1980.

Wright, Louis Booker, *Middle-Class Culture in Elizabethan England*, Chapel Hill, 1935; repr. 1964.

Yates, Frances A., *Astraea, the Imperial Theme in the Sixteenth Century*, London, 1975.

Young, David P., *Something of Great Constancy. The Art of A Midsummer Night's Dream*, New Haven and London, 1966.

Studies in Renaissance music and painting

Bousquet, Jacques, *La peinture maniériste*, Neuchâtel, 1964.

Chastel, André, *La grotesque*, Paris, 1988.

Cox, Angela, *Sir Henry Unton, Elizabethan Gentleman*, Cambridge, 1982.

Ehrmann, Jean, *Antoine Caron*, Geneva, 1955.

Fellowes, E.H., ed., *English Madrigal Verse 1588–1632*, Oxford, 1920; repr. 1967.

Fuzier, Jean, 'London and Country Cries: Elizabethan Life in Song and Music', *Cahiers Elisabéthains*, 8 (October 1975).

Gaignebet, Claude, 'Le combat de Carême et de Carnaval de P. Bruegel (1559)', *Annales*, 27:2 (1972).

Gaignebet, Claude and Jean-Dominique Lajoux, *Art profane et religion populaire au Moyen Age*, Paris, 1985.

Gibson, Walter S., *Bruegel*, London, 1977.

Kayser, Wolfgang, *The Grotesque in Art and Literature*, Bloomington, 1963.

Panofsky, Erwin, *Studies in Iconology*, Oxford, 1939.
Pieyre de Mandiargues, André, *Arcimboldo le merveilleux*, Paris, 1977.
Sadoul, Georges, *Jacques Callot miroir de son temps*, Paris, 1969.
Woodfill, W.L., *Musicians in English Society from Elizabeth to Charles I*, Princeton, 1953.

Addenda to the 1993 paperback edition

Berry, Edward and Linda Woodbridge eds., *Maimed Rites and True Rites*, Champaign, Illinois, 1992.
Billington, Sandra, *Mock Kings in Medieval Society and Renaissance Drama*, Oxford, 1991.
Blackstone, Mary, *A Survey and annotated bibliography of records research and performance history relating to early British Drama and minstrelsy for 1984–8, Records of Early English Drama* (REED), 2 vols. (1990).
Boose, Lynda E., 'Scolding Brides and Bridling Scolds: Taming the Woman's Unruly Member', *Shakespeare Quarterly*, 42 (Summer 1991).
Bristol, Michael D., 'In Search of the Bear: Spatiotemporal Form and the Heterogeneity of Economies in *The Winter's Tale*', *Shakespeare Quarterly*, 42 (Summer 1991).
Ericksen, Roy, 'Masque Elements in *Doctor Faustus* and *The Tempest*: Form and Function in the Literary Masque' in François Laroque ed., *The Show Within: Dramatic and Other Insets. English Renaissance Drama (1550–1642)*, 2 vols., II, Montpellier, 1992.
Marcus, Leah S., 'Levelling Shakespeare: Local Customs and Local Texts', *Shakespeare Quarterly*, 42 (Summer 1991).
Wiles, David, *Shakespeare's Almanac: A Midsummer Night's Dream*, London, 1993.

Index